D0407516

891.7 Struve, G
      Russian literature
under Lenin and
Stalin, 1917-1953

995

891.7 Struve, G
      Russian literature
under Lenin and
Stalin, 1917-1953

995

SAN DIEGO PUBLIC LIBRARY

ALW.YS BRING YOUR
CARD WITH YOU.

Russian Literature Under Lenin and Stalin

University of Oklahoma Press : Norman

Russian Literature under Lenin and Stalin 1917-1953

SAN DIEGO PUBLIC LIBRARY

by Gleb Struve

By Gleb Struve

Ekonomicheskie posledstvija mira (*The Economic Consequences of the Peace*), by John Maynard Keynes, 1921 (translator, with T. Lourié)
The Well of Days, by Ivan Bunin, 1933, 1946 (translator, with H. Miles)
Soviet Russian Literature, 1935
25 Years of Soviet Russian Literature, 1944
Practical Russian, 1946 (with E. A. Moore)
Histoire de la littérature soviétique, 1946
Russkij evropeec. Materialy dlja biografii i kharakteristiki knjazja P. B. Kozlovskogo (*A Russian European: Materials Toward a Biography and Portrayal of Prince P. B. Kozlovsky*), 1950
Skotskij khutor (*Animal Farm*), by George Orwell (translator, with M. Kriger)
Soviet Russian Literature: 1917–1950, 1951
Neizdannyj Gumilëv: "Otravlennaja tunika" i drugie neizdannye proizvedenija (*Unpublished Gumilyov: "The Poisoned Tunic" and Other Unpublished Works*), 1952 (editor)
Russkaja literatura v izgnanii. Opyt istoricheskogo obzora zarubezhnoj russkoj literatury (*Russian Literature in Exile: An Essay in Historical Survey of Russian Literature Outside Russia*), 1956
Geschichte der Sowjetliteratur, 1957, 1963
Russian Stories, 1961, 1963, 1965 (translator and editor, with Mary Struve)
Seven Short Novels, by Anton Chekhov, 1963 (editor)
Utloe zhil'jë. Izbrannye stikhi 1915–1949 gg. (*Frail Abode: Selected Poems, 1915–1949*), 1965
From Pushkin to Nabokov: A Century of Russian Prose and Verse, 1967 (editor, with others)
Rekviem (*Requiem*), by Anna Akhmatova, 1965, 1969 (editor)
Dva goda s simvolistami (*Two Years with the Symbolists*), by N. Valentinov, 1969 (editor)
Russian Literature Under Lenin and Stalin: 1917–1953, 1971

Co-editor with Boris Filippov:

Sobranie sochinenij (*Collected Works*), by Osip Mandelstam, 1955
Sobranie sochinenij v trëkh tomakh (*Collected Works in Three Volumes*), by Osip Mandelstam, 1965–69
Sochinenija (*Works*), by Boris Pasternak, 3 vols., 1961
Sabranie sochinenij v chetyrëkh tomakh (*Collected Works in Four Volumes*), by Nikolay Gumilyov, 1962–68
Stikhotvorenija (*Poems*), by Nikolay Zabolotsky, 1965
Sochinenija (*Works*), by Anna Akhmatova, 2 vols., 1965–68
Sochinenija (*Works*), by Nikolay Klyuev, 2 vols., 1969

INTERNATIONAL STANDARD BOOK NUMBER: 0–8061–0931–9
LIBRARY OF CONGRESS CATALOG CARD NUMBER: 68–31370

Copyright 1971 by the University of Oklahoma Press, Publishing Division of the University. Composed and printed at Norman, Oklahoma, U.S.A., by the University of Oklahoma Press. First edition.

I dedicate this book to the memory of

Osip Mandelstam

Isaac Babel

Boris Pilnyak

and all other Soviet writers who were
"illegally repressed" and died
"unrehabilitated"

This book is the outgrowth of several earlier works of mine. The first version, entitled *Soviet Russian Literature*, was published in England in 1935. A new edition, with a postscript covering the years 1935-43, appeared in 1944 under the title *25 Years of Soviet Russian Literature*. After the war the book was translated into French. In 1951 an updated and largely re-written version, *Soviet Russian Literature: 1917–1950*, was published by the University of Oklahoma Press. In 1957 it was translated into German, with some additional material again bringing up to date the story of Soviet Russian literature.

The present book is a considerably revised version of the 1951 book, with a great deal of new material carrying the story to 1953—that is, to the death of Stalin, which marks a watershed in the destinies of Soviet literature. It is my intention to follow this volume with still another in which the story of what happened in Soviet literature in the post-Stalin period will be told in detail. Some aspects of that story had to be anticipated in this volume, and this requires a word of explanation.

In the foreword to the book published in 1951, I wrote that at the time we could only presume the existence of a substantial body of unprinted literature which some Soviet writers were writing for their own desk drawers, without much hope of seeing them in print. The existence of such a "submerged" literature had been hinted at by Alexander Werth, the well-known British journalist of Russian extraction, who spent the years 1941–48 in the Soviet Union and who, in those days, was known as a staunch apologist of Stalin's regime.

Now we know that such literature did in fact exist, that there were many unpublished works by well-known Soviet writers. Their emergence is one of the most interesting and significant phenomena of the post-Stalin period, particularly of the 1960's. Anna Akhmatova's *Requiem*, a large body of Osip Mandelstam's poetry, two novels and several plays by Mikhail Bulgakov—all these works were written during the Stalin era but did not become known until long after his death. Chronologically speaking, they belong to the period covered in this book. But in another and more real sense they are part of the post-Stalin literary scene. This fact has presented a difficult problem. To discuss them out of the context of the period during which they were *published* seemed to me unjustifiable. It would have meant explaining in advance a number of events that were to occur after 1953, and especially after 1956. Moreover, most of those works, including some of the ones mentioned above, have so far been published only outside Russia, and this in itself represents another important phenomenon of the post-Stalin period—what I have described as *"émigré* books by non-*émigré* writers" (the best and most widely known example being, of course, Boris Pasternak's *Doctor Zhivago*). I therefore decided to defer the discussion of those works to the sequel to this volume. But here and there, mostly in footnotes, I found it necessary to allude to some of them and to anticipate certain biographical facts that did not become known until after Stalin's death.

In my earlier works about Soviet literature I thought it my duty to warn the reader that I was dealing with Russian literature alone—that is, with works written in Russian and not with national literatures in other languages of the Soviet Union. This warning was perhaps superfluous, because that limitation was implied in the titles of my books (at least in their English versions). The same is true of the present volume. It is only peripherally that I now and then touch upon the work of non-Russian Soviet writers, and only when those works played an important part in Soviet literature as a whole.

There are also two special fields of Soviet literature which for reasons of space I have excluded from my survey: literature for children and science fiction. While the former was part and parcel of Soviet literature from the very beginning and counted among its practitioners a number of well-known writers who made other contributions to literature, the latter is, in the main, a relatively recent development.

In conclusion, I should like to express my deepest gratitude to all those colleagues, students and former students, members of the staff of the University of Oklahoma Press, and others who, in one way or another, at one stage or another, have helped me in my work. Their names are too many to be listed here.

GLEB STRUVE

Berkeley, California
August, 1970

NOTE ON TRANSLITERATION

The system of transliteration of Russian names and words used in this book, which is meant for the general reader, is not the scholarly system with diacritical markings but a more popular one representing an admittedly inconsistent compromise between the system used by the Library of Congress and that used by the British Academy. The main departure from the Library of Congress system is the use of *y* instead of *ĭ* at the ends of names and the use of *y* instead of *i* in combinations with vowels to render Russian soft vowels. The *y* is also used to indicate a soft sign between a consonant and a vowel, as, for example, in Grigoryev. The soft sign in a final position, which stands for a palatalized consonant, is indicated by an apostrophe in transliterated names, titles, and words but is omitted from such commonly known names as Gogol and Babel, as well as from the titles of two well-known journals, *Oktyabr* and *Krasnaya Nov*. The soft sign in a medial position between two consonants is also omitted; for example, Pil'nyak is transliterated as Pilnyak. In some names of non-Russian derivation the original spelling is preserved, as in Ehrenburg, Eichenbaum, and Mandelstam. Some of the more common Christian names, such as Alexander and Peter, are also given in their English form.

NOTE ON TRANSLITERATION

CONTENTS

Part I. Literature in Transition, 1917–21

Chapter 1. LITERATURE ON THE EVE OF THE REVOLUTION

At the outset of the Bolshevik Revolution of October 25, 1917, Russian literature was in a state of disintegration—its outward shock accelerated and intensified the inner processes that had been going on for some time. The Revolution, contrary to the expectations of many of its opponents, but also of some of its leaders, was to weather all the storms and to inaugurate a new period of Russian history—the Soviet period.

It is usual to speak of two principal movements in pre-Revolutionary Russian literature of the twentieth century: Realism and Symbolism. Realism was a survival, and a continuation, of the great age of the Russian novel which, with Dostoyevsky and Tolstoy, had reached its point of saturation and then gradually degenerated, until it took a new lease on life—in a different form—in the subtle and peculiar art of Chekhov as a short-story writer, from whom nearly all the twentieth-century realists stemmed. Its greatest modern exponents were Maxim Gorky and Ivan Bunin.

Symbolism, on the other hand, whose origins in Russia can be traced back to the last decade of the nineteenth century, was a product of the general modernist movement in European art and literature, while at the same time it was closely bound up with, and affected by, important processes and changes in Russian cultural life at the turn of the century. Of the two, it played by far the more important and vital part in the period preceding World War I. Taken in a wide sense, Symbolism pervaded nearly everything that was talented and alive in modern Russian literature. It had renovated the very spirit of literature and raised the standards of literary technique—especially in poetry, which was its principal medium; it had opened new vistas before literature and freed it from the deadening influence of social and political tendentiousness, and from the narrow tenets of naturalism. The period between 1900 and 1912 can be rightly described as the period of Symbolism.

The important point about Russian Symbolism is that it was something more than a literary school. It implied a reversal not only of the literary technique but of the whole aesthetic and spiritual outlook; it was connected with the rise of individualism and of religious idealism; it was part of a general revaluation of the traditional values of the Russian intelligentsia, with its agnosticism, or even atheism, its cult of civic duty, and its stress on the social significance of art. Symbolism itself was a complex phenomenon. Some of its exponents, like Valery Bryusov, wanted to remain within the

3

narrower limits of art, stressing the aesthetic aspects of the changes effected by the Symbolists in Russian literature. Others, like Andrey Bely and Vyacheslav Ivanov, spoke of the "new consciousness," of "mythmaking," of a new religion. At the same time, within the Symbolist school itself, a reaction was born against both these tendencies—the cold aloofness and exclusiveness of the esoteric aestheticism of Bryusov and the metaphysical nebulousness of Ivanov. It was a reaction in the direction of realism, and its slogans were "Down to Earth" and "Closer to Man." It was represented by Alexander Blok, the greatest of all the Symbolist poets. In 1910 the conflict between these warring trends came to a head and found its expression in a heated controversy on the "crisis of Symbolism," in which Blok, Bely, Ivanov, and Bryusov took a lively part. Moreover, two movements came to attack Symbolism and its philosophy from the outside. One of them was an offspring of Symbolism. It took the name of Acmeism, and, as far as labels are of any use, it may be conveniently characterized as modern Neoclassicism, since Symbolism, *mutatis mutandis*, was a modern variant of Romanticism. Its principal representatives were Nikolay Gumilyov, Anna Akhmatova, and Osip Mandelstam, with Gumilyov, an earlier disciple of Bryusov, acting as the main theoretician and *maître d'école*.

Acmeism adopted and developed the slogan "Beautiful Clarity," which had been advocated by Mikhail Kuzmin in an earlier controversy with the Symbolists. Gumilyov was also fond of quoting Coleridge's description of poetry as "the best words in their best order." The Symbolists had emphasized the hidden, associative, musical elements in poetry; the Acmeists in reply asserted the elements of sense and logic in the art of words. The Symbolists had tended to disembody words as a medium of poetry; the Acmeists tried to clothe them with a new flesh. Their ideal was Adam, the first name giver, and at one time this new movement even thought of calling itself Adamism. To the growing tendency of Symbolism to regard the poet as a prophet, a mythmaker, or to stress his passive, mediumistic nature, the Acmeists opposed the conception of the poet as a craftsman. Their principal literary organization significantly bore the name Poets' Guild. Though romantic in some of its manifestations, Acmeism on the whole strove toward greater realism and simplicity. It made no attempt to revolutionize the poetic technique. Availing itself of the technical achievements and innovations of its predecessors, it developed the poetic diction in a different direction, by bringing it closer to the accents and intonations of everyday speech. This quality is particularly evident in the poetry of Anna Akhmatova.

The other movement which declared war on Symbolism and contributed to its ultimate disintegration was Futurism. Though in its origins it was allied to the Italian Futurism of Marinetti and its other European products,

Russian Futurism was a peculiar growth. It was essentially a negative, destructive, revolutionary movement. It waged war on bourgeois culture, on all conventions, on the art of the past, all in the name of the vaguely formulated art of the future.

Some of the Futurists combined revolutionary ideas about art with revolutionary ideology in politics, though this was by no means true of the movement as a whole at its inception. It was, however, true of one of the early spokesmen of the Futurist movement, Vladimir Mayakovsky, who was to become the acknowledged leader of post-Revolutionary Futurism when this school for a time attained literary supremacy.

When the Bolshevik *coup d'état* took place at the end of October, 1917, the great majority of the established writers, in common with the bulk of the Russian intelligentsia, took an uncompromisingly hostile attitude toward the new regime. In the course of the next few years, while the Civil War raged in Russia and immediately upon its conclusion, many of the writers found themselves on the other side of the fence and eventually became political exiles. At various times between 1918 and 1922 the following well-known writers left Russia: Ivan Bunin, Alexander Kuprin, Mikhail Artsybashev, Ivan Shmelyov, Boris Zaytsev, Leonid Andreyev, Dmitry Merezhkovsky, Alexey Remizov, Alexey N. Tolstoy, V. Ropshin (Boris Savinkov), and M. Aldanov, of the prose writers; and Konstantin Balmont, Zinaida Hippius, Vladislav Khodasevich, Ilya Ehrenburg, Marina Tsvetayeva, Georgy Ivanov, and Georgy Adamovich, of the poets.[1] Of these, Ehrenburg and Alexey Tolstoy returned in 1923 to Russia and won for themselves a place of honor in Soviet literature. Alexander Kuprin and Marina Tsvetayeva made their way back much later, in the mid-thirties, the former dying in 1938, and the latter committing suicide in 1941; neither made any important contribution to literature after this voluntary repatriation.[2] On the other hand, to the ranks of the exiles was added, in 1924, one of the leaders of the Symbolist movement, Vyacheslav Ivanov, who settled in

[1] For an evaluation of their respective places and roles in pre-Revolutionary literature, see D. S. Mirsky, *Contemporary Russian Literature: 1881–1925.*

[2] Much of Kuprin's pre-Revolutionary work was reissued in the Soviet Union after his return there, but he wrote practically nothing new. Some of the stories he wrote in exile were included in the six-volume edition of his works published in 1959. As for Tsvetayeva, even her earlier poetry was not republished during her lifetime; only one original poem of hers (not a new one) and a few translations were published, after her return, in Soviet magazines. More translations appeared after her suicide. A number of her poems were included in two literary miscellanies in 1956, and a volume of her selected verse was announced at the time, but it did not materialize until 1961. A much larger collection was published in 1965. To all intents and purposes, however, Tsvetayeva belongs to the pre-Revolutionary period and to Russian post-1917 literature in exile, not to Soviet literature. There is now an excellent study in English of Tsvetayeva's life and work: Simon Karlinsky, *Marina Cvetaeva: Her Life and Art.* For

Italy, became a convert to the Roman Catholic church, and died in Rome in 1949.

Of those who stayed behind, only a few welcomed the Revolution and openly took sides with the new order of things. The others submitted passively, continued writing and publishing, but often were latently hostile to the Soviet regime. The former included Gorky and Serafimovich, of the Realist group of writers; and Bryusov, Blok, and Bely, of the Symbolist poets, not to speak of some younger poets like Mayakovsky and Esenin. Among those who remained in Russia but did not "accept" the Revolution were the poets Fyodor Sologub, Nikolay Gumilyov, Anna Akhmatova, and Osip Mandelstam. Their work published in the early years of the Revolution belongs fundamentally with their pre-Revolutionary output and cannot be regarded as part of Soviet literature. Gumilyov was shot in 1921 on a charge of participating in a counterrevolutionary conspiracy. Sologub died in 1927, a broken and disillusioned man, unable to recover from the personal tragedy of his wife's suicide, which was a direct result of revolutionary conditions. Akhmatova's and Mandelstam's subsequent fate will be referred to later. Somewhat apart from the rest stood Maximilian Voloshin (1877–1932), who after 1917 wrote much poetry which had the Revolution for its subject. He stressed its national, anarchistic aspect and at the same time denounced its terroristic excesses. During the Civil War he lived under the Whites in the Crimea, where he remained even when the Reds came there. Regarded as a counterrevolutionary, he published nothing after 1925, but his villa at Koktebel was a popular meeting place of the literary and artistic intelligentsia. His poems about the Revolution enjoyed a great success with *émigré* readers.[3]

Some of the pre-Revolutionary prose writers who went into a temporary silence but re-emerged later and gradually adjusted to the new conditions will be discussed in Part III.

Through the Looking Glass

The adherence of Bryusov, Blok, and Bely to the Revolution was of some

the post-Revolutionary *émigré* work of Tsvetayeva and other pre-Revolutionary writers see also my *Russkaya literatura v izgnanii* (*Russian Literature in Exile*).

[3] For the early post-Revolutionary work of Sologub (1863–1927), Gumilyov (1886–1921), Akhmatova (1889–1966), and Mandelstam (1891–1938), see Mirsky, *Contemporary Russian Literature*. Much of Sologub's work of the last years remains unpublished to this day. A volume of Gumilyov's unpublished poems, as well as a collection of his stories and a volume of critical essays, appeared posthumously in 1922 and 1923. Since then, except for a few poems in anthologies in recent years, his work has been published only outside the Soviet Union. These publications culminated with the critical four-volume edition of his *Collected Works* (ed. by G. Struve and B. Filippov). The role of Mandelstam and Akhmatova in post-Revolutionary literature will be discussed in the proper chronological context. For Voloshin see Mirsky, *Contemporary Russian Literature*. Much of his poetry remains unpublished.

importance. All three had stood in the forefront of the Symbolist movement. Many of their friends and literary allies regarded their acceptance of the Bolshevik Revolution as an act of treachery, a betrayal of their ideals and of Russia. Blok especially many of his friends found it difficult to forgive. Bely had always been too irresponsible, morally and politically, to be taken seriously. In Bryusov's adherence to the Revolution the element of calculation and timeserving played a large part. Quickly forgetting the patriotic poems in which he had extolled Russian victories in the war, he now hastened to join the Communist party (of the three he alone took this step) and received an appointment under the new Commissariat of Education.[4]

Alexander Blok's welcome to the Revolution was a different matter: there was in it a note of deep and anguished sincerity. The Revolution to him was much more than just a political, economic, and social change. It was the crumbling of a whole world, of the old bourgeois, humanistic culture, the hatred for which is sounded so strongly in his pre-Revolutionary diaries and letters. As early as 1909 he wrote in a letter from Italy to his mother: "More than ever I see that to my dying day I shall not accept anything of contemporary life, nor submit to anything. Its disgraceful order makes me feel nothing but revulsion. No longer can anything be changed—no revolution will change it."

Blok (1880–1921)

But when the revolution did come at last, Blok saw it as a beneficial spiritual storm, the beginning of a great transformation. And he responded to it, early in 1918, with his two famous poems *Dvenadtsat'* (*The Twelve*) and "Skify" ("The Scythians"), which can be regarded as the starting point of post-Revolutionary literature. Both were first published in the newspaper *Znamya Truda* (*Banner of Labor*), the organ of the Socialist Revolutionaries of the left, at that time the only party, outside the Bolsheviks, adhering to the new regime. Both poems soon won great popularity and were recited at literary meetings. Two years later, in April, 1920, Blok wrote an explanatory note about the genesis of *The Twelve*, in which he said:

In January 1918, for the last time I yielded to the elements no less blindly than in January 1907 or in March 1914. If I do not recant what I wrote then, it is because it was written in accord with the elements: for example, at the time of writing *The Twelve* and after finishing it, for several days I felt physically, with my ears, a great noise around, a continuous noise (probably the noise of the crumbling of the old world). Therefore, those who see in *The Twelve* a political

[4] Valery Bryusov (1873–1924) wrote a great deal of poetry after 1917 and was also active as a critic. Although in his post-Revolutionary poetry there were new notes (he was the only one among the older Symbolist poets to succumb to the influence of Futurism and also to accept the Revolution unreservedly—at least on the surface), this later work adds nothing to the essential Bryusov, whose best poetry was produced before 1912. There are many Soviet editions of Bryusov's verse (though not of his prose) and several critical studies about him.

poem are either very blind to art, or are immersed ear-deep in political mud, or
are possessed by great wrath, whether they be enemies or friends of my poem.

The poem is now generally recognized as one of Blok's masterpieces and
one of the greatest works produced by the Revolution. It is a vision of the
streets of Petrograd in the early days of the Revolution, when murder,
looting, and drunkenness were rampant. A patrol of Red Guards, twelve
soldiers of the Revolution, is marching along the streets. The only "incident" in the poem is the killing of Katka, a prostitute, the faithless friend
of one of the soldiers. The rest of the poem consists of short, fragmentary
scenes of the Revolution in Petrograd, scenes imbued with irony and pathos.
Blok's familiar motif of the blizzard, here symbolizing also the Revolution,
runs through the poem. The combination of realism and symbolism, the
rich polyphonic quality of the poem, full of sudden rhythmical breaks and
transitions, the skillful use of the rhythms and language of factory songs
create a powerful and striking effect. This effect, however, does not depend
on any message. Did Blok intend any message? The poem ends with a
pointe which to many appeared as its real intended message. Here we see
the Twelve marching along, followed by the mangy dog which throughout
the poem symbolizes the old defeated world, and preceded by Christ:

> So they march with sovereign tread:
>   Behind them a hungry dog,
> Before them, with a bloodstained banner,
>   Unseen through the blizzard,
>   Unscathed by the bullets,
> With soft step above the storms,
> In a pearly whirl of snow,
>   With a white halo of roses,
>   Before them—Jesus Christ.[5]

The wording is ambiguous. Is Christ leading the Twelve (whose number
seems symbolically significant)? Or are they shooting at him, suspecting in
him an enemy lurking round the corner in the winter darkness? The
former interpretation is the more usual, and was probably the one intended
by Blok. When Gumilyov, in a lecture about Blok in June of 1919, reproached Blok for bringing in Christ and said it seemed to him artificial, aimed at a purely literary effect, Blok replied: "I don't like the ending
of *The Twelve* either. I wish it were a different one. When I finished it I
was myself surprised: 'Why Christ?' But the more I looked at it, the clearer
did I see Christ. And I wrote down then and there: 'Unfortunately,

[5] I give this passage in my own translation, aiming at the greatest possible accuracy
and disregarding the subtle beauty and music of the original. All the existing English
verse translations take some liberties with Blok's text. That of Babette Deutsch and
Avrahm Yarmolinsky, otherwise perhaps the best, destroys the effect of Blok's am-
biguity by making his Christ *lead* the Twelve.

Christ.' "[6] Actually what Blok wrote in his *Notebooks* was: "That Christ is marching before them is beyond doubt. The point is not whether 'they are worthy of Him': what is terrible is that He again is with them, and there is no other so far. But must there be the Other—?" These cryptic words still do not make the meaning of the poem's ending quite clear. Is Christ leading the Twelve? Are they marching toward him? If so, who is "the Other"? Antichrist? But the value of the poem, I repeat, is not in its message.

"The Scythians" is not one of Blok's great poems, though its popular appeal was—and in some circles still is—greater than that of *The Twelve*. It is an effective piece of rhetorical poetry, an impassioned appeal to the West, on behalf of the new Revolutionary Russia, to join the cause of peace and revolution. In form it bears a resemblance to Pushkin's famous poem "To the Slanderers of Russia," written after the suppression of the Polish insurrection in 1831. It exploits also the Dostoyevskian motif of the receptivity of the Russian genius, open to all outside influences and stimuli, as well as the motif of the "yellow peril" found in Vladimir Solovyov's poem "Pan-Mongolism." It strikes a Slavophile, and at the same time a pacifist, note. Those who believe in Russia's apartness from the West are fond of quoting it. It has some powerful lines and lends itself well to declamation. It is a modern revolutionary ode.

With those two poems Blok seems to have spent both his poetic power and his revolutionary ardor and enthusiasm. The last two years of his life were marked by silence and by growing disillusionment bordering on despair and accompanied by a rapid weakening of his physical forces. He died on August 7, 1921, in hungry, blockade-bound Petrograd, after all attempts by his wife and friends to obtain for him permission to go abroad to recuperate had failed. One of his last appearances before the public was some six months before his death, in February, 1921, when at the commemoration of the anniversary of Pushkin's death he delivered an address that, in the history of Russian literature, will be remembered alongside Dostoyevsky's famous address of 1880. Blok spoke of the "mission of the poet," and his speech, in which he enjoined his audience to remember a few truths and swear to them "in the gay name of Pushkin," was an almost deathbed profession of an ineradicable belief in the freedom and independence of art. Quoting Pushkin's line, "There is no happiness in the world, but there is peace and freedom," Blok said: "*Peace and freedom*. The poet needs them to release harmony. But peace and freedom are also taken away. Not the outward peace but the creative. Not the childish freedom, the freedom of being a liberal, but the freedom of creation, the secret freedom. And the poet dies because he can no longer breathe: life has lost its meaning." The same day he wrote his last poem, a wonderful short poem

[6] K. Chukovsky, *Aleksandr Blok kak chelovek i poèt* (*Alexander Blok as Man and Poet*), 27–28.

inscribed in the album of the Pushkin House of the Academy of Sciences and dated "February 11 [January 29], 1921." Here, just as in his Pushkin address, he referred to that "secret freedom" which Pushkin had sung.

Six months later Blok died because he, too, could no longer breathe and life had lost for him its meaning. His diaries and notebooks for the last two years are full of tragic references to the deafness which had suddenly submerged him who had been endowed with such a hypersensitive ear. Music was gone, not only out of the Revolution, but out of life.

Soon after Blok's death a man named A. Leo, who said that he was an artist friend of Blok's, published, in a Russian newspaper in Berlin, a letter from Blok containing an unfinished poem in which in effect he recanted *The Twelve*. The authenticity of the poem seemed plausible to many students and admirers of Blok's poetry. His authorship was never either confirmed or denied, no more was heard about it, and to this day the origin of the poem remains a mystery.

Bely Of all the great figures of the period of Symbolism, Andrey Bely (pseudo-
(1880–1934) nym of Boris Nikolayevich Bugayev) continued longest in post-Revolutionary Russia, and, although he failed to integrate himself in the new Soviet literature, some account of his post-Revolutionary work is necessary.

A revolutionary by temperament, and extremely sensitive to the flavor of the epoch, Bely was one of the few older writers who "accepted" the October Revolution. But, like Blok, he saw in it what he chose to see and not what it really was. He welcomed it not as a political, economic, and social revolution but as a great religious and cultural transformation; as an end of the old world, which fulfilled the Symbolists' eschatological expectations; as that catastrophe which he and his like never tired of predicting; as a national upheaval which would enable Russia to assume world leadership and fulfill her universal mission. A disciple of Rudolf Steiner, he visualized that mission through the prism of anthroposophy. But, unlike Blok, his acceptance of the Revolution did not achieve an adequate poetic expression. Its only direct outcome was his grandiloquent poem *Khristos Voskres* (*Christ Is Risen*), which can bear no comparison with Blok's *The Twelve*. During the years of War Communism, Bely, like many other writers who stayed behind in Russia, was active, teaching in various literary studios and giving public lectures. He founded the Free Academy of Philosophy (known under its abbreviated name Volfila) and was the leading spirit behind the publishing enterprise called the Scythians. His long poem *Pervoye svidanie* (*The First Meeting*, 1921), of frankly retrospective nature, recalling the atmosphere of his youth and giving a picture of life of the Moscow intellectual elite in the first years of the present century, is a work of great charm, combining effectively the two important elements of Bely's art: his irrepressible verbal inventiveness and his puckish, realistic humor. It is Bely at his best. On the other hand, the volume of lyrical poems, published in 1922 under the title *Posle razluki* (*After the Parting*), adds nothing to his stature as a poet.

More important is Bely's post-Revolutionary prose work. It can be divided into works of fiction and memoirs. Among the former the most original and significant is a short "autobiographical" novel *Kotik Letayev*, published in 1922 but written before 1917. This work inevitably calls to mind James Joyce, although there can be no suggestion of mutual influence. Its subject is the formation of a child's consciousness. It begins with prenatal experiences and shows the gradual process of the formation of the child's perception of and reaction to the external world. Written in Bely's customary rhythmical prose, full of musical associations, with more than his usual amount of daring word creation (and in this case more than ever justified), it has been rightly described as a work of genius,[7] though it can hardly be to the taste of many readers, and many of its anthroposophic implications will be understandable only to the initiated. Its sequel, *Prestuplenie Nikolaya Letayeva* (*The Crime of Nikolay Letayev*, 1921), later revised and renamed *Kreshchony kitaets* (*A Baptized Chinaman*), though full of typical "Belyisms," is much less abstruse and is set on a realistic plane.

These two works were meant as part of a larger autobiographical whole with which Bely did not, however, proceed. Instead, after 1923 he wrote three other novels, forming a sequence and also incomplete—*Moskovsky chudak* (*A Moscow Crank*), *Moskva pod udarom* (*Moscow Exposed*), and *Maski* (*Masks*). These works have a highly improbable, melodramatic plot, involving scientific secrets, German spies, and Communists, and the typical Bely mixture of realism and fantastic delirium. There are, however, some extremely effective nightmarish scenes. The plot, for all its improbability, is handled skillfully, but some of Bely's usual defects—the monotonousness of his rhythmical prose, the unreal abstractness of his psychological presentation, the rather tiresome puns and neologisms—are more conspicuous than in his earlier novels. The essential and irreconcilable dualism of Bely's nature—Bely the irrational dreamer and Bely the admirer of abstract and rational schemes—is apparent in them. Unlike *Kotik Letayev*, which, even if a failure, was a brilliant failure, and an anticipation of Joyce's most daring experiments in technique, these last novels of Bely did not constitute a step forward or open new vistas to literature.

In 1922, Bely went to live in Berlin, as did several other Soviet writers. There he edited the literary magazine *Epopeia*, took part in the *émigré* literary life, and at one time apparently contemplated remaining abroad. However, he went back to Russia in 1923. While in Berlin he continued working on his *Recollections of Alexander Blok*, parts of which had appeared before and which were now printed in *Epopeia*. This is one of Bely's

---

[7] Mirsky, *Contemporary Russian Literature*, 234.

most interesting works; for a student of Blok and of Russian Symbolism it is invaluable. On his return to Russia, Bely did his best to harness himself to the cart of the Revolution, but his efforts ended in a pathetic fiasco. His attitude toward the Revolution lacked consistency. Its political aspect was alien to him, and he could not possibly feel congenial to it. Despite his essential dualism and all his intellectual and spiritual vagaries, his outlook on the world was fundamentally religious and idealistic, and he could have no sympathy with dialectical materialism. All his professions to the contrary were insincere.

During the last years of his life Bely was engaged on his *Memoirs*, three volumes of which appeared between 1929 and 1933: *Na rubezhe dvukh stoletiy* (*On the Border of Two Centuries*), *Nachalo veka* (*The Beginning of a Century*), and *Mezhdu dvukh revolyutsiy* (*Between Two Revolutions*). In one of them he incorporated his *Recollections of Blok* in a thoroughly revised form. For a historian of Russian Symbolism these memoirs are a source of valuable information. For an understanding of Bely himself they are indispensable. As literature, they are a brilliant piece of work. All the best and all the most annoying of Bely is to be found in them. But their value as memoirs is more than doubtful. Veracity was never Bely's strong point; all who knew him well agree on this. In his account of the events of the past Bely is as elusive, as unaccountable, as subjective, and ultimately as untruthful as he was in life. The element of personal rancor is obvious (the way in which he revised the account of his relations with Blok is only the most glaring example among many). Throughout one feels a tendency—often undoubtedly dictated by political considerations—to read a new meaning, in the light of subsequent happenings, not only into the events of the past but even into the author's inward experience. Much of what he tells us in his memoirs has to be taken with more than a pinch of salt; his omissions and evasions are numerous; and even his factual statements have to be checked with other sources. Nevertheless, these three volumes remain a valuable and interesting document of one of the most brilliant and exciting periods in the history of Russian literature, in which Bely himself played one of the leading roles. Some of Bely's portraits of his contemporaries, bad history though they may be, are certainly brilliant literature.

Bely's place in Russian literature is important not only on account of his personal contribution to it but also because of the influence which he, especially through his prose fiction, exercised on the young generation of post-Revolutionary writers. The musical, contrapuntal prose of his *Symphonies*; the system of shifting, dislocated planes in his novels; his experiments with the Russian language, both in vocabulary and in syntax, have all left their traces in the work of Zamyatin, of Boris Pilnyak and his school, in Fedin's *Cities and Years*, in some of the early work of the young proletarian writers, in the historical novels of Yury Tynyanov, and so on. Bely's poetry had a great influence on Russian Futurists and Imaginists and on the so-called Cosmists, while his studies of Russian prosody largely determined the work of the Formalist school in literary science and criticism. In fiction, however, none of his disciples have produced anything equal to their master's best work. In the long run Bely's tradition in Russian prose fiction did not prove enduring; the influence of Leskov and Remizov, which went parallel with it, was more fruitful and lasting. Of late, as will be seen, there has been a reaction against all experimentation à la Bely. Whatever may lie in store for Russian literature, Bely will never be regarded as a typical figure of its "Soviet" period. His place, including his post-Revolutionary work, is in the age of Symbolism.

Chapter 2. **RUSSIAN FUTURISM**

Russian Futurism developed as a movement parallel to, but ideologically independent from, the Italian Futurism of Marinetti. Its beginnings can be traced to 1910. From the very first the movement lacked true homogeneity and split into a number of factions—the Cubo-Futurists, the Ego-Futurists, and others.[1] The factions had, however, one common denominator—a tendency toward innovation at all costs. Rejecting uncompromisingly all art of the past, they looked toward an art of the future. They spoke of throwing Pushkin and Dostoyevsky, Raphael and Michelangelo "overboard the ship of modernity." The movement was essentially revolutionary and, in ideal at least, cosmopolitan, though in some of its representatives (in Khlebnikov especially) there was a strong nationalist, "Slavophile" strain. Futurism as a whole was a reaction against both the leading currents of contemporary Russian literature: against Realism, with its "truthful" representation of reality, and against Symbolism, with its transformation of reality in the name of a higher one.

The object of art, said one of the early leaders of Russian Futurism, David Burlyuk (1882–1967), who was both a poet and a painter, was neither to reflect nature nor to transform it but "to *deform* it such as it is fixed in individual consciousness." Art was autonomous, it had no object outside itself, and it was not in any way "co-related" with the world. Fundamentally, this aesthetic credo, which implied an anticivic attitude, was much closer to Symbolism than to Realism, and it is possible, therefore, to say that Futurism was a continuation of Symbolism, with which it had some sources and antecedents in common (the poetry of Rimbaud and Mallarmé, for example). However, since Symbolism at the time dominated the literary stage in Russia, Futurism was also a revolt against some of the tenets and practices of Symbolism, and especially against all attempts to invest poetry with philosophical or religious meaning or message.

Some of the extreme Futurists went very far in their effort to revolutionize the very medium of art. In poetry that meant the language (there were parallel movements in painting and in music, and some of the Futurists, like the brothers Burlyuk, were active in more than one field). To revolutionize the language the Futurists were prepared to divest it of

[1] There is now a valuable detailed study of pre-Revolutionary Russian Futurism in all its ramifications, embodying a wealth of previously unexplored material: Vl. Markov, *Russian Futurism: A History.*

meaning. In one of their publications, *Troye* (Moscow, 1913), they proclaimed that words, "hitherto fettered to the meaning," must be freed from this dependence, and a new "trans-sense, or metalogical, language" (*zaumny yazyk*, or *zaum'*) was to replace the ordinary human speech. Among the Futurists, Khlebnikov and Alexey Kruchonykh (1882–1968) were the most prominent representatives of this trend.

Velimir (Victor) Vladimirovich Khlebnikov was one of the founding **Khlebnikov** fathers of Russian Futurism and one of its most colorful figures. His poetic **(1885–1922)** talent was recognized from the outset even by those who had little sympathy with Futurism. The Acmeist Gumilyov characterized him as a visionary and spoke of the "dreamlike" character of his verse and of the "persuasive paradoxicalness" of his ideas.

Khlebnikov did not play an important personal part in post-Revolutionary literature, although many of his poems appeared in the early years of the Revolution in various Futurist publications. He had always been rather careless about his own work, writing his poems on scraps of paper that came to hand and shoving them casually into a sack or a pillow case which he carried about with him. Even before the Revolution he had sometimes led the life of a tramp. "There were no material relations between him and the world," said Olesha.[2] This characteristic became even more pronounced after the Revolution. He wandered about Russia and at one time found himself with the Red Army in Persia. He died, at the same age as Pushkin, in misery and solitude in a country-hospital bed.

Before the Revolution, Khlebnikov had the reputation of an eccentric. Some people regarded him as a genius; others thought him a madman. He took a great interest in linguistics and in mathematics and made an attempt to forge a link between those two disciplines and history by working out what he called "Laws of Time" and drawing up "Boards of Destiny." He also founded a kind of Utopian International of his own and called himself "President of the Globe." During his lifetime his literary influence did not match Mayakovsky's, but by the mid-twenties he had emerged as one of the greatest poetic influences of the period, and something of a cult of Khlebnikov developed in highbrow Soviet literary circles. Many poets of the younger generation—Tikhonov, Selvinsky, Bagritsky, Zabolotsky, and Kirsanov, among others—were in various degrees influenced by him, and even such established poets as Mandelstam and Pasternak succumbed to some extent to his influence. A great interest in Khlebnikov was shown by some of the leading critics of the Formalist school, among them Tynyanov and Roman Jakobson. Some aspects of his life gave rise to a legend not unsimilar to that of Rimbaud. A group calling itself Friends of Khlebnikov was founded in the late twenties. Among its members were Pasternak and

[2] Yu. Olesha, *Izbrannye sochineniya* (*Selected Works*), 447.

Olesha, and the latter's prose fiction was to some extent influenced by Khlebnikov, who also had written some stories.

Five volumes of Khlebnikov's works were published between 1928 and 1933, with long and interesting introductory articles by Tynyanov and N. Stepanov. In 1936 a volume of *Selected Poems* was published, with a biographical sketch by Stepanov, and in 1940 a volume of previously unpublished works appeared. After World War II, in line with the new party policy (see Part VII for details), Khlebnikov came to be described as "a poet for the aesthetes," "a Formalist," and "a decadent."[3] Subsequently he was completely ignored until after Stalin's death. In 1956, Olesha devoted to Khlebnikov a page in the fragment of his diary (included in the volume of his *Selected Works*). A short entry on Khlebnikov appeared in one of the last volumes of the Soviet *Large Encyclopaedia* (which would not have been the case if the volume had been published between 1946 and 1953), and some of his poetry was included in the jubilee anthology of Soviet poetry, published in 1957.[4]

Oriented both toward the future and toward the past, Khlebnikov cut a strangely archaic figure among the Russian Futurists. His "trans-sense" language (*zaum'*), for which he drew upon Russian etymologies, differed radically from the purely arbitrary and artificial "invented" language of some of the extreme Futurists. And many of his poems were written without any trace of *zaum'*, even if the conventional *usus* of language was violated in them. He showed his "archaic" tendency also in his choice of pagan Slavic mythology as the background of many of his earlier poems.

As a poet Khlebnikov still awaits a thorough investigation. He will probably always remain a poet for the few, a poets' and critics' poet, without a wide appeal. Olesha said of him: "The reading of his verses is a very tough job—everything is so tangled, there is such a mess, but suddenly you light upon something of incomparable beauty."[5]

In addition to a large quantity of lyrical poetry, Khlebnikov wrote several longer works in verse, of which the following may be mentioned here: *Ladomir* (1920), a poem about a future Utopia; *Truba Gul-Mully* (*The Trumpet of Gul-Mullah*, 1921), based on his impressions of Persia; *Nochnoy obysk* (*The Nocturnal Search*, 1920), a strange and powerful work describing a clash between the two opposing camps during the early days of the Revolution, in which one can hear some echoes of Blok's *The Twelve*, but which strikes a tenser and more tragic chord and introduces an unexpected religious motif; and *Zangezi* (1922), a dialogue between a philoso-

---

[3] See B. Yakovlev, "Poèt dlya èstetov" ("A Poet for the Aesthetes"), *Novy Mir*, No. 5 (1948), 207–31.

[4] *Antologiya russkoy poèzii v dvukh tomakh, 1917–1957* (*An Anthology of Russian Poetry in Two Volumes, 1917–1957*), I, 168–74.

[5] Olesha, *Izbrannye sochineniya*, 447.

pher and the crowd, which Vladimir Markov has described as Khlebnikov's "confession" and an encyclopaedia of all his literary and poetic experiments.[6]

In the words of another Khlebnikov enthusiast, the Italian Slavist Ripellino, who described Khlebnikov as "a continent," the Revolution of 1917 was for Khlebnikov "a destruction of the old order, a rebellion of the poor, a retribution, a return of Razin and Pugachov." In this sense his approach had an affinity with that of Blok and Bely, as well as that of Esenin. The motif of retribution comes out clearly in *The Nocturnal Search*.

In a way the most outstanding and "representative" figure of the Russian Futurist movement was Vladimir Vladimirovich Mayakovsky, and it was his personal ascendancy that made the close alliance between Futurism and the new Soviet regime such an important factor in the history of the first decade of Soviet literature.

Mayakovsky (1893–1930)

Mayakovsky did not adhere at once to the Futurist movement, with its distinctly asocial tendency. At an early age he manifested an interest in political and social questions and, when still at school, joined the Bolshevik faction of the Social Democratic party. This act resulted in his expulsion from school. Later he studied in the Moscow School of Painting and Sculpture, showing considerable talent as an artist. In 1911 he became associated with Burlyuk and was drawn by the latter into the Futurist movement. In 1912 he was one of the signatories of the Futurist manifesto entitled *Poshchochina obshchestvennomu vkusu* (*A Slap in the Face of Public Taste*), and after that for some years he played the leading part in various activities of the Futurists intended to scandalize the philistine public. The bright yellow blazer he wore became the symbol of the Futurist challenge to all bourgeois conventions. He traveled about Russia, lecturing and giving recitals of his poetry.

Mayakovsky's work of 1912–13 came closest to the theoretical demands of Futurism, but, although it lacks the simplicity and mass appeal of his later work, he never composed trans-sense poetry or acceded to the other excesses of Khlebnikov and Kruchonykh. He shared, however, the Futurists' general aversion to realism and to any "message" in art and spoke slightingly of the writers who were being made into "harbingers of truth and posters of virtue and justice." All a writer does, he said, is "to mold a skillful vase, and it is of no account whether wine or slops is poured into it." This glorification of

[6] On Khlebnikov see R. Jakobson, *Noveyshaya russkaya poèziya* (*Recent Russian Poetry*); A. M. Ripellino, "Chlebnikov e il futurismo russo," *Convivium*, No. 5 (1949); and V. Markov, "O Khlebnikove: Popytka apologii i soprotivleniya" ("On Khlebnikov: An Attempted Apology and Retort"), *Grani* (Frankfurt), No. 2 (1954). Markov also wrote a detailed study of a certain area of Khlebnikov's work in *The Longer Poems of Velimir Khlebnikov* and discussed at some length Khlebnikov's place in Russian Futurism in *Russian Futurism: A History*. Both of Markov's books are provided with excellent bibliographies.

form and indifference to content were, in Mayakovsky's case, purely superficial—mere lip service to the tenets of the Futurist credo. Soviet students
of Mayakovsky are probably right when they say that what attracted him to
Futurism was its apparent revolutionary spirit ("Down with all accepted,
traditional values!") and its universalism. Even in his most individualistic
early works his great concern with the surrounding realities, his deeply
rooted revolt against them, is easily discernible. This is particularly true of
his first important long work, the tragedy *Vladimir Mayakovsky* (according to Korney Chukovsky, Mayakovsky changed its title from *I* to *Vladimir
Mayakovsky* after reading Chukovsky's translation of Whitman's "Walt
Whitman,"[7] and still more so of such poems as "Man" (1917), "A Cloud in
Pants" (1915), and "War and the World" (1916). The last-named was a
protest against the war (parts of it were banned by censorship), although
at first the war had inspired some exhilaration in Mayakovsky, as may be
seen in some of his 1914–15 articles. Together with other Futurists he saw in
the war an opportunity for the Futurists to assert their supremacy in literature, just as later he was to see—and seize—such an opportunity in the
Revolution. He even sounded some Slavophile, anti-Western notes à la
Khlebnikov.

With all the differences between the early and the post-Revolutionary
Mayakovsky, some of the essential characteristics of his poetry are already
to be found in this earlier period. Without going to the excesses of the
trans-sense poets, he made a more lasting contribution to the deformation
of the Russian poetic language than any other Futurist. He deformed the
syntax, by use of both archaic inversions and elliptical locutions. He took up
and systematically developed some of the prosodic innovations of the Symbolists and Acmeists, discarding the traditional tonicosyllabic versification

---

[7] "Walt Whitman" was the title of "Song of Myself" in the third (1860) edition of
Leaves of Grass. See K. Chukovsky's Introduction to his translation of Whitman's
Leaves of Grass, 6–7, and A. V. Fyodorov's very interesting essay "Mayakovsky i litera-
tura Zapada" ("Mayakovsky and the Literature of the West"), in *Vladimir Mayakov-
sky* (ed. by A. L. Dymshits and O. V. Tsekhnovitser), 113. Both Chukovsky and
Fyodorov make much of Whitman's influence on the pre-Revolutionary Mayakovsky.
On the other hand, David Burlyuk, who introduced Mayakovsky to foreign poets
(Mayakovsky's knowledge of foreign languages was poor), later denied any influence
of Whitman on him. See A. Kaun, *Soviet Poets and Poetry,* 51–52. It is possible that
Mayakovsky's attitude toward Whitman was ambivalent. In his poetry there is at least
one derogatory reference to Whitman where the latter is bracketed with Longfellow.
However, Chukovsky's testimony to Mayakovsky's interest in Whitman's "eccentrici-
ties" is sufficiently authoritative and convincing. Cf. also quotations from Chukovsky's
reminiscences about Mayakovsky in *Repin, Gorky, Mayakovsky, Bryusov. Vospominaniya (Repin, Gorky, Mayakovsky, Bryusov: Memoirs)* and from his article on
Mayakovsky and Whitman in V. Katanyan, *Mayakovsky: Literaturnaya khronika
(Mayakovsky: A Literary Chronicle).* Katanyan's book is the most nearly complete
record of Mayakovsky's literary life and is invaluable to a student of the poet.

and substituting for it a verse based solely on the count of stresses in a line, with complete disregard of the intervening unstressed syllables. Thus he succeeded in creating an instrument that was both unmistakably his and eminently suited to his purpose of "depoetizing" the language of poetry, of approximating it to the language of the street and of the tribune.

It is the effective combination of the conversational, verging on the slang, with the rhetorical and the declamatory that is characteristic of Mayakovsky's diction. His verses are made to be declaimed. In his hands Russian verse lost the melodiousness which the Symbolists had endeavored to give it, but it gained in virility and in rhythmical power. Mayakovsky's rhythms are his forte. This process of "depoetization" was further enhanced by the deliberate use of a coarse, vulgar vocabulary and of unpoetic imagery, especially where nature was concerned. This tendency was general among the Futurists, but no one displayed it more thoroughly and consistently than Mayakovsky. A title like "A Cloud in Pants," or a comparison of stars with spittle, is a typical example of this unpoetic treatment of nature. There is much in the early Mayakovsky that resembles E. E. Cummings.

Another characteristic feature of Mayakovsky is his inordinate love of hyperbole. Himself an outsize man, measuring well over six feet and endowed with a stentorian voice, he always dealt in outsize images, and many of his effects were achieved through a combination of the grandiose with the grotesque.

Mayakovsky's favorite device was a long and elaborate metaphor—what the Futurists called "a realized metaphor"—and more often than not his metaphors were blatantly coarse, stripped of all conventional poetic veneer. He would compare himself to a sun-scorched July pavement on which a woman throws cigarette stubs of kisses; speak of the unwanted, flabby moon wobbling beyond the suns of the streets or of the street being fallen in like the nose of a syphilitic, or compare a crowd to a hundred-headed louse bristling its legs and rubbing them against the butterfly of the poet's heart.

In the Bolshevik Revolution, Mayakovsky saw the opportunity he had been looking forward to—of placing his art in the service of the people. Although not an orthodox Futurist in the earlier sense of the word, he had become the acknowledged leader and spokesman of Futurism, which in its turn came to be regarded as the extreme left in art. The primary task of the Bolsheviks, when they won power in October, 1917, was to do away with the bourgeois institutions and the bourgeois mentality. The Futurists had always professed hatred for the bourgeoisie and all it stood for. Hence the natural tendency of Futurism not only to ally itself with the new regime but also to identify itself with the Revolution. Many of the Futurists cared little for the political or social revolution per se, but they saw in it a wonderful chance for carrying out under its cover their own revolution in the field of art. So they made a bold bid to secure a virtual monopoly in that field. Their official organ, *Iskusstvo Kommuny* (*Art of the Commune*), openly spoke of a Futurist dictatorship in the realm of art, parallel to the dictatorship of the proletariat on the political and economic plane.

In its first number this magazine printed an article by Osip Brik, a friend of Mayakovsky and one of the principal theoreticians of Futurism, entitled "The Draining of Art." New art, wrote Brik, must break completely with the bourgeois art of the past. The object of art was to create new and unprecedented things. Artists must go to factories and plants to learn new ways. Futurism and proletarian art were synonymous. In another article Brik wrote, "Art shall be proletarian, or there will be no art at all."

This bid for supremacy was, in the early phases of the Revolution, encouraged by the first Soviet commissar for education, Anatoly Vasilyevich Lunacharsky (1875–1933). Prominent Futurists like Brik, Punin, and others were appointed to leading posts in the Commissariat of Education and placed in charge of literary, artistic, and theatrical policy. It was all the easier for the Futurists to conquer these key positions because most of the other writers kept aloof from the new regime or hastened to emigrate. Among the exceptions was Valery Bryusov, who joined the Communist party and also received an appointment under the Commissariat of Education. But the Futurists were already so powerful that even Bryusov was forced to play up to them. The abnormal conditions of life which prevailed during this period—with Russia torn by the Civil War and cut off from the outside world—made the publication of books very difficult, if not impossible, and literature continued mostly in the oral form. Poets gathered in cafés and taverns, especially in Moscow, and recited their new works. These cafés were for the most part monopolized by the Futurists and their principal rivals, the Imaginists (of whom more below). The whole period is therefore often spoken of as the "café period" of Russian literature.

Mayakovsky threw himself heart and soul into the Revolution. He described himself as its "drummer," and was accepted as such. Whether his revolutionary ardor had anything to do with a real sympathy with the "toiling masses" is doubtful. The more perspicacious among the Communist critics were fully aware of the fundamental loneliness of Mayakovsky and of his immeasurable egocentrism. It is perhaps this ineradicable sense of loneliness, of utter isolation from the people, that gives such truly tragic accents to the best poems of this self-styled bard of the Revolution, whose "Left March" became for a time its anthem. They are all about himself. Mayakovsky's only real, live hero is Vladimir Vladimirovich Mayakovsky, a man of flesh and blood, with raw skin. His other characters are just puppets. And the Revolution, as we see it in his poetry, is, after all, a gigantic puppet show played out among the gaudy cardboard *décors* and Rosta[8] posters of his own designing. The Revolution was for him a means

[8] Russian Telegraphic News Agency.

of escaping from himself, though in the end it was he who escaped from the Revolution. Nevertheless, he welcomed the opportunity of placing his art in the service of the masses and began writing feverishly propagandistic verses, issuing "Orders of the Day" to "the Army of Art," giving pep talks to fellow artists and writers, and designing more posters for Rosta, which were displayed for the public in the agency's windows and were accompanied by terse epigrammatic lines on topical subjects in the style of popular factory ditties.

This "agit-poetry," as it was called, enjoyed a great success during the Civil War. In it Mayakovsky retained certain characteristic features but discarded some of his earlier sophistication. Simplicity and directness of appeal became his primary aims. Theater being regarded by the new regime as one of the most effective means of mass propaganda, and therefore particularly encouraged, Mayakovsky wrote for it his "dramatic poem," called *Misteriya-Buff* (*Mystery-Bouffe*), a glorification of the Bolshevik Revolution and a vision of the coming millenium, a sort of a cross between a grandiose parody of medieval mysteries and a Russian popular play, with a multitude of characters and elaborate stage machinery. It was first performed publicly in the Petersburg Musical Drama Theater on November 7, 1918. A later version, produced in 1921 in Moscow, was directed by Vsevolod Meyerhold.

In 1920, Mayakovsky published his long poem *150,000,000*. Full of bombastic Soviet patriotism and revolutionary spirit, it was primarily an invective against the capitalist West which was personified in President Woodrow Wilson. Soviet Russia, with her one hundred and fifty million inhabitants, was personified in the hyperbolically heroic and unlifelike figure of the peasant Ivan. Here the satirical note which had always been prominent in Mayakovsky is very strong.

Later his satire was to be directed at some of the aspects of the new regime. Although in general Lenin disliked Mayakovsky's poetry, preferring such old poets as Pushkin and Nekrasov, he is said to have particularly admired one of Mayakovsky's satirical poems ridiculing the early Soviet mania for official meetings and portraying Soviet officials who had to take part in so many meetings that they attended them in halves—the upper half of the body at one meeting and the lower half at another. The poem ended with a pious wish for "a meeting to abolish all meetings."

Mayakovsky's humor is somewhat on the heavy side, but his use of the hyperbolic and the grotesque for satirical purposes is very effective. Foreign themes were also treated by Mayakovsky in this satirical vein, especially after he had visited the United States and Mexico, as well as Germany, France, and other European countries. He lectured on his travels all over Russia, accompanying his talks with recitals of his new poems. His personal popularity was great and his manner of reciting effective, and his programs drew large crowds.

Of the later fortunes of Mayakovsky and of Futurism more will be said in subsequent chapters.

Chapter 3. PEASANT POETS, THE PROLETKULT, AND THE COSMISTS

In 1918–21, Mayakovsky's popularity was equaled, and later it was even surpassed, by that of Esenin. One can say that the two shared the literary stage in the early, "heroic" period of the Revolution.

Sergey Alexandrovich Esenin came of true peasant stock. He grew up in his native village in the Ryazan Region, in central Russia, in the family of his grandparents, who were "Old Believers," in an atmosphere of strong religious traditions. This early religious background is clearly reflected in Esenin's poetry, even though much of his work is not only profane but frankly blasphemous. After graduating from the local parish school, Esenin went to Moscow and enrolled in the Shanyavsky Free University, working at the same time as a proofreader in a printing office. In 1915, on the way to his grandfather in Riga, he stopped in Petrograd. A meeting with Blok, to whom he read some of his poetry, decided his fate. He remained in Petrograd and devoted himself to literature. Blok introduced him to the leading poets of the time, and he became a regular visitor at the Symbolist salons and literary gatherings. The Symbolists were attracted by the fresh accents they discerned in the poetry of this good-looking, blue-eyed, golden-haired peasant youth. The rustic sources of Esenin's early poetry, published before the Revolution, full of colorful imagery and religious symbols and showing an inborn gift of song, are indubitable. He was hailed as a peasant poet, and fame came to him rapidly. But he himself acknowledged the debt he owed to his Symbolist masters, especially to Blok and Bely. In a short autobiographical note which Esenin wrote in 1925, he said, "Bely gave me a great deal from the point of view of form, while Blok and Klyuev taught me lyricism."

When the Revolution broke out, Esenin welcomed it enthusiastically. Like Blok and Bely, he saw in it a spiritual upheaval, a renewal, and more particularly a victory of the peasant, "wooden" Russia. His acceptance of the Revolution was tinged with messianic expectations. The political and social aims of the Communist party were alien to him; he was more in sympathy with the Socialist Revolutionaries, who claimed to represent the peasantry and its aspirations. It was the antiurban, anti-Western aspect of the Revolution as he saw it that appealed to Esenin, and he voiced these sentiments in the picturesque, blasphemous imagery of his poem *Inonia*, a vision of the coming "peasant paradise."

**Esenin
(1895–1925)**

In 1919, Esenin moved to Moscow and joined the literary group which called itself the Imaginists,[1] signing on its behalf a manifesto in which the new group claimed the legacy of Futurism which it pronounced "defunct."

During the years of War Communism the Imaginists were, besides the Futurists, the only organized literary group. Their attitude to the new regime was much more independent—at times even defiant. They had their own cafés in Moscow (one of them was called Pegasus' Manger), and their noisy and truculent behavior was one of the features of the literary life of this period. Next to Esenin, whose connection with the group was somewhat loose, although he was regarded as its leader, its principal representatives were Vadim Shershenevich (a former Ego-Futurist), Anatoly Marienhof, and Alexander Kusikov. The theory of Imaginism, with its stress on striking and daring images as the principal element of poetry, had nothing original in it, while in their practice the Imaginists followed in the wake of the Symbolists and the Futurists. What they had in common with the latter was their utter disregard of all taboos—the use of the coarsest language and the crudest imagery. But, unlike Mayakovsky and his followers, they lacked even the semblance of any healthy or vigorous optimism. Their attitude toward life was thoroughly pessimistic. They reveled in morbidity and perversions. Both their poetry and their behavior were full of bohemian rowdiness, and they were often involved in all sorts of drunken rows and scandals. Works like Esenin's "Ispoved' khuligana" ("Confession of a Rowdy") and "Moskva kabatskaya" ("Tavern Moscow"), or Marienhof's obscene and blasphemous poems, were typical of this aspect of Imaginism. In outspokenness of language the Imaginists left Mayakovsky and the Futurists far behind; beside Marienhof, Kusikov, and Shershenevich, Mayakovsky looks almost respectable.

With some of the poets this coarseness was merely a literary pose, an affectation dictated by the desire to *épater les bourgeois*, like the yellow blazers, painted faces, and carrots for buttonholes of the earlier Futurists and Cubists. But in Esenin's case this mood of rowdy despair and nihilistic defiance had deeper roots. The Revolution had deceived his expectations ("The stern October has deceived me," he wrote in one of his poems); the dream of a peasant paradise had failed to materialize. When the antipeasant industrial, urban, and proletarian aspects of the Revolution came to the fore, he felt a bitter disillusionment, which gave his poems a note of tragic despair. His "tavern" poetry sounds poignantly sincere. His ill-starred and short-lived marriage to Isadora Duncan in 1922 and the subsequent world tour marked the culminating points of this period of drunken rowdiness

[1] The proponents of Imaginism may have heard about Anglo-American Imagism, but their poetic theories were not identical with those of Thomas Hulme and Ezra Pound, which were, in some respects at least, closer to Russian Acmeism, and it is therefore advisable to distinguish between the two terms.

and reckless abandon. When he sobered, repentance came, followed by desperate attempts to adjust himself to the new conditions of life and to recapture something of the old closeness to the native soil from which he had forcibly uprooted himself. This mood found its expression in a number of poems about "Russia of the Soviets." He revisited his native village, but the experience was rather bitter.

While some of his later poems reflect the renewed spell of "wooden" Russia and are full of fresh and charming imagery, there is also in them the sad awareness that this new and unfamiliar rural Russia has no use for him or his poetry. In some poems of this period we see Esenin trying to reconcile himself with the new Russia in the process of industrialization and proletarianization, the symbol of which he saw in the "iron steed" (the railways).[2] This attempt at adjustment to something to which he was instinctively hostile proved a failure, and Esenin's suicide on December 25, 1925, came as a tragic but natural denouement, as the only possible way out of hopeless contradictions and entanglements.

Esenin will be remembered for his earliest and his last poems, with their simple, wistful, and melodious evocations of the Russian countryside. He had a true gift of song, and in his poems the spirit of Russian folk poetry was revived, even though he made no conscious attempt to reproduce its meters. His diction was closer to Nekrasov, Blok, and Bely, and later to Pushkin, to whom he felt irresistibly drawn in the last two years of his life. Some of his latest poems have the Pushkinian limpidity. But the personal Esenin ring in them is unmistakable. The texture of his verse, simple and musical, is the very opposite of Mayakovsky's. Esenin was essentially a lyric poet, and his attempt to write a large-scale work (*Pugachov*) ended in a failure. This would-be "tragedy in verse" remained a series of disjointed lyrical fragments of uneven value.

Esenin enjoyed an enormous popularity during his lifetime, and his sensational suicide in a room in the Hotel Angleterre in Leningrad (he cut his wrists, wrote his farewell poem with his own blood, and then hanged himself) enhanced it still further. It came at the height of widespread disillusionment engendered by the New Economic Policy, when suicides were becoming a frequent phenomenon. People were reminded of the suicide, only a year before, of the twenty-year-old proletarian poet Nikolay Kuznetsov, which had been widely talked about. The death of the popular poet recalled also the tragically early end of Russia's two greatest poets,

---

[2] In his reminiscences of Esenin the Soviet critic A. Voronsky quoted the following words of Esenin: "Mind you, I know you're a Communist. I am also for the Soviet power. But I love Russia. I shall not allow myself to be muzzled, nor am I going to dance to anybody's tune. It won't do." Esenin said this when he visited Voronsky at his editorial office soon after returning from his trip abroad. *Literaturnye portrety* (*Literary Portraits*), I, 247.

Pushkin and Lermontov. Esenin's popularity was great among all the classes of the population, but he was particularly popular with the younger generation, including the young Communists, members of the Komsomol (League of Communist Youth). This popularity rested partly on his "hooligan" poetry, which impressed by the sincerity of its boundless despair and self-castigation; but it was mostly due to his slightly sentimental, wistful, and melancholy pictures of rural Russia, full of genuine and peaceful love for his native land. At one time this popularity caused considerable misgivings in the official circles. "Eseninism" came to be spoken of as a dangerous disease undermining the Soviet body politic, as a sign of degenerate and debile individualism, incompatible with the prescribed optimistic attitude toward life.[3]

Esenin was only one of a number of poets who were prominent in the early years of the Revolution and who voiced the sentiments and aspirations of the Russian peasantry. This class, despite the supremacy attained by the Bolsheviks, regarded the Revolution—not without some justification—as its own achievement.

**Klyuev
(1885–1937)** Among the peasant poets the most interesting and original was Nikolay Alexeyevich Klyuev. His first book, published in 1912, attracted attention in the Symbolist camp. The Symbolists saw in Klyuev a disciple of theirs, but at the same time he was genuinely of the people, steeped in the folklore and religious "dissenter" tradition of northern Russia and full of mystical revolutionary "Populism," which appealed particularly to Alexander Blok. Later Klyuev was to guide the first steps of Esenin. Like Esenin, Klyuev welcomed the Revolution as a kind of mystical revelation of the "peasant paradise." It was the national Russian, or "Scythian," aspect of the Revolution that fascinated him. He wrote much revolutionary poetry, and in his *Lenin* portrayed a legendary figure of the Bolshevik leader from the standpoint of religious revolutionism, likening Lenin to Archpriest Avvakum, the leader of the seventeenth-century dissenters.

Unlike Esenin's poetry, Klyuev's is heavy and ornate, with a strong bookish and traditional background, full of exotic imagery, of North Russian local color, and of symbols of religious ritual, which in his case have a deep significance and are not used for mere outward effects as they often are in Esenin's. It is somewhat monotonous in its single-mindedness, but at his best Klyuev is a genuine and powerful poet. His disillusionment with the Revolution, which did not fulfill his dream of a peasant paradise on earth, was inevitable. Also unlike Esenin, he was not a *déclassé* peasant, but was deeply rooted in the traditional soil. He therefore viewed Esenin's attempts to integrate himself with city life, and especially his "rowdiness," as a be-

[3] G. Gorbachov, *Sovremennaya russkaya literatura* (*Contemporary Russian Literature*), 61.

trayal. But Klyuev was regarded by the orthodox Communist critics as a true embodiment of the "kulak" spirit among the peasants, and he soon fell out of favor and was reduced to silence. In 1933 he was arrested and exiled to Siberia. He died apparently in 1937—according to one official version, on the way to Moscow after his release; according to another, while being transferred from one place of exile to another.[4]

Many other peasant poets who were active during those early years of the Revolution—Pyotr Oreshin (1887–1938), Rodion Akulshin (b. 1896), Sergey Klychkov, and others—disappeared later from the literary stage.[5]

The Proletkult and the Cosmists

Parallel with the encouragement which the new regime gave to the Futurists as the only organized literary force that was willing and ready to support it unconditionally, attempts were also made, from 1917 on, to foster a specific proletarian literature and to train budding writers belonging to the new ruling class of industrial proletariat. This task fell to the lot of the so-called Proletkult (an abbreviation of Proletarian Culture). Its leading spirit was Bogdanov (pseudonym of Alexander Alexandrovich Malinovsky, 1873–1928), one of the early theoreticians of Russian Marxism, whom Lenin had earlier charged with Machian heresy.[6] Bogdanov's conception of the Proletkult was based on the assumption that the working class should advance toward Socialism along three parallel and independent roads: next to the political and economic action, which belonged to the competence of the Communist party and the trade-unions, respectively, Bogdanov placed the

[4] See B. Filippov's Introduction to his two-volume edition of Klyuev's poetic works, *Polnoe sobranie sochineniy* (*Complete Works*), I, 105–107. This was the first more or less complete edition of Klyuev's poetry and contained some previously unpublished material, including the long poem "Pogorelshchina" ("Scorched Earth"), written about 1930. The reading of it at various private gatherings is supposed to have been one of the reasons for Klyuev's arrest. Rich in religious symbolism and imagery and couched in highly ornamental language reminiscent both of folk poetry and of the Russian Orthodox liturgy, it is an impassioned evocation of and lament for Russia robbed and defiled. A later, even more nearly complete edition of Klyuev's work (*Sobranie sochineniy*), containing a number of newly discovered poems, appeared under the general editorship of G. Struve and B. Filippov. It contains valuable introductory articles by Filippov and Emmanuil Rais in Russian, by Gordon MacVay in English, and by Heinrich Stammler in German. In his native country Klyuev is still under a ban.

[5] Both Oreshin and Klychkov, as it transpired much later, when they were "posthumously rehabilitated," became victims of the Stalin purges in the late 1930's. Akulshin emigrated during World War II and is now living in the United States and writing under the name Rodion Beryozov. The whole problem of "posthumous rehabilitation" of "repressed" writers will be dealt with in greater detail in the sequel to this volume, in the context of the post-Stalin period.

[6] Bogdanov was influenced in his views by Ernst Mach's philosophy of empirio-criticism, which was a heresy to the orthodox Marxists.

cultural action, which was to be exempted from the control of the political mechanism of the Communist party. The Proletkult was to be a separate, autonomous organization, using its own methods.

In 1917–20 the Proletkult displayed great activity. It published its own magazine, *Proletarskaya Kultura* (*Proletarian Culture*); it convened an all-Russian conference to discuss the issue of proletarian culture; it organized all over Russia a great number of literary and artistic studios or training centers for workers, where the latter were taught by bourgeois literary specialists how to write verse and prose. Among those who taught in the studios were some of the leading pre-Revolutionary writers: Bryusov, Bely, Gumilyov, Zamyatin, and others. The Prolekult succeeded in drawing into its sphere of influence a number of writers from among factory workers, soldiers, and sailors, as well as some peasants.

In 1920 several proletarian writers who had seceded from the Proletkult formed in Moscow a literary group called Kuznitsa (the Smithy). Their counterpart in Petrograd was called Kosmist (the Cosmist). Most of the writers were poets: Vasily Alexandrovsky (1897–1934), Alexey Gastev (1882–1941), Mikhail Gerasimov (1889–1939), Vasily Kazin (b. 1898), Vladimir Kirillov (1890–1943), and Sergey Obradovich (1892–1956). Some of them had begun writing and publishing before the Revolution. Several of them were industrial workers and could boast of proletarian "blue blood." It was, however, not so much the proletarian origin as the acceptance of Communist ideology that qualified one as a proletarian writer.

The ideological content of the work produced by these poets satisfied this demand. It was full of revolutionary fervor, it extolled collectivism, and factory labor was its principal theme. But there was little that was specifically proletarian in their poetry. Their form, their technique, their methods, and often their vocabulary were largely derived from Symbolism, with a slight admixture of Futurism and Imaginism. The revolutionary message of their poetry was strongly tinged with romantic heroism. Factory themes were treated by most of them not in terms of everyday factory life but on a cosmic, planetary plane. Cosmic terminology, grandiloquent, hyperbolic images characterized most of these poets. They were guilty of some of the worst sins of Symbolism, the only difference being that the old Symbolist dishes à la Balmont were now being served up with industrial and revolutionary seasoning. Compared with what was being offered by Mayakovsky and his disciples, or even the Imaginists, there was little that was fresh and novel in these proletarian poets. One exception among the Smithy poets was Vasily Kazin, who, besides the usual "cosmic" poetry, wrote also simple down-to-earth poems about workers and artisans, in which he struck a fresh note.[7]

[7] Many examples of the work of the proletarian poets belonging to the Smithy and other groups, as well as of their theoretical pronouncements, will be found in Kaun,

The Cosmists, as they were often called in those days, followed at first the Futurists in their wholesale rejection of the art of the past. One of the most talented among them, Kirillov, in a poem called "My" ("We") summoned his fellow proletarians to destroy museums and burn Raphaels "in the name of our Tomorrow." But this was only a temporary phase, and two years later the same Kirillov wrote a poem in which he spoke of "radiant Pushkin" and other Russian classics as friends and allies of proletarian poets.

The problem of the cultural heritage of the past—of the attitude to be taken toward it in the new proletarian state—occupied the leaders of Communism at this time. It was this problem that revealed the first serious rift between the new regime and its Futurist allies. As early as December, 1918, Lunacharsky gave a warning to the Futurists when he wrote in *Art of the Commune*: "It would be a nuisance if the vanguard artists were definitely to imagine themselves as a state-sponsored school of art, representing official art, which, albeit revolutionary, is dictated from above." And he went on to say that one of the alarming features of the extreme left in art was its purely negative and destructive attitude toward the art of the past. Equally dangerous was its claim to speak in the name of the government while representing a specific school.

Lunacharsky himself, while flirting with Futurism and other advanced movements, advocated a reverent attitude toward the artistic heritage of the past, insisted on the necessity of preserving its monuments, which the Futurists and the Cosmists were eager to destroy, and enjoined proletarian artists to learn from the old masters. He disapproved of a similar tendency manifested at first by the extreme wing of the Proletkult (although not by Bogdanov himself), but on the whole the latter also enjoyed his protection. In this he was at variance with the top leaders of Communism, for both Lenin and Trotsky looked with disfavor upon the attempts of Bogdanov and the Proletkult to assert their independence and to carry out an isolated cultural action.

For the time being, however, the leadership of the Communist party was beset with other and more urgent problems arising out of the Civil War and foreign intervention, and did not interfere with the Proletkult, which was allowed to proceed with its plans for building up proletarian culture. It was at the end of 1920, when the Civil War was over, that Lenin put his foot down, and a decree was promulgated placing the Proletkult under the direct control of the Commissariat of Education. Three years later an end was put to it, and "Bogdanovism" was denounced as a dangerous deviation from the party line. But in summing up the achievements of Soviet literature during the first post-Revolutionary decade, most Soviet critics admitted the beneficial role of the Proletkult in initiating workers and peasants into

Soviet Poets and Poetry. Of the writers named above, Gastev, Gerasimov, and Kirillov became victims of Stalin's purges in the 1930's.

the artistic and cultural life, even though they continued to regard it on the whole as a failure. However, before the days of the Proletkult were over, other methods of fostering proletarian literature and art were proposed, and the whole subject of a specific class culture, and of its role in the new society, gave rise to a violent controversy, which will be discussed in the next chapters.

Agit-Poetry

Bedny No history of Soviet literature can be complete without at least a brief men-
(1883–1945) tion of Demyan Bedny (pseudonym, meaning "Damian the Poor," of Efim Alexandrovich Pridvorov). A Bolshevik of old standing, a regular contributor to *Pravda* and other Bolshevik papers before the Revolution, during the first years of the Revolution he held the position of unofficial poet laureate of the new regime. His poetry is simple, even primitive, entirely "civic-minded," and devoid of all personal motifs. It is not so much poetry as rhymed journalism on topical subjects. Before the Revolution he excelled in political fables, a form that was particularly suited for dodging the vigilance of censorship. Many of his fables were frank but skillful imitations of the great Russian fabulist Krylov. There is also in his poetry a strong influence of Nekrasov's civic verse. After the Revolution he wrote more topical fables, as well as songs, ditties, and satirical poems.

A peasant himself by origin, Bedny regarded the alliance between the proletariat and the peasants as essential for the success of the Revolution, and much of what he wrote was meant for the peasant audience and clothed in simple, easily accessible language. In one of his poems, Esenin refers, not without some contempt, to the popularity of Demyan in the post-Revolutionary village. One Soviet critic described Bedny as "the trumpeter" of the Revolution's battles and victories. His verses breathe a violent, unquenchable hatred of the upper classes. There is also in them a strong antireligious bias, and at the height of the Communist party's campaign against religion Bedny was one of its principal spokesmen and a regular contributor to *Bezbozhnik* (*The Godless One*). Regarded as the quintessence of proletarian "agit-poetry," Bedny's work was equally removed from Mayakovsky's and the Futurists', with their "decadent" tendency to innovations, and from the Cosmists', with their "industrial romanticism." Taken as a whole, his output is monotonous, repetitious, and crude. As propaganda poetry it served its purpose well, and Bedny's official reputation stood very high until 1936, when he was snubbed for his play *Bogatyri* (*Epic Heroes*), to which reference will be made later. Although the war against Germany gave him a chance to write more propaganda poetry, he somehow never recaptured his erstwhile popularity.

Part II. **Revolutionary Romanticism, 1921–24**

Chapter 4. **FROM WAR COMMUNISM TO THE NEW ECONOMIC POLICY**

It was something of a miracle that literature continued to exist, even in an embryonic form, during the terrible years of War Communism. In a country torn by civil war, ravaged by hunger, suffering from lack of fuel, the intelligentsia—writers, artists, journalists—was hit perhaps more severely than any other single group. Victor Shklovsky has left a grim picture of the conditions prevailing in Petrograd in the winter of 1920, when "all was ruin and hopelessness," and "to live at all was a battle," when people "stood in a queue to get one degree of heat," or chafed their hands with ashes to cleanse themselves. The cold was even a greater scourge than the hunger:

What did we use for heating? A few of the surviving bourgeoisie, having turned traders in saccharine and other imponderable stuff, burned wood. As for us others, we burned everything. I burned my furniture, my sculptor's stand, bookshelves and books, books beyond count or computation. If I had owned wooden arms or legs I should have burned them and found myself limbless in the spring.

One of my friends burned nothing but books. His wife sat by the little smoky iron stove and stoked and stoked it with journal after journal. Elsewhere doors were burning and furniture from other people's dwellings. It was a festival of universal destruction by fire. . . . People slept in their overcoats and very nearly in their galoshes.

Everyone gathered in the kitchen; in the abandoned rooms stalactites grew. People drew close to one another and in the half-empty city they squeezed together as tight as toys in a playbox. Priests in churches conducted the services in gloves with the surplices put on over their fur coats. Sick school-children froze to death. The Arctic Circle had become a reality and its line passed through the region of the Nevsky Avenue.[1]

After reading this matter-of-fact description of Shklovsky's, one can feel better the full force of Zamyatin's surrealistic vision of Petrograd and its "cave dwellers" in "The Cave," one of his most effective stories and one of the best "documents" of this period:

Glaciers, mammoths, wildernesses. Pitch-dark, black rocks, somehow reminding one of houses; in the rocks—caves. And one cannot tell who trumpets of a night along the stony path amid the rocks and, sniffing his way, drives the white

---

[1] Shklovsky, "St. Petersburg in 1920," *Bonfire: Stories out of Soviet Russia: An Anthology of Contemporary Russian Literature* (ed. by S. Konovalov). This passage is taken from Shklovsky's *Khod konya* (*Knight's Move*).

33

snow dust before him. It may be the grey-trunked mammoth; it may be the wind; and it may be that the wind is only the icy roar of some super-mammothish mammoth. One thing is clear: it is winter. And one must clench one's teeth as tight as possible, to prevent them from chattering; and cut wood with a stone axe; and each night move one's fire from cave to cave, always deeper; and muffle oneself up in an always increasing number of shaggy hides.

The story is of a couple of such cave dwellers over whose life presides an insatiable god—the iron stove:

> In this cave-bedroom of Petersburg, things were like in Noah's ark: clean and unclean creatures in ark-like promiscuity. Martyn Martynych's writing-desk; books; cakes of the stone-age looking like pottery; Skryabin, op. 74; a flat-iron; five potatoes lovingly washed white; nickelled bed-frames; an axe; a chest of drawers; a stack of wood. And in the middle of all this universe was its god: a short-legged, rusty-red, squatting, greedy cave-god: the iron stove.[2]

These horrors of everyday life reached their apogee in the winters of 1919–20 and 1920–21. The spring of 1921 brought with it some relief. The Civil War was practically over by November, 1920. Sporadic hostilities still went on in the Far East, but the organized and centralized resistance to the new order was at an end. However, soon after this military victory, the Soviet government, under the growing pressure of economic necessities and faced with the specter of peasant discontent, had to beat a retreat on the home front. In February, 1921, Lenin promulgated his famous decree inaugurating the New Economic Policy, which came to be commonly known as the NEP. This meant a partial restoration of a bourgeois economy, a loosening of the taxation screw applied to the peasants, and a resumption of private trade—in other words, the end of War Communism.

The year 1921 also inaugurated a new period in Soviet literature. The main factors which determined the change were the reappearance of private publishing enterprises,[3] the growth of book-printing and bookselling facilities, the resumption of cultural intercourse with the outside world, and the entry into literature of many new writers. Some of them had been fighting in the Red Army, and were now demobilized. Others were civilians whom the conditions of War Communism had deprived of a chance of exercising their vocation.

By 1922 the literary scene had undergone a number of changes. Publish-

---

[2] E. Zamyatin, "The Cave" (trans. by D. S. Mirsky), *The Slavonic Review* (London), Vol. II, No. 4 (June, 1923). There is also a translation of this story by Alex M. Shane in *Russian Stories* (Bantam Dual-Language book) and by Richard Ravenal in F. D. Reeve (ed.), *Great Soviet Short Stories*.

[3] Not all private publishers closed down during 1918–20. But the State Publishing Company (Gosizdat) wielded a virtual monopoly, and writers who like Alexander Blok refused to work for it were placed under a handicap. See the editorial in *Literaturnye Zapiski* (*Literary Notes*) (Petersburg), No. 2 (June 23, 1922).

ing enterprises grew like mushrooms. Many of them, it is true, were of an ephemeral nature. But there were some that flourished and gradually extended their activities even beyond the borders of the Soviet Union, organizing branches in Berlin, where postwar inflation proved highly propitious for this kind of activity and where a number of Soviet writers (Gorky, Bely, Shklovsky) were living at the time. Many books by Soviet authors published during 1922–23 bear the double imprint "Moscow-Berlin" or "Petersburg-Berlin." Some firms even published Soviet and *émigré* authors indiscriminately. At no other time was intercourse so easy among Soviet writers, *émigré* writers, and "borderline" writers (that is, either those who, escaping to Berlin, lived there as Soviet citizens but later chose not to return or those who, while still officially *émigrés*, were contemplating a return to Russia).

In Russia itself, several new magazines were launched. Privately sponsored—although in 1922 still subject to censorship and bearing the official imprimatur—they strike one today by the variety and freedom of the opinions expressed in them and by their quick and ready response to cultural developments outside Russia. One of the most typical, and also one of the best, was *Literaturnye Zapiski* (*Literary Notes*), published by the Dom literatorov (House of Writers) in Petrograd. An institution organized earlier, chiefly for the purpose of relieving the material hardships of writers' life, it was the meeting point of the old intelligentsia, mostly liberal and radical writers and journalists whom the suppression of the independent press had thrown out of work. Every number of this magazine contained a chronicle of literature abroad and reviews of foreign books, in original and in translation. *Émigré* literature was often discussed in a detached, impartial manner, and in one article the well-known pre-Revolutionary critic A. Gornfeld went so far as to compare it favorably with what was being produced in Russia. The literary policy of the new government came in for a share of outspoken criticism, and the general tone was one of dignified independence.

The magazine often attacked the Futurists and other literary hangers-on of the new regime. This was another sign of the change that had set in; and although the Futurists, their rivals the Imaginists, and the Cosmists continued to be as vociferous as before—each group claiming to be the only one truly representative of Revolutionary art—they no longer held the floor alone. Other forces came into play. With new facilities for publication of books, the predominance of the poets ended.[4] Prose writers appeared on the scene and soon captured the attention of the public. A list of the "most

[4] One critic said significantly at this time that "the death agony of poetry" had begun with the death of Blok and Gumilyov in the autumn of 1921. I. N. Rozanov, "Khudozhestvennaya literatura za dva goda" ("Imaginative Literature During the Two Years"), *Literaturnye Otkliki* (*Literary Echoes*), 72.

interesting" prose works published in 1921–22 contains over thirty titles.[5] Many of the authors whose works, both prose and verse, appeared during these first years of the NEP were newcomers to literature, but there were also among them older writers, most of whom were soon either to emigrate (Shmelyov, Zaytsev, Muratov, Georgy Ivanov) or to go silent (Sologub, Akhmatova, Kuzmin). Two books of Gumilyov's poems and a book of his stories appeared posthumously in 1922.

There were also ephemeral magazines and almanacs which printed both prose and verse. Of these publications particular interest attaches to *Knizhny Ugol* (*Book Corner*), edited by Victor Khovin. Six issues were published in 1918–19 and just one more in 1921. It published some interesting critical material and also many pieces by one of the most original Russian philosophers and essayists, Vasily Rozanov (1856–1919), including some posthumous ones. Before the Revolution, Khovin had been associated with the Ego-Futurists and had edited a magazine called *Ocharovanny Strannik* (*Enchanted Wanderer*). In one of the issues of *Knizhny Ugol* he made a rather sharp attack on Maxim Gorky. His subsequent fate is not known (there were rumors that he emigrated), and even the dates of his birth and death could not be established.

A "fat" monthly review—that indispensable feature of the Russian literary scene before the Revolution—was launched in 1921. Called *Krasnaya Nov* (*Red Virgin Soil*), it was edited by A. Voronsky, one of the most broadminded of the Marxist critics. This review and its editor were to play a prominent part in Soviet literary life during its most flourishing period. Another important review to be founded soon, under the editorship of Vyacheslav Polonsky, was *Pechat' i Revolyutsiya* (*Press and Revolution*). The latter had an extensive book-review section, which included reviews of many books published outside Russia.

The Revolutionary Romantics

The period of Soviet literature between 1921 and 1924 is sometimes described as the period of Civil War literature. This is true in the sense that the Civil War—and, in general, the period of War Communism—became one of the main themes of literature during this period. For many young writers it was a great and harrowing experience which they sought to transmute creatively. More generally, one can say that from this moment on the Revolution became the principal theme of Soviet literature.

The new prose writers desired, in the first place, to describe the Revolution, to put on record their experiences and the impressions gathered during those fantastic years. Their interest was centered on the elemental and romantic aspects of the Revolution, and the main trend of this period can be described as revolutionary romanticism. The Civil War; the partisan activi-

[5] *Ibid.*, 79.

ties on the fringes of Russia, in the South and in the Far East; the terrible famine which befell eastern Russia and the Volga region in 1921; violent conflicts between the old and the new as the Revolution ate deeper and deeper into the traditional mode of life; the gigantic reshuffle of the population, resulting in thrilling adventures—such were the staple themes of this early post-Revolutionary prose fiction. Its form, its manner, and its style were in harmony with the quick, staccato tempo of life. These young Soviet writers, bent on hurriedly recording their rich stock of experiences, cared little for long, elaborate, slow-moving novels in the old manner, or for large canvases. A short story, an anecdote—told in a hurry, brimful with incident, devoid of all psychological probing or detailed analysis—became the favorite form. Often these stories were written in a high-pitched emotional tone.

In the case of longer works, such as some of the "novels" of Pilnyak, Nikitin, and Vsevolod Ivanov, there was no unity of plot, the narrative being conducted simultaneously on several planes and constructed according to the laws of a musical theme with refrains and variations. From the formal point of view these newcomers to literature were greatly influenced by two prose writers of the age of Symbolism, Andrey Bely and Alexey Remizov.

To Bely can be traced their tendency to rhythmical prose, with recurring leitmotifs; their broken, disjointed composition, with constant shifting and intersection of the narrative planes; and their feverish, strained, hyperbolic diction. Through Bely these writers go back to Gogol more than to any other of the older Russian writers.

Remizov's influence, on the other hand, is felt in their predilection for pure anecdote, for ornamental speech, for *skaz*—that is, an exact rendering of the peculiarities, local and individual, of the spoken language—and for folklore stylizations. Through Remizov these young prose writers looked back to Leskov, the great nineteenth-century master of *skaz*. Thus, somewhat paradoxically, Gogol and Leskov became the most powerful and vital factors of influence in the shaping of post-Revolutionary Russian literature.

The grim experience of the Civil War, when the price of human life had slumped so visibly, taught writers to face with fearless indifference the most horrible sights and to speak with cool detachment of gruesome and terrible things. Stark realism, bordering on naturalism, and outspoken cynicism characterize many of the works of this period. But their realism is often frankly fantastic. So fantastic, so gruesomely unreal had life become in those days, such unexpected adventures did it hold in store, that the border line between the real and the unreal seemed to be obliterated. In setting out to be matter-of-fact and realistic, these poets of the Revolution often achieved their most fantastic effects: life had indeed become "stranger than fiction."

It was only gradually that out of this welter of what came to be described as "dynamic" or "ornamental" prose there emerged, toward 1924, definite literary genres—first, the short, pointed *nouvelles* of Babel, and later the novel.

Chapter 5. PROSE AND POETRY

Prose Writers

The dominant figure in Soviet literature during the years 1921–23 was Boris **Pilnyak (1894–1937)** Pilnyak (pseudonym of Boris Andreyevich Wogau). Born in Mozhaysk, he was the son of a veterinary surgeon and was descended on his father's side from the Volga-German colonists. His first story appeared in print when he was only seventeen, but his real literary debut was a short story published in 1915 in the review *Russkaya Mysl* (*Russian Thought*). This story, "Tselaya zhizn'" ("A Whole Life"), had no human characters. It was about an owl couple and their life in the woods. It revealed a characteristic which later came very much to the fore in Pilnyak's work: his interest in biological, and even animal, manifestations of life. Several stories of Pilnyak's were published in various reviews and magazines between 1917 and 1921. But it was the publication in 1922 of his "novel" *Goly God* (*The Naked Year*) that brought Pilnyak fame, placed him at the head of a whole school, or movement, in Soviet literature, and made Soviet critics speak of "Pilnyakism." Until the early thirties Soviet critics and historians of literature gave Pilnyak the credit for being the first young writer who chose the Revolution and its impact on Russian life as his main subject.

Any student of Pilnyak who undertakes to write a monograph about him faces great difficulties. Not only is Pilnyak an intrinsically difficult, complex, and chaotic writer, but there is also the additional, purely external, difficulty of disentangling the intricate chronology and interrelation of Pilnyak's writings. Many of his stories were published under different titles in different collections and combinations, while many others were subsequently incorporated bodily into his "novels." He also made a considerable revision of earlier versions of his stories for the uniform edition of his *Collected Works*, which began to appear in 1929 and was then planned for eight volumes.

The Naked Year is, in a way, the most typical of Pilnyak's works. Although it set the pattern for his later novels, it is no novel in the traditional acceptance of the term, but a loose collection of episodes, of which many were actually included as complete, separate stories in the volume *Bylyo* (*The Bygones*). This incompleteness, this lack of any unifying plot, is one of Pilnyak's primary characteristics, both in his short stories and in his longer works which he arbitrarily designates as "novels": *Mashiny i volki*

(*Machines and Wolves*), *Tretya stolitsa* (*The Third Metropolis*), *Cherto-polokh* (*Thistles*), and *Rossiya v polyote* (*Russia in Flight*).

As a writer Pilnyak is a direct descendant of Andrey Bely and Alexey Remizov, though other, and often contradictory, literary influences, both formal and ideological, are readily discernible in his work: above all, those of Gogol, Dostoyevsky, Turgenev, Leskov, Chekhov, Bunin, and Zamyatin. The influence of Bely and Remizov on Pilnyak is very strong, and it is largely through Pilnyak that these modern Russian prose writers exercised such a powerful sway over early post-Revolutionary literature.

From Bely comes Pilnyak's predilection for "musical," rhythmical, con-trapuntal prose, for persistent repetition of verbal refrains (in *The Naked Year* whole pages recur verbatim in different parts of the book); for lyrical and historico-philosophical digressions; and for rhetorical questions and exclamations, as well as for the highly involved syntax with a complex ag-glomeration of parenthetical clauses, of broken, unfinished sentences full of hints and allusions. It was Bely who cultivated this difficult manner, re-quiring a creative effort on the part of the reader; and Pilnyak is one of those writers whose subtle allusive method, abounding in hidden clues and "signs," usually necessitates a second reading for the complete understand-ing of much that at first reading appears obscure or even unintelligible. Back to Bely goes also the involved chronology in Pilnyak's novels, the constant shifting and interlocking of temporal planes. Another point which Pilnyak has in common with Bely is his interest in the problem of Russia's historical destinies—of the East and West in Russian history and psycho-logical make-up. Such a story of Pilnyak's as "Sankt-Pieter-Burgh" is really a variation on the theme of Bely's famous novel *Petersburg*, while in *The Naked Year* there are indubitable echoes both of *Petersburg* and of *The Silver Dove*.

From Remizov, on the other hand, comes Pilnyak's use of the *skaz* man-ner, which consists in substituting for the author's narrative the individual manner and intonation of his fictitious characters. With Pilnyak, however, this *skaz* manner is never simple and straightforward. Not content with one fictitious narrator and a faithful rendering of the peculiarities of his speech, Pilnyak continually keeps changing his manner and style and adapting it to various characters.

To Remizov can also be traced Pilnyak's attraction for the old, pre-Petrine Russia and his use of old language and quotations from old documents. Quotations are one of Pilnyak's favorite devices. His narrative is interspersed with them, and he draws them from both old and modern sources, often without any acknowledgment. He likes also to introduce fictitious quota-tions from the writings of his own characters (the work on Russia and the Revolution, written in imitation of the Old Russian Chronicles, by Arch-bishop Sylvester in *The Naked Year* and the "statistical" treatise about the

Revolution of Ivan Alexandrovich Nepomnyashchy, the "hero" of *Machines and Wolves,* are examples). There is in Pilnyak something of the old Russian scribe or of the compilers of miscellaneous collections of stories and aphorisms known in Byzantine literature as the Bees. Pilnyak himself said that he was fond of "gathering trifles like honey." But some of his stories are so overweighted with such trifles that their balance is completely upset. In some, too, he lets his predilection for outlandish, obsolete, or dialect words run away with him; this is particularly true of his stories about Peter the Great.

To tell the story of *The Naked Year* is a hopeless task. It is fragmentary and disjointed, without a unified plot or a central character. Its separate parts have no organic connection, and the novel can be easily broken back into the separate stories which went into its making. Its subject is the early phase of the Revolution (1918–19) and its impact on Russian life, but apropos of it Pilnyak ventures in his digressions into a great variety of subjects. There is in it a little of everything—a picture of the decay and fall of the house of the Ordynins, an old degenerating princely family; a description of the life of an anarchist commune on one of the Ordynin estates; a terrifying, highly impressionistic vision of an overcrowded goods train in which starving people from the north of Russia travel southeast in search of bread; an equally impressionistic picture of true Bolsheviks—"leathern men in leather jackets"—feverishly rebuilding one of the plants in northeastern Russia laid waste by the Civil War; and so on; and so on. There is a multitude of characters who are purely episodic; often the author does not even bother to introduce them to the reader, and they flit in and out of Pilnyak's pages without the reader's being able to identify them. This is not to say, however, that beneath the chaos there is no central, unifying idea. Pilnyak is never content, as some of his contemporaries and followers are, with merely putting on record his experiences and impressions. He always philosophizes about them, for he has, or thinks he has, his own "philosophy" of the Russian Revolution. This philosophy may appear confused, contradictory, shallow, and unoriginal, but it gives unity and meaning to Pilnyak's chaotic productions.

Orthodox Soviet critics described Pilnyak's attitude toward the Revolution as purely aesthetic and emotional. That Pilnyak is an emotional writer, that his vision of the Revolution is always highly emotionalized and subjective, there can be no doubt. But his emotionalism is of a special kind, which distinguishes him from some of his closest followers in Soviet literature and allies him to Andrey Bely: it is intellectual emotionalism. One orthodox Communist critic characterized Pilnyak's attitude toward the Revolution as "a synthesis of Slavophilism and of kulak Neoanarchism and Neopopulism."[1] Pilnyak had no hesitation in "accepting" the Revolution.

[1] Gorbachov, *Contemporary Russian Literature,* 142.

But he accepted it much as did Blok, Bely, and Esenin—as a salutary destructive movement, as a blizzard which was to sweep away the rotten
fabric of the old bourgeois world, as that "Russian revolt, senseless and
ruthless"—to use the famous words of Pushkin—the roots of which are to
be sought in such popular movements as the revolts of Razin in the seventeenth century and of Pugachov in the eighteenth. References to both are
constant in Pilnyak's stories. Equally persistent is the theme of Russia's dual
face. In *The Naked Year*, just as in the stories about Peter and about Petersburg, one of the recurrent symbolical motifs is the symbol of Kitay-Gorod
(Chinatown) in Moscow and other Russian cities, and the contrast between
its truly Russian nocturnal life and its diurnal aspects dominated by Europeanized individuals in bowler hats. Echoing the Slavophiles and Merezhkovsky, Pilnyak speaks also of Peter the Great as Antichrist, who enticed
Russia away to Petersburg—the Revolution made her return to Moscow,
her veritable cradle, possible.

Judged by absolute standards, the work of Pilnyak has much in it that is
unsatisfactory: he has little sense of form; his confused composition is
further obscured by his shallow "philosophy of history" to which much in
the narrative is subordinated; his efforts at psychological analysis, especially
in the erotic genre, smack of a cheap imitation of Dostoyevsky; much of his
art is of bookish derivation and has a secondhand flavor, certain ready-made
patterns being merely cut to post-Revolutionary measure;[2] and his monotonous, shrill diction soon palls on the reader.

Judged in the general context of Soviet literature, however, there are in
Pilnyak many valuable elements: his keen sense of the Russian language
and of words in general; his interest in ideas, whatever may be their
intrinsic worth; his deep-seated humanism and sympathy with the suffering, which goes back to the best traditions of Russian literature. His courage
and independence were also conspicuous among his contemporaries. Whatever his later concessions to the demands of those in authority, and his
efforts to adjust himself to the new conditions, he was obviously sincere in
welcoming the Revolution at first. As he put it himself, he saw the artist's
"bitter duty" in being honest with himself and with Russia. Almost from
the outset this attempt at being honest involved him in troubles with the
powers that were. In the twenties he incurred displeasure with his story
"Povest' o nepogashennoy lune" ("The Tale of the Unextinguished Moon,"
1927), which was taken to be an allusion to the death on the operating table
of one of the outstanding Communist leaders in the Civil War, Frunze.
Pilnyak's later scrapes and his final undoing will be related in due course.

[2] Several Soviet critics have pointed out the close parallels between Pilnyak's picture
of the decaying Ordynin family in *The Naked Year* and the Karamazovs of Dostoyevsky on the one hand, and the Golovlyovs of Saltykov-Shchedrin on the other. There is
also much that goes back to Bunin, especially to one of his masterpieces, *Sukhodol*.

Another writer whose influence during this period was of paramount im- **Zamyatin** portance was Evgeny Ivanovich Zamyatin. Although his literary career had **(1884–1937)** begun long before the Revolution, it is his work published between 1922 and 1928 that will secure him a place in the history of Russian literature.

Born in central Russia in Lebedyan, Zamyatin studied in the Department of Naval Construction at the Polytechnic Institute in St. Petersburg and became a naval engineer by profession. As a student he belonged to the Social Democratic party and took an active part in political activities. In an autobiographical note, published in 1928, he wrote: "I was then a Bolshevik (now I am not)."

Zamyatin's first story appeared in print in 1908, but he did not take seriously to writing until 1911–12, when his "Uezdnoye" ("A Tale of Provincial Life") was written (it was published in 1913). A grotesquely realistic picture of life, it was strongly influenced by Gogol and Remizov. His next major story, "Na kulichkakh" ("At the Back of Beyond," 1914), led to judicial proceedings against him, and for several years he published nothing. In 1916 he was sent to England to supervise the construction of icebreakers for the Russian government. In two stories written and published after his return to Russia in 1917, "Ostrovityane" ("The Islanders," 1918) and "Lovets chelovekov" ("The Fisher of Men," 1922), the cant and smugness of English life were satirized in terms of an amusing grotesque.

During the years of War Communism and the first years of the NEP, Zamyatin played an important part in the literary life of Petrograd. His influence on most of the young writers was decisive. His own output was rather small, but it included some of his best stories: "Peshchera" ("The Cave"), "Mamay," and "Sever" ("The North"), as well as his short satirical tales in *Bolshim detyam skazki* (*Fairy Tales for Grown-up Children*, 1922), reminiscent of Saltykov-Shchedrin's satires. He also began writing for the theater. *Ogni sv. Dominika* (*The Fires of St. Dominic*, 1923) satirized the Soviet Cheka (Extraordinary Commission for Fighting Counterrevolution, the predecessor of the Ogpu) in the form of a historical play, with the action set in Spain during the Inquisition. *Obshchestvo pochotnykh zvonarey* (*The Society of Honorary Bell Ringers*, 1926) was a dramatic variation of "The Islanders," while *Blokha* (*The Flea*, 1926) dramatized Leskov's famous story "Levsha" ("The Left-handed Man"); the latter, done with great farcical verve in the style of the Italian *commedia dell'arte*, enjoyed a great success on the Soviet stage for many years.

Although Zamyatin continued some of the traditions of Russian nineteenth-century literature—part of his work goes back to Gogol and Leskov— he was essentially an innovator. He described himself as a Neorealist and in an interview he once gave to a French journalist made the following observations on his art:

What is after all realism? If you examine your hand through a microscope you will see a grotesque picture: trees, ravines, rocks—instead of hairs, pores, grains, and dust. . . . To my mind this is a more genuine realism than the primitive one. To follow up the comparison: while neo-Realism uses a microscope to look at the world, Symbolism used a telescope, and pre-Revolutionary Realism, an ordinary looking glass. This naturally conditions the whole imagery, the entire formal structure.

Zamyatin's method of microscopic realism results in a novel, grotesque vision akin to surrealism. His short stories, always very carefully constructed, revolve around a complex of interconnected metaphorical images, representing a concentric outgrowth of a central image, of a "mother metaphor," as Mirsky aptly called it ("The Cave" is a very good example of the effective use of this method). His mathematical interests are reflected in his predilection for geometrical images. Many of his characters appear to be drawn by a caricaturist. Like Gogol's, they are presented outwardly, with some particular feature grotesquely emphasized. The stories are deliberately pruned of all psychological apparatus. But it would be wrong to think, as some critics have suggested, that there is nothing in Zamyatin beyond his verbal mastery, his love of ornamentalism, and his delight in construction. In stories like "The Cave" and "Mamay" the tragic atmosphere of the years of War Communism is conveyed very effectively, and the stories only gain from being told with cold and fastidious detachment.

Zamyatin also advocated the method of broken narrative, conducted simultaneously on several parallel planes. He applied it most consistently in his most "surrealistic" story, "Rasskaz o samom glavnom" ("A Story About That Which Matters Most"), a complex multiplanar vision of the Revolution with an emphasis on its futility. It was denounced by Communist critics as "antirevolutionary" and, together with his novel *We* and his *Nechestivye rasskazy* (*Impious Tales*), contributed most to his reputation of being an "inside *émigré*" (Trotsky used this designation of Zamyatin as early as 1923—see *Literature and Revolution*, 24).

In *Navodnenie* (*The Flood*, 1929), a tense story of love, jealousy, and murder, Zamyatin proved his ability to write a good, straightforward story with human interest, free from any satirical intent.

As a craftsman, as a short-story writer, Zamyatin had a great influence on a number of young Soviet writers. Slonimsky, Nikitin, Olesha, Vsevolod Ivanov, and some others were indebted to his Neorealistic experiments. Of Olesha, who was not one of his direct "pupils," it is perhaps even more true than of the others who sat at his feet in the Revolutionary Petrograd of the early twenties.

By nature Zamyatin was a heretic, a nonconformist, a born rebel against the established order of things. Quite early he felt that, under Communism, Russia was not likely to produce a real literature, for "real literature can exist only where it is produced by madmen, hermits, heretics, dreamers, rebels, and sceptics, and not by painstaking and well-intentioned officials."

Long before Stalin consolidated his omnipotent totalitarian police state, Zamyatin saw the Revolution in Russia heading toward conservatism and stagnation. In 1923 he wrote: "Let the flame cool down tomorrow or the day after tomorrow. . . . But someone must see this today already, and heretically speak today of tomorrow. Heretics are the only (bitter) medicine against the entropy of human thought."[3]

Earlier he had put the same idea in the mouth of one of his characters in *My (We)*: "There are two forces in the world: entropy and energy. One means blissful repose, happy equilibrium; the other, the overthrow of equilibrium, painfully infinite movement."

The novel *We* is undoubtedly Zamyatin's most interesting and important work, if not necessarily his best. It was written in 1920–21, and a year later Zamyatin sent a copy of the manuscript to his agent abroad. The book was subsequently published in several translations. By 1924 it had become clear to the author that its publication in Russia would not be allowed. But its existence could not be concealed. Zamyatin himself had read it at a meeting of the Association of Soviet Writers, and the essay "On Literature" had some lines from it as a motto. Soviet critics were therefore forced to speak of it, and there are references to it in the articles on Zamyatin in the *Great Soviet Encyclopaedia*, in the *Literary Encyclopaedia*, and elsewhere. The *Literary Encyclopaedia* described the novel as "a base libel on Socialist future" and spoke of Zamyatin's "counterrevolutionary tendencies":

He is in favor of the Revolution but of an . . . infinite revolution. . . . He does not believe in a social revolution . . . because it spells the doom of his class. . . . Zamyatin's theories are merely a disguise for a very matter-of-fact and quite understandable pining of the bourgeoisie after the economic well-being which it has forfeited, and for its hatred of those who have deprived it of that well-being.

A Russian edition of *We* was ready for the press in France in 1939, but the outbreak of World War II prevented its publication. The book was at last published in Russian in New York in 1952 and reissued in 1967.

The novel is not, on the face of it, concerned with present-day Russia or

[3] E. Zamyatin, "O literature, revolyutsii, èntropii i prochem" ("On Literature, Revolution, Entropy, and Other Things"), *Pisateli ob iskusstve i o sebe. Sbornik statey No. 1 (Writers About Art and About Themselves: Collection of Essays No. 1)*, 68. There was apparently no second issue of this collection. Zamyatin's essay, together with his other critical articles, was reprinted in the posthumous volume *Litsa (Faces)*, published in New York in 1955 and reissued with two new introductions in 1967. These essays contain some very interesting judgments on the writers of those days, including the Serapion Brothers, whom Zamyatin claimed to have "invented." The volume, with the addition of some other essays, is now available in an excellent English translation by M. Ginsburg under the title *A Soviet Heretic: Essays by Yevgeny Zamyatin*.

the Soviet regime as such. It is a satirical fantasy set in an indeterminate future. One can see in it the influence of H. G. Wells's scientific romances (in 1922, Zamyatin published a short, sympathetic study of H. G. Wells) and perhaps of Anatole France. It bears a strikingly close resemblance to Aldous Huxley's *Brave New World*, which it preceded by twelve years (the English translation of Zamyatin's novel was published seven years before the appearance of Huxley's). The resemblance is particularly noticeable in some of the minor details, but there is also a similarity of general idea and of the over-all presentation of the standardized state of the future. There are differences, too, owing above all to Zamyatin's strong leanings to primitivism and Huxley's rationalist tradition.

In *We* the reader is transported at least a millenium ahead, into a perfect, modern, standardized state which has no name but is known simply as the Single State.[4] Its citizens have no names either, but are known by their letters and numbers, consonants denoting males and vowels, females. In this respect Zamyatin was even more logically abstract than Huxley. The latter could not withstand the temptation of showing to advantage his ingenuity and wit in the choice of names for his characters. In general, there is more local description and topical humor in Huxley's novel, while Zamyatin deliberately sticks to universal abstractions. All the citizens of Zamyatin's state wear identical blue-gray uniforms—the novel was written before the appearance of Mussolini's Blackshirts—and badges with their numbers. They are ruled over by the Benefactor (Huxley's World Controller), and their life is scientifically regulated down to the minutest details. Everything is mechanized and standardized in the Single State, though not quite to the same extent as in Huxley's Utopia. Zamyatin's men of the future have not yet learned to procreate new human beings by means of incubation. But in Zamyatin's state love is "dehumanized," too, and though promiscuity is the general underlying principle, it is controlled and "distributed," so to speak. Special pink counterfoil tickets are issued for its use, which is confined to certain fixed hours, but allows some latitude in the choice of partners. Every number of the Single State has also at his or her disposal a few "personal" hours a day, during which he or she is off duty. But even then

---

[4] In the very first entry in his diary the narrator, who is constructing a space ship for the Single State, quotes the following sentence from an announcement in the *State Gazette*: "A thousand years ago your heroic ancestors subjected the whole globe to the power of the Single State." This would place the action in the novel at least in the thirtieth century. See on this point Alex M. Shane's excellent and up-to-date monograph *The Life and Works of Evgenij Zamjatin*. The book is provided with a model bibliography of works by and about Zamyatin, comprising nearly eight hundred items, not counting some reviews of Zamyatin's books which are listed with the books themselves. There is also a reliable chronology of Zamyatin's fictional works. See also G. Woodcock's article in *Sewanee Review*. Another recent critical study of Zamyatin, less detailed than Shane's but also good, is D. J. Richards, *Zamyatin: A Soviet Heretic*.

the numbers are not free to do as they like, for the negation of freedom is
the very foundation of the Single State: "Freedom and crime are as in-
dissolubly bound up as, let us say, the motion of an airplane and its speed. . . .
If man's freedom equals zero, he commits no crimes. This is clear——"5
Thus runs one of the principles of the Single State.

Freedom and happiness are regarded as incompatible, and one must
choose between them: "Happiness without freedom, or freedom without
happiness—there is no alternative. Those fools [the men of old] chose
freedom—well, naturally, for centuries they yearned for chains."

The personal hours of the citizens of the Single State are accordingly subordinated to the same mathematically precise rules as the rest of their lives:

. . . in such weather the personal after-lunch hour is, as a rule, devoted by us to a
supplementary walk. As usual, the Music Factory played, with all of its pipes, the
march of the Single State. The numbers walked in regular ranks, four by four,
hundreds and thousands of numbers in bluish unifs, the golden badges on their
chests showing the official number of each one of them, male and female.

To look after the numbers' morals and behavior—mathematical morals
and mathematical behavior though they be—and to save them from all
"deviations," there are special "guardians" whose chief task is to spy upon
the numbers and who are assisted in this task by the voluntary zeal of the
well-intentioned numbers. To the law-abiding citizens of the Single State
these guardians appear as their guardian angels, and the character in whose
name the novel is written remarks with pointed, though unconscious, irony:
"It is extraordinary to discover the number of things of which the Ancients
[that is, men of the present era] dreamed and which we have turned into
reality."

In the Bureau of Guardians, Zamyatin undoubtedly anticipated the evolution of the Cheka (which did not provide him then with an actual
example of such thoroughness and efficiency) into the Ogpu and its successors and the parallel development of the Gestapo in the Nazi state.

The narrator of Zamyatin's novel is one of the chief mathematicians of the
Single State—the most privileged category of its citizens—No. D-503, who
is completing the construction of a new giant interplanetary flying machine
—the *Integral*—which will enable the Single State to establish communications with other planets and win them over to its way of life. He writes
"notes," as he calls them, for the benefit of the inhabitants of those other
planets. But as he writes them, they gradually become something quite

5 This and the following quotations are given in my own translation. The original
English version of *We* was unsatisfactory. A revised paperback edition of it appeared
in 1959. In 1960 a new translation, by B. G. Guerney, was included in his anthology
Russian Literature in the Soviet Period. German, Italian, and some other translations
appeared in the 1950's. A new Czech edition was announced in 1967, during the
"Czech Spring." It does not appear to have been published.

different from what he intended them to be, and we get an insight into a complex psychological change which he undergoes. To put it briefly, he reverts to the old human psychology, to individual consciousness. He discovers that he possesses a soul, something that is regarded in the Single State as an incurable disease. Numbers are supposed to have no souls and no individual consciousness. "No offense is so heinous as unorthodoxy of behavior," runs one of the guiding principles of the Single State. Soon he is led to discover that he is no exception—that there are other cases like himself.

The psychological transformation of D-503 is a result of his chance meeting with a woman—No. I-330—who fascinates him and with whom he soon falls in love in the way one is not supposed to fall in love in the Single State (until now D-503 has had a normal pink-ticket affair with another woman, O-90). She comes to exercise a strange influence on him. He obeys her slightest and queerest whims, even though they offend his sense of duty as one of the numbers of the Single State. She takes him to the Ancient House, which is preserved on the outskirts of the state as a historical monument, an illustration of the way the "Ancients" used to live before the introduction of modern transparent glass houses, where everything, with the sole exception of the sex act, is performed in everybody's sight (during the "sexual hour" the blinds are drawn).

In the meantime the process of "humanization," or individualization, of D-503 continues. He is now madly in love with I-330 and has to admit that "all this crazy stuff about love and jealousy was not confined to the idiotic books of old." He says of himself, "I no longer lived in our sensible world, but in the ancient morbid world, the world of the square root of minus one." He breaks with O-90 after getting her with child at her own request, for she also seems to have gone off the track and loves him in a way which is not regarded as normal, or approved, in the Single State. "Having a soul" turns out to be an infectious disease.

Then something quite unexpected happens, to the utter dismay and confusion of all law-abiding numbers. On the so-called Day of Unanimity, when all the numbers of the Single State are gathered in a huge auditorium to re-elect their Benefactor (the re-election is taken for granted; he has been unanimously re-elected thirty-nine times), some people, with I-330 at their head, dare raise their voice against him. There is a scuffle, I-330 is wounded but D-503 manages to rescue her and escape. She takes him through the Ancient House to the other side of the wall which circumscribes the boundaries of the Single State (the size and the location of the Single State is a point which Zamyatin leaves vague; one may imagine it as something quite small or as practically coincident with the whole earth). Beyond this wall no numbers are supposed to penetrate, nor do they know what is on the other side of it. Actually there we find nature untouched by the technical progress of civilization, a dwelling place of primitive, hairy men (which has its counterpart in Huxley's Savage Reservation). With these men I-330 and her accomplices, the other "revolutionaries," propose to launch a revolution in the Single State. They welcome the arrival of D-503, for they plan to make use of his *Integral* for their own ends. There are no very definite ideas behind the revolutionary action of I-330 and her friends, except a primitive, instinctive revolt against the standardized, planned life, in the name of freedom and of change and of newness.

When D-503, bewildered by the sight of naked men who live in natural and not mathematical surroundings, asks I-330 what it all means, her answer is, "It is the half we have lost," and she adds, "You must learn to tremble with fright, with joy, with wrath and fury, with cold, you must worship fire." But his love for this strange and fascinating woman clashes with his sense of duty and with the deeply absorbed doctrines of the Single State. A curious dialogue takes place between them:

He: This is unthinkable! This is absurd! Don't you realize that what you are preparing is a revolution?
She: Yes, it is a revolution. Why is it absurd?
He: . . . because . . . *our* revolution was the last, and there can be no more revolutions. Everybody knows that.
She: . . . There is no such thing as the last revolution. The number of revolutions is infinite.

This idea of "infinite revolutions," in which the Communist critics saw an echo of Trotsky's conception of "permanent revolution," was apparently very dear to Zamyatin. (Its political implications naturally alarmed the Soviet censors, who banned the book.)

In the last part of the book the tempo is accelerated almost to the point of incoherence. On the day before the proposed flight of the *Integral*, a proclamation is published in the official paper of the Single State, informing all the numbers that the real cause of all recent troubles has been discovered:

. . . you are ill. Your illness is called "imagination." It is the worm that gnaws black wrinkles on your foreheads. It is the fever that drives you on, further and further, even if this "further" begins where happiness ends. It is the last barricade on the road to happiness. Rejoice: it has now been blown up. The road is clear. The latest discovery of our State Science reveals that the center of imagination is a miserable little brain nodule in the region of the *pons Varolii*. A triple application of X rays to that nodule, and you will be cured of imagination—*forever*. You are perfect, you are equal to machines, the road to 100 per cent happiness is clear. Hasten ye, old and young.

The proclamation invites all numbers to undergo the Great Operation, which will deprive them of imagination, the source of all evil. D-503 sees at first a salvation in the operation, a way out of his inner conflict. He almost

decides to undergo it but changes his mind on realizing that the choice lies
between the happiness promised in the proclamation and I-330. The trial
flight of the *Integral* takes place, but the plot is thwarted—a woman, the
caretaker of D-503's house, who is also in love with him, reports the matter
to the guardians after prying into his manuscript notes. But she does so
without disclosing his own part in the plot. The Single State scores a victory
over the revolutionaries. All law-abiding numbers, including D-503, who is
not suspected, are subjected to the Great Operation, and their imaginations
are extirpated. I-330 and the other active revolutionaries are put to torture
according to the improved Single State method—they are first placed under
the Pneumatic Bell and then sent to the Machine of the Benefactor, a
modern-day guillotine. Speaking as a good citizen of the Single State, D-503
defends the Pneumatic Bell against the slander of the enemies thus:

> There were fools who compared our Operating Room to the old-time Inquisi-
> tion. But this is just as absurd as to put on the same level a surgeon performing
> a tracheotomy and a highwayman. Both may be using the same knife to perform
> the same operation—they cut the throat of a living man. Yet one is a benefactor,
> the other a criminal. One is marked with the "plus" sign, the other, with the
> "minus."

There is in Zamyatin's novel a prophetic note which distinguishes it from
George Orwell's vision in *1984*. Writing in 1948, Orwell had before him all
the essential elements of his Utopia, and one wonders even whether in
choosing the date for his title he did not simply play a joke on his readers by
merely reversing the last two figures—whether he had in mind not the
conditions mankind was heading for but those actually prevailing in a large
part of Europe in 1948. That would explain his seemingly arbitrary date.
Zamyatin in 1920 needed much greater imagination for his accurate portrayal of the totalitarian state. Some of his details anticipate the future with
striking fidelity.

The influence of *We* on George Orwell's *1984* is beyond all doubt. He had
heard about Zamyatin from me and had read about him in the 1944 edition
of my book on Soviet Russian literature, as well as the French version of
We which I had lent him (the American edition of it was unobtainable in
England during the war). He wrote about it for the London *Tribune* in
1946 (see Volume IV, of his *Collected Essays, Journalism and Letters*, where
his 1948 letter to me will also be found, and also Volume III).

Less witty and less scientifically elaborate than *Brave New World*,
Zamyatin's novel is more effective as a prophecy of things to come. Its very
bareness enhances its deadly seriousness.

The story of the campaign against Zamyatin which led to his subsequent
emigration will be told in Chapter 16.

The contrast between the new Stone Age, so strikingly depicted in Zamya- **Serapion**
tin's "The Cave," and the conditions created by the New Economic Policy **Brothers**
was great. The climate of the NEP proved propitious to a new florescence
of a more or less independent literature. For young writers this new flowering of literature was a novel and exhilarating experience. In the history of
post-Revolutionary Russian literature an important place belongs to a group
of young authors who called themselves the Serapion Brothers. Their
"brotherhood" was not a literary school held together by any real or fictitious
tenets. What united them was their youth, their zest for life, their eager
interest in literature, and their firm belief in the autonomy of art and in the
freedom of the writer. They were brought together more or less accidentally—partly topographically, so to speak—through the Dom Iskusstv
(House of Arts), which Gorky set up to counterbalance the influence of the
"bourgeois" House of Writers. The House of Arts was situated in the
former Eliseyev mansion at the corner of Nevsky Avenue and the Moyka.
Fedin in his memoirs says that in the House of Arts "everything was richer,
and some things even more distinguished, than in the House of Writers."
While the latter considered itself independent, the former was, through
Gorky, connected with the Commissariat of Education. According to Fedin,
the inhabitants of the two houses differed also politically. In the House of
Arts political views were either foolish or naïve; in the House of Writers
the old liberal tradition survived. Much later, Olga Forsh described the
House of Arts as "a mad ship."

Gorky and Zamyatin also helped to bring the Serapions together. Several
of them were Zamyatin's pupils in his House of Arts literary studio. They
looked upon Zamyatin as their master and older brother and learned from
him to use the tools of their craft. Their debt to him is incalculable, even
though today they cannot give him credit as their "teacher." All twelve
were quite young.[6] At the time the brotherhood came into being, in Feb-

[6] The number twelve is given by Vladimir Pozner in his *Panorama de la littérature
russe contemporaine*. K. Fedin in his book on Gorky speaks of ten Serapions, excluding
Shklovsky and Pozner. The latter he perhaps does not mention because he soon
became an *émigré* (and later, to all intents and purposes, a French writer), while he
says of Shklovsky that he "was, indeed, the eleventh, if not the first Serapion—by the
passion he brought into our life, by the wittiness of the questions he threw into our
debates." *Gorky sredi nas: dvadtsatye gody* (*Gorky in Our Midst: The 1920's*), 115.
Pozner's book contains a lively description of the atmosphere in which the Serapions
foregathered. It is quoted in W. Edgerton's valuable article "The Serapion Brothers:
An Early Soviet Controversy," *American Slavic and East European Review*, Vol. VIII,
No. 1 (February, 1949), 48–49. A monograph by H. Oulanoff, published in 1966, is a
recent addition to Western literature about this group. Some interesting letters to
Luntz from his fellow Serapions have been published in *Novy Zhurnal* (*New Review*,
New York) by Gary Kern. On the Soviet side some valuable material was published
in 1963 in the *Literaturnoe nasledstvo* (*Literary Heritage*) volume entitled *Gorky i*

ruary, 1921, the two oldest, Fedin and Shklovsky, were twenty-six and twenty-five respectively; most were in their early twenties, and three (Luntz, Kaverin, and Pozner) were still in their teens. Most of them were short-story writers; one (Luntz) specialized in drama but also wrote stories; three (Tikhonov, Polonskaya, and Pozner) were poets; and two (Shklovsky and Gruzdyov) were literary critics.

They took their name from the Hermit Serapion, a character in one of E. T. A. Hoffmann's tales, and the significance of this name was disclosed in their literary manifesto and in some of their writings, which made a great stir at the time.

In 1922 they published their first *Almanac*, a slender volume printed on wretched paper, which included stories by Zoshchenko, Luntz, Vsevolod Ivanov, Kaverin, Slonimsky, Nikitin, and Fedin. The *Almanac* attracted considerable attention, not because of the outstanding intrinsic value of its contents (though the talent of these young writers was immediately recognized by most critics), but simply because here were several young gifted writers, practically newcomers to literature, coming out as a group and attempting to revive Russian prose fiction. Another edition of the *Almanac* appeared almost simultaneously in Berlin. It differed from the Russian edition only in the inclusion of some poems by Tikhonov and Polonskaya, in addition to the stories. It was their prose fiction which attracted particular attention (of poetry there was more than enough in those years), and one of the critics greeted the appearance of the *Almanac* as heralding the rise of Soviet prose literature. Still, the *Almanac* in itself was hardly an event, and, unlike many of their predecessors, the Serapions did not preface it with any high-sounding declarations. It was only when attention had already been attracted to them that they came out with their literary credo. It appeared in the form of an article by one of the youngest of them, Lev Luntz, and was entitled "Why We Are the Serapion Brothers." It was published, together with their rather unusual, lively, and spirited biographical sketches, as a special supplement to *Literary Notes*, the publication of the House of Writers.[7]

Luntz's article was a courageous declaration of the essential freedom and independence of art. He began by protesting against all rules and regulations which signify coercion and boredom and explained the meaning of the group's name:

---

sovetskie pisateli. Neizdannaya perepiska (*Gorky and the Soviet Writers: Unpublished Correspondence*). The volume contains Gorky's correspondence with Serapions Fedin, Kaverin, Slonimsky, and Zoshchenko.

[7] "Serapionovy bratya o sebe" ("The Serapion Brothers About Themselves"), *Literaturnye Zapiski*, No. 3 (August 1, 1922), 25–31. Unable to procure this issue of the magazine, I quote here and below from Edgerton's article, with a few minor changes in translation that seemed advisable.

We have named ourselves the Serapion Brothers because we do not want coercion and boredom; we do not want everyone to write alike, even in imitation of Hoffmann. . . . We proclaim no new slogans, we publish no manifestoes or programs. But for us the old truth has a great practical meaning which has been misunderstood or forgotten, especially among us in Russia. We consider that the Russian literature of our day is amazingly sedate, stuffy and monotonous. We are authorized to write tales, novels, and tedious dramas in either the old or the new style—but by all means on contemporary themes. The novel of adventure is a pernicious phenomenon; classical or romantic tragedies are archaisms or conventions; and the dime novel is immoral. Therefore Alexander Dumas Senior is trash, and Hoffmann and Stevenson are children's writers.

But we consider that our gifted patron, creator of the unbelievable and the improbable, is equal to Tolstoy or Balzac; that Stevenson, the author of pirate stories, is a great writer; and that Dumas is a classic, like Dostoyevsky.

This does not mean that we acknowledge only Hoffmann, or only Stevenson. Almost all of us Brothers are writers of mores [*bytoviki*]. But we know that other things too are possible. A work may reflect the epoch, but it need not do so, and is none the worse for it. Now here is Vsevolod Ivanov, a confirmed realist, describing the revolutionary, oppressive, bloody countryside, who recognizes Kaverin, the author of foolish romantic short stories. And my ultraromantic tragedy lives in harmony with the noble, old-fashioned lyricism of Fedin. For we demand only one thing: that a work should be organic, real, should live its own life. *Its own life.* Not be a copy of nature, but live on a par with nature.

The crux of the "manifesto" was its proclamation of the writer's freedom from all regimentation and even from his age ("A work may reflect the epoch but need not do so") and the assertion of the organic and autonomous nature of a work of art. The manifesto contained even more daring statements, such as the following:

We have gathered together in days of powerful and revolutionary political tension. "Whoever is not with us is against us," we have been told from the right and from the left.—"Whom are you with, Serapion Brothers? With the Communists or against the Communists? For the Revolution or against the Revolution?"

Whom are we with, the Serapion Brothers?

We are with the Hermit Serapion.

That means—with nobody? That means—morass? Aestheticizing intelligentsia? Without ideology, without convictions? Standing aloof?

No. Each of us has his ideology, his political convictions; each paints his own hut to suit himself. Thus in life, and thus in our stories, tales and dramas. We all together, we the Brotherhood, demand only one thing: that the tone be not false. That we may believe in the work whatever its color.

And further:

Too long and painfully has the public welfare directed Russian literature. It is time to say that a non-Communist story may lack talent, but also it may show genius. And we do not care whom Blok the poet, author of *The Twelve*, was for; nor Bunin the writer, author of *The Gentleman from San Francisco*.

These are elementary truths, but every day convinces us that they must be said over and over again.

Whom are we with, the Serapion Brothers?

We are with the Hermit Serapion. We believe that literary chimeras are a kind of reality, and we will have none of utilitarianism. We do not write for propaganda. Art is real, like life itself. And, like life itself, it has neither goal nor meaning; it exists because it cannot help existing.

To anyone familiar with the history of the Soviet Union it must be clear that these defiant statements were a challenge to official ideology. And in 1922, Luntz's manifesto provoked the fury of several influential Marxist critics (Lebedev-Polyansky, Kogan, and others), who quite wrongly saw in it a vindication of "art for art's sake," and a stormy controversy arose in which Luntz took a lively part. In replying to his Marxist critics Luntz reiterated the Serapions' artistic credo when he wrote:

> Our brotherhood, our "unity of blood," does not lie in political unanimity. We do not care what political convictions each of us holds. But we all believe that *art is real and lives its own special life, independently of where it draws its material from. For that reason we are brothers.*[8]

All the Serapions echoed Luntz's declaration in their spirited autobiographies. Zoshchenko, who a little earlier had published some amusing and clever parodies of fellow Serapions,[9] made fun of the "precise ideology" demanded by Communist critics from writers:

> . . . being a writer is sort of hard. . . . Take ideology—these days a writer has got to have ideology.
>
> Here's Voronsky now (a good man) who writes: ". . . It is necessary that writers should have a more precise ideology."
>
> Now that's plumb disagreeable! Tell me, how can I have a "precise ideology" when not a single party among them all appeals to me?
>
> I don't hate anybody—there's *my* precise ideology. . . .
>
> In their general swing the Bolsheviks are closer to me than anybody else. And so I'm willing to bolshevik around with them. . . . But I'm not a Communist (or rather not a Marxist), and I think I never shall be.[10]

We shall see that this frivolous attitude of Zoshchenko's toward ideology

[8] Lev Luntz, "Ob ideologii i publitsistike" ("About Ideology and Journalism"), *Novosti* (*News*), No. 3 (October 23, 1922); reprinted in *Sovremennaya russkaya kritika: 1918–1924* (*Contemporary Russian Criticism: 1918–1924*) (ed. by I. Oksyonov), quoted in Edgerton, "The Serapion Brothers," *American Slavic and East European Review*, Vol. VIII, No. 1 (February, 1949), 54.

[9] See Mikh. Zoshchenko, "Druzheskie parodii" ("Friendly Parodies"), *Literaturnye Zapiski*, No. 2 (June 23, 1922), 8–9.

[10] Quoted by Edgerton, "The Serapion Brothers," *American Slavic and East European Review*, Vol. VIII, No. 1 (February, 1919).

was to be recalled, with dire consequences for him, twenty-four years later. At the time, however, this show of political and artistic independence went unpunished.

Several of the Serapions published individual books in 1921–22. These included three volumes by Vsevolod Ivanov, two each by Nikitin and Fedin, and one each by Zoshchenko and Slonimsky. All of them, as well as Kaverin and Tikhonov, were to play an important part in the general revival of literature, and their work will be discussed in greater detail in due place. More should be said here, however, about Luntz and Shklovsky.

Lev Natanovich Luntz (1901–24) came from a Jewish intelligentsia family. His childhood was happy and secure. At the University of Petrograd, which he entered soon after the outbreak of the Revolution, he studied Romance philology, specializing in Spanish literature. He was supposed to go to Spain on a postgraduate traveling scholarship. His parents emigrated to Germany after the Revolution, and in 1923 he joined them, but his main reason for going abroad was to undergo a cure for some unidentifiable illness which was probably due to undernourishment and privation during the terrible years of War Communism. He died in a sanatorium near Hamburg soon after his twenty-third birthday.

Luntz's most important contribution to Russian literature—apart from his lion's share in championing the freedom of art on behalf of the Serapions —is his play *Vne zakona* (*The Outlaw*, 1921). It is a romantic tragedy in the Western European tradition, full of incident, with a dynamic, swift-moving plot. Its action is set in Spain. The same "Westernism" characterizes Luntz's two other plays, *Obezyany idut* (*The Apes Are Coming*, 1921), and *Bertrand de Born* (1922). *Gorod pravdy* (*The City of Truth*, 1923–24), published posthumously in Gorky's *Beseda* (*Colloquy*), is a symbolical and philosophical play dealing in abstract terms with some problems raised by the Revolution. Its message is rather ambiguous. One critic has described it as a "courageous and pungent anti-Bolshevik play."[11] In the same number of *Beseda*, Gorky spoke of Luntz as a most promising dramatist who might have renovated the Russian drama and as a man of "rare independence and courage of thought."[12]

In his work, just as in his critical and theoretical pronouncements, Luntz rebelled against the "static" tradition of Russian literature, in drama as well as in prose fiction. He stressed, as we saw, the importance of construction, of plot and incident. His views were stated in a longish essay entitled "Na Zapad!" ("To the West!"), which also appeared in Gorky's *Beseda*[13] and which he had previously read at a meeting of the Serapion Brotherhood.

[11] Cf. V. Zavalishin, *Early Soviet Writers*, 226.

[12] Maxim Gorky, "Lev Luntz" (obituary), *Beseda* (*Colloquy*), No. 5 (June, 1924), 61–62.

[13] No. 3 (September–October, 1923), 259–74.

It is a brilliant and provocative piece of writing which today acquires an added significance. Luntz began by referring to a kind of literature which existed in the West but was regarded in Russia as "unserious if not harmful"—the literature of adventure. In Russia it was tolerated for children; but when the children grew up and were enlightened by their teachers, they hid their Rider Haggards and Conan Doyles in their bookcases and turned to the "most serious but most boring" Gleb Uspensky:

> We regarded as dime novels and childish fun that which in the West is considered classical. *The plot!* The skill in handling a complicated intrigue, in tying and untying the knots, in twining and untwining them—it is acquired by many years of meticulous work, is created by continuous and beautiful culture.
>
> And we Russians, we do not know how to handle plot, we ignore it, and therefore despise it. . . . We do not distinguish between the penny shocker Sherlock Holmes and the real.
>
> We ignore the plot and despise it. But this contempt is the contempt of the provincials. We are provincials. And we are proud of it. There is nothing to be proud of.

Speaking of the Russian theater, Luntz said that it had never existed. Five or six excellent, model comedies, a few partly forgotten, good dramas of manners did not count. Not a single tragedy. He ascribed this state of things to lack of system. Great writers for the theater appear in a bunch, they form a school. So it was in England, in Spain, in France. Intrigue and action are the main things in a play. A dramatic plot must obey rules of dramatic technique. Every dramatic system, whether classicist or romanticist, must have its canons. All these particular rules are subordinated to the general laws of economy of time, economy of space, and economy of action. The drama also demands tradition and training:

> That is why dramatic geniuses come out in schools, in pleiades, as a system. One cannot get off in drama with fine psychology, popular speech or social motifs. If the development of the action is defective, the play is no good at all, even though it contain psychological investigations and social revelations of genius.
>
> The Russian theater aspires, above all, after social motifs, after psychological truth, after mores. It ignores the technique of the intrigue, the tradition of the plot. That is why it does not exist. There are fine and original dramas for reading—Turgenev's, Chekhov's, Gorky's. Or there are Futurist, Imaginist and other plays based on mere tricks. Everybody in the theater is shouting about the crisis of the theater, and nobody laments the fact that with us no one knows or wishes to know how to handle the intrigue, to learn the plot tradition.

Things were different with the Russian novel, went on Luntz, in the sense that it did exist, that there was a Russian "system" of the novel, that the Russian novel had its own "face." This, he said, was due to the fact that, to begin with, there had been more "manure," more precursors, more bad imitators of the West. But the Russian tradition was one-sided: it was realistic. The fine tradition of the historical novel was diverted into juvenile literature. The tradition of the novel of adventure went underground. Dostoyevsky's brilliant attempt to drag it out remained a solitary one. Russian literature did not possess a single first-class historical novel or a single good novel of adventure.

After contrasting this situation with what he saw in the West, Luntz passed over to what he called the "practical" side of his paper—an attack on his fellow Serapions as "typically Russian, provincial, Populist, boring writers," who soon gave up their pious intention to learn how to write interestingly and fell back into the old rut. His behest to his literary brothers was as follows:

Do what you did before. Be revolutionary or counterrevolutionary writers, mystics or wrestlers with God, but don't be boring.

Therefore—to the West!

He who wants to *create* a Russian tragedy *must learn* in the West, for in Russia he has no one to learn from.

He who wants to *create* a Russian novel of adventure *must learn* in the West, for in Russia he has no one to learn from.

But even those who want to *renovate* the Russian realistic novel *I invite to look* to the West. . . . You can, of course, follow the Russian tradition, too, because the Russian novel is majestic and mighty. But I repeat: *Look* to the West, if you do not wish to *learn* from it.

A hard road awaits us. Ahead lies honorable death or true victory.

To the West! to the West!

Luntz's essay was the extreme expression of literary Westernism in Russia. There is much in his youthful ardor that may sound naïve and much that can be traced back to the influence of Shklovsky and the Formalists. Shklovsky in his *Gamburgsky shchot* (*The Hamburg Count*), published in 1928, wrote: "We miss Luntz very much now, with his mistakes, his despair, and his sure knowledge about the death of the old forms." Luntz's ideas had no lasting effect on Soviet literature. And even the fellow Serapions—with the exception of Kaverin, whom he excluded from his attack on them—did not heed his passionate appeal and went, on the whole, their own, Russian ways. But the appeal itself, in its very extremeness, was symptomatic of the moment when the newborn Soviet literature stood at the crossroads and the whole literary scene was in a state of turmoil. The editors of *Beseda* (Gorky, Bely, and Khodasevich) accompanied Luntz's essay with a note in which they said that, though not sharing Luntz's opinion about the advisability of "going to the other extreme," they thought his ideas worthy of attention.

Victor Borisovich Shklovsky is one of the most interesting figures in Soviet literature during its first decade. Born in 1893, he was of mixed

Jewish-German-Russian descent. His father, a teacher of mathematics, was a Jew. His paternal grandmother, who did not learn Russian until she was sixty, wrote her memoirs in Yiddish. His maternal grandfather was a German gentile, by profession a gardener, who married the daughter of a Russian Orthodox priest. Victor Shklovsky's brother also became an Orthodox priest, while his uncle was the well-known journalist, Isaac Shklovsky (Dioneo). At the outbreak of the 1917 Revolution, Shklovsky joined the Socialist Revolutionary party and served as a commissar of the provisional government with the armies, first in Galicia and later in Persia. After the advent of the Bolsheviks to power he both fought the Whites and conspired against the Reds. In 1920 he returned to revolutionary Petrograd but in 1922 escaped to Finland to avoid arrest on charges arising out of his conduct during the Civil War. For a time he lived in Berlin, participating in Russian literary life there, but in 1923, taking advantage of a partial political amnesty granted by the Soviet government, he returned to Russia and has lived there since.

His literary career began in 1914. While studying at the University of Petrograd, he became one of the leaders of the so-called Formalist movement and one of the founders of Opoyaz (Society for the Study of Poetical Language), which had close links with the Futurist movement in literature. Shklovsky's role in the Formalist movement, of which he was the principal theoretician, will be discussed in Chapter 15.

Arriving in Petrograd in 1920, he took quarters at Gorky's House of Arts and was appointed professor at the Institute of the History of Art, where among his students were several Serapions. His influence on them was very great. Like many other writers at that time, he led a hectic life between 1920 and 1922, managing to write a great deal despite great material hardships, contributing to various newspapers and magazines, lecturing at the institute and in a number of studios, launching new, and often short-lived, publishing enterprises. His first important book was published in Berlin in 1923, after he had left Russia. It was called *Sentimentalnoye puteshestvie* (*Sentimental Journey*)—the title was a tribute to Shklovsky's favorite writer. For many of his formalistic theories, especially his pet subject of "toying with the plot," he drew upon Sterne's *Tristram Shandy* ("I revived Sterne in Russia, for I knew how to read him," he once wrote). Shklovsky's *Sentimental Journey* is even less "sentimental" than its model. His approach in it to the Revolution and the Civil War and their horrors is as cool, as detached, and as matter-of-fact as that of his pupils, the Serapions, who probably learned their detachment from him. It is a documentary, autobiographical work, covering the period from 1917 to 1923. The first part ("The Front and the Revolution") deals with the author's experiences and adventures during the first year of the Revolution; the second, with his activities in southern Russia toward the end of the Civil War, his life in Bolshevik Petrograd, his escape to Finland, and his life in Berlin.

Shklovsky's manner derives both from Sterne and from Vasily Rozanov, one of the most original writers and thinkers.[14] His narrative is broken, fragmentary, full of digressions, irrelevancies and witty, scintillating paradoxes. His deliberate untidiness and casualness, his sprightly, nonchalant personalia may often annoy and even incense the reader, but as a document of that time the book is not only remarkable but unique. Shklovsky's terse, paradoxical appreciations of several of his contemporaries—Gorky, Blok, Gumilyov, and several of the Serapions—are well worth a close study.

Sentimental Journey was followed by another book of personal digressions, more or less in the same vein but much more affected and therefore less effective, called *Zoo, ili pisma ne o lyubvi* (*Zoo, or Letters Not About Love*, 1923; the title refers to the Berlin Zoological Garden in Tiergarten) and written in the form of an epistolary novel. In the same year there appeared in Berlin his *Khod konya* (*Knight's Move*), a small volume of short essays about art and literature, uneven, but mostly very interesting and clever, with the inevitable personal digressions. After his return to Russia, Shklovsky published another volume of "autobiographical fragments," *Tretya fabrika* (*The Third Factory*, 1926); one more collection of brilliantly paradoxical essays, many of them polemical, *Gamburgsky shchot* (*The Hamburg Count*, 1928);[15] and several theoretical books about literature in defense and illustration of his "formal method." When, after 1929, Formalism was proclaimed a dangerous doctrine, Shklovsky devoted himself to literary history and dramatic and film criticism and also wrote some scenarios. Much of his work between 1930 and 1953 is of little interest, and in his book of reminiscences, *Vstrechi* (*Encounters*, 1946), he is but a pale echo of his former self. After 1956 he was to write almost exclusively about literature, and his reputation as a literary scholar still stands high today.

The name Maxim Gorky (pseudonym of Alexey Maximovich Peshkov) is closely linked with Soviet literature and its fortunes. But his attitude toward the Revolution was by no means uniform, and the theme "Gorky and the Revolution" falls into several distinct periods. It also implies much that is still obscure, and it must be left to the future impartial historian of

Gorky (1868–1936)

---

[14] On Rozanov see Mirsky, *Contemporary Russian Literature*, 163–72; and R. Poggioli, *The Phoenix and the Spider*, 158–207. In 1920 Shklovsky himself published a curious little book about Rozanov as a writer, in which he of course drew parallels between Rozanov and Sterne. Rozanov is still taboo in the Soviet Union, but several of his books have been reissued in original Russian in the West.

[15] The title is taken from boxing terminology; its bearing on Russian literature is explained in a witty preface.

the Revolution, provided he has access to all its archives, to shed light on all
these blind spots.

Despite his long personal association with Lenin and with the Bolshevik
party in general, and his uncompromising pacifism during World War I,
which made him sympathize with the Bolshevik attitude on the question
of the war and its further conduct, Gorky was hostile toward the Bolsheviks
between the two revolutions in 1917 and in the early days of the new
regime. Later he exchanged this attitude for one of benevolent neutrality
(a Soviet critic described it as "benevolent incomprehension"),[16] and from
1918 to 1921 he devoted himself to the task of saving the remnants of Russian
culture and of helping its representatives. It was to him that such institutions
as the House of Arts and the House of Scholars (Dom Uchonykh) owed
their existence. He was also instrumental in organizing a vast publishing
undertaking known as Vsemirnaya literatura (World Literature), which
enabled Russian writers and scholars to earn their livelihood by translations
during the abnormal years of War Communism. Gorky's personal friendship with Lenin and his great fame and prestige outside Russia made it
possible for him to take at times an independent attitude toward the new
government's policy, and especially to exercise his influence on behalf of
some victims of the Red Terror in its initial stages. For instance, if we are
to believe Zamyatin, Gorky did all that he could to save Gumilyov from
execution and was terribly upset when his efforts in Moscow on behalf of
Gumilyov were forestalled by the authorities in Petrograd.[17]

Gorky was also responsible for helping and encouraging young writers,
in whom he had always taken a great interest. Many of the now-famous
Soviet authors remember with deep gratitude the encouragement they received from Gorky. It was he who "discovered" Vsevolod Ivanov and
helped Fedin to his feet, and in general, the Serapion Brothers as a group
owed much to Gorky's sympathetic interest and help.

In 1921, Gorky left Russia for reasons of health (the hardships of War
Communism and the heavy load of work he took upon himself in those
years had intensified his earlier tuberculosis) and went to live near Berlin,
where he started Beseda—"a review of literature and science"—while con-
tinuing to contribute to Krasnaya Nov. In 1924 he retired to his villa in
Sorrento, where he had lived before the Revolution, and there he remained
until 1928, in a kind of self-imposed exile. His attitude toward the new
regime during this period was ambivalent. He kept in touch with the
Soviet Union, and his works were printed there; he never relented in his

---

[16] Gorbachov, Contemporary Russian Literature, 36. Gorky's anti-Bolshevik articles
are now available in English in Untimely Thoughts (trans. and ed. by H. Ermolaev).

[17] Zamyatin's memoir of Gorky, originally published in French translation in La
Revue de France (August 1, 1936), was included in Litsa and is now available in
English in A Soviet Heretic.

hostility to its open enemies, both Russian and foreign; but on several occasions he spoke out in frank criticism of it, as for instance in connection with
the trial of the Socialist Revolutionaries. In his book published in 1929,
Gorbachov wrote of Gorky: "Gorky in his article about Vladimir Ilyich
Lenin [*Russky Sovremennik*, 1924] mentioned somewhat coquettishly . . .
the fact that he did not quite believe in the good sense of the masses. Gorky
hardly ever believed in it in earnest and was always a bad Marxist."

To Gorbachov, Gorky's "romantic Socialism" had little to do with the
militant tasks of the proletariat. He saw Gorky as "a revolutionary demo-
crat," a kind of Menshevik, interested above all in fighting for the "Euro-
peanization" of Russia, against the age-old backwardness of her masses.[18]

However, in 1928, Gorky made a short triumphant re-entry into the
Soviet Union and was feted there on the occasion of his sixtieth birthday. A
year later he went to Russia again, this time to remain there until his death.
His role as the *doyen* of Soviet letters and as an influential force in all
matters of literary policy, facilitated by his new-found friendship with
Stalin, was particularly great during the last four years of his life. Certain
aspects of Gorky's activities during this last period will be touched upon in
later chapters.

As far as his own contribution to Russian literature since the Revolution
is concerned, three points are to be noted: (1) quantitatively speaking, it
was not very great and cannot compare with Gorky's pre-Revolutionary
output; (2) it was almost entirely retrospective; and (3) its quality was on
the whole very high—some of his post-Revolutionary writings will undoubtedly rank among his best. This is true primarily of his nonfiction (I do
not mean, however, his political journalism of the last years). His *Vospominaniya o Tolstom* (*Reminiscences of Tolstoy*, 1919) is justly regarded as
one of his masterpieces and as one of the most interesting and penetrating
pieces ever written about the great Russian writer. It is not, as D. S. Mirsky
rightly pointed out, that Gorky is anything like Tolstoy's intellectual equal,
or that he understands Tolstoy better than did some others. It is rather the
vividness of his vision of Tolstoy the man, and the brilliant manner in which
he conveys certain aspects of Tolstoy to the reader, that matters. Very
interesting also, even if not so brilliant and revealing, are his reminiscences
of Andreyev and Chekhov, and his portraits of some other of his contemporaries, some of which are to be found in his *Zapiski iz dnevnika*
(*Notes From a Diary*, 1924). *Moi Universitety* (*My Universities*, 1923)
forms a worthy sequel to *Detstvo* (*Childhood*, 1913) and *V lyudyakh* (*In
the World*, 1915); the whole of this autobiographical trilogy, with its wonderful character drawing and its earthy realism, will remain for posterity as
Gorky's most memorable creation.

After leaving Russia, Gorky published several stories in *Beseda* from

[18] Gorbachov, *Contemporary Russian Literature*, 33–35.

1923 to 1925. They are also retrospective, but two of them reflect his preoccupation with the problems and inner workings of the Revolution. One is a very interesting study, in the form of a confession, of the mind of a schizophrenic, a revolutionary who betrays his comrades and turns secret-police agent. This is "Karamora" ("Daddylonglegs"). Another, "Rasskaz o geroe" ("The Story About a Hero"), is of a counterrevolutionary brought up on Carlyle's hero worship, who might just as well have been a revolutionary and who ends by becoming a bandit and a hangman. Both stories show Gorky's predilection for unusual characters, for people with a quirk, and both reflect strongly the influence of Dostoyevsky, for whom Gorky professed an intense dislike. There are also echoes of Dostoyevsky, especially of the latter's *Notes from Underground*, in "Rasskaz o bezotvetnoy lyubvi" ("The Story of an Unrequited Love"), one of Gorky's most effective stories.

Delo Artamonovykh (*The Artamonov Business*, 1925) was Gorky's first regular novel since *Matvey Kozhemyakin* (1911). It was better than any of his middle-period work and showed that, as a novelist, he was by no means a spent force. Its theme and atmosphere recalled *Foma Gordeyev*, but its structure was more firm and more compact. It is the story of three generations of a self-made bourgeois family. All the characters—the old Artamonov, the founder of the family's prosperity, a strong, self-willed man, one of those to whom Gorky, for all his hatred of the bourgeoisie, felt instinctively attracted; his sons and grandsons, in whom there are already signs of imminent degeneration; their wives; and other episodic characters—are portrayed with Gorky's uncommonly keen gift of observation. As is usual with Gorky, the element of healthy robustness and vitality is combined with an insight into the dark, somber side of life, not only in its outward manifestations but also in the inner workings of human nature. In spite of the lifelikeness and variety of its characters, of whom Gorky shows not only their darker sides, there hangs about the whole novel that atmosphere of gloom which makes him in his mature period, despite all his propensity to romanticism, a true representative of critical realism. The same is true of *Zhizn' Klima Samgina* (*The Life of Klim Samgin*, 1927–36). But this long epic of forty years of Russian life (it was to be continued) is one of Gorky's failures. With its multitude of characters and its extremely uninteresting hero, it is diffuse and dull, and it reveals glaringly Gorky's lack of constructive ability.

Gorky's two post-Revolutionary plays, *Egor Bulychov i drugie* (*Egor Bulychov and Others*, 1931) and *Dostigayev i drugie* (*Dostigayev and Others*, 1932), which are among his best realistic plays, are also retrospective in nature.

From the above it should be clear that, as an artist, the post-Revolutionary Gorky was looking back and seeking inspiration in the past. His few stories dealing with contemporary Soviet life are of little importance and interest.

The significant role which Gorky played in Soviet letters in the first years of the Revolution does not mean that as a writer he had any real influence on early post-Revolutionary literature, no matter what some of its representatives may say now. Mirsky was on the whole right when he wrote in 1926 that Gorky's work "is profoundly unlike all the work of the younger generation—first of all, for his complete lack of interest in style, and, secondly, for his very unmodern interest in human psychology."[19] The position, however, was reversed soon after Gorky's return to Russia, not because Gorky himself had changed in the meantime but because post-Revolutionary Russian literature had moved much closer to Gorky—to his realism tinged with revolutionary romanticism. This *rapprochement* will become evident in the further account of developments in Soviet literature.

When Gorky died on June 18, 1936, his death was lamented throughout the Soviet Union as an irreparable loss to Soviet letters. It was later ascribed to the evil machinations of the enemies of the Soviet Union, the "Trotskyites" and the "Fascists." In a volume of biobibliographical information about Gorky we read under the year 1936:

Winter and spring. Lives in Crimea, at Tesseli. On the instructions of the worst enemy of the people, the superbandit and international spy, Judas Trotsky, an anti-Soviet, "Right-Trotskyite" gang of traitors, spies and assassins sets about preparing the murder of Gorky.... *May 30.* As a result of the conceived plan of murder and the creation of harmful conditions for Gorky's health he fell ill with influenza at Gorki (near Moscow).... *June 8.* The illness took a turn for the worse in consequence of the saboteur methods of treatment applied by the murderers.[20]

This version of Gorky's death was generally accepted in the Soviet Union, and in a report surveying Soviet literature during a quarter of a century Alexey N. Tolstoy spoke of "the murder of Gorky, dictated by the Fascists to their direct agents."[21] This legend about Gorky's death is but part of the general mythmaking which played such an important part in Stalin's Russia. The true facts are still unknown and may not become known for many years to come.[22]

Victor Shklovsky once wrote: "Gorky's Bolshevism is ironic Bolshevism which does not believe in man. By Bolshevism I do not mean belonging to

[19] Mirsky, *Contemporary Russian Literature*, 120.

[20] S. Balukhaty and K. Muratova, *M. Gorky: Spravochnik (M. Gorky: A Reference Guide)*, 75–76.

[21] A. N. Tolstoy, *Chetvert' veka sovetskoy literatury. Doklad na yubileynoy sessii Akademii Nauk SSSR 18 noyabrya 1942 goda (A Quarter of a Century of Soviet Literature: Report Read at the Jubilee Session of the Academy of Sciences of the U.S.S.R. on November 18, 1942)*, 9.

[22] For some inconsistencies and fluctuations in Soviet accounts of the circumstances of Gorky's death see, for example, G. Herling, *Da Gorki a Pasternak: Considerazoni sulla letteratura sovietica*, 7–41.

a political party: Gorky never belonged to the Party"; and further: "Gorky does not at all believe in mankind. He does not like all men, but only those who write well or work well." These "paradoxes" of Shklovsky's are much nearer the truth than the official "icon" of Gorky the humanist which has been painted all too often. Gorky is still waiting for someone to strip his true face of artificial hagiographic varnish—to do for him what he did for Tolstoy.[23]

**Ivanov
(1895–1963)**

Vsevolod Vyacheslavovich Ivanov, one of the Serapion Brothers, was a typical revolutionary romantic. He was born in Siberia. His father, a village teacher and a drunkard, was killed accidentally by one of his sons. At the age of fifteen Ivanov ran away from school to follow a circus. He worked for it as a clown. After a short spell at an agricultural school he became a typesetter and during summers worked again for the circus in various capacities, including that of "fakir and dervish," under the name Ben-Ali-Bey. In his autobiography he wrote: "I read a lot, from Dumas to Spencer and from Dream Books to Tolstoy. Books never had a great influence on me, and I read them also from boredom, for I didn't drink vodka."[24]

In the autumn of 1916, Ivanov wrote his first story, and it was printed in the local Siberian paper. Encouraged by this success, he decided to send his next story to Gorky's *Letopis'* (*Annals*). Gorky liked the story and wrote Ivanov an encouraging letter, after which Ivanov sat down and wrote twenty stories within the next two weeks. Some of them he sent to Gorky, who thought them bad and advised Ivanov to study and read more before he again took to writing. Ivanov says that in the next two years he read more books than he would probably read during the rest of his life, but none of them were about politics, and that when the Revolution broke out in 1917, he did not know the difference between the Social Democrats and the Socialist Revolutionaries and so joined both parties at once! In the Civil War he fought first on the side of the Whites (apparently he was conscripted into Admiral Kolchak's army), when he was taken prisoner and barely escaped being shot. After that he fought with the Red guerrillas in Siberia. In 1919 his first book of stories appeared in Siberia, printed and published by himself; and in 1920, with Gorky's help, he went to Petrograd.

---

[23] Something toward this end was done by the poet Khodasevich, Gorky's friend, in his reminiscences of their life together at Sorrento. See *Sovremennye Zapiski* (*Contemporary Annals*), Vol. LXIII (1937), Vol. LXX (1940). Cf. also Gorky's letters to Khodasevich in *Novy Zhurnal* (Nos. 29-31, 1952) and their English version in *Harvard Slavic Studies*, Vol. I (1953). This period in Gorky's life has also been vividly described in the "autobiography" of Nina Berberova (Khodasevich's wife at the time), *The Italics Are Mine* (1969).

[24] *Pisateli. Avtobiografii i portrety sovremennykh russkikh prozaikov* (*Writers: Autobiographies and Portraits of Contemporary Russian Prose-Fiction Authors*) (ed. by Vl. Lidin), 145.

There he joined the Cosmist group of proletarian writers and, later, the Serapion Brothers. In 1922 he was expelled from the Cosmists for belonging to a nonproletarian literary organization. In 1921 there appeared *Partizany* (*Partisans*), a long story based on Ivanov's experiences in the Civil War. It was followed in 1922 by several books: *Bronepoezd No. 14–69* (*Armored Train No. 14–69*), *Loga* (*Gullies*, a book of stories), and *Tsvetnye vetra* (*Colored Winds*, a novel). Both Gorky and the Serapions regarded Ivanov as the most talented among them.

In these works and in the novel *Golubye peski* (*Skyblue Sands*, 1923) we find all the characteristics of Ivanov's early work: the spicy, ornamental language, full of dialecticisms; the jerky narrative, interspersed with lyrical refrains; the animistic attitude toward nature, which is made to participate in human joys and sorrows; the obvious influence of Russian folklore; the stress on the cruel, "bestial" aspect of the Revolution, its "blood and sweat"; and the utter detachment with which horrible things are related. Thus the story called "Polaya Arapiya" ("Hollow Arabia") tells of how the population of a whole village somewhere in eastern Russia, driven by hunger, moves southward to seek Hollow Arabia, a mythical country of plenty about which they have heard from a crazy woman; of how they are forced to eat rats and horse manure; and of how they suspect one another of anthropophagic intentions. The story ends with one of them, who is on the point of dying of starvation and exhaustion, hiding under a cart, with the greedy eyes of four of his covillagers on him, watching his every movement, ready to finish him off and devour him. The horror of this story is heightened by the author's detached, matter-of-fact manner.

In another typical story, "Dityo" ("The Child"), Red partisans kill two officers who are approaching them in a cart. One of the officers turns out to be a woman. In a basket tied under the cart they find a child. After some unsuccessful attempts to feed him on cabbage soup, chewed bread, and other unsuitable things, they decide to make a raid on a nearby Kirghiz camp and steal some cows. At the camp one of them decides also to kidnap a young Kirghiz mother, which he does. The kidnaped mother, without the knowledge of the raiders, brings along her own child. She starts feeding both babies, but soon the partisans discover that she is cheating them and giving preference to her own child. With little thought or hesitation they kill the "yellow" child so that the "white" one will get enough milk. And they laugh heartily when they see the child sucking vigorously at the breast of the impassive Kirghiz woman.

Shklovsky has pointed out that Ivanov's story may appear at first trite, that it reminds one of some stories by Bret Harte or Leonid Andreyev or Gorky, but that at the end Ivanov gives it a most unexpected and original twist. It was this *ostranenie* ("making strange"), of which Shklovsky regarded Tolstoy such a superb master, that the Serapions learned from

Shklovsky to value as one of the most effective weapons in a writer's arsenal, whether it be in the plot, in description, or in style. In all their early work they were deliberately aiming at this effect of "strangeness" and "freshness," and here there was no difference between the "Westerners," like Luntz and Kaverin, and the "Russians," like Ivanov and Nikitin. In fact, no one sought more these "strange" effects than the last two.

Ivanov's two novels (*Colored Winds* and *Skyblue Sands*) are novels in name only. They are shapeless, without plot, and full of "ornamental" writing and picturesque local color (of Siberia and Mongolia)—in fact, typical products of the Pilnyak school but devoid of Pilnyak's intellectualism and free of his historicophilosophical quests. Ivanov is much more genuinely primitive—he has a true pantheistic sense of nature and of man's fusion with it. He brings out forcibly the meaninglessness and aimlessness of life and of human behavior, emphasizing its obscure, inexplicable mainsprings. Characteristic of him is the combination of an instinctive zest for life with a fundamental pessimism. This quality imparts a somber note to his writings. Like all the Serapions, he is fond of unexpected situations and contrasts, of exoticism, and is given to overnaturalistic descriptions. Life, as Ivanov sees it, is cruel and senseless, and man, a toy manipulated by dark and blind forces. "A man's soul is like a bear's: it don't see its own path," says Ivanov in one of his stories.

In 1923, Ivanov published a short novel, *Vozvrashchenie Buddy* (*The Return of Buddha*), which marked a new departure for him. It was much less "ornamentally" written, was of a less localized interest, and had a plot of adventure. He also tried his hand at a "proletarian" political novel about factory life in *Severostal'* (*Northsteel*, 1925), but without success. His book of stories of village life, *Taynoye taynykh* (*Mystery of Mysteries*, 1927), had a mixed reception from Soviet critics. Here, in conformity with the general development of Soviet literature, Ivanov took a step toward psychological realism. His style became more simple and direct, and more room was given to the psychology of characters. But Ivanov's attitude toward life remained fundamentally the same. Again he showed human conduct as blind and senseless, human beings as possessed by dark and violent passions to which they in the end succumb. Most of the stories in this collection are pervaded with a sense of doom and destruction. As a result Ivanov was accused of mysticism and pessimism, of worshiping blind and cruel fate, of being unable to adjust himself to the Revolution. Some critics spoke of his fundamentally antirevolutionary tendency, in which they saw a legacy of his "petit bourgeois" past. Later, as we shall see, Ivanov did his best to live it down.

Nikitin
(1895–1963) Little is known about the life of another Serapion, Nikolay Nikolayevich Nikitin, except that he was born in the north of Russia, apparently in a

merchants' family, spent most of his childhood in Petersburg, and went to a high school and the university there. In his autobiography he says: "Then the War. Then the Revolution. It would take too long to write about this. Here I learned everything." It is to be assumed that Nikitin fought in the Civil War, but on whose side we do not know. His first story was published in 1922, after he had met Gorky, Shklovsky, Zamyatin (who taught him the art of writing), and the Serapions.

In many ways Nikitin is the typical representative of Russian prose fiction of this period—more typical even than Ivanov, because his scope is wider, because he is more bookish, and because his manner is less spontaneous and more experimental.

Nikitin's most characteristic early stories are to be found in the first two volumes of his *Collected Works* (1928), entitled respectively *Rvotny Fort* (*Fort Vomit*) and *Polyot* (*Flight*). It is not difficult to see in them the influence of Remizov, Zamyatin, and Pilnyak. To this list can also be added, either as direct or as indirect influences, Leskov and Gogol, and, as occasional influences, Dostoyevsky and Andrey Bely.

From Zamyatin and Pilnyak comes Nikitin's broken, disjointed narrative; from Pilnyak, the constant lyrical digressions, the author's personal interventions, the use of "documents" and quotations, the historical landscape, and the intense eroticism of many stories, among them "Fort Vomit," "Noch" ("Night"), and "Pella"; from Leskov and Remizov, the *skaz* manner, with a great variety of spoken intonations and styles—peasants', soldiers', gypsies', and so on; from them, too, the predilection for the anecdote, the folklore element, and certain characters such as the hermit Pim in "Fort Vomit." Stories like "Zhizn' gvardii sapyora" ("The Life of a Guards Sapper"), "Koshka-sobaka" ("Cat-Dog"), and "Chavaly" ("Romanies") read like Leskovian exercises on post-Revolutionary themes, like ingenious pastiches. In a highly concentrated form, nearly all the characteristics of the Russian prose fiction of this period are to be found in Nikitin: the elaborate, affected, mosaic-like style; the hysterically emotionalized diction; the prevalence of incident and action over psychology; the ideological detachment.

For a student of this "ornamental," "dynamic" prose with all its good points and all its defects, there is no better material than Nikitin's early stories, written in 1921–23. Many of these stories deal with the Civil War— in the north, in the south, and in the east. On the whole Nikitin is less interested in the war itself than in its effect on the life of remote Russian villages, where the old and the new clash. Several Soviet critics were right, however, in pointing out that Nikitin was concerned not so much with the new as with the old—with the resistance of the old rather than with the struggle for the new; and that he was much more successful in portraying the old, unchanging aspects of Russia than the new Revolutionary heroes.[25]

[25] See P. Medvedev's Introduction to Volume I of Nikitin's *Sobranie sochineniy*

Most of his stories served as an illustration of the thesis that the Revolution had touched only the surface of Russian life and that deep down everything remained as before, almost as it had been a hundred years ago.

One of Nikitin's most typical stories—both stylistically and "ideologically" —is "Night." It is full of literary reminiscences and looks like a mosaic where separate pieces can be traced to various sources: Zamyatin, Pilnyak, Leskov, Remizov, Gogol (in his famous comparison of Russia to a troika), Russian folklore, and so on. Its subject is an encounter between two armored trains during the Civil War in the south of Russia. Nikitin is little concerned with the military aspect of the situation, and the final clash is suggested rather than described. What he attempts to do is to suggest the atmosphere of doom, and to present a cross section of both trains—the Red, named after the Hungarian Communist Béla Kun, and the White, named after General Kornilov—and their passengers.

In a mixture of the tragic and the trivial, the mounting sense of the impending catastrophe (the events of the story take place in a single night) is conveyed very well. The portraits are dynamic and impressionistic: the old general who prays in the solitude of the train's bathroom while his wife is being unfaithful to him with a young subordinate of his whom the Revolution has reduced to drunken cynicism; the young White volunteer Neledin, who writes a naïve and touching letter to his mother and becomes indignant with the cynical, drunken officer; the commissar of the Red train, a rugged fellow from Siberia, who makes love to his American secretary. This last pair is, of course, a deliberate parallel to the general's wife and the young officer, illustrating the power which the forces of life have over men at all times.

Ideologically speaking, Nikitin refuses to take sides and shows an utter detachment. Both the Reds and the Whites are men—ordinary men—with all their qualities and all their failings. The old general and young Neledin are certainly meant to inspire sympathy in the reader, more so than any of the Reds. Moreover, the Whites are also shown fighting for their ideas, for the good of the country as they understand it. This is made particularly clear in Neledin's letter home, which has a genuine ring. To the Reds and the Whites are opposed the "neutral" Cossacks, who refuse to fight, who think only of their selfish interests, and after the final catastrophe try to profit by it, collecting scrap iron from the two burned-out trains. Nikitin calls them "the jackals of the Revolution." They are symbolized in Kuzma Fenogenov, a typical Cossack. Nikitin says:

History will call this rabble the jackals. The Revolution also had its jackals who

---

(*Collected Works*), 18–19. See also Gorbachov, *Contemporary Russian Literature*, 113–18, and *Ocherki sovremennoy russkoy literatury* (*Studies in Contemporary Russian Literature*), 93ff.

stood aside and waited for profits. But the Revolution itself was beautiful, elemental—like a powerful nocturnal thunderstorm. This is said not to justify it nor is it by any means a poetic image. It is the elements. And about the elements a song must be composed. And each one . . . will compose this song in his own, different way, but not one of them will sing the glory of Kuzma Fenogenov and his droves. . . . . Cursed be those who warmed themselves at the warm, after-battle ashes.

In another story, "Kamni" ("The Stones"), the implication is that the Revolution and the Counterrevolution, the Reds and the Whites, are equally bad and that both bring nothing but misery in their wake. But mostly the Revolution is shown by Nikitin as something mysterious, dark, and incomprehensible, greedy like the sea and intoxicating like the wind (in this respect the story is reminiscent of both Blok and Pilnyak). In the later stories the weekdays of the Revolution, after its comparative stabilization, are contrasted with its early, romantic period—those "wonderful, unforgettable days." Among these stories "Polyot" ("Flight"), despite its annoying stylistic mannerisms, its Pilnyakian tricks (sudden shiftings of planes, the use of documents and symbolic refrains), and its rather cheap eroticism, succeeds in conveying to the reader the drama of two average old-time officers caught in the revolutionary whirlpool. Some of the scenes describing the madness of Firsov, slightly reminiscent of Bely, are very effective.

Of all the Serapions no one perhaps aimed so persistently at strange, paradoxical effects as did Nikitin. In its most consistent and bare form the method of *ostranenie* is applied by him in "Daisy," the story of a young tigress in captivity and of her ultimate escape. This story, written in the name of the tigress and divided into short chapters, many of them less than half a page, can also be studied as a text illustrating certain favorite devices of the Pilnyak school in Russian literature.

Together with the rest of Soviet literature, Nikitin's work gradually evolved toward a more realistic treatment of the Revolution and its themes.

In 1923 a writer whose name was practically unknown attracted the attention of the critics and the public. He was Isaac Babel, soon to be hailed as one of the most talented and original among the younger Soviet writers.

Babel (1894–1941)

Born in Odessa in 1894 into a typical Jewish middle-class family with strong Jewish traditions, Isaac Emmanuilovich Babel was educated in one of the secondary schools of Odessa. While still at school he developed a great liking for French literature. Flaubert and Maupassant were his first literary masters, and his early youthful stories were written in French. This mingling of the traditional Jewish atmosphere, the study of the Talmud and of Hebrew, with the Latin precision and clarity of the French and their literature, the stylistic fastidiousness inspired by Flaubert (to which was later added the influence of the Revolution seen in its most elemental, "romantic," and cruel aspects), resulted in a strange product, full of contrasts and paradoxes.

Babel's literary career began in 1916, when Gorky, who was then editing *Letopis'*, published his first two stories. They were full of eroticism, and Babel and the magazine became involved in judicial proceedings under Article 1001 of the Russian Civil Code, which was aimed at pornography. Gorky, who was quick to see Babel's talent and ready to encourage him, was not satisfied, however, with the next stories which Babel sent him. Influenced by this adverse criticism, Babel stopped writing and did not reappear in literature until 1923. In the early years of the Revolution he took part in the Civil War and in 1920 fought against Poland with the famous cavalry army of Budyonny. Later he held various posts in Soviet administration and worked as a journalist in Tiflis and elsewhere. In an autobiographical note he wrote, "It was only in 1923 that I learned to express my ideas clearly and at not too great a length, and then I took to writing again." In 1923-24 he published a number of short stories. Many of them were included in his *Konarmiya* (*Red Cavalry*, 1926), a volume of stories for which he drew upon his experiences with Budyonny's army in the Soviet-Polish war. It was followed in 1931 by a collection of *Odesskie rasskazy* (*Odessa Stories*) and two longer autobiographical stories, "Istoriya moey golubyatni" ("The Story of My Dovecote") and "Pervaya lyubov'" ("First Love").[26]

The *Red Cavalry* stories brought Babel fame. Even outside Russia he began to be spoken of as the rising star of the young post-Revolutionary literature. It has been pointed out that Babel was the first among post-Revolutionary writers to revive a definite literary genre—that of the pointed, short *nouvelle* (in which, incidentally, the influence of Maupassant could be easily discerned). Babel's stories, with their clear and distinct outline, their brevity, and their fastidious style, came as something new after the welter of shapeless, loose productions of the Pilnyak school and of the other "dynamic prose" writers. Yet Babel had something in common with them and differed as much as they did from the realists who were about to make their appearance and revive the traditional psychological novel. He had the same predilection for *skaz*, for ornamentalism, and for the exotic and romantic aspects of the Revolution and the same aversion to psychological analysis. But he differed from Pilnyak and his followers in his feeling for form and his concern with style. Even his *skaz* was subordinated to a deliberate stylistic design in which the element of contrast and paradox played a great part. It has been rightly said that it is style which holds his stories

---

[26] It appears that some of the *Odessa Stories* were written before many of those in *Red Cavalry*. The chronology of Babel's writings—as distinct from publications—has not been completely ascertained. After Babel's posthumous rehabilitation it was discussed in an article by L. Livshits in *Voprosy Literatury*, No. 4 (1964), 110-35.

together, whether they be tales of the Revolution and the Civil War or pictures of Jewish life in Odessa.

Babel's attitude toward life can be described as purely sensuous and aesthetic. He is attracted by the bright, the picturesque, the unusual in life. His Jewish stories, for all their realism in the portrayal of the peculiarities of life and speech of Odessa Jews, are imbued with the same romanticism and exoticism. Instead of the familiar and traditional middle-class Jewish milieu, Babel shows us something quite out of the ordinary—the world of Jewish gangsters and bandits, who appear to us romantically glamorized and at the same time pathetic and humorous. In the center of this world stands the figure of Benya Krik, the "king" of Odessa gangsters, a character of almost legendary proportions, yet pathetically human and lovable.

In the Revolution, Babel's attention is also centered on the exotic and romantic aspects, on the unusual and paradoxical. All Babel's stories about life in Budyonny's army have this romantic streak. Babel's keen vision and great sense of line and color, combined with his extreme sensitiveness to cruelty and to all that is excessive and inordinate in life, enables him to depict graphically the Civil War in a series of Goyaesque scenes. He does this with great artistic economy and detachment. He dwells with a certain relish on scenes of plunders, riots, and executions—of senseless, instinctive, almost good-humored cruelty. It is the almost animal instinct of destruction that he shows above all in the Civil War, and this is why his *Red Cavalry* provoked a strong protest from Marshal Budyonny, who denounced it as a one-sided and distorted picture of his army and its exploits.[27] Babel's stories of the Red Cavalry are not, however, realistic snapshots of its everyday life— they are full of hyperbolism, of romantic contrasts, and of a peculiar pathos wherein the cruel and the heroic merge into each other. There is in Babel a strong element of eroticism, which, despite its apparent naturalism, is also treated romantically and hyperbolically. But many readers are revolted by the crude and outspoken physiological descriptions which abound in Babel's stories.

Babel's favorite method is that of contrast and paradox. Nearly all of his stories are based on contrasts, both psychological and stylistic. Throughout *Red Cavalry* there runs a contrast between the cruelty, the elemental blindness and crude sensuousness of the scenes described and their perception through the spectacles of the narrator, who obviously stands for Babel himself—an educated Jew, nearsighted, physically weak, and psychologically out of tune with his surroundings and the life he is forced to share and, in addition, burdened with a skeptical attitude toward the world. Parallel with

[27] Budyonny's short retort to Babel appeared in *Oktyabr* (*October*) No. 3 (1924), under the title "The Womanizing of Babel from *Krasnaya Nov*." In Russian there is a pun here, the Russian word for "woman" being *baba* and the verb "to womanize," *babnichat'*.

this is the contrast between Babel's poetic descriptions of nature, reminiscent of Gogol as well as of Imaginist poetry, full of color and hyperbole, and the crude physiological naturalism of many scenes. The crudeness and cruelty of human beings and their behavior are set off by this resplendent theatrical background. Babel's romanticism is tempered—one might almost say poisoned—by his irony and skepticism. An unusual "romantic" situation is often set off by small, matter-of-fact details. Here is a typical passage from the story "Berestechko":

Right in front of my windows a few Cossacks were executing an old silver-bearded Jew accused of spying. The old man was screaming and trying to tear himself loose. Then Kudrya, of the machine-gun section, seized his head and tucked it under his arm. The Jew hushed and spread out his legs. With his left hand Kudrya took out a dagger and carefully butchered the old man, without bespattering himself.

Babel is by no means a painter of everyday life, whether of the Red Army or of the Odessa Jewry; nor is he a psychologist. He saw the Revolution as a sort of romantic *décor*, and there is something romantically conventional in most of his characters. Among his contemporaries he showed himself a master of the short story. His stories are terse and compact and have an effective *pointe*. His attitude toward the Revolution is detached—he has no ax to grind, no message to bring. The Revolution appears to him as a great elemental force, blind and cruel, which sweeps along with no regard for the individual. This attitude is reflected in the story called "Gedali." Babel describes in it a conversation with an old Jewish owner of a curiosity shop during the Soviet-Polish war. The old man, Gedali, is ready to say yea to the Revolution, but he refuses to say nay to the Sabbath. He is at a loss to see a difference between the Revolution and the Counterrevolution. Both shoot and both are cruel to man: "Who can tell Gedali where is the revolution and where the counterrevolution? . . . all we learned men, we fall upon our faces and we cry out loudly: Woe unto us, where is the sweet revolution?"

Gedali asks the author to bring good men to his town. He wants "an International of good men":

". . . I want every soul to be kept on the register and be given first category rations. Here, man, pray, eat, and enjoy life. The International, mister comrade, do you know how it should be served?"

"It is served with gunpowder," I answered, "and seasoned with the best blood."

The story ends with Gedali—"the founder of a fantastic International"—going to the synagogue to pray, "small, lonely, dreamy, in a black top hat, a large prayer book under his arm."

Babel reached the height of his popularity in the late 1920's. His *Red Cavalry* and *Odessa Tales* went through several editions. In 1928 he published a very interesting play, *Zakat* (*Sunset*), with the life of Odessa Jews for its setting. During the period inaugurated in 1929 (to be discussed later), his reputation suffered a considerable setback. His romantic irony and detached individualism proved to be out of place. He almost ceased publishing and after 1938 disappeared from literature. In 1956 it was disclosed that he had died (apparently in a concentration camp) in 1941. The story of his subsequent "rehabilitation" will be told in its place.

Poets

With the re-emergence of prose fiction, poetry lost something of its monopolistic position. But books of poems continued to appear in great numbers, especially in 1921–23. Mayakovsky and Esenin, both of whom enjoyed great popularity during this period, were echoed by other Futurists and Imaginists. Proletarian and peasant poets were very active, too. Some of the former will be discussed in a later section, for much of their work is characteristic of the next phases of Soviet literature, as is that of Boris Pasternak, although one of his best and most important books, *Sestra moya zhizn'* (*My Sister Life*), appeared in 1922. It is, however, impossible to speak of this period of Soviet literature without saying something about Tikhonov and Aseyev, especially the former, who was not only a member of the Serapion Brotherhood but a true poetic counterpart of the Serapions as prose writers.

Nikolay Semyonovich Tikhonov was born into a lower-middle-class family. **Tikhonov** After studying at a trade school, he enlisted in the army as a volunteer and **(b. 1896)** fought with a Hussar regiment on the Riga front and later with the Red Army in the Civil War. Like many of his contemporaries he also tried his hand at various professions. In 1921 he joined the Serapion Brotherhood and a year later published his first book of poems, *Orda* (*The Horde*). Its principal theme was war. The influence of the Acmeists, especially of Gumilyov and to a lesser extent of Mandelstam, is quite obvious in it. Tikhonov can be described as a romantic realist. His verse of this period has a noble simplicity, there is no pursuit of novelty for novelty's sake. The choice of words is fastidious and precise, the structure of the phrase firm and compact, and the verse has a strong, metallic ring, in keeping with the dominant virile note of fearless acceptance of all the hardships of war, and even of death. Tikhonov's poetry is equally removed from Mayakovsky's coarse and strident rhetoric and from Esenin's mellifluousness. The following typical poem illustrates the influence of Gumilyov and at the same time reflects Tikhonov's fundamentally romantic attitude:

> Fire, rope, bullet and axe
> Like servants bowed and followed us.
> And in every drop a deluge slept,
> Mountains grew forth from little stones,

And in a twig crushed underfoot
Rustled black-armed forests.
Untruth ate and drank with us,
Church bells pealed from force of habit,
Coins had lost their weight and ring,
And children were not scared of corpses.

It was then we learned, for the first time,
Words beautiful, bitter and cruel.

Another illustration is the following famous lines about men of his generation, "simple like iron nails":

Life taught me with oar and rifle,
And a strong wind with a knotted cord
Lashed me upon my shoulders,
To make me both calm and nimble,
And simple like iron nails.

In Tikhonov's second book of verse, *Braga* (*Mead*), the heroic themes of the Civil War predominate, many of them treated in the form of ballads, in which can be seen the influence of English poetry and of Kipling in particular. This form of ballad was taken up not only by Tikhonov but also by several other disciples of Gumilyov (for example, Irina Odoyevtseva and Vladimir Pozner—the latter, like Tikhonov, a member of the Serapion fraternity). Tikhonov's ballads enjoyed great popularity, especially his "Ballad About the Blue Packet" and "Ballad About Nails." The latter, in eighteen laconic lines, sings the heroism of pre-Revolutionary Russian sailors. It ends with the lines:

Nails ought to be made out of these men:
There would be no stronger nails in the world.

The Oriental note, which was later to play a prominent part in Tikhonov's poetry, was introduced in the ballad called "Sami." Somewhat similar to Kipling's ballads in form, it is the story of a Hindu boy in Amritsar who is born to a new life, a new sense of his human dignity, after praying to "Lenni" (Lenin). After this a definite political note is sounded more clearly in the poetry of Tikhonov, who had earlier described himself as an incurable anarchist. It is conspicuous in his next book, *Poiski geroya* (*Quest for a Hero*), containing several poems in the nature of political satires. Even in Tikhonov's earlier lyrical poetry there was nearly always an element of "story," but with time this narrative element became more and more prominent. The three longer poems, written in 1924—"Krasnye na Arakse" ("The Reds on the Araks"), "Litsom k litsu" ("Face to Face"), and "Doroga" ("The Road")—are attempts at creating a new form of revolutionary narrative poem. They reflect the experimental stage in Tikhonov's poetry, when he not only strove after new compositional forms but also experimented with language and meters, becoming deliberately obscure and difficult. In this period the influence of Gumilyov and the Acmeists gave place to that of the Futurists, of Mayakovsky, and, even more, of Khlebnikov and Pasternak. Tikhonov is one of the very few Soviet poets who turned to creative account Khlebnikov's poetic experiments. Particularly characteristic of this tendency is the poem "Shakhmaty" ("Chess"), one of Tikhonov's most difficult and abstruse poems, in which he attempted to present the Revolution, as Gorbachov wrote, "through a strictly consistent reproduction of all the details of a game of chess."

The most important of Mayakovsky's followers during this period was **Aseyev** Nikolay Nikolayevich Aseyev, who began writing and publishing before **(1889–1963)** the Revolution. His early poetry was influenced by the Symbolists and Khlebnikov, and a romantic note of rebellious individualism was very strong in it. The influence of Khlebnikov was reflected in Aseyev's archaic stylizations. His acceptance of the Revolution was also colored with romanticism. His hatred of all bourgeois forms, of all philistinism, made him take a hostile attitude toward the NEP. His long poem "Liricheskoye otstuplenie" ("Lyrical Digression") reflects this post-NEP mood of bitter disillusionment.

From 1923 on, Aseyev took an active part in the so-called LEF (Left Front of Literature), of which Mayakovsky was one of the leaders and which united mostly Futurists, who sought in it a political basis for their action. In keeping with the program of "utilitarian" art proclaimed by the LEF in their magazine, Aseyev wrote a number of "industrial" and propaganda poems. But romanticism was too strongly ingrained in him, and his narrative poems about the Revolution—*Poema o 26 bakinskikh kommissarakh* (*The Poem About the 26 Baku Commissars*), *Poema o Budyonnom* (*The Poem About Budyonny*), and *Semyon Proskakov* (in which a Red Army soldier is contrasted with Admiral Kolchak)—are all full of romantic emotionalism. Aseyev's post-Revolutionary poetry was greatly influenced by Mayakovsky, but on the whole it is simpler and more emotional. Aseyev also took an active part in the literary controversies of the twenties. Some of his theoretical and polemical articles were collected, in 1929, in two volumes: *Dnevnik poeta* (*The Diary of a Poet*) and *Rabota nad stikhom* (*Working at Verse*).

Chapter 6. **LITERARY CONTROVERSIES**

With the revival of literature after the end of the Civil War, the antagonism between proletarian and nonproletarian literature reached a new and acute stage. The main part in that revival was played, as we saw, by nonproletarian and non-Communist writers who, in their own way, had "accepted" the Revolution and focused their artistic attention on its processes. Even most of the Serapions, despite their insistence on being free to choose their subjects, in point of fact wrote almost exclusively about the Revolution. All those writers who, without being Communists, vaguely sympathized with the Revolution and were certainly hostile to its enemies were dubbed "fellow travelers."

Onguardists Versus Fellow Travelers

The term "fellow travelers" was first used by Trotsky in one of the essays in his book *Literature and Revolution* (1923):

> Between the bourgeois art, which is living itself out in repetitions or in silence, and the new art, which has not yet arrived, a transitional art is being created, more or less organically bound up with the Revolution, but at the same time not the art of the Revolution.

After listing a number of writers representative of this art—including Esenin, Pilnyak, Vsevolod Ivanov, and Tikhonov—Trotsky went on:

> Their literary and, generally speaking, spiritual countenance is a product of the Revolution, of that angle of it which has touched them, and they all accept it, each in his own way. But in these individual acceptances they have one feature in common which marks them off sharply from Communism and always threatens to oppose them to it. They fail to grasp the Revolution as a whole, and its Communist aim is alien to them. They are all more or less inclined to look hopefully at the peasant over the head of the worker. They are not the artists of proletarian revolution but its artistic fellow travelers.

The term took root and came to be widely used in all the literary battles and squabbles of the next decade, though the definition was sufficiently vague to allow considerable latitude when it came to deciding whether this or that writer was or was not a fellow traveler. Thus, some critics treated even Mayakovsky as a fellow traveler. But in a very general way "fellow traveler" became synonymous with "non-Communist," just as "proletarian" came to mean "Communist."

Between 1921 and 1924, fellow travelers dominated the literary scene. Many of the Communist leaders came to look upon them in the way in which they looked upon non-Communist, bourgeois experts in various other fields—in economics, finance, technology, science, medicine, and the like—their superior specialized knowledge and ability made them indispensable. Thus fellow travelers in literature came to be treated as literary *spetsy* ("experts"). Many orthodox Communist critics willingly admitted their superiority and patronized them. Foremost among these was Alexander Konstantinovich Voronsky (1884–1943), the founder and editor of *Krasnaya Nov*, which became the principal outlet for fellow travelers. In the literary battles of 1923–24 it was Voronsky and his review which had to bear the brunt of the attacks on fellow travelers.

October

These attacks came from the group which called itself Oktyabr (October). Founded at the end of 1922, it took the place of the Proletkult. Among its founders were the poet Alexander Bezymensky and the novelist Yury Libedinsky, and its principal spokesmen in the early stages were Semyon Rodov and G. Lelevich (pseudonym of Labory Kalmanson, 1901–45). Affiliated with October were two groups of young writers which had earlier clashed with the Smithy: Rabochaya Vesna (Workers' Spring) and Molodaya Gvardiya (Young Guard). The former was composed of many non-Communist factory workers; the latter was connected with the League of Communist Youth. October itself had a 100 per cent Communist membership and came out in defense of ideologically pure proletarian literature. In June of 1923, it began issuing its own magazine, called *Na Postu* (*On Guard*); and in 1924 another monthly, *Oktyabr* (*October*). Both were edited by Lelevich.[1] This group came to be referred to usually as the Napostovtsy (Onguardists). In the first number of *Na Postu* appeared the "Ideological and Artistic Platform" of October. Its main points were as follows:

In a class society, imaginative literature, just as everything else, serves the objects of a specific class, and only through that class, of the whole of mankind; hence, that literature is proletarian which organizes the psychology and consciousness of the working class and of the wide toiling masses toward the final aims of the proletariat as the reorganizer of the world and the creator of Communist society....

[1] Lelevich, who wrote some poetry and in 1926 published a book on Bryusov, was expelled from the party in 1928 for "opposition." In the 1930's he became a victim of the purges and was apparently liquidated. In *Kratkaya Literaturnaya Entsiklopediya* (*Short Literary Encyclopaedia*), Vol. IV (1967), it is said that he was "slandered and illegally repressed" and was "posthumously rehabilitated." This has become the hackneyed formula for the victims of Stalin's purges. The period itself is described officially as that of "the cult of personality" (*kult lichnosti*).

Proletarian literature opposes itself to bourgeois literature as its antipode. . . .

The group "October" asserts the primacy of content. The very content of a proletarian work of literature supplies the verbal and artistic material and suggests the form. Content and form are dialectical antitheses: content conditions form and is artistically formalized through it.

The group refused to give preference to any particular form, or forms, and rejected the one-sided solutions offered by Imaginism, Futurism, and Symbolism. As its final aim it proclaimed the creation of "a new synthetic form of proletarian literature." But October, too, had its enemies within the ranks of proletarian literature. It fought and finally hounded out of existence the old Smithy. At the same time it aimed at creating a united front of proletarian literature and to that end utilized the earlier-founded All-Union Association of Proletarian Writers (known briefly as the VAPP),[2] with branches in Moscow (MAPP) and Leningrad, or Petrograd as it was then still called (PAPP, later LAPP). In these two cities other proletarian literary organizations, such as October itself, were allowed to exist side by side with the branches of the VAPP, but in all other cities the principle of centralization was strictly adhered to.

In January, 1925, was held the first All-Union Conference of Proletarian Writers, which passed a resolution, on the report of comrade Vardin (pseudonym of I. G. Mgeladze), emphatically proclaiming that literature in a class society, far from being neutral, actively serves a particular class. This, ran the resolution, was doubly true of the present time—in the age of wars and revolutions and in times of acute class struggle. Therefore, all talk about peaceful co-operation and competition of various ideologies in literature was a reactionary dream. In ideology and in literature laws of class struggle operated just as much as in any other field of social life. Hence the necessity of ideological "intransigence" and "intolerance." The resolution contained a violent attack on those who denied the possibility of a specific proletarian culture and literature, and especially on Trotsky and Voronsky as the most consistent opponents of proletarian literature. This negative attitude to proletarian culture was ascribed to the pressure of the petty bourgeois elements, which in 1922–24 found its expression in the opposition within the Communist party—those who were working toward the gradual liquidation of the dictatorship of the proletariat and a return to "democracy."

The resolution denied that fellow travelers, who according to Trotsky and Voronsky were to be the main force in literature, were a homogeneous group. It insisted on differentiating between those who honestly, and to the best of their ability, served the Revolution, and most fellow travelers, "who distort the Revolution in literature, often slander it, and are imbued with the spirit of nationalism, great-power-mindedness, and mysticism." These "antirevolutionary" elements among fellow travelers must be fought against. The better elements might be made use of, but this could be done only if they were influenced by proletarian literature, only if they were "grouped round a proletarian kernel." It was not enough, went on the resolution, simply to "recognize" proletarian literature; it was necessary to accept the principle of its "hegemony," in order to allow it "to swallow up all species and varieties of bourgeois and petty-bourgeois literature." The resolution ended with the following proud and militant declaration:

Proletarian literature in the Soviet Union has but one aim before it: to serve the cause of world proletarian victory, to fight ruthlessly all the enemies of the Revolution. Proletarian literature will conquer bourgeois literature, for the proletarian revolution will inevitably destroy capitalism.[3]

Throughout 1923–24 the Onguardists had kept attacking fellow travelers as distorters and detractors of the Revolution, as men who by their creative efforts tried to bridge the gap between the past and the present. In 1924 the controversy reached a high pitch of violence. Trotsky and Voronsky, who had stood in defense of fellow travelers, were attacked even more violently. Ivan Maysky, a former Menshevik who was later to become Soviet ambassador in London, opened the pages of his review *Zvezda* (*Star*) to a discussion of the whole subject of proletarian culture and literature. He introduced it with an article entitled "About Culture, Literature, and the Communist Party," in which he sided definitely with the Onguardists and appealed to the authority of Lenin. He was supported by Lelevich, Rodov, and Gorbachov. Among his opponents was G. Yakubovsky, of the Smithy group. A more cautious attitude was taken by Lunacharsky and by the old Marxist critic Peter Kogan.[4]

[2] After 1928 it was known as VOAPP (All-Union Union of Associations of Proletarian Writers).

[3] This resolution was printed in *Zvezda* (*Star*), No. 1 (1925).

[4] This discussion was subsequently published in book form under the title *Proletariat i literatura* (*Proletariat and Literature*). Maysky prefaced the volume with an Introduction on Lenin's views on art, adding also the articles of Trotsky and Voronsky which had triggered the discussion, as well as another polemical article by Voronsky which had appeared in *Krasnaya Nov* (*Red Virgin Soil*) in reply to those by Lelevich and himself. Much of this discussion smacks of pedantic scholasticism, while there is also a strong element of personal vituperation, but the issues at stake were of vital importance to a great many writers whose freedom to write more or less as they wished was directly involved. English-speaking readers will find a fuller account of this controversy and of Voronsky's subsequent skirmishes with the Onguardists in Hugh McLean, Jr., "Voronskij and VAPP," *American Slavic and East European Review*, Vol. VIII, No. 3 (October, 1949), 185–200. In my opinion there is little justification for describing Voronsky as one of the most original Soviet critics. Voronsky's chief qualities were his honesty, courage, and comparative broad-mindedness. There was nothing original or particularly sensitive in his approach to literature. Some of his essential ideas were derived from Plekhanov. A detailed and painstaking investigation of the whole of this controversy will be found in H. Ermolaev, *Soviet Literary Theories, 1917–1934: The Genesis of Socialist Realism*.

The Voronsky "Theses"

Since Voronsky's views were to prevail for some time in the official literary policy, his article which provoked the *Zvezda* discussion deserves some attention. Appearing originally in March, 1924, it represented a memorandum submitted to the Propaganda Section of the Central Committee of the Communist party, where the matters of literary policy were usually ventilated and decided. It was divided into twelve "theses," which can be briefly summarized as follows:

1. After 1905 the main current of Russian literature was individualistic and decadent. The October Revolution cut off the roots which fed this literature. The most prominent among the old writers fell silent, became anemic, or emigrated.

2. During the Civil War literature was naturally propagandistic. Its main task was to help the Revolution win over its enemies. The services rendered by this propaganda literature in the past were great, and since the Republic of the Soviets remained "a besieged camp" and was obliged to carry an incessant struggle against the bourgeoisie, propaganda literature retained its value.

3. Following upon the transition from War Communism to peaceful reconstruction, literature was now faced with the problem of reflecting more truly the Revolutionary reality. Propaganda and agitation were not enough. What was expected of literature was the artistic cognition of life. Hence the great revival of prose fiction. The first to reflect the new Soviet realities in prose fiction were the so-called fellow travelers, writers of lower-middle-class, peasant, or intelligentsia origin, who grew up during the Revolution, accepted its achievements, observed it at first hand, or even took part in it. They were afterwards joined by some of their seniors. Though motley, ideologically unstable, or even suspect, this literature produced some valuable and significant works reflecting the Revolution, its new men and new mores. Its methods were realistic, though tinged with a peculiar romanticism.

4. The NEP engendered "constitutional illusions" among a certain section of the bourgeois intelligentsia. These men tried to exploit the literary revival for their own class ends. There were attempts to infuse literature with clericalism and mysticism, to portray the Revolution as a senseless mutiny.

5. Various groups of proletarian writers were also affected by the literary revival. Many of them were brought down to earth from the heights of abstract industrial romanticism. Several proletarian prose writers emerged from the ranks of the League of Communist Youth.

6. The party fought vigorously against all attempts to utilize the NEP for reactionary ends. It gave active assistance to "intermediate," nonparty writers and encouraged the left wing of the fellow travelers. The main fault

of the fellow travelers was that they often understood the Revolution as a triumph of the peasants and disregarded the guiding role of the proletariat. Nor were they able to grasp the international character of the Revolution. In helping these writers, the party exposed the limitations of their outlook. On the other hand, it supported proletarian and Communist writers by helping their publishing enterprises, printing their works in Soviet periodicals, and in other ways. At the same time it combatted all alien influences on them (Andrey Bely, Cosmism, etc.).

7. Of late, some Communist writers grouped around the magazine *On Guard* began to campaign in favor of a unified party line in matters of art, in place of the alleged present chaos. They attacked the fellow travelers, the Smithy, the LEF, and even some Communist writers. Their main demand was that proletarian literature should be placed in the center of the picture, while fellow travelers should be relegated to the background. It was true that fellow travelers still held the central position in literary life. It was due to their numerical and qualitative superiority. But the problem was no longer acute, and the demand of the Onguardists for a "quota" for fellow travelers in literature was unreal.

8. The growth of Soviet literature in the last three years could not be doubted. The party's efforts to subordinate literature to its ideological hegemony and to make it serve the cause of the Revolution had borne fruit. But there were also signs of a crisis, of literature being "in the doldrums." They were to be seen in the drying up of romantic enthusiasm, due to the postponement of the social revolution in the West and the unseemly aspects of the NEP; in the artificial, showy optimism of some proletarian writers; in the drunken bohemianism of Esenin; and so on. The urgent problem facing Soviet literature was not the problem of fellow travelers, but the problem of getting out of these doldrums, of helping literature get closer to real life, of saving it from abstract romanticism and from Red hagiography. Vacillating nonparty writers must be oriented toward the Revolution, but their ideological shortcomings must not be glossed over. The sheep must be separated from the goats.

9. The party must continue to assist associations of proletarian writers and encourage young Communist writers. But the hothouse atmosphere prevailing in proletarian literary organizations handicapped normal developments. It was therefore desirable to aim at an association on a wider basis, which would include fellow travelers, without encroaching upon the independence of the existing organizations.

10. It was important to do away with the obvious absurdities and excesses of political censorship which interfered with the artistic evaluation of literary works, regarded satirical portrayal of life as an insult to the Revolution, and demanded Communist ideology from non-Communist writers. A special commission should be set up to mend this situation.

11. Steps should be taken to alleviate the material hardships of Soviet writers. The problem of living accommodations was particularly acute. Bohemianism in life and its reflections in literature should be combated.

12. Though allowing writers full freedom in their search for new forms and styles, the party considered realism, understood as cognition based on experience, to be most in keeping with dialectical materialism. At the same time the party called upon writers to produce clear, simple, and intelligible works for the new reading public.[5]

Such was Voronsky's moderate, but thoroughly orthodox, Marxist program of the party's literary policy. It will be seen later that in the main it anticipated the tenets of Socialist realism. He recognized unequivocally the party's "ideological hegemony" in literature and was uncompromisingly hostile to all alien influences. His thrust at Soviet censorship was mild enough. His desiderata received the implicit official approval when the Press Section of the Central Committee of the Communist party convoked a special conference which, on May 19, 1924, passed a resolution confirming the party's policy of benevolence toward fellow travelers and their literature. The resolution avoided any specific mention of proletarian literature, preferring to speak of "the art of those peasants and workers who, in the process of cultural elevation of the large masses of the people, become workers' and peasants' writers." But the resolution rebuked the Onguardists and proclaimed that "no literary current, school, or group must come forward in the name of the party." Most ranking Communist leaders opposed, at the time, the claim of proletarian literary organizations to a factual and legal supremacy in literature. Their point of view was tersely formulated by Bukharin when he told the Onguardists, "First you must build, then you can receive." Lunacharsky and Radek took the same attitude. Trotsky had expressed himself even more emphatically when he wrote earlier:

> There can be no question of creating a new culture . . . during the period of dictatorship. The cultural reconstruction, which will begin when the need for the iron clutch of a dictatorship unparalleled in history will have disappeared, will not have a class character. This seems to lead to the conclusion that there is no proletarian culture and never will be one. . . . Such terms as "proletarian literature" and "proletarian culture" are dangerous. . . . They falsify perspectives, violate proportions, distort standards, and further the arrogance of small circles.[6]

History has apparently failed to record Stalin's views on this problem.

The resolution of the Press Section of the Central Committee was embodied in a resolution of the Thirteenth Party Congress, which met in May,

[5] See A. Voronsky, "O tekushchem momente i zadachakh RKP v khudozhestvennoy literature" ("About the Current Moment and the Objects of the Russian Communist Party in Imaginative Literature"), in *Proletariat and Literature*, 45–52.

[6] *Literature and Revolution*, 185, 205. (The Russian edition of Trotsky's book appeared in 1923.) I have made slight changes in the translation.

1924. A year later it was laid at the basis of a more explicit resolution of the Central Committee. This resolution, of June 18, 1925, was to govern the official literary policy in the next four years, and more will be said about it in Part III.

LEF and Futurism

In the heated literary debates which raged during 1923–24, not the least noisy part was played by the former Futurists from the LEF who in 1923 launched a magazine under the same name. Apart from such well-known poets as Mayakovsky and Vasily Kamensky (1884–1961), its regular contributors included some Futurists from the Russian Far East, among them the poets Aseyev and Tretyakov and the literary critic N. Chuzhak (pseudonym of N. Nasimovich, b. 1876).[7] Chuzhak, Osip Brik (1888–1945), Boris Kushner (1888–1937), and Boris Arvatov (1896–1940) were the major theoreticians of the LEF group. In its program, published in the first issue of the magazine, LEF underlined the revolutionary nature of true Futurism and boasted of the services it had rendered to the Revolution in its initial stages:

> We produced the first things of art of the October era. . . . We organized the newspaper *Art of the Commune,* as well as visits to factories and plants, with debates and recitals. Our ideas won a working-class audience.

The program spoke slightingly and ironically of all rival groups and organizations. It accused proletarian writers of becoming "official" and "academic" and not learning from the Futurists and referred contemptuously to Pilnyak and the Serapions, as well as to Alexey Tolstoy, who was said to be "scrubbing the white horse of his *Complete Works* in anticipation of a triumphant entry into Moscow." The objects of LEF were formulated in a series of snappy sentences:

> . . . LEF will indoctrinate art with the ideas of the Commune, opening for it the road into Tomorrow.
> LEF will indoctrinate the masses with our art. . . .
> LEF will confirm our theories by active art. . . . It will fight for life-building art.
> We do not claim to monopolize the revolutionary mentality in art. We'll find it out by competition.

In a series of equally bombastic aphorisms LEF announced a revision of its tactics. The battle against the classical heritage in literature was declared to have lost its urgency, the classics having become the "ordinary textbooks" of the one hundred and fifty million Soviet citizens. But LEF promised to

---

[7] Aseyev, Tretyakov, and Chuzhak belonged to the group Tvorchestvo (Creation) in Siberia. Next to those in Moscow and Petrograd, it was apparently the most active Futurist organization in 1919–21. Tretyakov and Chuzhak were later "purged" and disappeared. Tretyakov was "rehabilitated" after 1956.

go on fighting dead methods in art and relics of the past in post-Revolutionary Russia, and waging war on all those "who for the poetry of one's home substitute the poetry of one's house committee."

We used to fight the bulls of the bourgeoisie. We shocked people with our yellow blazers and painted faces.
Now we are fighting the victims of those bulls in our Soviet society.
Our weapons are example, agitation, propaganda.[8]

Throughout the two years of its existence *LEF* magazine championed utilitarian, "purposeful" art, art conceived as "building of life" and "production of things,"[9] opposing this conception to Voronsky's idea of art as cognition of life, as well as to the Onguardists' stress on ideology. It was attacked both on the right and on the left. On the right, apart from Voronsky, its most outspoken critic was A. Lezhnev (pseudonym of Abram Gorelik, 1893-1938).[10] Lezhnev rejected the contention of LEF that realism was essentially a bourgeois form of art. For him it was the art of the rising class. "Every class," he wrote, "which comes to the forefront of history . . . asserts realism in art in one form or another." Soviet literature was therefore irrevocably moving toward realism. The "production art" proclaimed by LEF—art that "makes" life, instead of reproducing or reflecting it—was for Lezhnev a contradiction in terms. Its advocates were faced with the dilemma either of admitting their superfluity—of merging art with technology, of exchanging art workshops for workshops pure and simple—or of creating a new style, conventional and decorative; this was confirmed by the so-called "production" artists. Futurism was for Lezhnev a direct continuation of Symbolism,

---

[8] *LEF*, No. 1 (March, 1923).

[9] "Art is the production of values (things needed by the class and by mankind)" (Chuzhak). By way of explanation Chuzhak added that there existed two kinds of "things": material objects and "models of things (ideas)." Brik wrote that it was the "purpose" of a thing that determined "the organization of its color and form." In its insistence on form and its hostility to ideology LEF came very close to the Formalists. When Brik wrote that the "history of poetry is a history of the evolution of devices of verbal formalization" and further that "a poet is a craftsman of words, a word-maker," he was merely paraphrasing Shklovsky.

[10] Between 1924 and 1929, Lezhnev published several volumes of critical essays: *Voprosy literatury i kritiki* (*Problems of Literature and Criticism*, 1926), *Sovremenniki* (*Contemporaries*, 1927), and *Literaturnye budni* (*Literary Weekdays*, 1929). With D. Gorbov he also published in 1929 a survey of the first decade of Soviet literature, *Literatura revolyutsionnogo desyatiletiya* (*Literature of the Revolutionary Decade*). The year 1935 saw the publication of his book of reflections on literature, entitled *Ob iskusstve* (*About Art*). He was also the author of a good critical study of Pushkin's prose fiction (1937). In the late thirties Lezhnev disappeared from Soviet literature. He was rehabilitated posthumously, and his book on Pushkin was reissued in the 1960's. Gorbov published a volume of essays entitled *V poiskakh Galatei* (*In Search of Galatea*), as well as some essays on Russian *émigré* literature. In the late 1930's he turned to translating and managed to survive the purges.

for it implied hypertrophy of form. Futurism stood in the same relation to Symbolism as Symbolism to Naturalism. The so-called "left" art had no right to claim that it was realistic, for realism meant representation of reality and was opposed to formal, fantastic, and abstract art, while "left" art denied the very principle of representation.[11]

LEF was fighting a losing battle. Lezhnev was right in maintaining that Soviet literature was evolving toward realism. Attacked on both sides and aware of its precarious position, LEF, late in 1923, concluded a working arrangement with the Moscow Association of Proletarian Writers for the purpose of fighting "the demoralizing influence of the bourgeois-gentry and would-be fellow-traveling literature" and working out "a sound class policy in art."[12]

The attempt of Futurism to reassert itself in Soviet literary life proved a fiasco. Early in 1925 *LEF* magazine ceased publication. Apart from its vociferous campaign for "left" art, its contribution to literature was of small account. A few stories by Babel (whom it introduced into Soviet literature) and some poems by Pasternak, Mayakovsky, and Aseyev are probably all that will be remembered of its output. But, approached retrospectively, its shrill campaigning on behalf of a new art had the merit of freshness and daring. In 1927, *LEF* was revived under the title *Novy LEF* (*New LEF*), but its life was even shorter—more will be said about it in Chapter 13.

The Constructivists

A kindred group, with a rather vague program couched in appalling jargon (with such critical terms as *"gruzofikatsiya,"* or "loadification"), entered the literary scene in the autumn of 1924. It called itself the Literary Center of the Constructivists, or LTsC for short. Its manifesto defined Constructivism as "motivated art" and spoke of it as "a stage on the way to the art of Socialism" and as "a reflection of the organizational onrush of the working class."[13] The manifesto was signed by Ilya Selvinsky, Kornely Zelinsky, Vera Inber, Boris Agapov, Evgeny Gabrilovich, D. Tumanny (pseudonym of N. Panov), and Innokenty Oksyonov. They shared LEF's ideas about "purposeful, technicized" art but tried to be more specific in their demands on artistic form.

In December of 1924, the Constructivists, following the lead given by LEF, concluded an "agreement" with the MAPP for the object of fighting those literary groups which, "under cover of demands for the artist's technical freedom," tended to "obscure the meaning of our epoch and . . . dis-

---

[11] "Proletkult i proletarskoye iskusstvo" ("The Proletkult and Proletarian Art"), in Lezhnev, *Problems of Literature and Criticism.*

[12] *Literaturnye manifesty* (*Literary Manifestoes*) (ed. by N. L. Brodsky, V. Lvov-Rogachevsky, and N. P. Sidorov), 245–47.

[13] *Ibid.,* 258–60.

organize the cultural class effort of the proletariat."[14] This anxiety of the groups which claimed to stand for "left" art to reinsure themselves by an alliance with the extreme political left was significant, just as was the tendency of various groups to seek theoretical bases, no matter how vague and confusing, for their artistic practices. But it was soon clear that the highway of Soviet literature lay outside these various "fronts" and "centers."

[14] *Ibid.*, 261.

Part III. **The Emergence of a New Literature, 1924–29**

Chapter 7. THE CHARTER OF WRITERS' LIBERTIES

In June, 1925, just a year after Voronsky had won his signal victory over the Onguardists, the Central Committee of the Communist party, the supreme policy-making organ of the Soviet state, reaffirmed and clarified its literary policy in a special resolution which came to be spoken of as the "Magna Charta Libertatum" of Soviet writers.[1]

To be sure, the liberties the charter granted to Soviet writers were relative and limited. The fundamental principle of state and party interference in all matters of art and literature was reasserted quite clearly. The wording did not differ much from that of the resolution passed by the first conference of proletarian writers: point 4 of the 1925 resolution of the Central Committee laid down that "in a class society there is and can be no neutral art." This statement was, however, qualified by a reference to "the infinitely more varied forms" in which the class nature of art in general, and of literature in particular, is manifested, as compared with politics and economics. The resolution went on to say that it would be wrong to disregard this fundamental fact of Soviet social life—the fact that the working class had conquered power and set up a dictatorship of the proletariat.

During the period of proletarian dictatorship the party was confronted with a number of new problems: the problem of finding a *modus vivendi* with the peasantry while gradually transforming it; the problem of partial co-operation with the bourgeoisie, with a view to slowly ousting it; and the problem of enrolling the intelligentsia in the service of the Revolution and winning it over from the bourgeoisie. The proletariat, while retaining and gradually extending its leadership, must conquer various sectors of the ideological front. The process of infiltration of dialectical materialism into new fields (biology, psychology, natural sciences) had already begun. Sooner or later the proletariat would consolidate its position in literature, too. But this problem was infinitely more complex than many of the others, for "if the proletariat already possesses the unfailing criteria for evaluating the sociopolitical content of any work of literature, it lacks such ready-made answers to all the problems of artistic form." The resolution denied that proletarian writers had a "hegemony" in literature but pledged them the party's support in "*earning* the historical right to such a hegemony." Peasant

---

[1] *Literary Manifestoes*, 292–98. This resolution was published in all Soviet papers on July 1, 1925.

writers, said the resolution, must be treated benevolently and supported; their peculiarities must be respected.

With regard to fellow travelers the resolution insisted on bearing in mind (1) their differentiation, (2) the role played by many of them as skilled "specialists" in literary technique, and (3) the existence of vacillations among them. The general attitude toward them should be one of tactful care, in order to ensure their speediest adherence to Communist ideology. While sifting away antiproletarian and antirevolutionary elements and combating all signs of revived bourgeois ideology, the party must be tolerant toward "intermediate" ideological forms. All this was a restatement of Voronsky's program.

With regard to proletarian writers the resolution recommended that all possible support and assistance be given to them and their organizations, while at the same time all manifestations of pernicious *komchvanstvo* (Communist snobbery) on their part should be discouraged. "It is precisely because the Party sees in them the coming ideological leaders of Soviet literature that it must fight by all means against a frivolous and disdainful attitude toward the old cultural heritage and toward literary specialists." The resolution also declared war on all attempts at fostering a "hothouse 'proletarian' literature." Communist critics were told to give up their tone of "literary command" and, while fighting mercilessly against all counter-revolutionary tendencies in literature, be tactful and tolerant to "all those literary groupings which can and will march along with the proletariat."

Point 13 of the resolution confirmed the refusal of the party to commit itself to any particular literary form:

While guiding literature as a whole, the Party can no more support this or that faction in literature (classifying them according to their different conceptions of form and style) than it can solve problems of the family forms by resolutions, although it does and must guide the building of a new mode of life. Everything leads us to believe that a style in keeping with the epoch will be created by different methods, but the solution of this problem has not yet been suggested. All attempts to bind the Party in this respect, in the present phase of our cultural development, must be rejected.

The resolution therefore advocated "free competition of various groups and currents"; any other solution, it said, would be "a bureaucratic pseudo-solution." While pledging its moral and material support to proletarian and peasant-proletarian literature, the party refused to grant legal monopoly to any literary group or organization, not even to the most purely proletarian in its ideology, for this "would mean . . . the undoing of proletarian literature." Apparently taking its cue from Voronsky's memorandum, the party promised to "root out all attempts at crude and incompetent administrative interference in literary matters."

In a way the 1925 resolution of the Central Committee merely sanctioned the existing order of things. Its importance lay in the fact that the claim of proletarian literary organizations to play the leading role in literature and to control the literary production of non-Communists was firmly rejected. Fellow travelers were given more elbowroom and enabled to continue their work in peace. The resolution was interpreted by everybody as a clear-cut victory for them and a defeat for the Onguardists.[2] One of its immediate results was a split within in the Onguard group. Most members of the group loyally accepted the resolution as the guiding principle and decided to reorient its activities. The name of the group was changed to On Literary Guard, and its slogan became "Learning, Creative Work, and Self-Criticism." In its new work it was led by the young Communist novelist Libedinsky. The obdurate minority, with the critic Gorbachov at its head, withdrew from the group. It was also decided to create a Federation of Soviet Writers as a meeting ground for proletarian writers and fellow travelers. Expected to coexist with purely proletarian literary organizations, it does not seem to have played an important part in literary life in the years that followed. In 1929, in response to the party campaign against them, it expelled Zamyatin and Pilnyak from its membership.

The period during which the principles of the 1925 resolution governed literary life in the Soviet Union proved to be rich and fruitful. It was marked in the first place by the revival of the novel as a literary genre and by that return to realism which Voronsky and Lezhnev had advocated and predicted.

[2] For a somewhat different interpretation of the resolution, for which, in retrospect, there may be some justification, see Ermolaev, *Soviet Literary Theories*. According to this view, the 1925 resolution paved the way for RAPP's bid for control over literature.

Chapter 8. **THE REVIVAL OF THE NOVEL**

Chronological boundary lines marking off one period in the evolution of a literature from another are bound to be somewhat arbitrary. But there are sufficient reasons for regarding the year 1924 as the starting point of a new period in Soviet literature, for it was in 1924 that the Communist party definitely adopted a policy of benevolent encouragement toward non-Communist writers and fellow travelers. And it was the fellow travelers—both the comparatively young newcomers to literature, such as Fedin, Leonov, Kaverin, Slonimsky, Olesha, and others, and some of the older writers, like Alexey Tolstoy, Prishvin, and Ehrenburg—who made the greatest contribution to Soviet literature from 1924 to 1929. Indirectly, moreover, the party's decision to encourage fellow travelers and to snub proletarian writers helped also to stimulate the creative activity of the latter, and they, along with the fellow travelers, had their share in the revival of the novel as a literary form. It was during this period that the novel became the dominant literary genre in Soviet literature, definitely superseding the short story, which had dominated the preceding period. This new formal development implied thematic changes. While most of the writers of the preceding period had dealt with the period of the Civil War and concentrated on recording the incidents of the Revolution and their impressions of it, deliberately discarding the traditional method of psychological analysis and presenting the Revolution as a series of "purple patches," these new novelists aimed at grasping the Revolution as a whole, at analyzing its causes and effects, its makers and victims, at portraying—no longer impressionistically, but realistically—the new *byt* ("mode of life," "mores") and the sharp conflicts between the old and the new in post-Revolutionary Russia. The scope of literature was widened. Though it still dealt predominantly with contemporary themes, the very choice of its themes became wider. At the same time the writers' treatment of them underwent a considerable change. The earlier combination of ideological detachment and subjectivism no longer satisfied them. The new themes and the new approach favored the medium of the objective social-psychological novel. But thematic changes affected in their turn the character of other literary genres during this period. A number of writers appeared who can be best characterized as chroniclers of post-Revolutionary life, some of them with a strong satirical turn. The period also saw the revival of the historical novel as a legitimate and popular literary genre, no longer to be confined to the domain of juvenile literature.

The striking feature of this period is the richness and variety of its literary production, and an attempt to bring some unity into the picture inevitably involves certain simplification and overgeneralization. In the account that follows, I have bracketed some writers together according to certain common characteristics, departing from the strict chronological order.[1]

Although the rebirth of the novel as the dominant literary genre can be dated from 1924, when Fedin's *Cities and Years*, the first large-scale psychological novel in Soviet literature, was published, this does not mean that there had been no Soviet novels before that time. Some of them, however, were novels only in name (for example, those of Pilnyak, Nikitin, and Vsevolod Ivanov). Others (such as those of Semyonov, Tarasov-Rodionov, and Libedinsky) were not characteristic of the period during which they appeared, and will be discussed later in connection with their authors' subsequent work.[2] Two writers, however, who died in the early period of Soviet literature, may be introduced here—Neverov and Furmanov.

Alexander Neverov (pseudonym of Alexander Sergeyevich Skobelev) began writing and publishing before the Revolution. His stories of village life (he was of peasant stock himself) were in the tradition of Populist realism. During the famine of 1920–21 he went to Tashkent and later wrote what became his most celebrated work—*Tashkent gorod khlebny* (*Tashkent, the Bread City*, 1923). It describes the journey to Tashkent of two village boys who are driven from their home by the famine and gives a forceful picture of famine-ravaged Russia. Neverov also published several plays and stories. His village stories, especially "Andron Neputyovy" ("Andron Good-for-Nothing"), are a truthful reflection of the deep-seated social contradictions which were brought to light by the Revolution. The hero of "Andron" is a village Communist who in his fight for the new mode of life comes up against the stubborn opposition of the peasants.

Neverov (1886–1923)

Dmitry Andreyevich Furmanov also came from a peasant family but spent his childhood in Ivanovo-Voznesensk, the "Russian Manchester," where

Furmanov (1891–1926)

[1] The later works of several major writers dealt with in this chapter will be treated in their proper chronological place. In some cases, however, anticipation of later developments is unavoidable.

[2] The distinction of being regarded as the first Soviet novel belongs to Vladimir Zazubrin's *Dva mira* (*Two Worlds*, 1921). A Communist journalist, the author took an active part in the Civil War in Siberia, and it is with that phase of the Revolution that his novel deals. It enjoyed considerable popularity in the 1920's and early 1930's, but even Communist critics admitted that its propaganda value was greater than its artistic qualities. In 1958, in connection with the fortieth anniversary of the Revolution, it was suddenly brought out of oblivion and reissued. Lenin was quoted as having described it to Gorky as "not a novel, of course, but a good and needed book" (see the 1958 edition, 4). Zazubrin was later liquidated in the purges.

his father kept a pub. In the Revolution his sympathies lay at first with the Socialist Revolutionary party, then with the Anarchists. In 1918 he joined the Bolshevik party and became a member of a provincial executive committee. During the Civil War he served as a political commissar in the army of Chapayev, a colorful peasant guerrilla leader in the Ural Steppes. He earned fame with his *Chapayev* (1923), which Soviet critics often describe as the first important contribution to proletarian prose fiction. Though often referred to as a novel, it is really a piece of documentary literature. If its historical value is to be doubted, it is not because of any attempt on the part of Furmanov to "fictionalize" history but because of his definite political bias. Furmanov showed, however, considerable talent in the portrayal of Chapayev himself and of partisan psychology and methods of warfare. Much emphasis is laid on the political "education" of Chapayev. The novel was later made into one of the most successful Soviet films about the early period of the Revolution. Furmanov's second novel, *Myatezh* (*Revolt*, 1925), was also a semidocumentary account of the Civil War in central Asia.

Fedin
(b. 1892)   Born in Saratov, Konstantin Alexandrovich Fedin was older than most of his fellow Serapion Brothers. His early stories reflect the influence of Chekhov and Bunin. This is especially true of the first story of his to attract general attention, "Sad" ("The Orchard"), written in 1920. Its clear, transparent outline, its poetic descriptions, and its well-balanced prose remind one of Bunin, while the treatment of the theme and the characters resembles Chekhov. The subject of this story was one to which Fedin was to return again and again and which runs through much of the early Soviet literature: the clash of the old and the new in the Revolution. This theme gives the story, which is told in a quiet, measured tempo, a dramatic quality. The principal character is an old gardener, Silanty. His former masters, to whom he is unquestioningly devoted, have been scared away by the Revolution. The old manor house has been made over by the new regime into a children's home; new revolutionary songs echo through its rooms and sound a discordant note. The orchard, which is in Silanty's charge, goes to rack and ruin. In the end, Silanty, taking advantage of the absence of the new occupants, who have gone on some outing, and of his wife, whom he deliberately sends on an errand to a near-by town, sets the beloved house and orchard on fire.

The same tragic note is sounded in the story "Tishina" ("Stillness," 1924), which is about an old, dispossessed squire. The quiet, realistic flow of the uneventful narrative is broken by the almost fantastic scene of the squire's battle with a flock of rooks for the sake of an old lady whom he once loved and betrayed—the last romantic outburst of a man beaten down by life. "Muzhiki" ("The Peasants"), which relates several episodes in the

life of a village shepherd and his daughter, recalls Bunin in its somber portrayal of the cruel and brutal aspects of peasants' life and mentality. The
note of cruelty, gloom, and despair is sounded still more clearly in "Narov-
chatskaya khronika" ("The Chronicle of Narovchat"), told in the name of
a half-educated monk and by its *skaz* manner recalling Leskov and Remizov. All these stories deal with the post-Revolutionary period. There are
also a few others, such as "Anna Timofevna" (1922) and "Rasskaz ob
odnom utre" ("The Tale of One Morning," 1921), in which the Revolution
has no place.

A new and original note was struck by Fedin in his *Transvaal'* (1926), a
longish story of an odd character with an outlandish name (Swaaker) and
an obscure past, who settles down in a Russian village and gradually comes
to wield almost dictatorial economic power over the whole neighborhood,
marries the daughter of the former squire, and lords over the peasants. He
is shown as a cunning, enterprising, thrifty, selfish, and hardhearted kulak,
disliked and feared yet respected by all around him. On its publication the
story called forth a lively controversy among Soviet critics. Some of them
accused Fedin of idealizing his kulak; others spoke of his being "blind in
the left eye"—that is, of portraying Swaaker as much too powerful and not
opposing to him the revolutionary elements in the village.[3]

Fedin, who from the very first had shown that he had close links with the
traditions of nineteenth-century Russian literature, was to play an important
part in the revival of the novel as a literary genre. His first novel, *Goroda i
gody* (*Cities and Years*), published in 1924, represented the first attempt by
a Soviet author to depict the Revolution not in an impartially descriptive or
lyrically ecstatic vein—as did Pilnyak, Nikitin, Vsevolod Ivanov, and even
Babel—but as a large canvas, combining the elements of a novel of adventure with a social-psychological novel on a topical theme. For one of his
mottoes Fedin chose a quotation from Dickens' *A Tale of Two Cities*
("... we had everything before us, we had nothing before us ..."). The
novel was to be a picture of the first years of the Revolution, an attempt to
grasp and analyze its mainsprings and the forces at work in it. Orthodox
Soviet critics blamed Fedin for his one-sidedness, for dwelling on inessential
aspects of the Revolution and fussing too much about his hero, a spineless
and rootless intellectual.

The theme of *Cities and Years* is, in fact, the tragedy of a member of the
intelligentsia at grips with the Revolution. Its action covers a period of time
from before World War I to 1922. The hero, Andrey Startsov, a young
student, is caught by the war in Germany and remains there as a civilian
internee. (Here Fedin introduced an autobiographical element; his own
internment in Germany from 1914 to 1918 is the only incident in his otherwise uneventful biography.) Returning to Russia after the Brest-Litovsk

---

[3] Gorbachov, *Contemporary Russian Literature*, 170–71.

Peace, Andrey is drawn into the revolutionary vortex. He fails, however, to find a proper place for himself in the Revolution. His trouble is that he puts personal interests and values before the cause which he is expected, and wants, to serve. He is too sentimental, too vacillating—a modern variant of the *lishniy chelovek*—a superfluous man, a misfit, a square peg in a round hole—a character so beloved of the Russian novelists of the nineteenth century. This ultimately brings about his undoing. He is killed by his friend Kurt Wahn, but he is really finished long before physical death overtakes him.

Kurt Wahn, a man of strong will and of action is shown as a contrast to Andrey. A German by nationality, he is a gifted artist. He and Andrey first meet and become friends in Germany in prewar days, but the moment the war breaks out, Kurt's dormant German patriotism awakens, and he breaks with Andrey. Full of enthusiasm, he joins the army and is later taken prisoner by the Russians. They next meet in Moscow in 1918. The years spent by Kurt in Russia as a prisoner of war have turned him into an ardent revolutionary. He is now a prominent member of the Council of German Soldier Deputies, set up after the Bolshevik Revolution. As such he is sent to the small provincial town of Semidol, surrounded by villages with a backward Mordva population, to supervise the repatriation of German war prisoners. He takes Andrey with him.

Here one of the important episodes in the plot of the novel takes place. A group of German war prisoners, exploiting the backwardness of the Mordva peasantry and playing on their nationalist sentiments, organizes an anti-Bolshevik detachment. It is led by a German officer, a certain Markgraf von zur Mühlen-Schönau, who is linked with both Andrey and Kurt; the latter has his own reasons to dislike him, and the former, to be grateful to him. The rebels are defeated by a Soviet punitive detachment. During this short episode Andrey lives through something like a fit of revolutionary enthusiasm. He almost feels to be at one with the Revolution, but this feeling soon vanishes, and later he tries in vain to recapture it. Personal reasons lead him to betray the cause he is serving and help von Schönau escape, by providing him with papers which he steals from Kurt's desk. Before his deed is discovered, he is sent to Petrograd to take part in the defense against the approaching White Army of General Yudenich. The girl who has fallen in love with him at Semidol follows him there. Another girl, Marie Urbach, with whom he was in love in Germany, comes all the way from Germany to join him. Discovering that she has a rival, she decides to give way and withdraw from Andrey's life. Although Andrey himself could not really decide between the two, this is a great blow to him. Mad with grief, he wanders about Petrograd and afterward leads a strange, secluded life until ultimately Kurt's vengeance overtakes him—all this time Kurt has been dogging him as a traitor. In the end Kurt shoots him.

The construction of this novel is unusual. It begins with its own denouement—with Andrey's death in 1922 at the hands of Kurt. Then the narrative
is switched back to 1919, to Andrey's arrival in Petrograd and the visit
which von Schönau, on his way to Germany, pays him there. Much that
lies behind these incidents remains obscure to the reader, and this veil of
mystery and suspense is lifted only toward the end of the book. Havoc is
played with the traditional chronological order of the narrative; it is only
with the third chapter that Fedin takes up the exposition of events in their
chronological sequence and unravels for us some of the deliberately tangled
threads. We are shown Andrey in prewar Germany, his friendship with
Kurt Wahn, their life in Nuremberg, the outbreak of war, Andrey's life as a
civilian internee in the small Saxon town of Bischoffsberg, and his unsuccessful attempt at escape. There is a whole "chapter of digressions," as
Fedin calls it, relating in a flashback the childhood and youth of Marie
Urbach, the heroine of the novel, her love affair with von Schönau, her
meeting with and love for Andrey. Then the chronological order is re-
established once more, and we are told about the 1918 revolution in Germany; the repatriation of prisoners, including Andrey; his encounter with
Kurt Wahn in Moscow; their life in Semidol and the events there. Here
again there are some side episodes interpolated into the main story. One of
these, a whole novelette, has no direct relation to the main events of the
novel and was even published separately before the novel appeared. The
novel ends with a chapter describing what happened in Petrograd in 1920.
Its proper chronological place is between Chapters 1 and 2.

Although there is a certain disorder—partly deliberate—about *Cities and
Years*, it is a work of considerable originality and undoubted literary merits.
In point of time it was the first major work in Soviet literature which tried
to answer some questions raised by the Revolution. Fedin does not offer any
ready-made solutions; he merely shows us the tragedy of a typical member
of the intelligentsia caught in the Revolution and swept aside, after an
attempt to adjust himself to it and even to play an active role in it. The
general suffering and passive attitude of the intelligentsia is well conveyed
in a memorable chapter describing the compulsory digging of trenches
outside Petrograd, ordered by Trotsky at the approach of General Yudenich's army. The novel combines many traditional elements, which go back
to the Russian classics of the nineteenth century (the general theme, the
characters, and in parts the manner, recall Turgenev in particular), with
formal innovations, for some of which Fedin was indebted to Andrey Bely,
while some were his own. This first full-length novel by a post-Revolutionary author at once set quite a high standard.

Fedin's second long novel, *Bratya* (*Brothers*, 1928), has similar peculiarities of construction. It does not begin exactly where it should end, but
the real place of the opening chapter is just before the finale. In this opening

chapter Fedin introduces all the main characters with considerable dramatic skill, in a scene saturated with life and full of psychological intensity. We are shown at once all the knots of the plot ready to be untied. Fedin then proceeds to demonstrate at some length how these intricate and intertwined knots came into being and then to undo them in the last section of the book.

The theme of the novel is closely akin to that of *Cities and Years*, and the principal character, Nikita Karev, a gifted composer, is a variation on Andrey Startsov. But besides the issue of purely personal adjustment to the Revolution, he is faced with the additional problem of reconciling with it his artistic vocation. Like Startsov he fails; he cannot find in music an adequate expression for the Revolution, and he also ends by losing, in turn, all the women whom he loved or who loved him.

Fedin's second novel is much closer in manner to the Russian tradition of social and psychological realism, but it lacks the exciting novelty and the harmony between form and content of the earlier work.

Leonov (b. 1899) Another typical representative of the fellow travelers who played an important part in the revival of the novel is Leonid Maximovich Leonov.

Leonov was born in Moscow. His father was a peasant, a self-taught poet and journalist. In 1918, Leonov graduated from one of the high schools in Moscow, after which he served for three years in the Red Army. He began writing early, most of his youthful work being in verse. His first story to appear in print was "Buryga" (1922). His early stories are ingenious stylistic experiments. For some time Soviet critics spoke of him as a talented pasticheur. "Tuatamur," a weird and beautiful Oriental poem written in rhythmical prose; "Derevyannaya koroleva" ("The Wooden Queen") and "Bubnovy valet" ("The Knave of Diamonds"), two clever and charming stories where realism, Hoffmanesque fantasy, and quaint Andersenian humor are oddly blended; "Gibel Egorushki" ("Egorushka's Undoing"), a tale of primitive life in the Far North of Russia, with a strong element of fantasy —such are some of Leonov's early stories, published before 1924. The influence of Gogol, Leskov, Remizov, Zamyatin, and Pilnyak, together with that of some of the Western romantics, was obvious in most of them. In 1924 appeared two longer works: *Zapisi Andreya Petrovicha Kovyakina* (*Notebooks of A. P. Kovyakin*) and *Konets melkogo cheloveka* (*The End of a Petty Man*). The former, a story of provincial life in the early years of the Revolution, belonged to the Leskov-Remizov *skaz* tradition. *The End of a Petty Man* stemmed from Dostoyevsky and was still largely a pastiche, but it was of more than passing interest and marked the turning point in Leonov's literary career, for it contained some of the most significant elements of his later, mature work. Its theme was also one that was to play an important part in Soviet literature.

In it Leonov shows us one of the men cast overboard by the Revolution, floating helplessly and aimlessly in the middle of its turbulent stream. He is a scholar, a world-famous paleontologist, Likharev by name, who is engaged in epoch-making scientific work and is impervious to what is going on around him. The action is set during the worst years of War Communism, famine, and misery, against the nightmarish background of revolutionary Petrograd. Likharev is joined by his sister, a consumptive old maid, who comes to minister to his daily needs. He falls ill and is haunted by hallucinations. Every night he is visited by his double, a distant relation of Ivan Karamazov's devil, who comes to converse with him and mock him. There is a powerful rhythm in the succession of mad and terrible scenes. One of the most memorable passages is the description of a gathering of all sorts of *ci-devant* men, the flotsam and jetsam of the Revolution, who engage in futile or crazy discussions of the events. It is after this party that Likharev suddenly becomes aware of the realities and sees that his sister is dying, that there is no bread, nothing left in his larder, that the whole country is going the way of its appointed sufferings. Suddenly there is peace and light in his mind. He is ready to die. But to make his sacrifice complete he must destroy the manuscript of his work. His double also urges him to burn it—"maybe something will grow out of its ashes." And there is a note of mockery in the parting words of Likharev's demon when he paints before him a vision of the coming millenium: "Now Russia will rise high, very high. The sky will be paved with concrete, streetcars will furrow the clouds. Bread will be made of air . . . people will wear velvet trousers." At these words Likharev flings himself at his visitor, slips, and loses consciousness. After that, Likharev, who burns his manuscript, is "transformed" and "prepares himself" for death.

Everything in this story—its diction, its characters, its situations—reminds the reader of Dostoyevsky. There are passages that read like plagiarisms but are probably deliberate parallels—for a long time Leonov, in his treatment of the Revolution, continued to be obsessed by Dostoyevsky and his visions. But for all its dependence on Dostoyevsky, *The End of a Petty Man* is an interesting and powerful work, one of the most interesting in this early period.

Leonov's first long novel, *Barsuki* (*The Badgers*), was published in 1925, soon after Fedin's *Cities and Years*. It reflected the same tendency— away from pure verbal ornamentalism and emotional lyricism, back to psychological and social realism. It had, however, closer ties with the Gogol-Remizov-Zamyatin-Pilnyak tradition. Its language is highly emotional and often stylized; it has frequent lyrical digressions and interpolated stories that have obvious symbolical significance; like Pilnyak, Leonov often suddenly interrupts his narrative to apostrophize the reader or studs the narrative with exclamations and rhetorical questions. The main theme of the novel is the deep cleavage between town and village, which from this point becomes one of Leonov's favorite motifs. It probably reflects his own background, the double nature of an urbanized offspring of peasant stock.

The novel is a diptych. It falls distinctly into two parts, unequal in length. The first, a shorter one, has for its setting a typical merchant quarter of Moscow not long before the Revolution, a corner of the old world where life runs along a well-established rut. The two heroes of the book, the brothers Semyon and Pashka, grow up amid these surroundings, to which they were brought as small boys from their native village to learn urban ways and be trained in business. But their characters are different, and they soon part ways. The elder, Pashka, lame, sullen, unsociable, and willful, rebels against the oppressive, stifling atmosphere of Bykhalov's store where he and Semyon work as errand boys. He runs away, joins the ranks of the proletariat, and becomes a factory worker. During the greater part of the novel the reader loses sight of him, but he reappears toward the end of the book as a Soviet commissar and plays an important part in the dramatic denouement. The real hero of the book is Semyon. Although he shows himself more adaptable than his brother and remains in Moscow until he is drafted into the army, he cannot erase from his mind the early reminiscences of village life and is nostalgically drawn toward it; at heart he remains a peasant. The Revolution brings him back to his native village as one of the many deserters from the army.

In the second part of the book Leonov shows us Semyon's native village under the impact of the Revolution. The local peasants rise against the Soviets, and on Semyon devolves the leadership of the rebellion. The causes of the rising are to be sought partly in the squabble between two neighboring villages, the squabble that goes back to the pre-emancipation days (this gives Leonov an opportunity for painting some Gogolian scenes of the age of serfdom), and partly in the peasants' grievances arising out of the food tax levied by the new government. The rebellion is ultimately crushed—it fails for lack of any real general purpose and plan behind it and, consequently, of any genuine fighting spirit.

Semyon is the only one among the rebels who is actuated by an idea, the idea of an irreconcilable conflict between village and town; the only one who rises above those petty local grievances, who has dreams of a peasant uprising on a national scale, and who is not disheartened by the hardships and privations to which the rebels expose themselves when they retire to the surrounding woods and dig themselves in there (hence their name "Badgers"). But Semyon, too, when all his followers betray and desert him, is forced to capitulate. In the final scene we see Semyon back from the woods and meeting with his brother. Pashka, now known as "Comrade Anton," heads the punitive detachment sent to suppress the rebellion. Not a word is spoken between them on this occasion (the two brothers have, however, met earlier in the woods and talked matters over), but the reader is left with the impression that, although capitulating in fact, Semyon does not do so in spirit; his hatred for the town and all that it stands for remains as strong as ever. In a new disguise and under a new name, that of Nikolka Zavarikhin, a young peasant who is on the way to become rich under the NEP, he will come to life again in Leonov's next novel, to personify the same idea and the same everlasting conflict. In *The Badgers*, however, the conflict remains unsolved, and upon that silent meeting between the two brothers, Leonov characteristically lets the curtain fall.

Leonov's love of *skaz* is felt in *The Badgers* in the interpolated stories which the Badgers tell as they while away time around a campfire. One of these stories, "The Tale of the Furious Kalafat," has interesting political implications. The story is told by an old man who says that his grandfather heard it from his father and that the latter had had it read aloud to him from a book by an Old Believer. The action in the story is placed in time immemorial, when there was still plenty of room on earth and forests, fields, and rivers teemed with animals, birds, and fish. Kalafat was the son of an old king who ruled over one of those vast old kingdoms. When he was nine years old, he went to his father and told him that he was not leading a good life and that there was no order in his kingdom.

"Can you tell me, for instance, how many blades of grass grow in your fields, how many trees there are in your forests, how many fish there are in the rivers, and how many stars in the sky?" he asked his father, adding that every single blade of grass must be counted. When his father scratched his head and said that twenty generations before them had lived in that way, the son answered that that was wrong, for there was a science called 'eometry and people must live according to it. All the fish and all the stars and all the blades of grass must be numbered. And he announced to his father that he was going into the mountains to study 'eometry.

After eleven years in the mountains Kalafat came home, and his father was surprised to see how enormously he had grown. When storm clouds were gathering, he could easily dispel them with his cap. The son dismissed his father, took over from him, and began to work "in the sweat of his brow," branding all the fish, issuing passports to birds, registering every blade of grass. "And everything around grew sad and dull. . . . Even the bear is pining, for he no longer knows, now that he has been given a passport, whether he is human or animal."

Thereupon Kalafat conceived the idea of building a tower which would reach the sky, so that he could also number the stars. "This idea meant the beginning of the end of our earth," says the narrator. To begin with, Kalafat assembled all his peasants and went to war with the neighboring countries. He conquered seven of them, and two more surrendered of their own accord rather than starve. Kalafat marched on to the sea and on the way conquered another small nation. He needed all these prisoners of war to build his tower. As he was marching back with them, he met in the woods an old man with a bag who advised him to dismiss his army, abstain from doing evil, and take to making boots—and in whom one could easily recognize Tolstoy. Kalafat refused to follow this advice and said he wanted to build his tower and also grow still larger. And everything in Kalafat's kingdom began to grow and swell, and so did his tower. After twenty years it began to reach the sky, while it took a whole year to go around it. The foreman complained to Kalafat that the construction had become difficult, that it was very damp up there, and that all sorts of rogues were trying to get there first.

In the spring Kalafat decided to try to climb the tower. Taking with him seven rogues, the most honest among them, he locked the tower so that none of the common folk could get in and began to climb. It took them five years before they could at last see light—five of the rogues had in the meantime died from dampness. When, with a last effort, Kalafat came out to the top and looked around him, he howled as no one had howled before him:

The whole 'eometry was blown to pieces!

As he was climbing up the tower, it could not stand his weight and kept sinking into the ground. He had not mounted an inch: he would take one step up and the tower would sink one step down, into the ground.

And all around were forests again, and in them were foxes. The fields were bright and fragrant, and in them were birds.

Thus nature had rejected Kalafat's passports.

And nothing came out of the whole thing.

In his whimsical legend Leonov was, in a way, echoing Zamyatin's prophecy of the standardized state, although the ending was somewhat different: with Leonov, nature triumphed over man's machinations. The story can also be viewed as a further development of the theme of opposition between town and country, and this interpretation was pointed out by Soviet critics. It is interesting to note that in the recent editions of *The Badgers* some cuts have been made in the "Tale of Kalafat." All the references to the conquest of foreign lands by Kalafat have been removed (they might have sounded awkwardly prophetic after World War II), and so has the reference to the ambitious rogues. In the episode with the old man in the woods the mention of boots, which made the allusion to Tolstoy too obvious, is no longer there.[4]

The Badgers was followed in 1927 by another long novel, *Vor* (*The Thief*), still more ambitious in size and scope, though lacking perhaps the single-mindedness of the earlier novel and the definiteness of its social theme. The Revolution is less obviously felt in it, partly because the novel deals with a period—the era of the NEP—when the Revolution abandoned some of its principles and made a temporary retreat. The hero is Mitka

[4] Cf. L. Leonov, *Sobranie sochineniy* (*Collected Works*), I.

(Dmitry) Vekshin, who recalls Rocambole, the adventurer hero of Ponson du Terrail's countless popular romances, and at the same time has a great deal in common with some of Dostoyevsky's characters, especially with his namesake in *The Brothers Karamasov* and with Raskolnikov. He is one of the "disillusioned" of the Revolution. From a prominent figure in its early stages—a commissar in the Red Army—he becomes under the NEP regime the ringleader of a formidable gang of burglars with a worldwide reputation.

No sooner does the reader begin *The Thief* than he becomes aware of the influence of Dostoyevsky on Leonov. In *The Badgers* it is possible to trace it here and there, but on the whole this novel belongs to a different tradition. In *The Thief*, however, the impact of Dostoyevsky on Leonov is as obvious as it is in *The End of a Petty Man*. Apart from the general morbid tone and heightened, hysterical style, the predilection for psychological complications and perversities and for delving into the darker sides of human nature, many of Leonov's characters have their models in Dostoyevsky. Thus Masha Dolomanova, nicknamed the "Blizzard," is a direct descendant of Dostoyevsky's "infernal" women—of Nastasya Filippovna in *The Idiot* and of Grushenka in *The Brothers Karamazov*. In old Manyukin there is an obvious resemblance to the old Karamazov. The relation between Mitka and Leonty parallels the relation between Ivan Karamazov and Smerdyakov. Chikilyov, even in name, recalls Shigalyov in *The Possessed*. Pukhov, however, a homespun philosopher with a strong religious coloring, seems to stem from Gorky's "truth seekers" (just as does Katushin in *The Badgers*—the two have much in common); but when Pukhov tells Mitka to steel himself by suffering, one is again reminded of one of Dostoyevsky's favorite ideas. The opening scene of the novel, which takes place on a train, suggests the opening scene in *The Idiot*.

The structure of the novel, with its criminological interest, its complicated crisscross plot, its great number of multifarious characters—representatives of the underworld, former bourgeois, small Soviet employees—is also reminiscent of Dostoyevsky. Leonov still further complicates the already complex structure of the novel by introducing, and making a very clever use of, the device of a novel within a novel, as did André Gide in his *The Counterfeiters*: one of Leonov's characters, the writer Firsov, is writing a novel about the characters of *The Thief*. Thus sometimes the reader gets a double vision of the whole thing, through the eyes of Leonov and through the eyes of Firsov.

Leonov excels particularly in drawing the underdogs of life, the "humiliated and injured," the downtrodden representatives of the old world; these he portrays with great insight and much compassion. This compassionate note also allies Leonov with Dostoyevsky and makes him fit in well with the main tradition of Russian literature. *The Thief* is free from political

bias, and Leonov is not concerned with any "messages." It is true that the
novel ends on an optimistic note. Mitka gives up his gangster life and goes
into seclusion somewhere in the country, from where he returns, we gather,
a "reformed" character, though how and to what purpose reformed Leonov
does not tell us. This inconclusive ending is typical of Leonov. He is interested not in Mitka's social re-education but in Mitka as a man, in Mitka's
ethical problem, which is to know whether a man has the right to kill a
fellow being—the problem that occupied Raskolnikov and Ivan Karamazov.
In his revolutionary past Mitka had committed a cold-blooded murder,
killing his prisoner, a White officer, in retaliation for killing his favorite
horse. This incident came to be the turning point in Mitka's revolutionary
career and the real cause of his subsequent downfall and of all his torments
and sufferings.

Leonov is concerned in his novel not with any specific problems of the
Revolution but with life in all its many-sided complexity—life that is reluctant to follow any ready-made grooves and obeys its own laws. Firsov,
the novelist in Leonov's novel, says: "After all we [writers] know life better
than anyone else. It tastes nice: you eat it—and die without noticing."
Through Firsov it is Leonov himself who is speaking, just as to him can be
applied the following words: "Firsov was fond of life, of its acrid and coarse
smell, of its tart and bitter taste, of its flimsy bulkiness, even of its sense-
lessness." It is this smell and taste of life that Leonov tried to convey in his
novels, and no wonder Communist critics accused him of "irrationalism."
Moreover, to Firsov's irrational zest for life Leonov opposed the views of a
certain Chikilyov. The resemblance to Dostoyevsky's Shigalyov is not only
in the name. Like his quasi namesake in *The Possessed*, this insignificant
Soviet official, a tax inspector who likes to pry into other people's affairs,
preaches the idea of a society based on absolute equality where thought
control will be carried to perfection through an all-round system of mutual
espionage. Leonov's Chikilyov says:

Here we are seeking happiness. But we have not yet bethought ourselves of
cutting the whole human race to one pattern. Let men be born equal in height,
length, weight, and so forth. As soon as someone starts pushing up, we'll cut his
wings short. There will be no trouble, all will dance to the same tune. . . .

In the future state, which will come in a thousand years, there will be no
secrets. Anyone, you see, will be able to come to anyone else and watch the other
man's life at any time of day or night, say through a magnifying glass. Suppose
you are secretly planning to ruin mankind. With those modern scientific achievements—the ray of death, the sneezing gas—you could blow up the whole globe
in no time. You must watch the humans, they must not be left to themselves. No
little secrets, citizens, come out, come out into the open, and make a clean breast
of what you are up to. Then willy-nilly all will be honest. Want it or not, you'll
have to stick to it. Suppose I were the ruler of the world, I would fix on to every-

body's head a sort of machine, with a kind of telegraph tape. In the morning a specially appointed official would take the reading and affix his resolution. . . . And everybody would be able to peer in the same way into his controller's mind. Thought—that's the source of all suffering.

Chikilyov's words about "the future state which will come in a thousand years" may be a conscious echo of Zamyatin's *We*. At the same time, there is here an intentional parody of Shigalyov's idea of a society which "proceeds from unlimited freedom and arrives at unlimited despotism," as Verkhovensky explains it to Stavrogin:

He has espionage. He has every member of society watching the others, and under an obligation to inform on them. Each one belongs to all, and all belong to each one. All are slaves, and equal in slavery. If need be, slander and murder, but above all—equality. The first thing is to reduce the level of education, knowledge, and talent. A high standard of learning and talent is within reach of higher abilities only—down with higher abilities! Higher abilities at all times seized power and became despots. . . . Slaves must be equal. There has never been freedom or equality without despotism. But there must be equality in a herd, and that's what Shigalyovism means.

In *The Thief*, Leonov also reintroduced his favorite theme of the irreconcilable cleavage between city and village. He personified it in Nikolka Zavarikhin, a rival of Mitka in the affections of Masha Dolomanova. Nikolka is young, cunning, energetic, and ambitious. He hates the city and its "idle" inhabitants who sponge on the peasants and their toil, and he dreams of domineering them. He symbolizes peasant vitality and at the same time the unconquerable bourgeois spirit, the lust for wealth and power.

On its publication Leonov's second novel was acclaimed by Soviet critics as a work of indubitable talent and power. But the more orthodox among them stressed Leonov's fundamentally pessimistic attitude toward the Revolution. In the words of Gorbachov, "The 'potent poison of Manyukin's disillusionment' in the 'epoch of unheroic weekdays' is diffused throughout Leonov's book."

The Thief was reissued four times, the last time in 1936. In 1959, Leonov published a thoroughly revised version of the novel. In this form it is now included in the editions of his collected works.

In 1927 there appeared one of the most interesting and original works in the whole of Soviet literature. Its title was *Zavist'* (*Envy*), and its author, Yury Karlovich Olesha. Olesha was born in Elizavetgrad and grew up in Odessa and was thus a countryman of Babel, Katayev, Bagritsky, and other young writers. Until 1927 he was practically unknown beyond the confines of daily journalism; and even there his activities were limited to the railway men's paper, *Gudok*, for which he wrote topical verse, which he

**Olesha
(1899–1960)**

signed "Zubilo" ("Point-Tool"). His name was quite new to most of the critics, but with the publication of *Envy* his literary reputation was established at one stroke. *Pravda* wrote that it had placed Olesha "in the front ranks of those writers who stand close to the circles of proletarian artists." *Molodaya Gvardiya* called it "a brilliant and profound work." *Revolyutsiya i Kultura* spoke of the significance of its theme, "one of the central themes of our time." Outside Russia the novel was hailed with equal enthusiasm by several *émigré* critics. The overnight success of this first novel by a hitherto unknown writer could be compared only to that of Dostoyevsky's *Poor Folk*.

There is nothing new in Olesha's theme, however. It was the rather hackneyed theme of the conflict between the old and the new in the Revolution, a conflict which had been explored by Fedin and Leonov, by some of the early revolutionary romantics, by Gladkov, and by many third-rate proletarian novelists. The novelty of the work lay in Olesha's treatment of this theme, in the freshness of form and manner. Instead of portraying this conflict in terms of actual episodes and concrete political or economic problems of Soviet life, Olesha succeeded in raising it to a higher level, in giving it a deeper and more universal meaning.

Envy is a short novel, especially as Russian novels go—some 120 pages. It has only six characters, of whom three stand as it were for the old world and three for the new. This bareness and simplicity of structure, reducing the theme to an almost algebraic and symbolic baldness, is obviously deliberate. The characters are Andrey Babichev, director of a Soviet Food Industry combine; his adopted son, Volodya Makarov, a member of the Young Communist League and a noted football player; Valya, a young girl of sixteen, Andrey's niece—these three representing the new world; and Ivan Babichev, Andrey's brother and Valya's father; Nikolay Kavalerov; and Anichka Prokopovich—these representing the old world. Andrey is a kind of "Americanized" Communist, an embodiment of physical fitness and of moral and intellectual smugness. Volodya Makarov is a typical young Communist—narrow-minded and strongly oriented toward a machine-made civilization. In the eyes of Andrey he personifies the new generation, the coming man. Valya has also in her something of the modern young woman, healthy and realistic, but at the same time she is endowed with the charm of the eternally feminine. She and Volodya are in love. Ivan Babichev is a gifted good-for-nothing romantic, cast out by the Revolution, who describes himself as "the last dreamer on earth." Kavalerov is also a romantic and a dreamer, but of a different cast. Anichka Prokopovich, a repulsive widow in her fifties, is an incarnation of *poshlost*, mean vulgarity.

From a formal point of view, the book falls into two parts. In the first, Kavalerov is the narrator; in the second, the author himself takes over. At the beginning we see Kavalerov as an inmate of Andrey Babichev's house, where he is, in his own words, the latter's buffoon—one night Babichev, moved by a sentimental recollection of Volodya, his temporarily absent adopted son, had picked him up in the street where he was lying drunk and had taken him to his home. Kavalerov is quite young, only twenty-seven, but the reader thinks of him as ageless. An individualist who feels out of harmony with his epoch and with the order of things in revolutionary Russia, he dreams of attaining personal fame—of some way of bequeathing his name to posterity—but he can see no opportunity in Communist Russia. His overwhelming, all-consuming emotion is envy. He both envies and hates Andrey, all the more since he realizes that he, Kavalerov, for all his inefficiency, is more intelligent and more gifted than the prosperous and self-satisfied director of the Food Combine—the "sausage maker," as Kavalerov contemptuously calls him. Babichev, on the other hand, feels for Kavalerov a pity bordering on contempt. One day Kavalerov decides to leave Babichev's house and go back to his old life as a down-and-out loafer. He writes a long, sarcastic letter to Andrey, giving vent to his hatred for him and proclaiming his superiority over him. He also expresses his conviction that Volodya, of whom Babichev seems to be so fond, is really in the same position and will never come back. As he takes the letter to Babichev's apartment, Volodya arrives, and Kavalerov sees for himself that Volodya is very much at home there, that there is no similarity in their positions. Realizing his foolishness, he decides to take his letter back, but by mistake picks up Volodya's recent letter to Babichev about himself and thus learns the true motives behind Babichev's hospitality. This makes him hate the "sausage maker" all the more. He vows vengeance upon him.

During his subsequent wanderings through Moscow he comes across Babichev's brother Ivan, whom he had only just seen and overheard in an argument with Andrey. He hails him as his friend, his master, his comforter, for Ivan is Andrey's avowed opponent. A romantic liar who throughout his childhood kept inventing fantastic gadgets and telling fantastic lies, he speaks also of having invented himself. He laments the disappearance of ordinary human feelings in the new society and wants to organize their parade—"a conspiracy of feelings," as he calls it. In one of the disreputable beerhouses which he now frequents and where he does card tricks, reads people's characters by the lines on their palms, sketches customers' portraits, displays feats of memory, and engages in other dubious occupations, Ivan holds forth before an audience of similar good-for-nothings:

We are human beings who have reached the uttermost limits of life. Men with strong personalities, men who want to live life in their own way, egoists, single-minded men—it is you I am addressing, for you are the intelligent ones: you are my advance guard! Listen, you in the vanguard! An age is dying. A wave is breaking against the rocks, it seethes and then it begins to froth. What do you want? To disappear like the foam of the wave? No, my friends, this should not be your end! No! Come to me and I will teach you. . . .

Be proud! I am your leader, I am king of the rabble. Any man who sings, weeps, rubs his nose on the table when all the beer is drunk and they won't serve him with more—his place is here, by my side. Come, all of you who are laden with grief, all you borne on song. You who are bursting with jealousy and you who are tying a hangman's noose for yourself—I call on you all, children of a doomed age, come to me, vagabonds and dreamers, fathers of families who cherish your daughters, honest bourgeois, men faithful to tradition, who acknowledge the norms of decency, duty and love, who shun the sight of blood and disorder, my dear friends—soldiers and generals alike—let us march out to war.[5]

Babichev is talked about as a new prophet. Marvelous stories are told about him, and rumors make their way "into government offices, the rest homes, and markets."

One story concerns an actual episode when Ivan Babichev tries to stop his brother driving in an official car, obstructs the traffic, and is arrested by the Ogpu. It is to the Ogpu examining magistrate that he tries to explain what he means by his "conspiracy of feelings." He says that many human feelings are about to be done away with. They include compassion, tenderness, pride, zeal, love—"in short, almost all the emotions which constituted the soul of man in the age which is now dying."

"I take it you understand me [says Ivan]. Stung by the serpent of jealousy, the communist is a prey to persecution. . . . We know that the grave of a Young Communist who has committed suicide is alternately covered with wreaths and the curses of his colleagues. The man of the new world says: 'Suicide is the deed of a decadent.' But the man of the old world says: 'He must have committed suicide to save his honor.' Thus we see that the new man schools himself to scorn sentiments that are hallowed by poets and by the muse of history herself."

To him, says Ivan, has fallen the honor of leading the last parade of human feelings.

The examining magistrate asks Ivan whether he has managed to find any followers. Only one, says Babichev, adding that his name is Nikolay Kavalerov and that the emotion he represents is envy.

So Ivan and Kavalerov fight their battle against Andrey together. There is something of a modern Don Quixote in Ivan. When his "conspiracy of feelings" fails, he falls back upon the marvelous, all-round machine of his own invention to which he gives the name of Ophelia—"the most human, the most touching of all names, . . . the name of a girl who went mad from

---

[5] This and the following quotations are taken, with some alterations, from the English version of *Envy* (trans. by P. Ross). There have since been other translations of which the one by A. R. McAndrew, strangely entitled *The Wayward Comrade and the Commissars*, is perhaps the best.

love and despair." He intends to use this machine for the eternal dishonor of the modern, inhuman, mechanized world, and in particular for the destruction of his brother's "Dime," a gigantic model canteen which is to provide cheap and hygienic meals for the population of Moscow and to free housewives from kitchen drudgery.

In the imaginary speech which Ivan Babichev holds at its inauguration he exclaims: "Do not call upon us. Don't beckon to us, don't tempt us. What can you offer us in the place of our capacity for loving, hating, hoping, weeping, pitying, and forgiving? Here is a pillow. Our coat-of-arms. Our banner." And Ivan brandishes the pillow as a symbol of family life, of the traditional home.[6]

Kavalerov, who acts as a Sancho Panza to Babichev's Don Quixote, is in fact more romantic, more of an individualist. An obvious kinship binds him to Dostoyevsky's Man from the Underground. He is worried by the same problem of self-assertion. The following monologue of his is reminiscent of the Man from the Underground with his "twice two is five," of Ivan Karamazov with his "everything is permitted," and of Raskolnikov's challenge:

I want to argue. I want to display the force of my personality. I want the fame to which I am entitled. . . . If only one could go out into the open, do something with oneself, make one's bow: I have lived, I have done something I wanted to. . . . If it were only committing suicide for no reason. Just out of mischief. To show that everyone has the right to act as he thinks fit. Today, let us say. Hang myself on your front door . . . .

As a side theme Olesha also introduces the Dostoyevskian theme of the opposition of Russia and the West. It is not without significance that Kavalerov, the romantic rebel, the individualist who dreams of asserting his personality, regrets that he was not born in the West "in some small French town." "In our country," he says, "the roads to fame are barred. A gifted man must either dim out or dare lift the barrier with a great row." It is this last that Kavalerov and Ivan Babichev attempt to do. They end, however, by capitulating and resigning. The conspiracy of feelings falls flat—even the "Ophelia" fails Ivan. They are also defeated in their efforts to save Valya from Andrey and Volodya, and come to realize that she does not want to be

---

[6] In an interesting article entitled "Potomki ludditov" ("The Descendants of the Luddites"), *Zvezda* (1934), R. Miller-Budnitskaya discusses the different, and sometimes contradictory, aspects of the persistent "antimachine" theme in Soviet literature, with reference to Pilnyak, Zamyatin, Alexey Tolstoy, Ehrenburg, and Olesha. In some of them she traces the Western roots of this theme. In this connection it is worth noting that H. G. Wells's *The Invisible Man* was one of Olesha's literary favorites. An attempt to juxtapose it with Olesha's own *Envy* and to interpret the latter in this light was made by D. G. B. Piper in an article in *Slavonic and East European Review*, Vol. XLVIII, No. 110 (January 1970).

saved, that she herself is part of the new world. For Kavalerov this is the greatest blow, for he is romantically in love with her and imagines himself her knight protector, destined to save her from the usurping designs of Andrey and Volodya.

In the person of Valya, Olesha may have intended to bridge the world of emotions and the world of new realities. In spite of her modernity and her earthliness, which are seen especially in the scenes of the football match and of the sporting exercises in the courtyard of her house, Valya is drawn in romantically ethereal colors. The sentimental romantic pink is the color accompaniment of her theme. Behind the exterior of a modern Soviet girl, keen on sports and physical culture, Olesha stresses her "eternal-feminine" substance. The key to her personality is in the following phrase which Kavalerov addresses to her and which is repeated as a refrain: "You swept past me like a branch laden with flowers and leaves." Yet, it is not only Andrey and Volodya but also Valya herself who laughs at it. Kavalerov's realization of his failure and defeat lead to his final and utter degradation: he returns to the huge, comfortable double bed of the Prokopovich widow. The same fate awaits Ivan Babichev. In a way, the new triumphs over the old. But only in a way.

Olesha's fundamental theme is the same which occupies many searching minds today, especially among former Communists. We find it restated in Arthur Koestler's *Darkness at Noon* and *The Yogi and the Commissar*. Andrey Babichev, the "sausage maker," the "model of masculinity," is an embodiment of Koestler's commissar type. When Rubashov, the hero of *Darkness at Noon*, writes in his diary "We have thrown overboard all conventions, our sole principle is that of consequent logic; we are sailing without ethical ballast," he states, in my opinion, the problem which tormented Olesha and which leads Ivan Babichev to organize his conspiracy of feelings. What will be the place of personal ethics, of human emotions and human dreams in this new mechanized, planned, totalitarian society which has discarded all ethical ballast and has proclaimed that the end justifies the means, a society which is represented by Andrey Babichev and his "Dime," that soulless ideal of material comfort and hygiene, and by Volodya Makarov with his cult of "unfeeling, proud machines" and his "Japanese grin"? Such is the main problem of *Envy*.

Olesha's romantic rebels are portrayed in all their vulgarity and unattractiveness (one of the merits the Soviet critics saw in it, when they praised the novel on its first appearance, was this showing up of the "enemies of the Soviet regime" in all their naked ugliness). Yet the unprejudiced reader cannot help being aware that Olesha has a sneaking regard for them—that it is not unintentionally that he endows Kavalerov with talent and imagination, that he sympathizes with his assertion of the worth of the individual and his proud rejection of a fame derived from the manufacture of improved sausages, just as he does with Ivan Babichev, for whom "invention is the beloved of reason." For all their vulgarity and meanness the two "negative" characters of *Envy* are human, while the two main spokesmen of the "new world," the world of sausages, machines, and model canteens, are both vulgar *and* inhuman. When Kavalerov returns to Anichka and falls ill, he has a symbolic dream in which he sees Ivan killed by his own "Ophelia." Just as the machine, with a needle protruding from its head, is about to pin Ivan to the wall, he exclaims: "Save him! Surely you are not going to allow a machine to kill a human being?" There is no answer to his agonized cry. "My place is with him," says Kavalerov. "Master! I shall die with you." This dream of Kavalerov is also a symbolic triumph for Valya, the romantic, idealized Valya. Charming and beyond reach, she soars above the crowd and the orchestra—"ribbons flew over her head, her dress billowed, her hair streamed upwards." She is apparently the only pledge of redemption for the "new world."

Although Olesha's novel is by no means a perfect work, in it he succeeded raising one of the staple themes of early Soviet literature to the level of a modern myth and produced one of the few works which, because of this universal significance, may remain when many other novels about the Russian Revolution will be studied only as documents reflecting a certain interesting period in Russian history.

Among contemporary Soviet fiction the novel also stands out because of Olesha's concern with formal design and verbal texture. Not only has Olesha a keen eye for the world, especially for its material externals, but he also has the gift of presenting them in striking and unexpected images, of making us see them, as it were, with new eyes. There is in his prose a freshness of outlook and vision combined with a freshness and felicity of expression. Like his Ivan Babichev, he is fond of the picturesque and sometimes allows himself to be carried away by his colorful imagery. Some Soviet critics have spoken of the influence of Giraudoux on Olesha's style.

In contrast to the deliberate simplicity of its structure and plot, the verbal texture of *Envy* is rich and complex—at times a little too rich, perhaps. The nervous dynamic style harmonizes well with the tempo of modern urban life, and *Envy* is essentially an urban novel. To the influence of Bely and his school may be ascribed the frequently recurring motifs. Thus Olesha enjoys mirrorlike, reflecting effects, which make ordinary things look new and fresh. Kavalerov himself speaks of the childlike character of his perceptions, of enjoying the vision of things through the wrong end of the binoculars. One of the central moments in the novel is the scene where Kavalerov meets Ivan Babichev, while watching his surroundings reflected in a street mirror. This bizarre, backward, refracted vision of the world, in which normal rules of optics and geometry are violated and distorted, is the leitmotif of the whole work, in which the planes of reality and fantasy are displaced and interlocked and the borderline between waking and dreaming obliterated. We are not in the least surprised, therefore, when to Kavalerov's question about his sudden appearance out of nowhere, Ivan Babichev replies, "I invented myself." The motifs of refraction and invention are subtly woven into the very texture of the novel.

That the problem which occupied Olesha in *Envy* continued to interest him is proved by the volume of his stories which appeared in 1929 under the title *Lyubov'* (*Love*). Two of the three stories in this volume, "Love" and "Liompa," are elaborations of some of the motifs of *Envy*. In "Love" we see a young Marxist, Shuvalov, who falls in love with a girl and whose vision of the world is suddenly transformed by love. Not only does he see the world differently from the way he saw it before, but his vision of it goes against the grain of his reason. Love turns him from a sober Marxian realist into a romantic. As a foil to him Olesha shows an anonymous, color-blind, black-hatted "citizen" whose vision of the world, except for his color-blindness, echoes the reality. There comes a moment when Shuvalov is so desperate that he is ready to exchange places with his counterpart, to give up the romantic green, the color which has become the dominant color of his world, and to see pears as inedible blue objects. But in the end romantic feelings triumph, and Shuvalov remains with his love and his green vision of the world.

In "Liompa" Olesha develops one of the side motifs of *Envy*—that of the relation between man and the objects which surround him. In *Envy* he contrasted Kavalerov and Andrey Babichev. "Things don't like me," says Kavalerov. "Furniture tries to play nasty tricks upon me. Once I was literally bitten by some varnished angle. My relations with blankets are always involved. My soup never cools. If some silly object, like a coin or a stud, falls off the table, it usually rolls under a piece of furniture which is hard to move. I crawl on the floor and, when I lift my head, I see the sideboard smirk." In "Liompa" we find this theme developed into a whole story. It is the story of a sick man who gradually loses his hold on things and is betrayed by them. Lying on his sickbed the hero of the story, Ponomaryov, thinks:

> I thought the outside world did not exist. I thought it would cease to exist with me. But now . . . I see everything turning away from me while I am still alive. After all, I still exist. Why, then, don't things exist? I thought it was my brain which gave them shape, weight, and color, but here they are gone from me, and only their names—useless names having lost their masters—are swarming in my mind.

To this dying man's nominalist vision of the world is opposed the healthy and joyous realism of a small boy: "Objects rushed to meet him. Without knowing a single name he smiled to them. As he went away a sumptuous trail of objects would flap after him."

In 1931, Olesha published another book of stories, *Vishnyovaya kostochka* (*The Cherry Stone*). It included the stories from *Love* as well as some new ones. Nearly all developed some of the motifs and secondary themes of *Envy*. Also closely related to the main theme of *Envy* was *Tri tolstyaka* (*Three Fat Men*, 1928), a novel supposedly written for children. It is an adventure story, full of delightful whimsicality, telling of certain happenings during a revolution in an imaginary country. The key theme of this novel, which was actually written before *Envy*, is to be found in its concluding lines:

> The three fat men told me: "Take out the boy's heart, and make an iron heart in its place." I refused to. I said that one must not deprive a man of his human heart; that no other heart—whether of iron, or of ice, or of gold—should be given man in the place of the simple, real, human heart.

This theme of the "simple, real, human heart" is also the leitmotif of Olesha's *Strogiy yunosha* (*A Strict Youth*), "a play for the cinema," to which reference will be made later.

Several Soviet critics rightly described Olesha as a writer of a single theme. One of them (Lev Levin) defined it as "the theme of a lonely human destiny" and the theme of the "ugly duckling." Both definitions were in fact Olesha's own and occur in his play *Spisok blagodeyaniy* (*A List of Blessings*, 1931), which will be treated at length in Chapter 17. Another critic (Zelinsky) spoke of Charlie Chaplin's "little man" as the real hero of all Olesha's works, and it is true that both Ivan Babichev and Kavalerov have in them something of Chaplin's hero (Babichev's "bowler" is an outward sign of his "Chaplinism"), while in *A List of Blessings* the Chaplin motif plays a very important part. But it would be better to say that all Olesha's writings represent the writer's dialogue with his epoch. This dialogue is significant because it epitomizes the fate of a nonconformist writer in Communist society, and to its later stages we shall return in Part IV and Part V.

Veniamin Kaverin (pseudonym of Veniamin Alexandrovich Zilberg) has some affinity with Olesha. But his success was less rapid and spectacular, and he proved to be much more adaptable, so that his literary career was more steady and durable. Kaverin played some part in all the phases of Soviet literature from 1922 to this day.

Coming from a family in which musical talent had been conspicuous for four generations, he also began by studying music. Later he studied Oriental languages and history of literature at the University of Petrograd. He began

Kaverin (b. 1902)

writing at the age of fifteen and in 1920 sent Gorky his first story, "Odi-nadtsataya aksioma" ("The Eleventh Axiom"). Soon after that he joined the Serapion Brotherhood, in which, together with Luntz, he represented the "Westernizing" tendency. In his autobiography he described Luntz as his best friend, and also wrote facetiously: "So far I have not had time to make for myself a biography fit for a Russian writer. I neither have tried to shoot myself nor to hang myself, nor did I once go mad."[7] Kaverin's story, printed in the Serapions' *Almanac*, stemmed from E. T. A. Hoff-mann, and the whole of his first volume, *Mastera i podmasterya* (*Craftsmen and Apprentices*, 1923), showed the influence of that German romantic and of Edgar Allan Poe (later Kaverin described himself as "a young man who had read Edgar Allan Poe and took every barrel for a cask of Amontilla-do"). His early stories were often clever experiments for experiment's sake. His interest in plot and composition contrasted sharply with the plotless ornamentalism and shapelessness of most of the writers of this early period. The tendency toward a novel of adventure—this time one can speak of the influence of R. L. Stevenson, another of his and Luntz's idols—is particular-ly pronounced in Kaverin's first major work, *Konets khazy* (*The End of a Gang*, 1926). It is an exciting story of the Leningrad underworld, of gangsters and anarchists.

Elements of romanticism and grotesque realism à la Gogol are mingled in the stories in *Bubnovaya mast* (*Diamond Suit*, 1927), while the frankly surrealistic *Revizor* (*The Inspector General*) is a parody of Gogol's "The Nose," with a deliberately obscene twist.

On the other hand, the novel *Devyat' desyatykh sudby* (*Nine-Tenths of Fate*, 1926) reflected the general trend toward reviving the psychological novel. Its theme—the place of the intelligentsia in the Revolution—is remi-niscent of Fedin's *Cities and Years*, but the treatment is much more super-ficial and immature.

In *Skandalist, ili vechera na Vasilyevskom ostrove* (*The Troublemaker, or the Evenings on Vasily Island*, 1928) Kaverin portrays the academic and literary milieu in Leningrad. Into it he manages to introduce the element of adventure. Much of it reads as a topical pamphlet in the form of a novel *à clef*. One of the main characters appears to have been modeled on Victor Shklovsky, and the literary battles around Formalism are parodied. A note of protest against all restrictions on creative freedom, against all chaperon-ing of literature, is cautiously sounded, but at the same time Kaverin seems to be settling some personal accounts with the Formalists. The whole tone is too facetious and the message too ambiguous. The problem of the artist's freedom and independence and of his place in society was treated more seriously by Kaverin in his next novel, *Khudozhnik neizvesten* (*The Un-

[7] See *Writers About Art and About Themselves*, 157.

known Artist), which appeared as late as 1931 but was apparently written in 1929–30 and, in spirit, belongs to the earlier period.

There is a great affinity between this novel and Olesha's *Envy*. The similarity can be seen not only in the parallelism of their themes but also in their form: their brevity, their small number of characters (Kaverin's has only three characters that matter; the rest are mere episodic figures), their simplicity of outline (which, however, in Kaverin's case is complicated by his Sternean toying with the plot), and their concern for form and verbal effects.

The motto of the novel was taken by Kaverin from *Don Quixote*: "And they marveled at the wisdom and folly of this gentleman." With equal appropriateness Kaverin could have chosen for his motto Ivan Babichev's formula: "Invention is the beloved of Reason," which would have suited his hero very well. At the core of *The Unknown Artist* lies the problem of artistic consciousness. But it is coupled with the problem of ethics in Communist society. Like *Envy, The Unknown Artist* is a contemporary myth. Its hero, the artist Arkhimedov, is a modern Don Quixote, an old-fashioned romantic idealist who fights a lonely, losing battle against the new society in the name of forgotten moral values, of artistic freedom and independence. There is a family air of resemblance between him and Olesha's Kavalerov and Ivan Babichev, and one can easily imagine him being drawn into Babichev's "conspiracy of feelings." But, though piteous and ludicrous, he is, unlike them, a lovable character and a tragic figure. The conflict between what Arkhimedov stands for and the new "technocratic" society is presented in terms of a personal clash between him and his friend Shpektorov, the new-world realist, the man of the Five-Year Plan, a younger and less bourgeois variation on Andrey Babichev. He does not care a hang for Arkhimedov's moral preoccupations and qualms and attaches more value to a pair of trousers than to any moral principles. He is too busy "building Socialism" to bother about such "trifles." He reproaches Arkhimedov for wishing to "incorporate Middle Ages in the Five-Year Plan." It is indeed to the medieval guilds that Arkhimedov looks back for the ideal of collective ethics, when he says:

In the fifteenth century not a single workshop would accept an apprentice until he swore to perform his work honestly in accordance with the statutes and the aims of State. The weavers of those days used to burn publicly any cloth which had an admixture of hair. Guildsmen guilty of giving false wine measures were thrown off the roofs into sewers. Just imagine the next session of the Central Executive Committee passing a decree on labor morality. With us there wouldn't be enough sewers for all the unscrupulous guildsmen.[8]

[8] This and the following quotations are taken, with some changes, from Ross's English translation of *The Unknown Artist* (published in the same volume as Olesha's *Envy*). The exact translation of the title is *Artist Unknown*.

This in a way anticipates Arthur Koestler's definition, in his essay "The Yogi and the Commissar," of one of the vaguely formulated but distinct trends of our times as "anti-materialistic nostalgia": "It is allergic to the rationalism, the shallow optimism, the ruthless logic, the arrogant self-assurance, the Promethean attitude of the nineteenth century; it is attracted by mysticism, romanticism, the irrational ethical values, by medieval twilight." "Rationalism," "shallow optimism," "ruthless logic," and "arrogant self-assurance" are precisely the attributes of Shpektorov and of the mentality he represents, just as they express the very essence of Andrey Babichev.

Arkhimedov is not an enemy of the new regime. But, like Ivan Babichev he is conscious—though much more acutely—of a great lacuna in it which must be filled in. To use again Koestler's later definition, he realizes that "a society with no incentives and ethical values will, whatever its economic structure, either dissolve into chaos and anarchy, or become a dumb mass under the whip." Of course, Arkhimedov does not formulate this idea in so many words; after all, Kaverin had to write with an eye on censorship. But it is implicit in Arkhimedov's refusal to surrender his soul and his artistic consciousness to Shpektorov's "new world." It needed great courage on Kaverin's part in 1931 to put into the mouth of one of his minor characters, an art student and an admirer of Arkhimedov, the following vehement defense of free art:

Real art is a perilous business, ruthless, with successes and failures, with revolts against the teachers, with veritable battles in which not only canvases are destroyed but human beings too. It is a battle for one's eye, for an honest eye which will yield to no laws or prohibitions. For its sake, one must accept hunger, cold and mockery. One must pocket one's pride or clench it between one's teeth, and if there is no canvas one must use one's own bedsheets to paint on.

Equally courageous was the denunciation of "little" artists, of typical "conformists":

There are artists who find it easy to work these days. They are the lucky ones who are convinced that time works for them. They seize with a ready hand upon whatever comes their way, because in their artistic household everything seems timely and necessary. There are among them worthy men who have an exceptionally strongly developed instinct of historical self-preservation. And there are the boys who arrive when the meal is over . . . .

Arkhimedov and Shpektorov clash throughout the book. Too much stress, says Arkhimedov, is being laid in Soviet Russia on technique, with the result that morality lags hopelessly behind. "Personal dignity," he contends, "must be an essential ingredient of Socialism." He defends romantic illusions. To Shpektorov, who says that for Soviet Russia "the West is a box of tools without which it is impossible to build even a wooden shed, let alone Socialism," Arkhimedov retorts: "A box of tools is not enough to launch a new era." He insists on fighting "the decline of honor, hypocrisy, baseness, and boredom." Shpektorov just shrugs his shoulders: "Morality? I have no time to stop and think over that word."

The ideological conflict between Arkhimedov and Shpektorov is complicated by their personal relations. Arkhimedov's wife, Esther, and Shpektorov are in love with one another, and a little boy, whom Arkhimedov believes to be his son and whom he named Ferdinand (after Lassalle), is in fact Shpektorov's son. When Esther is faced with the choice between her love for Shpektorov and her pity (and, perhaps, secret admiration) for Arkhimedov, she commits suicide by jumping out of a window. Arkhimedov's clash with Shpektorov ends with Arkhimedov's defeat: he is forced to give up his last and most precious possession, his son and only prospective follower (as in Olesha's *Envy* there is a stress on the childlikeness of romanticism). The boy is officially adopted by Shpektorov, and Arkhimedov renounces all claim to him. This is the crowning blow dealt to him, for he is pathetically attached to Ferdinand. But the epilogue to the novel suggests that his defeat is only on the outward plane. Spiritually he is the winner, and his passionate and selfless defense of free art is vindicated by his picture—a picture painted by "an unknown artist." The description of that picture, conceived during Arkhimedov's aimless wanderings about the streets of Leningrad after Esther's suicide, forms the epilogue to the novel. It is a picture representing his wife's suicide and the impressions gathered during his wanderings:

Only an artist whose free genius had rejected the cautious, dishonest standards of modern art with its aloofness from the people could have made a success of it. The mixture of the grand style with the trifles, of everyday details with a deep feeling for time, was something which neither living nor dead masters could have taught him.... To paint such a picture one had to crush to death.

Arkhimedov's defeat and downfall on the plane of life lead to his triumph as an artist and to the glorious vindication of his conception of true and heroic art. Such was the untimely message of Kaverin's novel.

Like *Envy*, Kaverin's novel is unusual in form. It is begun in the third person, but from the second chapter—Kaverin calls his chapters "encounters," and, in fact, they all center round some crucial encounter—the author himself intervenes, and after that we see Arkhimedov either through his eyes or as described by those who meet him. Shpektorov is portrayed as the author's former schoolfellow, and it is through him that the author meets Arkhimedov. The novel is interspersed with frankly autobiographical material, seemingly irrelevant to the story. Kaverin keeps toying with the plot and resorting to what the Formalist school calls "laying bare the device," which results in some original effects. Some of the most important conclusions about Arkhimedov are reached by the author during a performance

of Dickens' *A Tale of Two Cities*; and in general the theater plays a significant part in the unfolding of Arkhimedov's story. Some important scenes
are laid behind the wings of the School Youth Theater, and here the important motif of Don Quixote is introduced, thus emphasizing the unreal,
romantic, quixotic, "theatrical" nature of Arkhimedov's crusade for true art.

Slonimsky
(b. 1897)

Mikhail Leonidovich Slonimsky was one of the seven young writers who in
1920 formed the nucleus of the Serapion Brotherhood (the others, according
to him, were Zoshchenko, Luntz, Nikitin, Gruzdyov, Polonskaya, and
Pozner; the rest joined them a little later).[9] Like Kaverin and Luntz, he was
a Jew and came from a highly cultured family. His father was for many
years a regular contributor to the Liberal monthly *Vestnik Evropy*
(*Messenger of Europe*); his mother was the sister of the literary historian
Vengerov; his older brother was a pianist; and the Polish poet Antoni
Słonimski is his cousin. His childhood was spent in a literary and musical
milieu. In 1914 he joined the army as a volunteer. When the Revolution broke out in February, 1917, he was still a private in an engineer-
ing regiment stationed in Petrograd. The regiment was one of the first to
join in the revolt, and more than half its officers were killed by the men.
About this time Slonimsky began to write. In 1918 he was released from
military service, and when the House of Arts was founded by Gorky, he
began to attend Zamyatin's and Shklovsky's lectures there regularly.

His early stories, collected in the volume *Shestoy strelkovy* (*The Sixth
Fusiliers*, 1922), show a very strong influence of Zamyatin's manner and
style. In Slonimsky the training received in Zamyatin's studio is more
obvious than in any other of the Serapions. Broken, elliptical narrative;
intense aversion to all psychological motivation and analysis; eccentric, odd
characters involved in strange situations where the real and the fantastic
are intermingled; a predilection for unusual, dramatic incidents—such are
the characteristic features of these stories. Nearly all of them have the war
and the impact of the Revolution on the army for their setting. The subject
is treated in terms of stark realism bordering on the grotesque, and the
paramount impression is that of powerful irrational forces playing havoc
with human destinies, of senseless cruelty and inescapable doom. One of
Slonimsky's merits—especially if we compare him with his two fellow
Serapions, Nikitin and Vsevolod Ivanov—is his ability to tell a story without unnecessary comment.

In 1923, Slonimsky spent some time in the Donets coal basin, editing a
miners' paper there. One of the stories he wrote at the time, "Mashina
Emery" ("The Emery Machine"), marked, thematically speaking, a new
departure. Its hero is a certain Oleynikov, an ascetic Communist of the
builder type, for whom personal life is completely overshadowed by his

[9] See *Writers About Art and About Themselves*, 313–14.

sense of duty toward the collective. Slonimsky fails to make his portrait of this Communist visionary—especially his relations with the girl whom he marries for the sake of her brother's memory—psychologically convincing. But it was one of the first attempts on the part of a typical fellow traveler to portray an "ideal" Communist. Oleynikov is shown as a dreamer who lives not so much in the present as in the future when all human emotions, sensations, and desires, everything except man's thoughts, will be mechanized, so that "machines will not only work for men but also rejoice and suffer for them," and human thought, thus freed, "will be able to take mechanized life apart, to separate joy from suffering, and to do away with suffering."

One of the most interesting passages in the story is the letter which Oleynikov receives from his friend Grisha, who, about to commit suicide, asks Oleynikov to marry his sister. Grisha's letter is the confession of a disillusioned Communist who cannot bring into harmony the two planes of his existence, the two "floors" of life, as he puts it—the ideological and the everyday one. No longer capable of living on the upper floor only and rejected by the lower floor, he chooses death. Slonimsky shows Grisha as a direct contrast to Oleynikov. As was usual with the Serapions and other writers of this period, he does not go into their biographical antecedents, leaving it to the reader to reconstruct them, but it is clear that Grisha is also a Communist and that their friendship is not purely personal, that they have had a common revolutionary experience. To Oleynikov's single-minded optimism Grisha opposes his doubts and qualms. His schizophrenia is due to ordinary human pity:

My vision has changed. I used to look at the present through the future and was never sorry for anything. But now I look at the future through the present, and doubts assail me: Are we right? I've been corrupted by the oldest motif in the world—by pity. I remember with horror all I did in 1919. For the future, which you and I know, it was necessary, but what is one to do with pity? Everyday life has eclipsed the aim for which I lived. I feel sorry for all sorts of people— White Guards, Communists, all. I want everything to come true now and everybody to be happy. Hence the snag, the vicious circle: in order not to pity anyone, you must rebuild life; in order to rebuild life, you must kill; in order to kill, you must have no pity for anyone; in order to have no pity, you must rebuild life. I can't get out of this vicious circle. I am not up to living on both floors at once. I find myself outside space and time.

Let my case be a lesson to you. Stand on firm ground, don't hang in the air. I know: you'll be up to both floors, you're a strong man.

Here Slonimsky states concisely and bluntly the problem which must have been a very real one for many a Communist. Whether he has succeeded in making his readers share Grisha's faith in the ability of Oleynikov to cope with the problem is another question. For, while Grisha, who does not even appear in the story, is real and human, Oleynikov remains an abstraction.

The story retains many characteristic features of Slonimsky's earlier work —the rapid narrative packed with incident, strange characters whose actions are disconcerting and unmotivated, rapid dialogue, and little description. Grisha's letter, with its ideological and psychological motivations, is like a foreign body. But in it may be seen a germ out of which Slonimsky's later novels grew.

In 1926 appeared Slonimsky's first novel, *Lavrovy* (*The Lavrovs*). It depicts the disintegration of an intelligentsia family. The action of the novel begins on the eve of World War I and goes on into the first years of revolution. Much of the background—the war scenes, the early days of the Revolution which find the hero serving as a private in Slonimsky's own regiment in Petrograd—is obviously autobiographical and strictly documentary. The novel centers around the figure of Boris Lavrov, who straight from school joins the army as a volunteer, goes through some harrowing experiences at the front, and then is caught in the whirlpool of the Revolution and tries to fix a place in it for himself. To him are opposed, on the one hand, the other members of his family—his vulgar, domineering mother; his meek, henpecked father; his vain, futile brother—and on the other, Foma Kleshnyov, a true Bolshevik, active, sober-minded, resolute, who has a strong influence on Boris and is responsible for the latter's ultimately siding with the Revolution and becoming a small cog in its mechanism.

Boris Lavrov has been described by some Soviet critics as a new variety of "superfluous man," once so popular in Russian literature and revived, after the Revolution, by Fedin. That is true up to a point, but at the end Boris is shown on the way to becoming a useful member of Soviet society. However, for a long time he flounders about, unable to grasp the meaning of what is going on around him. The more he thinks about it and about his own actions, the more meaningless it all appears to him. At one moment he thinks that in siding with the Revolution he has attained full freedom, but "later he realized that there was no freedom anywhere on this earth, not in a single corner of it, and that of all the available unfreedoms he had chosen the one in which his wishes and actions coincided."

Lavrov's search for a place in the Revolution is erratic and psychologically not very convincing, his hold on it rather precarious. One has the impression that in portraying Lavrov's search Slonimsky either was vacillating, afraid to probe deeper into his own hero, or, true to his method of eschewing psychological motivation, was unable at this time, in a novel which purported to be a large-scale picture of the Revolution and its processes, to make a convincing and effective use of his customary medium.

Five years later Slonimsky was to return to his heroes in *Foma Kleshnyov* (1931), a chronological sequel to *The Lavrovs*. Here Kleshnyov, a good, straightforward Communist, is the hero, while Boris Lavrov plays a secondary part and is shown chiefly through his personal preoccupations (his love for Kleshnyov's wife, Liza, and his relations with another girl, Nadya Zhilkina). As a novel the book is a failure.[10] In between *The Lavrovs* and *Foma Kleshnyov*, Slonimsky wrote another novel, *Sredniy Prospekt* (1927).[11] It is quite short and in manner much closer to the early stories than to the Lavrov novels. Its plot is somewhat shadowy; certain rather interesting possibilities remain unrealized, leaving loose ends that stick out here and there. But in the main it is a novel of incident, involving unusual or even absurd situations, and strange, disconcerting people, who have a habit of appearing from nowhere and vanishing into thin air. The background is the "unheroic" NEP period of the Revolution. One of the characters, Mikhail Shchegolev, is a distant relation of Leonov's Mitka Vekshin—a former Red commissar turned smuggler. Utterly disillusioned, indifferent at bottom to everything, he calmly walks to his doom. The principal character in the novel is a certain Pavel Lebedev, a "petty man" who becomes a typical hanger-on of the Revolution. His "success" in life is a combined result of luck and the animal instinct of adaptation. Though hardly a good novel, *Sredniy Prospekt* is a good picture of a certain period in Soviet life and a certain section of Soviet society.

Voobrazhaemy sobesednik (*The Imaginary Interlocutor*, 1928), by Ovady Savich, appears to be the only work of interest written by this author, about whom Soviet reference works are silent.[12] It is one of the very few Soviet novels dealing almost entirely with personal problems and without political implications. Its hero bears the symbolical name Obydyonny, which could be rendered as something like "Mr. Everyday" or "Mr. Everyman," and is apparently meant to represent an average specimen of Soviet humanity. He is a very ordinary man, an employee of a provincial trust. The background

Savich (b. 1896)

[10] In 1949, Slonimsky reissued *The Lavrovs* under a new title: *Pervye gody* (*First Years*). It is a considerably revised version of the original novel, with a number of new characters and new episodes, some of them transferred bodily or in new combinations from another short novel by Slonimsky, *Proshchanie* (*The Farewell*, 1937). *The Farewell* was meant to complement the picture of the Revolution given in *The Lavrovs*, where Slonimsky had concentrated on the democratic February Revolution, by scenes describing in greater detail the October coup d'état. Neither the Lavrovs nor Kleshnyov appeared in it. In *First Years* these scenes were woven into the framework of the original version and the new characters tied by new ties to Boris Lavrov and Foma Kleshnyov. Some of these changes were obviously dictated by Slonimsky's desire to round off and clarify his main hero; others were of a purely "ideological" nature and will be mentioned in Chapter 29.

[11] The novel is so called from the name of a street in St. Petersburg. The title (*The Middle Avenue*) has both a direct topographical and a symbolical meaning.

[12] The only other major work by Savich known to me, besides some magazine stories, is *My i oni* (*We and They*, 1932), which he wrote with Ilya Ehrenburg. It is an anthology of Russian opinions, mainly from literature, about France and the French. As far as I know, it was never reissued—perhaps because it was colored to some extent by Ehrenburg's pro-French sentiments.

of the novel and its secondary characters are all realistic—the daily routine of a Soviet trust, Obydyonny's domestic life, and his relations with his insignificant colleagues. But beyond this background a second, symbolical plane is felt constantly. The novel is really the story of Obydyonny's gradual transition, on his way to death, to a different plane—of his meaningless, unmotivated actions, his deep boredom, and his estrangement from those who surround him. The symbolism is enhanced by the introduction of Obydyonny's "imaginary interlocutor," who now appears as his double, as an exteriorization of his own thoughts and forebodings of death, and now is materialized in the real but mysterious person of a young dancer, Obydyonny's lodger. The novel ends with Obydyonny's death, for which all the rest was merely a preparation. There are in this curious and unusual novel echoes of Tolstoy's *Death of Ivan Ilyich* and also of Dostoyevsky, but the calm, unhurried narrative is quite unlike Dostoyevsky's.

Budantsev
(1896–1939) Sergey Fyodorovich Budantsev began writing before the Revolution, but his first important work, the novel *Myatezh* (*The Revolt*), was published in 1923. Renamed later *Komandarm* (*The Army Commander*), it has for its subject an anti-Bolshevik rising in a provincial town, led by a certain Kalabukhov, a Socialist Revolutionary of the left. He is shown as an individualist, a reckless adventurer, capable of personal heroism but opposed to all organization and discipline. He has his own conception of the Revolution which borders on anarchism, and he refuses to accept the Soviet government, just as he refused to accept the Brest-Litovsk Peace with the Germans and went on fighting them at their rear with his guerrillas. He says:

Your revolution is swallowing me. Yours. Not the one of which I became aware at the front after Brest when I withdrew to the Germans' rear. That revolution was mine, it was eternal, it was against death, it fought death. And yours, which you have mastered in two months, the Communist one, is a change from one form of economic activity to another. A transition, no more.

The somewhat pretentiously named *Povest' o stradaniyakh uma* (*A Tale of the Sufferings of Mind*) was written in 1929 and first published in *Novy Mir*. The action of this short novel is set outside Russia and sometime in the past, but it has nothing to do with historical fiction. It has but few characters, and the only one that really matters is the hero, Mikhail Grekov, a brilliant young scientist of the 1860's, a follower and admirer of Darwin. The story of his childhood, of his scientific and academic career, and of his ill-fated marriage is given in a long flashback. The action proper takes place within a very short time in a Swiss boardinghouse, whose occupants are briefly introduced to the reader as a kind of grotesque backdrop. The narrative centers around Grekov's two attempts at suicide. The first time he takes morphine, but is saved. The second time he proceeds more elaborately. He takes a scalding bath and then, dressed very lightly, walks out of the boardinghouse with the intention of catching cold. This time he is saved in a not very plausible way—through the combined agency of a friend's timely intervention and—his own suddenly aroused scientific interest in some insects. This artificially contrived rescue ends the novel, leaving the reader to assume that Grekov's suicidal intentions are over and that he will now resume life with a new zest.

The main interest of the novel—an altogether unusual work in Soviet literature—lies in the thorough dissection of Grekov's mind and in the account of his past life. Budantsev was criticized for his unhistoricity and his failure, despite many references to Herzen and other contemporary figures, to portray Grekov as a typical man of the sixties. One Soviet critic spoke of Budantsev's "reactionary individualism." It appears, indeed, that Budantsev's choice of his period was quite arbitrary, or that he chose it by way of disguise, to avoid placing his hero in a contemporary setting. For the problems that occupy him are of no particular time or place; in fact, they might very well be those of a Soviet scholar. Grekov deliberately opposes himself, his personal problems, his meditations on life and death, to the interests of the society at large. In a conversation with his brother he tells the latter that for him his personal problem (the blindness which threatened him at the time) is of infinitely greater consequence than any social injustices. He says:

> Any social cruelty can be straightened out and mitigated. How many institutions that used to oppress mankind have fallen during the past seventy years! But this mitigation did not affect my lot. And the chief thing is: How will you mend the cruelty of Nature, its basic cruelty—death?

The novel is concerned largely with Grekov's grappling with the problem of death. His second attempt at suicide is the result of the cerebral tug of war that goes on within him. His decision to seek death is really a challenge to fate. Instead of a simple suicide he must try something which will either finish him off or reawaken in him the desire to live. The ending of the novel suggests this latter outcome, but it is not very convincing.

Budantsev continued to write and publish stories and plays in the thirties. One of his later plays, *Kollektsiya mednykh monet* (*A Collection of Copper Coins*, 1932), reads almost like a vivid parody of a Communist "morality" play.

Sergey Klychkov (pseudonym of Sergey Antonovich Leshenkov) was originally known as a peasant poet. His poetry had points of affinity with Klyuev's and Esenin's, but it lacked the religious and messianic note. Some of its essential themes and motifs are to be found in the volume *Domashnie* **Klychkov (1889–1940)** *pesni* (*Domestic Songs*), which is saturated with Russian folklore. The folklore motifs form also an important element of his prose fiction, on which he concentrated after 1924. His novels *Sakharny nemets* (*The Sugar German*), *Chertukhinsky balakir'* (*The Prattler of Chertukhino*), and *Knyaz' mira* (*The Prince of Peace*), published in the late twenties, are parts of a vast epic of peasant life before the Revolution. Written in rich language, now ornately poetical, now colloquial, they combine a realistic portrayal of village life and types with unbridled fantasy rooted in popular legends, and are peopled with all sorts of quaint goblins, wood spirits, and other whimsies, side by side with peasant characters whose intonations and peculiarities of speech are meticulously reproduced. The best of these novels is *The Prattler of Chertukhino*, in which Klychkov gives free rein to his fantasy. Communist critics, while admitting Klychkov's mastery of the peasant *skaz*, his feeling for Russian folklore, and his clever handling of the plot, stressed his "archreactionary romanticism" and his idealization of old Russia.[13] Klychkov was arrested in 1937, and there are reasons to believe that he died in a concentration camp.

Lavrenyov (1897–1959)   Boris Andreyevich Lavrenyov began writing poetry about 1913. In those days he belonged to various Futurist groups. His later poetry, which he went on writing till 1924, was composed under a very strong influence of Gumilyov and, in its romantic and exotic aspect, of Acmeism in general. In 1916, while serving as a cavalry officer in the Russian Army, Lavrenyov wrote his first short story ("Gala Peter"), which, though a little too carefully "made," showed considerable promise. After a spell of revolutionary activity, military and otherwise, he devoted himself entirely to literature, joining the Leningrad group Sodruzhestvo. After 1924 his stories and plays earned him an important place in Soviet literature.

In an autobiographical note, published in 1928, Lavrenyov wrote that for him literature filled a gap in life, since there was no longer any romance in life itself.[14] In a later autobiography (1930) he wrote ironically and somewhat defiantly:

I know my qualities. Also my shortcomings. European literary culture is too strong in me. "Literaturizing." Too much of an inveterate intellectual. Too much of an un-Russian writer. Bred and brought up on French and English writers. I like a sound and firm pattern. I don't like our "literature. . . ."

Literature must be brief, clear and improbable to the point where it can be believed. For truth, there are newspaper reports and chronicle. Literature must excite and captivate. . . .

Literature must master *above all* the plot. I have mastered it. To master the rest, is my task for the coming years.[15]

13 See Gorbachov, *Contemporary Russian Literature*, 125–26.
14 *Writers About Art and About Themselves*, 193.
15 B. Lavrenyov, *Sobranie sochineniy* (*Collected Works*), I, 45–46.

Robust romanticism and concentration on the plot are the salient features of Lavrenyov's work between 1924 and 1926. Quick, dynamic action; plenty of incident; unusual situations; tense, romantically heightened collisions; and romantic yet lifelike characters with clearcut social characteristics— these are the essential elements of Lavrenyov's stories, some of which are more like short novels. In many of them the Civil War and the period of War Communism, romantically portrayed, form the background. "Veter" ("Wind," 1924) is the story of the adventures of a sailor whom the experiences of the Civil War turn into a class-conscious revolutionary. After a period of peaceful civilian work, however, he soon gets bored and returns to the romantic life of the front, there to meet death after another exciting (and somewhat improbable) adventure. In "Rasskaz o prostoy veshchi" ("The Story About a Simple Thing," 1924) the hero is an old Bolshevik, chairman of the local Cheka, who is left behind to carry on underground work in a town occupied by the Whites and, after some breath-taking adventures, is caught by them and ordered to be shot. The story, divided into short chapters, proceeds with cinematographic speed from one exciting and psychologically tense situation to another. "Zvezdny tsvet" ("The Starry Flower," 1924) combines an exotic setting (the action takes place in Turkestan) and an exciting story with a sharply contrasting social situation.

The best of these Civil War stories by Lavrenyov is "Sorok pervy" ("The Forty-first," 1924), the heroine of which is a young girl, Maryutka, daughter of a Volga fisherman, who joins a Red partisan detachment and becomes a first-class sniper. The story tells of the partisans' encirclement by their enemies and of their laborious retreat through the salt steppes east of the Caspian Sea. On their way they meet a caravan of camels led by some Kirghizes and accompanied by six "Whites." One of these, an officer who was to have been Maryutka's forty-first victim but whom she had missed, is taken prisoner by the partisans. Later, she is stranded alone with him on a desert island in the Aral Sea, and they fall in love. The story ends with Maryutka shooting her lover when a party of White officers approaches their island—her orders were not to let him go alive. Here, as in some other stories, Lavrenyov makes effective use of some stock literary situations (there are in this story some deliberate echoes of *Robinson Crusoe*), which he instills with fresh content and treats in an original and exciting way. "The Forty-first" was made into a highly successful motion picture.

In some of Lavrenyov's stories the influence of Bely and Pilnyak can be discerned—for example, in the lyrical digression about Petersburg in "Wind" and a similar digression about the wolves prowling in the steppe in "The Forty-first." The lyrical paraphrase of passages from *The Lay of the Raid of Igor*, used as an inset in "Wormwood," is likewise reminiscent of Pilnyak. In "Wind" the general symbolism—the wind motif—is also Pilnyakian. But the differences are more striking than the similarities. The digressions are more coherent, more organized. They resemble vignettes worked into the general pattern of the narrative, and Lavrenyov never lets himself be carried away by these irrelevancies, but always has the story in mind. He also knows how to tell a story—rapid, dynamic, well knit, tense, full of incident. However, for all his avowed aversion to psychological probing and "mystical poking around in one's navel," he is interested in individual characters, and his stories are also social-psychological studies. But he prefers to show his characters in action and dialogue.

After 1926, Lavrenyov turned to subjects taken from everyday Soviet life. His vision of it, however, remained colored by his romanticism. A typical story is "Mir v styoklyshke" ("The World in a Bit of Glass"), subtitled "A Sentimental Story." The characters in it are all "small" people—some of them relics of the world gone by, who live in the past; others live on more or less good terms with the present but away from the mainstream of events. The Revolution serves as a backdrop to the story, but in the center of it stand ordinary human beings and their interwoven human tragedies.

In the stories included in the volume *Shalye povesti* (*Crazy Tales*, 1926), everyday-life subjects are treated in terms of whimsical humor or grotesque. "Nebesny kartuz" ("The Skyblue Cap"), subtitled "An Improbable Story," is an amusing parody of a Sherlock Holmes story in a Soviet setting. "Vozdushnaya mechta" ("An Airy Dream") is a facetious Leskovian *skaz* of queer happenings in a godforsaken village which the Revolution takes five years to reach; the improbable and the grotesque are intermingled with touches of everyday reality. "Thalassa" (1926), with the ironic subtitle "A Sober Story," tells of the adventures of a meek and modest Soviet employee who gets involved with a pretty smugglers' agent and takes part in a smuggling expedition along the coast of the Black Sea. Beneath its frivolity, however, one can feel Lavrenyov's romantic nostalgia, his aversion to the humdrum realities of Soviet life (which Soviet critics accused him of voicing openly in the short, autobiographical story "Marina").

Sedmoy sputnik (*The Seventh Satellite*, 1927) was regarded by some critics as a turning point for Lavrenyov. Here he takes the reader back to the period of the Civil War. But his manner is different from his earlier stories of the same period. The narrative is quieter and slower; the accent is on psychology rather than on incident. It is the story of the gradual transformation of an old general, a former professor of the Academy of Military Jurisprudence, who is arrested as one of the hostages for the murder of Uritsky in 1918 but, unlike many of his fellow prisoners who are shot, is eventually released, only to find that his apartment and all his belongings, by the sale of which he lived before, have been confiscated and he has nowhere to live. After an unsuccessful attempt to get a temporary refuge with one of his old school friends, he goes back to the prison and gets engaged as a laundryman. Later, when a high-ranking commissar discovers his presence there, he is given a judicial post in the Red Army and sent to the front. By this time his sympathies are already on the side of the new regime, and he "accepts" the Revolution out of patriotism, though he does not become a Communist. He admits this when he is taken prisoner by General Yudenich's White Army and is ordered to be shot. Lavrenyov's General Adamov, portrayed sympathetically by the author, is probably not untypical of a certain section of the old technical intelligentsia when faced with the Revolution. The story is told in a quiet, subdued manner. The scenes in a Petrograd square, where representatives of the old propertied classes are selling their personal belongings, and in the prison, where some of them are led out to be shot, are very well done.

A place apart in Lavrenyov's work belongs to his novel *Krushenie respubliki Itl* (*The Downfall of the Republic of Itl*, 1925). It describes, in terms of a fantastic satire, foreign intervention in the south of Russia and the establishment there, with the help of England (which is disguised as "Nautilia"), of a democratic republic. Lavrenyov demonstrates here his narrative skill and sense of humor, but, although he was influenced by Anatole France's *Penguin Island*, his work lacks France's earnestness and has more of a Ruritanian musical comedy about it, as was rightly pointed out by some Soviet critics.

Mikhail Emmanuilovich Kozakov came from a bourgeois Jewish family and spent his childhood in the south of Russia. Before the Revolution he studied medicine in the University of Kiev but left without graduating and became a journalist. Later he graduated from a law school and worked as a defense counsel in a Soviet tribunal. In his autobiography he wrote: "I shall not hide it, I always feel a great moral satisfaction at having been able, in those days, to save a few human lives: acquitted by the Soviet authorities, these people are now, I know, being useful, each in his own way, to state and society." In Kozakov's work there are many echoes of his legal work.

Kozakov (1897–1954)

In 1922, Kozakov settled in Petrograd and joined the Sodruzhestvo literary group, which was supposed to represent the left-wing fellow travelers. His first book of stories, *Popugaevo shchastye* (*Parrot's Luck*), appeared in 1924. In the choice and treatment of characters it showed a considerable influence of Dostoyevsky. Kozakov approached the Revolution as a landslide which had wrought great changes in the course of daily life and specialized in the portrayal of the "humiliated and injured" in it. His stories abound in odd characters on whom destiny plays odd tricks. He also shows people in whom the kicks and blows dealt by the Revolution awaken primitive biological instincts and strengthen their instinctive grip on life. Among the more curious characters is Vitos, chairman of the revolutionary tribunal in the story "Tsygarka" ("A Cigarette"), a Dostoyevskian mixture of saintliness and sadism. A good Communist, Vitos displays a great interest in his victims and, after sentencing them, often to death, spends hours questioning them in prison, trying to find out all about them. The author describes this interest as "man's greediness for man."

Kozakov's second book of stories, *Povest o Karlike Makse* (*The Tale About Max the Dwarf*, 1926), contained a longish story called "Abram Nashatyr', the Innkeeper." The setting is a Russian provincial town during the NEP period. It is a good picture of everyday Soviet life of that period, but it is also something more than that. The main interest is in the central character, a hardhearted, unscrupulous Jew who rises to wealth and importance through a murder committed, at his instigation, by his brother and ends by calmly killing that very brother when he reappears on the scene and threatens his peace and happiness.

Kozakov's most interesting work of this period was the short novel *Meshchanin Adameyko* (*Adameyko the Philistine*, 1927). Its dependence on Dostoyevsky is obvious; it is a psychological detective story, and both its theme and its form recall *Crime and Punishment*. The plot revolves round the murder of Adameyko's neighbor, a well-to-do widow. She is a usurer (a deliberate parallel to Alyona in *Crime and Punishment*), and Adameyko is a kind of modern Raskolnikov who conceives and plans the murder in order to give life to his idea—his "social fancy" as he calls it—that social justice demands the elimination of all "superfluous" people, of all the "parasites" who have survived the Revolution. Adameyko describes them as the "proud flesh" of life. This is how he formulates his idea to Sukhov, an unemployed printer whom he wants to use as his instrument:

There are people who should not live. Yet they live, because the Revolution overlooked them, and the Revolution itself is over and will not hurt anyone now: it lies like a cartridge taken apart—the cap here and the case there. . . .

I have in mind—let me put it scientifically—a social fancy. Some people may think it crazy. But why not collect all this "proud flesh" and expose it to one bullet, and use the goods that will be left behind for the benefit of those whom life has injured? . . . I say to myself: If, indeed, it comes to justice, then you, Ardalyon Porfiryevich, justify murder.

(Even the name and patronymic of Adameyko have a Dostoyevskian ring.)

When Sukhov asks him point-blank whether he is personally capable of killing, Adameyko's answer is evasive. He speaks of being capable of "justifying" a murder and of "taking part" in it, but his real intention is to use Sukhov. He does so, and the murder comes off, though actually the victim dies of heart rupture before she is killed.

The narrative follows an unusual pattern. The story is told in jerky zigzags, with constant anticipations of things to happen; but these anticipations and chronological shifts, which do away with the element of "mystery," enhance rather than diminish the psychological interest and suspense. Kozakov's attitude toward his hero is noncommittal—he remains true to his maxim: "From myself and from other writers I demand one main thing—that they be *honest* in the literary sense."[16] Adameyko's "idea" has obvious political implications, but his own approach is rather ethical. His attitude toward the Revolution is ambiguous: he is clearly an individualist with Nietzschean leanings, but he is not against the Revolution and emphasizes that he is not of the ruling class, but a "philistine," a man-in-the-street.

Equally original in structure is Kozakov's story "Chelovek, padayushchy nits" ("The Man Who Prostrates Himself," 1928), where newspaper documentation is cleverly worked into the framework of a fictional story. But here the "laying bare of the device" is a trifle too obtrusive. The story is also interesting for its subject matter—various manifestations of anti-Semitism in Soviet life.

In 1929 appeared the first volume of Kozakov's long "historicopolitical" novel *Devyat' tochek* (*Nine Points*), portraying the Russian liberal and revolutionary intelligentsia on the eve of World War I. It was to cover also the post-Revolutionary period, and a sequel to it was published later, but the novel remained unfinished.

[16] *Writers About Art and About Themselves,* 180.

Chapter 9. PROLETARIAN NOVELISTS

As mentioned earlier, the official policy of slighting proletarian writers in the 1924–29 period had the effect of stimulating them to greater literary activity. Among this group were such novelists as Libedinsky, Gladkov, Fadeyev, and Sholokhov.

Libedinsky (1898–1959) Yury Nikolayevich Libedinsky was, chronologically speaking, one of the first proletarian novelists. Born in Odessa, he spent his childhood at one of the big plants in the Urals. In 1921 he joined the Communist party and for several years was engaged in political work for the Red Army. He became one of the most active members of the October and the Onguard groups. In 1922, *Molodaya Gvardiya* published his first short novel, *Nedelya* (*The Week*). It was followed in 1924 by *Zavtra* (*Tomorrow*), and in 1926 by *Komissary* (*The Commissars*). All three novels deal with the inner life of the Communist party, and their principal characters are average Communists shown in connection with their party work.

In *The Week* the action takes place in Chelyabinsk in 1920. Libedinsky shows us a number of Communists with different backgrounds who run the town and have to tackle various problems facing the new government. The central episode is the anti-Bolshevik rising organized by the Whites with the help of the discontented peasants. The rising is suppressed, but most of the Communist leaders perish in it. The novel is interesting as an illustration of the inner workings of the Communist party and as a gallery of lifelike portraits of Communists, drawn objectively though superficially. Its weakest point is its style. Libedinsky himself admitted that he was influenced by Bely, who at one time was his favorite writer. But his attempt to write rhythmical prose, with constant syntactical inversions, in the manner of Bely and Sologub, produces ludicrous results, quite out of keeping with the subject matter and the general realistic manner of the narrative. The descriptions are either vapid or forced and affected. When Libedinsky tries to show his Communists outside their party activities, he fails signally. As party members they are sufficiently differentiated, but as human beings most of them lack individuality.

In *The Commissars*, written some three years later, Libedinsky adopted a more simple manner, free from all stylistic pretensions. The action is set in a large provincial town in 1921, at the critical time of transition from War Communism to the New Economic Policy. The occasion is a refresher course for Red Army political commissars. All the main characters are Communists who played an active part in the Civil War. They are of different social origins: some are factory workers and old Bolsheviks; some are peasants who joined the party in 1917; while a few come from the middle class. The director of the course is a former officer who was a Menshevik before the Revolution but who is now a good Bolshevik. Some of these former commissars find it difficult to adjust themselves to new conditions, to the discipline which is demanded of them now. Others reveal their essential "bourgeois" nature and have to be purged. The novel is a good picture of a microcosm of the Communist party at a time when the new policy decreed by Lenin produced great bewilderment and confusion among its rank and file. There are scenes of party meetings, of purges, and of political lectures that have considerable documentary value. Once more Libedinsky is at his best when he shows his characters in their party environment. However, as soon as it comes to showing them as human beings facing personal problems, his limitations as an artist become more obvious. Neither Lobichev's quest for love nor Mindlov's mental illness, caused by overwork and by separation from his wife, who is dying of consumption in the Crimea, is presented in a convincing way. The bourgeois wife of Alferyev, the stern and cold director of the refresher course, is a hackneyed stock character, devoid of flesh and blood. But the psychological conflicts and the clashes of opinions within the Communist elite are shown with considerable objectivity, and for a student of the Communist party and its history and of a certain period of Soviet life, the novel has much to offer that is of undoubted interest.

Tomorrow, which appeared between *The Week* and *The Commissars*, was regarded by Libedinsky himself and by his Communist critics as a distinct failure and, what is more, a great ideological mistake. It reflects Libedinsky's dismay, which he shared with many good Communists, at the sight of the rapid *embourgeoisement* consequent upon the introduction of the New Economic Policy. The action is set in Moscow in 1923. There is a vivid picture of the "demoralization" brought about by the NEP. The plot—if a plot it can be called—is centered around the news of a successful Communist revolution in Germany, which has a heartening effect on many Communist old-timers in Russia. The title of the novel and the way in which the effect of this news is presented justified the critics' inference that for Libedinsky the only way of saving the Revolution in Russia from the morass of the NEP lay through its extension beyond the boundaries of Russia. This was, of course, the way many Communists felt at the time. The novel was therefore denounced as pessimistic and ideologically erroneous. In a postscript to it, entitled "Why My *Tomorrow* was a Failure," which accompanied a later edition, Libedinsky admitted that in contemplating the Soviet reality of those days he had arrived at Trotskyism.

In its over-all manner *Tomorrow* is closer to *The Week* than to *The Commissars*. The influence of Bely and of ill-digested modernism is felt in the hysterical, staccato style. Characters are even less individualized, while there is an unsuccessful attempt to show the masses in action. There are some unnecessary episodes which slow down and lengthen the narrative. A failure artistically, *Tomorrow* does not possess the documentary interest of the two other novels.

Gladkov (1883–1958) Fyodor Vasilievich Gladkov came of a poor peasant family. His early life, amid poverty, squalor, and wanderings about the country, bears some resemblance to Gorky's. At the age of sixteen he wrote his first story, which was printed in a provincial newspaper. In 1901 he came across Gorky's stories and after that began to imitate him in his work. In 1905–1906, Gladkov took part in the revolutionary movement and was arrested and exiled for three years to Siberia. On returning from exile, he lived in Novorossiysk and there wrote his long story "Izgoi" ("The Exiles"). He sent it to Korolenko, who called it a "lunatic asylum"[1] but advised Gladkov to offer it to the review *Zavety*, where it was accepted. Until 1917, Gladkov worked as a village teacher in the Kuban region. With the outbreak of the Revolution he was again drawn into active political work and stopped writing.

After 1922, Gladkov devoted himself entirely to literature, becoming a member of the Smithy and of other proletarian literary organizations. His first major post-Revolutionary work was *Ognenny kon'* (*The Fiery Steed*), a rather pretentious novel combining revolutionary ideology with a morbid, amorous psychology à la Dostoyevsky and a cheap imitation of modernist style.

However, with the publication of the novel *Tsement* (*Cement*) in 1925, Gladkov's literary reputation was assured. The novel was enthusiastically received by the Communist critics. It was translated into several European languages, and its sales quickly reached the unheard-of figure of 500,000 copies. On the title page of its early editions one could read the following recommendation, reminiscent of the good old times when certain books were approved by the Ministry of Education for inclusion in school libraries: "Recommended by the Chief Department of Political Education for mass public libraries. Admitted by the State Learned Council into school libraries."

In *Cement*, Gladkov tried to write a monumental proletarian novel about the Revolution. Its subject is the transition from the Civil War period, which had disorganized and dislocated the life of the country, to the period of peaceful but unromantic reconstruction. The action is set in a big Black

---

[1] *Writers About Art and About Themselves*, 91.

Sea port (which is easily recognized as Novorossiysk), and the novel describes the resumption of work in a well-known cement plant there. Parallel with the story of this reconstruction is shown the disintegration of the old framework of life—the dissolution of family relations, the birth of a new morality and new ways of life. The novel is full of enthusiasm for revolutionary reconstruction, but one cannot reproach Gladkov for looking at things only through rosy spectacles, for he does not shirk from exposing the seamy side of this new life as well. Gladkov's realism is, however, blended with romanticism. He is fond of contrasts and striking situations, often at the expense of verisimilitude.

The principal characters in the novel are the cement worker Gleb Chumalov and his wife, Dasha. Chumalov has spent nearly the whole Civil War at the front and has been decorated with the Order of the Red Banner. On returning to his home town, he takes upon himself the initiative of restarting the cement work. Before he triumphs, he has to overcome a great deal of inertia, red tape, and open opposition; much of the novel is concerned with his battle for the cement plant. At the same time Gladkov shows us Gleb's inner conflicts. A good Communist, he has not yet succeeded in discarding some of his old moral instincts and "prejudices." This conflict between his political and his moral nature is one of the psychological pivots of the novel. Gleb clashes first with his wife, who, during his absence at the front, has been drawn into social work for the party and has become an "emancipated" woman who believes in "free love," and she now refuses to submit to Gleb's old-fashioned notions of morality and woman's duties. The conflict between Gleb and Dasha is interlinked, through a complex net of relationships, with other characters in the novel: with Badyin, chairman of the local Executive Committee, a drunkard and a debauchee, but a good party administrator; and with Kleist, an old engineer at the cement plant, an avowed class enemy, who had earlier ordered Gleb's execution but had saved Dasha from death and who in the end is won over to the cause of restoring the cement plant.

The novel is an interesting document, reflecting a critical period in the life of the Soviet Union and of the Communist party. The atmosphere of confusion and bewilderment is conveyed with great objectivity, and many of the secondary characters are well portrayed. Gleb and Dasha are much less convincing. They lack individuality. Dasha especially sounds stilted, while many incidents in her life touch on cheap melodrama. The principal defect of the novel lies, however, in its style. It is an incongruous mixture of old-fashioned realism, naturalism, and ill-digested modernism, in which the echoes of Dostoyevsky and of Leonid Andreyev are only too obvious. The diction is often shrill and hysterical, and many of the dialogues— especially of the workers—represent an untenable mixture of coarse, naturalistically reproduced dialect and high-sounding, sophisticated rhetoric.

Gladkov lacks all sense of measure. In a later, revised edition he tried to smooth out some of these stylistic incongruities.

Among Gladkov's stories written after *Cement* should be mentioned three satirical studies of three different types of "kibitzers" in the Communist party: "Golovonogiy chelovek" ("The Cephalopodous Man"), "Neporochny chort" ("The Immaculate Devil"), and "Vdokhnovenny gus'" ("The Inspired Goose"). Written between 1928 and 1930, they were republished together in 1936 under the title *Malenkaya trilogia* (*A Little Trilogy*). Told in the first person as episodes in the career of a director of a Soviet plant, they give grotesque portraits of an insolent climber and plotter, a hypocritical prig, and a popular windbag. All three are successfully exposed by the narrator.

Fadeyev (1901–56) The revival of psychological realism in proletarian literature found its principal expression in the work of Alexander Alexandrovich Fadeyev. Fadeyev was born in a peasant family in the province of Tver, but most of his childhood was spent in the Far East, where his father worked as a surgeon's assistant. In 1918 he became a member of the Communist party and took an active part in the Civil War, fighting against Admiral Kolchak, Ataman Semyonov, and the Japanese. In 1921 he participated in the suppression of the sailors' rising in Kronstadt and was wounded there. From 1921 to 1926 he was engaged in party work in various parts of the Soviet Union.

Fadeyev's first two stories, "Razliv" ("The Flood," 1924), and "Protiv techeniya" ("Against the Current," 1925), did not stand out from the general run of "dynamic" prose fiction of that period. Of the former, which had all of the worst stylistic and compositional defects of such writers as Vsevolod Ivanov and Nikitin with none of their merits, Fadeyev himself said later that it was "a slovenly work." "Against the Current" (later renamed "The Birth of the Amgun Regiment"), for all its imperfections, had a greater clarity of design. But it was Fadeyev's third work, the short novel *Razgrom* (*The Rout*), written in 1925–26 and published in 1927, that brought Fadeyev to the forefront of young "proletarian" literature. *The Rout* was very well received and has since gone through many editions. It is now regarded as one of the classics of Soviet literature.

There was nothing new in the subject of Fadeyev's novel. It is the story of a Red guerrilla detachment fighting against the Japanese and Admiral Kolchak's White forces in the Far East. The story covers a short period of time and is well constructed. The narrative begins during a lull in the fighting, and this enables Fadeyev to introduce the reader, in the first seven short chapters which form the exposition of the novel, to his main characters. Beginning with Chapter 8, which is entitled "The First Move," the narrative gathers dramatic momentum and is brought to its inexorable climax when the detachment, at the cost of enormous losses, makes a risky crossing of a bog and breaks out of the enemy encirclement. The surviving eighteen men and their leader are ready for new adventures and new battles.

Unlike Vsevolod Ivanov, Nikitin, and other writers of the Pilnyak school, Fadeyev shows the Civil War not in terms of an elemental movement and a clash of impersonal forces but in terms of individual psychology. In his novel men play a more important part than episodes of fighting or ideological problems. His characters are not symbolic tokens, but flesh-and-blood human beings. Levinson, the red-bearded, blue-eyed Jew who leads the detachment; Morozka, the reckless, daredevil miner with rebellious, anarchistic leanings; Varya, his wife, the only woman in the detachment, at once motherly and lascivious, ready to bestow her love on almost anyone; Mechik, a young boy from the intelligentsia who joins the detachment more or less by chance and deserts it at the critical moment; the old man Pika, who reminds Mechik of a picture of a Russian saint; the powerful giant Goncharenko—all are live figures. The only touch of conventional stylization may be seen in the shepherd Metelitsa and his heroic death at the hands of the Whites. Fadeyev himself confessed later that Metelitsa was a kind of afterthought, a complement to Levinson, an embodiment of those characteristics which Levinson lacked for an ideal leader. Hence the disproportion, the hyperbolism of the whole Metelitsa episode.[2] Apart from this, however, the story is remarkable for its objectivity and its psychological verisimilitude, though again there is one jarring note—the final desertion of Mechik, who is shown throughout as a "foreign body" among the partisans—not because the reader does not believe in it, but because here Fadeyev renounces his calm, objective method and passes judgment on Mechik.

Soviet critics lost no time in pointing out that both for his method and his style Fadeyev was indebted to Tolstoy. *The Rout* was, indeed, the first Tolstoyan work in Soviet literature, and, significantly enough, it came from a proletarian novelist. Tolstoy's influence was felt in Fadeyev's method of psychological analysis, in his style, in his descriptions of the battle scenes, and in the very structure of his sentences. Some overenthusiastic Soviet critics went so far as to place Fadeyev on a par with Tolstoy. Fadeyev, they said, had mastered Tolstoy's technique while remaining free from Tolstoy's ideological fallacies, thus giving his work the true proletarian orientation. Other Communist critics were more cautious and refused to see in Fadeyev anything more than a gifted disciple of Tolstoy. They were right, of course.

Fadeyev's limitations were clearly revealed in his first large-scale, multivolume work, the novel *Posledniy iz Udege* (*The Last of the Udege*), which he began writing parallel with *The Rout* (he even thought of incorporating the latter as an episode in the novel). The title must have been suggested to

---

[2] See Fadeyev, "Moy literaturny opyt nachinayushchemu avtoru" ("My Literary Experience—to Beginner Authors"), *Literatura i zhizn'* (*Literature and Life*), 158.

Fadeyev by James Fenimore Cooper's *The Last of the Mohicans* (the Udege are a curious, almost extinct native tribe of Siberia). The novel was planned as an ambitious social-psychological novel with a multitude of characters and a complex, multiplanar plot, involving the Siberian intelligentsia, coal miners, members of the Communist party, and some representatives of the Udege. One of the themes of the novel is the cultural "rehabilitation" of the Udege by the Soviet government and their incorporation into the collective-farming system. In the first volumes the action takes place during the Civil War in the Far East (with some flashbacks into the pre-Revolutionary period); in the concluding volume the transformation wrought by the Revolution was to be shown. Fadeyev himself said that the Udege theme of the novel was suggested to him by Engels' *The Origin of the Family, Private Property, and the State.*

The novel was planned in six parts, or volumes. The first installments were published in 1930, and the completed four parts appeared in book form in 1930, 1933, 1935, and 1940. Some chapters of Part 4 were published in 1956, and in 1957 appeared a posthumous revised edition of all that had been written. The earlier parts had in the meantime undergone considerable revision. As late as 1951, Fadeyev voiced his dissatisfaction with the novel, saying that, while it had been meant as a historical novel, it did not contain enough history. Earlier he had said that he had found the work on this novel very difficult going: "Evidently one must possess a greater artistic experience than I have to write a big novel with a complex idea, such as I have planned."[3]

Sholokhov (b. 1905) Soviet critics and historians of literature usually include among proletarian writers Mikhail Alexandrovich Sholokhov. This inclusion is justified since "proletarian" was always taken to refer not to class origins (neither Libedinsky nor Fadeyev was a true proletarian in this sense) but to ideological sympathies and Communist party attachments.

Sholokhov was born in the Don Cossack region. His mother was half-Cossack, half-peasant. His father belonged to the lower middle class and came from central Russia. Sholokhov has lived most of his life among the Don Cossacks, and nearly all that he wrote is about their life. His secondary education was interrupted in 1918 by the Revolution. Throughout the Civil War, when the Don Cossack region was the main scene of hostilities and a large section of the Cossacks actively supported the anti-Bolshevik movement, Sholokhov lived there. There is no evidence that he fought on either side, but after 1920 he apparently joined the Communist party and

[3] *Ibid.,* 162. Cf. also K. Zelinsky, *A. A. Fadeyev. Kritiko-biograficheskiy ocherk* (*A. A. Fadeyev: A Critical-Biographical Study*). For a bibliography of Fadeyev's works and literature about him see N. Nikulina, *A. A. Fadeyev. Seminariy* (*A. A. Fadeyev: A Seminar*).

worked in Soviet administration. He began writing in 1923, and his first book of stories appeared in 1925.

It was his novel *Tikhy Don* (*The Quiet Don*), however, that made Sholokhov famous throughout the Soviet Union.[4] He began work on it in 1926, and the first three volumes appeared between 1928 and 1933 (a fourth volume was added in 1940). The novel went through a great number of printings, and several million copies of it were sold in Russia and abroad. There is no doubt that Sholokhov became the most popular writer in the Soviet Union. In 1936 he was elected deputy of the Supreme Soviet and in 1939 awarded the Order of Lenin. He was also elected to the Soviet Academy of Sciences.

Like Fadeyev's *The Rout, The Quiet Don* was an expression of the "back to Tolstoy" trend in Soviet literature. It is a vast canvas of Cossack life on the eve of World War I, during that war, and in the first five years of the Revolution—in fact, all things taken into consideration, a Cossack *War and Peace*. It is a realistic novel, brimful with life, with a great number of characters. It is a chronicle of the war and the Revolution, with a particular stress on their effect on the Cossacks and their life. Without a plot in the strict sense of the word, it is written in a colorful, racy language that is sometimes spoiled by an excessive tendency toward ethnographical naturalism. Sholokhov is particularly good when he deals with the Cossacks and their life, a subject with which he is particularly familiar. Much weaker are those parts where the non-Cossack element is introduced. Here one feels Sholokhov losing his grip on his material and realizes the enormous distance that separates Sholokhov from Tolstoy.

Like *War and Peace, The Quiet Don* is a combination of family chronicle and historical epic (with the difference, however, that Sholokhov has a clear-cut central hero in the person of Grigory Melekhov). Alongside a multitude of fictitious characters there appear several historical personages, such as Generals Kornilov and Alexeyev, the Cossack Ataman Kaledin, the Bolshevik leader Podtyolkov, and other prominent actors of the Civil War drama. Unlike Tolstoy, Sholokhov avoids philosophizing about history. His presentation of the period is on the whole objective and balanced. He neither idealizes all his Reds as heroes nor portrays all the Whites as un-

---

[4] The author of a fundamental and very sympathetic study of Sholokhov and his work reveals that Sholokhov had some difficulty getting his now-famous novel accepted by *Oktyabr*. There was a persistent rumor at the time, which even found its way into the press in Sholokhov's native Don Region, that Sholokhov was not the real author of *The Quiet Don*, that it was written by a White Army officer who was killed in battle and on whose body the manuscript was found. Sholokhov was said to have appropriated it. See I. Lezhnev, *Mikhail Sholokhov*, 12. (This Lezhnev, who at one time was an *émigré* but returned to the Soviet Union, is not to be confused with Abram Lezhnev-Gorelik, the well-known critic. The story is not very plausible, and in any case it could be true only of the first volume of Sholokhov's epic.

mitigated villains. One of the most idealized figures is the Communist agitator Bunchuk, who becomes leader of a machine-gun section and is in the end shot by several Cossacks who have gone over to the Whites. But even Bunchuk is shown as a three-dimensional figure—with all the human failings—and not as a paragon of Communist virtues. Nor does Sholokhov attempt to deny heroism to the opponents of Bolshevism. There is a touch of grandeur in the description of the death of the Cossack officer Kalmykov, who is shot by Bunchuk. The Cossack Ataman Kaledin, who collaborated with the Whites, is also portrayed without the usual prejudice and hostility, and there is a sense of real tragedy in the scene preceding his suicide. Sholokhov's principal character, Melekhov, with whom the author is obviously very much in sympathy, personifies the deep cleavage among the Cossacks. He is shown changing sides and deserting the Reds, and in the third volume we even see him fighting on the side of the Whites. The fourth volume was written with the specific object of setting this straight and of showing Melekhov's final change of heart, but the ending is somewhat ambiguous, and Melekhov's adherence to the new order of things somehow incomplete. Throughout the novel one feels that Sholokhov himself, while his reason approves the Communist Revolution, cannot help subconsciously regretting the loss of much in the traditional mode of the Cossack life which the Revolution has swept away. While the novel has unquestionably been overpraised and many defects of its language and composition overlooked, it is, if not a classic, a work of great breadth, giving a truthful and impartial picture of the revolutionary blizzard that swept over Russia, carrying with it many human lives and affecting individual destinies.

Sholokhov's second major work will be discussed in Chapter 18.

Tarasov-Rodionov (1885–1937?) Alexander Ignatyevich Tarasov-Rodionov, a Bolshevik from 1905, took an active part in the 1917 Revolution and commanded Red Army divisions in the Civil War of 1919–20. After demobilization he worked for a time as examining magistrate attached to the Supreme Tribunal of the Republic. His novel *Shokolad* (*Chocolate*, 1922) was one of the first Communist contributions to the revival of prose fiction. Its theme aroused a good deal of controversy. It is the story of the framing of a certain Zudin, chairman of a local Cheka, who becomes innocently entangled with a beautiful girl, a former ballerina and a counterrevolutionary agent, to whom out of pity he gives a job in his office. Suspicions are aroused among his colleagues, and an investigation is ordered from the center. Although Zudin's friends and colleagues who are appointed to the commission that is to investigate his "crimes" are convinced of his fundamental innocence, they agree with the investigator sent from Moscow who demands that Zudin be shot. Their motives are rather involved. The working masses, they say, will never believe in Zudin's innocence, and it is their duty to impress on the masses that the Revolution spares no one who betrays its cause, no matter how highly placed. The novel ends with Zudin bidding farewell to his wife. To comfort her, he pretends that the party, while announcing his execution, is sending him on a long and secret mission to Australia. Soviet critics regarded the author's main thesis—the sacrifice of a good and honest Communist to the ignorance and prejudice of the masses—as an ideological error, and the novel was attacked for being untrue to life. While not without interest for the light it throws on the early workings of the Cheka, *Chocolate* is poor literature. The characters, beginning with Zudin himself, are unreal; the story smacks of cheap melodrama; the style is poor. Tarasov-Rodionov's hashed, pseudopoetic prose obviously belongs to the Pilnyak school, but he lacks utterly Pilnyak's sense of language.

In 1928, Tarasov-Rodionov published *Fevral'* (*February*), the first volume of *Tyazhelye shagi* (*Heavy Steps*), which was intended as a vast chronicle-novel about the Revolution of 1917. The second volume, *Iyul'* (*July*), appeared a few years later. The third volume (presumably to be called *October*) apparently remained unpublished, and probably unfinished. A volume of stories, *Svetly kray* (*Bright Land*), published in 1934, seems to have been his last published work. In 1937 he was denounced as a Trotskyite and disappeared.

Malyshkin (1890–1938)

Alexander Georgievich Malyshkin attracted attention in 1924 with his *Padenie Daira* (*The Fall of Dair*), which was written in 1921. As its subject it had one of the principal episodes of the Civil War—the Red Army break-through at Perekop, which brought about the end of the last organized center of anti-Bolshevik resistance in the Crimea. This work is a typical specimen of "dynamic" prose. There is no psychology in it, no individualized characters; the center of interest is in the masses, in the clash of the Red and White forces, which is shown with something of epic grandeur. The heightened, rhythmical diction is derived from Bely and Pilnyak; however, along with other Soviet writers, Malyshkin later evolved toward realism. In his novel *Sevastopol* (1929), he gave a picture of the Revolution as it affected the Black Sea fleet. Its hero, Shelekhov, is a sailor from the intelligentsia who gradually, but not without some relapses, comes to espouse the cause of the Communist Revolution. Malyshkin's main thesis is that men like Shelekhov can find their place in the Revolution, provided they give up aspiring for high positions and accept being useful but inconspicuous pawns in the new order.

Vesyoly (1899–1939)

Artyom Vesyoly (pseudonym of Nikolay Kochkurov) is one of the few true proletarians in the ranks of proletarian literature. His father was a Volga stevedore, and Vesyoly himself worked as a factory hand and drayman. A member of the Communist party, he fought in the Civil War, and most of his work before 1928 has the Civil War as its subject. His characters are soldiers, sailors, peasant guerrillas, and other "instinctive" revolutionaries. In his stories, which are collected in two volumes, *Gorkaya krov* (*Bitter Blood*) and *Dikoye serdtse* (*The Wild Heart*), Vesyoly concentrates on the elemental, irrational, and destructive aspects of the Revolution. He prefers the first person narrative and the *skaz* manner. In his novels, *Strana rodnaya* (*My Country*) and *Rossiya krovyu umytaya* (*Russia Washed in Blood*), verbal ornamentation plays a more important part than the plot. Of all the proletarian writers he stands closest to Pilnyak (except for his Communist orthodoxy), while in some of his earlier stories his short staccato sentences recall Mayakovsky's verse. *Russia Washed in Blood* is a colorful picture of the first phase of the Revolution, in the center of which stands the mass desertion of soldiers from the front. Like many other writers of the same type, Vesyoly was purged in 1937.

Semyonov (1893–1942) Sergey Alexandrovich Semyonov, son of a Petersburg factory worker, is another true proletarian. He joined the Communist party in 1917 and made his debut in literature in 1922 with the novel *Golod* (*Hunger*), written in the form of a diary and giving a naturalistic description of starving workmen in revolutionary Petrograd. This was followed by a number of stories of workers' life. Considerable attention was aroused by Semyonov's long work *Natalya Tarpova* (1927). It is a social-psychological problem novel, dealing with the life of the Communist party and with the problems of marriage, family life, cultural work, ideology, and so on. Its heroine is a woman, an active member of a Communist organization, who is shown in both her political and her private life against the background of the NEP. As in the case of Libedinsky's novels, its value is mostly documentary.

Chapter 10. SOME PRE-REVOLUTIONARY WRITERS

After 1921 several pre-Revolutionary prose writers whom the Revolution had at first silenced or driven away made a gradual reappearance in literature. There were also those who from the very first had sympathized with the Revolution but did not come to play a part in post-Revolutionary literature until it had reverted to traditional realism. The work of the most important among these older writers, who can now be justly regarded as part of Soviet literature, will be discussed in this chapter.

Count Alexey N. Tolstoy joined the ranks of Soviet writers in 1922. Before **Tolstoy** that, he had taken sides with the anti-Bolshevik White movement. In 1919 **(1882–1945)** he emigrated abroad and lived first in Paris and then in Berlin. His return to Russia in 1923 was dictated largely by personal considerations, in which the purely financial difficulties of *émigré* existence played not a small part. But it was also connected with the so-called "Change-of-Landmarks" movement among the *émigrés*, when a comparatively small number of them—scholars, writers, and journalists—decided to bow before the Revolution as a force that had won the day and accept it as a fact, without, however, subscribing to its Marxist ideology. Tolstoy's return was a great acquisition for the young Soviet literature. A man of great natural gifts, a master of excellent Russian prose, one of the principal representatives of that Neorealism which combined the best traditions of nineteenth-century Russian literature with some modernist achievements, Tolstoy could certainly count on being lionized in the country where the dearth of good prose fiction was still badly felt.

However, it took Tolstoy a long time to find a real place for himself in Soviet literature. He was always at his best in describing real life, especially the life he knew well. His pictures of the decaying gentry in *Khromoy barin* (*The Lame Squire*), and in numerous pre-Revolutionary stories and plays, were his best work. His post-Revolutionary work was handicapped for a long time by his inability to hit upon a congenial theme. Fundamentally a man of the past, a cross between a country gentleman and a literary bohemian, he felt lost in the melting pot of post-Revolutionary Russia. As a former *émigré* he had to tread warily. Reluctant to draw upon the recent past, he wisely abstained at first from portraying and interpreting the unfamiliar present. Hence his escapes into the realm of fantasy and attempts to clothe fantastic plots with revolutionary ideas.

In *Aelita* (1922), a combination of a Wellsian scientific romance with a Russian psychological novel, the plot revolves round the arrival of a Soviet scientific expedition on Mars and an attempt to start a social revolution there. Upon this social fantasy are superimposed two other themes: of love as stronger than death or than any sense of revolutionary duty, and of elemental, irrational revolt. The former, one of Tolstoy's favorite themes, is exemplified in the love affair between the leader of the expedition, the engineer Los, and the beautiful Martian woman Aelita. The second theme is embodied in Gusev, a demobilized Red Army man who joins the expedition out of sheer boredom and thirst for adventure and places himself at the head of the Martian proletariat. Soviet critics objected, however, that Gusev was neither a proletarian nor a Communist. Actually, Gusev is a true Russian. When he arrives on Mars, his first thought is to proclaim its annexation to Soviet Russia. In his Bolshevism there are elements of anarchism, and one feels that it is his nationalism and anarchism that make Tolstoy sympathize with him.

The same strain runs through *Rukopis', naydennaya pod krovatyu* (*A Manuscript Found Under a Bed*, 1923), in which an old, degenerating squire cannot help admiring the broad, elemental, purely Russian sweep of the Revolution, although he really hates all that it stands for. The same idea dominates *Golubye goroda* (*Skyblue Cities*, 1925), where two forces are shown at grips in post-Revolutionary Russia: the force of rational organization and planning and the force of elemental, biological life. In the end it is the irrational force of life that triumphs, and the hero, a Communist dreamer and planner, has to admit his defeat. Any other solution would have been contrary to Tolstoy's nature. In a sympathetic essay on Tolstoy, Voronsky once pointed out that Tolstoy's main characters were often dreamers and idealists who came to a bad end after a clash with reality. Tolstoy's most infectious quality is his zest for life, his craving for full-blooded things, his earthy realism, which is excellently served by his rich, racy, full-blooded Russian.

During this period Tolstoy continued also to work on his long novel *Khozhdenie po mukam* (*The Way Through Hell*), which he began when still an *émigré* (the last volume was completed in 1941). It is a vast canvas of Russian life on the eve of World War I, during the war, and in the first year of the Revolution. The story is well told, the characters are lifelike and varied. The picture of pre-Revolutionary Russia is painted in dark colors, with a strong emphasis on its futility, its spiritual confusion and disorientation. The work is spoiled by the author's persistent tendency to philosophize about the historical destinies of Russia and the meaning of the Revolution, and by his petty spitefulness in the portrayal of the literary Bohemia.

Infinitely more satisfactory is *Detstvo Nikity* (*Nikita's Childhood*, 1921), written shortly before Tolstoy's return to Russia. This story of a child's life on a pre-Revolutionary Russian estate, of obviously autobiographical inspiration, is worthy to stand beside Leo Tolstoy's *Childhood* and Aksakov's autobiography. Here Tolstoy the realist, who is in love with life and its pleasures and knows how to describe it truthfully and yet poetically, is at his best. Its beautiful Russian—simple, limpid, and yet picturesque—makes it one of the unquestionable masterpieces of post-Revolutionary Russian literature. It was first published outside Russia but has since been reissued many times in the Soviet Union and has come to be considered part and parcel of Soviet literature—the one and only true example in it of the old gentry tradition and therefore hardly in keeping with the rest of it.

Tolstoy's literary output in the late twenties was large and uneven. Constant attacks on him as a "bourgeois" writer forced him to look frantically for the right line to follow. In the fantastic genre *Aelita* was followed by *Giperboloid inzhenera Garina* (*Engineer Garin's Hyperboloid*, 1925), later revised and renamed *Garin the Dictator* (1927). Garin is a "superman," a "Fascist," who dreams of organizing and ruling the world on the principle of caste division. The upper caste will govern and create; others will perform the function of procreation; still others, free of all emotions and ideas, will be mere robot slaves; and the unnecessary surplus will be exterminated.

Sem' dney v kotorye byl ograblen mir (*Seven Days in Which the World Was Robbed*) is a mixture of social satire with science fiction. It tells the story of a conspiracy of a group of American capitalists who succeed in scaring the world into submission by bombing and splitting the moon. In the end their dictatorship is overthrown. Written with gusto, it is one of Tolstoy's lighter works. The same may be said of *Priklyuchenia Nevzorova ili Ibikus* (*The Adventures of Nevzorov, or Ibicus*, 1925), a grotesque picture of *émigré* life within the framework of an adventure story. *Émigré* life is also the subject of *Chornoye zoloto* (*Black Gold*), later revised and renamed *Emigranty* (*The Émigrés*). Here foreign and *émigré* intrigues around Soviet oil form the center of a melodramatic plot. The picture of *émigré* life is one-sided, and some of the characters are not very real. Everyday Soviet life of the NEP period was handled by Tolstoy in "Vasily Suchkov," the story reflecting the widespread mood of disillusionment during the aftermath of the heroic period of the Revolution.

Another pre-Revolutionary writer who came to play a conspicuous part in Soviet literature was Ilya Grigoryevich Ehrenburg. A Jew of middle-class origin, from 1909 to 1917 he lived abroad, mostly in Paris. In 1911 appeared his first book of poems. At the time he felt an aesthetic attraction toward Roman Catholicism and even thought of entering a monastery. During World War I, after an unsuccessful attempt to join the Foreign Legion in France, he covered the war on the French front for one of the big Russian

Ehrenburg (1891–1967)

dailies. The Bolshevik Revolution inspired him to write "A Prayer for Russia," a powerful poetic diatribe against the Bolsheviks as modern barbarians. During the Civil War, Ehrenburg lived in the south of Russia under the Whites. On his return to Moscow he was arrested but soon released. *Razdumya* (*Meditations*), a book of poems published in 1921, marked his "acceptance" of the Revolution. But Ehrenburg was none too anxious to remain in Russia, and in the same year he went back to the bohemian haunts in Montparnasse where he had spent his carefree, happy-go-lucky exile. Soon, however, he was deported by the French police. After a short stay in Belgium he went to Berlin, where he also contributed to the periodical *Nakanune*. In 1923 he was back in Russia. Later he was allowed to revisit France and for several years lived in Paris. In 1936–37 he covered the Spanish Civil War on the Loyalist side for Soviet newspapers, and the outbreak of World War II found him again in Paris. Of all Soviet writers, Ehrenburg knew Western Europe best and was at heart attached to Western ways of life, feeling particularly at home in the café land of Montparnasse.

The work which started Ehrenburg's career as a successful, versatile, and prolific Soviet novelist was *Neobychaynye pokhozhdeniya Julio Jurenito i ego uchenikov* (*The Extraordinary Adventures of Julio Jurenito and of His Disciples*), written in 1921, during his enforced stay in Belgium, and published in Berlin in 1922.[1] It is perhaps Ehrenburg's best work, the one in which he managed to find the most adequate form of expression for his cynical nihilism, his unprincipled mockery of everything. In a note he contributed to a collection of autobiographies of contemporary Russian writers, Ehrenburg said of it: "It is my only book 'in earnest'; it seems that neither the critics, nor the readers, nor I myself, nobody can define precisely where mockery ends in it." It is primarily a ruthless, satirical indictment of modern European civilization, in which no country, no nationality, and no aspect of that civilization is spared. But Soviet Russia—where Ehrenburg's "Master," the Mexican Julio Jurenito, the great *agent provocateur*, whose mission is to unmask the sham and evil of modern civilization, ends his life—does not fare any better at Ehrenburg's hands.

It is this corrosive, all-pervading nihilistic cynicism, apparent in all his best work, that is Ehrenburg's principal attribute as a writer. It is the only thing in him that seems genuine and sincere. All the rest—his enthusiasm

---

[1] The full title of Ehrenburg's novel is extremely long and elaborate: *The Extraordinary Adventures of Julio Jurenito and of His Disciples: Monsieur Delhaie, Karl Schmidt, Mr. Cool, Alexey Tishin, Ercole Bambucci, Ilya Ehrenburg, and Aysha the Negro, in the Days of Peace, War and Revolution in Paris, Mexico, Rome, Senegal, Kineshma, Moscow and Other Places; as Well as Various Opinions of the Master About Pipes, About Death, About Love, About Freedom, About the Game of Chess, About the Jewish Race, About Reconstruction, and About Many Other Things.* According to Jürgen Rühle, Jurenito was modeled on Diego Rivera.

for Soviet achievements on various "fronts," which he voiced later in *Den' vtoroy* (*The Second Day*) and in *Ne perevodya dykhaniya* (*Without Pausing for Breath*), or his patriotic effusions during the Soviet-German War—are mere pose. And yet behind this cynical, wholesale negation one senses the tragic dualism of a man whose real roots are in that very civilization he so ruthlessly yet lightheartedly exposes.

To give here even a brief analysis of all Ehrenburg's writings between 1921 and 1929 is impossible. All I can do is mention a few of the more important ones, leaving some of the later ones to be mentioned in due course. *Zhizn' i gibel' Nikolaya Kurbova* (*The Life and Undoing of Nikolay Kurbov*, 1923) is the story of an "ideal" Communist, purposeful and rigidly ascetic, who succumbs in a clash with the irrepressible "biological" forces of life. *Trest D. E.* (*Trust D. E.*, 1923) is an "inverse Utopia," telling the story of how Europe is conquered, in 1940, by the soulless capitalist civilization of America. Ehrenburg's versatility is illustrated by such works as *Lyubov' Zhanny Ney* (*The Love of Jeanne Ney*, 1923), a sentimentally melodramatic story of a love affair between a respectable French girl from a bourgeois family and a Russian Communist, and *Rvach* (*The Grabber*, 1925), a satirical picture of the Soviet scene during the NEP. The same period is depicted in *Leto 1925 goda* (*The Summer of 1925*, 1926), which is the most personal, sincere, and earnest of all Ehrenburg's works. It was denounced by Soviet critics as a cynical expression of the post-NEP mood of depression and disenchantment. One of Ehrenburg's novels was even proscribed in Russia and its Russian editions appeared in Paris (1928) and in Berlin (1929) without any unpleasant consequences for the author. It was *Burnaya zhizn' Lazika Roytshvantsa* (*The Stormy Life of Lazik Roitschwanz*), a picaresque and ultrasatirical story of a little Jewish tailor.

Ehrenburg's talent is undeniable, but too often the journalist was to the fore in him, and some of his novels and stories are clever pamphlets in fictional form. But he knew how to handle a thrilling plot and undoubtedly learned from Western detective fiction. His caustic intelligence made his satires witty and pointed. He was good at parody—in *Julio Jurenito* there is some obvious parody of Dostoyevsky and Anatole France. But his characterization was crude and simplified. He was fond of sharp contrasts and often used stock characters who are either paragons of abstract virtue or unmitigated scoundrels. Although violently denounced by orthodox Communist critics as a typical degenerate bourgeois, a cynic who held nothing sacred, Ehrenburg enjoyed in the twenties considerable popularity among Soviet readers, which was in no small measure due to the "exoticism" of his non-Russian subject matter and his ability to tell a good story in a rapid cinematographic tempo. There were periods when Ehrenburg played quite an important role in the fortunes of Soviet literature, and we shall have to return to him more than once in the account of them.

Prishvin
(1873–1954)
Mikhail Mikhailovich Prishvin was something of a Russian W. H. Hudson. A trained specialist in agriculture, he first attracted attention in 1907 with *V krayu nepugannykh ptits* (*In the Land of Unscared Birds*), which contained some wonderful descriptions of nature and animal life in the Far North of Russia. A poet of nature, he was also a great master of racy and picturesque Russian. His first important post-Revolutionary work was *Kurymushka* (1924), which he described as his first "real story of a man." It is a novel of obviously autobiographical inspiration, though written in the third person, and describes the hero's childhood with remarkable insight into the inner workings of a child's mind. Further parts of it appeared later under the title *Kashcheyeva tsep'* (*Kashchey's Chain*). In Russian folklore Kashchey is the legendary embodiment of evil, and the title symbolizes the fetters of moral and social prejudices from which man must free himself. Prishvin's manner resembles Remizov's, but his outlook of manly and robust optimism marks him off from some of the dominant tendencies of Russian literature. He was a passionate hunter and at the same time an animal lover, and in many of his stories of the Soviet period he continued to explore the theme of nature. Some of them—for example, those in the volume *Lesnaya kapel'* (*Forest Thaw*, 1945)—are more like short poems in prose, combining descriptions of nature with lyrical meditations.

Veresayev
(1867–1946)
V. Veresayev (pseudonym of Vikenty Vikentievich Smidowicz) was before the Revolution a typical old-school realist, a scrupulous and observant witness of the social and psychological processes of his time. He gained fame with his nonfictional *Memoirs of a Physician* (1901). A documentary value attaches also to his two post-Revolutionary novels. In *V tupike* (*In a Blind Alley*, 1922) he draws a picture of the democratic and socialist intelligentsia confronted with the Revolution and with the problem of its terroristic excesses. It is a painstakingly objective work. Veresayev shows both the young and the old, both those who accept the Revolution and those who reject it. The heroine, Katya, a typical young girl from the revolutionary intelligentsia, morally pure and intellectually honest, frank in her democratic rejection of the antidemocratic Bolshevik Revolution, is a memorable creation. To her is opposed Leonid, a Bolshevik who justifies the Red Terror on grounds of expediency, rejects contemptuously the "old yardsticks" of "our dear, sensitive intelligentsia," and recognizes but one criterion: "Does the Revolution need it?" The novel is a truthful, if by no means comprehensive, picture of the period and its problems.

The same can be said of Veresayev's *Syostry* (*The Sisters*, 1933), which portrays two girls from the old intelligentsia who belong to the Young Communist League and their reactions to the policy of forcible collectivization. The novel is written in the form of their joint diary. One accepts Communism unquestioningly; the other passes through a crisis of individualism and becomes a prey to doubts. But it is the latter who, with her intuition and common sense, proves to be more farsighted than her sister, who adheres blindly to party instructions and finds herself behind the times when Stalin springs upon the country his famous article "Giddiness from Success," which denounces the excesses of collectivization and decrees a slackening of its tempo. The novel was at first warmly acclaimed by Soviet critics, but soon it was realized that Veresayev's picture of the inner life of the Young Communist League was far from flattering, while the ending seemed to suggest that party members had better ignore instructions and follow their own intuition.

The Sisters was Veresayev's last contribution to fiction. After 1933 he concentrated on literary history, publishing *Pushkin in Life* and *Gogol in Life*, and wrote his *Memoirs*, which are characterized by the same scrupulous veracity. He also returned, toward the end of his life, to his old love (he was a classical scholar besides being a doctor of medicine) and undertook a translation of *The Iliad*.

Sergey Nikolayevich Sergeyev-Tsensky, one of the outstanding representatives of Neorealism in pre-Revolutionary literature, published in 1923 *Valya*, first in a series of novels meant to constitute a vast canvas of Russian life between the eve of World War I and the present day. Gorky thought it one of the best works in modern Russian prose fiction. It is a work of intense psychological realism, with many interesting, uncommon characters and a rather intricate plot. It was followed at rather long intervals by other volumes of the same series. Several of them dealt with World War I and will be discussed later. Their connection with *Valya* is somewhat tenuous, and the general pattern of the whole series—the title of which is *Preobrazhenie (Transfiguration)*—remains obscure. Of Sergeyev-Tsensky's post-Revolutionary stories, *Rasskaz professora (The Professor's Tale*, 1924), is a narrative within a narrative. Although told in 1920 by a Red Army commander, it has a pre-Revolutionary subject and is a psychological study of the makings of a murderer. In the volume called *Zhestokost' (Cruelty)*, the long title story tells of the death of six Bolshevik commissars in a clash with peasant rebels during the Civil War.

> **Sergeyev-Tsensky (1876–1959)**

Sergeyev-Tsensky also wrote several historical novels, which will be discussed later.

Andrey Mikhaylovich Sobol began his literary career shortly before the Revolution. A member of a Jewish middle-class family, he left home at the age of fourteen, worked as a prompter in an operetta theater, and tried several other professions. In 1905–1906 he took part in revolutionary activities. Sentenced to four years of penal servitude in Siberia, he managed to escape and emigrate. In 1915 he returned to Russia illegally and enlisted

> **Sobol (1888–1926)**

in the army under an assumed name. His first novel, *Pyl'* (*Dust*), was published in 1915 and acclaimed by critics. After the Revolution he wrote a number of stories. Some of the best are to be found in the volume *Oblomki* (*The Wreckage*, 1923). Many of them are psychological studies of "superfluous men"—of revolutionaries disappointed in the Revolution, or of counterrevolutionaries who no longer believe in their cause. Sobol is a realist, but his realism has a nightmarish, fantastic quality, and his manner is impressionistic. His fantastic realism is particularly effective in such stories as "Oblomki" ("The Wreckage"), describing a group of odd inmates of a Crimean boardinghouse during the Civil War, in whose midst appears a Dostoyevskian "petty demon" in human disguise; or "Panoptikum" ("Panopticon"), a story of strange happenings in a commune organized by "egocentric anarchists" in a provincial town, where human beings and wax figures are equally real (or unreal). The whole Revolution appears to Sobol as a gigantic panopticon.

The longest story in the book, "Salon-vagon" ("The Pullman Car"), is more deeply psychological, though also told in a rapid succession of impressionistic scenes. It is the story of an old special railway coach which was once upon a time at the disposal of a governor-general in central Asia and which is now (in 1917) occupied by a special commissar of the Provisional government, an old revolutionary, who travels to and fro over the whole vast expanse of Russia, from one front to another, in a desperate effort to stem the wave of mass desertions and save the Russian Army from complete disintegration. Sobol succeeds in conveying both the fantastic nature of events and the inner drama of the commissar, who sees his long-desired Revolution turn into a grim and cruel reality. When the hero of the story tells the girl with whom he falls in love and for whom the blue Pullman car is a symbol of her happy childhood, that "one must not be afraid of pity. It is, perhaps, the most beautiful of all human sentiments bequeathed to us," it is the author himself who speaks through him. Nearly all of Sobol's stories are imbued with pity for those whom the Revolution has crushed or led off the track. In this he was a true heir to the traditions of nineteenth-century Russian literature.

One of Sobol's last stories, "Povest' o golubom pokoe" ("The Tale of a Blue Chamber"), was an unexpectedly light-hearted picture of non-Russian life, which had nothing to do with the Revolution. Soon after writing it, he committed suicide in a Moscow street, himself one of the spiritual victims of the Revolution.

Shaginyan Before the Revolution, Marietta Sergeyevna Shaginyan was known as a
(b. 1888) minor poet of the Symbolist school and author of modernistic stories. Of Armenian descent, she had a variety of interests and studied philosophy, music, science, and later textile weaving; after the Revolution she taught

some of these subjects. Most of her post-Revolutionary work consisted of prose fiction. The novel *Svoya sudba* (*One's Own Fate*), written before the Revolution but published in 1923, described life in a mental home. *Peremena* (*The Change*, 1924) and *Priklyuchenie damy iz obshchestva* (*The Adventure of a Society Lady*, 1925) are pictures of Soviet life during the Civil War. Considerable interest was attracted by her attempt to create a Soviet detective novel by combining a thrilling plot with revolutionary ideology.

Strange though it may appear today, in 1925–26 Soviet critics kept complaining that the public preferred foreign novels to the home product. In 1925 the magazine *Zhurnalist* (*Journalist*) lamented the fact that the statistics of lending libraries and railway newsstands showed that Soviet readers preferred translations of foreign fiction to works by Soviet writers. None other than Gorky volunteered the following interesting explanation of this state of things:

Jack London, Conrad, and O. Henry are read more readily . . . because they write more "romantically," with more stress on the plot, and about unfamiliar things. . . . The reader wants romanticism, no doubt about it. He wants to be told about things familiar in an interesting and unfamiliar way, he wants his own experiences to be somehow deepened and beautified. He can see that contemporary reality is more interesting than its representation in books, and he feels that books leave something unsaid, while some of them gloss over or hide certain things.[2]

Three years later the Soviet critic Lezhnev had to admit that foreign fiction still constituted the bulk of Soviet reading and that Jack London and Upton Sinclair remained "the most widely read authors." The demand for "romanticism" which Gorky mentioned was satisfied in part by such writers as Ehrenburg. It was with this need in mind that Marietta Shaginyan wrote her two novels, *Lori Len—metallist* (*Laurie Lane, the Metal Worker*) and *Mess Mend ili yanki v Petrograde* (*Mess Mend, or the Yankees in Petrograd*). They appeared in 1925 and 1926 under the pen name Jim Dollar, their supposed narrator being an American worker in Russia. The novels caused some stir and enjoyed popularity with the public at large, but Soviet critics disapproved of this attempt to "sovietize" Nat Pinkerton. In Gorbachov's opinion Shaginyan's detective novels were neither fish nor fowl. For good thrillers there was too much propaganda in them; at the same time the author failed to overcome her "bourgeois" approach. Thus the attempt to produce a literature both entertaining and ideologically sound ended in a fiasco.

In 1929, Shaginyan published a curious experimental novel called *K. i K.* (*K. and K.*). The story of a missing Soviet commissar was told in four different versions by four authors, who were themselves characters in the

[2] No. 10 (1925). Quoted by A. Lezhnev, *Literary Weekdays*, 10.

novel. The epilogue contained an amusing critical examination of their works—a poem, an unfinished *nouvelle*, a verse melodrama, and a "scientific film"—which was put into the mouth of the missing commissar. The work was marked by original composition, clever handling of the plot, and good characterization.

Grin
(1880–1932) "An anomaly in Soviet literature" is how a Russian literary critic, a World War II *émigré*, and a great admirer of Alexander Grin, has described him.[3]

Like Ehrenburg, Grin was a "westerner," perhaps even more so because he seems to have had almost no ties with the Russian literary tradition. His real name was Alexander Stepanovich Grinevsky. He was the son of a Russian mother and a Polish 1863 insurrectionist who was exiled to Siberia at the age of sixteen. Before the 1917 Revolution his career was checkered. At one time and another he was a sailor, a fisherman, a gold digger, a tramp, a semiprofessional revolutionary, a soldier.

Grin's literary career began in 1906, and in 1912 he settled in St. Petersburg. He lived there until 1924, spending the rest of his life in the Crimea, where he became something of a literary legend. His place in pre-Revolutionary literature was not conspicuous, most of his work—short stories and novellas—being published in popular magazines and newspapers, though sometimes they found their way into better journals like *Russkaya Mysl'*. But he was a prolific writer, and by 1917 he had three volumes of collected works to his credit. Several more were added between 1922, when he resumed literary work, and 1932.

In his *Avtobiograficheskaya povest'* (*Autobiographical Story*, 1929), Grin wrote that the favorite writers of his youth had been Mayne Reid, James Fenimore Cooper, Gustave Aimard, and Arthur Conan Doyle, to whom were later added Jack London, H. Rider Haggard, Edgar Allan Poe, and Knut Hamsun. Before the Revolution, Grin was not taken very seriously and was regarded as an imitator of writers of western adventure stories and thrillers. But it was precisely this undisguised predilection for romance and adventure that assured him popularity in the late twenties and thirties, not only with the general public but also with many fellow writers. Among his great admirers were Olesha, Paustovsky, who painted a word portrait of him in one of his stories, and Leonid Borisov, who wrote a whole book about him entitled *Volshebnik iz Gel'-Gyu* (*The Wizard from Gel-Gyu*, 1945).

Grin's principal post-Revolutionary novels were *Alye parusa* (*Scarlet Sails*, 1923), *Serdtse pustyni* (*The Heart of the Desert*, 1923), *Begushchaya po volnam* (*Scudding the Waves*, 1928), and *Doroga nikuda* (*The Road to Nowhere*, 1930). The action is usually set in a country of his invention, named Grinland. According to Zavalishin, it was a "whole continent acces-

[3] See Vyacheslav Zavalishin, *Early Soviet Writers*, 311–12.

sible only by climbing high mountain ranges or by sea, dotted with towns and villages and large ports bearing such exotic names as Zurbagan, Liss, Gel-Gyu, and populated by sailors, dreamers, and good and loving women, with a proper admixture of scoundrels, brutes, and ladies of easy virtue."

Grin's fiction was unique in one respect. At least ostensibly, none of it had anything to do with contemporary Soviet themes and problems. During the post–World War II spell of "anticosmopolitanism" this fact made him a target for a vicious posthumous attack (see Chapter 28).

Of the proletarian pre-Revolutionary writers the best known was Alexander Serafimovich (pseudonym of Alexander Serafimovich Popov), who began writing in 1888, when he was a political exile. A Don Cossack by origin, he stood close to the Social Democratic party and was one of the pillars of Gorky's *Znanie* group of writers. One of the first to adhere to the new regime, he contributed to the *Izvestia* of the Moscow Soviet and wrote various political leaflets. For this he was expelled from the literary society Sreda and from the Writers' Publishing House in Moscow, a fact that serves to illustrate the anti-Bolshevik mood which prevailed among Russian writers in 1918–21.

Serafimovich (1863–1949)

Serafimovich's principal post-Revolutionary work is the novel *Zhelezny potok* (*The Iron Torrent*, 1924), now regarded as a Soviet classic. It tells of the march of a partisan army across the Caucasus during the Civil War. Their leader is something of a legendary figure, but the real hero of the novel is the partisan mass, the object of the author being to show mass action and mass mentality. He depicts the heroic exploits of these fighters for the Revolution but also shows their calm, unreflecting cruelty. In form it has been compared to an Eisenstein film. Mass scenes alternate with brief close-ups, with no attempt to treat the characters psychologically or to show their antecedents; we see them only in action and as parts of a bigger whole. Communist critics praised the novel for its "truthfulness" and its "clear understanding of the class essence of the Civil War."

Chapter 11. WRITERS ABOUT EVERYDAY LIFE AND SATIRISTS

Among the many fellow travelers who lent richness and variety to the Soviet literary scene during this period were several writers whose main interest lay in their reflection of Soviet mores. They did not belong to any single literary school and reflected different aspects of Soviet life. Some of them were straightforward chroniclers of post-Revolutionary Russia; others approached life from a satirical angle. It is somewhat arbitrary to bracket them together and to discuss some of them apart from those who contributed to the revival of the novel. They had, however, this in common: they were out to chronicle the everyday realities of the Revolution, with the emphasis on its second, unromantic phase. Most of them specialized in short stories rather than in novels. Their literary merits are unequal, but many of them held at one time an important place in Soviet literature, and some were long active in it.

Chroniclers of the Revolution

Seyfullina
(1889–1954)

Lydia Nikolayevna Seyfullina entered literature rather late. Of mixed Russian-Tartar descent, she was a schoolteacher by profession. Her first stories appeared in 1921 in the local press in Siberia. One of them was favorably reviewed by Petrograd and Moscow critics, and in 1923 she moved to Moscow and devoted herself to writing.

Most of Seyfullina's early stories had for their setting the village during the Revolution and portrayed its social conflicts. Her best-known work, which went through several editions, was *Peregnoy* (*Mulch*, 1923), a long short story. Its hero is a good-for-nothing peasant who is completely transformed by the Revolution. Parallel with his inner transformation, Seyfullina shows the general impact of the Revolution on village life. In *Virineya* (1924), a counterpart to *Peregnoy*, Seyfullina portrays the new type of peasant woman emancipated by the Revolution. Both stories were written in the old-time realistic manner and differed greatly from the romantic portrayal of the Revolution in the work of Vsevolod Ivanov and Nikitin. They set a pattern for many stories about the beneficent effects of the Revolution on the backward Russian peasant. Both were later dramatized and successfully staged. In *Pravonarushiteli* (*Lawbreakers*, 1921) Seyfullina gave an equally unpretentious, realistic portrait of a homeless boy, one of the great army of waifs and strays who wandered about Russia in those years. Although lacking imaginative power, Seyfullina had a gift of observation, and her stories of post-Revolutionary rural Russia retain a documentary value.

Panteleimon Sergeyevich Romanov was even older than Seyfullina, but only a few of his stories appeared in print before the Revolution. He wrote two long works, one an autobiography—*Detstvo* (*Childhood*, 1928)—the other a long and ambitious novel about pre-Revolutionary Russia entitled *Rus* (*Russia*, 1924–26); but it was his novels and stories of contemporary Soviet life that gave him a place of his own in Soviet literature and made him widely known outside Russia. The best-known of these was the novel *Tovarishch Kislyakov* (*Comrade Kislyakov*, 1930), known to non-Soviet readers under the title *Three Pairs of Silk Stockings*. This novel, and the earlier *Novaya skrizhal'* (*The New Table of Commandments*, 1927), as well as many of Romanov's short stories which are collected in the volumes *Bez cheryomukhi* (*Without Cherry Blossoms*) and *Voprosy pola* (*Problems of Sex*), deal with Soviet youth, with love and marriage, and with the problem of reconciling the romantic impulses of human nature with the new morals and the stern demands of Communist ideology. Problems of sex particularly interested Romanov. He showed the new type of young men and women, mostly students, reflecting sexual laxity and cynicism characteristic of the early period of the Revolution, when new Communist morality was equated with the lifting of all taboos and inhibitions. As the heroine of "Without Cherry Blossoms," one of Romanov's most typical stories, puts it: "Among us there is no love, there is only sexual intercourse, because we relegate love contemptuously to the domain of 'psychology,' and it is only physiology that counts."

In most of Romanov's stories there is a touch of vulgarity and unhealthy sensationalism, and their success was largely due to their subject matter, but there is no doubt that they mirrored faithfully a certain phase in the evolution of Soviet society when traditional moral values were held in contempt and the old family and marital relations were rapidly disintegrating.

Romanov (1884–1938)

Vladimir Lidin (pseudonym of Vladimir Germanovich Gomberg) made his debut in literature shortly before the Revolution with some stories in the Chekhov manner. After the Revolution he wrote several novels and numerous stories. In these he often described the milieu of the Soviet employees, of the old and the new bourgeoisie—the so-called "Nepmen," the new rich of the NEP period. He is pre-eminently a short-story writer and owes much of his technique to Chekhov, Bunin, and Maupassant. One of his would-be novels, *Idut korabli* (*Ships Are Sailing*, 1926), is really a collection of short stories running alternately, loosely connected with one another, with settings in Moscow, Italy, Germany, and the Arctic region. The two most important of these stories have for their respective heroes a

Lidin (b. 1894)

certain Ivan Kostrov, a convinced and sincere Communist, and Glotov, the cashier of the plant of which Kostrov is the manager. The interest of the Glotov story lies mainly in the vivid picture of a somewhat unusual aspect of life in Soviet Moscow: the racecourse, the restaurants and night clubs, and so on.

In *Otstupnik* (*The Renegade*, 1928), a regular problem novel, Lidin portrayed the milieu of Soviet students. Its hero, Bessonov, is involved in a murder and passes through a series of moral trials. The novel ends with his regeneration. At the last moment he gives up his plan of escaping abroad and decides to make a clean breast of his part in the murder. When he makes this decision, he suddenly realizes anew the beauty of life and rejoices at the thought of going back to his own world, where he will learn "the values of life, of human blood, of toil, and of love." Once more the novel is an interesting picture of Soviet life and mores of the NEP period.

Katayev (b. 1897) Valentin Petrovich Katayev was born in Odessa, where his father was a schoolmaster. He began writing at the age of nine, and his first poem was printed when he was twelve. In 1914 he met Ivan Bunin and, in his own words, became Bunin's "conscientious pupil." In 1915 he joined the army as a volunteer, and was wounded, shell-shocked, and gassed. During the Civil War in the Ukraine he was tossed between the Reds and the Whites and spent at least eight months in various prisons. In 1922 he settled in Moscow and devoted himself to literature.

His early post-Revolutionary work consisted of short stories about everyday life and stories of adventure. Some of his best early stories are to be found in the volume *Otets* (*The Father*, 1928). The title story is about an old man who carries on a quiet but joyless existence in one of the great South Russian ports, where he is a schoolmaster. His sole joy in life is his son, a former officer who is imprisoned in the same town as a counter-revolutionary. When he is at last released, he turns out to be unworthy of his father's care and affection. He manages to get a snug job for himself and lives comfortably while the old man loses his job and is forced to drag out a miserable existence and die a lonely death. The story is a study of two different types—men of two different generations. It also gives a good picture of daily life in a large provincial city under the Soviet regime.

There is in many of Katayev's stories a strong lyrical strain which distinguishes him from other everyday-life writers. He is also more versatile and has tried his hand at other genres. *Ostrov Ehrendorf* (*Ehrendorf Island*, 1924) is a novel of adventure, while *Rastratchiki* (*The Embezzlers*, 1927) is a gay satire describing the adventures of two employees of a Moscow trust who abscond with a sum of money and go on a spree. Justice overtakes them in the end, but in the meantime the two men have plenty of fun and meet all sorts of queer people. Told in a quick tempo, full of amusing incidents, this novel treats Soviet life in light-hearted, satirical terms. About the same time Katayev wrote several gay, farcical plays about everyday Soviet life and its problems, some of which will be mentioned in Chapter 14.

Considerable attention was aroused in 1926–27 by *Dnevnik Kosti Ryabtseva* (*The Diary of Kostya Ryabtsev*). Its author was N. Ognyov (pseudonym of Mikhail Grigoryevich Rozanov). His earlier stories, such as "Shchi Respubliki" ("The Cabbage Soup of the Republic") and "Evraziya" ("Eurasia"), were written under a strong influence of Pilnyak, whom Ognyov once acclaimed as a daring challenger and destroyer of old forms. The interest of *The Diary of Kostya Ryabtsev* lay, however, not in its form but in the novelty of its subject. Written in the form of a schoolboy's diary, it gave an extremely interesting and vivid picture of life in revolutionized Soviet high schools at the time when the old principles of education and methods of instruction were cast to the winds and schools became miniature revolutionary republics run by the students. The picture was based on a thorough inside knowledge—Ognyov himself had taught in Soviet schools —and for a historian of Soviet education it is a document of great value, all the more interesting since the principles of education in the Soviet Union have since undergone a radical change. Ognyov also wrote a sequel to it, *Iskhod Nikpetozha* (*Exit Nikpetozh*), describing Kostya Ryabtsev's college days, but it is less interesting either as literature or as a document of the period.

Ognyov (1888–1938) and Others

The life of Soviet students, with an emphasis on its more unsavory aspects, is the subject of *Kommuna Mar-Mila* (*The Mar-Mila Commune*, 1926), a novel by Sergey Grigoryev (real name Grigoryev-Patrashkin, 1875–1953).

An equally somber picture of the mores of the Young Communist League was given by Nikitin, one of the Serapion Brothers, in his novel *Prestuplenie Kirika Rudenko* (*The Crime of Kirik Rudenko*, 1928), in which drunken debauchery, sexual license, and crime play a prominent part. The novel gave rise to a controversy, Communist critics accusing Nikitin of laying on the black paint too thickly.

Provincial life was vividly portrayed in Sergey Zayaitsky's *Baklazhany* (*Eggplants*, 1928), in which he introduced some members of the clergy under the Soviet regime—a subject seldom touched upon in those days by Soviet writers.

The Satirists

Mikhail Mikhailovich Zoshchenko, one of the original Serapions, was for many years the most widely read Soviet writer, and his popularity among the Russians outside Russia rivaled his popularity in the Soviet Union. In the biographical dictionary of Soviet writers published in 1930, we read: "The name of Zoshchenko, a most popular Soviet humorous writer, enjoys

Zoshchenko (1895–1958)

widest fame. His stories are read even by those who, as a rule, do not follow contemporary literature."[1]

Born in 1895 in Poltava, Zoshchenko was the son of an artist. He studied at the Law School of the University of St. Petersburg but did not graduate and in 1915 enlisted as a volunteer in the army. He was wounded and gassed, but this did not prevent him from volunteering again, in 1918, for the Red Army. His literary career began in 1921, when he joined the Serapion Brotherhood.

Zoshchenko gradually evolved a style and manner of his own, which mark him off from all other Soviet writers and make his writings easily and instantly recognizable. It was based on *skaz*, which was popular in the early period of Soviet literature. But of all the writers who, in the years 1920–23, used the *skaz* form so lavishly and with so little restraint, Zoshchenko was the only one who stuck to it after it had gone out of fashion with the revival of the novel and a return to psychological realism. Zoshchenko not only retained the *skaz* form, but modified it and put it to a new use.

His early stories, included in the book *Rasskazy Nazara Ilyicha gospodina Sinebryukhova (Stories Told by Nazar Ilyich Mr. Sinebryukhov,* 1922), were typical of that period. They were about the war and the Civil War, and were put into the mouth of a semieducated noncom whose language was a mixture of natural raciness and a hideous, artificial lingo. Both the subject and the language were exotic and the presentation highly stylized. It is obvious that Zoshchenko's masters were Leskov and Remizov and to a certain extent Zamyatin; but beneath these influences it is possible to discern individual notes and unmistakable signs of literary mastery.

With both the *skaz* manner and the exotic subjects going out of fashion, Zoshchenko had to evolve a new manner to suit both his artistic personality and the requirements of the times. He passed through an intermediate period, writing a number of short stories in which the comic effects were achieved through the subject matter, through improbable and ridiculous situations, involving comic characters. These stories were written in the third person, in the ordinary, "educated" language. Then he began writing short humorous stories which stood on the border line between imaginative literature and newspaper *feuilleton*. Their subjects were usually topical; they exposed the so-called "minor defects of mechanism" in various branches of Soviet administration and satirized Communist red tape, corruption, inefficiency, and so on. Gradually Zoshchenko evolved a new manner, a combination of his earlier *skaz* stories and his purely comic anecdotes. It

---

[1] V. Tarsis, *Sovremennye russkie pisateli (Contemporary Russian Writers),* 86. The name of the compiler of this little reference book cropped up thirty-odd years later in an unexpected and sensational context when two of his novels, smuggled out of the Soviet Union, were published abroad. They were followed by the author himself, who became a defector.

was largely a question of finding a proper "mouthpiece" for the *skaz*—a good substitute for the author—who would no longer be exotic but would fit in with the normal course of daily Soviet life. Such a mouthpiece was found by Zoshchenko in the Soviet man-in-the-street, the average Soviet citizen who passively accepts the Revolution but vaguely regrets the good old times and longs for bourgeois comforts. Zoshchenko's narrator speaks the inimitable jargon of a semieducated man, with a strong admixture of the specific Soviet journalese which was at the time rapidly inundating and disfiguring the Russian language. He is a synthetic portrait of the Soviet philistine.

Although Zoshchenko's situations are often improbable and grotesque, the label "everyday-life writer" suits him more than it does anyone else of the period. He gives a true picture of Soviet weekdays, stripped of all romantic and heroic varnish, of all pretension and make-believe. Some of the orthodox Soviet critics were from the outset at a loss what to make of Zoshchenko. In turn they praised him for exposing so mercilessly the petty-bourgeois weaknesses of the average Soviet citizen—the spirit of *embourgeoisement* invading large circles of Communist society, including the party itself—and denounced him as a vulgar "bourgeois," identifying him with his own characters.

Zoshchenko was a prolific writer. His stories, most of them quite short, fill many volumes, some of whose titles are *Uvazhaemye grazhdane* (*Esteemed Citizens*), *O chom pel solovey* (*What the Nightingale Sang About*), *Nervnye lyudi* (*Nervous People*), and *Siren' tsvetyot* (*Lilac Is in Bloom*). Most of them went through several editions. Their popularity with the mass of Soviet readers rested probably on their outward comic effects and on the familiarity of the subject matter. But it is their second, hidden meaning and their technical excellence that make the best among them real literature. Stylistically, some of them are gems. At his best Zoshchenko reminds one simultaneously of two great masters of Russian literature, Gogol and Chekhov, so dissimilar on the whole, but so alike in their keen vision of the mean vulgarity and insipidity of life. It is the pettiness, the vulgarity of life, the essential incomprehensibility of one man to another, that forms the keynote of Zoshchenko's stories. In some of the best—in "Wisdom," for instance—one can sense a deep feeling of tragedy beneath and beyond the humorous and grotesque presentation of a humdrum, vulgar life. The most hilarious of modern Russian writers was at heart a thorough pessimist, and for a discerning reader his comic stories must inevitably leave an after-taste of sadness. Often one feels that Zoshchenko is speaking with his tongue in his cheek, and it is not surprising that Communist critics were baffled by him.

Like Gogol and Leskov, Zoshchenko is one of the most difficult Russian writers to translate, for so many of his effects are based on verbal jugglery, on inimitable peculiarities of speech. It is as difficult to translate Zoshchenko into English or American as it would be to translate Damon Runyon or Edward Lear into Russian.

Since Zoshchenko's work is all more or less of a piece, it is not improper to discuss here one of his later works—his first "novel," *Vozvrashchonnaya molodost'* (*Youth Restored*, 1933). Although he called it a novel, it differs little, except in length, from his typical stories. It is written in the same colloquial, facetious style. Its very short chapters, each containing a typical Zoshchenko situation or anecdote, make it into a succession of short stories, held together by the unity of characters and a slender plot. It falls into two parts, the first seventeen chapters forming a kind of preface in which the author makes his pseudoscientific and subtly irrelevant comments on the subject of his story. The work was written at the time when the need to bring science and literature together was urged by Soviet critics. In reading Zoshchenko's "preface," the reader cannot help feeling that the author is laughing at science, at Soviet critics, at his own ridiculous characters, and at the reader. Describing his "novel" as a cross between an ordinary novel which the reader picks up of an evening "in order to dispel his daily worries and become engrossed in other people's lives, other people's emotions, and other people's thoughts" and a scientific treatise written "in the simple, incoherent, everyday language," Zoshchenko goes on in the same would-be naïve but actually jeering vein:

Well, if this is not a scientific work, if, suppose, the Academy of Sciences or, say, the Section of Scientific Workers, having come to an agreement with the Municipal Committee and the Writers' Union, refuses to find here any evidence of a scientific work, or, while finding such evidence, will not regard the author as having duly mastered the Marxist-Leninist conception, then, in such a case, this book could be described by a more neutral name, a more harmless one, so to speak, which would not offend the eyes and ears of certain citizens and organizations. Let this book, say, be called an educational film. Let it be, say, such an educational film as we have had on the screen: *Abortion*, or say, *Why Does It Rain?* or *How Silk Stockings Are Made*, or finally *What Is the Difference Between Man and Beaver?* There are such films on great contemporary scientific and industrial subjects, worthy of study. Just as in those films, we shall first have a scientific argument with various footnotes and references to this and that, and all sorts of comments which will definitively clear up the matter. And only after that the reader, slightly tired and dazed by other people's thoughts, will receive his share of entertaining reading matter, which will serve as a sort of visual illustration to the above-mentioned thoughts and considerations.

The story itself concerns an aging, almost decrepit Soviet professor of astronomy, vaguely hostile to the present regime but just as vaguely in sympathy with Socialism in general. He laments his lost youth and finally succeeds in restoring it by an effort of will. He deserts his wife, marries a young girl, flighty and vulgar, who "at the age of nineteen has already managed to change five husbands and undergo seven or eight abortions," and goes away to the Crimea with her. Soon she tires of him and begins to flirt with young men. One day the professor finds his Tulya in the arms of one of these young men. He has a stroke, and one side of his body is paralyzed. In the end he is cured and even manages to preserve his restored youth. He returns to his wife and family, but deep in his heart never ceases to pine after Tulya.

All the situations and characters in the novel are grotesque, and the work reads like a sort of synthetic parody of many Soviet works, with their stock situations and ready-made themes. Here is Zoshchenko's description of the happy marriage of the professor's daughter, Lida, who, herself an enthusiastic Communist, marries a Communist. For reasons of work they have to live apart, meeting once in every five days:

Lida, feeling a little sorry at heart, and at the same time surprised by the haste with which he had married her, consented to wait a little, agreeing that the search for an apartment, the removal, and various domestic affairs and cares might unfavorably affect the course of his work. He praised her for her common sense and political maturity, saying that he now realized quite well that he had made no mistake in choosing her, and that, indeed, he would perhaps be unable to find at present a better wife. And Lida, pleased with his praises, looked at him with admiring eyes and said that, maybe, she too could not have a better husband. They were happy in their own way, and in no hurry to disturb their happiness with kisses and embraces.

The most amazing thing about Zoshchenko's novel is that it was taken seriously as an attempt to introduce science into literature and bring the two together. Several discussions were organized on this subject, in which some eminent Soviet scientists, such as Professor Yoffe, the famous physicist, took part, and it did not occur to anyone that Zoshchenko was pulling everybody's leg.

The element of parody and legpulling played also a large part in Zoshchenko's *Golubaya kniga* (*Light-Blue Book*, 1934), which he dedicated to Gorky, who had first suggested that Zoshchenko should write a humorous "history of civilization." In a letter to Gorky with which he prefaced the book, Zoshchenko said that what he had written was not so much a "history of civilization" as "a short history of human relations." It is a collection of usual Zoshchenko stories, over forty of them, written in the inimitable chatty style of Zoshchenko's semiarticulate philistine protagonist. The stories are arranged under five main headings: "Money," "Love," "Perfidy," "Failures," and "Remarkable Happenings," and are linked together by historical and pseudohistorical anecdotes, illustrating the part played in human life and relations by money, love, and so on. Each section has a short "preface" and "postface," in which Zoshchenko gives free play to his irony. The book ends with a short "postface" to the whole volume, and two sections entitled "Taking Leave of the Bourgeois Philosopher" and "Taking Leave of the Reader." The unity which Zoshchenko tried to impart to this volume of some four hundred pages gives his humor a "monumental" quality. The reader is free to take these humorous stories at their face value or to read into them a deeper meaning and message. Zoshchenko himself refrains from laying his cards on the table, and some of his cards are certainly marked. His delight in laughing at life and at the follies of mankind knows no bounds. But, as usual, his is not a simple, hearty laughter, and the reader cannot help feeling uncomfortable.

The subsequent fortunes of Zoshchenko in Soviet literature will be discussed in Chapters 23 and 26.

Bulgakov (1891–1940) Among the writers in the late twenties and early thirties who, like Zamyatin, acquired the reputation of inside *émigrés* was Mikhail Afanasyevich Bulgakov. Born in Kiev, he came from an intelligentsia family with clerical antecedents, studied medicine but did not practice it for long, and engaged in journalism before turning to literature. His first work to attract attention was the novel *Belaya gvardiya* (*The White Guard*), which in 1924 was serialized in *Rossiya* (*Russia*), one of the more independent magazines which had certain associations with the *émigré* Change of Landmarks movement. Bulgakov had earlier contributed to that movement's paper in Berlin. Apparently the novel did not meet with approval in the higher spheres, for it was never published in book form in the Soviet Union; several editions of it were, however, issued outside Russia. Later it was dramatized by Bulgakov and, under the title *Dni Turbinykh* (*The Days of the Turbins*), had a somewhat checkered career on the Soviet stage. By 1930, Bulgakov had the reputation of a "neobourgeois writer" belonging to the "right wing" of Soviet literature.

Bulgakov used to say that of all his works he liked *The White Guard* best. But its value as literature is not very great. It is written simply, in the realist manner, without any stylistic or compositional refinements. Its interest lies in its subject matter and in the author's attitude toward his characters. The action is set in Kiev in 1918, when the Ukraine was under the semi-independent, German-sponsored government of Hetman Skoropadsky. The novel describes the events leading to Skoropadsky's downfall and the subsequent occupation of Kiev, first by the Ukrainian nationalists of Petlyura and then by the Bolsheviks. In Soviet literature it has the unique distinction of having no Communists in it, all its principal characters being White officers, some of them monarchists, and all avowed enemies of Bolshevism. They are portrayed sympathetically—as honest, chivalrous, disinterested men who fight the Bolsheviks not for personal, selfish reasons, but in the name of patriotism and of their principles. This is true above all of the brothers Turbin, who stand in the center of the picture: the liberal-minded but disillusioned Alexey, the elder brother, chivalrous and courageous, but lacking in will power; and the young, romantically inclined Nikolka, who bears a certain resemblance to Petya Rostov in *War and Peace*. Bulgakov's approach is detached and objective, and not all the Whites are painted in these attractive colors. The Turbins end by accepting Bolshevism, but Bulgakov shows them doing so for purely patriotic reasons, as the lesser of the two evils, for in the struggle between the Bolsheviks and Petlyura's bands the former stood for the unity of Russia.

Bulgakov's novel apparently enjoyed a great success with the readers. Communist critics tried to explain it away by the craving of the average Soviet reader for "exotic" and "thrilling" matter. But there was probably more to it than that, and a still greater success awaited the dramatization of Bulgakov's novel on the stage of the Moscow Art Theater. Here the alleged counterrevolutionary elements of the novel, especially the chivalry and personal heroism of its White heroes, were brought into still greater relief. The success of this play, which included the performance on the stage of the old Russian National Anthem, was so staggering that after a time the government was forced to ban the play, at any rate in Moscow. The ban was later lifted for a time, but two other plays of Bulgakov's, both of them satires, one on the contemporary theater—*Zoykina kvartira* (*Zoyka's Apartment*, 1926) and *Bagrovy ostrov* (*Crimson Island*, 1928)—came under heavy attack.

Bulgakov's book of stories, *Dyavoliada* (*Devilry*, 1925), was also denounced as hostile to the Revolution. It consists of five stories of uneven length. Both in subject matter and in manner these stories differ from *The White Guard*. They all deal with contemporary Soviet life, but with two small exceptions do so in terms not of realism but of fantasy or of satirical grotesque. It is these stories which entitle Bulgakov to be regarded as a satirist.

The first story, which gave the book its title, begins on a realistic plane but passes imperceptibly into the realm of fantastic satire, where the real and the unreal are hopelessly intermixed. It is based on a trifling anecdote about Soviet red tape and tells the story of the undoing of a small Soviet clerk who gets fired because he mistakes the name of his new boss for the word "pants," and issues, as a result of that mistake, a nonsensical instruction. In his efforts to vindicate himself he loses his name and identity and encounters all sorts of queer and grotesque people. His fantastic adventures give us odd glimpses of the Soviet bureaucratic mechanism. Bulgakov deliberately discards here all realism and psychology. His characters are grotesque puppets; his world, the Gogolian world of fantastic reality. The story particularly calls to mind Gogol's *Nose*. But "Devilry" is at the same time a satire on the inefficiency of Soviet bureaucratic institutions, told with almost too much gusto.

There is a more clearly drawn boundary line between the real and the fantastic in the longest story in the book, "Rokovye yaytsa" ("The Fatal Eggs"). It is a sort of scientific satire, and the reference in it to H. G. Wells's *Food of the Gods* is not accidental. The story is told against the background of a satirically presented picture of Moscow life in 1925, but its plot is purely fantastic. A certain Professor Persikov, a zoologist of worldwide reputation, in the course of his routine work makes an important scientific discovery— a new kind of red ray possessing an enormous life-giving and procreating capacity. His experiments with it, conducted on frogs, coincide with a mysterious epidemic which almost wipes out the poultry population of the Soviet Union. Against Persikov's wish and at the suggestion of a Communist whose name is Rokk (the name sounds exactly like the Russian word *rok*, "fate"—hence the untranslatable pun in the title), it is decided to use Persikov's discovery in the breeding of new hens in the Soviet Union. A special farm is allotted for this purpose, and Rokk is placed in charge of it. Hens' eggs are ordered from Germany, and the experiment begins. It ends, however, in disaster. Because of an error on the part of some Soviet institution, Rokk receives, instead of hens' eggs, several crates containing eggs of ostriches and huge anacondas and crocodiles, which Persikov had ordered for his scientific experiments. The hens' eggs arrive at Persikov's address after much delay, when it is too late to avert the disaster. Snakes, crocodiles, and ostriches, hatched artificially on the Red Ray Farm, come out of the eggs, grow within a few hours to giant dimensions, multiply with unheard-of rapidity, and cause havoc, panic, and destruction all around. They begin by swallowing Rokk's wife and killing all the inhabitants of the farm. They then proceed to invade the province of Smolensk, laying eggs by the thousands as they move eastward toward Moscow, and procreating at an extraordinary rate.

All the resources of the Republic—the Red Army, the Air Force, the Chemical Warfare Society, the fire brigades—are mobilized to fight this terrible invasion. Towns and villages on the way to Moscow are seized with panic; thousands of people perish; Moscow itself is in a state of alarmed expectation. The anger of the mob turns against Persikov, who is held responsible for the disaster. A crowd led by Rokk, who has gone mad after his wife's death, storms the Zoological Institute and kills Persikov and his faithful attendants. In the end the terrifying progress of the gigantic reptiles is stopped by an unexpected circumstance: a severe frost grips Russia one night in the middle of August, and the reptiles and their eggs freeze to death. Nature intervenes to save the Soviet Union from complete destruction. This climax in itself sounded a counterrevolutionary note.

Apart from the fantastic plot, in "The Fatal Eggs" there is no such mingling of the real and the fantastic as in "Devilry." But the reality is portrayed from a satirical angle. Beginning with Rokk—an antiquated Communist, in the past a flutist in a cinema orchestra, who in 1925 still wears the symbolical leather jacket of a hidebound Communist—down to the episodic figures of several Soviet journalists, all the characters in the story are obviously satirized. Irony permeates the whole story, but Bulgakov's own attitude is difficult to make out. He uses this all-round irony as a sort of safety valve.

The third important story in this collection is entitled "The Adventures of Chichikov" (the title which the censors imposed on Gogol's *Dead Souls*). The subtitle is "A Poem in Ten Points with Prologue and Epilogue" (Gogol also called his *Dead Souls* "a Poem"). The story introduces Chichikov and several other characters from Gogol's immortal work and transplants them to the Soviet Union, the obvious implication being that in contemporary Russia there is plenty of scope both for cunning rascals and rogues like Chichikov and for some of Gogol's inefficient bunglers. The point which Bulgakov seems to make here is that, beneath the surface and beyond the Communist appearances, life in Russia remains much as it used to be in Gogol's days. On entering the gate of the very hotel which he left one hundred years ago at the end of Gogol's novel, Chichikov finds that everything is much the same, if not worse:

Cockroaches were peeping out of the crevices and even seemed to have become more numerous. But there were some slight changes, too. . . . Thus, for instance, the sign bearing the word "Hotel" was now replaced by a poster with the inscription "Hostel No. So-and-so." Also, needless to say, dirt and filth were such as Gogol could never have imagined.

Chichikov's adventures in modern Russia are humorously described, though the humor is a trifle too obvious and superficial. He easily adjusts himself to the new surroundings and circumstances and plays a number of cunning tricks on the silly and inefficient Soviet administration. The first thing they ask him to do is to fill out a questionnaire containing one hundred tricky questions. It takes him only five minutes to do so, but when he hands it in, his hand trembles:

"Well," he thought, "presently they will read it and will see what sort of a bird I really am, and . . . ."

But nothing happened at all.

First of all, no one read the questionnaire. Secondly, it got into the hands of the filing clerk who did the usual thing with it: she entered it as an outgoing document instead of an incoming, and then immediately shoved it somewhere, so that the questionnaire vanished into the thin air, as it were.

Chichikov grinned and started upon his job.

It was only after Chichikov had played all sorts of ingenious tricks and they had been laid bare, thanks to Nozdryov, that his questionnaire was unearthed with great difficulties, and this is how it ran:

Name: Paul. *Patronymic*: Ivanovich. *Surname*: Chichikov. *Social standing*: Gogol's character. *Pre-revolutionary occupation*: Buying up dead souls. *Relation to military service*: Neither this nor that nor devil knows what. *To what party are you affiliated?* Sympathizer (but with whom, goodness knows). *Have you been under trial?* Curved zigzagging line instead of an answer. *Address*: Turn into the courtyard, third floor on the right, ask at the enquiry office for the officer's wife Podtochina, and she will know.

Finally the author himself intervenes, volunteers to catch Chichikov, has him dissected, finds inside him stolen "people's milliards" in the form of diamonds, and orders him to be drowned in an ice hole. As a reward he asks for Gogol's *Complete Works*.

Then follows the ironical epilogue, which dismisses the whole story as a bad dream:

... of course, I woke up. And there was nothing: no Chichikov, no Nozdryov, and what is more, no Gogol. ...

"Well, well," I thought to myself, and began to dress. And once more life paraded before me in its everyday attire.

Commenting on Bulgakov's picture of Soviet life, Communist critics said that it boiled down to the assertion that the Revolution had changed nothing below the surface of Russian life, and they compared Bulgakov to his countryman Shulgin, with his famous formula: "Everything the same, but slightly worse."[2]

During the last years of his life Bulgakov was associated with the Moscow

[2] In 1926, Shulgin, the former editor of the Kiev right-wing daily *Kievlyanin*, one of the leaders of the "Progressive Bloc" in the Fourth Duma and one of the most brilliant of the *émigré* journalists, paid a sensational "secret" visit to the Soviet Union and published an interesting account of it in the book called *Tri stolitsy* (*Three Capitals*). Later it turned out that the organization which had arranged Shulgin's "conducted tour" of the Soviet Union was an offshoot of the Soviet secret police, organized for the purpose of infiltrating the anti-Soviet groups abroad, and that the manuscript of Shulgin's book was actually edited and proofread in the offices of the Moscow OGPU. The same organization was later responsible for the kidnaping of General Kutepov, one of the leading White Army generals, in Paris. After the revelations about his visit to the Soviet Union (which, incidentally, he undertook mainly with the object of finding his son, who had been missing since the end of the Civil War), Shulgin lived in almost complete seclusion in Yugoslavia. At the end of the war he was arrested by the Russians, taken to Moscow, and sentenced to long-term imprisonment. When he was set free under Khrushchev (he was about eighty years old then), he appeared to have been brainwashed by his captors. Appeals over his signature were published in Soviet papers, calling upon Russian *émigrés* to return to their native land. He also published a book of memoirs.

Art Theater, for which he dramatized Gogol's *Dead Souls* and wrote a play about Pushkin's duel and death for the centenary of the poet's death (1937). But he had virtually stopped publishing. Much of his unpublished work came to light only in the 1960's and belongs thus to the post-Stalin period. It also became known that, like Zamyatin, he had sought permission to go abroad but had been refused.

In 1928 appeared a long novel which was soon to become one of the favorites of the Soviet public. It was called *Dvenadtsat' stulyev* (*Twelve Chairs*) and was signed by two unknown names: Ilf and Petrov.

Ilf (1897–1937) and Petrov (1902–42)

Both Ilya Ilf (pseudonym of Ilya Arnoldovich Fainzilberg) and Evgeny Petrov (pseudonym of Evgeny Petrovich Katayev, younger brother of Valentin Katayev) were born in Odessa. But they first met in Moscow, where they began their literary careers as journalists on the railwaymen's paper *Gudok*. Almost everything they wrote between 1927 and 1937 was written jointly. In their joint humorous "autobiography" (which contained a great deal of truth, said Petrov later) they wrote:

> It is very difficult to write together. It was easier for the Goncourts, we suppose. After all they were brothers while we are not even related to each other. We are not even of the same age. And even of different nationalities: while one is a Russian (the enigmatic Slavic soul), the other is a Jew (the enigmatic Jewish soul).

In his "Recollections of Ilf" (written in 1939), Petrov told the curious story of the genesis of *Twelve Chairs*, their first joint product. One day Valentin Katayev, who used to write comic verses for *Gudok*, came to the editorial offices and announced, "I want to become the Soviet Dumas-père." To Ilf's question, "Why?" he answered:

> It is high time to launch a Soviet novel workshop. I'll be the Dumas-père and you'll be my Negroes. I'll give you the themes, you will write the novels, and I'll polish them up. I'll just go over your manuscripts once or twice with my master's hand—and there it is. Like Dumas-père. Eh? Who's game? But remember, I'll give you a rough treatment.

They exchanged a few more jokes on the subject, and then Katayev said quite seriously: "Here is an excellent theme: chairs. Imagine that money is hidden in one of the chairs. It must be found. Isn't it a good adventure novel? There are also other themes. Eh? Do agree. Seriously. Let Ilya write one novel, and Zhenya, another."[3]

Thus was born the idea of *Twelve Chairs*. But Ilf and Petrov decided to write it together and the very same day drew up the plan. This was in August or September, 1927, and by January, 1928, the novel was completed.

[3] E. Petrov, "Iz vospominaniy ob Ilfe" ("From My Recollections of Ilf"), in I. Ilf, *Zapisnye knizhki* (*Notebooks*), 14–15.

It was written together by the two of them, in the most literal sense of the word—that is, they sat beside each other and collaborated on every sentence. When the first part of the novel was shown to Katayev, he liked it and said: "You'll do without the Dumas-père. Continue to write on your own. I think the book will be a success."[4] And so it was.

Twelve Chairs is a gay, picaresque novel. It is also a satire. In the center of it stands the irrepressible Ostap Bender, who was originally meant as a purely episodic character, but grew into a real hero. He is one of the most memorable creations in Soviet literature, a modern Chichikov, a cunning and ingenious rogue, who leads the fantastic, breath-taking race for the diamonds which their pre-Revolutionary owner hid in one of a set of twelve chairs. The set having been dispersed, the search for the right chair takes Bender, his assistants and his rivals, among whom is a former priest, through all sorts of fantastic and farcical adventures, against the background of grotesquely satirized Soviet life of the NEP period. The hunt for the chair has an appropriate ideological ending: the chair with the diamonds in it turns out to have become the property of a Soviet club and the money used for cultural purposes. As for Bender, he is killed by one of his fellow diamond hunters just before the denouement of the novel. The authors afterward regretted having disposed of their hero and decided to bring him back to life in their second novel, Zolotoy telyonok (The Little Golden Calf, 1931). This sequel to Twelve Chairs is just as entertaining and just as recklessly fantastic, while the satire in it is even more serious and biting. It also has a neater and better balanced plot, revolving around several competing pretenders to the role of the son of Lieutenant Schmidt, the famous hero of the Potyomkin mutiny in 1905, with Ostap Bender acting as the sponsor and impressario of one of these pretenders. Here again everyday Soviet life can be seen through a grotesquely distorting mirror.

In Twelve Chairs and its sequel we see a procession of Soviet gangsters, confidence men, corrupt and unscrupulous officials, and gullible, ordinary citizens. The authors let their fancy run loose, while at the same time drawing upon real life for their characters and situations. As the Communist review Oktyabr put it, life in Twelve Chairs is "grotesque, confused, improbable, and yet real."

Ilf and Petrov also wrote together a number of humorous and satirical stories, again for the most part satirizing various aspects of Soviet life. However, two of the stories in the volume Tonya (1935) are satires on American life. "Tonya" describes the first steps of a young Soviet couple in America and contrasts American and Soviet life (it is written more seriously than is usual with Ilf and Petrov and is spoiled by its obvious didacticism), while "Kolumb prichalivayet k beregu" ("Columbus Puts To") is an amusing short skit on modern-day United States, describing what happens to

[4] Ibid., 19.

Christopher Columbus when he rediscovers twentieth-century America, with her reporters, her publicity, her burlesques.

Ilf and Petrov's last major joint work, *Odnoètazhnaya Amerika* (*One-Storied America*, 1936), is also about the United States. It is a witty, satirical account of their visit to the United States and their transcontinental automobile trip. In writing it, they adopted a new method: twenty chapters were written by Ilf, twenty by Petrov, and seven by both of them in the old way. The original intention of the authors was to take Ostap Bender, the "Great Combiner" of their two novels, to the United States and describe his adventures there—they even sold the idea in advance to their American publisher[5] —but instead they described, in a mildly satirical vein, their own impressions of American life, many aspects of which obviously appealed to them.

This successful tandem team came to an end in 1937, when Ilf died of tuberculosis. Left to himself, Petrov did not produce anything worthwhile. He was killed in 1942 in the Crimea, while reporting the war for Russian and American newspapers.

In 1939 appeared posthumously Ilf's *Zapisnye knizhki* (*Notebooks*), short notations of an observant artist containing both the laboratory material for satires and "lyrical" fragments.

[5] I owe this information to the late Charles Malamuth, who translated both this book and *The Little Golden Calf* into English.

Chapter 12. **THE HISTORICAL NOVEL**

Strange though this may appear at first glance, historical fiction as a specific literary genre took a new lease on life in post-Revolutionary Russia—a Russia which was supposedly looking to the future and doing away with the past. Some of the historical novels published in the Soviet Union during the period under review represented a new departure and constituted a distinct contribution to literature. To understand this, a brief survey of Russian historical fiction before the Revolution may not be out of place here. It was the influence of Walter Scott and the quickening of national-patriotic sentiments after the Napoleonic wars that gave rise to historical novels in Russia. The novels of Zagoskin (who was often called the Russian Walter Scott, though he was certainly inferior, both in talent and in scope of historical vision, to the famous Scots novelist) as well as Pushkin's historical novels and Gogol's *Taras Bulba*, much as they differ from each other, represented the fruits of Scottism on the Russian soil. The well-known Russian critic Apollon Grigoryev (1820–64) went so far as to say that the whole of the National-Romantic period in Russian literature was influenced by Sir Walter Scott.

Zagoskin had several successors. The best known of them was Lazhechnikov, whose novels were built on more solid historical foundations than Zagoskin's costume pieces and were at the same time readable. But the traditions of Scottism were not carried on in great Russian literature. Turgenev's six major novels, while "historical" in the sense that they mirror successive stages in the evolution of Russian society, do so in terms of imaginary characters and do not come within the strict meaning of historical fiction. The only instance of a historical novel in the great Russian literature of the second half of the nineteenth century is Tolstoy's *War and Peace*. But *War and Peace*, this "river of a novel" (*roman fleuve*), is a genre in itself. While it is, of course, a historical novel, it is also something more than that—a vast epic of Russian life, a family chronicle, and a masterpiece of individual characterization. What is more, this "historical" novel is eminently antihistorical in spirit and sets out to shatter the traditional view of history. Tolstoy's great work has therefore remained a solitary, isolated fact in Russian literature, even though it did influence some second- and third-rate novelists. After Tolstoy, historical fiction was for a long time relegated to the lower regions of literature or regarded as juvenile reading (typical examples of it are Alexey K. Tolstoy's colorful costume novel *Prince Serebryany* and the novels of Vsevolod Solovyov). More important was the handling of historical themes in the drama, where the Shakespearean tradition of Pushkin's *Boris Godunov* was continued by the same Alexey K. Tolstoy in his famous trilogy *The Death of Ivan the Terrible, Tsar Fyodor Ioannovich*, and *Tsar Boris*. Alexander Ostrovsky, the principal representative of Russian dramatic realism, also wrote some historical plays.

An attempt to revive and renovate historical fiction and give it a higher status in literature was made by the Russian Symbolists—in the novels of Merezhkovsky and Bryusov and in the stories of some less important writers like Kuzmin, Sadovskoy, and Auslaender. The interesting new element in Merezhkovsky's historical novels—those which form his celebrated trilogy, *Christ and Antichrist*, as well as his later novels from Russian history—was that, contrary to the traditional historical novel brought into fashion by Walter Scott and to Tolstoy's great masterpiece, the central parts in them were assigned to historical, not fictitious, characters. Julian the Apostate, Leonardo da Vinci, Peter the Great, and Alexander I of Russia are the key characters in Merezhkovsky's novels. But in Merezhkovsky the novelist was subordinated to the thinker. In terms of historical facts and characters he gave expression to his historical, philosophical, and religious ideas. His novels were "historiosophical" novels *à thèse*. They combined an attempt—not always successful—at archaeological accuracy with a modernization of history, but they lacked true historicity. This is particularly obvious in the last part of the trilogy, *Peter and Alexis*. In a way it was therefore natural for Merezhkovsky to give up, finally, the historical-novel form and turn to a nonfictional treatment of historical themes and characters.

In Bryusov's historical fiction (*The Fiery Angel* and *The Altar of Victory*) the impulse was purely literary. The novels were an outlet for the general tendency of the Symbolists to get away from contemporary life, which in their eyes lacked color and variety, and to seek inspiration in the past or in exoticism, as did the romantics. Into the first-named novel Bryusov also introduced a purely autobiographical element. After Merezhkovsky and Bryusov came a new interval which lasted until after the Revolution, when the historical novel was once more revived both in Soviet Russia and in *émigré* literature (as in the work of Mark Aldanov).

The Social-Historical Novel

It is possible to distinguish two principal varieties of historical fiction in post-Revolutionary Russia: the social-historical novel and the biographical novel. The former originated in the desire to relate the present to the past; the latter was prompted largely by a desire to escape from the present into the past.

It is also necessary to bear in mind that the general orientation and significance of Soviet historical fiction underwent a considerable change in

the mid-thirties. In the present section, going beyond the strictly chronological limits of this chapter, I shall discuss the novels which appeared
before 1937; those which appeared later will be mentioned in subsequent
chapters.

It has been said that revolutions are propitious to historical studies and to
the spirit of history.[1] It is very doubtful, however, whether this statement,
without serious qualifications, is applicable to the Russian Revolution. In
its later phases especially, the Revolution proved to be much more propitious
to the revision, and even falsification, of history. It is nevertheless true that,
so far as the literature of the Revolution tried to grasp the meaning of
events and not merely to record them, it had to analyze their genesis and
treat them in historical perspective. A Soviet critic stressed the influence of
the present on the interpretation of the past when he wrote in 1936:

> Popular mass movements are legitimately becoming the principal theme of
> the Soviet historical novel. The *reassessment of the historical role of the people*,
> the rehabilitation of its past heroes—all this has been suggested to our novelists
> by the present-day practice of millions of toilers.[2]

The same critic said that "the pedigree of the Revolution" was naturally
one of the main subjects of Soviet historical fiction.[3]

Hence, during the period under examination, especially in its early part,
there were a number of Soviet novels containing historical material about
the Revolution of 1917 itself and of purely historical novels about its more
or less distant antecedents. The first type of novel is exemplified by Tarasov-
Rodionov's *February* and Sholokhov's *The Quiet Don*.

The Revolution of 1905 and the revolutionary movement which preceded
it also quite naturally attracted the attention of Soviet novelists. It was the
subject, for instance, of *Kolokola* (*The Bells*, 1926), by Ivan Evdokimov
(1887–1941), and of *Goryachiy tsekh* (*Hot Workshop*, 1932), by Olga Forsh
(of whom more will be said later).

The same period is treated in *Tsushima*, a novel about the Russo-Japanese
War by Alexey Novikov-Priboy (1877–1944). A professional sailor, he began
writing long before the Revolution, but his first book of stories did not
appear until 1917. He was known mostly as the author of vivid but unpretentious sea yarns written from a revolutionary standpoint. The subject
of *Tsushima* is the notorious disaster of the Russian fleet. The novel is an
eyewitness account of the progress of Admiral Rozhestvensky's fleet around
the world toward its doom at Tsushima. The first part gives a detailed,
realistic picture of the sailors' daily life and routine. The second part is

[1] D. S. Mirsky, "Der russische historische Roman der Gegenwart," *Slavische Rund-schau*, No. 1 (1932).

[2] M. Serebryansky, *Sovetskiy istoricheskiy roman* (*The Soviet Historical Novel*), 50–51.

[3] *Ibid.*, 53.

centered around the battle itself, in which the author was taken prisoner by the Japanese. It is almost nonfictional in its documentary character and does not aim at a creative interpretation of history.

Some Soviet writers sought subjects for their historical novels in the revolutionary movements of the more remote past. Their novels are more strictly historical, but they are also essentially revolutionary in inspiration and approach. To these historical-revolutionary novels belongs *Odety kamnem* (*Clad with Stone*, 1927), by Olga Dmitrievna Forsh (1875–1961), who before the Revolution wrote stories under the pseudonym A. Terek. *Clad with Stone* is a novel about the Russian revolutionaries of the 1870's and 1880's, written in the form of a diary. In Forsh's approach to historical fiction may be seen some influence of Merezhkovsky and the Symbolists, and her historical novels are never purely historical, for they also contain philosophical and psychological elements.

Alexey Pavlovich Chapygin (1870–1937), a pre-Revolutionary writer of peasant origin, first attracted attention in 1915 with his novel *Bely skit* (*White Hermitage*), of which Gorky thought very highly. In 1926–27, Chapygin made a spectacular comeback to literature with his thousand-page-long historical novel *Stepan Razin*, about the picturesque brigand leader of the Cossack rebellion in the seventeenth century, who is one of the favorite heroes of Russian folk poetry. Chapygin painted a vast canvas of one of the most turbulent periods in Russian history, a period which he not only knew but also felt. The novel is spoiled, however, by overminute descriptions and a highly stylized language, while the figure of Razin is also stylized and idealized. Chapygin's second historical novel, *Gulyashchie lyudi* (*Itinerant People*, 1935), also had the seventeenth century for its setting and a popular revolt for its subject. Almost as long as his first novel, it gave an interesting picture of the religious struggle and social unrest in that period.

In *Povest' o Bolotnikove* (*The Tale About Bolotnikov*, 1929), by Georgy Storm, we are taken still further back in Russian history. Bolotnikov was one of the leaders of the rebel Cossacks and peasants during the "Time of Troubles" on the threshold of the seventeenth century. Storm's novel is much shorter than Chapygin's and the writing much more impressionistic. It is a series of graphically told episodes set against a background of rapidly changing scenery. Most of its characters are historical, but since historical documentation is often wanting for them, the author took some liberties in attempting their psychological reconstruction. This is especially true of the colorful figure of Bolotnikov himself. History and fiction are skillfully blended, and ingenious use is made of passages from historical documents. Freely used archaic terms lend the language a spicy flavor, but on the whole stylization is kept within bounds.

Another historical "mass" novel is Artyom Vesyoly's *Gulyay-Volga*

(*Volga on the Spree*, 1934), which is a chronicle of Ermak's expedition to Siberia. Written in a lyrical vein, as is usual with Vesyoly, it is stylized to resemble folk songs, while Vesyoly's characters are patterned on his revolutionary partisans and unfortunately lack both individuality and historical verisimilitude.

The life of runaway Siberian peasants and of workers in state mines under Catherine II was the subject of a novel by Anna Karavayeva (b. 1893), entitled *Zolotoy klyuv* (*The Golden Beak*). Karavayeva belonged to the proletarian October group and had earlier specialized in describing social collisions in the post-Revolutionary village. In her historical novel she made considerable use of little-known historical documents.

Non-Russian revolutionary subjects came in for a lesser share of attention. Among the novels which dealt with the French Revolution may be mentioned Ehrenburg's *Zagovor ravnykh* (*The Conspiracy of Equals*, 1928), the subject of which is the Babeuf movement; and *Chorny konsul* (*The Black Consul*, 1931), by Anatoly Vinogradov (1888–1946), which tells the story of Toussaint L'Ouverture's rising in Haiti. The Paris Commune of 1870 is the subject of Peter Pavlenko's short novel *Barrikady* (*Barricades*, 1932).

The Biographical Novel

To the second group of Soviet historical novels of this period belong many novelized literary biographies or novels about prominent figures in literature, art, and science. Many of them were "escapist" in character; that is, their authors did not feel inclined or capable to deal with contemporary life and its problems—either because they feared to walk where angels tread or because, like their predecessors the Symbolists, they failed to find inspiration in contemporary life.

It is interesting to note, however, that the authors of these biographical novels included several literary scholars. The novel which launched the fashion for literary-historical novels—the Soviet counterpart of Lytton Strachey and André Maurois—was *Kyukhlya* (1925), by Yury Nikolayevich Tynyanov (1894–1944). A literary historian of note, one of the leaders of the Formalist school in literary science and an authority on the Pushkin period, Tynyanov brought to this new genre of fiction his great literary erudition and his feeling for the period. The hero of *Kyukhlya* was Wilhelm Küchelbecker, one of Pushkin's schoolfellows and friends, himself a poet and playwright, who became implicated in the Decembrist conspiracy of 1825 and was exiled to Siberia. Tynyanov's work was based on a meticulous study of the documents. But with all its unquestionable historicity, the novel was also an interesting psychological study of a literary and political Don Quixote, a kindhearted but muddleheaded idealist, lovable and ridiculous, whose life contained the seeds of tragedy. Because of the discrepancy between his lofty aspirations and his inadequate powers of self-expression, he ended in failure and frustration. Küchelbecker's fate is shown also as part of the social pattern of the period. Pushkin, Griboyedov, Zhukovsky, and other well-known historical figures appear in the novel, and the whole background picture is excellently drawn.

Tynyanov's second novel was *Smert' Vazir-Mukhtara* (*The Death of Wazir-Muchtar*, 1929). Wazir-Muchtar was the official Persian title of Alexander Griboyedov, the famous author of *The Misfortune of Being Clever* and Russian minister to Persia, one of the most interesting and enigmatic figures in Russian literature. Tynyanov's novel, published in connection with the centenary of Griboyedov's death (he was assassinated by the Teheran mob in 1829), was not a full-length biography but covered only the last year of Griboyedov's life, from the moment when he returned from Persia with the Treaty of Turkmanchay in his pocket. At that moment his reputation as a diplomat—so different from his posthumous fame as a writer—had reached its climax.

By concentrating on this last year of Griboyedov's life, which marked the beginning of a steady progress toward the inevitable doom, Tynyanov tried to emphasize the tragic essence of Griboyedov's personality, to convey that "acrid smell of fate" which Griboyedov diffused around him. But he failed in what André Maurois regarded as the essential thing in the art of biography—namely, discovering the keynote to the life and personality of the model. Instead of a portrait, Tynyanov gives us a mirror broken into many fragments, in which we see reflected separate features of his model, but no synthesis is achieved. Instead of conveying a sense of doom, Tynyanov relates but a series of disjointed anecdotes in which can be discerned only a persistent tendency to caricature and to mock. Tynyanov's historical characters are helpless puppets and his attitude toward history a caricature of Tolstoy's. The style is reminiscent of Andrey Bely's, but Tynyanov's "Belyisms" are at times annoyingly obtrusive. For all its defects, however, *The Death of Wazir-Muchtar* is an interesting and original work, more original in fact than *Kyukhlya*. Its very defects result from the author's attempt to rise above the ordinary level of historical fiction, to present the problem of Griboyedov as the tragic problem of the individual battling with his own destiny, and at the same time to renovate the novel structurally.

Tynyanov's third and last historical novel was *Pushkin* (1936–37), a full-length fictional biography of the great Russian poet. As the new fashion demanded, it was written more simply and realistically than the Griboyedov novel, but lacked the latter's originality as well as the poetic unity and inevitability of *Kyukhlya*. Tynyanov also wrote three shorter historical stories, "Podporuchik Kizhe" ("Lieutenant Kizhe"), "Maloletny Vitushishnikov" ("Minor Vitushishnikov"), and "Voskovaya persona" ("The Wax Figure"), set respectively in the reigns of Paul I, Nicholas I, and Peter the Great. All three stories are highly stylized; the author's primary concern in them is neither with history nor with psychology but with style.

Tynyanov's *Kyukhlya* had a large progeny. Within the next few years appeared several novels and stories about Lermontov (by Pilnyak, Sergeyev-Tsensky, Pavlenko, and others), but none of them matched the high standard set by Tynyanov's work. Pushkin, too, naturally attracted attention, especially in connection with the centenary of his death, which occurred in 1937. Among the more satisfying biographical novels about him may be mentioned *Pushkin v Mikhaylovskom* (*Pushkin at Mikhaylovskoye*) and *Pushkin na yuge* (*Pushkin in the South*), by Ivan Novikov (1879–1959), a pre-Revolutionary writer of the Turgenev-Bunin landed-gentry school. *Zapiski d'Arshiaka* (*Memoirs of d'Archiac*, 1937), by Leonid Grossman (1888–1967), a noted literary scholar, was based on the fictitious memoirs of the Vicomte d'Archiac, who was Danthès's second in his duel with Pushkin. Severely criticized by Soviet critics, it was a well-told story of the last months of Pushkin's life. Grossman also wrote a novel about Dostoyevsky's gambling in Germany (*Roulettenburg*, 1932) and a novel about Loris-Melikov and the last years of Alexander II's reign, *Barkhatny diktator* (*The Velvet Dictator*, 1933).

After Tynyanov, the most important contribution to the literary-historical novel was made by Olga Forsh, mentioned earlier. In *Sovremenniki* (*The Contemporaries*, 1927) she describes Gogol's life in Rome and his friendship with the religious painter Alexander Ivanov. The theme of the novel is the artist's place in society, and to present it more completely the author introduces the fictitious character of another painter, Bagretsov, but the interest is focused on Ivanov. In *Simvolisty* (*The Symbolists*, 1933) Forsh's subject is the Russian literary scene before the Revolution. It was intended as part of a wider work about that epoch in Russian life. In *Sumasshedshy korabl'* (*The Mad Ship*, 1930–31) Forsh portrayed the literary and artistic life in Petrograd in the early 1920's. The scene is set in the House of Arts, and most of the protagonists are easily recognizable under their fictitious names. The work is a kind of documentary satire, witty and incisive. It was not included in Forsh's collected works, but in 1964 was reissued in the United States, edited by Boris Filippov. Social-historical and biographical elements were combined in her later three-volume novel *Radishchev* (1934–39): *Yakobinsky zakvas* (*The Jacobin Leaven*), *Kazanskaya pomeshchitsa* (*The Squiress of Kazan*), and *Pagubnaya Kniga* (*The Nefarious Book*). Its hero is Alexander Radishchev, the author of *A Journey from St. Petersburg to Moscow* (for which he was exiled to Siberia by Catherine II). The novel has a definite bias, to fit in with the official Soviet view of Radishchev as a precursor of the Russian revolutionary movement, but is well written and gives an interesting picture of the period.

Another combination of the social-historical and biographical novel is

Storm's *Trudy i dni Mikhaila Lomonosova* (*Labors and Days of Mikhail Lomonosov*, 1932), in which Lomonosov's life is projected against the contemporary Russian and European scene.

Russian and foreign literary figures were brought to life in Anatoly Vinogradov's novels *Dva tsveta vremeni* (*Two Colors of Time*, 1930) and *Povest' o bratyakh Turgenevykh* (*The Tale About the Brothers Turgenev*, 1932). The former is about Stendhal and his part in Napoleon's Russian campaign. It is an entertaining narrative. Vinogradov is better as a fiction writer than as a scholar, for his studies of Mérimée, Stendhal, and Franco-Russian literary contacts are full of errors. The novel about the brothers Turgenev, based in part on unpublished material, is centered around the lives of Nikolay and Alexander Turgenev and their associations with Russian freemasonry. Vinogradov also wrote a novel about the life of the famous Russian chemist Mendeleyev, *Khronika Malevinskikh* (*The Chronicle of the Malevinskys*, 1934).

Tynyanov's and Vinogradov's literary novels are connected with a large nonfictional literature of literary biographies constructed on the principle of montage, of piecing together bits of contemporary evidence from letters, diaries, memoirs, and the like. To a certain extent all these literary biographies reflected the same tendency: to escape from contemporary, topical themes.

Tolstoy's Peter the First

A place apart among Soviet historical novels belongs to Alexey N. Tolstoy's ambitious but unfinished novel *Pyotr Pervy* (*Peter the First*). In 1931, Gorky called it "the first real historical novel in our literature." Romain Rolland admired this "gigantic epic, huge, dense and intricate like a forest with its roads, bogs, gaps of sky and shadows."

From the time of Pushkin, the outsize figure of Peter the Great, the reformer of Russia, had attracted Russian writers. Pushkin's unfinished *The Negro of Peter the Great, Poltava*, and *The Bronze Horseman*, not to speak of several lyric poems, have Peter for their hero. Toward the end of his life Pushkin was collecting material for a history of Peter's reign, and, just as his *Captain's Daughter* was a by-product of his historical study of the Pugachov revolt, this historical work might well have produced a novel dealing with Peter's times. Leo Tolstoy also thought of writing a historical novel about Peter but gave up the idea. Most of the minor historical novelists of the nineteenth century felt drawn toward this exciting period in Russian history, and in many of their novels Peter appears as a secondary character. Merezhkovsky made Peter the central figure in the last—and least satisfying —part of his trilogy, but with him the historical personality of the great emperor was distorted and twisted to suit his own ideas about Russian history. This is even more true of Boris Pilnyak, whose stories about Peter are made to fit in with his neo-Slavophile concepts.

Pilnyak's attitude toward Peter was frankly hostile and closer to Merezhkovsky's than to Pushkin's and the nineteenth-century literary tradition. The same hostile approach is obvious in Alexey Tolstoy's two early stories from Peter's times: "Navazhdenie" ("Obsession") and "Den' Petra" ("Peter's Day"), both written in 1917. In the first Peter himself does not appear; in the second he is the hero. The story describes an ordinary day in Peter's life. Tolstoy deglamorizes Peter, stressing all his bad qualities, both physical and spiritual: his ugliness, his coarseness, and his almost bestial cruelty. Peter's reforms are interpreted as the personal whim of a willful barbarian despot. This story was strongly denounced by the great Russian historian Platonov as a distortion of historical truth. Yet much of this early hostile attitude can still be seen in Tolstoy's play *Na dybe* (*On the Rack*, 1929), where, like Merezhkovsky and some of his predecessors, Tolstoy contrasts Peter and his son Alexis and builds the tragedy out of the conflict between personal and impersonal forces. Here, however, Peter appears as already a statesman for whom the good of his country is the supreme law to which everything else must be sacrificed.

In the same year, 1929, Book 1 of Tolstoy's novel was serialized in *Novy Mir*. Book 2 was published in 1933. Book 3 did not appear until 1944–45. After Tolstoy's death in 1945 the remaining part (six chapters) was published in the same year. During this period Tolstoy also wrote dramatic versions of the first two parts, and the scenario for a film which enjoyed great success in Russia and abroad.

Unlike most traditional historical novels, *Peter the First* is primarily a biography of a great historical figure set against the vast background of the period. There are in it some fictional characters who help diversify the plot, but the main interest is centered on Peter and the Russia of his time. Peter is the true hero of the novel. The story begins with his childhood and is carried down to the battle of Narva (1701). Tolstoy apparently intended to end the novel with the great victory over Charles XII of Sweden at Poltava (1709).

The Peter of the novel is quite different from the Peter of the earlier story and the play. He is portrayed as a great man, a genius, who performed great deeds and changed completely the face of Russia. Without idealizing his hero, Tolstoy no longer shows him as an assemblage of physical and other monstrosities. This change of attitude may have been in part due to a change in the official Soviet approach to Peter (which, however, came to light only when Tolstoy was engaged on the second part of the novel), but in part it was no doubt the result of a more careful and thorough study of historical sources. It is clear that extensive research underlies Tolstoy's novel, although, unlike Merezhkovsky's work, it never gives the impression of a wax museum or a record office.[4] Nor, on the whole, are Tolstoy's characters mere vehicles for certain ideas and points of view. They are alive and real. He is equally good in individual characterization and in the portrayal of this turbulent and critical period in Russian history, which he paints with great gusto. The novel is brimful with life; it has a multitude of characters, a richness and variety of settings, and a great width of social, historical, and geographical scope. Written in excellent, full-blooded Russian, with no attempt at reproducing pedantically the language of the period, it is a fine example of historical realism.

The question whether Tolstoy tried to read the present into the past and deliberately suggested parallels between Russia in the process of "sovietization" and Russia being forcibly "Europeanized" by Peter is not easy to answer. The first volume is, on the whole, free from such a tendency. In the subsequent volumes it is felt here and there, especially in the treatment of Peter himself. But in the end Tolstoy's artistic sense and flair for life saved him from the pitfall of reading too much of the present into the past, which cannot be said of his later play about Ivan the Terrible (see Chapter 26).

[4] For an appraisal of Tolstoy's handling of documentary sources see I. I. Veksler, *Alexey Nikolayevich Tolstoy. Zhiznenny i tvorchesky put (Aleksey Nikolayevich Tolstoy: His Life and Work)*, 359–72. Cf. also M. Karpovich, "Soviet Historical Novel," *Russian Review*, Vol. V (1946), 53–63.

Chapter 13. THE POETS

After 1925, poetry, which had dominated the earlier Soviet literary scene, receded into the background. Some poets, in keeping with the prevalent trend in literature, turned to prose fiction (Tikhonov and, to a lesser extent, Pasternak) or to play writing (Mayakovsky), or tried to bring poetry and prose closer to each other, either in content or in style (Pasternak in his narrative poems and Selvinsky). Few new poets captured the attention of the critics and the reading public. That does not mean, however, that no good poetry was produced during the period.

Of the poets who had made names for themselves earlier, the most notable were Mayakovsky, Pasternak, Mandelstam, and Tikhonov.

Mayakovsky The last five years of Mayakovsky's life were uneasy and hectic, and his poetry was full of contradictions. No longer unequivocally recognized and accepted as the leader of revolutionary literature, he was attacked by orthodox Communists for his individualism and "formalism." In 1927 he revived the magazine *LEF* under the title *Novy LEF*, but a year later parted ways with it and issued the slogan "To the Left of LEF." In 1929 he organized the group REF (Revolutionary Front), but the attacks on him did not cease, and in February, 1930, two months before his death, he joined the Russian Association of Proletarian Writers, the bulwark of Communist orthodoxy, which at that time called the tune in Soviet literary life. After 1926 he took an active part in daily journalism, becoming a regular contributor to *Komsomolskaya Pravda*, for which he wrote political and propaganda verse.

In 1923, Mayakovsky wrote the most personal of his longer post-Revolutionary poems, "Pro èto" ("About This"). A tragic poem about love, into which are woven the motifs of expiation and of resurrection of the dead, it echoes the earlier *Cloud in Pants*. After that, personal motifs continue to crop up in Mayakovsky's poetry, but most of his longer works—"Vladimir Ilyich Lenin" (1924), "Khorosho!" ("It's Good!" 1927)—are essentially political, imbued with enthusiasm for the achievements of Socialist reconstruction. Lyricism and social-political motifs are intertwined in the unfinished "Vo ves' golos" ("At the Top of My Voice"), published posthumously in 1930. A tragic note is sounded in this last major work of Mayakovsky: he speaks here of having "trampled underfoot the throat of [his] own song."

A counterpart to Mayakovsky's poems glorifying the new order of things may also be seen in his satirical poems and his two biting and clever satirical plays, *Klop* (*The Bedbug*, 1928) and *Banya* (*The Bathhouse*, 1929). In these two plays he gave vent to his passionate protest against the smug philistinism that was invading Soviet life and against the hypertrophied bureaucratism that was becoming increasingly characteristic of the new state. In *The Bathhouse* the figure of Pobedonosikov, the director of the Department of Co-ordination, is a brilliant satire on Soviet bureaucrats. Both plays are "expressionistic" and full of unusual scenic devices. Mayakovsky himself took an active part in their production.

Mayakovsky is also said to have been writing a poem entitled "It's Bad," but none of it has ever been published. It is to be assumed that it was to present the reverse of the picture painted in "It's Good!"

Between 1926 and 1930, Mayakovsky made three trips abroad and regularly toured the Soviet Union, giving lectures and recitals of his poems in fifty-two towns. Toward the end of this period a personal, lyric note reappeared in his poetry—a note of unwonted bitterness and disillusionment. It may have been in part due to personal complications in his life,[1] but the attacks of those who still doubted his wholehearted attachment to the Revolution and regarded him as a mere fellow traveler must have had some share in it, too. A few days before his death he stated in public: "They hang so many dogs on me, and accuse me of so many sins . . . that at times I feel like going off somewhere for a couple of years, only not to listen to abuse." On April 14, 1930, Mayakovsky shot himself through the heart. He left a note, addressed to his mother, his sisters, and his comrades, in which he apologized for what he was about to do and asked them to abstain from gossip, and a poem in which he spoke of his "love boat" having smashed against "everyday life" (*byt*) and of being "quits" with life.

This suicide of a man who, five years earlier, had in a poem severely reprimanded Esenin for taking his own life and had written, paraphrasing Esenin:

> In this life it is not hard to die—
> To mold life is far more difficult

came quite unexpectedly to his many friends and admirers—as well as to the official circles in the Soviet Union. The immediate reaction was one of shocked stupefaction. The keynote of all the obituaries in the Soviet press was that the very idea of suicide was "incompatible" with Mayakovsky. Lunacharsky, Koltsov, Khalatov, Demyan Bedny—all with one voice re-

---

[1] In 1928, on a visit to Paris, Mayakovsky fell in love with a young Russian *émigrée*. The next year he intended to rejoin her, but was denied a passport. For more details of this episode and its reflections in Mayakovsky's poetry see R. Jakobson, "Novye stroki Mayakovskogo" ("Unpublished Verses by Mayakovsky"), in *Russky Literaturny Arkhiv* (ed. by D. Čiževsky and M. Karpovich), 173–206.

peated that they never expected it from Mayakovsky.[2] The official version attributed the suicide to Mayakovsky's illness: a disease of the throat combined with overwork and nervous breakdown. Unofficially it was blamed largely on disappointment in love. But there can be no doubt that, his professions of official optimism notwithstanding, Mayakovsky was feeling at the time more and more out of tune with the surrounding realities.

Today Mayakovsky's "individualistic" and "formalistic" deviations are forgotten, as is his final "un-Communist" act of escaping from the insoluble tangle of his own contradictions through voluntary death. He is regarded as the greatest Soviet poet—an estimate which had the sanction of Stalin— the classic of Soviet literature, the bard of the Revolution. Although timid attempts to question his poetic heritage and his value as a model for young Soviet poets were made at times after World War II, they were quickly cut short and his detractors immediately called to order. Whether all of Mayakovsky's work could be fitted in with the narrow tenets that came to govern literature and art in the Soviet Union after his death, and whether he himself would be at home in present-day Soviet society, are altogether different questions. The fact remains that he took his voluntary exit from that society in 1930.

Pasternak (1890–1960) Boris Leonidovich Pasternak is undoubtedly one of the most significant modern Russian poets. The son of a well-known portrait painter who was a friend and illustrator of Leo Tolstoy, Pasternak grew up in a refined artistic and intellectual atmosphere in Moscow. His mother was a concert pianist, and he too devoted several years to a serious study of music. Later he studied philosophy at the University of Moscow and at Marburg, the center of German Neo-Kantianism. As a young man he joined one of the many factions of the Futurist movement.

Pasternak's first two books of poetry—*Bliznets v tuchakh* (*A Twin in Clouds*, 1913) and *Poverkh baryerov* (*Over the Barriers*, 1917)—showed considerable talent, but it was only after his third book, *Sestra moya zhizn'* (*My Sister Life*), published in 1922 but written some five years earlier, that he was hailed as a new star on the Russian poetical horizon. A year later, with the appearance of his next book of verse, *Temy i variatsii* (*Themes and Variations*), Pasternak was recognized as the outstanding younger poet of post-Revolutionary Russia.

[2] Among the many reactions to Mayakovsky's death one of the most interesting is R. Jakobson's essay "O pokolenii, rastrativshem svoikh poètov" ("About the Generation Which Squandered Its Poets"), *Smert' Vladimira Mayakovskogo* (*The Death of Vladimir Mayakovsky*). This little book also contains an essay by D. S. Mirsky. One of the early leaders of Russian Formalism and a personal friend of Mayakovsky, Jakobson stresses the persistence of the suicide motif in Mayakovsky's poetry and gives an interesting analysis of his "mythology," which included a belief in bodily immortality, somewhat akin to Nikolay Fyodorov's religion of resurrection.

In 1925 he published a book of short stories, some of which had earlier appeared in magazines. In 1927 appeared *Devyatsot pyaty god* (*The Year 1905*), consisting of two more or less independent fragmentary poems dealing with the Revolution of 1905 ("The Year 1905" and "Lieutenant Schmidt"), and in 1931, a narrative poem *Spektorsky*, in which much of the background is clearly autobiographical (parts of this short "tale in verse" had appeared earlier in periodicals). Related to *Spektorsky* through the main character was a fragment in prose published in 1929 in *Novy Mir* under the title "Povest' " ("A Story"; separately issued in 1934). In 1931, too, appeared Pasternak's partial autobiography, titled *Okhrannaya gramota* (*Safe Conduct*). In the same year he collected some of his early poetry and the poems written since the publication of *Themes and Variations* in a volume whose title repeated that of his 1917 book (*Poverkh baryerov*). In 1932 was published a new volume of lyrical verse, *Vtoroye rozhdenie* (*The Second Birth*). Between 1933 and 1936 there were several editions of Pasternak's collected and selected poems, and in 1933 several of his early stories, together with "Povest'," were reissued.

In 1936, Pasternak came under attack for being out of tune with his times, and after that not a single volume of his original poetry was published until 1943, and almost none appeared in the periodicals. He did, however, engage extensively in translating Georgian poets, both old and modern (the translations were made not from the originals but from word-for-word prose versions). In 1940 a volume of his translations from English, French, and German was published; it included Kleist's *Prinz von Homburg* and poems by Shakespeare, Byron, Keats, Verlaine, and others. And between 1941 and 1945 Pasternak published translations of Shakespeare's *Hamlet, Romeo and Juliet, Anthony and Cleopatra,* and *Othello* (*King Lear, Macbeth,* and *Henry IV* were added to this list later).

A romantic and an individualist, Pasternak was never quite at home in Soviet literature. His talent was never disputed; his influence on a number of young Soviet poets, as well as on several *émigré* poets, was very great (among those who were influenced by him at this or that stage of their career may be named Tikhonov, Bagritsky, Selvinsky, Sayanov, and Antokolsky); but he was periodically attacked for being out of tune with the new Soviet state, for his individualism, for his "chamber" poetry. Unlike so many other Soviet writers, he was constitutionally incapable of prostituting his muse, of writing to order. Hence his long silences, his translations of Georgian poets, and his escape into Shakespeare.

Pasternak is not a poet for the many; rather, he is a poets' poet. He is neither easy nor simple, and many people find him obscure. His capricious syntax, his elliptical language, his associative method, which involves sudden metaphorical jumps, all demand an imaginative effort on the part of the reader. His rhythms are vigorous, infectious, and varied; his poems have a long breath. His startling freshness and originality are due both to the novelty of his vision and to the originality of his idiom. Things that may appear ordinary and trite he approaches from a new perspective and presents in a new way. To use Coleridge's words, he "lends the charm of novelty to things of every day." The Formalists would say that his favorite method is that of *ostranenie* ("making strange"). He likes unexpected contrasts and bold and paradoxical metaphors. He has no fear of vulgarisms, of prosaic locutions, or of technical terms, but uses them without destroying the poetic, and even the romantic, effect.

In a way quite different from Mayakovsky's, without recourse to purely tonic verse, without doing violence to classical meters, Pasternak approximates poetry to prose, gives his verse the intonations and cadences of ordinary colloquial speech, and yet achieves wonderful musical and rhythmical effects. He is nothing if not a musical poet. Some of his best poems (for instance, the remarkable short lyric beginning, "The boat is thumping in my drowsy breast") may appear to defy normal semantic analysis, but as the reader is carried along on the waves of their sound magic, their hidden and profound meaning is revealed to him. Yet there is in Pasternak nothing of the effeminate musicality of a Zhukovsky, a Fet, a Balmont, or a Verlaine. The texture of his verse is taut and muscular. His prosaisms, his bold enjambments, his paradoxical juxtaposition of poetic and unpoetic words and lavish use of metonymy, destroy the automatism of perception and enhance the effect of novelty and freshness. He has been compared with Donne, with Gerard Manley Hopkins (without his religion), and with Rilke (without his mysticism), but one might as well find in him parallels with T. S. Eliot and Dylan Thomas—and if poetry could develop untrammeled in the Soviet Union, his influence on the younger generation of poets would certainly be comparable to Eliot's in England and America.

In passionate intensity Pasternak has also been compared with Lermontov. His kinship with the romantic tradition in Russian poetry is beyond question. He has something of Tyutchev's intense cosmic feeling, and the ordinary phenomena of nature—the succession of seasons, the rain, the snow, the thunderstorm—receive in his poetry a novel and original response. One cannot say of Pasternak, as one can of many other poets, that he is a poet of thought alone or of feeling alone. In him the two are blended. In this he is akin, among the Russian poets, to Baratynsky. Allusive and elusive, he is yet never vague. He is infinitely more sophisticated, more cultured, more subtle than Mayakovsky. At times one can feel the burden of culture weighing down on him, and one can see him trying pathetically to escape his own complexities and contradictions. It is easy to realize that the literary climate of the Soviet Union was for most of the time hardly propitious to such a poet.

It was especially in his two longer narrative poems, *Spektorsky* and "The Year 1905," that Pasternak tried to overcome the pure individualism of his lyrical poetry, in which nature and the spiritual, rather than social life, were the principal source of inspiration. *Spektorsky* is a kind of lyrical auto-biography unrolled against the background of contemporary life, a tale in verse, relating some episodes in the life of a young Moscow intellectual and introducing facts of Pasternak's own life. Here and there Pasternak shows a fine gift of observation and description, but in the main he is concerned with the inner life of his hero, his amatory and intellectual preoccupations. Once or twice he apologizes, as it were, for having chosen as his hero an "insignificant" personage. The lyricism of the poem, full of happy dis-coveries, is characteristic of Pasternak, but the narrative thread is both too slender and too involved, and as an attempt to outgrow lyricism and create a modern epic, the poem is a failure. It is nothing more than one of Paster-nak's extended lyric poems, a sequence of lyrical scenes.

"The Year 1905" and "Lieutenant Schmidt" are parts of a fragmentary poem about the Revolution of 1905. They represent Pasternak's most signal attempt to break out of the confines of his chamber poetry, and as such they were particularly welcomed and always singled out by Soviet critics. But although in "The Year 1905" the famous *Potyomkin* mutiny and the De-cember uprising in Moscow play a conspicuous part, the poet is at his best in the autobiographical and purely lyrical sections of the poem. In "Lieutenant Schmidt" the stress is more on the hero's psychology and inner qualms and battles than on the social-political implications of the events in which he played the central part. Both poems are marked by a much greater metrical freedom and variety than most of Pasternak's other lyrical poems.

Attempts to get outside himself, to reconcile his own personal views with the demands which Soviet society makes on its poets, were reflected also in some poems in *The Second Birth* (1932), but they too ended in failure. All that Pasternak could say of Socialism was that its remoteness appeared to him "close by." But this ambiguous and paradoxical statement did not satisfy his Communist critics, who again accused him of keeping aloof from the problems of the day.

Many of the poems in *The Second Birth* have the Caucasus and its majes-tic nature for their background and echo Lermontov. One of the best describes, with true Pasternakian felicity and freshness of expression and an acute sense of sound associations, a vision of Tiflis from the mountains. But it is characteristic of Pasternak that from the majestic splendors of the Caucasus he longs to go "back home, to the vastness of the sadness-inspiring apartment," that he is yearning for "the sedate life, such as it is." He aspires to simplicity and even dumbness, voicing these sentiments in a poem which echoes Tyutchev's famous "Silentium":

> There are, in the experience of great poets,
> Elements of such naturalness,

That, once having tasted of them,
It is impossible not to end in utter dumbness.
Having established one's relationship with all that is,
And being familiar with life in the future,
It is impossible not to fall, ultimately, as into a heresy,
Into an unheard-of simplicity.

For more than ten years after the publication of *The Second Birth*, Pasternak published little other than translations. But in 1934–35 his reputation in the Soviet Union stood at its highest. He was often spoken of as the greatest living Soviet poet. In 1935 he was chosen, with Ehrenburg, Babel, and others, to represent Soviet writers at the International Anti-Fascist Congress in Paris (which he attended very reluctantly). But the next year saw the unleashing of a campaign against him in the press and within literary organizations (more about this campaign will be said in Chapters 21 and 25, while Pasternak's wartime poetry will be discussed in Chapter 25).

Pasternak's prose is very much like his poetry. It is characterized by the same freshness of vision and felicity of expression. His book of short stories, of which the earliest was written in 1915 and the latest in 1924, was published in 1925 under the title *Rasskazy* (*Stories*) and reissued in 1933 as *Vozdushnye puti* (*Aerial Ways*). In the 1933 edition one of the earlier stories was omitted and its place taken by a fragment called "Povest'" ("A Tale"), first published in 1929 in a literary magazine and later issued in book form. It is an episode, of obviously autobiographical inspiration, connected through its hero with *Spektorsky*, Pasternak's narrative poem. Of Pasternak's early stories, only one, "Aerial Ways," has any relation to the Revolution, and in this the Revolution forms only the background to its psychological theme. Of the others, the longest, the most characteristic, and the most satisfying is "Detstvo Luvers" ("The Childhood of Luvers"). It is a story of a few years in the life of a girl on the verge of puberty. The story is plotless. Outward events are described only so far as they are in correspondence with the inner states of the heroine's mind. In portraying them, Pasternak alternately proceeds from the inside outward and from the outside inward, thus recording the deep subterranean currents in the girl's mind while at the same time describing the objects outside her that take part in her life and affect her. He uses the method of accumulating infinitesimals, somewhat reminiscent of Proust's, but Pasternak is both more concise and more elliptical. There is also some influence of Rilke's *Aufzeichnungen des Malte Laurids Brigge*. As a boy, Pasternak met Rilke when his father painted Rilke's portrait. Later Rilke corresponded with the elder Pasternak and followed with interest the beginnings of his son's career. For his part, Boris Pasternak was always a great admirer of Rilke's poetry, some of which he translated. In his prose, Rilke's influence is very strongly felt in *Povest'*. It was to the memory of Rilke that Pasternak dedicated his "autobiographical tale" *Okhrannaya gramota* (*Safe Conduct*, 1931). Written in highly personal style which, in its associativeness and ellipticalness, is close to that of his poetry, it is by no means a conventional autobiography (it is only about one hundred pages long) but rather a record of inner experiences set against the background of a few salient episodes, of which the main are Pasternak's acquaintance with the composer Scriabin; the year spent in Marburg studying philosophy under Hermann Cohen; the short trip to Berlin which followed upon a rejected marriage proposal; the visit to Venice; the return to Moscow and the first steps in literature, including the acquaintance with Mayakovsky. After that there is a big chronological jump, and the book ends with a dramatic personal account of Mayakovsky's sensational suicide and its impact on Pasternak. According to Pasternak, who at one time was greatly fascinated by Mayakovsky, the latter "had the novelty of the times climatically in his blood" and was "strange with all the strangeness of the epoch, as yet half unfulfilled." *Safe Conduct*, in which Pasternak's individualism is given free play, met with cool reception on the part of Soviet critics.

One of the leaders of pre-Revolutionary Acmeism, Osip Emilievich Man- **Mandelstam** delstam was one of the major poets of the pre-Soviet period of Russian **(1891–1938)** literature. But he was also one of the few poets of that brilliant period who not only survived the Revolution but continued to hold a small but distinguished place on the Soviet literary scene. Mandelstam's first two books of poems, *Kamen'* (*The Stone*, 1913; second, enlarged edition, 1916) and *Tristia* (1922), revealed him as a poet of great originality, a subtle and fastidious craftsman, steeped in classical and Western European culture. In the words of Mirsky, "Mandelstam's diction attains sometimes to splendid 'Latin' sonority that is unrivaled by any Russian poet since Lomonosov."[3] His poetry had at times a somewhat "bookish" appearance—he was often stimulated by literary and historical themes, by music and architecture —but these themes were lyrically reinterpreted and transmuted, and through them pierced a profound personal concern and experience. Their form was always original and arresting.

The Revolution found in Mandelstam a detached and somewhat bewildered spectator. Not a prolific writer at any time, he published relatively little after 1923, when the poems from *Tristia*, together with some new ones, were brought out under the simple title *Vtoraya kniga* (*The Second Book*). In 1928 appeared his last volume of poetry, just as simply entitled *Stikhotvoreniya* (*Poems*). It contained poems from the earlier collections and some new ones, written between 1922 and 1925. In some of the recent poems there were distant and very personal echoes of the Revolution, but on the whole it seemed to have had little impact on the poet. Here and

[3] Mirsky, *Contemporary Russian Literature*, 259-60.

there a certain affinity with Pasternak could be felt, but Mandelstam remained throughout a more careful, more restrained, and more classical artist. Until 1933, Mandelstam continued to publish his work now and then in different Soviet magazines that were broad-minded enough to print a poet so obviously out of tune with the Revolution. Some very interesting poems appeared in 1931 and 1932 in *Novy Mir*, and in 1933, *Zvezda* carried a very personal account of his travels in Armenia (earlier he had published in *Novy Mir* a sequence of twelve magnificent poems inspired by Armenia).

Like Pasternak, Mandelstam wrote some interesting prose, but mostly nonfictional. Of his pre-Revolutionary essays Mirsky said that they contained "perhaps the most remarkable, unprejudiced, and independent things that have ever been said on modern Russian civilization and on the art of poetry."[4] Some of those essays, together with some new ones, were included in the volume *O poèzii* (*On Poetry*, 1928).

Earlier Mandelstam had published a little volume of prose under the title *Shum vremeni* (*The Noise of Time*, 1925). It consisted of autobiographical pieces in most of which Mandelstam recalled his childhood and adolescence, trying to recapture the flavor of that period—"the noise and growth of an epoch." The Russian *fin de siècle*, the stately splendor of Imperial St. Petersburg, the peculiar, stuffy atmosphere of the bourgeois Jewish home in which he grew up, the modern "Anglicized" school (the same school to which Vladimir Nabokov went) in which he was educated—everything was brought to life in a distinctive, personal, inimitable manner. One of the best pieces in the book is "Knizhny shkap" ("The Bookcase"). Here, through a description of the family bookcase and its successive "geological strata," Mandelstam paints a suggestive synthetic portrait of the Russian and Russian-Jewish intelligentsia of the nineties. This picture grows out of a recollection of a volume of Nadson's poems, which Mandelstam aptly calls "the key to the epoch." Like many of his poems, the book reveals Mandelstam's keen sense of history and of the passing of time. It is his ability to encompass the general within the concrete that gives particular value to his picture of *le temps perdu*.

In 1928 a new edition of *The Noise of Time* appeared under the title *Egipetskaya marka* (*The Egyptian Stamp*), so named after an additional longish piece, which was different from the rest in that it contained some elements of fiction, even though it could not be pigeonholed in any genre. Unlike the shorter pieces in *The Noise of Time*, it is a sort of novella, with a first-person narrator, who is Mandelstam himself, and a third-person protagonist, who is both Mandelstam and another, vaguely identifiable, person. According to one Soviet critic, "The Egyptian Stamp" is stylized in the manner of a manuscript containing two texts, of which the second consists

---

[4] *Ibid.*, 260.

of "marginal notes," the autobiographical asides.[5] The over-all effect is that of a novella with an autobiographical underlayer and surrealistic overtones.

After 1933, Mandelstam disappeared from the literary scene, and nothing was known about him for certain in the outside world. After World War II there were all sorts of stories and rumors about his fate, including one which reported that he had perished at the hands of the Germans in a concentration camp overrun by them in central Russia. One thing that seemed to be certain was that he was no longer alive. Gradually, by the early sixties, his story had been pieced together. It turned out that he had been arrested in 1934 for writing an anti-Stalin epigram and exiled to a small town in northeastern Russia. There he made an attempt to commit suicide by throwing himself from a window, whereupon his wife appealed to the powers that be and asked permission for him to choose another place of exile. Mandelstam was then allowed (the permission, it is said, emanating from Stalin himself) to go to Voronezh, a large town in central Russia with some nineteenth-century literary associations. His term of exile expired in 1937, and he returned to Moscow, where he and his wife led a rather precarious existence for just under a year. Then he was rearrested in a sanatorium in which he was undergoing treatment. Accused of counterrevolutionary activity during the height of the Stalin purges, he was sentenced to five years of exile in one of the Far Eastern camps. He did not reach his final destination and died in a transit camp in Vladivostok on December 27, 1938, while awaiting the opening of navigation. From the *Memoirs* of Mandelstam's widow, smuggled out of Russia and published abroad in 1970, one can see that various stories about Mandelstam having survived beyond 1938 and having reached the Magadan forced-labor camp were current in Russia.

A great deal of Mandelstam's unpublished poetry, as well as some prose, came to light and was smuggled out to the West in the 1960's, leading to the publication of his *Collected Works* in three volumes, under the editorship of Boris Filippov and me. A small number of the poems was also published in various Soviet periodicals and collections, while his essay on Dante, written about 1931, appeared in Moscow as a separate booklet in 1967.[6] However, a volume of Mandelstam's collected poetry announced several times for publication in the Soviet Union in the course of the past ten years,

[5] See N. Berkovsky, *Tekushchaya literatura* (*Current Literature*), 176. Cf. also Clarence Brown's fine Introduction to his *The Prose of Osip Mandelstam: The Noise of Time—Theodosia—The Egyptian Stamp*.

[6] Prior to its publication in Volume II of Mandelstam's *Collected Works* (in Russian), it was published in English (unfortunately in a translation from a somewhat defective manuscript) in the special "Homage to Dante" issue of *Books Abroad* (May, 1965). In 1967 it was published in book form, with some critical comments, in the Soviet Union. There was also a Spanish translation, apparently made from the English, in a volume published in Madrid in 1965 in conjunction with *Books Abroad: Dante en su centenario*.

has never materialized. There have been many translations of Mandelstam's work, both poetry and prose, into other languages, not only Western but also Polish, Czech, Serbo-Croatian, and so on. Mandelstam is thus one of those Russian writers whose work is better known outside his own country than within it. But, of course, in Russian literary circles his unpublished work is known in manuscript (and partly through the Filippov-Struve edition), and his reputation stands higher than ever. He is recognized as one of the most significant modern Russian poets and one of the very few who straddle the pre-Revolutionary and post-Revolutionary periods and transcend that division.[7]

Tikhonov
Nikolay Tikhonov's development in the late twenties was complex and devious. Constantly on the lookout for new forms, he fell under a strong influence of Khlebnikov, Mayakovsky, and Pasternak. At the same time he tried to move closer to Soviet realities. Temperamentally romantic, he fell in love with the Soviet East, and many of his poems of this period have for their setting the Caucasus and central Asia. He was attracted both by their exoticism and by the pioneering efforts to bring modern civilization to Lermontov's "drowsy East." The old Orient satisfied his romantic craving for the picturesque, while the work of the new Soviet "Kulturträgers" appealed to his innate desire for adventure. Even when he voiced orthodox Communist sentiments and glorified the civilizing mission of the Soviets, he romanticized and hyperbolized the reality.

In the late twenties Tikhonov tried to combine technical experimentation with a satirical handling of contemporary social-political themes. In the book, characteristically entitled *Poiski geroya* (*Search for a Hero*, 1927), one can hear echoes of Pasternak, Mayakovsky, and Khlebnikov (compare, for instance, the poem "The Slaughter of Drones"). Tikhonov's poems of the early thirties (*Yurga, Pesni o Kakhetii*), in their "exoticism," once more recall Gumilyov, but in their ideological orientation are irreproachably orthodox. Their background is the sovietization of central Asia and the Caucasus. This romantic Oriental theme was prominent in the literature of the First Five-Year Plan. Like Pasternak, Tikhonov at one time specialized in translating Georgian poets.

In 1935 Tikhonov published a book of poems called *Ten' druga* (*The Shadow of a Friend*). Its title was suggested by the well-known poem of Batyushkov, an early-nineteenth-century poet, and the first poem had a line from it for its motto ("I was leaving the misty shores of Albion"). The book

---

[7] For a fuller account of Mandelstam's post-Revolutionary period see the introductions to the three-volume edition of *Sobranie sochineniy* (*Collected Works*, 1964–69) by Clarence Brown, Gleb Struve, and others. See also his widow's remarkable memoirs, published in 1970 in New York both in Russian and in translation under the title *Hope Against Hope*.

recalls Batyushkov (as well as the Acmeists) by the plasticity of its imagery and the classical clarity of its diction. But its spirit is quite different from Batyushkov's. It is a lyrical diary of a visit to various European countries— Poland, France, Belgium, and England—which are seen through Soviet spectacles. In the last poem, called "The Gas Mask," the poet sees the mask —"this head, neither a fish's nor a bird's, looming, tongueless, on man's shoulders" replacing "the living human countenance"—as the uncanny symbol of the epoch:

> Gas mask!
>   within your sticky rubber
>   Enclosed is Europe's head,
>   And there is no more laughter or smile,
>   The forests do not murmur, and the grasses do not rustle.

There are evocations of Parisian crowds, of English miners, of Nazi victims in Germany, of "Asturian heroes," and of Abyssinians sharing the last drop of water with the deceived Italian soldiers. Beside all them the poet places the name of "the land of lands" and voices his faith that the day will come when, stuffed with straw, the gas mask will be hung on the door as a target for children's games, just as the Assyrians used to hang motley masks "to drive away sickness and the devils." This optimistic faith, rooted in Soviet patriotism, inspires the whole book. Europe is shown as a contrast to "the land of lands." But, whether or not one shares Tikhonov's political outlook, one cannot help appreciating the poetic quality of the best among these poems.

It was also in the late twenties—and parallel with his development toward realism—that Tikhonov began to use more and more frequently the medium of prose. He wrote once, "When a poet writes prose he merely extends the range of his work," and these words can well apply to him. In his prose he remains true to his romantic realism. He showed this in his first book of stories, *Riskovanny chelovek* (*The Venturesome Man*, 1927). Not content with the elementary, superficial truth of real life, Tikhonov perceives beyond it another and different truth. It is, in his own words, "the truth of artistic perception which merges into the subtle art of artistic lie" and which transforms everyday life, so that from a mere accident it is turned into something many-sided and general. Tikhonov's art is based on a vision of reality, but the reality is condensed and turned into something almost fantastic. He likes sharp, definite outlines, bright colors, and dramatic situations, and he prefers to show his characters in action. Like the earlier revolutionary romantics of the dynamic-prose period, he has an aversion to psychological analysis. Curiously enough, while in his poetry he tended to become less of a romantic and more of a realist, in his prose he was moving in the opposite direction. A story like "Klyatva v tumane"

("An Oath in the Fog," 1933), with its Caucasian setting, is full of romanticism, of adventures, of unusual characters. What distinguishes Tikhonov from writers like Vsevolod Ivanov and Nikitin is his interest in the plot, his careful construction, and his orderly narrative. This is particularly noticeable in his stories about the war and the Civil War—in *Voyna* (*War*) and *Klinki i tachanki* (*Blades and Chariots*).

Tikhonov's style is in keeping with his romantic realism. It is compact, robust, and picturesque; in its wise economy one feels the influence of his poetic training, of his Acmeist heritage. He is also in no small degree indebted to Kipling, both in the technique of his stories and in the spirit of romantic realism which pervades them. Like Kipling's, many of his stories deal with military life, and often their action is set on the eastern fringes of Russia. His characters also have a Kiplingesque touch.

Selvinsky (1899–1967) and Constructivism The movement in poetry away from the romantic and lyric toward the realistic and concrete found its expression in the late twenties in the school of Constructivism. Its chief theoretician and critic was Kornely Lutsianovich Zelinsky (1896–1970); its principal exponent in poetry, Ilya (Karl) Lvovich Selvinsky. Born in a bourgeois family in Simferopol, Selvinsky studied at first in a Catholic monastery school in Constantinople, then in the high school at Evpatoria. He took part in the Civil War, served as a sailor and worked in a factory, and then went to the University of Moscow. His first book of poems was published in 1926, and he soon became the acknowledged leader of the Constructivists.

Constructivism as a movement was rather vague and heterogeneous. It had some points in common with Futurism, especially in its admiration of modern technology, but it did not share the Futurists' wholesale rejection of the art and culture of the past. It laid a great stress on the principle of "organization" in a poetic work and tried to introduce into poetry the methods of prose. It advocated what it called the "local method," which consisted in subordinating the word pattern of a poem to its subject, in "localizing" it stylistically. Of all the nominal practitioners of Constructivism, Selvinsky was the only one who tried to practice consistently what he preached.

His principal works during this period were *Ulyalaevshchina* (*Ulyalaevism*, 1927), *Zapiski poeta* (*Notebooks of a Poet*, 1928), *Pushtorg* (1929), and *Pao-Pao* (1932). They are all long, narrative poems, with plots and a number of characters. *Ulyalaevshchina* is almost a novel in verse, with a complicated plot line, describing the partisan and bandit movements in eastern Russia and portraying several cleverly drawn and sharply individualized characters. The plot is somewhat blurred in its complexity—this is one of the defects of the poem—but in itself the tendency toward plot, away from purely lyric forms, is characteristic of Constructivism as it was understood by Selvinsky. Selvinsky is a realist, or more precisely, a naturalist, and *Ulyalaevshchina* reveals his greediness for life. One critic has described him as a "temperamental rationalist." His vocabulary, his syntax, and his irregular meters were strongly influenced by Mayakovsky. But he also introduced some innovations of his own, such as using queer typographical devices, punctuating his words with periods and question marks to indicate pauses and changes of intonation, and mixing Latin characters with Russian. Some of these innovations looked like experiments for the sake of experiment, but some had inward justification and showed a feeling for words and a sense of rhythm. Both in *Ulyalaevshchina* and in the autobiographical *Notebooks of a Poet*, Selvinsky resorts to dialogues and introduces long discourses on political and aesthetic subjects. In *Notebooks of a Poet* he displays his gift as a parodist in clever and pointed parodies of several Soviet poets.

Pao-Pao is a play in verse and was supposed to be a contribution to the Five-Year Plan literature. It is the story of an ape, who symbolizes simultaneously the low, animal instincts of men and bourgeois culture. Introduced into the beneficent proletarian environment of a Soviet factory and discovering there Marxism, the only true ideology, Selvinsky's ape becomes human. Taken at its face value, the poem, though it has some clever points, is absurd. But Selvinsky may have written it tongue in cheek.

Another Constructivist was Eduard Bagritsky (pseudonym of Eduard Georgievich Dzybin), a Jew and a native of Odessa, one of the most talented and attractive poets of his generation. His first poems appeared in print in 1914. In 1917 he was with the Russian Army on the Persian front and during the Revolution fought in the Red Army. His first volume of poetry, *Yugozapad* (*South-West*, 1928), in some points resembled Tikhonov's early romantic realism. It was possible to trace in it the same influences—of Gumilyov and the Acmeists, of the English ballads (which he translated), and of Kipling. One of his favorite heroes seems to have been Tyll Eulenspiegel. A decided romantic who looked at the Revolution from outside, Bagritsky saw it as something strange and alien but recognized its elemental, sweeping force. In one of his best lyric poems, in which one feels the winds of the Revolution blowing about, he speaks of "strange constellations rising above us," of "strange banners unfurling over us," and likens himself to "a rusty oak leaf" bound to follow in the wake of these strange banners. In some of his poems, however, he tried to draw closer to the Revolution and to portray it other than subjectively. Such is his famous *Duma pro Opanasa* (*The Lay About Opanas*), which for a long time was regarded by Soviet critics as one of the masterpieces of Soviet poetry. It is a long poem, in which the lyric and the narrative elements are intermingled, telling the story of a simple Ukrainian peasant, Opanas, who flees from a Communist food-

Bagritsky
(1897–1934)

requisitioning detachment commanded by Kogan, a Jew. While fleeing, Opanas encounters the "Green" anarchist band of Makhno and is forced to join it. When Kogan falls into the hands of Makhno, Opanas is ordered to shoot him. He decides to let Kogan escape, but Kogan refuses the offer and chooses death, which he faces with proud indifference. Later on, the Makhno bands are defeated by the Reds, and Opanas is taken prisoner. Questioned by the Red commander Kotovsky, he admits having shot Kogan and submits docilely to his own execution.

The Lay About Opanas is a heroic revolutionary poem. The underlying romanticism of its conception is unquestionable. In form it has been influenced by Ukrainian folk poetry and by Taras Shevchenko, the national poet of the Ukraine. Its free and quick-changing meter recalls Ukrainian folk songs. There are in it some beautiful evocations of the Ukrainian landscape. In its combination of naïve simplicity and romantic hyperbolism it also derives from folk poetry.

In his later poems, collected in *Pobediteli* (*The Victors*) and *Poslednyaya noch* (*The Last Night*), Bagritsky tried to identify himself even more closely with the Revolution and Socialism, but at heart he remained a romantic; his sense of life, and zest for it, saved him from becoming didactic or doctrinaire. In the autobiographical narrative poem *Fevral'* (*February*), which was published posthumously, the romantic note is again sounded very clearly. But *South-West* (for which Bagritsky made a careful and small selection from the poems written during the first ten years of his poetic activity) remains, I think, his best book, full of genuinely spontaneous poetry and striking a distinct personal note. Such poems as "Pigeons," "The Watermelon," and "The Cigarette Box" deserve a place in any anthology of modern Russian poetry.

Bagritsky belonged nominally to the Constructivist group, but his connection with it was rather tenuous, though he did apply the "local method." His premature death in 1934 was a distinct loss to Soviet poetry.

Zabolotsky (1903–58) An even more original and interesting phenomenon in the literature of the late twenties was Nikolay Alexeyevich Zabolotsky. He first appeared in print in 1926, soon after graduating from the Herzen Pedagogical Institute. His first book of poems, *Stolbtsy* (*Columns*, 1929), met with sharp criticism and was apparently withdrawn from circulation. An even more violent controversy arose over his poem "Torzhestvo zemledeliya" ("The Triumph of Agriculture," 1933), in which some Communist critics saw a lampoon on collective farming. It is difficult to say whether in it the poet was mocking the Soviet society or the modern world in general or laughing at his readers.

More than any other poet of his generation, Zabolotsky was impressed and influenced by Khlebnikov, and in several of his poems there are references and allusions to him. To Khlebnikov can be traced his sophisticated primitivism and the liberties which he takes with conventional meters, without abandoning the syllabic principle and resorting to Mayakovsky's accentual verse. He often makes use of parody, and at times some of his serious poetry reads almost like nonsense verse. His mastery of his medium and his originality are beyond dispute, and he had and still has great, even enthusiastic, admirers, but his stature as a poet is still a moot question.

In the thirties Zabolotsky's poetry became a subject of heated debate. At a meeting of the Leningrad writers, to whom Zabolotsky belonged, Nikolay Tikhonov suggested that Zabolotsky would have to choose between "committing an artistic suicide" and "revamping his poetic household" by coming to closer grips with Soviet realities. Whether or not of his own volition, Zabolotsky disappeared from literature for several years. He made a brief comeback in 1937 with *Vtoraya kniga* (*The Second Book*), in which there was not much left of his earlier bizarre, surrealistic world or of prosodic experiments. The grotesque urban and suburban settings of his earlier poems were replaced by pictures of nature pure and simple or of nature overcome by man on the road to technological progress. The verse was now characterized by Neoclassical, "Acmeistic" limpidity and sonority. In some of the nature poems there was an undercurrent of symbolism, reminiscent of Tyutchev, while at times the poet seemed to be carrying on a *sotto voce* dialogue with Tyutchev.

The publication of *The Second Book* was followed by another and even longer disappearance from literature. Little is known about Zabolotsky's life during the next ten years. It is known, however, that he was arrested and exiled during the purges. A letter he is alleged to have written to Tikhonov, asking the latter to intercede on behalf of himself and his fellow prisoners, seems to have circulated in literary circles.[8] Some of the poems published subsequently indicate that he was in exile in Siberia,[9] while others written about the same time obviously originated in the Caucasus (and it may be noted that Zabolotsky later became one of the most popular Soviet translators of Georgian poetry).

Zabolotsky made his final reappearance in Soviet literature in 1947–48, with some poems in literary magazines and, later, a book unpretentiously entitled *Stikhotvoreniya* (*Poems*). It included some poems from *The Second Book*, as well as poems written in the 1940's, and also a translation into modern Russian of the famous twelfth-century work *The Lay of the Raid of Igor*. After that, although he continued to write original poetry, for five years Zabolotsky published nothing but translations. His own poems began to appear again in 1953. In 1957, a year before his premature death (his health had been undermined by the years of exile), another volume

---

[8] See R. Ivanov-Razumnik, *Pisatelskie sudby* (*Writers' Destinies*), 51.

[9] See B. Filippov's Introduction to Zabolotsky's *Stikhotvoreniya* (Poems) (ed. by G. Struve and B. Filippov).

called *Poems* was published. It contained both earlier and recent original work and many translations from German and Georgian. The original poems ranged from 1932 to 1956. Some of the earlier ones were printed there for the first time. The volume also contained a revised version of the curious long poem "Lodeynikov," which had been severely criticized at the time of its original publication in 1933.

All of Zabolotsky's late poetry displays the same fastidious craftsmanship. Most of it has, at least on the surface, a Neoclassical ring and scarcely reminds one of the early disciple of Khlebnikov; but here and there, under the surface, one glimpses the old ironic undertones and curious semantic shifts. In many ways the late Zabolotsky is just as unlike the overwhelming majority of his Soviet contemporaries as was the early one, and Soviet critics are sometimes at a loss what to make of his poetry, though willing to give its due to his mastery.[10]

Bezymensky (b. 1898) and Other Proletarian Poets

Unlike the earlier Cosmists of the Smithy group, the younger proletarian poets—those born between 1898 and 1904—represented the realistic trend. At one time the leading role among them was played by Alexander Ilyich Bezymensky. Born in Zhitomir, he began working for an underground Social Democratic organization in 1916 and a year later joined the Communist party. He played an active part in various proletarian literary organizations and in the early twenties was one of the ringleaders of the opposition to fellow travelers. He became the recognized bard of the Communist party and the Young Communist League and the principal rival of Demyan Bedny for the unofficial poet-laureateship.

If the nineteenth-century "civic" poets followed the famous dictum of Nekrasov that "a poet you need not be but you must be a citizen," Bezymensky went one better, proclaiming that he was first a member of the Communist party and only then a poet. In one of his poems he uses the much publicized formula: "I carry my Party membership card not in my pocket but inside myself." To the traditional "sentimental" themes of the

---

[10] See I. Rodnyanskaya, "Poèziya N. Zabolotskogo" ("The Poetry of N. Zabolotsky"), *Voprosy Literatury* (*Problems of Literature*), No. 1 (1959). The author of this interesting appraisal of Zabolotsky suspects the Acmeistic polish of some of his poems to be tongue-in-cheek. A very interesting discussion of the principal motifs of Zabolotsky's poetry will be found in the above-mentioned article by B. Filippov and in the English Introduction to the same volume by A. Rannit, who sees Zabolotsky as "a visionary at the crossroads of Expressionism and Classicism." Cf. also V. Markov's preface to his anthology *Priglushonnye golosa* (*The Suppressed Voices*) and his "Mysli o russkom futurizme" ("Thoughts About Russian Futurism") in *Novy Zhurnal*, No. 38 (1954), where he describes Zabolotsky as "the last major Russian Futurist." Editions of collected works of Zabolotsky appeared in 1965, almost simultaneously, in the Soviet Union and in the West. The Soviet edition did not, however, include some important early poems.

"bourgeois" poets he opposed the matter-of-fact realities. Let others think of spring, he said,

> But I, as I walk along, keep thinking
> Of the cost price of Soviet goods.

He expressed his contempt for love poetry when he wrote defiantly:

> Some fear for girlish lips,
> And I, for smoking stacks.

His predominant mood was one of joyful optimism. In one of his poems he wrote that "if the heart of a Communist cell could for a moment become a fifty-kopeck piece, it would contain two kopecks' worth of bitterness and forty-five kopecks' worth of joy" (what happens to the remaining three kopecks is not clear). One of his books was called *Tak pakhnet zhizn'* (*That's What Life Smells Like*). But he saw the chief aim of a proletarian poet as the discovery of world revolution "behind every small trifle."

Bezymensky was strongly influenced by Mayakovsky and did his best to imitate the latter's declamatory style and coarse language. In his longer poems, such as *Komsomolia*, he uses, like Mayakovsky, a rapid succession of different contrasting meters. But he totally lacks Mayakovsky's sense of rhythm and keenness of vision: he explains and describes things rather than shows what he sees. Much of his poetry is mere rhymed journalism. In his earlier verse the life of the Communist party was almost the only subject. Later, in *Puti* (*Pathways*, 1925), his field of vision was somewhat enlarged and his official optimism mitigated by the sudden realization of the tenacity of old-world instincts beneath the Communist surface of Soviet life.

Bezymensky reached the height of his popularity in 1929–31. His play in verse, *Vystrel* (*A Shot*, 1930), caused a sensation—but of a political, rather than a literary, nature—and gave rise to a general discussion about the methods of proletarian literature. It was deliberately apsychological and propagandistic; its characters were schematic embodiments of various problems of Soviet life. It was meant as a satire but lacked the pungency and brilliance of Mayakovsky's satirical plays. *Noch nachalnika politotdela* (*The Night of a Chief of Politsection*) was another purely political poem, dealing with the work of the political instructor on a collective farm. It lacks structural and stylistic unity and is a rather incongruous mixture of Mayakovsky with Koltsov and Nadson. It is both more realistic and more sentimental than Bezymensky's earlier work. In line with the general evolution of Soviet literature Bezymensky discarded his earlier experimental proclivities and called upon Soviet poets to learn from Pushkin and other Russian classics.

Closely akin to Bezymensky was another poet of the Young Communist League, Alexander Zharov (b. 1904). His early poetic style also derived from Mayakovsky, while his choice of themes was similar to Bezymensky's, with more stress on everyday realities.

More talented, and at the same time less political and more personal, were Mikhail Golodny (pseudonym of Mikhail Epstein, 1903–48) and Mikhail Svetlov (1903–64). Svetlov's Civil War poem "Grenada," with its folk-song accents and lilting rhythm, enjoyed great popularity and foreshadowed the later trend toward songs.

Iosif Utkin (1903–42), a Jew born in Manchuria, attracted attention with his poem *The Tale About the Redheaded Motele, Mr. Inspector, Rabbi Isaiah, and Commissar Bloch*, which described the impact of the Revolution on provincial Jewish life and was full of Jewish local color. Utkin's lyric poetry was characterized by heightened emotionalism. Soviet critics spoke of the influence of Esenin on him. He was killed in the Soviet-German War.

Somewhat apart from these proletarian poets stood Vissarion Sayanov (pseudonym of Vissarion Makhnin, 1903–59). Son of a political exile in Siberia, he joined the Communist party as a young man and fought in the Civil War. Later he was active in the LAPP. His early poetry had little in common with Bezymensky's. His main theme was the Civil War, and he treated it romantically and heroically, in a spirit of virile optimism reminiscent of Gumilyov. His careful handling of form was also influenced by the Acmeists. His predilection for classical meters, at the time when most young poets followed Mayakovsky and took liberties with Russian prosody, singled him out among his contemporaries. Later he turned to political and social themes, but in these poems (which include the inevitable poem about Lenin) one misses the attractive personal accent of his more youthful poetry. Sayanov also wrote a narrative poem, with a detective adventure plot, called "Kartonazhnaya Amerika" ("Cardboard America").

Inber (b. 1893) and Others It is impossible to enumerate all the poets who were active in the late twenties and early thirties. Some of them we shall meet later, but a few may be mentioned here briefly.

Vera Inber began publishing before the Revolution, imitating Akhmatova but lacking Akhmatova's sincerity and depth. In the twenties she joined the Constructivists, but her connection with the movement, like Bagritsky's, was superficial. She exchanged her intimate lyricism for revolutionary themes and showed a tendency toward narrative poetry, which is particularly noticeable in the book entitled *Synu, kotorogo net* (*To the Son Who Does Not Exist*, 1927).

Another Constructivist was Vladimir Lugovskoy (1901–57), whose first book of poems, *Spolokhi* (*Sheet Lightnings*), appeared in 1926. Most of his early poems were about the Civil War, and there were both Acmeist and Futurist influences in them, but like so many others he later moved toward revolutionary realism and in 1930 joined the RAPP. He wrote some charming poems about children.

Pavel Antokolsky (b. 1896) is another poet on whom the Acmeists (in his case Mandelstam rather than Gumilyov) had a considerable influence. He is a man of culture, and his poetry wears a somewhat bookish air: he often draws inspiration from history and world literature and has made many translations. Soviet critics of the thirties often treated him as a typical representative of "Western" orientation in Soviet literature. One of his major works is a poem about François Villon.

Futurism during this period had lost much of its appeal and popularity. Next to Mayakovsky and Aseyev it was represented by Sergey Tretyakov (1892–1939), who was in the twenties one of the principal theoreticians of the LEF group and an ardent advocate of "factual literature," about which more will be said later.

Among the younger followers of Mayakovsky one of the most talented was Semyon Kirsanov (b. 1906). Kirsanov followed Mayakovsky both in his Soviet thematics and in his interest in formal innovations. Such books of his as *Pritsel* (*Taking Aim*, 1925), *Stikhi v stroyu* (*Verses in Formation*, 1930), and *Udarny kvartal* (*The Shockworkers' Quarter*, 1931), and such longer poems as *Pyatiletka* (*The Five-Year Plan*, 1931) and *Tovarishch Marks* (*Comrade Marx*, 1932) are full of enthusiasm for the Revolution and socialist reconstruction. On the other hand, a book like *Opyty* (*Experiments*, 1927) abounds in technical experiments. The best evidence of Kirsanov's formal inventiveness is to be found in his poem *Zolushka* (*Cinderella*, 1935), in which the "political" element, by no means unimportant, is disguised in the form of a variant of the famous fairy tale, while the author gives free rein to his verbal acrobatics and obviously enjoys them.

Chapter 14. THE DRAMA

Those who visited the Soviet Union in the twenties left with the impression that it was the only country in Europe where there was no crisis in the theater. Theatrical life seemed to be in full swing and the art of the theater blossoming. The names Stanislavsky, Meyerhold, and Tairov were known all over the world, and their art was discussed in Paris, Berlin, and London.

It must be noted, however, that the different and even diametrically opposed tendencies they represented were not purely of Revolutionary growth, that they were all rooted in the pre-Revolutionary Russian theater, and that some of them merely received a fresh impetus from the Revolution. The intense psychological realism of Stanislavsky's Moscow Art Theater, with its tendency to extend the psychological treatment of characters in a play beyond its actual limits and to create, as it were, their personal biographies; the Constructivism of Meyerhold, with his sharply pronounced tendency to subordinate the author and the actors to the supreme will and caprice of the director; the "pure" theater of Tairov, which was just as hostile to psychological realism and naturalism as Meyerhold's but differed from the latter in its tendency toward aesthetic "theatricalization" of reality—all these different theatrical currents had in substance existed before the Revolution. As far as Stanislavsky and Tairov are concerned, the Revolution did not affect to any noteworthy degree their main line of development. But it was not quite so with Meyerhold; the Revolution supplied him with new social and political contents, resulting in what came to be known as "socio-mechanics." The Constructivist technique was subordinated to the class idea.

Soviet Theater

Stanislavsky (with the Moscow Art Theater), Tairov (with the Kamerny Theater), and Meyerhold (with the theater which bore his name) represented the three main currents in modern Russian theater. All the other theaters, especially those which sprang up after the Revolution, were either extensions of them or represented attempts to combine some of their principles. Thus the Vakhtangov Theater combined the methods of Stanislavsky with those of Meyerhold, while the Theater of the Revolution (Alexey Popov), the Realistic Theater (Ohklopkov), and the Leningrad Dramatic Theater (Akimov) followed more or less in the path of Meyerhold, though the influence of Tairov on them could also be discerned. The Theater of the Revolution in particular aimed at a synthesis of different methods. It was also the most consistent in choosing for its productions modern plays with a definite social and political significance. The same stress on modern repertoire was given by the Trades Unions' Theater, but there the method was more realistic.

The Revolution undoubtedly gave a new impetus to theatrical life in Russia. There were several reasons for this. There is no denying, of course, the efforts expended by the Soviet government in fostering theatrical culture, especially in the first years of the Revolution, when it was clearly conscious of the power of the theater as a weapon of propaganda. But one must also take into account the inherent theatrical instinct of the Russian people, with its love of the spectacular. If anything, this theatrical instinct was intensified in the first years of the Revolution, when the theater became one of the means of escaping from the hard and sordid realities of life. Even during the worst years of famine and general misery, theaters in Moscow were crowded, and the numerical increase in theaters and in the number of theatergoers after the Revolution was remarkable. Factory and village-club theaters, children's theaters, theaters of various national minorities (Jewish, Georgian, Armenian, Gypsy, and others)—all these represented either a new departure or a new development in the life of the Russian theater.

The weak spot of the post-Revolutionary Russian theater was the lack of good new dramas. The Russian theater as such has always been infinitely more interesting and significant than the dramatic literature on which it had to rely, but never was the scarcity of good dramatic literature so strikingly laid bare and exemplified as in the modern Russian theater, especially since the Revolution.

The problem of creating a new revolutionary repertoire worried the leaders of the Soviet theater from the very outset. Even before the Revolution the Russian theater, more than any other, had to rely to a large extent on foreign repertoire plays; and what there was of original dramatic literature was, with a few exceptions (such as Gogol's *Government Inspector*), eminently undramatic and untheatrical. Such was, after all, practically the whole theater, not only of Chekhov, but also of Ostrovsky. This explains, in a large measure, the fact that the modern Russian theater, in aspiring toward "theatricalization," went so far in denying the role of the playwright in the art of the theater and either tried to do without him or took the utmost liberties with the dramatic text; hence Meyerhold's well-known fanciful and often distorted adaptations or "stylizations" of classical Russian plays such as *Government Inspector* and Ostrovsky's *Forest*. Foreign plays— for example, those by Ibsen—were similarly distorted. Meyerhold proclaimed the supremacy of the director over the author and the actor. In this he was not alone. His ideas were echoed by Max Reinhardt in Germany and Granville-Barker in England, both of whom saw the way to a rebirth of the art of the theater in its emancipation from the author. This tendency was further increased by the competition which sound motion pictures offered to the theater. But it was Meyerhold who not only pioneered the idea but tried most consistently to bring it to life.

In the Soviet Union, however, parallel with Meyerhold's experiments on this "authorless" path and with the development of the theater along the line of mass performance and of revolutionary festivals (which in a way meant the revival of the ancient and medieval conception of the theater as a mass mystery), the problem of a new repertoire continued to preoccupy those who were concerned with the destinies of the Soviet theater.

In 1927, surveying the achievements of the Soviet theater during the first revolutionary decade, Vladimir Wolkenstein, one of the leading Russian dramatic critics and himself a dramatist of some merit, wrote: "The problem of the new theater is above all the problem of a new repertoire." In summing up the results of ten years of dramatic activity, he was rather optimistic, emphasizing especially "the growing interest taken by the public in the new plays." But Wolkenstein undoubtedly erred on the side of official optimism. Three or four years later Cecil B. De Mille was still asking Zamyatin, "Where are your new plays?" and Zamyatin had to agree with him that there were none. In 1933 the dearth of good contemporary plays was still the keynote of Soviet dramatic criticism. And while Wolkenstein had earlier noted that the public clamored for new plays, Soviet critics now admitted that the theatergoers were tired of what they were being offered in the way of new Soviet plays and showed a renewed interest in classical drama.

Soviet Playwrights

Soviet dramatists of the twenties can be roughly divided into three principal groups. The first and largest group consisted of older writers who had established themselves before the Revolution and represented different currents: Realism, Neorealism, Romanticism, and Futurism. Among them we find Maxim Gorky, Alexey Tolstoy, Zamyatin, Mayakovsky, Trenyov, Lunacharsky, and Wolkenstein. For most of these, playwriting was only a sideline to their other activities. In fact, of those named above, only Wolkenstein devoted himself entirely to the drama. Lunacharsky was more prominent as a literary critic and as the man who in the first years of the Revolution was responsible for the new government's literary and artistic policy. In this capacity he contributed measurably to the development of theatrical culture in the rural areas. His own plays, now justly forgotten, are full of high-sounding revolutionary rhetoric and cheap symbolism; their literary and dramatic value is mediocre. Of the remaining authors, it can be said that their contribution to the post-Revolutionary drama was secondary to the rest of their literary output. Gorky's two post-Revolutionary plays, *Egor*

Bulychev i drugie (*Egor Bulychev and Others*) and *Dostigayev i drugie* (*Dostigayev and Others*), are frankly retrospective in character and represent variations on one of Gorky's favorite themes: the decadence of the Russian bourgeoisie. In technique they are superior to some of Gorky's earlier plays and in sureness of characterization recall some of Gorky's best prose fiction, such as *The Artamonov Business,* to which they are allied in theme. The success of *Egor Bulychev* was greatly helped by the excellent productions of the Moscow Art Theater and the Vakhtangov Theater. But neither of these plays represents a new development in drama.

Alexey Tolstoy's plays written in the twenties are, on the contrary, greatly inferior to those of the earlier period when, of all the Neorealists, he showed himself the most capable of handling well the dramatic form. Two of these post-Revolutionary plays, *Zagovor imperatritsy* (*The Empress' Conspiracy*) and *Azef,* were written in collaboration with the literary historian Pavel Shchogolev and dealt with recent Russian history, which was distorted to suit the official interpretation. Later Tolstoy specialized in historical drama, writing a play about Peter the Great and dramatizing his novel about him. Toward the end of his life he wrote a play about Ivan the Terrible, of which more will be said later.

Mayakovsky's *Mystery-Bouffe* was the first signal success of Soviet drama. It was an impressive grand-scale political satire, with a multitude of characters, both real and allegorical, and was designed for mass action. Its first production provided Meyerhold with an opportunity for bold experiments in stagecraft, but it did not hold its place on the Soviet stage for long, partly because of the technical difficulties of production and partly because its spirit was soon no longer in harmony with the prevalent tendency for realism. Mayakovsky's two pungent satires, *The Bedbug* and *The Bathhouse,* were technically more manageable, but also contained a number of ingenious tricks and novel devices. These fitted in well with Meyerhold's idea of "sociomechanics" and were fully exploited on the stage.

Konstantin Andreyevich Trenyov (1884–1945), who before the Revolution was known as a second-rate realist of the Gorky school, scored a great success with his *Lyubov Yarovaya,* a tense psychological drama enacted against the background of the Civil War. Its heroine is a village teacher, a convinced Bolshevik, who is married to a White officer. This play was one of the big successes of the Moscow Art Theater. Trenyov also wrote some historical plays.

The second group of playwrights consisted of younger writers, mostly fellow travelers, who came into literature after the Revolution. For most of them, too, playwriting was subsidiary to other activities. Among these were Vsevolod Ivanov with his *Bronepoezd No. 14-69* (*Armored Train No. 14-69*), a dynamic play of the Civil War, the first purely Soviet play to be produced by the Moscow Art Theater and one of its greatest post-Revolu-

tionary successes; Bulgakov with his *The Days of the Turbins*; Katayev
with *Kvadratura kruga* (*Squaring of the Circle*) and other satirical plays
of Soviet life; Lavrenyov with *Dym* (*Smoke*; originally called *Revolt*) and
Razlom (*The Break*), two well-constructed plays portraying the dramatic
conflicts arising during the Revolution and the Civil War; Fedin with his
Bakunin v Drezdene (*Bakunin in Dresden*); Seyfullina with her dramatization of *Virineya*; Olesha with his dramatized versions of *Envy* (retitled
A Conspiracy of Feelings) and *The Three Fat Men*, and his *Spisok blago-
deyaniy* (*A List of Blessings*); Gladkov with his *Vataga* (*The Gang*);
Neverov with his dramatization of his own novels, *Baby* (*Womenfolk*) and
Smert' Zakhara (*Zakhar's Death*); Babel with his symbolically realistic
plays of Jewish life, *Zakat* (*The Sunset*) and *Maria*; Leonov with his
Untilovsk and *Usmirenie Badadoshkina* (*The Taming of Badadoshkin*)
and the dramatizations of his novels (*The Badgers* and *Skutarevsky*);
Zayaitsky with several plays for the Children's Theater; and others.

Katayev's plays were for the most part gay, light-hearted comedies satirizing various aspects of Soviet life. *Squaring of the Circle*, which had a great
though not lasting success in the Soviet Union and was well received abroad
(in Paris, for instance, it was successfully revived in the 1949–50 season), is
an amusing skit about Soviet marriage and a grotesquely realistic picture of
the post-Revolutionary student milieu. Other aspects of Soviet life were
treated by Katayev in the same farcical vein in *Doroga tsvetov* (*The Prim-
rose Path*) and other light plays.

The satire in Bulgakov's plays *Zoykina kvartira* (*Zoyka's Apartment*)
and *Bagrovy ostrov* (*The Crimson Island*) was more grim and serious; as a
result both these plays were soon taken out of the repertoire, and Bulgakov
was forced to dramatize other people's works (Gogol, Dickens). His
dramatization of Gogol's *Dead Souls* enjoyed a great success at the Moscow
Art Theater, but was never published in Russia. He also wrote a play and a
novel about Molière. Bulgakov's "rediscovered" dramatic works will be
discussed in their proper chronological context.

The third group of playwrights consisted of younger writers who more
or less specialized in writing for the theater. The most prominent among
them were Alexander Afinogenov (1904–41), Vladimir Kirshon (1902–38),
Nikolay Pogodin (1900–62), Vsevolod Vishnevsky (1900–51), Alexey Fayko
(b. 1893), Boris Romashov (1895–1958), and Nikolay Erdman (b. 1902).
Most of the writers of this group continued to write in the thirties, and some
of them we shall meet later. All were realists and wrote almost exclusively
about contemporary Soviet subjects. Of plays popular in the twenties may
be mentioned Fayko's *Chelovek s portfelem* (*The Man with the Briefcase*),
a social-psychological problem drama, and Erdman's *Mandat* (*Mandate*), a
satirical comedy full of Gogolian verve, produced by Meyerhold. Its author

became later a victim of one of the purges but after Stalin's death reappeared in Moscow.

On the whole, the evolution of the Soviet drama followed the general trend of developments in literature. In the early period the romantically heroic treatment of revolutionary themes prevailed. There was also a large number of naïve and primitive propaganda plays, most of which soon vanished into oblivion. They dealt with topical subjects, were stuffed with political speeches, and portrayed crude black-and-white characters. Among the later propaganda plays of better quality may be mentioned Sergey Tretyakov's *Rychi, Kitay!* (*Roar, China!*), influenced by Mayakovsky's conception of poster art.

The second period was marked by pronounced realistic tendencies in the treatment of contemporary subjects—the Civil War, the changed ways of life, and various problems raised by the Revolution. As in fiction, there was a reversion toward psychological realism in the drama.

Chapter 15. LITERARY CRITICISM AND CONTROVERSIES

In keeping with the quantitative and qualitative growth of Soviet literature in the mid-twenties, and with the variety of currents represented in it, the period was characterized by a variety of critical opinions and by sharp clashes of conflicting points of view.

The Formalists

Not a small part in these literary controversies was played by so-called Formalism, or, as some of its adherents preferred to call it, the "formal method" in the science of literature and in literary criticism. Until the end of the twenties the Formalists were the most consistent and active opponents of the officially sponsored Marxist, sociological approach to literature.

The origins of Formalism can be traced back to two main Russian sources. On the one hand, it was influenced by the two schools in the Russian *Literaturwissenschaft*, which are linked respectively with the names of two great nineteenth-century scholars: Alexander Veselovsky (1838–1906), of St. Petersburg, and Alexander Potebnya (1835–1891), of Kharkov. The former initiated in Russia the so-called school of "historical" poetics and made an important contribution to the study of comparative literature. The latter, who was primarily a specialist in linguistics, founded the school of linguisticopsychological poetics. Both broke sharply away from the prevalent nineteenth-century tradition, felt equally in literary criticism and in literary scholarship, which had attached paramount importance to the social content and message in literature.

On the other hand, Formalism was greatly indebted to modern Russian poetry, to Symbolism and its subsequent outgrowths. Chronologically speaking, Formalism as a distinct school in the science of literature originated more or less simultaneously with Futurism, and some of its more extreme representatives were closely connected with the latter. But the bases of the formal method, in the broad sense of that term, had been laid down first by the literary-historical and linguistic studies of Veselovsky and Potebnya—as well as the kindred movements outside Russia, especially in Germany—and second by the poetry and poetics of Symbolism, more particularly in the person of Andrey Bely (and, to a lesser extent, Bryusov). Bely's studies of Russian prosody marked an epoch and exercised a decisive influence. Despite Bely's errors in some particulars and the fallacy of some of his too-sweeping conclusions, his work in this field, based on formal analysis and statistical evaluations, still retains its value and interest. The method first applied by him to the study of Russian verse was further exploited and extended by the Formalists.

What in the case of the Symbolists had been a more or less casual and limited expression of their natural interest in problems of literary form and had been confined almost exclusively to poetry, Formalism as a school tried to work out into a theory applicable to all literary facts. Its aim was to construe the science of literature along the same lines which are adopted in approaching other arts. It viewed literature as an evolution of literary styles and genres and was bent on rejecting all extraliterary criteria and approaches —ideological, sociological, psychological, biographical, or any other. Literature, the Formalists maintained, was primarily one of the arts, and therefore literary science and literary criticism must in the first place deal with the specific devices (*priyom*) of that art and not with its philosophical, sociological, psychological, or biographical contents and implications. In the main, their approach was analogous to Croce's formula: "Lo fatto estetico é forma e niente che forma."

The beginnings of Formalism as a distinct school date from the early years of World War I, when a group of young students of literature organized in Petrograd the so-called Opoyaz (Society for the Study of Poetic Language) and began to issue its nonperiodical publication, *Poetics*. The leading role in it was played at the time by Victor Shklovsky, who later became the principal theoretician of extreme Formalism. Among other regular contributors were Roman Jakobson (b. 1896), L. Yakubinsky, O. Brik (1888–1945), and others. In the first miscellany published by Opoyaz there appeared Shklovsky's article entitled "Trans-Sense Language and Poetry," which testified to the close relationship between Formalism and Futurism as a reaction against Symbolism, in the name of what the Futurists called the "self-sufficient word." In their revolt against all literature in which words were subordinated to meaning, the Futurists went so far as to demand a universal "trans-sense" language. One of the best Soviet literary scholars, Boris Eichenbaum (1886–1959), who in the twenties joined the Formalists, said that "the main slogan which brought together the original group of Formalists was the slogan of the emancipation of poetic words from the fetters of philosophical and religious tendencies to which the Symbolists were more and more succumbing."

The principal tenets of Formalism are stated with great dogmatic clarity, fullness, and detachment in Boris M. Engelhardt's little book *Formalny metod v istorii literatury* (*The Formal Method in the History of Literature*, 1927). The main fallacy of the traditional approach to art is seen by Engelhardt in our failure to overcome the dualistic conception of the "object expressed" and the "means of expression," or—to use the ordinary terminology—of form and content. The result is that, instead of studying a beautiful *work of art*, we study *the beautiful* in a work of art. It is necessary, says Engelhardt, to do away with this dualism:

In a work of art, studied on the aesthetic plane, there can be neither a system of means of expression nor an expressed object, and this not only in the sense of the famous opposition of form to content, but also in the sense of the broader anti-thesis of the "language of art" and the aesthetically significant object of expression. From this point of view there is no such thing as an aesthetically significant object expressed in one or another way in a work of art, but only the work of art as an object of aesthetic study.

In every such object, continues Engelhardt, two elements must be dis-tinguished: (1) the aesthetic significance as such and (2) the work itself as a concretely determined structural entity. Thus approached, the process of artistic creation is reduced to the molding of an aesthetically indifferent concrete material (the object of creation) into an aesthetically significant one (the work of art).

Defining the object of aesthetic study as actual material *plus* aesthetic significance, the Formalists determine the boundaries of the science of litera-ture and its auxiliary branches. The problem of aesthetic significance per se belongs to the competence of general aesthetics. The material as it exists before it is subjected to the process of aesthetic remolding must come within the corresponding nonaesthetic branch of study. Since the material of litera-ture is words, it falls within the purview of linguistics. The object of the specific aesthetics of a given art is to assess the aesthetic function of different elements of the organized concrete material. Thus the object of the aesthetics of literature is, first, to define, on the basis of general aesthetics, the meaning of aesthetic significance per se; second, on the basis of general and specific linguistics, to establish the primitive characteristics of verbal material in its preaesthetic state; and, finally, to elicit the specific meaning of that material in its aesthetically organized form. Therefore, the study of a literary work consists in demonstrating how the aesthetic factor transforms original verbal material into a work of art.

In their definition of aesthetic significance the Formalists follow the school of Hamann and Jonas Cohn, which defines it as "self-value." There are, they say, two ways of perceiving an object: the nonaesthetic, which has a practical purpose behind it; and the aesthetic, which is purposeless. This may be illustrated by the different ways in which the same river landscape is seen by the pilot who is piloting the boat and by the passenger of that boat who simply enjoys the view. For the pilot each detail of the river has a meaning and an interest so far as it has a bearing on his task. For the passenger the whole landscape is interesting and valuable in itself. In order to turn the raw material into a self-valuable work of art, it is necessary first to eliminate all collateral meanings attached to it, while, at the same time, since an object devoid of collateral meanings ceases to attract attention to the same degree as before, it is necessary somehow to increase its power of being perceived. Thus the process of aesthetic reshaping is a twofold one: it implies aesthetic *neutralization* and aesthetic *condensation*. The aesthetic interpretation of a work of art consists in explaining this twofold process.

For the solution of the problem of the other element of an aesthetically organized entity—the element of words—the Formalists turn to linguistics. Accepting the theory that language is an organ of communication, they distinguish in it two elements: (1) that which is being communicated and (2) a system of means of communication. These means or vehicles of communication consist of words. Therefore, for the Formalists a poetical work is a complex of words. This leads one of the theoreticians of Formalism, Roman Jakobson, to the statement that poetry is indifferent to the object of expression, that it is concerned only with the shaping of self-valuable words which stand in the same relation to it as sounds, colors, and lines stand to music, painting, and architecture.

In practice, therefore, the extreme Formalists reduce the study of a work of art to the study of its devices, by which they mean words or the separate elements of verbal structure in their aesthetic function, for example, the rhyming words taken as rhymes or the syntactical patterns taken as an element of construction. Devices, as the Formalists understand them, include also the choice of subjects and the treatment of plots, and Formalism has done much for the study of these aspects of prose fiction. According to Zhirmunsky, who did not share all the excesses of left-wing Formalism, the unity of these devices constitutes the style of a literary work. Before that, Shklovsky had coined his provocative formula, proclaiming that a work of literature represents "the sum of its stylistic devices" and nothing else. The Formalists reject automatically Potebnya's theory of poetry as "thinking in images." Words, they say, not images or emotions, are the real material of poetry. Their poetics is built on the opposition of two systems of language— the poetical and the everyday. To the ordinary everyday speech, which aims at the greatest possible economy, fluency, and accuracy, they oppose the deliberately obstructed, complicated, and twisted poetical speech, which aims at creating the greatest possible effect by overcoming the automatism of perception. In accordance with this, they lay stress in literature on what they call *ostranenie* ("making strange"), the object of which is to enhance the effect by presenting ordinary things in an unusual form or in an unusual perspective. Shklovsky took pains to demonstrate how frequently Tolstoy had resorted to this device. The Formalists naturally welcomed the same tendency in Mayakovsky and Pasternak. Some of the younger Soviet writers, such as Kaverin and Slonimsky, both of whom were influenced by Shklovsky's ideas, practiced the *ostranenie* method on an extensive scale and shunned simplicity.

Tynyanov, one of the leading Formalists in the twenties, evolved the theory of verse language as a constant violation of automatism through the ascendancy of one specific factor which dominates all other elements and tends to deform them. Thus the meter of a poem tends to deform its syntax and meaning. According to Tynyanov, poetic language implies a continuous clash of various elements. The impression of a deliberate verbal whole is achieved through various violations, interruptions, brakings, and digressions, all of which help to destroy the automatism of perception.

The more extreme Formalists not only disregarded altogether the element of content in the usual sense of the word and studied the naked form of a work of literature but also had a tendency to deny all causal connection between literary facts and all the other concomitant facts. Above all, they denied all connection between a work of literature and the personality of its author. Thus, Boris Eichenbaum in one of his articles wrote:

> The mind of the artist, as someone who experiences this or that mood, remains, and must always remain, outside his work. A work of art is always something made, shaped, invented, not only artistic but artificial in the good sense of that word, and therefore there neither is nor can be any place in it for the reflection of the inner empiric world of its author.[1]

Just as emphatically Eichenbaum denied all causal connection between art on the one hand and life and social environment on the other.

For the Formalists the evolution of literature consisted primarily in a succession of styles, forms, and genres. Boris Tomashevsky (1890–1957), in his *Teoriya literatury* (*Theory of Literature*), said that the value of a work of literature lay above all in its novelty and originality. Shklovsky, in his *Teoriya prozy* (*Theory of Prose Fiction*), wrote: "Forms of art are accounted for by their artistic lawfulness [*zakonomernost'*]. A new form appears, not in order to give expression to some new contents, but in order to replace the old form which has lost its artistic value." The same idea was voiced by Eichenbaum when he said that art subsisted "by crossing and contrasting its own traditions, by developing and modifying them on the principle of contrast, parody, shifting, and sliding." This is why the Formalists were particularly interested in certain minor writers in whom the new genre characteristics were more conspicuous.

But in laying down this principle, the Formalists failed to specify the laws which govern this dialectics of art, this "lawful" succession of forms. Nor did they bother to explain why this or that particular form, and not another, succeeds and supplants this or that old form. This gap in the theory developed by Shklovsky, Eichenbaum, Tomashevsky, Tynyanov, and Jakobson was pointed out by their "fellow traveler," the most moderate and

---

[1] "Kak sdelana 'Shinel' Gogolya" ("How Gogol's 'The Overcoat' Is Made"), *Poètika* (1919), 161.

cautious among the Formalists, Victor Zhirmunsky (b. 1891), the author of a number of valuable theoretical and historical studies and originally a specialist on German Romanticism. It was he who drew a distinction between the broadly understood "formal" method and the "extravagances" of Shklovsky and consorts, which he described as "formalistic." In his introduction to the Russian translation of Oskar Walzel's little book *Die künstlerische Form des Dichtwerks* (1919), Zhirmunsky set forth a number of points on which he disagreed with his fellow Formalists.

The formula of art as device seemed to him acceptable only as a method of aesthetic study. Side by side with it there could exist other equally legitimate formulas: art as a product of mental activity; art as a social fact and factor; art as a moral, religious, or educational fact; and so on. Syncretic forms of art are to be met not only in the primitive stages of civilization. Zhirmunsky cited some works of Novalis, Nietzsche's *Zarathustra*, and the writings of Andrey Bely as examples of philosophicopoetical syncretism in modern literature. The same is true of all so-called tendentious literature, where the artistic object is coupled with moral or social sermonizing. Zhirmunsky even conceded that "tendentiousness" in a wide sense—that is, understood as a certain moral tendency or orientation—was characteristic of a great majority of literary works.

Once it is granted that device is not the only thing that matters in a poetical work, it follows that it is not the sole factor of literary evolution. Zhirmunsky therefore flatly rejected Jakobson's formula of device as "the sole hero of literature." He maintained that Joseph Bédier was perfectly right when, in his standard work on French heroic legends, he studied the influence of monastic civilization, the problems of monastic and ecclesiastical policy, and the way of life in monasteries. One would be equally justified, when studying Nekrasov as a poet, in considering the influence of Belinsky's ideas on him.

Zhirmunsky objected also to the explanation of the succession of literary forms on the principle of contrast. Such an explanation, he said, was too broad and meaningless; it did not account for the direction of the historical process, since most widely dissimilar trends could arise by contrast. Nor did Zhirmunsky accept the view of literature as a purely formal, objectless art. Poetry, he said, just as painting and sculpture, and as distinct from music and ornamental drawing, is one of those arts which *have* an object. Modern poetics was wrong in giving preference to problems of composition over those of thematics. Poetics cannot be confined to problems of prosody, instrumentation, syntax, and plot construction. The aesthetic evaluation of a work of literature is not complete unless it embraces poetic themes—what is known as "content" or "message"—considered from the point of view of their aesthetic effectiveness.

Finally, Zhirmunsky established another important point of divergence between himself and the extreme Formalists and thereby introduced some clarity into the area where great confusion had reigned before. He refused to treat a lyric poem and a modern psychological novel on the same footing, insisting that the relation between composition and theme in the two is quite different. While a lyric poem is, indeed, a work of verbal art, wholly subordinated to the aesthetic design, a novel by Tolstoy or Stendhal makes use of words in their neutral capacity and subordinates them, as in everyday speech, to their communicative functions. Such a work, even if it is considered a work of verbal art, can be so regarded only in a sense quite different from the one which applies to a lyric poem. Zhirmunsky admitted the existence of purely formal prose fiction, in which the elements of style and composition predominated, and cited examples of such "ornamental" prose fiction in modern Russian literature (Gogol, Leskov, Remizov, Andrey Bely). But it was precisely when confronted by such "ornamental" works that one became fully aware of their fundamental difference from the novels of Tolstoy, Stendhal, or Dostoyevsky, in which words are used "neutrally" or, to use the Formalist terminology, are perceived not in their "self-valuable" meaning but with all the collateral accretions of meaning.[2]

Zhirmunsky's strictures on his erstwhile colleagues were a stab in the back of Formalism. It came at a time when Formalism, under the growing impact of hostile criticism on the part of orthodox Marxists, was beginning to disintegrate. For a few years the Formalists were able to voice their views more or less freely, but the great majority of orthodox Communist critics, including the most moderate among them, not to speak of the party leaders, were openly hostile to them. It was under this pressure that the Formalists gradually modified their views. The change became more or less imperative when it came to expressing their attitude toward contemporary literature.

All that has been said above of the Formalist views refers primarily to Formalism as a school of literary science, and not as literary criticism properly speaking. But the Formalists' theoretical views were bound to influence their judgments on contemporary literature—and so much was admitted by Engelhardt in his book—although he drew a distinction of principle between the science of literature and literary criticism. The latter, he said, does not investigate literature but is its complement, its final stage. Its object is to assimilate a given work of literature to the artistic consciousness of the reading public. The criterion of scientific objectivity cannot be applied to criticism; it is always subjective, for the criticized work has to be sifted through the personality of the critic, who represents a certain historical and social environment. Yet it would be absurd to deny the inevitable connection between literary science and literary criticism and to demand

---

[2] Zhirmunsky's views are quoted by B. Engelhardt in *Formalny metod v istorii literatury* (*The Formal Method in the History of Literature*). There is now an English edition of Zhirmunsky's *Introduction to Metrics*.

that they use totally different criteria. Literary criticism need not be absolutely objective; it can introduce certain modifications into the hard-and-fast rules laid down by the literary historian, and it can take into account facts and elements which literary history leaves out. But how can a literary critic who accepts in principle the theory of Formalism resist the temptation of applying purely formal criteria in his own critical work? In the second half of the nineteenth century, Russian literary historians were strongly influenced by the "civic" and utilitarian tendencies of literary criticism. Now it was the turn of literary history or science to exercise its influence on literary criticism.

But the upholders of Marxist views on literature could not eye with indifference the attempts of the Formalists to apply their theoretical views to the criticism of contemporary literature. Nor did the Formalists themselves dare approach Soviet writers with purely formal criteria. So, after 1927, they began to modify their theory. We have already seen the important reservations that were made by Zhirmunsky. Shklovsky and Eichenbaum, too, made concessions to the sociological method and began to include within the scope of their studies problems concerning the social and historical genesis of literary facts. This change of attitude found an expression in a number of articles by Eichenbaum and in Shklovsky's work on Tolstoy's *War and Peace* (1929). Eichenbaum spoke openly of combining the formal method with the sociological. But the enemies of the Formalists remained wary and suspicious. A certain Efimov, a professor in Smolensk, in a pamphlet entitled *Formalizm v russkom literaturovedenii (Formalism in Russian Literary Science*, 1930), showed himself very skeptical of the value of the Formalists' "sociologism." It was not real, he said, for it denied the causal genetic connection between social and economic facts on the one hand and literary facts on the other.

Some of the early extreme Formalists, including Shklovsky and Brik, tried at one point to conclude an alliance with proletarian literature and to direct the latter into their channels. Both were regular contributors to Mayakovsky's *LEF* and *Novy LEF*, and Shklovsky even came to advocate the "literature of fact," of which the LEFists became the most ardent partisans.

Whatever may have been the errors and excesses of extreme Formalism with its one-sided and unrealistic deification of form in literature, there can be no doubt that, in its uncompromising reaction against the social-utilitarian tradition of the nineteenth-century criticism and the subjective impressionism of some modern critics, its effect on Russian literary studies was on the whole beneficent. It drew attention to many problems traditionally despised by Russian literary historians and critics; it studied actual literary facts, instead of indulging in extraliterary investigations and futile generalizations; and finally, it tried to put literary history and literary criticism on a sound scientific basis and do away with critical dilettantism. In

the twenties it was the most productive school in literary science, and even
its adversaries could not but succumb to its influence. With a few exceptions
the representatives of the sociological school of the twenties and early
thirties paid infinitely more attention to problems of form than did their
"civic-minded" predecessors in the nineteenth century. At no other period
was the study of literature in Russia so productive, so rich in both theoretical
and historical works, as when Formalism reigned supreme. Among the
theoretical works published between 1921 and 1927 we find Zhirmunsky's
The Rhyme, Problems of Poetics, Introduction to Metrics, and *The Structure of Lyrical Poems*; Shklovsky's *Theory of Prose Fiction*; Tomashevsky's
Theory of Literature; Tynyanov's *The Problem of Verse Language*; Grift-
sov's *Theory of the Novel*; Grossman's *Method and Style*; Vsevolodsky-
Gerngross' *Theory of Intonation*; Reformatsky's *An Essay in the Analysis
of Novel Composition*; and Eichenbaum's *Verse Melody*. Works dealing
with Russian literature and its specific problems include Zhirmunsky's study
of Pushkin and Bryusov; Eichenbaum's books on Tolstoy, Lermontov, and
Akhmatova; Grossman's, Dolinin's, Tseytlin's, and Victor Vinogradov's
books on Dostoyevsky; and Vinogradov's studies of Gogol and Akhmatova.
Major works in the field of comparative literature include Zhirmunsky's
Byron and Pushkin, Piksanov's *Griboyedov and Molière*, and Shklovsky's
Pushkin and Sterne, not to count many essays on Pushkin in his relation to
English and French literature by Yakovlev, Yakubovich, Tomashevsky,
Alexeyev, and others.[3] Though not all these works came from the pens of

[3] This list is far from complete. Further references will be found in S. Balukhaty's
and B. Tomashevsky's books on theory of literature and in I. Vladislavlev's *Russkie
pisateli (Russian Writers)*, which has a special section on "Problems of Poetics."
English-speaking readers now have an excellent account of Russian Formalism, with
a look at its reverberations in Poland and Czechoslovakia and its relation to the Anglo-
Saxon New Criticism, in V. Erlich, *Russian Formalism: History—Doctrine*. Two
essays by Shklovsky and one each by Eichenbaum and Tomashevsky will be found in
Russian Formalist Criticism (comp. by L. T. Lemon and M. J. Reis). Unfortunately,
the translation is unsatisfactory. The literary output of the Formalist school, especially
in the field of theory, dwindled after 1927, but some interesting works continued to
appear, among them A. Bely's *Ritm kak dialektika i Medny Vsadnik (Rhythm as
Dialectics and "The Bronze Horseman")* and *Masterstvo Gogolya (Gogol's Craftsmanship)*. The publication of works on literary history went on undiminished, but a
large body of pre-Revolutionary literature, branded as "decadent," was, on the whole,
neglected. Many new literary documents and memoirs of great value have been published since the Revolution. Of particular value are such publications as *Literaturnoye
nasledstvo (Literary Heritage)* and *Zvenya (Links)*. The former, launched in 1931,
is a nonperiodical publication which still continues to appear. Among its volumes,
usually of several hundred pages, were special ones devoted to Pushkin, Lermontov,
Griboyedov, Belinsky, Saltykov-Shchedrin, Goethe and Russian literature, and Franco-
Russian literary ties—to mention a few published before 1953. *Zvenya*, also nonperiodical, appeared between 1932 and 1936 and contained a number of valuable
studies and previously unpublished documents about Russian literature and culture.

Formalists, it was Formalism which gave the impetus to all the studies of this kind, and therein lies its undoubted merit.

The Marxists and Other Sociological Critics

The sociological method in literary criticism and history and theory of literature, which was the principal method opposed to Formalism, was comprised of several trends of which orthodox Marxism was only one. Among its not strictly Marxian followers were to be found some of the older historians of literature, such as Pavel N. Sakulin (1868–1930)[4] and Nikolay K. Piksanov (1878–1968). Both accepted the teachings of the Formalists up to a point, and Sakulin even tried to combine the formal method with the sociological approach. He agreed that history of literature was primarily a history of styles and forms, but looked for a sociological explanation of their succession.

In the 1920's the older orthodox Marxist critics were represented by, in addition to such pillars of the Communist party as Trotsky, Bukharin, and Lunacharsky, Mme Lyubov Axelrod-Orthodox (1868–1946), Vladimir M. Fritsche (1870–1929), Peter S. Kogan (1872–1932), Alexander Voronsky, Vyacheslav Polonsky (1886–1932), Valerian Polyansky (pseudonym of P. I. Lebedev, 1882–1948), and Vladimir F. Pereverzev (b. 1882). Among the younger ones were Isaac M. Nusinov (1889–1950), Pavel N. Medvedev (1891–1938), A. Lezhnev (1893–1938), Dmitry A. Gorbov (b. 1894), G. Gorbachov (1897–1942), and Leopold L. Averbach (1903–38). Some older Marxists, especially Kogan and Fritsche, took an uncompromisingly hostile attitude toward Formalism and stuck to their old-fashioned guns. Thus Kogan, author of *Literature of These Years* and of several other works, voiced this crudely anti-Formalist view when he wrote: "I am little attracted by formal investigations. I take no interest in Mayakovsky's syntax or in discussions about composition, imagery, epithets, etc. I could never understand why these boring questions should be thrashed out in public."

Kogan thus came closest to the traditional attitude of Russian "utilitarian" criticism, with its neglect of, and even contempt for, problems of form—an attitude that had already been discarded by Plekhanov, the founder of Russian Marxism and the first to apply consistently Marxist principles to the study of literature. Kogan's attitude was not, however, shared by all the older Marxist critics. Both Trotsky and Lunacharsky recognized the value of some of the Formalists' studies. This was even more true of the younger Marxist critics. Some of them attached great importance to questions of

Some valuable materials were also published under the auspices of the State Literary Museum, including the correspondence between Alexander Blok and Andrey Bely.

[4] Sakulin's works include a book about Russian literature and Socialism and an ambitious sociological study of the evolution of literary styles in Russia, published as Volume I of his *Russkaya literatura i sotsializm* (*Russian Literature and Socialism*).

form and style but sought to explain different forms and styles by economic and social causes and stressed the class nature of art.

All their differences apart, those who adhered to the Marxist method had a common ground. They all proceeded, of course, from the doctrine of historical materialism. As distinct from the aesthetic method in all its varieties, which *describes* aesthetic facts, the Marxists aimed at *explaining* and *interpreting* literature. For them, each given complex of literary facts is a product of the social environment in which the literary work is produced. The Marxist approach implies, therefore, three consecutive stages. It begins by analyzing the economic structure of society. Thence it proceeds to explain social conditions and class differentiation. Finally, from the economic and social data it deduces the social psychology of a given society, its mental and intellectual state, which is a result of the complex interaction of economic and social factors. Where the Marxists vary is in the assessment of the relative importance of those three elements—the economic basis, the social structure, and the social psychology. For some of them the social psychology of a society is the immediate source of its art and literature, while economic and social facts have no direct bearing on literature but exercise their influence through the intermediary of the psychological factor and merely condition the society's psychology. For others the economic factor pure and simple, especially the "prevalent form of production," is the one that directly influences and determines the evolution of art and literature.

This latter extreme wing of Marxism was represented in the Soviet Union by Pereverzev, the author of works on Gogol and Dostoyevsky. Pereverzev did not neglect problems of style and even studied the stylistic "devices" of the authors with whom he was concerned, but he sought to explain them by the underlying economic conditions and, above all, by the process of production. Dostoyevsky's art, for instance, became, in his interpretation, an expression of the grievances and aspirations of the lower middle class. For a short time Pereverzev's Marxist interpretation of Russian classical literature was very much in vogue, but soon he was attacked by leading Marxist critics, who accused him of "vulgarizing" and distorting Marxism. "Pereverzevism" was proclaimed a dangerous heresy that had to be stamped out, and he and his followers were hounded off the literary scene. The campaign was carried on with great vituperation, the word Pereverzevism was bandied about in the columns of Soviet periodicals, and Marxist critics of various brands vied with each other in denouncing those who were guilty of it. Not the least vocal in this campaign were the faithful watchdogs of the proletarian purity of Soviet literature from the former Onguard group. Particularly vicious attacks on Pereverzev were made by Gorbachov, one of the early pillars of that group and one of the most intelligent younger critics. The precariousness of a Soviet critic's position was strikingly illustrated by the speedy fall from grace of Gorbachov himself, whose name was joined to the list of "missing" in the late thirties.[5]

As in the case of Formalism, it is necessary to distinguish between the application of the sociological method to the study of literature, especially of its past phenomena, and its manifestations in current literary criticism. As far as the former is concerned, the sociological school has produced some interesting and valuable works (those of Sakulin, Piksanov, and even Pereverzev). But its critical output is of little value, for it was too much influenced by the constant variations in the official literary policy of the Communist party.

Literary Controversies

We have seen that when in 1925 the conflict between the Onguardists, those extreme partisans of proletarian hegemony in literature, and the more moderate elements within the party, who took the fellow travelers under their wing, came to a head, the moderates won. Fellow travelers were given elbowroom and enabled to work more or less unhampered. It was their share in Soviet literature that made the period discussed in this chapter a period of fruitful diversity.

The new orientation of the Onguard group, known now as On Literary Guard (with a magazine of the same name), brought it closer to the principal spokesmen of the fellow travelers in literary criticism. They spoke of raising the quality of proletarian literary production, of learning from the classics of nineteenth-century realism and from Tolstoy especially, and of showing the "live" Soviet man instead of ideological abstractions. Their enemies delighted in pointing out how little difference there was now between some of the critics of On Literary Guard (for example, V. Ermilov) and such advocates of fellow travelers as Voronsky, Polonsky, and Lezhnev. These enemies turned up on the extreme left of literature, in the LEF group, which, after an interval of four years, in 1927 launched *Novy LEF*. Its pillars were Chuzhak, Tretyakov, Brik (all former Futurists), and Victor Shklovsky, and its slogan became "literature of fact" (or "factography," to use the word later coined by them). They attacked equally the fellow travelers and the proletarian psychological realists, and spoke no less slightingly of Gladkov's *Cement*, Fadeyev's *The Rout*, and Semyonov's *Natalya Tarpova* than of Leonov's *The Thief*.

In 1929 appeared a volume of their articles written during the two previous years. Edited by Chuzhak, it was called *Literature of Fact*[6] and

---

[5] On Pereverzev see E. J. Brown, *The Proletarian Episode in Russian Literature: 1928–1932*, and Ermolaev, *Soviet Literary Theories*.

[6] *Literatura fakta. Pervy sbornik materialov rabotnikov LEF'a* (ed. by N. Chuzhak). Page references for further quotations are given in the text.

contained articles by the editor, Brik, Shklovsky, Tretyakov, V. Pertsov, P. Neznamov, V. Trenin, and T. Grits, most of them contributing several articles (there were five by Chuzhak, seven by Tretyakov, and eight by Shklovsky). All spoke of the death of fiction, of "plot literature," and acclaimed the advent of "factual literature." Chuzhak called fiction "opium for the people" and saw in factual literature an antidote for it (page 28). He spoke of "activizing," "concretizing," "technicizing," and "rationalizing" literature—of shifting the center of gravity from human emotions to the organization of society. It was no use, he said, learning from the classics, for old literature was throughout individualistic and idealistic. There was no room for inspiration in art, since art was a matter of "skill" and of "knack" (the old Formalist notion of art as "a sum of devices," presented from a class angle).

Tretyakov ridiculed both the pessimists who were lamenting the absence of "Red Homers and Red Tolstoys" and the optimists who regarded the appearance of Communist Tolstoys as a question of time. His answer to those who demanded or expected Soviet Tolstoys was: "There is no need for us to wait for Tolstoys, because we have our own epics. Our epics are the newspapers." Tretyakov wrote:

What the Bible was for the medieval Christian—a guide for all occasions of life; what the novel with a message was for the Russian liberal intelligentsia, the newspaper is today for the Soviet activist. . . . What is the good of talking about bookish novels, about something called *War and Peace*, when every morning as we snatch our newspaper we turn over a new page of the most astounding novel called *Our Today*. The characters in this novel, its authors and its readers are we ourselves [pages 31 to 33].

Chuzhak rejected emphatically the idea that the object of literature was cognition of life and repeated the old LEF slogan about literature as "life building." Most Soviet novels were no more than conscientious attempts at "cognizing" life and proceeded from the obsolete notion that literature must approach life at a certain distance in time in order to allow life to settle down before it became the subject of literature. This notion was shared by Gorky, and this was the great defect of his fictional work, though Chuzhak had nothing but praise for Gorky the publicist. Among post-Revolutionary writers, Chuzhak singled out for praise Furmanov and Tynyanov who came quite close to factography, the former in his *Chapayev*, the latter in his historical novels. The field of factography, as Chuzhak and his fellow LEFists understood it, was wide. It embraced newspaper sketches and reports, biographies, memoirs, autobiographies and human documents, diaries, essays, law reports, travelogues, reports of meetings, speeches, pamphlets, parodies, satires, and even "artistic (that is, masterful) scientific monographs" (page 60). Chuzhak listed some achievements in this field, allocating the first place to John Reed's *The Ten Days That Shook the World*. His list also included Veresayev's *Pushkin in Life*, Shklovsky's *Sentimental Journey*, Mayakovsky's *How I Wrote My Esenin*, the memoirs of the old revolutionaries Nikolay Morozov and Vera Figner, Voronsky's autobiography (although as a literary critic Voronsky was one of the bugbears of the factographers), Tretyakov's books about China, and Arsenyev's *In the Jungles of the Ussuri Region* (a book of travel and hunting adventures in the Russian Far East which was often cited by the factographers as superior to much of Soviet fiction and as a proof that fiction was dying out). He also named purely journalistic writings of Koltsov, Zaslavsky, Radek, Zorich, and others (pages 61 to 62).

Similar ideas were developed by Shklovsky, Tretyakov, and Pertsov. Shklovsky insisted on the importance for the writer of having another profession which would provide him with material for writing. Journalists and reporters therefore had an advantage over professional fiction writers. He also raised his voice against the prevalent tendency to imitate the classics, saying that "the traditional psychological novel is not easily acclimatized in Soviet conditions, for its plot formulas are of no use in the conditioning of new material" (page 130).

Tretyakov demanded "biographies of things" and wrote: "Such books as *Forest, Bread, Coal, Iron, Flax, Cotton, Paper, Railway Engine, Factory* remain unwritten. We need them, and they can be done most satisfactorily by using the method of 'a biography of a thing'" (page 70). As an example of this factographic literature he quoted the French writer Pierre Hamp, whose novels were popular in Soviet Russia in the 1920's (one of them was translated by Mandelstam).

The idea of "artistic realism" as the proper style of proletarian literature was rejected by Pertsov, who said that the critics of On Literary Guard did not know the meaning of realism, let alone of "proletarian realism"; all that they could say was that it meant the way the classic authors wrote, Tolstoy in particular.

Literature of Fact contained a number of sarcastic judgments about some of the greatest successes of Soviet literature. Thus Brik wrote that in Gladkov's *Cement* all the ingredients were taken from the best cookery books, but the result was "inedible," because the ingredients were not cooked— "only for appearance' sake were they kneaded into a kind of literary paste" (page 87). Similar attacks were made on Fadeyev and Leonov, on Bagritsky and Utkin.

Tretyakov, in *Novy LEF*, accused all the leading fellow travelers and proletarian novelists of being "passeists," of looking toward the past instead of the present and the future.

Novy LEF, attacked on all sides, ceased appearing in 1928, and the LEF group soon came to an end. Its place was taken by the REF (Revolutionary

Front), launched by Mayakovsky. But its independent existence was of short duration, and it ended by merging with the RAPP (Russian Association of Proletarian Writers) as part of a larger body of proletarian literary organizations.

In May, 1928, the first congress of all associations of proletarian writers (VOAPP) took place. Its leading lights were Fadeyev, Libedinsky, Averbach, and Ermilov, and its proceedings were reflected in a volume of articles edited by Averbach.[7] Fadeyev's report, read at the congress, was later reissued as a separate pamphlet, under the title *The Highway of Proletarian Literature*.[8] It contained attacks both on Voronsky and Lezhnev and on LEF. The former were attacked for their "irrationalism," their interest in the subconscious. The same charge was leveled against a number of writers, including Pilnyak, Leonov, and Vsevolod Ivanov. The LEFists were criticized for their ultrarationalist approach to literature. Their worship of facts was ascribed to their inability and reluctance to interpret the world that surrounded them. "We must take down what we see, let others come and make it all out"—such was, according to Fadeyev, the LEF formula. Their proclamation of the supremacy of form over content and their insistence on "ideological form" were ascribed to the same reason. Fadeyev defended against LEF the two main tenets of the proletarian Neorealists: the portrayal of "live" men instead of schematic abstractions and the learning from the classics of realism, from writers like Tolstoy and Flaubert, who, for all their "bourgeois" limitations, had attained the maximum objectivity that was possible under the circumstances. Learning from the old literature was not, however, enough in itself, said Fadeyev. The foremost duty of a Soviet writer was to learn from life itself.

[7] *Tvorcheskie puti proletarskoy literatury. Vtoroy sbornik statey (The Creative Paths of Proletarian Literature: Second Collection of Articles)*. An earlier collection had appeared in 1928, containing reports and addresses delivered at the 1927 Moscow Conference of Proletarian Writers by Averbach, Libedinsky, Bezymensky, Fadeyev, Zonin, and Ermilov.

[8] *Stolbovaya doroga proletarskoy literatury*.

Part IV. **Literature Puts on Uniform, 1929–32**

Chapter 16. SOCIAL COMMAND

In 1929 fellow travelers and all independent writers came once more under concentrated fire, this time with results that were disastrous to Soviet literature as a whole. The period of comparative freedom was at an end, and to it succeeded what came to be known as the dictatorship of the RAPP, which was headed unofficially by that most virulent of critics, Leopold Averbach. This period lasted about three years and coincided with the early years of the First Soviet Five-Year Plan of industrialization and collectivization, to which everything else in the country was subordinated. Literature, too, was enlisted in its service. The leading role in it was given to Communist writers and purely "proletarian" organizations. RAPP assumed dictatorial powers and laid down the policy which all writers had to follow if they cared to survive in literature.

The inauguration of this policy of subordinating literature (and other arts) to the requirements of the Five-Year Plan was preceded, in 1928–29, by a lively controversy in the Soviet press on the subject of "social command," in which a number of prominent writers and critics took part.

In a sense, "social command" (*sotsialny zakaz*) had always been taken for granted in the Soviet Union. But it was understood broadly as the implicit command of the ruling class. Even some orthodox Communist critics were ready to admit, for instance, that Pilnyak and the Serapions, in describing the Revolution and its impact on Russian life, were carrying out this implicit social command, despite their own studiedly detached attitude. But this time social command was to be understood much more narrowly— as specific assignments to be executed by writers. The first to use the formula and to give it this meaning were the former Futurists from LEF. The RAPP extremists, led by Averbach, followed suit, though Averbach himself was moderate at first and did not recommend "dictating directly" to writers. Most of those who took part in the 1928–29 controversy, writers and critics alike, protested against this narrow interpretation of social command. Gladkov, himself a Communist, described the LEF formula as "fundamentally alien" and harmful to proletarian literature. The point of view of its opponents was clearly voiced by Polonsky, the editor of *Pechat' i Revolyutsiya*, who wrote:

The theory of "social command" marks an attempt, on the part of a group of writers and artists of the extreme left, who are severed from the proletariat, to establish a link with it, while preserving their independence as makers of ideological values. Having assigned to the working class the role of "social commander," . . . they keep for themselves the humble role of "artisans," . . . of producers of "ideological" things. . . . It is easy to notice that while they throw a sop to the working class they remain in reality on the other side of the fence. For the theory of "social command" does not furnish that organic link with the proletariat which . . . is precisely what our epoch demands of the master who aspires to be the proletarian artist of the proletarian revolution and the proletarian spokesman of our wonderful age.[1]

Polonsky opposed the theory of social command from the Marxist point of view. But before a few months had passed he was himself proclaimed a counterrevolutionary and divested of his leading position in Soviet magazines. The theory of explicit social command, sponsored by the extremists of RAPP, then received official approval. It was decided to place literature in the service of the Five-Year Plan, to make use of writers in the furtherance of it, and to involve them in "Socialist emulation" which was becoming so popular in industry. Writers were expected to become "shock workers" (*udarniki*), to form "artistic brigades," to join various construction projects and collective farms and describe them in factual sketches (*ocherki*). In fact, RAPP, which had hitherto fought LEF, now took a leaf out of the latter's book and proclaimed the superiority of "literature of fact" to all other forms. Fiction was frowned upon, and several leading fellow travelers—Tolstoy, Kaverin, and others—turned their attention to documentary literature. Those who continued writing novels and stories had to reflect various aspects of the Five-Year Plan. Collective writing also became fashionable. The idea was encouraged by Gorky, who sponsored two large collective literary undertakings—a *History of the Civil War* and a *History of Factories and Plants*. As part of the latter a volume appeared describing the construction of the Stalin Canal linking the White Sea with the Baltic and built with forced labor of common-law criminals and political prisoners.

---

[1] V. Polonsky, "Spor o sotsialnom zakaze" ("The Controversy About Social Command"), *Pechat' i Revolyutsiya* (*Press and Revolution*), No. 2 (1929), 23. This article served as an introduction to a discussion in which O. Brik, P. Kogan, G. Gorbachov, Z. Steinman, I. Nusinov, V. Pereverzev, and N. Zamoshkin took part. In the same number appeared short statements on the same subject by Gladkov, Leonov, Pilnyak, Selvinsky, Fedin, and Karavayeva. All of them protested against the idea of social command. In the next issue (No. 3, 1929) Polonsky replied to his critics, of whom Brik, Kogan, and Pereverzev were the most outspoken. Some objections have been raised to rendering the word *zakaz* as "command," and it has been suggested that the real meaning implied in the term *sotsialny zakaz* would be better expressed by the word "demand." While that may be so, I do not wish to abandon the use of the term that has taken such firm root. In speaking of the "command" emanating from the ruling class (or the state or the party) the buyer-vendor or patron-artist relationship is implied. The word "order" (in the dictionary sense of "a direction to provide or furnish something") could be substituted just as well.

Several well-known writers and critics collaborated on this volume (Tolstoy, Zoshchenko, Katayev, Inber, Zelinsky, Averbach, and others).[2]

Averbach and Bezymensky, who played the leading roles in RAPP, set about infusing new political blood into a literature that had become too objective and apolitical. The old dream of the Onguardists came true: the supremacy of proletarian literature was officially recognized. RAPP was to set the line, and everybody had to toe it. The result was a drying-up of the creative sources of Soviet literature, a narrowing-down of its themes, and a tightening of controls over individual writers.

Pilnyak in Hot Water

Two literary incidents of 1929, involving Pilnyak and Zamyatin, served well to illustrate the limitations on the writer's freedom in the U.S.S.R. The Pilnyak incident resulted from the publication of the author's short novel *Krasnoye derevo* (*Mahogany*). Following the not unusual practice—for reasons of foreign copyright—Pilnyak had his novel first published (in Russian) in Berlin, by a firm which had contacts with the Soviet State Publishing House. In the meantime the book was apparently turned down by Soviet censorship[3] and its publication abroad unleashed furious attacks on Pilnyak, which led to his expulsion from the Association of Soviet Writers.[4] Later Pilnyak tried to redeem himself by revising *Mahogany* and incorporating it in his Five-Year Plan novel, *The Volga Flows into the Caspian Sea.*

In more than one way *Mahogany* is a typical work of Pilnyak's, with no plot and almost no action. It is a static picture of the two-faced modern Russia—of the old world encased within the new, with the main attention on the old. The scene is set in an old small town in provincial Russia, which Pilnyak describes as "Russian Bruges and Russian Kamakura." In the center of the novel stands the Skudrin family. Yakov Skudrin himself is a typical relic of the past, a cunning embodiment of the surviving counter-revolutionary tendencies. With a quaint irony he lists the tsars he has out-lived, from "Nikolay Pavlovich" (Nicholas I) to "Nikolay Alexandrovich" (Nicholas II), adding to them "Vladimir Ilyich" (Lenin) and concluding:

[2] A detailed account of the way in which literature was placed in the service of the Five-Year Plan will be found in H. Borland, *Soviet Literary Theory and Practice During the First Five-Year Plan: 1928–1932.*

[3] The exact workings of Soviet censorship are surrounded with mystery, and its history offers many puzzles. In the main its functions are exercised by Glavlit (Central Department of Literary Affairs). Some information, though inadequate, about its procedures will be found in G. Reavey, *Soviet Literature Today.* Interesting data about the activities of Soviet censorship will be found in the article by a former Soviet citizen, V. Zavalishin, "Sovetskie tsenzory za rabotoy" ("Soviet Censors at Work"), *Narodnaya Pravda* (*People's Truth*, Paris), No. 11–12 (November, 1950). See also A. Gayev, *Tsenzura sovetskoy pechati.*

[4] For details of this incident see Eastman, *Artists in Uniform.*

"I am also going to outlive Alexey Ivanovich"—that is, Rykov, then chairman of the Council of People's Commissars, who was later to perish as a victim of the opposition purges. Skudrin develops a counterrevolutionary theory—behind which one can feel Pilnyak's own views—of the imminent extinction of the proletariat as a result of the progress of mechanization: "All proletarians will become engineers." His brother Ivan, who hates Yakov and has changed his last name to Ozhogov, is a romantic revolutionary for whom the clock stopped in 1919. With a few others like himself he has founded a primitive commune. Its members live in a dugout in a factory yard and preach a variety of Communism based on charity. Ivan says, lamenting the loss of this genuine Communism: "Communism is primarily charity, an eager interest of one man in another, friendship, cooperation, collaboration. Communism means giving up things, and for a genuine Communist love, respect for men, and men as such stand above all other things."

Yakov's youngest son, Akim, an engineer, whose short visit to his native town forms the single "incident" in the otherwise static story, has some affinity with Ivan. He is also a Communist but belongs to the Trotskyite opposition and has fallen out with the "general line" of the party. At heart he is, in Pilnyak's own words, "the flesh of the flesh" of his uncle. The reader can feel that Pilnyak's own sympathy lies with these two romantic revolutionaries, and it was this tendency toward romantic idealization of Trotskyism that led to the banning of the book. When, later, Pilnyak transposed a good deal of *Mahogany*, as a minor episode, into his novel *The Volga Flows into the Caspian Sea*, he excluded the whole episode with Akim and opposed several other characters, bourgeois wreckers and ideal Communists, to Ivan Ozhogov, the last of the idealists of romantic Communism. In *Mahogany* we see only the representatives of the old world, relics of seventeenth-century Russia, and those two antiquated Communists. At the end of the book their obsoleteness is symbolized by Akim's missing his train: "Akim the Trotskyite missed his train just as he had missed the train of time."

Apart from the two romantic revolutionaries, who in 1929 sounded anachronistic and frankly counterrevolutionary, critical notes crop up here and there in the book. Thus Pilnyak emphasizes the inefficiency of Soviet provincial administration based on "the slow squandering of pre-Revolutionary wealth." The trade-union membership card is represented as the pivot of the town's life and a key to its elementary comforts: "Those who are disfranchised receive no bread, nor do their children."

In *Volga vpadayet v Kaspiyskoye more* (*The Volga Flows into the Caspian Sea*, 1930) Pilnyak set out to put right the ideological fallacies of *Mahogany*. Yet the real significance of the novel had little to do with the avowed task of glorifying the Five-Year Plan. It is true that the Five-Year

Plan forms the background of the book. But it is not by chance that Pilnyak conceives his industrial project on a somewhat fantastic and hyperbolical scale. The novel tells the story of the building of a gigantic dam at Kolomna, not far from Moscow, with the object of reversing the Volga and making the Moscow River navigable to big Volga steamers (on a more modest scale this project was realized a couple of years later in the form of the Volga–Moscow Canal).

The book is interspersed with a great deal of technical matter. It opens with a long passage which would be more in place in a textbook on hydraulics (a good example of the "factual literature" demanded by Chuzhak and Tretyakov). One of the chapters even has attached to it in the form of an appendix a complete issue of the wall newspaper published at the Kolomstroy, which the gentle reader is politely asked to read but which, from the point of view of the story, can be just as well left unread. But Pilnyak is interested not in the technical achievements of the Five-Year Plan but in the clash of the old and the new world in Soviet Russia. His artistic attention is centered on the depiction of the forces which the old world arrays in this battle.

Side by side with the Soviet Union of the Five-Year Plan, Pilnyak shows us the half-Asiatic, pre-Petrine Russia. This Russia is symbolized in the Marina Mniszek Tower in Kolomna, which forms a sort of refrain running throughout the book. Pilnyak develops here his favorite conception of the historical duality of Russia, her Januslike face turned simultaneously toward West and East. But Pilnyak does not confine himself to a symbolical demonstration of the essential duality of Russia. With a picturesqueness which reminds one of Gogol, he depicts, next to the model Communist city of Kolomstroy, built according to plan, the little old town of Kolomna, which drags on its unchanging, sluggish, sleepy life, with pigs wallowing in the mud in the middle of the streets—just as in Gogol's Mirgorod. (Here again Pilnyak was in fact repeating himself, for in one of his earlier stories he had written: "In the market square a puddle, not a Gogolian, but an all-Russian one. At the corner of the puddle the inn called 'Europe.'")

And side by side with the ideal Communist Sadykov, simple and straightforward, and therefore the least interesting for the author, Pilnyak shows us a number of complex and twisted characters who obviously attract him much more. Some of them are outspoken enemies of the Soviet regime, counterrevolutionaries and wreckers (an important part in the novel is played by a wreckers' conspiracy—a fashionable and topical subject in nearly all Five-Year Plan novels and plays).

But the most important character—and the one who is obviously nearest and dearest to Pilnyak's heart—is again Ivan Ozhogov, old Skudrin's brother, half-workman and half-tramp, who introduces himself as "a Communist of the year 1919." He is one of the characters brought over from

Mahogany, but in the framework of this novel he acquires an added symbolical significance. He personifies the romantic and heroic period of the Revolution, the period of storm and stress when the elemental forces were let loose and swept like a gale across Russia. Pilnyak's Ozhogov is not the only representative of this type of romantic Communist in Soviet literature. In Gladkov's *Cement* two ardent Communists, the young girl Polya Mekhova and the typical intellectual Sergey Ivagin, are possessed by the same mood, the same disillusionment, and the same pining after the epoch of War Communism. But *Cement* was written at the very beginning of the NEP when, from the Communist point of view, such moods were much more comprehensible and excusable. With Pilnyak, this revolutionary romanticism is opposed not to the semibourgeois reality of the NEP but to the realism, both heroic and everyday, of the Five-Year Plan, of Socialist reconstruction. His Ozhogov is therefore, from the point of view of an orthodox Communist, an unpardonable anachronism. Yet Pilnyak cannot conceal his sympathy with Ozhogov. The latter embodies for him all that is best in the Revolution. His death in the waters of the river when the new dam is opened, while it fittingly disposes of an anachronistic relic of the past, symbolizes also the death of those best elements in Communism.

Pilnyak went all out to glorify the Five-Year Plan and to remove the bad impression which *Mahogany* had created in Communist circles. But filled with romanticism and heavily flavored with Dostoyevskian scenes, the novel misfired completely.

Pilnyak's recantation after the publication of *Mahogany*, which has been described as "abject," was not the only one in his literary career. In 1926 he went to Japan, one of the objects of his visit being to set up the Japanese branch of the Russo-Japanese Literary Society. A result of this trip was a book entitled *Korni yaponskogo solntsa* (*The Roots of the Japanese Sun*). It was full of the usual Pilnyakian fireworks, of relevant and irrelevant reflections, of interesting observations and half-baked generalizations. With his *Kitayskiy dnevnik* (*A Chinese Diary*) it was included in the seventh volume of his *Collected Works*, issued by the State Publishing House. In 1932, Pilnyak revisited Japan, and in 1934 appeared another book, this time entitled *Kamni i korni* (*Rocks and Roots*). It consisted largely of quotations from the earlier book, with additions, comments, and self-refutations. It also contained a renunciation of the earlier book, worded so astonishingly that one might easily suspect Pilnyak of speaking with his tongue in his cheek. Pilnyak wrote here:

The writer Pilnyak informs his readers that his *Roots* (1926) are no good. The writer Pilnyak of 1932 asks his readers to throw out from their shelves the seventh volume of the GIZ edition of his *Collected Works*. As for the translations of this book, Pilnyak asks that its Japanese translation be destroyed first of all. This must be done out of respect for the author.[5]

Not content with this formal disavowal of his book, Pilnyak went on to advocate in even more astonishing terms a strict control of writers:

A writer is like a geologist or a traveler to uninhabited and undiscovered lands. . . . Writers must be treated like geologists, for writers can certainly muddle up things no less than the latter. In Soviet literature, too, it is necessary, after re-registering all writers and cutting down their number, . . . to create an Institute of Literature, an Institute of Artistic Prospecting and Equipment, without whose diploma writers could not have the status of a writer and get published, by analogy with the Institutes of Mining Prospecting which equip the geologist for his work. This institute, in qualifying a writer, should demand from him, beside the ability to write and general knowledge, moral good faith which characterizes the writer in his public work and his home life. . . . And if a writer makes a mistake (this also happens to geologists), his mistake will be an accident and a matter for regret rather than abuse. For, given the diploma of the Literary Prospecting Institute and the writer's honesty, there will be no doubt about the accidentally vexatious nature of the mistake. And the mistakes will be much fewer, although God alone is never mistaken because He does not exist, . . . while those who make most mistakes are the geologists because they discover things hitherto undiscovered and because they are not tourists who follow beaten paths. Tourist writers, in particular those who travel from Moscow to the Dneprostroy of Socialism in the mail coaches, dormeuses and railway carriages of Tolstoy, Dostoyevsky and Bunin, travel like tourists and will never get anywhere (pages 57–58).

This amazing passage, which is a good specimen of Pilnyak's elaborately nonchalant manner (popularized at one time by Victor Shklovsky and going in part back to Rozanov), defies comment. The actual nature of Pilnyak's mistakes, factual and "political," which he made in 1926 and deemed it necessary to rectify in 1932, is immaterial. One is left wondering whether Pilnyak was making here an abject act of submission to whatever control the omnipotent Soviet state had chosen to exercise over him as a writer or, like Slonimsky's hero, Boris Lavrov, merely electing "the best of all available unfreedoms" or simply pulling his readers' and censors' legs by piling up subtle irrelevancies. The only possible way of commenting upon his unprecedented proposal is by juxtaposing it with the following extracts from Pilnyak's 1923 diary, published in 1924 in lieu of a special article in the volume entitled *Writers About Art and About Themselves*:

I am not a Communist and therefore do not admit that I have to be a Communist and write as a Communist, while I admit that the Communist power in Russia is determined, not by the will of the Communists, but by the historical destinies of Russia, and, inasmuch as I want to trace those destinies (as best as I can and as my conscience and my intellect prompt me), I am with the Communists, that is, inasmuch as the Communists are with Russia I am with them, too. . . . I admit

[5] *Rocks and Roots*, 51. In the 1935 edition this and similar passages were transposed from the third person to the first.

that I am much less interested in the fortunes of the Russian Communist party than in the fate of Russia, the Russian Communist party being for me only a link in the history of Russia. I know that I must be absolutely objective, must not bring grist to anyone's mill, must not delude anyone, and I admit that I may be wrong in everything, but I also know that I cannot, nor know not how to, nor ever shall, write otherwise than I do, even if I wanted to do violence to myself. . . . In recent years our state has been setting up incubators for Party literature, providing them with food rations, and nothing came of it, or rather bad things came of it, for when these people touched art they stopped being politicians, without becoming artists. . . . Hence another conclusion: I believe that a writer must care only about his manuscripts, about their being *good*, and the honesty and validity of his Party-school-social membership card is his own personal business which has nothing to do with literature.[6]

Pilnyak's pathetic attempts at adjusting himself also included *O-Kay* (1931). Described as an "American novel," it was really not a novel at all but the usual Pilnyakian assortment of facts, impressions, and relevant and irrelevant reflections, all gleaned on his short visit to the United States. In the main it was a denunciation of capitalist America, one-sided and biased, and Pilnyak had no reason or occasion to refute it, although here and there his admiration for the achievements of American material civilization can be felt. This admiration did not, however, conflict with the party line of the moment, for one of the popular slogans of the Five-Year Plan period was, "Let us catch up and overtake America," and the stress was very much on technical progress.

The Zamyatin Incident

The incident with Zamyatin, which led to his resignation from the All-Russian Writers' Association, also happened in 1929. It was caused by the publication of his novel *We*, in a shortened Russian version, in the *émigré* magazine *Volya Rossii*, published in Prague. The publication was preceded by an editorial note explaining that the Russian version represented a re-translation from the Czech. Unlike Pilnyak, Zamyatin behaved in this incident with great dignity. He disclaimed all responsibility for the publication of this Russian version, and when the Writers' Association, yielding to the vociferous campaign launched in the Communist press, passed a vote of censure on him, he resigned his membership. In a letter he wrote to the association he said that it was impossible for him "to belong to a literary organization which, albeit indirectly, takes part in the persecution of a fellow member."[7]

---

[6] *Writers About Art and About Themselves*, 83–85.

[7] For details see Eastman, *Artists in Uniform*. In the Preface to the 1959 revised American edition of *We*, Mark Slonim, the former editor of *Volya Rossii*, explains that he had actually used Zamyatin's manuscript but made some deliberate alterations in it to make it look like a retranslation.

But the campaign against Zamyatin, led by RAPP, continued. He was denounced as an "inside *émigré*" and reduced to silence. In 1931, as a result of a personal outspoken letter to Stalin, and probably thanks to Gorky's intervention with the latter, Zamyatin was allowed to leave the Soviet Union. Zamyatin wrote to Stalin:

If I am indeed a criminal and deserve punishment, I still think that it should not be such a heavy one as literary death, and I therefore beg to have this sentence commuted to banishment from the U.S.S.R., with the right for my wife to accompany me. But if I am not a criminal, I ask for the permission, for myself and my wife, to leave the country temporarily, let us say for one year—on the understanding that I shall be able to return as soon as it becomes possible in our country to serve great ideas in literature without being subservient to little men.

Zamyatin concluded by expressing his hope that he would not have to wait long and assured Stalin that he had no intention of joining "the reactionary *émigrés*."[8] He settled down in Paris, where, until his death in 1937, he published some critical articles in French periodicals and the first part of his novel about Attila, *Bich Bozhy* (*The Scourge of God*). His four-act tragedy about Attila, which had been accepted by a Leningrad theater just before his disgrace but was not produced, was published posthumously in New York in Volume XXIV of *Novy Zhurnal* (1950). His novel *We* and a collection of literary essays, *Litsa* (*Faces*), also appeared posthumously in New York. Unlike many others, he has never been "rehabilitated."

The Campaign Against Voronskyism and the Pereval Group

The year 1930 was marked by violent attacks on all the more or less independent writers who failed to follow the party line. One of the most bitterly attacked groups was Pereval (the Pass, in the sense of "mountain pass"). Pereval came into existence in 1924 as a result of the secession of a number of younger writers, mostly poets belonging to the Young Guard, from the October group. These writers disagreed with the anti–fellow-traveler policy of October and went over to Voronsky's *Krasnaya Nov*. The group was later joined by some older writers, such as Prishvin; by several peasant writers, including Klychkov; and others. Among its most talented younger members were Ivan Katayev (1902–42; no relation of Valentin Katayev); Andrey Platonov (1889–1951) who changed his real name, Klimentov, in 1921; and Nikolay Zarudin (1899–1937). Voronsky was for several years associated with the group and supported its policy of *rapprochment* between proletarian writers and fellow travelers (in fact, the group itself represented an attempt to merge the two).

In February, 1927, Pereval published its literary declaration in *Krasnaya Nov*. The members' ideas were influenced by Voronsky. They invoked the

[8] See Zamyatin's *Litsa* (*Faces*), 177–82; English translation, *A Soviet Heretic*.

humanistic traditions of Russian and Western European literature and opposed the pedestrian *bytovism* (from the word *byt*, "mores") that was invading a certain section of Soviet literature. Like Voronsky, they saw a creative act as a process of "tearing off the veils." To them the immediacy of impressions was the basis of all artistic creation. Their slogans were "intuition" and "sincerity," and one of the charges later laid against them was that of "Bergsonian intuitivism." Two major critics of those days, Gorbov and Lezhnev, both of them close associates of Voronsky, often came out as spokesmen for Pereval. An important role in their aesthetic conception was played by the notion of "craftsmanship," which found its programmatic expression in Peter Slyotov's novel of that name (*Masterstvo*, 1929) and in Gorbov's volume of critical essays entitled *V poiskakh Galatei* (*In Search of Galatea*, 1930).

The campaign against Voronsky reached its climax in 1927, when he was expelled from the party and apparently banished to Siberia. Later he recanted, was allowed to return to Moscow, and in 1930 or 1931 was even readmitted to the party. In 1933–34 he published some autobiographical fiction and a biography of the well-known revolutionary Zhelyabov. But he no longer played any important part in Soviet literature and in 1937 was again arrested and disappeared from the literary scene. Like many victims of Stalin's purges he was "rehabilitated" in the late fifties. The date of his death is now officially given as 1943. Some of his work, including his autobiography, has been reissued.[9]

After Voronsky's downfall "Voronskyism" came to be used as a term of abuse in the campaign against Pereval and other nonconformists. It was identified with "Bergsonian idealism," and several Pereval writers and critics were accused of "idealistic humanism," "irrationalism," subjectivism, betrayal of the principles of class war, softness toward class enemies, and support of the kulaks. Among the Pereval writers particularly violently attacked were Ivan Katayev, for his novel *Moloko* (*Milk*, 1930); Zarudin, who wrote *Tridtsat' nochey na vinogradnike* (*Thirty Nights in a Vineyard*, 1932); and Platonov, for his sketches entitled *Vprok* (this title is not easy to translate—it means something like "for future, or eventual, use"). These sketches gave a graphic, frank, unvarnished firsthand picture of collectivization and various problems it raised in a typical rural area. They were pub-

---

[9] For an account of the 1927 campaign against Voronsky see McLean, "Voronskij and VAPP," *American Slavic and East European Review*, Vol. VIII, No. 3 (October, 1949), 199–200. Robert A. Maguire's recently published *Red Virgin Soil: Soviet Literature in the 1920's* is a valuable contribution to the study of Soviet literature of that period, of Voronsky's role in it, and of the important place occupied in it by *Krasnaya Nov*, even though the author, like some of his predecessors, seems to me to overestimate the intrinsic value of Voronsky's literary criticism. A great deal of fresh documentation has recently become available; but the last years of Voronsky's life are still shrouded in darkness, and the circumstances of his death are not known.

lished in *Krasnaya Nov* in 1931, when it was no longer edited by Voronsky and when its editorial board included such a staunch champion of proletarian literature as Alexander Fadeyev. It was nevertheless the same Fadeyev who, two months later, in the same *Krasnaya Nov*, published an article in which he called *Vprok* a slander on collective-farm leadership and denounced Platonov as an agent of the kulaks.[10]

Platonov found it difficult to live down this attack and was practically forced to cease publishing. In 1936 the magazine *Literaturny Kritik* (*Literary Critic*) did an unprecedented thing and published two of Platonov's stories (normally it published nothing but literary criticism and scholarly papers on literary history and literary theory). The editors explained that they were publishing two stories by a talented writer which had been rejected by all the literary magazines (one of them was accepted by the annual *God XIX* [*Year XIX*], where it would have had to wait a long time before publication). The stories were entitled "Bessmertie" ("Immortality") and "Fro" and are now regarded as among Platonov's best. The next year *Literaturny Kritik* had to defend Platonov against a vicious attack by *Komsomolskaya Pravda* in connection with another story of his. And in the same year *Krasnaya Nov* published a long critical article by A. Gurvich, who spoke of Platonov as a writer obsessed by themes of misery, orphanhood, and death and thus completely out of tune with what was then expected of a Soviet writer.[11] It is surprising, indeed, that Platonov did not share the fate of so many other Pereval writers (Ivan Katayev, Zarudin, Klychkov, Boris Guber, Nasedkin, and others) who became victims of Stalin's purges, and managed to survive. For a time Platonov came again into his own during the war, but one of his postwar stories was once more violently attacked, and he was reduced to silence. His literary legacy includes some unpublished work, including a long early novel.[12]

While it existed, Pereval published eight annual collections of poetry, prose fiction, and criticism by its members. The last two were brought out in 1930 and 1931 under the title *Rovesniki* (*Contemporaries*, or *Coevals*). As an organized group, it more or less ceased to exist in 1930 (some had begun to defect even earlier) and was finally disbanded in 1932, together with other "factional" organizations (see Part V).

But there was no unity within RAPP itself, and the charge of Voronskyism was readily used in inter-RAPP polemics. Thus, an article in *Pechat i Revolyutsiya* brought this charge against Libedinsky for his theory of

[10] See "Ob odnoy kulatskoy khronike" ("About a Kulak Chronicle"), *Krasnaya Nov*, No. 5–6 (1931), 206–209. Platonov had subtitled his sketches *A Pauper Chronicle* and introduced his narrator as a "soulful pauper."

[11] "Andrey Platonov," *Krasnaya Nov*, No. 10 (1937), 193–233.

[12] For some further details about Pereval and its writers see G. Glinka, *Na Perevale* (*At the Pass*). Glinka, a poet and story writer, was one of the minor Pereval writers who found himself in the West during the war.

"direct impressions"—for opposing art to science and saying that "direct impressions lie at the basis of art; they are the common link uniting the creator at the moment of creating a work of art and the perceiver at the moment of perception."[13] Similar charges were brought against such a hidebound RAPP stalwart as Ermilov, who had praised Libedinsky's new novel *Rozhdenie geroya* (*The Birth of a Hero*, 1930). This novel, which Ermilov and some other RAPP critics had described as "a model of proletarian literature," aroused bitter controversy. It was written as a specific response to the demand for showing the "live" Soviet man.

Libedinsky's hero was Shorokhov, a Communist commissar. The author showed him in his personal and family life (thus supplementing, as it were, his earlier novel *The Commissars*) with all his foibles and contradictions— with all the temptations, especially of the flesh, lurking in wait for him. In the end the author made him overcome these temptations and foibles. Shorokhov was "reborn" as a true proletarian hero, a living example to the men of the future. One RAPP critic described the novel as Freudian and characterized Shorokhov's experience as a fight with his libido. Calling Shorokhov "a newfangled Party Hamletkin," the critic wrote, "All Libedinsky's characters are pale and impotent shadows of reality, for whom the material world, class struggle, Socialist reconstruction in our country are merely the idealistic creation of self-developing shadows."[14]

Those who criticized Libedinsky's novel won the battle, and the author himself had to admit that it was one of his greatest failures, better to be forgotten.

The attacks on Libedinsky and Ermilov came from the left-wing opposition within RAPP, which for a short period in 1930 was consolidated under the name Litfront (Literary Front). Among its prominent adherents were the former Onguardists Gorbachov and Rodov, the poet Bezymensky, the playwright Vishnevsky, the critics I. Bespalov and M. Gelfand (both former disciples of Pereverzev), and the Komsomol leader Taras Kostrov, to whom Mayakovsky had dedicated his poem "A Letter About Love." The main object of the Litfront was "to bring literature in line with the progress of Socialist reconstruction."[15] The Litfront attacked the RAPP theory of the "live man," which, it said, led to excessive preoccupation with individual problems. It criticized Fadeyev and some other "proletarian" writers for their excessive "addiction" to Tolstoy and Flaubert and their neglect of such revolutionary representatives of bourgeois literature as Schiller and Heine (one of Fadeyev's polemical articles in 1929 was entitled "Down with

[13] See D. Tamarchenko and N. Tanin, "Napostovstvo ili voronshchina?" ("Onguardism or Voronskyism?"), *Pechat' i Revolyutsiya*, No. 5–6 (1930), 40–47.

[14] See A. Kamegulov, "Pismo tovarishcham" ("A Letter to Comrades"), *Pechat' i Revolyutsiya*, No. 5–6 (1930), 29–40.

[15] See Ermolaev, *Soviet Literary Theories, 1917–1934*, 210.

Schiller!"). Litfront also championed Mayakovsky as a truly proletarian writer, while RAPP's official attitude toward him was much more guarded.

The leadership of RAPP had no difficulty in defeating the Litfront, and the latter was soon disbanded. Some of its stalwarts disappeared from literature. The struggle within RAPP went on, however, while at the same time some of RAPP's policies came to be criticized by the party. Among other things, curiously enough, RAPP was reprimanded in *Pravda* for supporting Demyan Bedny in connection with his poem "Slezay s pechki!" ("Get off the Stove!"), in which the poet was said to have slandered the Great Russian branch of the Russian people. The poem provoked a letter from Stalin to Bedny, in which one can see a foretaste of Soviet nationalism to come.[16]

[16] Stalin's letter was dated December 12, 1930. It is to be found in his *Sochineniya* (*Works*), XII, 23–27. For a detailed discussion of the Litfront episode see Brown, *The Proletarian Episode in Russian Literature*, and Ermolaev, *Soviet Literary Theories, 1917–1934*.

Chapter 17. OLESHA'S INNER DIALOGUE

To recount in detail the RAPP campaign of vituperation against all non-comformist writers and critics would be an impossible and dreary task. But the tragic plight of a talented Soviet author trying to preserve his artistic individuality and to reconcile his conception of literature with the demands of the "ruling class" on him may well be illustrated by the case of Yury Olesha.

The publication of Olesha's *Envy* in 1927 was hailed by nearly all Soviet critics as an event of great literary importance. Even diehard proletarian critics from VAPP and RAPP joined in the chorus of praise. Particular enthusiasm was displayed by V. Ermilov, who missed Olesha's irony and chose to see in Andrey Babichev a portrait of a good Communist and of the new Soviet man. The fallacy of this view was soon exposed by more perspicacious critics. Ya. Chernyak, in an article in Volume V of *Pechat i Revolyutsiya* (1928), wrote that Communism would ultimately reject Babichev, although for the time being it still needed him and his model canteen. In 1929, Lezhnev spoke of Babichev as "an Americanized business-man," while Polonsky called him a "parody" and said that he was as much of a bourgeois as his antipode Kavalerov. Polonsky continued to regard *Envy* very highly as a work of literature and voiced the opinion that Olesha's artistic success in "objectivizing his own inner lyrical world" (which meant, of course, identifying Olesha with Kavalerov) implied "the possibility of conquering it."[1] Olesha's subsequent works, however, showed that he was obsessed by but one theme—and that an essentially individualistic one.

In his story "The Cherry Stone" (written in 1929), in which there are many allusions to his "controversy" with his age, Olesha compared art to wandering in an invisible country, "the country of attention and imagination." The wanderer is not alone. He is accompanied and held by the hand by two sisters: "One sister is called Attention, and the other, Imagination." There is also much that is revealing in Olesha's autobiographical fragments. In his very interesting "Zapiski pisatelya" ("Writer's Notes"), written in 1931 and included in the 1934 volume of his *Selected Works* (which also included *Envy*), Olesha speaks of the artist as a magic photographer who sees the world afresh and transforms it: "One must see the world in a new

---

[1] V. Polonsky, "Preodolenie zavisti" ("Overcoming of Envy"), *Novy Mir* (*New World*), No. 5 (1929), 196. Later Olesha himself admitted this when he said: "Yes, Kavalerov looked at the world with my eyes."

way. It is very good for a writer to engage in this kind of magic photography. This is not a trick, nothing to do with Expressionism. On the contrary, it is the purest, the healthiest Realism."

Two other autobiographical fragments, both written in 1928 and included in *The Cherry Stone*—"Ya smotryu v proshloye" ("I Look into the Past") and "Chelovechesky material" ("Human Material")—showed that Olesha was eager to overcome his individualism, to unburden himself of his "bourgeois" past, and to attune himself to the Revolution. In the latter he wrote:

I seize myself in myself, I seize by the throat the me that wants to turn suddenly and stretch its hands toward the past. The me that thinks that the distance between us and Europe is but a geographical distance. The me that thinks that everything that is going on is only his life, unique and unrepeatable—*my* all-embracing life, the end of which cuts short all that exists outside me.

I want to crush within me my second I, my third I, and all the I's that are crawling out of the past.

I want to destroy all small feelings within me.

If I cannot be an engineer of the elements, I want to be an engineer of human material.

In "I Look into the Past," Olesha spoke of solitude, of "a lonely human destiny," and of "being alone everywhere and in everything." Such a lonely man, he said, is called a dreamer. People laugh at him and make him laugh, too, and then explain it by characterizing him as "worthless and officious," while he

walks on, lonely, his head drawn into his shoulders, and in his mind vanity, haughtiness, self-humiliation, contempt for human beings, alternating with tenderness, and thoughts about death produce a never-subsiding storm. It never breaks out of this sickly skull, the man tames it, drawing his head into his shoulders, but now and then he turns round to look at those who laughed, and they see then that the face which always made them laugh is bared in a dog's scowl.

This tragic self-portrait of a lonely artist appeared in print when optimism and collective enthusiasm were the order of the day in Soviet literature, and it is no wonder that Soviet critics began to speak of Olesha's lack of harmony with "the great era of Socialism."

In 1931 appeared Olesha's play *Spisok blagodeyaniy* (*A List of Blessings*). Its dramatic structure had many weak points, but it was interesting as a further development of the theme of loneliness and of other favorite motifs of Olesha's. Full of literary reminiscences and allusions (motifs from *Hamlet*, from Andersen's "The Ugly Duckling," and from Chaplin's films play an important part in it), it was quite unlike the contemporary run-of-the-mill Five-Year Plan plays, with their glorification of Socialist construction and their vilification of its enemies, the wreckers, and their sharp, black-and-white division of characters into heroes and villains. Olesha's play, with its Symbolist undercurrents and its close interweaving of personal and social motifs, reminded one rather of Ibsen.

The central figure of the play is a famous Soviet actress, Elena Goncharova. The play is divided into eight scenes. It begins with a prologue in the theater after a performance of *Hamlet*. The performance has been followed by a post mortem, and now Goncharova, who played the title role and who is about to leave to go abroad, has to answer written questions. Her answers to some of them represent clues to certain problems, which Olesha then sets out to develop in dramatic form. One of the questions is: Why is *Hamlet*, this old foreign play, which was "evidently written for the intelligentsia" and which the working-class spectator cannot understand, being shown? Goncharova's answer is: "*Hamlet* is the best thing produced by the art of the past. So I believe. In all probability, *Hamlet* will never again be shown to Russian audiences. I decided to show it to our country for the last time." To the questions: "Why produce *Hamlet*? Are there no contemporary plays?" Goncharova answers: "Contemporary plays are schematic, false, devoid of fantasy, rectilinear." On the note which reads: "In the period of reconstruction, when everybody is seized by the frenzied tempo of building, it is disgusting to listen to your Hamlet's wearisome soul-searchings," Goncharova's comment is: "I believe that in the period of quick tempi an artist must think slowly." More personal questions, which run: "You're a famous actress; your earnings are good. What do you miss then? Why in the photographs is there such a restless expression in your eyes?" elicit the following candid reply from Goncharova: "Because it is very difficult for me to be a citizen of the new world." One of the notes handed to her Goncharova tears up without reading. The last note contains a request to repeat the flute scene between Hamlet and Guildenstern. She accedes to it, and this gives Olesha an opportunity to state, in Shakespeare's words, his own artistic credo. Goncharova recites Hamlet's answer to Guildenstern:

Why, look you now, how unworthy a thing you make of me. You would play upon me; you would seem to know my stops; you would pluck out the heart of my mystery; you would sound me from my lowest note to the top of my compass; and there is much music, excellent voice in this little organ, yet cannot you make it speak. 'Sblood, do you think I am easier to be played on than a pipe? Call me what instrument you will, though you can fret me, you cannot play upon me,

But it is Olesha himself who answers his epoch, his country, and its Guildensterns from the Communist party.

Just as Goncharova finishes the monologue, one more note falls on the stage at her feet. She picks it up and reads: "What was written in the note which you tore up? Answer honestly." She says that she was asked whether she would return from abroad and that her honest answer to that question is: "I shall."

Scene 2 shows Goncharova and a friend of hers, Semyonova, also an actress, preparing a farewell party on the eve of Goncharova's departure for Paris. On the wall hangs a large portrait of Charlie Chaplin. Goncharova asks her friend to dust it from time to time and then addresses the portrait: "Chaplin, Chaplin! Little man in frayed trousers. I am going to see your famous films. Katya, . . . I shall see "The Circus" and "The Gold Rush." The whole world went into raptures about them. . . . Years have passed, and we still have not seen them. . . ."

She visualizes herself arriving in Paris on a rainy day, when sidewalks, umbrellas, and capes will shine "in Maupassantish slush," and she will go to see and cry over a Chaplin film in some small Parisian cinema. Then she remembers a notebook she wants to entrust to her friend's care during her absence. She wonders whether she should not take it with her and sell it abroad. Semyonova thinks it must be her diary, the diary of an actress, but Goncharova corrects her: "No, it isn't the diary of an actress. It is the secret of the Russian intelligentsia, . . . the whole truth about the Soviet world." Goncharova shows her friend the book and explains: "Look, the book is divided into two halves. Two lists. Here is the first half: a list of crimes of the Revolution."

Semyonova advises her to hide the book, but Goncharova retorts:

Don't be afraid. You think, these are crude complaints about the shortage of provisions? Don't be afraid, it's something different. I speak about the crimes against personality. There are many things in the policy of our government which I cannot put up with. Come here. Look: here, on the other side is a list of blessings. You think I can't see and understand the blessings of the Soviet government? Now let us put the two halves together. This will be me. You see? It is my anxiety, my ravings. Two halves of one conscience, a confusion which drives me crazy. I'll hide it in this suitcase. It mustn't be left here. Anything may happen. Someone will find it. Awful. They'll interpret it in a vulgar way, they'll say: "A counterrevolutionary."

"Why not really sell it abroad?" suggests Semyonova. Goncharova is indignant:

What? Tear off one half? Only the crimes. For abroad they won't pay a penny for a list of blessings of the Soviet government. Show only the items of malice and pass over in silence the items of enthusiasm? No. This notebook cannot be torn. I am not a counterrevolutionary. I am a creature of the old world who is arguing with herself.

The scene ends with the appearance of the director of the theater and a young man who brings Goncharova a large bouquet from workers as a token of gratitude for her acting. Goncharova asks the young man to thank them and tell them that she will soon be back and that she is proud to be an actress in the land of the Soviets.

In the next scene the action switches to Paris and becomes rather melodramatic. Paris is shown as a city of contrasts, typical of the crisis that eats away at the heart of capitalist Europe—of luxury and pleasure hunting on the one hand and poverty and unemployment on the other. The contrast is symbolized in the International Artists' Ball, organized by the banker Lepelletier as a diversion amidst the economic slump, and a demonstration by the unemployed that is being prepared simultaneously. Goncharova, the famous Soviet actress, is expected to appear at the ball. She is tempted to buy on credit a beautiful evening dress from a Russian *émigré* dressmaker; and a White Russian journalist, who accidentally discovers and steals her secret notebook with its two lists, publishes in his paper her list of crimes of the Soviet government, alleging that Goncharova sold it to him for four thousand francs (the price of the evening dress). In support of this allegation he produces Goncharova's receipt written on the back of the newspaper's letterhead paper. This receipt he sends, together with the notebook, to the Soviet embassy, and some Soviet officials whom Goncharova meets in Paris believe the whole story and treat her as a traitor.

There is also a grotesquely improbable scene between Goncharova and Margeret, the director of a French music hall in which she hopes to appear in the flute scene from *Hamlet* and thus earn the money she owes for the dress. The whole dialogue between them is at cross-purposes. Margeret has no use for the scene from *Hamlet*. Thinking that Goncharova is a flutist, he suggests that she appear as a special attraction on the program. She will begin by playing a minuet on the flute and then swallow the flute. The audience will gasp. "Then you will turn your back to the audience and it will appear that the flute is sticking out from a place from which flutes never do. This will be all the more piquant since you're a woman. . . . Then you will begin to blow on the flute from the other end, so to speak—and this time not a minuet, but something jollier." The scene ends with Goncharova leaving the theater alone, depressed and humiliated, and soliloquizing. She wants now to go home, back to the country which is "rebuilding the world."

In the street she meets a lamplighter and a man who turns out to be a workman dismissed by Margeret. She gives him some money. When she is gone and the lamplighter has lit the street lamp, the other man turns out to be a perfect likeness of Chaplin—with his shock of hair, his mustache, his bowler, his big boots, and his cane.

The play ends on a rather shrill, melodramatic note with Goncharova's death in an attempt to protect a Communist leader of the unemployed from the police. She is killed by a crazed Russian *émigré* who was hired to assassinate the Communist leader.

As a drama the play has, I repeat, many weak points, while, ideologically speaking, it lacks consistency, and the symbolic ending is rather artificial. However, the very fact that Olesha uses the method of symbolic realism is significant. But the main interest lies in those bits of dialogue in which Olesha carries on the argument with himself. One of the most important passages is a conversation between Goncharova and Fedotov, a Soviet trade official who is on his way home from the United States. Fedotov asks her about her pastimes in Paris. She says she just walks about, and then goes on:

Sometimes I stop and look. I see my shadow lying. I gaze at it and I think: my shadow is lying on the stones of Europe. I live in a new world. Now tears well up in my eyes when I see my shadow on the stones of the old world. I recall my personal existence in the world which you call new. What did it consist of? Only of thinking. The Revolution deprived me of the past and did not show me the future. So my thoughts became my present. To think. Think. I did nothing but think—with my thought I wanted to grasp what I could not grasp with my senses. A human life is natural only when thoughts and sensations are in harmony. I was shorn of that harmony, and therefore my life in the new world was unnatural. With my thought I fully grasped the idea of Communism. With my brain I believed that the triumph of the proletariat was natural and lawful. But my feelings spoke against it. I was torn asunder. I fled here from this double life—had I not done so I would have gone crazy. In the new world I was like a broken sliver of glass of my country. Now I have come back, and the two halves have been joined together. I live a natural life, I have recovered the present tense verbs. I eat, I touch, I look, I walk. . . . A speckle of dust of the old world, I am deposited on the stones of Europe. They are ancient, mighty stones. They were laid down by the Romans. No one will move them.

To which Fedotov replies with true Communist fervor: "They will soon be wrenched out of the ground, and barricades will be built of them." He is indignant when Goncharova tells him that for three weeks she has been resting from thoughts of the Revolution and that it is natural for a human being to think about his or her own self. When Fedotov denounces this as "a man-in-the-street's attitude," Goncharova corrects him: "In other words, human." I am an actress, she says, and "an actress becomes great only when she gives flesh to a democratic theme, which everybody understands and by which everybody is moved."

When Fedotov retorts that Socialism is such a theme, she disagrees, and to his question: "What is, then?" replies: "The theme of a lonely human destiny. Chaplin's theme. An ugly man wants to be good-looking. A beggar wants to be rich. A lazy man wants to receive a legacy. A mother wants to join her son."

There is no doubt that much of what Goncharova says reflects Olesha's own innermost thoughts. It is he who suffers from the dichotomy of thoughts and feelings, he who yearns for a "democratic theme" by which all would be moved. This was understood by many Soviet critics and more or less admitted by Olesha himself.

There is also much that is interesting in what Tatarov, the White Russian journalist, says of Goncharova:

She was allowed a great deal. She produced *Hamlet*. Think only: *Hamlet* in a country where art has been reduced to the status of propaganda for pig-breeding, for digging silage pits. . . . And yet . . . her most ardent desire was to flee here. . . . Through her . . . I shall prove once again, and most convincingly, that there is slavery in Russia. There has been talk of it throughout the world. But what does the world hear? It hears the grievances of lumberjacks, the obscure bellowing of slaves who can neither think nor shout. And now I can extract a complaint from a highly talented creature. . . . A famous actress from the country of slaves will shout to the world: Don't, don't believe my fame! It was a price paid for my refusal to think. Don't believe my freedom; I was, after all, a slave.

This passionate denunciation of Soviet slavery is put, of course, into the mouth of the enemy, of one of the villains of the play, but it has a ring of sincerity.

On the face of it, the play was a denunciation of the old decadent bourgeois world which Goncharova (just as Kavalerov) had idealized from afar. At contact with it she experienced a change of heart. For her list of crimes of the Soviet government she substituted a list of the crimes of capitalism. And Olesha made her into a tragic victim who, by her death on the ancient stones of Europe, expiates her temporary betrayal of the new world. But subsequent events showed that for Olesha himself the tragic dilemma was by no means solved, and the inner dialogue went on.

In 1932 the magazine *30 Dney* (*30 Days*) published a short piece by Olesha entitled "Something from the Secret Notebooks of the Fellow Traveler Sand."[2] Modest Sand, a Soviet writer, a fellow traveler, is obviously Olesha's alter ego, and the whole piece must be (and was) taken as a barely disguised personal confession. Sand-Olesha begins by saying that he is very fond of looking at himself in a mirror, that while some men never even dream of doing it, he would not miss a cupboard with a looking glass that was being loaded on to a furniture van. This introduction sets the appropriate note of extreme individualism and introspection. Sand continues:

When you think that you are a writer and that you live in an epoch when a new class is rising, and when you begin to check yourself, to look around, to weigh up what you have done, it becomes clear that your doings, which at moments seem to you so important, are in fact extremely insignificant by comparison with the majestic character of all that forms the history of these years and days.

[2] "Koe-chto iz sekretnykh zapisey poputchika Zanda," *30 Dney* (*30 Days*), No. 1 (1932), 11–17. I have chosen the spelling "Sand" in English because of a reference in the "Notes" to George Sand.

Sand mentions a picture at which he likes to look. It shows Schiller being given a triumphant ovation by the people after the first performance of his *Kabale und Liebe*:

It is the rising class greeting its poet. . . . I am a poet, too. How can I help dreaming about my own *Intrigue and Love*—about a new drama which would shake the proletariat just as once upon a time Schiller's drama shook the burghers? How can I not dream about strength? Not to crave passionately, to the point of howling, to the point of tears, for strength which a writer must have when a new class rises?

Quoting Benvenuto Cellini's words about his envy of other masters, Sand speaks of his own "noble envy" of several writers: of Jack London ("I could write equally fine things, since life itself, by creating such circumstances, favors me in this"); of Balzac ("the wizard who sees the way all the people around him live, what they want, and what they think"); of Pushkin ("He should be envied more than anybody, because when he was twenty-four, he wrote *Boris Godunov*, a tragedy . . . which attains such perfection as has not existed either before or after him"). There is also Tolstoy, says Sand, but one cannot envy him, "because he just *was*, as natural phenomena are—stars or waterfalls," and he chose the mightiest adversaries to fight, before whom the rest of mankind lay prostrate: Napoleon, Death, Christianity, Art, and Life itself, since he wrote *The Kreutzer Sonata*. "Envy and ambition are forces that aid creation," says Sand. He describes then his friend Kolotilov, a strong man, a scientist: "I think, for instance, that art is the most important thing in life. Like the sky it envelops my life. But Kolotilov asserts that life is vast, and that art is only part of it, just as his science is."

That man is strong, continues Olesha, whose attention is focused on the outer world. For Kolotilov this outer world is experiment, matter:

While for me, a writer, this outer world is the epic. Yes, yes, the epic! To portray events, characters, passions—to be outside.

Passions? But how can I portray another man's passion without inoculating myself with its germ? If I wish to portray greediness or something else, . . . I must stir up in myself, pull out, and straighten out the sprout of that passion! The sprout, unless it is already flowering in me! And in stirring it up I shall set in motion all the others—all the tissues of my mind. So it means again turning the attention to oneself, to the inner world. That's what it is. My very profession—the profession of the writer—is such that my attention cannot belong to the outer world alone.

Sand-Olesha states here his dilemma with the utmost clarity and candor and exclaims passionately: "I don't want to be a writer." Then he makes a vow:

Never to look in a mirror! Never! To get away from the miserable, infantile

242 LITERATURE PUTS ON UNIFORM, 1929–32

habit of scrutinizing oneself. It is a characteristic of the weak. A child in a bath-tub examines its hands, its feet, its little body. . . .

I want to cross out of my consciousness everything that bespeaks weakness. I want to become completely re-educated.[3]

At the end of his "Notes" Sand introduces his friend Bazilevich, a Bol-shevik newspaper editor. Sand tells him of the difficulty of being a writer, of his "lofty desires" and his "agonizing perplexity." Bazilevich does not look long for an answer. "You must merge yourself with the life of the masses," he says. Sand comments upon this answer:

An official phrase. . . . But he utters this phrase with living conviction. Then, if a phrase is official, it does not mean yet that it is not an expression of life. I exclaim that I want to write a new *Intrigue and Love*. It is a highsounding phrase. But I utter it with living conviction, and this phrase is part of my life. . . . A high-sounding phrase is then also an expression of life. And these two phrases meet.

The fragment ends with a variation of Bazilevich's phrase: "You must fuse with the masses!"

In the same number of *30 Dney* appeared a Communist critic's reply to Olesha.[4] He accused Sand of "slandering history" by implying that it used to be more lenient and that now it "oppresses and debases man." Sand was also slandering his country and depreciating that "majestic something which constitutes the history of these years and days." He demanded the right to utter high-sounding phrases—"*any* high-sounding phrases!" exclaimed the critic indignantly. In his opinion the whole thing was "quite simple." In-stead of repeating after Bazilevich that "you must fuse with the masses," Sand should say, "*I* must fuse with the masses."

Olesha's dialogue with himself was now brought into the open, and the same magazine printed an "Open Letter" which a workers' literary group addressed to him. They wrote:

Instead of helping us, you are actually hindering us. You sow panic. You raise alarm. Instead of joining the proletariat in the depiction of the petty bourgeoisie, you share the attitude of Sand, you pull out of yourself the "sprouts" of his passions and "straighten them out" in yourself. . . . In your works, comrade Olesha, there is still no working class, you have not shown our production. . . . You are now concerned with problems of art and of fellow-traveling. . . . You stand before a mirror, consumed by Benvenuto Cellini's "noble envy."[5]

Two months later Olesha published his reply to this letter. It was entitled

[3] In the Russian the word *perestroitsya* is used (literally, "to reconstruct oneself").

[4] I. Bachelis, "Nash otvet poputchiku Zandu" ("Our Answer to the Fellow Traveler Sand"), *30 Dney*, No. 1 (1932), 18–20.

[5] "Otkrytoe pismo rabochego litkruzhka 'Dvoretsstroya' pisatelyu Yuriyu Oleshe," ("Open Letter of the Workers' Literary Group of 'Dvoretsstroy' to the Writer Yury Olesha"), *30 Dney*, No. 3 (1932), 63–64.

"The Necessity of Re-educating Myself Is Clear to Me."[6] Here are the salient points from this candid and courageous statement:

In the course of years themes grow and develop inside the writer. Suddenly, one fine day, he sees that the themes which were his life are not wanted. This is a monstrous shock to him. One theme turns out to be unwanted, another untimely, still another reactionary or demobilizing, and so on.

The writer deletes those themes from his notebook, but this is really no solution:

A deleted theme can rise and stand athwart the brain. A graveyard of themes arises. They rot—these individualistic corpses—and poison the brain. They cannot be brought out. . . .
Half the talent consists of memories. And what is a memory? It includes the philosophy I read, under the influence of which I was brought up—I who was born into the world of private property. . . . One must accumulate new memories, . . . learn to know the workman as I know Sand. . . . This cannot be done all at once. . . . I realize clearly the necessity of re-educating myself. But I am first of all a writer. In other words, imagination has a great power over me. I am even ill with the elephantiasis of imagination, that is, hyperbolism. . . . Do not identify me with Sand. He is only one half of my memories. The other half began to be accumulated by Zubilo.[7] I am still young, there is plenty of time ahead of me, many victories. . . . I know that I shall reach this future . . . along my own ways but I shall reach it. . . . And there is nothing more important for an artist than his own ways.

But this was precisely what the Communist supervisors of literature would not grant Olesha. They wanted him to follow their ways. The editors of *30 Dney* prefaced Olesha's confession with a statement that, while admitting the necessity of re-education, he continued "to think and feel along the old lines." They expressed the hope that the tempo of Olesha's "re-education" would be speeded up by this discussion.

In the next number the same magazine published a scene from Olesha's new play, *Chorny chelovek* (*The Black Man*), the hero of which was to be Modest Sand, the author of the "Secret Notebooks." In a short note Olesha explained the idea of the play. Sand dreams of becoming the writer of the ruling class. To attune himself to his epoch he must reject a number of themes, themes that may be wonderful in themselves but are "not wanted for our times" or are even harmful—"reactionary, pessimistic, demagnetizing." A writer must delete such themes from his notebook. But this is not a solution, for, cast out of the writer's notebook, the theme will dwell in his brain and interfere with his creative effort:

[6] "Neobkhodimost' perestroyki mne yasna: Otvet Yuriya Oleshi litkruzhku. Dvoretsstroya," *30 Dney*, No. 5 (1932), 67–68.
[7] This was Olesha's pen name when he wrote satirical verse for *Gudok* (*The Whistle*). At that time he enjoyed a great success with his many working class readers.

Driven in, it will twist itself and crawl out onto the paper.

If Sand tackles a new, great, living, joyful, "sunny" theme, that black lizard of a theme will nevertheless, one way or another, thrust out its stinking tail or its venomous head through his new work. . . . How is one to kill the lizard theme? . . . The severed parts of the lizard's body will grow again. There are many such themes, a whole nest of poisonous lizards.

Olesha's Sand is obsessed by the theme of murder. He wants to kill a man and does so in a dream. To rid himself of that obsession he decides to consult the Black Man, a graphologist and chiromantist ("a cynic, a quack, a poisoner," adds Olesha). This symbolic character was to be, according to Olesha, a synthetic parody of Freud, Spengler, and Bergson, and of their ideas, a caricature of decadent European thinkers, "a parody of those who write today about the doom of progress and the end of mankind which lies prostrate at the feet of machines." The idea of the play was to show Sand's clash with the Black Man—"the conflict of the idea of death in creation with the idea of rebuilding the world through creation." Whether or not the play was ever finished, no more of it was published, and Olesha's inner dialogue went on in silence.[8] We shall return to its last stages later.

[8] In an article about Olesha's art this play is spoken of as "unfinished." See Lev Levin, "Tema odinokoy sudby" ("The Theme of Lonely Destiny"), in *Literaturny Sovremennik* (*Literary Contemporary*), No. 7(1933), 119–42. In this article, written a year after the above discussion, the author, after analyzing Olesha's obsession with his "lizard themes," comes to the conclusion that Olesha has not yet rid himself of them and advises him to "open the window" and let in "the fresh wind of real life." Levin himself was later accused of "Trotskyism." A Soviet literary critic and scholar, Arkady Belinkov, who defected to the West in 1968 and died two years later, spoke of Olesha's "evolution" as a typical instance of "capitulation and undoing" of a representative of the Soviet intelligentsia. Extracts from his book about Olesha appeared early in 1968 in the Siberian magazine *Baykal*. The book, in its entirety, was to be published in the United States.

Chapter 18. SOME FIVE-YEAR PLAN NOVELS

Among the outstanding Five-Year Plan novels, apart from Pilnyak's *Volga*, were those of Leonov, Katayev, and Sholokhov.

In Leonov's *Sot'* (1931), the Five-Year Plan forms the background of the story, which deals with the construction of a huge paper mill on a small river among the dense forests of northeastern Russia, in a remote, out-of-the-way country, barely touched by civilization and preserving its old way of life. In carrying out their industrial project, the Communists come up against the resistance not only of nature but also of the forces representing the old world. As in his earlier works, it is in this conflict between the old and the new that Leonov is primarily interested. The old is represented by three main elements. First, there is the large mass of conservative peasants who instinctively stick to the old and fear the new. They are supported and inspired by the monks from a neighboring forest hermitage, who represent the force of religion and superstition and its sway over the peasant mass. Finally, there are some individual enemies of the Soviet regime who are engaged in deliberate sabotage.

Leonov

Among the monks Leonov places a young man, Vissarion by name, a former officer of the White Army. He is an active ideological enemy of Communism, with strange and confused ideas of his own. He preaches the coming of a new Attila, the destruction of modern mechanistic civilization, and the resurrection of the "human soul." The reader cannot help feeling that to some extent Leonov sympathizes with these ideas, that they echo the antiurban utterances of Semyon in *The Badgers* and of Zavarikhin in *The Thief*.

The principal Communist in the novel, Uvadyev, combines belief in reason with revolutionary instincts. "Everything is all right," he says, "everything is always all right in the world, but there are still some things in it that need blowing up."

Among the several types of technical specialists in the novel the most interesting is the old engineer Burago, a man of great culture and intelligence who loyally serves the new government but is far from sharing its ideology. The worm of culture is eating away at his heart. But he believes in Russia as a country where anything is possible (Gorky's formula, which many fellow travelers used to justify their acceptance of the Revolution).

245

Another engineer, Renne, is shown as a selfish, narrow-minded enemy of Communism, a saboteur, whose only aim is to wreck the construction.

In the end, Socialism triumphs—all technical and political obstacles are surmounted, Vissarion is murdered, and Renne commits suicide when he realizes that his plans of sabotage have failed. But Leonov is interested not so much in showing the technical success of the Five-Year Plan project as in depicting a tense social conflict, against the background of which he weaves a complex pattern of individual psychology.

Leonov's second Five-Year Plan novel, *Skutarevsky* (1932), has a much more primitive pattern. The social command is more clearly felt in it, and the plot has a touch of melodrama. Leonov introduced into it the fashionable element of industrial sabotage organized from abroad. Its topical character was further emphasized by the fact that Leonov chose for the subject of his novel the wrecking activities in the electrical industry—at the moment when the famous trial of British engineers in Moscow was taking place. Again, however, Leonov was primarily interested in the psychological conflict. There is the inevitable element of family clash. The hero of the novel is Professor Skutarevsky, an old man of pre-Revolutionary training and an international celebrity in the field of electricity. The saboteurs include his son.

Skutarevsky's proletarian origins are duly emphasized. He is not a Communist but is vaguely in sympathy with the new regime and works for it as the head of the Institute of High Frequencies, which has been created at Lenin's personal wish and which is now engaged in secret research work. But Skutarevsky's mentality is on the whole alien to the official Communist ideology (though he is not quite so much of a "fossil" as Pilnyak's Professor Poletika), and Leonov's main purpose is to show how he gradually but inevitably rallies to it and even joins the party. His ideological transformation is closely interwoven with the events of his personal life— the discovery of his son's implication in the sabotage plot, and his own strange and abortive love affair with a young Communist. But as is often the case with Leonov, the novel ends abruptly at the moment when Skutarevsky is about to turn over a new leaf in life.

Katayev   Katayev's *Vremya, vperyod!* (*Forward, O Time!*) is a more genuine Five-Year Plan novel, concerned primarily with production processes and not with social and individual psychology. Instead of inventing a fictitious setting, Katayev described one of the real industrial projects, the gigantic coke-chemical combine at Magnitogorsk. This element of reality was introduced deliberately—Katayev even called his novel a "chronicle." Where in Pilnyak's *Volga* the wall newspaper was merely a literary trick (similar to those which the avant-garde painters before World War I used when they introduced three-dimensional objects into their pictures), the insertion by Katayev of a long article from one of the Soviet papers about the production of high-grade concrete has a different function, and the article is in all probability authentic. Generally speaking, purely technical matter plays a large part in Katayev's novel.

Forward, O Time! differs also from Pilnyak's and Leonov's novels in that it is imbued with real enthusiasm for Socialist reconstruction, with that somewhat naïve Americanism, that cult of machinery bordering on fetishism which was characteristic of Russian Communism at the time. While Pilnyak and Leonov were concerned primarily with human beings and their intellectual and emotional problems, in Katayev's novel purely technical problems play the major part in the plot. The subject is the breaking of the world record for concrete mixing by an enthusiastic brigade of Magnitogorsk workers. All of the action of the novel takes place in one day. Around this subject Katayev has strung a number of diverse characters, drawn vividly but superficially, without any attempt at deep psychological probing. The description of how the brigade of a certain Ishchenko, under the supervision of the young Communist engineer Margulies, breaks the record set by the workers of Kharkov, is vivid and dynamic.

The whole novel, with its quick, cinematographic tempo, its rapidly shifting scenes, bears traces of the influence of John Dos Passos, who at the time enjoyed great popularity in the Soviet Union and was regarded as a revolutionary, not only ideologically but also technically speaking. The saboteurs, who had become almost a fixture in the Five-Year Plan literature, are absent from Katayev's novel, and this in itself is a refreshing feature. By comparison with Pilnyak and Leonov, the general tendency of Katayev's theme is much more optimistic. There is no hint of the sharp cleavage between the old and the new in the Soviet Union.

It is significant that to the enthusiasm and zeal of his 100 per cent Communists Katayev opposes the philosophy of an American industrial magnate who visits Magnitogorsk as a guest and tourist. The magnate lacks faith precisely in that in which the Russian Communists have come to believe with the zeal of converts—in the power of machinery, in mechanized civilization. For him the salvation of mankind lies in a return to God and Nature. The American capitalist does not sound very convincing, but it is perhaps on purpose that Katayev put those unpopular ideas into the mouth of a foreigner and a capitalist. Among his Russians the skeptical note is sounded only by the old engineer Nalbandov, but he is just an opportunist who easily adjusts himself to all conditions and circumstances and not an active enemy of Communism. Only one of the workers, Sayenko, a drunkard and a gambler, is shown as a negative character and a real counterrevolutionary. All the rest are full of Socialist enthusiasm and willing to sacrifice their interests to the common cause. Occasionally there is a slight touch of satire, but there is a great difference between this novel and *The*

Embezzlers or Katayev's satirical plays, and one feels that Katayev must have deliberately blunted the point of his satire. The satirical element is most conspicuous in the conversations between the American millionaire and Nalbandov, where the author treads on safe ground.

Sholokhov   Another aspect of the Five-Year Plan is depicted in Sholokhov's long novel *Podnyataya tselina* (*Virgin Soil Upturned*), the first volume of which appeared in 1931. Written in a more simple, less picturesque style than his vast Cossack epic, it gives a striking and powerful picture of forcible collectivization of agriculture among the Don Cossacks, and of the Cossacks' overt and covert resistance to it—when they hid their stocks of grain, slaughtered their cattle, and so on. As a work of literature this novel may be inferior to *The Quiet Don*, but its interest and value as a social document are unquestionable. It is written with the maximum possible objectivity. There is nothing of Katayev's light-hearted optimism in it. The tragedy of the dispossessed peasants, the conflict between their inborn proprietary instincts and the doctrine of Communism, and the harsh process of so-called dekulakization are shown in all their stark reality and acuteness. Most of the characters are Cossacks, and there are many finely drawn portraits of various types. The only outsider is Davydov, a workman from Leningrad, whom the party sends to supervise and speed up the collectivization campaign and who becomes involved in sharp clashes with the Cossacks. It has been rightly said that this novel of Sholokhov's does more to help one understand the realities of collectivization than all the official Soviet literature on the subject put together.

Panfyorov   A more orthodox treatment of this subject we find in *Bruski*, a long novel
(1896–1960)   by Fyodor Ivanovich Panfyorov, the first two volumes of which appeared in 1930. Its success at first was enormous; it had very large sales, and the Soviet press was almost unanimous in praising it. Several literary groups claimed Panfyorov as their spokesman. Officially, he stood closest to Libedinsky's On Literary Guard and was regarded as a true proletarian writer.

Bruski is a long, rather tedious, and almost plotless novel with a multitude of characters (most of whom fail to come to life) and a strong political bias, since one of the main objects of the author was to demonstrate the advantages of collective farming over individual tenure of land. The novel takes its title from the name of an estate somewhere on the Volga. Its owner died before the Revolution, and it was on the point of passing into the hands of a rich peasant, a kulak, when the Revolution occurred. It was then seized by the village poor, who eventually turned it into a collective farm. The hero is a certain Kiril Zhdarkin. Demobilized after the war, he returns to his native village and is struck by the poverty and ignorance of his fellow villagers. He takes to his farming with great zest but gradually comes to realize that if he limits his interests to it, he will himself degenerate into a kulak. He gives up his farm, goes to the city, and becomes a factory worker. Here the truth dawns on him, and he understands that the only salvation for the peasants lies in doing away with individual ownership of land and organizing farming on collective lines. Returning to his village, Zhdarkin organizes a commune in Bruski.

Although biased, the novel is not grossly one-sided and is of some documentary value. It portrays minutely and faithfully the class conflicts and differentiation among peasants. But its value as a work of art is insignificant. Speaking of the third volume, then still in preparation, Panfyorov said somewhat defiantly that he had more to learn from technical works on peat industry than from Tolstoy or Dostoyevsky. Panfyorov's artistic shortcomings were from the very first realized by some critics, but this did not prevent them from proclaiming his novel a classic of Soviet literature. But *habent sua fata libelli*, and a few years later, during the campaign to raise the standard of Soviet literature (of which more will be said in the next chapter), Panfyorov's novel became one of the principal targets for attack. The signal was given by Gorky, who singled out *Bruski* as a glaring example of the low standard of craftsmanship and language in contemporary Soviet literature. A controversy ensued in which Gorky was opposed by Serafimovich and several others, but the great majority of Soviet writers and critics sided with Gorky, and a veritable hurricane of criticism and even abuse was unleashed against Panfyorov and his novel.

Among the novels dealing with the industrial aspects of the Five-Year Plan may be mentioned also Gladkov's *Energiya* (*Power*) and Shaginyan's *Gidrotsentral* (*Hydrocentral*), both describing, at great length and with minute detail, vast construction projects.

There were also numerous Five-Year Plan plays, all of them built more or less on the same pattern—with good, honest Communists for heroes, and spies, wreckers, and saboteurs for villains. All had the inevitable happy ending, the villains being unmasked and duly punished. Of these plays, Kirshon's *Bread* and some others enjoyed a considerable if ephemeral success. In poetry, too, the Five-Year Plan subjects were exploited by Bezymensky, Selvinsky, Aseyev, Kirsanov, and other poets. But the end of the RAPP period in literature came about soon in a sudden and spectacular fashion.

Part V. **Literature in the Doldrums, 1932–41**

Chapter 19. THE "REFORM" OF 1932

The reversal of literary policy came as a bolt from the blue on April 23, 1932, when the Central Committee of the Communist party made what was almost immediately described as its "historic" decision. In substance it meant the disbanding of all proletarian (and other) literary organizations and the creation, in their place, of a single Union of Soviet Writers. This step was motivated by the "achievements of Socialist reconstruction," which made the existence of separate proletarian literary and artistic organizations superfluous. The party decided that, having succeeded in breaking in literature and subordinating it to its plan, it had achieved a sufficient degree of homogeneity which could be maintained in future.

This reversal of policy meant doing away with the very conception of fellow travelers. For some time the more moderate among the Communist writers and critics had been insisting that it was wrong to lump all fellow travelers together—that those who were known under this name could really be divided into two main groups: (1) enemies of the Revolution, whether open or disguised, and (2) its allies. This was in substance the point of view advocated from the very first by Voronsky; and just as, on the political and economic plane, Stalin, after denouncing Trotsky's views and disposing of him, adopted much of the policy championed by the latter, so now, on the literary plane, much of the denounced and abused "Voronskyism" was actually carried into practice. Most of the fellow travelers were raised to the rank of full-fledged allies. Averbach and his followers were completely disavowed, their policy was declared harmful, and those who had suffered in silence from the mailed fist of their dictatorship now felt free to attack them and heap abuse on them. Soviet newspapers and magazines for the latter part of 1932 were full of violent denunciations of "Averbachism." It was only later, however, that Averbach's activities were officially connected with those of the enemies of the Soviet regime, the Trotskyites and "Fascist agents," and Averbach's literary dictatorship presented in a new light as part of a Machiavellian plot against the very foundations of the Soviet state and its internal and external security. What happened to Averbach personally is not known for certain. Officially his name did not figure in any of the opposition purges.[1]

[1] Nor is it to be found in the new *Kratkaya Literaturnaya Entsiklopediya* (*Short Literary Encyclopaedia*) which began to appear in 1962 and of which five volumes were published by 1969 (ending with the entry *Pripev*). Each volume contains a

The 1932 resolution of the Central Committee did not explicitly denounce the literature of the Five-Year Plan period. On the contrary, it emphasized that in the past few years literature and art in the Soviet Union had grown, both quantitatively and qualitatively speaking, and this growth was ascribed to the successes of Socialist reconstruction. The resolution recalled how, a few years earlier, when "alien elements" were still active in Soviet literature and proletarian literature was still weak, the party had helped, by every means in its power, in the fostering of special proletarian organizations. "But now," went on the resolution, "that the rank-and-file of proletarian literature has had time to grow and assert itself and that new writers have emerged from factories, plants, and collective farms, the framework of the existing proletarian literary and artistic organizations is becoming too narrow and hinders the proper development of artistic work." There was a danger, therefore, that these organizations might be turned into a means of cultivating exclusive coteries and of diverting a large body of writers and artists from contemporary political problems. It can be seen, then, that behind the Central Committee's "historic" decision lay not so much the concern for the writers' and artists' freedom as the realization that Averbach's tactics of dictatorial regimentation of art were not bearing fruit and that other methods had to be tried to ensure that literature should follow the party line, without at the same time impairing its quality.[2]

An important role in this reversal of policy was played by Gorky. He was one of the first to draw attention to the noticeable lowering of literary standards after 1929. In his campaign for raising the standard of literature he was supported by the most talented among the Communist writers, such as Sholokhov and Fadeyev. After the passage of the 1932 resolution Gorky's voice became particularly authoritative in all literary matters and more than ever he came to be looked upon as the *doyen* of Soviet letters.

From the practical point of view, the most important part of the 1932

----

number of names of writers who were "illegally repressed during the period of the cult of personality" and "posthumously rehabilitated" (this is the formula which, with slight verbal variations, is used throughout). There have been no signs of Averbach's "rehabilitation." But the year of his death as given elsewhere (1938) suggests that he was probably purged. More will have to be said about this whole problem of unpersons in the account of the post-Stalin period.

[2] For a good analysis of the RAPP period in Soviet literature and a complex picture of relations both within RAPP and between RAPP and the Party, see Brown, *The Proletarian Episode in Russian Literature, 1928–1932*. From Brown's retrospective account of all the controversies of the period, RAPP itself emerges as one of the victims of party policies aimed at still further *Gleichschaltung*. It is true that toward the end of this period RAPP was getting out of hand and showing signs of impatience with the dead, schematic literature which had resulted from excessive regimentation. It is also true, however, that independent nonparty writers had come to associate RAPP with the party and to look upon it as the main instrument of controls.

resolution of the Central Committee was that which decreed the creation of a single Union of Soviet Writers. This step was designed primarily to put an end to factional squabbles and to create a body that would be more or less homogeneous, held together by officially approved bylaws and hence more easily controllable. The union was to comprise all Soviet writers who accepted the general policy of the Soviet government, supported Socialist reconstruction, and adhered in their work to the method of Socialist Realism. This last restriction was the most important. However ill-defined may have been this method (as we shall see presently), its use circumscribed the writer's scope by imposing on him the obligation to deal in his work with "Socialist realities." By the very act of adhering to the Union of Soviet Writers—and this act, though formally a voluntary one, was too closely bound up with all sorts of material and other advantages to be really regarded as such—a Soviet writer limited the range of his creative work of his own accord and agreed to serve the Soviet state and its ultimate policies in his capacity as a writer.

In a way this restriction meant going back on the amount of freedom which the famous resolution of 1925 had accorded to those who were then termed fellow travelers, not to speak of the earlier period of more or less spontaneous literary creation, when such a document as the manifesto of the Serapion Brothers, proclaiming that literature need not reflect the epoch and that a writer had a right to be politically detached, was still conceivable. Henceforth it was enough to prove that a work of literature (or any other work of art, for that matter) was incompatible with the spirit of Socialist Realism—that it contained a slight admixture of "poisonous idealism," or "Formalism"—to place it outside the pale of Soviet literature. This a priori imposed on the writers a great circumspection in their choice of themes and their treatment of them. The political factor remained decisive, and although writers were no longer expected to write purely industrial or political novels, they were expected to adhere to Socialist Realism or face ostracism. The Union of Soviet Writers was thus a typical by-product of totalitarian regime. It was not an ordinary professional organization, for all its members were not only obliged to subscribe to a definite political program but also tied down to a specific literary method.

Since one of the principal objects of the 1932 reform was to ensure homogeneity in Soviet literature—or, in other words, complete compliance of the writers with the demands made on them by the party—considerable importance attaches to the Literary Institute which was created as an adjunct to the Union of Soviet Writers. Its function was to train and indoctrinate young Soviet writers. Many of the younger writers later active in Soviet literature (Simonov, Aliger, and others) studied at this institute, of which Gorky was the principal sponsor.

Chapter 20. SOCIALIST REALISM: THEORY

The statute of the Union of Soviet Writers provided that all its members should apply in their work the method of Socialist Realism. As with everything else in the Soviet Union, the coining of this formula was ascribed to Stalin himself, who was also said to have formulated the role of Soviet writers as "engineers of human minds."

The same statute defined as the object of Socialist Realism "the creation of works of high artistic significance, saturated with the heroic struggle of the world proletariat and with the grandeur of the victory of Socialism, and reflecting the great wisdom and heroism of the Communist party . . ., the creation of artistic works worthy of the great age of Socialism."

In itself this directive was, apart from the obvious political implications, sufficiently vague to allow a variety of interpretations; and, to begin with, Socialist Realism was interpreted by Soviet commentators as implying a considerable latitude of styles. However, so far as the stress was on the word "realism," this formula was directed against "romanticism," on the one hand, and against all sorts of "formalistic" experiments, on the other. Thereby it merely sanctioned the tendency which had already been dominant in Soviet literature ever since 1925. "Back to Realism" was the slogan, launched by Voronsky and Lezhnev, underlying the revival of the novel after 1924. As time went by, this tendency became even more pronounced in the work of the proletarian writers, most of whose novels were nearer to old-fashioned realism than the early works of Fedin and Leonov, let alone of Pilnyak. It is significant that the invitation to learn from the classics came not only from Gorky and Fadeyev but also from Bezymensky, the early proletarian disciple of Mayakovsky.

But if, by proclaiming realism to be the dominant trend of the new age, Soviet leaders merely consecrated the status quo, by qualifying it as "Socialist" they hardly helped make matters clearer. The question arose at once wherein lay the difference between Socialist Realism and realism pure and simple? Was it only in the Socialist contents of a work, in its Socialist message? But why, then, was it necessary to speak of a new literary method and style? Some Soviet critics drew a parallel between Socialist Realism and what a Russian critic of the 1870's, Shelgunov, had described as "popular realism," which he opposed to the "aristocratic realism" of most Russian writers of the nineteenth century (Turgenev, Tolstoy, Goncharov, Pisemsky). A typical representative of popular realism was seen by Shelgunov in one of the minor "populist" novelists of the sixties, Reshetnikov. He described the essence of popular realism as preoccupation with social psychology above all. Instead of individuals and representatives of the upper classes its writers focused their attention on the "masses," on the middle class, and on the peasants.[1] According to Soviet critics, popular realism, which had survived in different forms till the October Revolution, could no longer meet the situation. And like their predecessors in the 1860's, after the emancipation of the peasants, the realist writers were now confronted with the task of discovering a new realistic method that would fit in best with the historical realities of the moment. First of all, they had to realize that this new variety of realism must oppose itself to popular realism as typical of the obsolete small-bourgeois mentality. Socialist Realism was called upon to reflect *Socialist* realities and *socialistic* mentality. It was thus, historically speaking, a legitimate successor of popular realism. In the opinion of Pereverzev, who advanced this view, the value of the term "Socialist Realism" lay in the fact that it naturally and inevitably presupposed its historical antithesis which was at the same time its inexorable premise, namely, popular realism. One can see that this attempt at tying Socialist Realism with its historical antecedents did not lead very far.

Other critics opposed Socialist Realism to bourgeois, or critical, realism. The traditional bourgeois realism, they said—the realism of a Balzac and of the great Russian nineteenth-century novelists—was rooted in a critical, more or less negative attitude toward reality. It was born of a protest against that reality and was therefore potentially revolutionary. Socialist Realism, on the contrary, was founded on a positive attitude toward the new realities of a collectivized society. It was fundamentally optimistic; it said "yea" to life, while the old bourgeois realism was fundamentally pessimistic and often implied an unhealthy, morbid attitude toward the world.

Gorky, in his report to the First Congress of Soviet Writers in 1934, said:

> While we do not at all deny the vast and enormous work performed by critical realism and highly appreciate its formal achievements in the art of word-painting, we must understand that we need this realism only for throwing light on the relics of the past, for fighting them, for eradicating them. But this form of realism has never served and cannot serve to educate a socialistic personality, for, while criticizing everything, it never affirmed anything or, at worst, it went back to the affirmation of what it had criticized.[2]

[1] *Populisme* in France in the early 1930's was somewhat similar to Popular Realism thus understood. One of its exponents, Eugène Dabit, author of *Hôtel du Nord*, was very popular in the Soviet Union and died while on a visit there.

[2] M. Gorky, *O literature. Statyi i rechi 1928–1936 (About Literature: Articles and Addresses, 1928–1936)*, 471. A translation of this report will be found in H. G. Scott (ed.), *Problems of Soviet Literature: Reports and Speeches at the First Writers' Congress.*

One of the fervent Marxist critics, Nusinov, whom we shall meet later in a different context, contrasted Socialist Realism with the methods of psychological realism used by Dostoyevsky and Tolstoy. The aim of Socialist Realism was the exact opposite, he said, of Dostoyevsky's psychologism, for Dostoyevsky reduced man's actions to the struggle within him between the forces of good and evil and sought for it a religious solution and explanation. But it was wrong to think, as did some Soviet writers, that Tolstoy's psychological method was any nearer to Socialist Realism. There was only one point in which they met, and that was Tolstoy's moral optimism. But Tolstoy, too, like Dostoyevsky, showed human beings as individuals and not as parts of a social body. For Tolstoy, man was an embodiment of good as long as he was left to himself but became an agent of evil whenever he was, or felt himself to be, part of a social whole. This made Tolstoy's method even more dangerous than Dostoyevsky's, for the latter at least "showed the man of the past in all his iniquity." A Socialist writer, before assimilating Dostoyevsky's and Tolstoy's psychological methods, must substitute for their nonclass and unhistorical attitude, rooted in religious pessimism and abstract ethics, his own social and historical interpretation. Therefore, of the classics of bourgeois realism, Balzac and Stendhal, with their social and historical approach to their themes, were much closer to Socialist Realism than either Tolstoy or Dostoyevsky. For Nusinov, Socialist Realism was called upon to portray "the whole of the reality," both present and past, "in the light of the struggle for Socialism," and its first distinctive characteristic was its "proletarian party-mindedness." We thus see that Socialist Realism and party-mindedness were coupled at a very early stage in the debate.[3]

Finally, an attempt was also made to oppose Socialist Realism to the revolutionary romanticism which characterized the work of many Soviet writers in the early period and to which some of them still clung. There was a long and heated discussion on the relation between Socialist Realism and revolutionary romanticism, the outcome of which was that the latter was recognized as an essential ingredient of Socialist Realism. This view was advocated by Gorky, in whose own work elements of revolutionary romanticism had always been prominent, and he was supported by such romantically inclined Soviet writers as Lavrenyov. Gorky himself went even further when, in one of his articles published in 1934, he proclaimed that revolutionary romanticism was merely "a pseudonym of Socialist Realism."

After gallons of ink had been spilled in fruitless and somewhat scholastic attempts at defining Socialist Realism, a compromise formula, which reconciled Socialist Realism with revolutionary romanticism, was agreed upon, but the dispute about the relation between them was revived again after the war.[4]

[3] I. Nusinov, "Dvoryansko-burzhuazny i sotsialisticheskiy realism" ("Gentry-Bourgeois and Socialist Realism"), *Novy Mir*, Vol. V (1934), 253.

From the very first it was clear that the negative aspects of Socialist Realism were more tangible than the positive. It was fundamentally a re-action against certain existing trends and practices (or malpractices) in literature—as it turned out, a two-pronged reaction. It was a product of the "reform" which had swept away "proletarian" literary and artistic organi-zations and aimed at raising the general level of Soviet literature. Those who were instrumental in bringing about that reform had in mind an all-round improvement of Soviet literature. They wanted to improve the lan-guage and style which had become slipshod and sullied with colloquialisms and dialecticisms (this was one of the chief reproaches Gorky made to Panfyorov); they wanted to do away with the barrenness resulting from the uniformity of themes and their one-sided treatment; and they also wanted to reinstate *man* to his rightful place. Novels, stories, and plays about production and productive processes, about new construction projects and collective farms, were to give place to works which would focus their main interest on human beings, on ordinary Soviet men and their personal life. This element of humanism in Socialist Realism was strongly empha-sized by several speakers at the first Pan-Soviet Congress of Writers, of which more will be said in Chapter 21. Theoretically speaking, Socialist Realism aimed at greater objectivity. By comparison with the immediately preceding period it did enlarge the writer's scope. On the other hand, by imposing on the writer the task of portraying the new Socialist reality and the new Soviet man, and by emphasizing at the same time the heroic nature of the new era of Socialism, it set them on a hunt for new heroes. If, in 1930, Libedinsky had called his novel *The Birth of a Hero*, the usual title for a critical article or a book about Soviet literature in the late thirties be-came "In Search of a Hero." There were, however, very few heroes who satisfied the exacting Communist critics, and the frantic search for "a hero of our times" continued.

Nevertheless, so far as Socialist Realism contributed toward greater ob-jectivity and helped raise the literary standards, it showed its progressive facet. But it had also a conservative, or even reactionary, aspect, for it was also a reaction against what was described, sweepingly and therefore mean-inglessly, as "bourgeois Formalism." This phrase was used to include all experiments with form and technique, and much of earlier Soviet literature came under this description. While in the first stages of the Revolution the avant-garde artists were treated as its natural allies, now those who were responsible for running the most "advanced" state in the world suddenly

---

[4] A meticulous study of all the literary and philosophical debates of the twenties which preceded the formulation of Socialist Realism, as well as of the discussions that took place between the April Resolution of 1932 and the convocation of the First Con-gress of Soviet Writers in August, 1934, will be found in Ermolaev, *Soviet Literary Theories, 1917–1937*, which also contains a valuable bibliography.

turned conservative and began to look askance at all revolutionary experiments in art, dubbing them "bourgeois Formalism." The formula was widely used in the thirties and applied to all fields of art. In visual arts the ban on Formalism and the insistence on representational realism led to a frank revival of stiff and lifeless "Academicism" of the worst variety. In the theater Meyerhold and Tairov, who were responsible for the most interesting and daring theatrical experiments, became the principal targets for attack. Tairov after a time managed to work his way back into the fold, but Meyerhold, who was first deprived of his theater, eventually disappeared from the scene and met his end in a concentration camp. In music one of the first conspicuous victims was Dmitry Shostakovich, whose opera *The Lady Macbeth of Mtsensk*—until then regarded as one of the most notable achievements of Soviet music—seems to have incurred the displeasure of Stalin himself in 1935, with the result that a storm of criticism was unleashed against Shostakovich in the Soviet press, both general and musical, and various musical bodies passed resolutions condemning the opera as an expression of "rotten bourgeois Formalism." For some time Shostakovich was forced into retirement, but he emerged later with his Fifth Symphony, winning back his place in Soviet music. During the war he reaffirmed his position by his Seventh Symphony (*Leningrad*). His subsequent tribulations are well known. Since Shostakovich was highly regarded outside the Soviet Union and his opera was performed with success in several European countries, his case aroused much interest. It was the first clear demonstration of what Communist totalitarianism in art meant.[5]

[5] For some details of the Shostakovich case see the interesting article by G. Abraham, "Shostakovich: A Study of Music and Politics," *Horizon*, Vol. VI, No. 33 (September, 1942). In the light of what happened to Shostakovich and Meyerhold—and since then to so many others—it is interesting and appropriate to recall what Gorky wrote in 1930 apropos the Pilnyak incident and similar ones: "We have a stupid habit of dragging people up to the belfry of fame and throwing them down into the mud after a while. No need for me to specify examples of such absurd and cruel treatment of people; everybody knows them. They remind me of the scenes of 'lynching' of pickpockets in 1917-18." See Gorky, "The Working Class Must Rear Its Masters of Culture," in *About Literature*, 49.

Chapter 21. THE FIRST CONGRESS OF SOVIET WRITERS

In August, 1934, the new Union of Soviet Writers called its first Pan-Soviet Congress in Moscow. The government spokesman at the congress was Andrey Alexandrovich Zhdanov (1896–1948), who later the same year replaced the murdered Kirov as head of the Communist organization in Leningrad and subsequently acquired great notoriety by his cultural "purges."

Literature as the Handmaiden of the State

In his inaugural address at the congress Zhdanov stated quite plainly that literature in the Soviet Union could not but be tendentious. He said:

> Our Soviet literature is not afraid of being accused of tendentiousness. Yes, Soviet literature *is* tendentious, for in the age of class struggle a nonclass, nontendentious, would-be apolitical literature does not and cannot exist.
>
> And I think that every Soviet man of letters can say to any thick-headed bourgeois, to any philistine, to any bourgeois writer who will talk of the tendentiousness of our literature: "Yes, Soviet literature is tendentious, and we are proud of its tendentiousness, because our tendency consists in liberating the toilers, the whole mankind from the yoke of capitalist slavery."[1]

Zhdanov went on to emphasize the fact that the congress was convening at a moment when the main obstacles on the way to Socialist reconstruction had been overcome, when the policy of industrialization and collectivization had been vindicated, when the Socialist system had "finally and irrevocably triumphed in our country under the guidance of the Communist party, under the leadership of genius of our great leader and teacher, Comrade Stalin." The international weight and prestige of the Soviet Union was growing, said Zhdanov, and so was "its importance as the shock brigade of the world proletariat, as the mighty bulwark of the coming proletarian world revolution." The difficulties still facing the Soviet Union would be overcome with the aid of "the great and invincible doctrine of Marx-Engels-Lenin-Stalin." Soviet literature was the youngest of all literatures of the world, but it was also the richest in ideas (*samaya ideynaya*; the word *ideynaya* defies exact translation), the most progressive, and the most revo-

[1] A. Zhdanov, *Sovetskaya literatura—samaya ideynaya, samaya peredovaya literatura v mire* (*Soviet Literature—The Richest in Ideas, the Most Progressive Literature in the World*), 12. This pamphlet reproduces Zhdanov's address at the congress. An English version of it will be found in Scott, (ed.), *Problems of Soviet Literature.*

lutionary. Its successes reflected the achievements of the new Socialist system. It was superior to bourgeois literature which reflected faithfully the decline and decay of the capitalist system, was characterized by "an orgy of mysticism, clericalism, and pornography" and for its "heroes" had thieves, detectives, prostitutes, and hoodlums. Things were different in the Soviet Union:

Our Soviet writers draw for the material for their works of art, their themes, their images, their speech, upon the life and experience of the men of Dneprostroy and Magnitostroy. . . .

In our country the chief heroes of literary works are the active builders of a new life: working men and women, collective farmers, engineers, members of the Komsomol, pioneers. . . . Our literature is saturated with enthusiasm and heroism. It is optimistic, but not through any zoological instinct. It is fundamentally optimistic, because it is the literature of the rising class of proletariat, the only progressive and advanced class.

Zhdanov gave the following definition of Socialist Realism:

Comrade Stalin described our writers as engineers of human minds. What does it mean? What duties does this title impose on you?

It means, above all, to know life in order to depict it truthfully in works of art, to depict it not scholastically, not lifelessly, not just as "objective reality," but to depict real life in its revolutionary development.

In so doing, truthfulness and historical concreteness of artistic depiction must be combined with the task of ideological remolding and re-education of the toiling people in the spirit of Socialism. This method in fiction and in literary criticism is what we call Socialist Realism. . . .

To be an engineer of human minds means to stand with both feet firmly planted on the ground of real life. This, in its turn, means breaking away from old-type romanticism, from that romanticism which depicted nonexistent life and nonexistent characters, diverting the reader from the contradictions and oppressions of life into a world of the impossible, a world of Utopia. Our literature . . . must not shun romanticism, but it must be a romanticism of a new type, revolutionary romanticism. . . . Soviet literature must know how to portray our heroes, it must be able to look into our tomorrow.

Declaring the proletariat to be the only heir to the best treasures of world literature, Zhdanov called upon Soviet writers to "collect, study, and critically digest" the literary heritage "squandered" by the bourgeoisie. He also warned them that Soviet literature had still to live up to the demands of its epoch. Its weak spots reflected "the lagging of consciousness behind economics." But all the prerequisites for producing "works attuned to the epoch" were there.[2]

Zhdanov's address set the keynote to the congress. Most of the writers who took part in its deliberations subscribed to his thesis about the "ten-

[2] All these quotations are from Zhdanov, *Soviet Literature*, 6–14.

dentiousness" of Soviet literature. Vsevolod Ivanov, who as a member of the Serapion Brotherhood had earlier protested against all tendentiousness in literature and demanded from the latter only one thing—"that its voice should not ring false"—could be heard confessing that life had taught him wisdom and that he realized now that "Bolshevik tendentiousness" was an indispensable weapon in a Soviet writer's literary armor.

The principle that literature was *ancilla rei publicae*, which underlay Zhdanov's speech and had always been in fact the unshakable basis of the Communist party policy in literary matters, was fully endorsed by the congress. The latter paid special attention to the problem of producing "national defense literature" to help the Red Army and boost its martial spirit. Vsevolod Vishnevsky, a Communist playwright, author of several plays dealing with the Red Army and Navy life, urged his "friend Olesha" not to overlook, "amidst his dreams about a better future," the more immediate need of being ready to defend, arms in hand, the Soviet Union against the imminent "imperialist" aggression. In its address to Voroshilov, the commissar for defense, the congress undertook "to arm the country and the Red Army with new models of literature," depicting both the Red Army in all its "heroic simplicity and unmatched strength," and its potential enemies, the nature of their objectives and their "antihuman" aims.

Olesha's Plea for Humanism

Vishnevsky's appeal to Olesha referred to Olesha's speech at the congress, one of the most sincere and interesting. Once again, it was a candid personal confession of a Soviet writer who, while doing his best to adjust himself to the new world and meet its demands, was conscious of his ties with the "old world," of the "Kavalerov" in him. It was both frank and pathetic. Olesha began by saying that in every human being there were both good and bad things and that he could not visualize a man incapable of understanding what it meant to be vain, cowardly, or selfish. In an artist this characteristic is particularly developed, and he knows how to pull up the seedlings of the most diverse human passions and turn them into trees. An artist cannot describe a character without becoming that character, at least momentarily. Very often the artist is asked how he knows this or that or whether he has just "invented" it. The answer is that the artist "invents" everything. He cannot invent that which does not exist in Nature, but Nature has no secrets from him, it is more communicative with him than with anyone else. It would be possible to write a book called *The Machine of Transmutations*, which would demonstrate how life impressions are transmuted by the artist into images of art. An artist's relations with the good and the bad, with vice and virtue, are none too simple. When he portrays a negative character, all that is negative in him comes up to the surface. Goethe is reported to have said: "I felt like rereading *Macbeth* but dared not. In the state in which I then was, I was afraid that this reading might kill me." That was true, added Olesha: "An image can kill an artist." He recalled his own *Envy* and what was said about the kinship between the author and his hero. He admitted that Kavalerov's vision of the world was his own and that he was shocked when Kavalerov was denounced as an epitome of vulgarity:

I could not believe that a man with a keen eye and a gift of seeing the world in his own way could be vulgar and worthless. I said to myself: "It means that all this ability, all these things of your own, which you regard as your strength, are worthless and vulgar. Can that be so?" I wished to believe that the comrades who had criticized me (they were Communist critics) were right, and I believed them. I began to think that what I took for a treasure was in fact a sign of poverty. Thus the conception of a beggar was born in me.... My artist's imagination came to my aid, and under its impulse the naked concept of social futility began to take on the form of fiction, and I decided to write a novel about a beggar.

The novel remained unwritten.[3] It was only later that Olesha understood why he did not write it, understood that it was not he who mattered but that which was around him:

While I was thinking over the theme of the beggar and recapturing my youth, my country built factories. It was the First Five-Year Plan. . . . This was not my theme. I could have gone to a construction project, lived at a factory among workers, described them in a reportage, even in a novel, but it was not my theme, it wasn't the theme that was connected with my bloodline, with my breath. I wouldn't have been a true artist had I chosen this theme. I would have lied and invented. I did not have what is known as "inspiration." It is difficult for me to understand a worker, a revolutionary hero. I cannot become one. It is beyond my power, beyond my comprehension. That is why I don't write about it. I felt terrified and began to think that I was unwanted, . . . and thus arose in me the terrifying image of the beggar, the image that was killing me.

Meanwhile, continued Olesha, there grew up a young generation that knew nothing of the old world, and the sight of this new generation brought about the miracle of his own rejuvenation. As an artist he became fascinated by these new, young Soviet men and women:

. . . a young Soviet man is growing up in our country. As an artist I rush to him. "Who are you? what colors do you see? do you ever have dreams? what do you daydream about? what do you feel yourself to be? how do you love? what feelings do you have? what do you reject and what do you accept? what predominates in you—feeling or reason? do you know how to cry? are you tender? have you understood all the things that terrified me and that I could not grasp?

[3] This novel was even announced for publication in one of the Soviet magazines in 1931.

what are you like, young man of the Socialist society?" I cannot write without discovering an analogy between us. I want to create the type of the young man, endowing him with all that was best in my own youth.

Declaring that a writer must be "an educator and a teacher," Olesha announced his intention of writing plays and stories about young people who will be concerned with moral problems and added:

Somewhere there lurks in me the conviction that Communism is not only an economic but also a moral system, and the first to embody this aspect of Communism will be our young men and young women.

I shall endeavor to embody in these works all my sense of beauty, of gracefulness, of nobility, my whole vision of the world . . . in order to prove that the new socialistic attitude to the world is a human attitude in the purest sense of the word. Such is my rejuvenation. I did not become a beggar.

To many sober-minded Communists, Olesha must have appeared a dreamer and an idealist. But his plea for humanism struck some responsive chords. Shklovsky, the one-time cold and calculating Formalist and later an ardent advocate of "factography," spoke of the birth of new proletarian humanism, of the coming era of "a new sensibility." Vera Inber, the former Constructivist, stressed the failure of Soviet literature in portraying "positive" characters and attributed it to the tendency of Soviet writers to draw their characters flat, without all their human flaws and foibles.

A curious and somewhat naïve document was quoted by one of the delegates from Georgia, the novelist Dzhavakhishvili (pseudonym of Mikhail Adamashvili, 1880–1937).[4] It was a "letter of instructions" to the congress from a group of readers, subscribers to a municipal lending library in Rostov-on-Don. Among other things it urged writers

to write more about love, about marriage, to depict ordinary life, without exaggeration, but also without underrating its importance. . . . Give us striking and unforgettable types of heroes of our days, both positive and negative. . . . More historical novels are wanted. The reader needs them greatly. . . . What is more, we want to laugh. Give us a chance to laugh heartily and not just smile gingerly. . . . We want a literature that would be read and that one would feel like reading. . . . Write in simple, correct language. Learn it from the classics.

This document seems to be a fair reflection of the desiderata of the average Soviet reader who was bored by Five-Year Plan literature with its

---

[4] Delegates of various national minorities played an important part at the congress, which proclaimed, as one of the urgent tasks, a closer interpenetration of Russian and other national literatures of the Soviet Union. The differences of languages, it was said, should not conceal the *ideological unity* of Soviet literature thus widely understood. Similarly, a closer intercourse with international revolutionary writers was urged by the principal spokesmen of the congress. Dzhavakhishvili became one of the victims of Stalin's purges.

ready-made patterns, its neglect of ordinary human beings and of their personal problems, and its overemphasis of the ideological element. Dzhavakhishvili himself, in commenting upon this letter of instructions, said that he would put an end to all talk about "forbidden" subjects which was still sometimes heard. To his mind all subjects were good—if treated in the spirit of Socialist Realism.

Many of the speeches at the congress reflected the widespread dissatisfaction with the state of things in Soviet literature in the period preceding the "reform" of 1932. An official statement by Nakoryakov, of the State Publishing House, described 75 per cent of the literary works produced during the years 1929-31 as worthless![5] It will be seen that much of what was produced in the years that followed went to satisfy the demands of the Rostov-on-Don library subscribers.

Olesha himself tried to give life to his idea of the artist's duty to portray young people and their problems in his short film scenario *Strogy yunosha* (*A Strict Youth*), published in 1934 in *Novy Mir*. Its hero was a young Communist, and its theme the problem of "qualitative inequality" in Socialist society, of the place which talent and brains must occupy in it. Olesha's thesis here was that Socialism means inequality and that one must "live up" to those who create spiritual values—music, pictures, ideas, and beauty. Olesha also brought in his favorite theme of "feelings." His young Communist champions some of the feelings which Communists have come to regard as "bourgeois prejudices" but which, he maintains, are really all-human. He devises a new code of Komsomol ethics, based on such qualities as modesty, truthfulness, generosity, altruism, and even sentimentality. This skeleton of a play, almost masquelike in its symbolic delineation of characters, was received coolly by Soviet critics, who detected in Olesha's conception of ethics a dangerous touch of idealism. The film, though made, was never shown. This "play for the cinema" was Olesha's last major prewar contribution to Soviet literature.

Bukharin Sums Up Soviet Poetry

One of the most interesting reports at the congress was made by Nikolay Ivanovich Bukharin (1888-1938), the ablest and most erudite of the theoretical exponents of Soviet Communism, who four years later was to be arrested, tried, and executed on charges of conspiring against the security of the Soviet Union.

Bukharin surveyed the development of Soviet poetry and examined the problems facing it in the era of Socialist Realism. He distinguished three

[5] This statement was quoted by Gorky in his address at the congress (*About Literature*, 480). It is curious to note that L. Timofeyev, in attacking the British edition of the earlier version of this book in the Soviet periodical *Kultura i Zhizn'* (*Culture and Life*, March, 1947), referred to this statement and called it "unfounded."

main periods in the evolution of Soviet poetry. The first period was a period of new slogans, when new principles of life were proclaimed to the working masses of all countries. Its poetry was declamatory, full of sweeping ideas, of cosmic concepts. But it had no flesh and blood; it was a kind of "poetical blueprint," heroic and abstract—"insofar as one can speak of abstract poetry at all." The second period was characterized by a transition to constructive everyday work when specialized knowledge and skill were in demand. Poets turned their attention to the minutiae of life. Cosmic visions of "World Sovnarkoms" gave place to minute depiction of empiric realities. It was a dialectical negation of the preceding period. Universalism passed into its opposite; synthesis gave place to analysis. The third period was just beginning. It was conditioned by the growing complexity of life:

> The problem of mastering the technique of production has not been solved yet, though much has been done. Cultural needs have expanded to an extraordinary degree. Interests have become incomparably more diversified. There is a tremendous desire to know everything, a desire to *generalize*, to rise on a *new* basis to the understanding of the process as a whole. Hence the need that is felt for synthesizing poetry and synthesizing literature in general. . . . This is not just a return to the starting point, not a reversion to declarative, schematic poetry, but a new synthesis which can only arise out of previous analytical work.[6]

Bukharin also examined in detail the work of individual Soviet poets. While admitting that Pasternak shunned topical themes, he spoke of him as "one of the most remarkable craftsmen of verse in our days" and made flattering references to his formal achievements. At the same time he criticized such orthodox Communist poets as Demyan Bedny and Bezymensky for being "elementary" and "old-fashioned" and even made some strictures about Mayakovsky. Underlining the need for raising the general level of poetic culture, he pointed out that those poets who were ideologically above suspicion often tended to be "elementary" and went on as follows:

> Yet one of the hallmarks of a significant work is the wealth of associations and emotions it evokes, of ideas and allusions it contains. If you compare the work of many of our poets with that of Verhaeren you will see how many ideas the latter has . . ., how much culture he possesses. And with us a rhymed slogan often passes for poetry. You may mention Mayakovsky. But to some extent time has set its stamp on him, too, for life has grown infinitely more complex, and we must march forward. Culture, culture, and once more culture!

Bukharin's strictures about Demyan Bedny, Bezymensky, and even Mayakovsky, especially next to his praise of Pasternak, Tikhonov, and

---

[6] This and subsequent quotations are taken from N. Bukharin, *Poèziya, poètika i zadachi poèticheskogo tvorchestva v SSSR* (*Poetry, Poetics and Tasks of Poetic Creation in the U.S.S.R.*). An English version of Bukharin's report can be found in Scott (ed.), *Problems of Soviet Literature*, 185–260.

Selvinsky, and his derogatory references to certain aspects of "proletarian" poetry, provoked some spirited protests from several delegates. Bedny and Bezymensky rose to defend themselves, while others, whom Bukharin in his reply described sarcastically as "Mayakovsky's poor relations," took up the defense of the late poet. Replying to Kirsanov, Surkov, and others who had accused him of brushing aside Mayakovsky's propaganda poetry, Bukharin said:

> Pardon me, but I rate Mayakovsky very highly, and I used a formula which says that he has become "a classic of Soviet poetry"; but this does not mean that even such a great man as Mayakovsky must be idolized. For you are idolaters and fetishists if you do not understand that *life keeps moving forward.* I am not against propaganda poetry as such, I am not against tendentious poetry in the good sense of that word. . . . I said that propaganda itself must undergo a change now, that the conception of topicalness has changed, that a mere rehash of editorials and minute operative slogans in verse satisfies no one, that we must aim at a synthesis, at creating a powerful, rich, and diversified art.[7]

Besides his Marxist analysis of various trends in Soviet poetry, Bukharin made an attempt at clarifying the concept of Socialist Realism. He said that it was absurd to oppose romanticism to Socialist Realism; that while old realism was to a certain extent antilyrical and old lyric poetry to a certain extent antirealistic, there was no such discord between Socialist Realism and lyric poetry; that Socialist Realism, while definitely anti-individualistic, must be "oriented toward man." Bukharin rejected flatly the formula of "Communist individualism" suggested by André Gide in a letter he addressed to the congress; such a formula, he said, was a contradiction in terms.

Socialist Realism versus James Joyce

Another very interesting and controversial report was read before the congress by Karl Radek (1885-?), who, like Bukharin, was subsequently "purged" as a Trotskyite and "Fascist agent." The report was entitled "Contemporary World Literature and the Tasks of Proletarian Art."[8] Three capital events of recent times, said Radek, determined the evolution of contemporary world literature: the World War, the October Revolution in Russia, and the advent of Fascism to power in several European countries. In the light of these events and their reflection in literature, Radek pro-

[7] It is significant that the pamphlet reproducing Bukharin's report, as well as his "Last Word" in reply to his opponents, also contains a "Statement" in which he apologizes for his polemical brusqueness and says that his estimates of individual authors must not be understood as "directive and compulsory."

[8] Like the other important reports at the congress, it was immediately issued in pamphlet form, together with Radek's reply to his opponents (Karl Radek, *Sovremennaya mirovaya literatura i zadachi proletarskogo iskusstva*). An English translation can be found in Scott (ed.), *Problems of Soviet Literature*, 73-184. All the quotations that follow are translations from the original Russian text.

ceeded to analyze the contemporary literary scene. He spoke of the birth of a young proletarian literature in Western Europe and in Asia, of the bourgeois writers who were rallying to the cause of the proletariat, such as André Malraux and Jean-Richard Bloch in France, Johannes Becher and Ludwig Renn in Germany, and Theodore Dreiser in the United States.[9] He referred sympathetically to such proven friends of the Soviet Union as Romain Rolland, Bernard Shaw, and Upton Sinclair and mentioned the recent "change of heart" on the part of André Gide, whom he called "a great French poet." He analyzed the output of Italian Fascist literature and admitted the possibility of Fascism's producing talented writers. In his reply to his critics he stressed the split in bourgeois literature, its division into openly Fascist literature and literature attempting to defend bourgeois democracy but "slowly creeping toward Fascism," while there was also a group of bourgeois writers who were openly siding with Soviet Communism. As a typical example illustrating the disintegration of bourgeois literature, Radek quoted Céline's *Journey to the End of the Night.* Tomorrow, he said (prophetically, it may be added), Céline might become a Fascist. But today he was reflecting the despair of those elements of petit bourgeois intelligentsia which saw no way out of the crisis and were profoundly disappointed in capitalism. This was something to be welcomed:

> Literature of disintegration is not our literature, but it is a good thing when your enemy is disintegrating, when one part of the petite bourgeoisie ceases to believe in bourgeois leadership. . . .
> Literature which is still hostile to the revolution but is already hostile to Fascism is of great importance to us.

But particularly interesting was what Radek had to say about the advanced antibourgeois writers of the West and the desirability of learning from them. For some time this problem had been occupying Soviet writers and critics. Several of them were looking for models in the West. This was especially true of some of the fellow travelers. Many critics pointed out the debt which Olesha's vision and method of presentation owed to Jean Giraudoux. Some influence of Proust could also be discerned in his work. (Olesha himself admitted his admiration for H. G. Wells's *The Invisible Man.*) And in his novel *Forward, O Time!* Katayev was certainly influenced in his technique by John Dos Passos. But the most discussed literary figure in the West was naturally James Joyce, although little of his work was at the time accessible to those Soviet writers and critics who could not read him in the original. Joyce came to be regarded as the epitome of the antibourgeois spirit in bourgeois literature and as a literary revolutionary,

---

[9] Several foreign writers, including Jean-Richard Bloch, André Malraux, and Theodor Plievier, attended the congress as guests. André Gide sent his greetings.

and in the early thirties a bitter controversy about his significance for Soviet literature flared up.

Paradoxically, the campaign against Joyce and what he stood for was launched by Prince D. S. Mirsky (1890–1939?). During the Civil War, Mirsky fought in the ranks of Denikin's and Wrangel's White Armies. With their collapse he emigrated and with the help of Maurice Baring, who knew his family well, found his way to London. There he became lecturer in Russian literature at the School of Slavonic and East European Studies and in 1926–27 published his excellent two-volume book on Russian literature. He also contributed articles on Russian literature to the *Times Literary Supplement* and to various highbrow and avant-garde English and French periodicals such as *Echanges*. A man of great erudition, broad views, and pungent personal style, he was at home not only in Russian but also in classical and Western European literature and soon won for himself a position of respect and authority in English letters. To many people his conversion to Communism (in about 1931, when he became a member of the British Communist party) came as a surprise. But to some who knew him well this about-face seemed a natural result of his love of intellectual mischief and his instinctive nonconformism, and when in 1932 he went back to Russia, these people confidently predicted that he would end badly. At first Mirsky's knowledge of European, especially English, literature and his personal ties with a number of English and French left-wing intellectuals were taken advantage of. He was entrusted with editing English classics, writing introductions to various volumes, and acting as liaison officer for various foreign guests of honor who visited the Soviet Union. He also published in England a malicious book about the British intelligentsia.

In 1934, however, just before the Congress of Soviet Writers, he got into a bad scrape as a result of an article which he printed in the June 24, 1934, issue of *Literaturnaya Gazeta* (*Literary Gazette*). In the article, about Fadeyev's novel *The Last of the Udege*, he reproached Fadeyev for trying to win back the sympathies of the intelligentsia whom he had "offended" by his portrayal of Mechik in *The Rout*. Mirsky spoke slightingly of Fadeyev's part in Soviet literature and called his novel "an artistic blunder." Fadeyev's novel was at the time freely criticized by various critics, and the article did not attract much attention. But a month later *Literaturnaya Gazeta* was obliged to recant and "accept the responsibility for Mirsky's blunder." Mirsky himself was taken severely to task by some orthodox Communist critics, who pointed out that a recent convert from "White Guardism" had no right to criticize Communist writers. The fact that Mirsky had criticized Fadeyev from the ultraleft standpoint and had showed himself to be *plus royaliste que le roi même* was disregarded.

For a time Mirsky's name disappeared from *Literaturnaya Gazeta*, but in January, 1935, somewhat belatedly, none other than Gorky came to his defense. He pointed out that Mirsky had been quite right because "everyone knew" that Fadeyev's novel was bad, and anyway it was not Mirsky's fault that he had been born a prince. Gorky was answered by Panfyorov, who in an article published simultaneously in *Pravda* and *Izvestia* once more accused Mirsky of unfair methods of criticism. The controversy around this incident gradually died out; but in the summer of 1935, Mirsky was arrested on unspecified charges. A few months later, apparently as a result of intervention from abroad, he was released. In 1936 and 1937 his signature was still appearing under some articles in Soviet publications. In the latter year he was arrested and exiled to Siberia.[10] Apparently he died in a concentration camp.

The anti-Joyce campaign took place before the Fadeyev incident. Early in 1933, Mirsky published several articles on the problem of the relationship between Soviet literature and contemporary European writers.[11] He charged some "formalizing" Communists with trying to interest Soviet writers in Joyce's decadent art and with regarding newfangled art forms as an absolute virtue. Among those whom he criticized was the Communist playwright Vsevolod Vishnevsky, and the latter replied in an article entitled "We Must Know the West!"[12] He reminded his readers that one of the first to raise the issue of mutual Western and Soviet influences was the famous film producer Sergey Eisenstein, who met Joyce in Paris and became interested in Joyce's methods. Eisenstein himself said that he realized, while working on the film based on Dreiser's *An American Tragedy*, that new methods and new devices were needed for a deeper understanding of images and characters and that the new social treatment of images had a great effect on purely formal devices. It was from this idea, he said, that his conception of "inner monologue" in films had originated.

Propping himself on the authority of Eisenstein, Vishnevsky boldly took up the cudgels on behalf of Joyce. He described *Ulysses* as "a perfectly outspoken portrayal of men of the capitalist era" and spoke of Joyce as having

[10] In 1936, Mirsky came out in defense of Pasternak, who was being attacked by orthodox Communist writers and critics. An ultra-Marxist article by Mirsky appeared in the Pushkin volume of *Literaturnoye nasledstvo* (*Literary Heritage*) (1937). In the same year the Leningrad magazine *Zvezda* began publishing Mirsky's biography of Pushkin, about which it even printed a special advance notice. After the first two installments, however, publication of the biography was discontinued without any explanation, and Mirsky's exile apparently soon followed. *The Short Literary Encyclopaedia* now speaks of him as one of those writers "illegally repressed" and "posthumously rehabilitated." The year of his death is given as 1939, though according to private information he died later.

[11] For instance, "Dos Passos, sovetskaya literatura i zapad" ("Dos Passos, Soviet Literature and the West"), *Literaturny Kritik* (*Literary Critic*), No. 1 (1933); and two articles about Joyce and Proust in *God Shestnadtsaty* (*The Year Sixteen*), Nos. 1 and 2 (1933).

[12] "Znat' Zapad!" *Literaturny Kritik*, No. 7 (1933), 80–95.

"revealed the amazing secrets of the life and mentality of the people of the dying epoch." Free from all usual literary tricks, from an entertaining plot, from Zolaesque naturalistic twists, *Ulysses* was "a stunning, avalanche-like, epochal work" which faithfully recorded the epoch and its human multitude. It gave rise to new literary currents in France, England, the United States, Italy, and other countries.[13]

Ulysses is remarkable for the great tension in which it holds the reader. It is the nervous tension . . . of Western life. *Ulysses* is musical. It creates multiplanar life, and makes you aware not only of the "hero" but also of the world, of cosmos. *Ulysses* is amazingly exact, often scientifically exact, opening the road to a kind of supernaturalism. . . . *Ulysses* reflects a tremendous linguistic culture—Joyce is a rare linguist.

Six hundred pages of Joyce's book are brimful with hatred for the old capitalist Britain. Joyce is one of those "witnesses" of whom Lenin spoke. Lenin knew very well how to handle any material with which literature, journalism and statistics provided him. How barbarous and medieval Mirsky sounds when he says, "We have no use for Joyce and Proust." Another step and Mirsky . . . will evidently make a bonfire of their books.

Describing Joyce as "a monstrously powerful realist," Vishnevsky accused Mirsky of failing to understand the objective value of what one found in Joyce and his followers, "decadents" and "nihilists" though they were; for, socially speaking, their experiments were parallel to those of the Russian Futurists, and, like the latter, these Western intellectuals, "these lonely souls," these "dissenters" were still blind to the fact that their real "customer" was the revolutionary proletariat. But, he wrote, "time will come when they will see it. Some of them will join the revolution, others the counter-revolution. It is a great pity that Mirsky in advance brands all these seeking, embittered, radical lonely souls as candidates for the camp of the counter-revolution."

Vishnevsky also defended Dos Passos and mentioned a questionnaire circulated by *Literaturnaya Gazeta* which showed that among Soviet writers Dos Passos was the most widely read author.

The controversy about Joyce and Dos Passos, and the value of literary innovations in general, continued throughout the year.[14] Radek's report to

[13] Vishnevsky gave here a rather strange assortment of names representing the Joyce "school" in European literature. His list included Valery Larbaud, Montherlant, Drieu de la Rochelle, Dos Passos, Hemingway, Walter (Waldo?) Frank, Thornton Wilder, Virginia Woolf, and Aldous Huxley. It would be interesting to know whether Vishnevsky's knowledge of Ulysses was first hand and, if so, in what language he had read it.

[14] Several articles about Joyce, of whom little was really known in the Soviet Union (in this respect Mirsky had an enormous advantage over his opponents), appeared about this time in Soviet magazines. Among them may be mentioned a detailed and serious study by R. Miller-Budnitskaya in *Literaturny Kritik*, No. 1 (1934).

the 1934 Congress of Soviet Writers contained a summing up and the final verdict. One section of Radek's report was entitled "James Joyce or Socialist Realism?" With his usual biting irony Radek said that Soviet writers were not familiar with foreign literatures and when they heard of this or that novelty they asked "with morbid interest" whether it might not contain "a great key to art." Whenever they heard that a book eight hundred pages long, without full stops or commas, appeared abroad, they said, "Maybe this is the new art that is being born out of chaos?" It would be absurd, went on Radek, for Soviet writers to refuse to learn from foreign artists. From the point of view of form an average French writer certainly wrote as well as a very good Soviet writer. There was nothing surprising in this— a French or English workman also could handle his tools better than his Soviet comrade. Therefore there was much that Soviet literature could learn not only from the old classics but also from the literature of dying capitalism. The question was not whether one should learn from a great artist like Proust the art of depicting all the minutiae of man. The question was whether Soviet literature should go along its own "highway" or follow in the footsteps of foreign "seekers."

Two names represented the search for new forms in literature. One of them was Marcel Proust, who "wants to present the psychology of his heroes, the heroes of the French drawing room, by laying bare their minds, by subtly dissecting their tissues, by sniffing at all their motions." Compared to Proust's, however, even the meanest of Dostoyevsky's characters are giants of suffering: "The drawing-room heroes of Proust seem to be saying that there is no need to analyze them, that no analysis will get anything out of them."

The other "hero" of contemporary bourgeois literature was James Joyce, "the mysterious author of *Ulysses*, a book which is loudly discussed but little read." His "originality" consisted in attempting to depict a day in the life of his characters "motion by motion—the motions of the body, the motions of the mind, the motions of the feelings in all their shades—from conscious feelings to those which rise up in the throat like a spasm."

Dismissing Joyce's "intricate web of allegories and mythological allusions," his "madhouse phantasmagorias," Radek went on to examine the essence of the "new method," which in his opinion "reduced naturalism to clinical observation, and symbolism to delirious ravings." He saw the quintessence of Joyce in

his conviction that there is *nothing great in life—no great events, no great people, no great ideas,* and that the writer can give a picture of life by just taking "any hero any day" and photographing him carefully. *A heap of dung, teeming with worms and photographed by a motion-picture camera through a microscope— that is Joyce.*[15]

[15] The italics in this and subsequent excerpts are Radek's.

Radek denied that Joyce, for all his minute portrayal of every single motion of his hero, was an impartial recorder of life:

He has selected the piece of life which he is portraying. His selection is determined by the fact that his entire world lies between a bookcase full of medieval books, a brothel, and a pothouse. For him, the national revolutionary movement of the Irish middle class does not exist, and therefore the portrait which he draws is wrong, despite its semblance of detachment.

While the Joycean method might be considered fit for depicting small, insignificant, worthless people and their actions, thoughts, and emotions, it "would prove utterly bankrupt the moment the author were to approach the great events of the class struggle, the gigantic conflicts of the modern world."

Radek attributed the "morbid interest" some Soviet writers evinced in Joyce to the fact that he was almost untranslatable and practically unknown in the Soviet Union, but added also the following significant explanation:

This interest in Joyce reflects unconsciously *the craving of the right-wing writers, who have adjusted themselves to the Revolution but do not understand its greatness, to get away from Magnitogorsk and Kuznetskstroy, to get away from the great deeds of our country to "great art" which shows small doings of small men; to escape from the stormy seas of the Revolution to the stagnant waters of a little marshy pond where frogs live.*

Radek ended his report by advising Soviet writers to learn from the best masters of proletarian literature abroad and to portray not only Soviet factory workers and collective farmers but also the underground revolutionaries in Nazi Germany and the Chinese coolies.

Radek's report provoked several retorts, mostly from foreign guests at the congress. His chief opponent on the subject of Joyce was Wieland Herzfelde,[16] who said that Joyce was a great artist who photographed not a heap of dung but "his own inside." Radek thought this correction immaterial and provoked general laughter and applause by pointing out that "a man's inside also contains various component parts of a heap of dung." In a more serious vein he said that an artist had no business to look into his inside at the moment when the Fascists were preparing "to stifle the last remnant of culture" and "to throttle the Soviet Union." For Radek the historic role of Joyce lay not in any inventions of literary technique:

Joyce's form is in keeping with his content, and *his content is a reflection of all that is most reactionary in the petty bourgeoisie.* Joyce may curse at God, he may curse at imperialist England, but he does not lead the artists the right way. . . . *The only things that appeal to Joyce are the medieval, the mystical, the reactionary in the petty bourgeoisie.*

[16] A German writer, connected with the left-wing Malik Publishing House. After the advent of Hitler he went to live in Moscow.

As for Dos Passos, Radek admitted that he was "a great revolutionary artist." If he had not yet reached his full stature, it was because he was under the influence of Joyce and not under the influence of Marx and of the great artists of realism. His formalistic innovations, which some Soviet writers admired so much, were his main weakness: "He inserts newspaper clippings in order to paste together the background which he is incapable of portraying."

Radek finished by opposing Socialist Realism to all these bourgeois attempts to find new forms. Socialist Realism did not mean indiscriminate photographing of life. It selected what was essential, as its very name implied.

Joyce stands on the other side of the barricades. . . . There is nothing fundamental we can learn from Joyce. If you mean learning from Joyce his technique, I am not going to argue. I don't write novels, but if I did I think I would learn how to write them from Tolstoy and Balzac, not from Joyce.

I wish to say to Soviet and foreign writers: *Our road lies not through Joyce but along the highway of Socialist Realism.*

Radek, not yet "exposed" as an agent of Hitler and an enemy of the Soviet Union, was speaking as an official representative of the party, and his verdict on Joyce, Proust, and Dos Passos bore the stamp of finality. Soviet writers accepted it in silence, or even joined in the attack on Joyce and the "decadent" bourgeois literature. Even Vishnevsky did not rise in defense of Joyce, preferring to rebuke his friend Olesha, to whose opinion about Joyce he had appealed against Mirsky.

Thus the "highway" of Soviet literature was clearly traced: a close alliance with revolutionary proletarian literature abroad; learning from the old masters like Balzac and Tolstoy; and no traffic with modernists and innovators who were in search of new forms.

Chapter 22. CHANGES IN SOVIET OUTLOOK

Socialist Realism was but one of the manifestations of far-reaching changes in the official Soviet outlook which took place between 1932 and 1939. These changes could not but affect the development of literature. Some of them were determined by external factors—by Hitler's advent to power and the growth of the Nazi state in Germany and of what came to be known as the "Fascist menace" to the existence of the Soviet Union. In the face of it Soviet leaders began to look for allies among the Western democracies. Hence the more conciliatory attitude toward the Socialist parties in Europe and the encouragement given to the policy of the so-called "popular fronts"; hence also the entry of the Soviet Union into the hitherto despised League of Nations.

On the Road to Totalitarianism

To what extent this policy of international co-operation was sincere and genuine and to what extent it was dictated by the desire to play out the opposing camps in Europe cannot be discussed here. What matters is that, from 1933 on, the Soviet Union and its leaders became increasingly "national-minded." While it would be a gross mistake to think that the old idea of world revolution, which inspired the Bolsheviks in 1917 and underlay the conception of both Lenin and Trotsky, was now given up, there is no doubt that for the time being it gave place to Stalin's conception of "Socialism in one country." The survival of the Soviet regime in Russia was no longer regarded as contingent on the immediate social revolution in other countries, the chances of which appeared remote. It was therefore important to ensure the external security of the Soviet Union and to increase its military might, while at the same time consolidating the Soviet regime internally. It was in the thirties that the Soviet Union became the thoroughgoing totalitarian state it is now. Viewed retrospectively, the literary "reform" of 1932, which did away with proletarian and other organizations and set up a homogeneous writers' organization pledged to support the domestic and international policies of the Soviet government, was a clever step in the direction of suppressing all nonconformism and establishing a totalitarian control over all manifestations of spiritual and cultural life.

Revising Russian History

In 1934 the leadership of the Communist party launched a significant cam-

paign against the views of the leading Soviet historian, Mikhail Nikolayevich Pokrovsky (1868–1932). For many years Pokrovsky, who had received
his historical training before the Revolution, was the principal exponent of
the Marxist interpretation of history. He was fond of describing history as
"politics projected into the past" and of denying the very existence of such
a thing as "objective history." In the words of his followers, "All scholarship
is Party scholarship, the tenet about non-Party scholarship is one of the
most harmful perversions of Marxism, pregnant with direst consequences.
As for history, it must be politically oriented to the maximum degree and
more Party-minded than any other science." The years 1929–31, which in
literature were marked by the RAPP dictatorship, witnessed a violent and
concentrated attack on the "class enemy on the history front."[1] Eminent
historians were accused of "bourgeois objectivism." Several of them, including Platonov and Tarle, were arrested and exiled. By 1930, with the
reorganization of the Soviet Academy of Sciences on the Marxist basis, the
school of Pokrovsky had won the battle. Under Pokrovsky's influence the
teaching of history was practically discontinued in Soviet schools and col-
leges and replaced by vulgar sociology. Such things as chronology, facts,
and historical personalities were completely disregarded. In the words of a
later critic, "living people have almost disappeared from our curriculum
and teaching."[2]

The reaction came in 1934. It was a complete about-face. Pokrovsky, by
now dead, was denounced as a "vulgarizer" of Marxism, guilty of empty
sociological schematism, of perverting and distorting Russian history, of
failing to see the positive achievements of the Russian people, and of approaching the past solely from the point of view of vulgar opposition between the people and the state. Pokrovsky's works, which had hitherto
served as the principal textbooks of Russian history, were discarded, and
Stalin himself, assisted by Kirov and Zhdanov, drew up observations that
were to guide the compilers of new textbooks. A contest for a new school
textbook of Russian history was announced, with several prizes. None of the
contestants was adjudged worthy of the first prize, but the second prize
was awarded to Professor Shestakov, whose *History of the U.S.S.R.* became
the officially adopted textbook.

The attitude toward Russia's past was fundamentally revised. A good
Soviet citizen had to be a Soviet patriot. And patriotism no longer meant
pride in the "conquests of the Revolution" (the popular phrase of the

[1] The title of a book by R. Seidel and M. Zwieback: *Klassovy vrag na istoricheskom
fronte: Tarle i Platonov i ikh shkoly* (*The Class Enemy on the History Front: Tarle
and Platonov and Their Schools*).

[2] From an article by Yu. Bocharov in *Istorik-Marksist* (*The Marxian Historian*),
quoted by B. H. Sumner, "Soviet History," *Slavonic and East European Review*, Vol.
XVI (April, 1938), 601.

twenties); it also implied pride in Russia's past, in her military glory, in her territorial expansion, in her historical achievements, and in her military heroes. This new patriotic spirit and new attitude toward the past brought forth a number of historical novels which differed greatly from the earlier Soviet historical fiction, especially in their choice of subjects. The interest was now focused on critical moments in Russian national life, on the periods when Russia fought for her very existence against external enemies.

Historical Novels with a Difference

Among these new historical novels, one of the earliest and most ambitious was Sergeyev-Tsensky's *Sevastopolskaya strada* (*The Ordeal of Sevastopol*), which was first serialized in 1937–38. The author set himself the task of painting the picture of Russia in 1854–55 against the general background of contemporary history, of doing for the Crimean War what Tolstoy did for the Napoleonic wars of 1805–12. The result was a novel of some fifteen hundred pages. There is in it, of course, more war than peace, because, unlike the period covered by Tolstoy, the whole of the period chosen by Sergeyev-Tsensky was taken up by the war. We see Sevastopol preparing for the attack, the scuttling of the Russian fleet in the bay, the battles of Alma and Inkermann, the siege of the city, and the famous Charge of the Light Brigade. We also see the background of the war—in St. Petersburg, London, and Paris, with Nicholas I, Queen Victoria, and Napoleon the Little all making their appearance on the scene. There are full-length portraits of several historical figures, including Pirogov, the great Russian surgeon who was responsible for the activities of the first Russian Red Cross nurses at the front. Some of the battle scenes are well done; the description of the scuttling of the Russian fleet is particularly good. Interlocked with the historical narrative are stories of some personal destinies, in the course of which the author takes the reader to the "rear," to an estate in the province of Kursk, and shows us provincial Russia and its reactions to the war. The novel is not free from an anti-British bias, but is on the whole much more objective than some of the earlier Soviet novels on historical themes.

The period of the Napoleonic wars and its leading individual figures naturally attracted the attention of Soviet novelists and playwrights. Here, perhaps, the existence of Tolstoy's unique masterpiece deterred many writers from attempting to treat the subject on a large scale (even Sergeyev-Tsensky's novel about the Crimean War invites some invidious comparisons). But there were many works dealing with individual figures and separate episodes. One of the most successful was Vladimir Solovyov's play *Fieldmarshal Kutuzov* (1939). There were also novels and plays about Suvorov and Bagration.

Of the earlier periods in Russian history, the one to attract particular at-

tention was the period of the struggle against the Tatars, with its climax in
the famous Battle of the Kulikovo Field (1380) in which Prince Dmitry
Donskoy defeated the Tatar host of Khan Mamay and paved the way for
Russia's final liberation from the Mongol yoke. Dmitry Donskoy is the
central figure in the historical novel of that name by Amir Sargidzhan
(pseudonym of Sergey Borodin), but its real hero is the Russian people.
For his novel Sargidzhan was awarded a Stalin Prize. He also wrote a short
biography of Dmitry Donskoy which enjoyed wide circulation during
the war.

The struggle with the Tatars, seen partly from the other side and on a
vaster plane, was the subject of a historical trilogy by V. Yan (pseudonym
of Vasily Yanchevetsky). The first two parts (*Genghiz-Khan* and *Batu*)
had the two great Mongol war captains for their central figures, while the
third part dealt with Alexander Nevsky. The whole was a colorful work for
which the author drew on various historical sources, both Russian and
Oriental, also making large use of Russian folklore.

Of the later rulers of Russia, the two that were now reappraised and extolled were Peter the Great and Ivan the Terrible. Peter was seen both as a
man who revolutionized Russia from above and did not stop before harsh
coercive measures and as the creator of Russian military might—the man
who made Russia a powerful factor in European politics. Soviet literature
paid tribute to him through Alexey Tolstoy's novel, which has been discussed in an earlier chapter. As for Ivan, he was acclaimed as a precursor of
Peter, who realized the necessity of westward expansion of Russia, and
as a great Russian patriot and a wise statesman.

Exterminating the Enemies

In the approach to Ivan as a farsighted patriot and great statesman and not
merely a cruel and perverse tyrant, there was nothing essentially novel. This
view had already been advanced by some nineteenth-century Russian historians. If there was anything new in the Soviet approach, it was the
tendency to idealize the personality of the tsar and to justify his ruthless
treatment of his enemies. This vindication was not accidental, for under
Stalin's absolute, despotic rule Russia was in many respects going back to
the times of Ivan the Terrible, even though those who stress this parallel
are often guilty of forgetting the historical perspective and of drawing
unwarranted conclusions.

In literature the glorification and idealization of Ivan found its expression
during and after the war, and more will be said of it in Part VII. Here it
should suffice to point out that this particular piece of historical revision was
closely bound up with one of the cardinal features of the Soviet scene during
this period: the consolidation of Stalin's absolute power, the cunning and
ruthless extermination of all opposition in a series of framed-up trials,

during which Lenin's Old Guard, the leading figures in the Comintern and the Communist party, and the front-rank generals of the Red Army were eliminated on fantastic charges of conspiring with the Germans and the Japanese for the destruction of the Soviet Union. Not the least fantastic feature of these trials was the abject docility with which the accused themselves confessed to their fantastic crimes and the readiness and violence with which the intelligentsia, including writers, denounced them. In September, 1936, the leading article in *Oktyabr*—entitled "The Vermin is Squashed!"—denounced the sixteen accused in the trial of the "Trotskyite-Zinovievite gang" in the following terms:

There were sixteen of them in the dock. Sixteen base hirelings of Fascism. Sixteen active members of the Trotskyite-Zinovievite gang. Sixteen murderers, who had stained their hands with the blood of the best son of the people, Sergey Mironovich Kirov, came on trial before the people, before history.... The Fascist curs confessed their criminal deed. They admitted that they were direct agents of the Gestapo, that they had co-operated with the Fascists....

The despicable gang of murderers, whose names will be cursed through ages, has been crushed. The sentence of the Court has been carried out. It is easier to breathe now that the Trotskyite-Zinovievite vermin has been squashed.

And so on and so forth, with many bloodthirsty quotations from Vyshinsky, who acted as the chief prosecutor in the trial. The same article denounced the enemies of the people who had "entrenched themselves on the literary front." Among these were included the dramatic critic Pikel', who "for many years operated in the field of 'criticism,' carrying out with impunity his counterrevolutionary deeds" (and who was sentenced to death by the court); the writer Galina Serebryakova, author of a biographical novel about Marx, who organized a literary salon "with the object of covering up her filthy deeds and connections"; Tarasov-Rodionov, author of *Chocolate*, described now as "a graphomaniac Trotskyite"; the influential critics Selivanovsky and Maznin; the novelists Ivan Katayev, Boris Guber, and N. Zarudin (all of whom belonged to the Pereval group), who "gave material assistance to the Trotskyites and 'visited' them in exile."

The editors of *Oktyabr* continued indignantly:

Enemies of the Party and the people infiltrated themselves into the editorial boards of magazines, into publishing houses, into the Union of Writers, wherever they could, carrying out their infamous, vile, base deeds, taking advantage of rotten liberalism and sometimes of direct connivance.

Then came the inevitable element of self-accusation:

It was a bad mistake on our part and a sign of blunted vigilance when the counterrevolutionary degenerate Friedland and the inveterate Trotskyite terrorist Ter-Vaganyan took part in the discussion about the historical novel organized by *Oktyabr* in the spring of 1934, and when their speeches were published in our magazine; or when our magazine published *Marx's Youth* by the enemy Serebryakova.

In 1934 Kamenev's henchman Chernyak worked for several months in *Oktyabr* magazine. The editorial board unmasked and expelled him, but he was immediately invited to work in *Krasnaya Nov....*

Were not a number of bad mistakes, committed by the *Krasnaya Nov* magazine, and consisting in the publication of insolent, frankly counterrevolutionary articles by Vaganyan, due to the blunting of vigilance? Or the publication of such works as *Seekers of Glory* by Orlov, etc., about which *Pravda* wrote indignantly?

To this day Kamenev's henchman Elsberg, who prints his articles in *Krasnaya Nov* and works in the *Academia* publishing house, is active in literature.

The article ascribed these and other facts, which testified to "lack of Bolshevik vigilance," to the "group spirit" which prevailed in literature and overshadowed broad political interests, and proclaimed (in capital letters) the following principle:

The interests of the Party and of the people are the immutable supreme law governing the work and conduct of every truly Soviet writer. There is no justification for our mistakes, for the blunting of Bolshevik vigilance. We are taught vigilance every day and every hour by our Party, by our leader of genius—Stalin.

Joining their voices to the national chorus of wrath against the Trotskyite-Zinovievite gang, Soviet writers have with one accord condemned the Trotskyite agents on the literary front and expelled them from their ranks.[3]

A few months later another Soviet periodical published a special article on "Trotskyite Agents in Literature," in which several literary critics were specifically denounced as Trotsky's agents. Voronsky was called "Trotsky's armsbearer," Mirsky was described as "Averbach's henchman," Lev Levin as "Averbach's envoy in Leningrad," and Oksman (1894–1970, a distinguished historian of literature and specialist on the Pushkin period) as "a swindler and adventurer."[4]

The Cult of Stalin and Mythmaking

The *Oktyabr* article ended on a note that was becoming more and more usual in Soviet literature in those days—of undisguised adulation for Stalin:

Workers on the literary front—writers, critics, editors, publishers—together with the entire people, are turning their eyes, full of affection and devotion, toward Stalin.

All the thoughts and feelings of our great people are turned toward him, the father of the Soviet Union, the bright sun of humanity, the greatest genius of

[3] See "Gadina razdavlena!" *Oktyabr*, No. 9 (1936), 3–8.
[4] L. Plotkin, "Trotskistskaya agentura v literature" ("Trotskyite Agents in Literature"), *Zvezda*, No. 7 (1937).

our age, toward our dear Stalin. His name is uttered by the toilers of the whole globe with immense affection and joy, as a symbol of new and beautiful life.

With the banner of Stalin our country is vigorously and confidently striding from victory to victory.[5]

This cult of Stalin, which gradually acquired truly mythological proportions, became a distinctive feature of Soviet society in the thirties. No parallel to it can be found in the early history of the Soviet Union during Lenin's lifetime, and even the posthumous myth of Lenin paled before the living legend of Stalin. The idolatrous sentiments for Stalin were voiced on all possible occasions, but more especially in connection with the trials and purges of his enemies and on the occasion of the promulgation of the Stalin Constitution in 1936, which provided the Soviet Union with a democratic façade and a most liberal constitution on paper (never, however, had the gulf between what was decreed on paper and the reality been so wide). This cult of Stalin found also its reflection in literature. In the poems of Prokofyev, Shchipachov, Dolmatovsky, Lebedev-Kumach, Surkov, and many others whose reputation was established in the thirties will be found numerous adulatory references to Stalin. Older writers, too, could not escape the contagion. A few of those who apparently refused to "conform," in one way or another, to the new ideological outlook were forced to silence and eventually disappeared from the literary scene. They included those who were openly denounced as "Trotskyite agents" and "enemies of the people," but there were also some who "faded out" silently, without much ado.

It was in those years, and particularly in 1937 and 1938, that a number of writers became victims of wholesale purges. How many of them were liquidated outright and how many died in prison or in exile is not known. Their biographies in reference works speak merely of "illegal repression" (in some cases indicating the year) and "posthumous rehabilitation." These victims of Stalin's terror included well-known writers (Babel, Pilnyak, Mandelstam, and Klyuev), many representatives of "proletarian" and "peasant" literature (Aleksandrovsky, Tarasov-Rodionov, Gastev, Gerasimov, Kirillov, Tretyakov, Kirshon, Klychkov, Oreshin, Kornilov, Pavel Vasilyev), members of the Pereval group (Ivan Katayev, Boris Guber, Zarudin), and prominent critics and journalists (Voronsky, Mirsky, Lezhnev, Gorbachov, Lelevich, Koltsov, Selivanovsky), as well as many writers belonging to non-Russian literatures (Ukrainian, Georgian, and so on). A few cases are known in which major men of letters survived long terms of imprisonment and exile and made a comeback in the 1950's (Zabolotsky, Oksman, Galina Serebryakova). In such cases their official biographies are usually silent about their "repression" (for example, the entries on Zabolotsky and Oksman in *The Short Literary Encyclopaedia*). There were also

5 "Gadina razdavlena!" *Oktyabr*, No. 9 (1936), 3–8.

instances when well-known writers would fade out of literature and then reappear without any explanation of their prolonged silence. Such seems to have been the case of Olesha between 1938 and 1946.[6]

Connected with the cult of Stalin and the denigration of his enemies, particularly of Trotsky and the alleged Trotskyites, was the falsification of recent history undertaken in literature. A typical example was Alexey Tolstoy's novel *Khleb* (*Bread*, 1937), written obviously for the purpose of glorifying the role of Stalin in the Civil War at the expense of Trotsky. History was travestied in a similar way in a film called *The Defense of Tsaritsyn*, which dealt with the same period of the Civil War. Needless to say, all more or less complimentary references to Trotsky in the early works of Soviet literature were expunged from later editions.

After the 1937 trial of the "right-wing" opposition, in which the principal accused—Bukharin, Rykov, Krestinsky, and Yagoda—were described as "the frenzied slaves of the German-Japanese-British-Polish intelligence services" (this hyphening in itself was a priceless example of Soviet "incantation formulas") and accused, among other crimes, of the murder of Kirov and Gorky, the theme of foreign "spies" and "diversionists" provided many a Soviet novelist and playwright with exciting material, and even some of the best writers hastened to make use of it.

The Soviet Union Going Conservative

Parallel with the growing conservatism in art, the rehabilitation of the historical past and its heroes, the emergence of Soviet patriotism, and the sedulous cultivation of the Russian species of "Führerism" ("*vozhdizm*"), went the process of what has been described as the birth of the new respectability.[7] It meant, in the first place, the restoration of the family as

[6] Without access to all Soviet periodicals and other publications it is impossible to ascertain the exact dates of all these "disappearances." The last story by Pilnyak that has come to my notice was published in *Literaturny Sovremennik*, No. 2 (1937); the last story by Babel, in *Krasnaya Nov*, No. 7 (1937). Several short stories and sketches by Olesha (of little intrinsic interest), appeared in 1936 in *30 Dney*, a magazine devoted to short stories, poetry, and literary criticism. In 1937, both *30 Dney* and *Zvezda* published fragments from a film scenario by Olesha and A. Macheret. It was called *Walter*, and its subject was the persecution of political enemies in Nazi Germany. In 1938 there appeared in *30 Dney* (No. 4) a short, journalistic piece by Olesha entitled "Nasha rodina—Rossiyskaya sotsialisticheskaya respublika" ("Our Country—The Russian Socialist Republic"). Ironically, it appears that it was after this loyal (and trite) expression of Soviet patriotism that Olesha disappeared for a long time from Soviet literature.

[7] The expression is not mine. It was used by the late Sir John Maynard, a benevolent British student of the inner processes in the Soviet Union, as a chapter heading in his book *Russia in Flux*. He borrowed it from J. D. Littlepage and D. Bess, who in their book *In Search of Soviet Gold* say: "A new kind of respectability is emerging, which sometimes seems almost as extreme in one direction as the previous ideas in the other." This phrase aptly describes the Soviet processes in the thirties.

an object of respect and as the mainstay of the state. Divorce laws were tightened, abortions made illegal, and sexual laxity strongly condemned. In matters of education there was a marked return to old-time, pre-Revolutionary methods. An end was put to all experimenting with progressive education. Discipline came back into its own and with it such old-fashioned "bourgeois" institutions as grades, examinations, certificates, gold medals, uniforms, segregation of sexes, military schools modeled on the old cadet academies and named after Suvorov, and so on. This retrogressive process was slow and gradual, and some of the changes mentioned here were effected only in the forties. It goes without saying that, under the new dispensation, one of the distinctive features of the early Soviet educational system—the large part allotted to students in the management of schools—went overboard. Today Ognyov's novel about a Soviet school of the twenties (see Chapter II) reads like a glaring anachronism.

The reappearance of economic inequality was another feature of the period. It was the natural result of the encouragement given to personal incentive in industry and collective farming which is associated with the famous Stakhanov movement. It is also curious to note that in the pre–World War II world the Soviet Union was the only country in Europe where domestic servants were not a vanishing institution but a fixture of everyday life—not a privilege within the reach of a few rich but a right to which the Soviet intelligentsia, officialdom, and technocracy felt justly entitled.

This is not the place to study all these new facts and trends in detail; they belong to the domain of the sociologist and student of politics. But they must be recorded, for they not only were reflected in Soviet literature of this period but also affected its character. The official slogan, "Life has become gayer, comrades!" was taken up by Soviet writers who vied with each other in describing "the new and beautiful life."

It should also be mentioned that this period saw a gradual relaxation of the antireligious campaign which had reached its climax in the early thirties. A characteristic incident occurred in 1937 when the one-time poet laureate of the Soviet regime, Demyan Bedny, was officially rebuked for the opera libretto he wrote, entitled *Bogatyri* (*Epic Heroes*), because in it he spoke slightingly of Russia's conversion to Christianity in the tenth century. The authority of Karl Marx was invoked to show that this historical event was a progressive factor of great moment. The opera was withdrawn.

These processes, which have sometimes been described as the Russian Thermidor (though they bore little resemblance to the original French Thermidor), were of dual nature. Up to a point, they represented a genuine concession to the unspoken desires and sentiments of the masses which had grown tired of the Revolution and the sacrifices it imposed on them in the name of long-distance goals—hence the promise of gayer life, of less austerity, and of greater personal comforts and amenities, which played such an important part in the official propaganda of the late thirties. To some extent the fostering of national feelings and the rehabilitation of the past also represented a sop to the population which could not be roused by the prospect of the world triumph of Communism. On the other hand, these processes meant a tightening of the party's totalitarian hold on the country —by strengthening the discipline and by suppressing all manifestations of nonconformism while at the same time creating new large groups of people interested in the maintenance of the existing regime. Behind all these ideological changes could be detected the one all-powerful motive which demanded the preservation of the totalitarian single-party dictatorship. The worship of the Soviet state had replaced the worship of the old abstract ideal of world revolution. But the ideal remained. And the importance of literature as a docile instrument of the party policy was realized more clearly than ever. A repetition of the literary chaos of the twenties could not be allowed.

Chapter 23.   SOCIALIST REALISM: PRACTICE

One of the objects of Socialist Realism in literature was described by some of its advocates as the creation of *types*—of typical characters of the revolutionary epoch—a task in which until then most Soviet writers were believed to have failed. On the other hand, there were also those partisans of Socialist Realism who stressed the search for *heroes* and the reflection of the heroic features of the great Revolutionary age, again maintaining that literature had hitherto failed to do so. These two aspects of Socialist Realism, as it was understood by Soviet writers and critics, were reflected in the literary output which followed the "reform" of 1932.

Types and Heroes

Among the early achievements of Socialist Realism Soviet critics counted Sholokhov's *Virgin Soil Upturned*, although it was largely written and even published in the earlier period of the Five-Year Plan. Among the works of that era it stood out through its greater objectivity. Sholokhov succeeded in realistically depicting a whole sector of Soviet life and in portraying a number of typical characters. Davydov, a Leningrad workman whom the party sends into the South to supervise collectivization and who has to fight the petit bourgeois, possessive instincts of the Cossacks; Nagulnov, who represents the left-wing deviations within the party and ends by being expelled from it; Ostrovnov, a thrifty farmer who, in joining the collective farm and even becoming its manager, in reality pursues his personal ends; and the colorful old man Shchukar'—all these are memorable character creations, typical and individualized at the same time. Davydov was probably meant by the author to serve as the embodiment of revolutionary heroism, but as a model hero he did not come off.

Another achievement of Socialist Realism was seen by the critics in Bruno Jasieński's novel *Chelovek menyaet kozhu* (*A Man Sloughs His Skin*, 1934). Jasieński (1901–38) was one of a number of international Communists who found their spiritual, and later also physical, home in Moscow. Of German-Polish descent, he apparently belonged to the cosmopolitan group of artists in Paris and wrote his first works in French (among others, *Je brûle Paris*, a Utopian revolutionary novel). His fate was not unlike that of many other foreign Communists who came to worship at the shrine of Lenin. He was accused of Trotskyism and "liquidated."

The principal character in *A Man Sloughs His Skin* is a young American engineer who is shown as gradually shedding his bourgeois nature and becoming a true friend of the Communists. The action of the novel is set against the background of Socialist reconstruction in central Asia, with flashbacks into the pre-Revolutionary past. There are many diverse characters, including several American engineers, one of whom is a disguised British intelligence agent (in his story Jasieński deliberately mixed facts— or what he believed to be facts—and fiction). The novel had a well-organized plot and was competently written (the author wrote it in Russian).

A place apart belongs to *Kak zakalyalas' stal'* (*That's How Steel Was Tempered*, 1935) by Nikolay Ostrovsky (1904–36). Like Furmanov's *Chapayev* and Serafimovich's *Iron Torrent*, it is regarded as a major Soviet classic. Frankly autobiographical, though not told in the first person, it describes the formation and growth of a young Communist of working-class origins, his childhood, his part in the Civil War, and his share in the subsequent reconstruction effort. The hero, Pavel Korchagin, an embodiment of true-red Communism and revolutionary heroism, became one of the most popular characters in Soviet fiction, at least if one is to believe official Soviet information. The element of Socialist "uplift," which came to be regarded as one of the indispensable ingredients of Socialist Realism, played an important part in Ostrovsky's "novel," in which the influence of Gorky can be clearly seen. Its popularity was partly due to the appeal of the author's personality. Blind and bedridden during the last years of his life, he battled heroically against these handicaps, dictating his novel, taking an active interest in life, and receiving visitors. At the seaside resort of Sochi in the Caucasus, where he lived, he became almost an institution and an object of devout pilgrimages. To what extent Ostrovsky's nationwide popularity was spontaneous and what part was played in it by deliberate myth-making is difficult for an outsider to say.

Among the other works boosted during this period may be mentioned Anton Makarenko's semifictional *Pedagogicheskaya poema* (*Educational Epic*, 1934) and its sequel, *Kniga dlya roditeley* (*A Book for Parents*, 1938). Makarenko (1888–1939) was a noted Soviet pedagogue who specialized in juvenile delinquents, of which there were a great many in the Soviet Union. *Educational Epic* (translated into English as *Road to Life*) described in detail Makarenko's educational venture in the famous Gorky colony for the waifs and strays of the Revolution. For the most part it has a sincere ring and is of considerable interest to a student of Soviet education, though probably it does not tell the whole story or the whole truth. In its sequel the tendency to idealize the reality is much more pronounced. This is even more true of Makarenko's novel *Flagi na bashnyakh* (*Flags on Towers*, 1939).

Older Writers' Contributions

Leonov   Leonid Leonov's only major prose fiction during this period—his first since *Skutarevsky*—was a long novel entitled *Doroga na Okean* (*The Road to the Ocean*, 1935). Like nearly everything Leonov wrote, it is an interesting work. Its complex, unwieldy structure, with many intersecting lines of plot and a great number of characters bound together by intricate ties, is further complicated by the curious superimposition of three temporal planes in the narrative: the present, the past, and the future. Leonov is in fact carrying three parallel narratives. In the first, which unrolls in the present—about 1934—the background for the action is provided by the life, political and other, of the Volga–Revizan Railway, of which Kurilov, the novel's principal character, is the political director. The railway, however, forms only the setting; the main interest of the novel is psychological, and as usual Leonov is concerned primarily with complex human relationships.

Kurilov takes a notable place in Leonov's portrait gallery. It was his first attempt to place a dedicated Communist in the center of the picture, to make him the pivot round which the story revolves. Kurilov is an active Communist with a distinguished party and Civil War record, with a past that obliges and a responsible position in the present. He is an *otvetstvenny rabotnik*, a high-ranking Communist official. Communist critics reproached Leonov for underrating the political aspect of his "hero" and dwelling on his "human, all too human" feelings and failings. But it is no accident, perhaps, that Leonov shows us Kurilov from this "human" angle, at grips with an incurable disease and gradually realizing, at the approach of death, how little personal enjoyment he has had from life. Hence his mild platonic "affairs," his interest in other people's lives, his unexpected tolerance for one of his bitterest class enemies, his brother-in-law Omelichev, whom he discovers among the employees of his railway. Kurilov dies after an unsuccessful operation performed by the famous surgeon Ilya Protoklitov.

Leonov's characteristic predilection for showing human relationships as complex tangles is revealed in the fact that Ilya is the husband of Liza, in whose life Kurilov comes to play a very important part. After meeting him, her whole life and outlook are completely transformed. Ilya also has a brother, Gleb, who after Kurilov is the most important character in the book. A former White Army officer, he is an active enemy of Communism. By clever deceit he worms his way into the Communist party and secures for himself an important post under Kurilov. In Kurilov he sees the main danger to his far-reaching designs and by a series of clever moves tries to forestall him. Later Gleb very nearly suggests to his brother Ilya (who as Liza's husband has a personal grudge against Kurilov) the idea of a surgical murder. Gleb's undoing comes during a periodical purge in the Communist

cell of his railway depot. Despite his clever tissue of lies, despite an artistically faked proletarian autobiography, he fails. At the last moment his own
brother unmasks him.

Parallel with this plane runs the story of the past, which is concerned
with the pre-Revolutionary antecedents of the same railway, with its construction and the concomitant interplay of private interests and unsavory
speculation. Leonov introduces a young Communist journalist, Peresypkin,
a friend of Kurilov's, who unearths this past story of the Volga–Revizan
Railway from forgotten archives and oral legends. The link which connects
the past story with the present is a certain Pokhvisnev, who happens to be
the uncle of Liza Protoklitova. But this story of the past, told with many
unsavory details, in that Dostoyevskian vein of which Leonov is so fond,
seems a rather artificial adjunct to the main story, and its *raison d'être* is not
very easy to detect.

Superimposed on these two stories, which jostle and interfere with each
other and make the reader at times lose his bearings among the welter of
names and incidents, is a third story. This is a utopian picture of the world
of the future, of Ocean, "the mother of the cities of the future" (situated
apparently somewhere in the Far East), to which the author himself
accompanies Kurilov and Peresypkin and which is presented simultaneously as the author's and Kurilov's vision and as a reality of the future. Much
of this story is given in long footnotes which sometimes run into pages—
an original but annoying device. Particular stress is laid on the military
events of the future, on the war between the Federated Soviet Republics
and the non-Sovietized remainder of the world. Soviet critics reproached
Leonov for having thus circumscribed his vision and failed to visualize the
man of the future and the kind of life he was going to live. Even more
important was Leonov's failure to blend organically his utopia with the rest
of the novel; the footnote device was clear evidence of this. As a whole, the
novel was a failure, but even so it was more interesting than some of the
so-called achievements of Socialist Realism.

Fedin's principal work published during this period was *Pokhishchenie* **Fedin**
Evropy (*The Rape of Europe*, 1934–35). The interval which elapsed between the publication of the first and the second volume accounted for a
certain shift of emphasis and the resulting lack of unity.

Originally one of Fedin's objects seems to have been to contrast the bust-
ling Soviet Union of the Five-Year Plan with the quiescent and decadent
bourgeois West. In the first volume the action is set in Western Europe—
in Norway, Holland, and Germany. Europe is shown through the eyes of
a Communist journalist, Rogov, who has some traits in common with two
of Fedin's earlier heroes, Startsov and Nikita Karev, with the difference,

however, that he is a Communist and is not faced with problem of adjusting himself to the Revolution.

The bourgeois world is personified in the van Rossoems, a family of Dutch timber merchants who held vast interests in Russia before the Revolution and obtained from the Soviet government a concession for their former forests. Philip van Rossoem, the younger brother, who is responsible for the firm's dealings with the Soviet Union, stands for modern progressive spirit in business. Knowing Russia and the Russians well, he likes the country and has no prejudice against the new regime. To him is opposed his older brother and partner, Lodevijk, who dislikes the very idea of trading with "those godless Bolsheviks" and looks askance at the extension of the firm's trading business in Russia, especially as the affairs of the concession run far from smoothly and there are growing signs of the Soviet government's unwillingness to prolong it on the old basis. But Lodevijk's health is failing (he dies later in the book), and Philip is allowed to have his way. The third representative of the van Rossoem family is their nephew, Frans, who is the firm's agent in Russia and is married to a Russian woman with a somewhat romantic past. Dissatisfied with her drab life in the Soviet Union, Klavdia Andreyevna escaped across the Finnish border and joined the émigrés, adopting the career of night-club dancer. Frans van Rossoem met her in a Riga night club, fell in love with her, and took her back to Russia as his wife. At the time Rogov arrives in Holland she is there on a visit to Philip van Rossoem. Rogov falls in love with her, and they go back to Russia as lovers.

To Philip and Lodevijk van Rossoem—one of them modern, progressive, broad-minded, the other conservative and old-fashioned but a model of gentlemanly urbanity—Fedin opposes another capitalist type in the person of Sir Justus Elderling-Geyser, in whom Soviet critics saw an intentional likeness of Sir Henry Deterding. It is true that although Fedin took some pains to disguise his name, that of the Shell Oil Company appears in the novel without any disguise. Whereas the van Rossoems are portrayed as three-dimensional human beings with their individual characteristics, Elderling-Geyser resembles a crude *Pravda* cartoon of a capitalist "shark."

There is little incident or movement in the first volume of the novel. Much of it is taken up with descriptions, some of which—such as the urban landscapes of Bergen and Amsterdam, done in the Flemish manner—are very good. But there is about the whole novel that static quality which also characterized Fedin's second novel, *The Brothers*. If anything it is more accentuated.

In the second volume the pace is even slower, while the action moves to Russia to a place on the White Sea coast and then to Leningrad and Moscow. At the end of the first volume Philip van Rossoem sails for Russia to discuss the affairs of his concession; the second volume opens with his arrival. There we see Philip and Frans fighting a losing battle over their concession, which is finally annulled. The Soviets are now strong enough to dictate their own terms, and Philip has to be satisfied with the role of a mere timber broker for the Soviet Union. His business defeat is compensated by his "conquest" of Klavdia, whom, after Frans's death in a motor accident (or was it suicide?), he takes back with him to Holland.

The main defect of the novel is the lack of unity of design between the two parts, with the result that the second volume represents a series of scenes with no backbone to them. In the first volume such a backbone is supplied by the satirical picture of decaying Europe. But there is no corresponding counter-picture of the Soviet Union. The mythological title is somewhat obscure and sounds farfetched. In the first volume it might have referred to Rogov's "abduction" of Klavdia, but in the second volume Klavdia is in turn "abducted" by Philip van Rossoem. At the same time, there is no real justification for the title if it is to be understood politically or ideologically.

Another work Fedin wrote during this period was a very short novel (rather a novelette) called *Sanatoriy "Arktur"* (*Sanatorium "Arcturus,"* 1936). Its action is set in Davos in a sanatorium for tubercular patients. The principal character is a young Russian who is recovering from tuberculosis. He is one of Fedin's favorite "reasoning observers." There is very little action—Fedin's static technique is suited by this picture, painted in subdued tones, of semireal existence on the confines of death.

Kaverin The element of personal life, the portrayal of which was implied in Socialist Realism, played a large part in Kaverin's new novel, *Ispolnenie zhelaniy* (*The Fulfillment of Desires*, 1934-35). The problem of the individual's integration in society had always interested Kaverin, but this time he showed more interest in the people themselves and their personal problems. The hero of the novel is Trubachevsky, a young student of literature who makes a literary discovery. His friend Kartashikhin, who is of proletarian origin, is contrasted to him and shown as a more useful and purposeful member of society. Another character, Nevorozhin, introduces the political-detective element, for he is an enemy in disguise, a secret agent of some anti-Soviet *émigré* organization (the persistence of this motif in the Soviet novels of the mid-thirties serves well to illustrate the potency of social command). The characters include also an old professor of literature for whom Trubachevsky works, his son (another class enemy and a friend of Nevorozhin), and his daughter. The daughter is in love with Kartashikhin and supplies the romantic element.

The novel is much more simple and straightforward in outline than *The Unknown Artist*. There is no toying with the plot of which Kaverin used to be so fond and which now might easily have been interpreted as "bourgeois

Formalism." The message of the novel, if any, is not very obvious. Perhaps it is to be sought in the ultimate winning back to the community of Trubachevsky, who for a while goes astray and is shown as preoccupied too much with things of little importance in a Socialist society.

This novel of Kaverin's was followed by *Dva kapitana* (*Two Captains*, 1939). It is a story of adventure, with a mild detective interest, woven around the pre-Revolutionary Arctic explorations of a Russian captain, but involving also its post-Revolutionary echoes and aftermath. Compared with the majority of contemporary Soviet novels, it has a pleasant accent of freshness and novelty. Kaverin's interest in the plot, in adventure, is certainly refreshing. The book is somehow reminiscent of Arthur Ransome's juvenile sea yarns (plus the inevitable ideological element), and although it first appeared in a regular literary magazine, most of its subsequent editions were issued by the Children's Section of the State Publishing House (Detizdat). It is, in fact, a book for the young which can be read and enjoyed by grown-ups.

Katayev Katayev's *Beleyet parus odinokiy* (*The Lone White Sail*, 1936) is one of this author's most attractive works. Its autobiographical background is obvious. The action is set in Odessa, where Katayev himself grew up and where his father was a schoolmaster. The principal characters in the book are two boys: Petya Bachey, the son of a high-school teacher, and Gavrik, a little fisherman. The novel takes place in 1905, against the background of the first Russian Revolution, and this gives Katayev a chance to introduce elements of exciting adventure. We catch glimpses of the Potyomkin mutiny, of a typical Jewish pogrom, of street fighting and strikes in Odessa. But these revolutionary activities merely form the background; the main interest and charm of the novel derive from the fresh and delightful presentation of the two boys—one of them a typical intelligentsia boy, the other a little Odessa street Arab—and of their half-childish, half-adult experiences and adventures.

In Petya's case the grown-up element is introduced by the Revolution, which suddenly encroaches upon his uneventful everyday life. Here and there the author forgets that he is showing us the Revolution of 1905 through the eyes of two nine-year-old boys, and there are passages—for example about religion and the Church—which must put readers on edge whatever their views. But such passages are few, and against them can be set such wholly delightful pages as the opening description of Petya's last day on a seaside farm in Bessarabia; the picture of Petya's school entrance examinations when he is deeply disappointed by not being allowed to recite right through Lermontov's poem about "the lone white sail"; the whole episode of the street game of "buttons," of which Gavrik is a recognized champion, and how it involves Petya in petty larceny, lies, and other misdeeds; and the wanderings of the two boys about the city in the early days of the Revolution, when Petya unwittingly carries in his school satchel cartridges which he believes to be Gavrik's spoils at "buttons." These and other scenes have about them an accent of freshness and spontaneousness and in their genuinely deep insight into children's psychology are worthy to rank with some of the best things written about children in Russian literature. The novel was turned by Katayev into a very successful play for the Children's Theater in Moscow and was later made into a film which had some memorable acting by child actors in the principal roles.

Katayev's short novelette *Ya, syn trudovogo naroda* (*I, the Son of the Toiling People*, 1937), based on his experience in the early days of the Civil War, is of little interest.

Tolstoy Alexey Tolstoy's chief contribution to the literature of Socialist Realism—apart from his historical novels and plays—was the last part of his long novel *The Way Through Hell*. Another work, the novel *Bread*, mentioned earlier, revealed an important and distinctive aspect of Socialist Realism: the tendency to rewrite recent history to fit in with the latest party line. There is no doubt that in writing *Bread* Tolstoy was carrying out an assignment. Its subject was the Civil War, more specifically the defense of Tsaritsyn (Stalingrad) against the Whites in 1919. The author's principal object was to glorify the role played by Stalin and Voroshilov and to expose Trotsky's "treacherous" conduct. This Tolstoy did to the best of his considerable natural ability, but despite some good characterizations and vivid descriptions the novel did not add any new laurels to his crown. It remains one of the most glaring examples of literature placed in the service of the party, and even Soviet admirers of Tolstoy seem to be ashamed of it.

Zoshchenko The statute of the Union of Soviet Writers stipulates that Socialist Realism must aim not only at describing the realities of the new world but also at remolding men and educating them toward Socialism. Its literature must provide edifying examples. This "Socialist uplift" became an integral part of Soviet literature in the 1930's. Several writers tackled the theme of moral and political "reformation" of hostile elements. Thus Zoshchenko, in *Istoriya odnoy zhizni* (*The Story of One Life*, 1935), chose for his setting the construction of the White Sea–Baltic (Stalin) Canal, which was built with the forced labor of common-law criminals and political prisoners under the supervision of the Ogpu, and described the moral regeneration of an ordinary criminal working on that construction. Soviet critics welcomed Zoshchenko's book as a new step toward the portrayal of a positive character and a renunciation of his customary satirical method and approach. But the book, with its sentimental idealization of the Ogpu men, is one of Zoshchenko's weakest; he was obviously out of his element. The same subject, on a wider scale, was dealt with in Pogodin's play, of which more will be said later.

Malyshkin The "reforging" of hostile or indifferent elements—to use the formula popular in the Soviet press of the time—was also one of the themes of Malyshkin's *Lyudi iz zakholustya* (*People from the Backwoods*, 1938). This work was planned as a long and ambitious novel, with a great number of characters and two parallel lines of action, one in Moscow, the other at a big construction project in the Urals. The action is set during the First Five-Year Plan at the height of the reconstruction fever. Unfortunately, only the first volume was written, the author dying soon after its publication. It is an interesting, though uneven, work. Several of the characters—Peter Soustin, Zhurkin, and Tishka—are well done, and most of the chapters dealing with the Krasnogorsk project and its life are good—well written, vivid, and free from all idealization.

Ehrenburg Ilya Ehrenburg also made his contribution to the Five-Year Plan literature. His two novels *Den' vtoroy* (*The Second Day*, 1935; the title is an allusion to Genesis) and *Ne perevodya dykhaniya* (*Without Pausing for Breath*, 1937) have for their background the industrial construction in the outlying parts of the Soviet Union. Ehrenburg is, however, interested mainly in personal problems and attitudes, especially in the first novel. One of his characters in *The Second Day*, Volodya Safonov, a maladjusted young man who ends by committing suicide, seems to have walked into Ehrenburg's novel out of one of Dostoyevsky's.[1] In the second novel there was much less of the Dostoyevskian element, and it was more orthodox.

Nikitin and Ivanov In the late thirties two former Serapions, of whom little had been heard for some time, made a comeback. Nikolay Nikitin published a long novel, *Eto nachalos v Kokande* (*This Began at Kokand*, 1940), describing the period of Socialist reconstruction in central Asia; and Vsevolod Ivanov wrote a long and colorful autobiographical novel entitled *Pokhozhdeniya fakira* (*The Adventures of a Fakir*, 1935). In 1938, Ivanov published *Parkhomenko*, a biographical novel about a noted Civil War leader, which heralded a revival of the Civil War theme in literature. The new approach to it, however, contrasted sharply with the romantic hyperbolism of Pilnyak and his followers. It was more realistic and more historical, even though history, as in Alexey Tolstoy's *Bread*, was often distorted to suit the official party line of the moment. Among these "socialist-realistic" novels about the Civil War

---

[1] Cf. R. Jackson, *The Underground Man in Russian Literature*. One Soviet critic described Safonov as younger brother of Olesha's Kavalerov, a relation of Ehrenburg's own Julio Jurenito and at the same time a descendant of Ivan Karamazov.

may be mentioned another biography of a Red Cossack leader, *Kochubey* (1937), by Arkady Perventsev (b. 1905).

Some Newcomers

At the 1934 Congress of Soviet Writers great stress was laid on the need for creating special "national-defense literature." Several works were written to meet this demand. A typical example was *Na vostoke* (*In the East*, 1937), by Peter Andreyevich Pavlenko, once a member of the Pereval group.

Pavlenko (1899–1951)

Pavlenko was not exactly a newcomer to Soviet literature. Born in the oil city of Baku, he spent his childhood and youth in the Caucasus. Between 1919 and 1924 he was engaged in active Communist work in Baku, developing there a strong hatred for Britain and the British. In 1924 he went as a delegate to the Communist party congress in Moscow, and in the summer of the same year was sent on some vague mission abroad which took him to Turkey, Syria, Greece, Italy, and France. About this time he also made his literary debut with a book called *Aziatskie povesti* (*Asiatic Tales*), exotic in subject matter and florid in style. Among his later works mention has already been made of *Barricades*, a novel about the Paris Commune. But it was not until 1937, when *In the East* appeared, that he made a real hit in Soviet literature.

Pavlenko's novel has no "hero" in the ordinary literary sense of the word. In a different sense, most of its many characters—with the obvious exception of the enemies of the Soviet Union—are heroes in their respective walks of life. Its underlying idea is that small and seemingly inconspicuous doings are just as "heroic" under the circumstances as the most startling exploits. The real hero of Pavlenko's novel is the Soviet Far East with its spirit of daring, enterprise, and enthusiasm. Soviet men are shown here, on the remote fringes of the vast Soviet territory, blazing new trails and building a new life. The book had a definite propaganda object and value since it portrayed the work of reconstruction and military preparations on the Soviet Far Eastern frontier in anticipation of a Japanese attack. To many people in the Soviet Union the menace of Japanese aggression seemed at the time more immediate and real than the menace of Nazi Germany.

The first two parts of the novel, the action of which starts in 1932, deal mostly with peaceful activities—with the building of new cities in Siberian forests, the carrying out of new and daring projects by young Soviet men whom Pavlenko characterized in the following words:

And so they came out there in hundreds of thousands and in millions in order to keep pace with the Revolution and not lag a step behind it. Their fathers had burned down estates, had defended scores of fronts, had lost their wives and become disused to their children, while the sons were building cities and setting up stable families, were getting used to sleeping eight hours and eating three meals a day.

It is a picture of stabilization, of the Revolution settling down to peaceful work after a hectic period of struggle and destruction, yet losing none of its zest and enthusiasm. A whole procession of builders, explorers, collective-farm managers, military commanders, and Ogpu officials, passes before our eyes, while we also get glimpses of frontier skirmishes, of Chinese and Korean guerrilla leaders, and of Japanese and White Russian spies who cross the frontier from Manchukuo. In fact, peaceful reconstruction is but one side of the picture. Gradually, military activities and military prepara-tions are thrust to the forefront. Part 4 of the novel, where the action is set at some future though not very distant date ("the year 193-") describes the war between the Soviet Union and Japan, started by the latter and won by the former. Tokyo is bombed and destroyed from the air, the Japanese fleet is defeated by Soviet submarines, while the Japanese land attack fails thanks to some mysterious and deadly new weapon invented by the Soviets. The rising of the Japanese workers and the insurrection in China combine to make the military rout of Japan complete and final. The last part of the book describes the feverish building of a new town, to be called Sen Kata-yama after the well-known Japanese revolutionary, which is to house seventy thousand Japanese, Chinese, Korean, and Manchu war prisoners, as well as its Russian builders, and thus symbolize the triumph of international brotherhood. One of the episodes of this last part of the novel describes the trial, in Sen Katayama, of the chief villain, the old and astute Japanese arch-spy Marusima, but strangely enough the outcome of the trial is not mentioned.

Pavlenko's novel gives some interesting glimpses of Soviet life and activi-ties in the Far East, but it shows traces of hasty writing, and the episodes dealing with the Japanese and White Russian spying activities smack of a cheap thriller and are unconvincing.

It is interesting to note that although the novel appeared at the time when the outside world labored under the illusion that the Soviet Union had abandoned its dream of world revolution and was evolving along purely nationalist lines, Pavlenko did not hesitate to sound the "internationalist" note. "There are a million Communists in Europe—the war will be to the bitter end," says one of the characters in the novel. England is shown by Pavlenko as the symbol of the old capitalist world which is bound to collapse:

Whole nations were dying before people's eyes. Political systems established in the course of centuries crumbled to pieces. England was tossing in agony, and the young nations, her laborers, stood by, their mouths agape with joy and happiness. With England, a whole era in the history of mankind was passing away. If it were possible to impersonate political systems we would have seen a decrepit gentleman posing as a diplomat and an educator, who, after his death, turned out to be only a secondhand dealer and usurer. And as always happens in the life of men, no sooner had this enterprising merchant died than a hungry shoeblack emerged and, on the strength of a certain similarity in their biographies, claimed to be the historical successor of the deceased.

Pavlenko's "hungry shoeblack" was Japan.

Yury Pavlovich Herman published his first major work in 1936, when Socialist Realism was in full swing. It was a novel called *Nashi znakomye* (*Our Friends*). The book had an immediate success, partly because it satisfied a widespread demand for pictures of everyday life and ordinary people. Its very title was apparently designed to convey the idea that people in the book were the kind that every reader could meet in everyday life. Almost throughout the book—which is long, somewhat old-fashioned in construction, and tries to be very "true to life"—the author succeeded in maintaining an accent of quiet, unobtrusive veracity and only toward the end fell to the temptation of sliding into sentimental idealization.

Herman (1910–68)

Our Friends is a story of an unattractive Soviet girl, Antonina Staroselskaya, a dreamer in search of a meaning of life. This she finally finds in social work and in a marriage (her third, the first two having been failures) to an Ogpu official, who twice crosses her path before she really gets to know him.

The story begins in 1925, during the NEP period (there is a clearly detectable undercurrent of hostility in the author's portrayal of NEP conditions, reminiscent of the attitude of Gladkov's ideal Communists). Antonina, a sixteen-year-old girl, is left alone after the death of her father, an accountant in a Soviet institution. She gives up school, sells her father's belongings, and starts looking for work. At one of the labor exchanges she meets a famous and popular actor and falls in love with him, dreamily and romantically. He takes her to supper in a luxurious restaurant, and this event constitutes the climax of Antonina's romance. The next day the actor goes away, leaving Antonina to her dreams of him.

After that she drifts, more or less against her will, into marriage with Skvortsov, a merchant seaman who is engaged in smuggling. She becomes his unwilling accomplice. When Skvortsov is caught by the Ogpu, Antonina is summoned and questioned by Altus, the Ogpu official, whom she had met casually before. Skvortsov is sentenced to three years of hard labor, but Antonina is let off. She finds work as a hairdresser's assistant but continues to lead the same half-dreamy, half-real existence, unconscious of its purpose but vaguely feeling that some purpose will be found. A neighbor of the Skvortsovs, Pal Palych Shvyryatykh, a former waiter, maître d'hôtel and director of restaurants under the old regime, now in charge of one of the Soviet canteens, falls in love with Antonina. An elderly man who lost in the Revolution not only his fortune but also his dream of becoming a landowner, he is at bottom not bad and is full of gentle and genuine solicitude for Antonina and her little son. In his friendship Antonina finds an outlet from her solitude.

Skvortsov, whom Antonina had divorced in the meantime, returns after having served his term, and she has not the heart nor the will to refuse him. For a time they live together; then Skvortsov is run over by a car, and, just as she had drifted into marriage with Skvortsov, Antonina now drifts into marriage with Pal Palych. Outwardly their marriage is happy at first. He is full of love and tenderness for her, while she, without loving him, feels that she owes him a debt of gratitude. But at heart she is still dissatisfied with life and tormented by vague yearnings.

All this leads to a stupid affair with one of Pal Palych's former customers, a representative of the old bourgeoisie. It culminates in a repulsive scene during which Pal Palych beats his rival almost to death, while Antonina realizes how stupid and undignified her behavior was. She and Pal Palych are reconciled, and she falls back into the old, smooth groove. They plan a journey to the Crimea, but suddenly this frail structure of Antonina's existence is upset by an unexpected visit from Tatyana, former caretaker of the house where she used to live. Tatyana is also Skvortsov's former mistress, but now is running a stockbreeding farm somewhere in the country. For a few days Tatyana—this new and changed Tatyana, a useful member of society—stays with Antonina, and after seeing her off, the latter decides to break with Pal Palych. This escape from Pal Palych and the atmosphere of peaceful smugness concludes the second part of the novel. The third part tells of Antonina's "regeneration" through learning and work and of the ultimate happiness she finds in her marriage with Altus. The dreamer becomes a socially useful member of the community. The ending strikes a false note, and Altus himself, this guardian angel from the Ogpu, cuts a very unreal figure. Nor is the novel by any means free from tearful sentimentality.

Of Herman's other works the most interesting is a long story called "Alexey Zhmakin." Its hero is an escaped criminal who is tracked down by an energetic and virtuous Ogpu official, Lapshin, bent on "reforming" his quarry rather than on bringing him to bay. Both the character of Zhmakin and the situations in this story are unusual; there is an atmosphere of tension, and the interest is sustained throughout, even though the reader can hardly believe in Herman's virtuous Ogpu man. Lapshin also appears in another story, where he is the principal character and is even less credible.

Virta
(b. 1906) Another newcomer to Soviet literature in this period was Nikolay Evgen-yevich Virta.[2] He made his name with his first novel, *Odinochestvo*

[2] Virta's real name was apparently Severtsev. His father was a village priest in the province of Tambov and appears to have been involved in the Antonov uprising.

(*Solitude*, 1936), which was to be the first part of a trilogy dealing with some important phases of the political history of the Soviet Union. In *Solitude* the subject is the famous peasant rising, led by Antonov, in the province of Tambov in 1920. At the time it was a cause of great concern to the Soviet government, and its suppression was regarded as a matter of prime importance. The troops sent to crush it were commanded by Tukhachevsky, the future marshal and the principal victim of the Red Army purge in 1937.[3]

In Virta's novel the hero is a real person—Peter Storozhev, a well-to-do peasant who becomes one of Antonov's principal lieutenants. The interesting subject, the acuteness of the conflict portrayed, the variety and wealth of characters involved, and the skillful handling of the material make *Solitude* a memorable first novel. Its last part, entitled "The Wolf," has true accents of tragedy. It describes the collapse of the Antonov movement and shows Storozhev roaming like a lonely wolf around his native village, striking the last desperate blows at his enemies. Although Virta was at pains to present Storozhev as a villain and an enemy of the people, he could not deny him a certain grandeur. Nor is Antonov himself painted in uniformly black colors.

Soviet critics were at first cautious in their comments on Virta's book, but it appears that soon the word went round that Stalin himself thought very highly of it, and praises were showered on the practically unknown writer. The novel went through several editions in a short time. In 1937, Virta wrote a play based on it, entitled *Zemlya* (*Land*). Later he was awarded a Stalin Prize for the novel.

The second volume of Virta's trilogy appeared in 1937 under the title *Zakonomernost'* (*Lawfulness*). Through several characters and plot threads it is connected with *Solitude*. Storozhev himself does not appear in it except in a flashback but hovers in the background and is an important factor in the story. The same part of Russia is the scene of action, but at a much later period, in the late twenties. There are frequent references to Antonov and his movement, and the survivals of "Antonovism" among the peasants and the anti-Soviet elements of Soviet intelligentsia and officialdom are stressed. Their links with the old Socialist Revolutionary party are pointed out.

At the beginning of the novel we are introduced to the household of Nikita Kagarde, a village schoolmaster and one of Antonov's former henchmen, and are told his story, which involves his relations with Storozhev. His son, Lev Kagarde, who is shown first as a boy and then as a young man, is the main character. An ambitious youth, who inherits his father's hatred for the Soviet regime, he becomes the center of a sabotage group in the small town of Verkhnerechensk. Intelligent, unscrupulous, with a gift and

[3] In later editions of *Solitude*, after Tukhachevsky's liquidation, his and Uborevich's names were expunged from the book.

a craving for leadership, he succeeds not only in drawing into his net some of the anti-Soviet elements in Soviet institutions, but also in corrupting several representatives of the younger generation who, dissatisfied with drab realities, are on the lookout for ideals and adventures. Kagarde provides them with both. Most of these young people, who ultimately find their way back into the fold, are shown as innocent victims of Kagarde's charms and cunning. Kagarde himself, unmasked and held at bay, disappears in the nick of time from the town. He goes to Moscow, where for a time he changes his methods and tactics, without, however, giving up his final anti-Soviet aims. He imagines himself to be safe, while in fact all the time his footsteps are dogged by the vigilant organs of political security. He meets his end while on his way to a tryst with Storozhev on the Polish frontier. Storozhev, according to the novel, has been living in Poland all this time, awaiting a signal from his partisans to cross over into Russia and lead a general anti-Soviet uprising.[4]

This novel of Virta's was the first important Soviet work of fiction to deal with the background of the wreckers' and opposition trials that swept the country in the late thirties. It is very interesting in that it shows the variety of characters involved in anti-Soviet activities and especially the diversity and complexity of the motives ascribed to them. It is true that Virta does his best to show Lev Kagarde—this miniature caricature of Trotsky and embryonic "Führer"—in all his repulsiveness. But some of Kagarde's victims, willing and unwilling, are very attractive. The picture painted by Virta is on the whole objective but, of course, is far from complete. Some of the riddles presented by the famous "trials" are left unsolved, and certain aspects of the affair are completely ignored. The moral of the tale, as the author sees it, is given in the purely political epilogue, which has for its motto a line from Sophocles: "That which is coming. . . ." Here is a passage from it:

We have come out on the right road and we know where it leads us. Everything is behind and everything is ahead, everything is known, everything is understood, time has lifted its veils.

The Bogdanovs, murderers and hirelings of murderers, have been caught and brought to book from their stinking underworld, and the world recoils in horror

---

[4] Actually, Storozhev never seems to have gone to Poland, and he is said to have been shot soon after the publication of Virta's book. Virta must have known him as a boy. From the scanty biographical data attached to the 1947 edition of *Solitude* we learn that in 1921 the village in which Virta grew up joined the Antonov rebels and that his father's house, the best in the village, was used by the rebels as their headquarters. Of Virta's father this short biography says that he was "more inclined to politics than to priestly duties." There is also a dark hint at a family tragedy which took place in 1921, after which Virta became the head of the family. Apparently Virta's father was shot with other rebels. In his novel the village priest is shown as an enemy of Communism and a friend of Storozhev.

from this abyss of baseness. Their repugnant road is ended—they died the death of mad dogs. But have all of them been caught and brought to trial before the people?

We must learn to distinguish between enemies and friends, learn to search and to find, to love and to hate. Let us be prepared—storms are still ahead of us.

The epilogue explains the title of the novel: it refers to the lawful course of the Revolution and the relentless lawfulness of its nemesis.

Virta's novel may be regarded as a good specimen of what was expected of Socialist Realism, for it combined edifying purpose with a sufficiently detached portrayal of realities.

Another younger writer whose first novel was a great success was Yury Krymov (pseudonym of Yury Solomonovich Beklemishev). Born in Petrograd, he came of a family of the intelligentsia (his mother was a writer, too), but before entering literature, he worked for many years as a technical expert in various branches of Soviet industry. His first novel, *Tanker "Derbent"* (*The Tanker "Derbent,"* 1938), was greatly praised by Soviet critics and was soon translated into several foreign languages. Its setting is laid in a Caspian Sea port and on board an oil tanker which is engaged in "Socialist emulation," or "Stakhanovism," so popular in those days. Krymov succeeds in making the story of the tanker's part in this contest not only readable but even exciting. His characters are sufficiently original and interesting. The hero, Basov, is somewhat unusual. Surly, quarrelsome, seemingly unattractive, he is snubbed by his superiors and disliked or mistrusted by most of those who work with or under him, which does not prevent him from showing his mettle in the end and proving a true Stakhanovite hero. The central episode in this short realistic novel, based on a thorough knowledge of the life it describes, is the fire on another tanker whose survivors are rescued by the *Derbent*. In keeping with what was regarded as one of the essential features of Socialist Realism, the story of human relations, and in particular of Basov's matrimonial mishaps, is cleverly interwoven with the social aspect of the novel.

Krymov (1908–41)

Krymov's literary career was cut short when he was killed in battle with the Germans in September, 1941. His biography mentions that on the eve of his death he joined the Communist party.

Chapter 24. SOCIALIST REALISM IN DRAMA AND POETRY

Drama

During the Five-Year Plan period the drama, more than any other form of Soviet literature, suffered from the deadening effects of social command. And with the advent of Socialist Realism the reaction against it took a two-fold form. On the one hand, there was a tendency toward greater objectivity in the portrayal of social collisions and toward a more realistic presentation of complex characters, instead of aligning them in two opposite camps, as flawless Soviet heroes and unmitigated anti-Soviet villains. On the other hand, to plays dealing with purely social themes and situations were added plays about ordinary Soviet citizens and their everyday personal problems. Some of them struck a gay note and were built around farcical situations. A typical example was *Chuzhoy rebyonok* (*Another Man's Child*), by Vasily Shkvarkin (b. 1893), a mediocre comedy which enjoyed a great success and brought its author a fortune.

Pogodin
(1900–62) Representative of the new trends in the Soviet drama were the plays of Nikolay Pogodin (pseudonym of Nikolay Fedorovich Stukalov) and Alexander Afinogenov. Pogodin came into literature by way of journalism, and all his plays reflect an interest in topical problems of Soviet life. The first three, *Temp* (*Tempo*), *Poema o topore* (*Poem About an Axe*), and *Sneg* (*Snow*; all 1930), were written before the advent of Socialist Realism. *Tempo* and *Poem About an Axe* are, in the main, typical Five-Year Plan production plays. *Tempo* has for its subject the construction of the Stalingrad tractor plant, and its characters, all of whom are superficially drawn, include Communist enthusiasts, anti-Communist saboteurs, and an American engineer, who is at first horrified by the Russians' slovenly methods and then amazed by the tempo of construction which eclipses all American records. The play actually lacks all plot; Pogodin's method is that of documentary naturalism. Thus, since the American, Mr. Carter, knows no Russian, his speeches are given in English, but to make them understandable to Russian readers and spectators each sentence is duplicated in Russian. Pogodin himself, in writing of *Tempo*, said that nothing in his play was "invented"—that Carter was modeled on a Mr. Kidler, who built the Stalingrad plant, that other characters were also drawn from life, and that everything that happened to Carter had actually happened in real life. And, in keeping with the views prevalent at the time, Pogodin declared: "The theater has to do

with documentary dramaturgy, and it would not be a bad thing to try to bring this documentariness, this truthfulness home to the spectator."

Poem About an Axe deals with the discovery of nonrusting steel at a Soviet plant and was built in much the same way as *Tempo*, with almost the same assortment of characters. *Snow* has for its subject a scientific expedition somewhere in the Caucasus (the location is deliberately vague), with the object of "conquering" mountain snows and utilizing them for industrial purposes. There are the usual stock characters: the enthusiastic Communist leader of the expedition; the skeptical, egocentric, absent-minded professor who ends by espousing the Communist cause; the engineer who as a class enemy tries to sabotage the whole expedition; a young Communist girl journalist who keeps unmasking "enemies"; two young natives, brother and sister, who defy their tribe's hostility to the expedition; an operatically wicked native sheikh; and so on. *Snow* differs from the two earlier plays in being less "documentary"; it even has a touch of symbolism. Another novel feature in it is the inclusion of a prologue in which the two leading actors give humorous comments on the play and its characters. They also reappear several times during the play, interrupting the action with their comments and humorous asides. In Act 2, after a slapstick scene in which the wicked sheikh is duped by the girl journalist, they intrude with the following dialogue to make fun of the run-of-the-mill Soviet plays:

The Second: I don't like this play.
The First: Why?
The Second: This play is like nothing on earth. In fifteen years I have got used to plays which resemble each other like a pair of overshoes. The spectators know in advance where to clap, where to laugh, and where to go to sleep.
The First: What about crying?
The Second: Nowadays you don't cry during the play, you do so after the play.

Generally speaking, Pogodin's Five-Year Plan plays differed from the typical products of that period by their element of humor, though more often than not this humor was somewhat primitive.

Pogodin's first play written after the 1932 "reform" was *Moy drug* (*My Friend*). Written in 1932, it was produced by the Theater of the Revolution in 1934. It largely repeats the pattern of his earlier plays. It shows a Soviet plant under construction and the efforts of its director to overcome all sorts of difficulties. But the play is less episodic, less journalistic, and dramatically more compact. There is also an attempt to give a more rounded portrait of the central character, Gay, the director of the plant. He is the new Soviet man, the positive hero, one of the builders of Socialism. All the other characters are there merely to set him in relief and are for the most part as conventional as those in Pogodin's earlier plays. This is particularly true of Gay's enemies, those who, guided by various motives, hinder the construction. In the words of one of the leading Soviet dramatic critics, Yuzovsky, who was on the whole quite favorable to Pogodin, "Pogodin's negative characters do not come off. . . . They are mannequins disguised as saboteurs and wandering about the play because one can't dispense with them."

In *Posle bala* (*After the Ball*), written in 1933 and produced also in 1934, the negative characters are either comic or melodramatic, and the whole play is a rather incongruous mixture of kolkhoz heroics, slapstick humor, and melodrama, with a dash of romantic calf love—all set against the background of a hectic sowing campaign on a collective farm.

Pogodin's most successful play was *Aristokraty* (*Aristocrats*). Described as "a comedy in four acts," it was produced in 1934. The scene is the construction of the White Sea–Baltic (Stalin) Canal, which, as mentioned earlier, was dug with forced labor. The main characters are three Cheka-men (*chekisty*), as they are described in the list of characters, and numerous prisoners, of whom four are described as "specialists" and the rest as "bandits, thieves, prostitutes, fanatics, kulaks, etc." The play lacks real plot. In a series of rapid, colorful episodes, some of which no doubt must have been very effective on the stage of Okhlopkov's Realistic Theater, it tells the story of the winning over of these class enemies and social outcasts, most of whom refuse at first to work or submit to discipline. Psychologically it is unconvincing, and the Cheka-men, in their saccharinity, are particularly unreal. But many of the minor characters are real enough, and the dialogue, spiced with thieves' slang, is vivid. Among the multitude of characters are two who stand out. One is Sadovsky, an engineer sentenced to forced labor for his anti-Soviet wrecking activities; the other, Kostya the Captain, a glib, irrepressible gangster, full of humor and vitality. While Sadovsky is a pale abstraction, Kostya is real enough as long as he refuses to work, behaves rebelliously and cracks his gangster's jokes, but his conversion into an enthusiastic Stakhanovite is not very easy to believe. Van Gyseghem, in his book *Theatre in Soviet Russia*, has described Pogodin's *Aristocrats* as "a modern miracle play," giving a very interesting account of its production by Ohklopkov's Realistic Theater, which he called "the last word . . . in the direction of a stylized convention."

In *Chelovek s ruzhyom* (*The Man with the Rifle*, 1937) Pogodin tried to apply the principles of Socialist Realism to recent history. The play represents a series of episodes which show Lenin (or the Soviet myth of Lenin) in October, 1917. The play owed its great success largely to the lifelike performance of Lenin's role by Shchukin. In 1941 Pogodin followed this up with another play about Lenin, *Kremlyovskie kuranty* (*The Kremlin Chimes*). Whereas in *The Man with the Rifle* the stress was on Lenin the man, here Lenin the statesman was to the forefront. Another play, *Tretya*

Pateticheskaya (*The Third Pathetic*), was added in the fifties to make the plays into a trilogy.

Afinogenov, who belonged to the Proletkult, began by writing a number of mediocre plays in the twenties. Typical of them was *Malinovoye varenye* (*Raspberry Jam*, 1926), a Communist melodrama, complete with bourgeois villains, spies arriving from abroad, camouflaged telephones, invisible ink which a hysterical woman drinks instead of sedative drops, and a young Komsomol heroine. The artistic value of this play (and some other of Afinogenov's early plays) is nil; its characters are unreal, and its humor is often in poor taste. It has, however, some documentary value, since it sheds considerable light on certain aspects of Soviet life of that period. This is still more true of *Chudak* (*The Eccentric*, 1928), whose hero is a young enthusiast of Soviet production who has to fight against indifference, red tape, favoritism, anti-Semitism, and other evils rampant at a Soviet paper mill. Though not free from some melodramatic moments and occasional lapses of taste, this play gives a more realistic picture of life, and its characters are psychologically more plausible.

Afinogenov (1904–41)

Afinogenov's first popular success was scored with *Strakh* (*Fear*, 1931), a somewhat overpraised problem play about an old scientist who becomes a more or less willing tool of anti-Soviet elements but ends by repenting. The play has some interesting ideological moments since it deals with the problem of freedom of science, but the characterization is poor and the form conventionally old-fashioned.

A great success awaited also the play *Dalyokoye* (1936; in English translation *Distant Point*; actually the title is the name of a small railway siding on the Trans-Siberian Railway). It is in the true Chekhovian, undramatic tradition: a record of twenty-four hours in the life of several inconspicuous Soviet people working at a tiny station lost in the Siberian forests at which the special coach of a high-ranking Red Army commander, proceeding from Vladivostok to Moscow, is forcibly delayed. There is a refreshing absence of saboteurs and class enemies, and although there is the inevitable amount of declamatory phrases and breezy official optimism, several of the characters are sufficiently attractive as ordinary human beings. Afinogenov has more psychological finesse than Pogodin, but he lacks Pogodin's sense of the theatrical.

One of the principal figures in proletarian literary organizations in the twenties and early thirties, Afinogenov was expelled from the party in 1937, but did not disappear from literature. Of his last three plays one, *Vtorye puti* (*The Second Track*, 1939), was a sequel to *The Distant Point*; the second, *Mashenka*, was a light comedy of everyday Soviet life; and the last, *Nakanune* (*On the Eve*, 1941), was about the early phase of the Soviet-German War. Afinogenov himself was one of its first casualties. He was

killed in October, 1941, during an air raid on Moscow, just before he was
to go abroad on an assignment from the Soviet Information Bureau. In the
last years of his life a close friendship bound him and his English wife with
Boris Pasternak. Two volumes of his articles and enlightening excerpts from
diaries, notebooks, and letters were published in 1957 and 1960.

Leonov   Much more interesting are the plays of Leonov. His dramatic works before
1932 included a dramatization of his own novel *The Badgers* and three
original plays: *Untilovsk* (1928), *Provintsialnaya istoriya* (*A Provincial
Episode*, 1928), and *Usmirenie Badadoshkina* (*The Taming of Badadoshkin*, 1929). In all three the theme was the survival of the "old Adam" in the
new world. Just as in his novels, Leonov's approach to this theme was psychological and ethical, rather than social or political. The most characteristic
feature of his plays was their tenseness, their strain. There was nothing
ordinary about them. Strange, unusual, often pathetic characters, full of
quirks and twists, were involved in strange situations and engaged in
weird conversations, full of allusions, of symbolic undercurrents, in which
things left unsaid mattered more than what was actually said—a mixture
of Chekhov, Ibsen, and Dostoyevsky.[1] It was this symbolism and this tendency to generalize that raised Leonov's plays above the level of the average
Soviet dramatic productions. In *Untilovsk*, for instance (the name itself—
that of a small town—is significant), Leonov tried to portray in a microcosm
the vulgarity of life. The characters are a gallery of has-beens and castaways,
some of them pathetic, some despicable, but all of them drifting futilely
away from the mainstream of life. Chervakov, who is described in the list
of dramatis personae as "an Untilovsk homunculus," was apparently meant
by Leonov as the embodiment of all that was mean and evil in the old world.
Soviet critics saw in him "the psychological quintessence of counterrevolution," but Leonov was not really interested in any political issues, and there
is very little in the play to indicate when its action takes place. Untilovsk
itself is a psychological symbol, not a geographical term, while Chervakov is
a distant descendant of the Karamazovs, a cross between the old Karamazov
himself and Smerdyakov.

    Both dramatically and ideologically speaking, Leonov's plays are incon-
clusive; there are too many loose ends in them and too little unity of action.
But his superiority to such acknowledged Soviet dramatists as Pogodin and
Afinogenov is revealed in his characters and his dialogues. His characters
may strike one as queer, as too complex and twisted, too Dostoyevskian, but

---

[1] Leonov himself once said that in his plays words mattered less than what was
hidden under them. See *"Zolotaya kareta": Materialy k postanovke* (*"The Golden
Carriage": Materials for Its Production*), 24, quoted by A. M. Galanov in his article on
Leonov in *Problemy sotsialisticheskogo realizma* (*Problems of Socialist Realism*), 111.
Zolotaya kareta is Leonov's post–World War II play.

they are infinitely more interesting, especially in *Untilovsk*, than those of Pogodin and Afinogenov. And Leonov is a master of Russian. His language is rich and flexible; his dialogues remind one at once of Leskov and Dostoyevsky; however, he sometimes lets these stylistic elements run away with him to the detriment of purely dramatic considerations. His plays also run a gamut of moods, from tragic pathos to grim humor. In *Polovchanskie sady* (*The Orchards of Polovchansk*, 1936–38) and *Volk* (*The Wolf*, 1938)— the latter also known as *Begstvo Sandukova* (*Sandukov's Flight*)—the dramatic effect is achieved by a close interweaving of family and social conflicts. In both Leonov comes somewhat closer to the Soviet realities of the day, but his method remains that of symbolic realism. There is an obvious influence of Ibsen and Chekhov, while at least one Soviet critic has noted an affinity between Leonov's plays and the symbolic theater of Maeterlinck.

In *The Orchards of Polovchansk* there is an almost classical unity of place and time, the drama unfolding within a day or two during a family reunion of the Makkaveyevs. The old man, Makkaveyev, is director of a famous state orchard. In addition to the two children who live with him, he has five sons by his first marriage, who represent the flower of Soviet manhood and a variety of occupations. One of them does not appear in the play, although he is mentioned in the list of characters. But in a way he is the real hero of the play. The news of his death while on an important mission in the Arctic comes during the family-reunion celebrations, over which he presides in spirit as it were, a symbol of patriotic duty and vigilance. The dramatic knot of the play is tied around the appearance during the reunion of a former friend of the family who turns out to be an enemy agent. There are some well-drawn, slightly grotesque, minor characters, but on the whole the play differs from Leonov's earlier ones in that nearly all the characters are wholesome and more or less attractive people and not a collection of cranks and monstrosities. Even the villain is not too overdone. However, despite the excellent dialogue and the subtle atmosphere of suspense, as drama the play fails. Is it because, as one Soviet critic has suggested, Leonov is at his best only when he portrays unhappy people?

The Wolf has many points in common with *The Orchards*, but here the theme of the exposure of enemy agents is more to the fore and is handled much more melodramatically. With it again is interwoven the theme of family conflict. The play is full of symbolism, of significantly allusive dialogues, of understatements and mysterious hints, but one cannot help feeling that Leonov has been wasting these Ibsenian subtleties on a theme that was not worth it. As usual with Leonov, there are several finely drawn characters, especially some of the minor ones. All Leonov's characters have depth and leave scope for the actor's imagination, so that his plays must gain considerably on the stage.

In *Metel'* (*Blizzard*, 1940) Leonov portrayed another "enemy of the people." The play was not published and was soon taken off the stage. More than twenty years later, in 1963, Leonov was to write a new version of it, as he did also of his novel *The Thief*.

Throughout this period Soviet critics continued to complain about the dearth of good Soviet plays. With one or two exceptions Soviet theaters preferred to produce plays by pre-Revolutionary or foreign authors, and this undoubtedly reflected the playgoers' preference. In his book on the Soviet theater André van Gyseghem, the well-known British theater director who paid four visits to the Soviet Union and spent a year working with Soviet producers, gives a list of plays which ran in the leading Moscow theaters during the 1935–36 season. If we exclude the Jewish State Theater and the Gypsy Theater with their specific repertoires, there were forty-nine Soviet productions as compared with seventy-two foreign and pre-Revolutionary Russian productions. They represented forty individual plays by thirty-one Soviet authors. The only authors with more than one play running were Afinogenov, Fayko, Kirshon, Pogodin, Pervomaysky, and Mikitenko. Of these, the last two were Ukrainian-language writers, while Kirshon was soon to be "exposed" as a Trotskyite and an enemy of the people, and his plays banned.

Poetry

Simplicity, realism, and accessibility to the masses came to be regarded also as the main virtues in poetry, and several new poets whose work satisfied these requirements gained recognition and popularity in the thirties.

Prokofyev
(b. 1900) Alexander Andreyevich Prokofyev came of northern peasant stock (his father was a fisherman on Lake Ladoga). He joined the Communist party in 1919 and fought in the Civil War. His first books of poetry appeared in 1931, but he became particularly popular in the latter part of that decade. In 1939–40 he took part in the war against Finland as a newspaper correspondent. During World War II he worked in the Political Administration of the Leningrad front. In 1944 he was awarded a Stalin Prize for his poem "Russia."

Prokofyev's early poems were written under the influence of Mayakovsky and were characterized by bombastic diction, by "grand" revolutionary themes, and by affectedly crude language. There were also in them some survivals of proletarian Cosmism, with its grandiloquence and its predilection for capital letters. In a poem called "The Epoch," Prokofyev spoke of "the young Epoch overtaking constellations in the impetuous train of Fame." In the poem "We" (1930) he referred to his generation of Soviet men as being famed "from the White Sea to San Diego." Referring to the Allied intervention in Russia in 1919, he recalled "Lord Churchill" who "led the bandits" and expressed the pious wish that "the entrails of his swinish soul may be scattered by the wind," that in his hour of death "he may tear the earth with his teeth," for "such vermin must be quartered." In the same poem Prokofyev spoke of the existence of "two Englands," one of which could not live while the king was alive, and so "the second England will emerge after hanging the king."[2]

In the late thirties Prokofyev became less political-minded and began to write simple poems about his native country, about village life, and about love, in which he revealed his unquestionable inborn gift of song. It is in these simple poems, strongly influenced by folk songs and village ditties and asking, as it were, to be accompanied on the accordion, that Prokofyev is at his best. His range is limited, he is often naïve and sentimental, but his poems are infectiously melodious.

Shchipachov (b. 1899)

The emphasis on simplicity and melodiousness became pronounced during this period, and several of the poets who gained popularity in the late thirties developed along the same lines as Prokofyev. Many of them were of humble origin and had joined the Bolsheviks when still quite young. One of these, Stepan Petrovich Shchipachov, came of a poor peasant family and began earning his living when still a boy. In 1919 he volunteered for the Red Army and joined the Bolshevik party. Later he taught in military schools but in 1931 enrolled in the Institute of Red Professors, where he studied literature. His poems began to appear in print in 1926, and his first book was published in 1931. By 1947 he had some twenty books of poetry to his credit. During World War II he worked for an army newspaper at the front.

Shchipachov's poetry is simple in themes, in structure, and in rhythms, but his simplicity is more studied than Prokofyev's, and his lines lack melodious infectiousness. Soviet critics have spoken of the "philosophic note" in Shchipachov's poetry, but his "philosophy" is elementary and shallow—one should rather speak of his inclination to rationalize, of which Prokofyev at his best is free.

Dolmatovsky (b. 1915)

A much younger poet is Evgeny Aronovich Dolmatovsky, a true offspring of the Revolution. His first poem appeared in *Pionerskaya Pravda* when he was fifteen. In 1933 he worked as a volunteer on the construction of the Moscow subway, about which he wrote several poems. A year later his first book of poems was published. In 1937, after graduating from the Gorky Literary Institute, he went to the Far East and published a book of *Far Eastern Poems*. In 1939 he took part in the Soviet invasion of Poland, and in 1940 he served in the war against Finland as a war correspondent. During World War II, Dolmatovsky served again as a war reporter on various fronts, received nine decorations, and published several books of poems. Like

[2] In the 1947 edition of Prokofyev's *Selected Poems*, this passage about "Lord" Churchill and the two Englands was omitted.

Shchipachov, he is simple and unsophisticated, but more virile and optimistic. He is the author of many popular songs that became part of the everyday Soviet repertoire. They are typical of the tendency, prevalent in the thirties, to return to simple, traditional forms and to write poetry with mass appeal.

Surkov
(b. 1899) Alexey Alexandrovich Surkov also came of a poor peasant family. His childhood was spent in his native village in the province of Yaroslavl. From 1912 to 1918 he worked at various trades in St. Petersburg; later he served in the Red Army and did party work in the Volga region. In 1934 he graduated from the Institute of Red Professors. In the invasion of Poland, the war with Finland, and World War II, Surkov did political and newspaper work at the front. His first book of poems appeared in 1930 and has since been followed by nearly thirty others. In Surkov's prewar poetry reminiscences of the Civil War play a large part, and woven into them is the motif of implacable hatred for the enemies. The fighting note is clearly sounded in his poems. He speaks of "the joy and fatigue of battle" and of the "acrid smoke of unquiet campfires"; he has no use for "warmth and quiet." In a programmatic poem entitled "The Hero," Surkov speaks of himself as "a soldier of world revolution," "an anonymous guardsman of the rebel class," who learned under fire "to hold his rifle and his heart at ready." In another war poem, "Sovremenniku" ("To a Contemporary") dedicated to his friend and fellow poet Mikhail Isakovsky, Surkov wrote:

> We grew old before we realized it,
> As though we had been fighting all life.

The poem spoke of their generation as having suffered enough for five generations, and ended on a defiant note:

> Let the roads into the new epoch
> Be unexplored and dangerous.
> We refuse to exchange for anything
> Our draughty destiny.

This stern acceptance of one's lot, coupled with Communist loyalty and patriotic pride, is the keynote of Surkov's poetry. It is free from that mawkish sentimentality which colors much of Shchipachov's and Dolmatovsky's work. There is in it a manly note, reminiscent of the early Tikhonov and going back to Gumilyov. The very texture of his verse is firm and compact. His military songs were among the most popular in the Red Army.

Tvardovsky
(b. 1910) Alexander Trifonovich Tvardovsky lived until the age of eighteen in a backwoods village. In 1928 he went to Smolensk and began writing for newspapers. His first book of poems, *Put k sotsializmu* (*The Road to*

Socialism), describing the rise of collective farms, appeared in 1930. Fame came to Tvardovsky in 1936 with the publication of his long poem *Strana Muraviya* (*The Land of Muravia*); in 1941 he was awarded a Stalin Prize for it. In the meantime Tvardovsky graduated from the Institute of History and Philosophy in Moscow and, joining the Red Army, took part in the invasion of Poland and in the war against Finland as a war correspondent. In 1941, when Hitler invaded the Soviet Union, Tvardovsky resumed his work for army newspapers. He did not become a member of the Communist party until 1938.

Tvardovsky's principal prewar work, *The Land of Muravia*, is a narrative poem of over two thousand lines, divided into nineteen chapters. Its hero is a "middling" peasant, Nikita Morgunok, who refuses to join a collective farm. Leaving his family, he sets out with his horse and cart in search of the fabulous land of Muravia, the Land of Cockaigne of peasants' dreams where he can truly own and till his own land, where everything will be his, where he need not ask anyone's permission, where there will be no communes and no collective farms—a land that is true to peasant traditions. The poem describes Nikita's fruitless quest and the various adventures and incidents that befall him on the way. He partakes of the carousing of the dispossessed kulaks, who hold a wake for their deported fellow villagers. His horse is stolen by a former kulak, who sells it to an itinerant priest, and Nikita has to drag his cart for the rest of his journey. In a prosperous collectivized village he attends a wedding feast. And he sees with his own eyes the misery and poverty of a village where individual tenure still prevails. His last encounter is with an old man who had gone on the last pilgrimage to the holy places of Kiev but is now returning without having reached his destination, suddenly convinced that even if God exists He has no more power in this world. The old man tells Morgunok that there is no such thing as Muravia Land, that it has "grown over with grass and sward." "Why should anyone need this Land of Muravia when there is such life all around you?" he asks.

Thus the only thing that is left to Morgunok is to join a collective farm. The political moral of Tvardovsky's poem is therefore orthodox. But it is not a propaganda poem. The author has an understanding for and sympathy with the personal proprietary instincts of the average Russian peasant, personified in Morgunok. The scene of the carousing dispossessed peasants has a tragic accent. One of them sings a song about a little bird which refuses to eat or sing and asks for its cage to be opened. The charm of the poem lies in its blend of realism and whimsical fancy, of spicy satire and gentle humor. It is a modern counterpart of Nekrasov's great epic of peasant life, *Who Lives Happily in Russia?* Like the latter it is saturated with the genuine spirit of folk poetry. Tvardovsky not only uses the racy peasant speech which fits naturally into his easy-flowing verse but also handles skillfully various folklore devices and especially the motifs and meters of the *chastushka* (village ditty). For instance, folklore motifs are worked into the imaginary speech which Morgunok addresses to Stalin, asking to be allowed to keep his holding for a while and promising to join the kolkhoz later.

Tvardovsky's later work will be discussed in its proper place.

Lebedev-Kumach (1898–1948)   The genre of song became the specialty of several poets who wrote almost exclusively poems that were meant to be sung rather than read. Some of them were written in collaboration with the composers who set them to music or as lyrics for popular films. This is especially true of Vasily Lebedev-Kumach, author of the popular "Pesnya o Rodine" ("Song of the Motherland"), which was treated as a sort of unofficial national anthem and became the signature tune of Radio Moscow. He also wrote such popular "hits" as the song about the wind in the film *The Children of Captain Grant* and the march in the film *The Gay Kids*. They are simple, catchy, and melodious.

Isakovsky (b. 1900) and Gusev (1909–44)   Great popularity was also enjoyed by the songs of Mikhail Isakovsky and Victor Gusev. Both were influenced by Russian folk songs and were responsible for some successful imitations. Isakovsky's humorous "I kto ego znayet?" ("Why on Earth?") and Gusev's "Polyushko," popularized by the Red Army Choir, found their way back to the people, just as did some early-nineteenth-century imitations of folk poetry by Merzlyakov, Neledinsky-Meletsky, Tsyganov, and others.

In the thirties there also began to appear in Soviet magazines the names of three poets, Simonov, Bergholz, and Aliger, who were to become much better known during the war. The poetry of all three reflected the new interest in personal themes now not only tolerated but even encouraged from above. At the same time all three were more sophisticated and technically more fastidious than song writers like Dolmatovsky or Lebedev-Kumach.

Simonov (b. 1915)   Konstantin (Kiril) Mikhailovich Simonov from the outset divided his attention between personal love themes and historical-patriotic subjects. Typical of the former is the poem entitled "Pyat stranits" ("Five Pages," 1938), which tells, in the form of an unmailed letter forgotten in a hotel room, the story of the unfolding and withering of a love affair. It reveals a feeling for form and words and is emotionally tense, though at times it smacks of cheap sentimentality. Its refreshing feature is its complete freedom from all political and social didacticism. Simonov's patriotic poems included a long poem about Suvorov (1939), a poetic re-creation of several episodes in the career of the great Russian soldier, and a poem about the famous "Ice Battle" which Alexander Nevsky won against the Teutonic Knights. In Simonov's handling of his material, in his stress on visual imagery, there was some influence of Acmeism and of its leader, Gumilyov.

Another Acmeist, Akhmatova, influenced the early poetry of both Olga Bergholz and Margarita Aliger. Both poets sounded clearly a personal, feminine note. Bergholz, who represented the Leningrad school of poets, was more austere and intellectual; Aliger, more emotional. Both occasionally introduced a topical social note. Of their and Simonov's war poetry more will be said in the next chapter.

Bergholz (b. 1910) and Aliger (b. 1915)

Two poets who enjoyed considerable popularity in the early thirties disappeared from literature before the end of that decade. They were Pavel Nikolayevich Vasilyev and Boris Petrovich Kornilov. Both had some affinity with the peasant poets, although they were not true peasants themselves (Vasilyev was a descendant of Siberian Cossacks, and Kornilov was the son of a village teacher and the husband of Olga Bergholz).

Vasilyev (1910–37) and Kornilov (1907–39)

Vasilyev came to be compared with Esenin and Klyuev, and like the latter he was accused of sympathizing with the kulaks. In 1934 a veritable campaign was launched against him. He was charged with idealizing the backward countryside and told to "reform." Vasilyev's poems published in 1936 testify to his efforts to adjust himself. At the same time, like Esenin, he began to drink heavily. After 1936 his name ceased to appear in the Soviet press. His death in 1937 was admitted in 1956, when some of his work was reissued and some new poems were published for the first time. Both in his lyrical poetry and in his narrative poems on social themes—for example, "Solyanoy bunt" ("The Salt Riot") and "Kulaki" ("The Kulaks") —Vasilyev gave evidence of powerful, if somewhat uncouth, talent. While it is true that, like Klyuev and Klychkov, he was hostile to the city, this hostility proceeded from his aversion to provincial philistinism and not from any opposition to the Soviet regime.

Kornilov's first book of poems, *Molodost'* (*Youth*), was published in 1928. His early poetry was imbued with revolutionary romanticism and showed a close affinity to Bagritsky's. It had freshness and vigor. In the late thirties Kornilov became one of the victims of the purges. Like Vasilyev, he was among those who were "resurrected" after Stalin's death.

Part VI. Literature on War Service, 1941–46

Chapter 25. LITERATURE AND THE WAR EFFORT

In the late 1930's the theme of Fascism and its evils (the term National Socialism was deliberately avoided in the Soviet Union) and of the implied Hitler threat to the Soviet state became one of the staple themes of the Soviet press. There were also frequent references to it in Soviet literature—mostly, however, in its internal aspect, the stress being laid on the activities of "Fascist agents" in the Soviet Union.

Prelude to the War

The indirect effect of the Nazi menace was felt in the growth of patriotic literature—of novels and plays dealing with great national crises in Russian history and extolling the heroism of the Russian people and even of its leaders and rulers. In 1939, however, appeared a curious little book by an almost unknown author, which described the first twenty-four hours in the coming war between the U.S.S.R. and Germany. It was called *Pervy udar* (*The First Blow*), and its author was Nikolay Shpanov.[1]

The First Blow is a short novel. It has a somewhat tenuous love story, but its center of gravity is in the description of the air-war operations. All the characters are members of the Soviet Air Force, bomber pilots and navigators, paratroopers, and others. Shpanov shows a Soviet bomber force undertaking, within a few hours after the outbreak of the war, a long-distance raid on important industrial targets in Nuremberg. Great havoc is wrought there, and after returning safely to their base, the Soviet bombers prepare for another raid. The book gives some interesting glimpses into the life of the Red Air Force, but the characterization is slight and superficial. An introductory chapter describes the international situation which precipitates the war. Here Shpanov was as wide of the mark as he was in his description of the initial air operations. According to him, the Soviet Union, the first victim of the Nazi aggression, had to face this aggression alone, although at the end of the introduction there is a hint that at the very last moment France, under the pressure of the "Popular Front" movement, is about to throw in her weight on Russia's side. Great Britain, on the other hand, is shown as taking an attitude of friendly neutrality toward Germany, while Poland comes in on Germany's side as her half-willing ally. An

---

[1] I could find no biographical data about Shpanov. Soviet magazines published several stories of his in the thirties, and during the war he wrote war stories and sketches.

interesting point about Shpanov's book is that it does not mince words. Although some of the names of German generals are fictitious, Germany herself as the aggressor is named *en toutes lettres*, and the description of the first Soviet raid on Nuremberg is given with an abundance of topographical detail.

It is to be presumed that three months after its publication (it was signed for the press in May of 1939) Shpanov's book, copies of which had just had time to reach foreign countries, was withdrawn from circulation, for Shpanov's forecast of events had completely miscarried. The Stalin-Hitler friendship pact, which shocked the outer world, probably surprised the Soviet people themselves. The Soviet attack on Poland was presented as a move to liberate the oppressed Russian and Ukrainian minorities from the yoke of Polish Fascists, and this war of liberation was glorified in many poems, stories, and sketches. The delicate topic of the Molotov-Ribbentrop pact and of Nazi-Communist collaboration was studiously avoided by Soviet writers, but many of them had no difficulty changing their tune and replacing their denunciations of German Nazis by attacks on Polish "Fascists" and Anglo-French "Imperialists."

Literature as a Weapon

Less than two years later (with the Soviet-Finnish War interlude again giving rise to considerable "patriotic" literature), the tune had to be changed again. For most Soviet writers the Nazi attack on the Soviet Union was probably as much of a surprise as the friendship pact of August, 1939, but there can be no doubt that this time they faced about more willingly and sincerely.

From June, 1941, on, literature in the Soviet Union, as behooves that of a totalitarian country, became part of the total war effort. It was regarded as an important war weapon. Many Soviet writers joined the fighting forces as war correspondents and devoted themselves almost entirely to war reportage. Those who for various reasons remained behind wrote stories, poems, and sketches about the war or boosted morale by writing patriotic historical novels, biographies of national heroes, patriotic pep articles, and the like. The place and function of literature in wartime were clearly and succinctly defined by *Literatura i Iskusstvo* (*Literature and Art*), the official mouthpiece of the Union of Soviet Writers and of the government Committee on Arts, when it wrote:

What is of paramount importance today, as it has never been before, is the *activizing* function of art which possesses the invaluable faculty of inspiring men to fight, of helping them in the struggle.

The expression "military theme" is inaccurate. What we need is not military literature, but *militant* literature. We want not just ordinary "military" art but *fighting* art [*voyuyushcheye iskusstvo*].[2]

In another leading article the same official journal wrote:

Always bound up closely with the life of the people, Soviet art had entered, since the outbreak of war, upon a new phase of its development. From now on, it was called upon to serve one single aim—the cause of victory over the enemy. It was meant to become a weapon in the hands of the soldiers who rose to defend their country. It had to foster the fighting spirit of the people, to consolidate the force of patriotism, to fan the hatred for German-Fascist invaders, to call for revenge. It was to show the moral greatness of the Soviet people, their tenacity, their faith in the coming victory.[3]

War Fiction

Soviet wartime literature is enormous in bulk. Much of it is of that ephemeral variety of which Ehrenburg wrote in one of his wartime articles: "A writer must know not only how to write for the centuries but also how to write for the one short second if the fate of his people is to be decided in that second." Most of this literature consists of short works—short stories and front-line reports. But there are also many plays and several novels, mostly written in the latter part of the war. In the list of war authors many well-known names will be met, though some strike one by their absence. There were also a few newcomers.

Among the few fictional works about the war written while it was still fought should be mentioned those of Simonov, Fadeyev, Leonov, Sholokhov, Nekrasov, Gorbatov, Grossman, and Perventsev.

Simonov's *Dni i nochi* (*Days and Nights*, 1944) is a story of the Stalingrad battle. As a picture of one of the most important and decisive events of the war it is quite good. But it is not great literature and cannot even stand comparison with Plievier's novel about Stalingrad. The characters are conventional, and the fictional story, especially the love episode, is trite. But there is throughout an appealing absence of bombast.

Another novel about Stalingrad is *V okopakh Stalingrada* (*In the Trenches of Stalingrad*), by Victor Nekrasov, written in 1945 and published in 1946. Free from Simonov's fictional adornments and based on firsthand experience, it is of greater documentary value, simple, sincere, and free from politics.

Fadeyev's *Molodaya gvardiya* (*The Young Guard*, 1945) is centered around the activities of an underground group of members of the Young Communist League under German occupation. It is based on actual facts that were disclosed during the war. Fadeyev succeeded in investing his

---

[2] *Literatura i Iskusstvo* (*Literature and Art*), September 19, 1942. This publication represented the wartime merger of *Literaturnaya Gazeta* and *Sovetskoye Iskusstvo* (*Literary Gazette* and *Soviet Art*). Toward the end of 1944 they resumed separate publication.

[3] *Literatura i Iskusstvo*, October 17, 1942.

heroes (in both the real and the literary sense of the word) with flesh and blood and creating memorable characters. The novel is competently written and well put together. It was enthusiastically hailed by Soviet critics but later came in for criticism on the ground that the author had minimized the role of party leadership and overrated that of his young patriotic heroes. Fadeyev was even forced to revise it in 1951 (see below).

Sholokhov, a slow-working writer, was much less prolific than most of his colleagues, though during the war he did publish some war stories and sketches, of which "Nauka nenavisti" ("The Science of Hatred," 1942) attracted considerable attention. He also published a few chapters of his much-publicized war novel *Oni srazhalis' za Rodinu* (*They Fought for Their Country*), but it remains uncompleted twenty-five years after the end of the war. On the eve of Stalin's death Sholokhov brought out a new version of his *The Quiet Don*, which he revised in a "conservative" spirit, both ideologically and stylistically (especially linguistically) speaking.

Of the other front-rank Soviet writers, Leonov wrote, in addition to his war plays, which will be discussed later, *Vzyatie Velikoshumska* (*The Taking of Velikoshumsk*, 1944). Only 150 pages long, it can hardly be described as a novel. It deals with an episode in the life of a Soviet tank corps during the Red Army's successful offensive in the Ukraine. The writing is fragmentary and impressionistic. As in Leonov's earlier work, the realism has a symbolic quality. Even such a small, and on the whole natural, detail as the fact that the commander of the tank corps, the driver of one of his tanks, and a peasant woman in one of the liberated villages all have the same name—Litovchenko—is apparently meant as a symbol of the unity—nay identity—of the Soviet people in the hour of national calamity. Leonov begins by describing the tour of inspection which General Litovchenko makes of the sector of the front to which his corps has just been assigned. He finds himself near his native town of Velikoshumsk, recently taken by the Red Army, retaken by the Germans, and now about to be recaptured from them.

The description of the general's journeyings and encounters with various people is reminiscent of Leo Tolstoy's manner. Suffering from a feverish chill, he is in that state of befuddlement where, although he retains complete lucidity of thought when it comes to military matters, as soon as he is left to himself, recollections of childhood, impressions of gruesome reality, and dreamlike anticipations of a meeting with his old teacher in Velikoshumsk mingle together. In the course of his peregrinations we are introduced to tank No. 203, which, with its crew of four men and one kitten, becomes the main character in the story. The greater part of the story describes the nocturnal progress of this tank and her final destructive but suicidal attack on a German column, in which two members of her crew meet their end. The characters of the four members of the tank crew are etched very sharply.

One of the best passages in the story is the whimsical fairy tale which the tank commander tells his crew while they are holding night watch over their temporarily disabled tank.

Nepokoryonnye (*The Unconquered*, 1943)—also known as *Semya Tarasa* (*Taras's Family*)—by Boris Gorbatov (1908–54), deals with the war reactions of a Soviet family in the Kuban region after it has been overrun by the Germans. The author seems to have deliberately modeled his family —an old father and two sons—on that in Gogol's famous romance *Taras Bulba*. There are some descriptions of the fighting, but Gorbatov is primarily concerned with human beings and the heroism and patriotism of ordinary Soviet citizens.

On the other hand, in *Narod bessmerten* (*The People Immortal*, 1943), by Vasily Grossman (1905–64), are portrayed various types of Soviet fighters —officers, political commissars, and ordinary soldiers. Grossman entered the ranks of Soviet writers in 1934 and before the war began the publication of a long novel (*Stepan Kolchugin*) dealing with pre-Revolutionary times and World War I.

Valentin Katayev's short novel *Syn polka* (*The Son of a Regiment*, 1945) tells the adventures of an orphan boy adopted by a front-line regiment.

The only major novel dealing with the war in the West was Ehrenburg's *Padenie Parizha* (*The Fall of Paris*, 1941). Written before the German invasion of Russia, it gives a picture of France between 1935 and 1940, together with an analysis, through a variety of characters representing various strata of French society, of the causes of France's collapse. It is a social-political novel, and the journalistic approach, always present in Ehrenburg's novels, is evident. A man of no strong or stable convictions, Ehrenburg had a keen, versatile, and observant mind and was quick to respond to topical themes. Having lived in France off and on for years, he knew the country and on the whole loved the people. He stayed in Paris throughout the tragic days of the debacle and was able to see much for himself. His character studies of French politicians of various shades, of industrialists, intellectuals, and workers, are fundamentally true to life, even if they are psychologically not very profound. The over-all picture is, however, colored by a definite bias, his thesis being that the salvation of France lay in her working class and, more especially, in the Communist party as its most vocal and active spokesman.

Most of Ehrenburg's characters serve to illustrate and prove this thesis. Michaud and Denise Tessat (who gives up her own class and family to work for the people) and Pierre Dubois and Agnès who, though belonging to the middle class, also come to be with the people, are those who represent true France. To them are opposed most of the politicians (those of the People's Front are shown in an even more unpleasant light than some of the right-wing ones like Ducamp, in whom there is at least a healthy core of deep-seated French patriotism), industrialists, and unhinged young intellectuals like Lucien Tessat, who moves from one extreme to another and from a left-wing intellectual Communist becomes a Fascist and an admirer of Franco.

Of those whom Ehrenburg portrays sympathetically, Denise and Michaud, who love each other, are the only ones to survive. Unswerving in their loyalty to Communism, they look forward to coming battles and the better future which will be forged in them. Much stress is laid by the author on their unshakable faith in the distant land of Socialism. But the picture drawn by Ehrenburg is incomplete and ambiguous, since he deliberately passes in silence such an important factor in the situation as the Soviet-German pact of 1939 and the havoc it wrought in the ranks of European Communists, especially in France. The problem of reconciling their hatred of the Germans with their allegiance to Moscow simply does not arise for Ehrenburg's good Communists.

Wartime short stories were numerous, but few of them have literary distinction and lasting interest; usually, the less fictional, the more documentary, they are, the greater is their value. Such are, for instance, Tikhonov's sketches of Leningrad during the siege—*Cherty sovetskogo cheloveka* (*The Traits of the Soviet Man*, 1943). In one of the stories an old history teacher, in a conversation with a chance street acquaintance, compares Leningrad to ancient Troy, and most of the stories tell of the simple heroism of its defenders and are more like documentary sketches.

In *Morskaya dusha* (*Soul of the Sea*, 1942), a volume of stories by Leonid Sobolev (b. 1898), are to be found portraits of typical Soviet sailors and episodes of naval war. Sobolev had earlier written, among other things, a long novel about the pre-Revolutionary Russian navy—*Kapitalny remont* (*Capital Refitting*, 1933). Volumes of stories by Kaverin, Pavlenko, Paustovsky, Gabrilovich, Ilyenkov, and Stavsky may also be mentioned here.[4]

Some interest attaches to Yury Herman's story "Be Happy!" (the original title is English, transliterated into Russian characters). It is written in the form of a diary of a Russian girl attached to an aerodrome used by the British near the supply port of Murmansk, and its characters include several RAF pilots who are portrayed with considerable sympathy and warmth.

---

[4] Of Paustovsky, who had been publishing much earlier but whose literary reputation grew by leaps and bounds after the war, more will be said in the sequel to this book. Evgeny Gabrilovich had early connections with the Constructivists but first attracted attention with his Five-Year Plan sketches of collective farming. Vasily Ilyenkov wrote one of the much-discussed Five-Year Plan novels, *Vedushchaya os* (*Driving Axle*, 1933), and another novel about Socialist reconstruction, *Solnechny gorod* (*The Sun City*, 1935). Vasily Stavsky, author of lively war reports, particularly from the Moscow front, was one of the early casualties of the war.

War Plays

Of the many war plays the most interesting are those of Leonov: *Nashestvie* (*Invasion*, 1942) and *Lyonushka* (1943). For each of them the author was awarded an annual Stalin Prize for literature.[5]

Written in Chistopol on the Kama, the great and majestic tributary of the Volga, far from the turmoil of the war, *Invasion* is full of dramatic tension and poignant scenes. Most of the action is set within the household of Dr. Talanov, a slightly Chekhovian country doctor, in a small town situated along the road of the German advance on Moscow in 1941. The central character is Fyodor Talanov, Dr. Talanov's prodigal son who has been serving a sentence for a criminal offense and returns to his native town, unexpected by his family, on the eve of the Germans' entry. Broken physically and morally, he adopts a cynical pose behind which can be felt the tragedy of a man who has lost himself and his place in life and is capable now only of some desperate action, for good or for evil. Beneath this cynical bravado he is trying to conceal his despair and emptiness. It is around Fyodor's spiritual rebirth that Leonov ties the main knots of his play. The Germans in the town are terrorized by the underground activities of a group of partisans led by Kolesnikov, the former secretary of the local executive committee. Every day some Germans in the town are killed, and a note is pinned to their bodies with the words, "*Dobro pozhalovat*" ("Welcome to you"). This phrase becomes the symbolical leitmotif of the play. It is used by different people under different—and sometimes dramatic—circumstances. Fyodor Talanov, whom Kolesnikov refuses to take into his group, kills some German officers on his own and when caught poses as Kolesnikov—a deceit in which his parents bravely concur. The play ends with the Russian paratroops retaking the town just after Fyodor and two other partisans have been hanged by the Germans.

Even if Leonov's play does not quite hit the mark, it has the makings of a fine play, with effective dramatic situations, emotional suspense, and tense, significant dialogues which convey more than their surface meaning. As usual with Leonov, the play has depth, an undercurrent of symbolism, and it is this that saves Leonov from lapsing into cheap melodrama, although at times he skirts dangerously close to it.

Some of Leonov's characters and situations will be familiar to readers of

---

[5] Annual Stalin Prize awards for outstanding works of fiction, drama, poetry, and literary criticism were instituted at the end of 1939. There were parallel prizes for outstanding achievements in other fields of art and various branches of learning. In each category there were several awards, the first prize the handsome sum of 100,000 rubles. Among the early recipients of prizes for literature were Alexey Tolstoy (for the third part of his *A Way Through Hell*), Sholokhov (for the third volume of *The Quiet Don*), Ehrenburg (for the *Fall of Paris*), Virta, Simonov, and Tikhonov. After Stalin's death the prize came to be called simply the State Prize.

his novels and earlier plays. Fyodor, for instance—a man with no place in life, with an empty soul, lost but not beyond recall—is a distant relative of Mitka Vekshin in *The Thief*. The homecoming of the prodigal son also recalls similar situations in Leonov's plays (Pylyaev in *The Orchards of Polovchansk*, Sandukov in *The Wolf*, and Syrovarov in *Blizzard*, though in Fyodor's case the "ideological" nature of his "crime" had to be guessed by the reader; it was later spelled out by Leonov in the revised version of the play). Another character who can be traced back to Leonov's earlier works is Fayunin, a former local capitalist who returns with the Germans and becomes the mayor of the town under them. He can claim more or less direct descendance from Manyukin in *The Thief* and *Untilovsk*. But Fayunin is more clearly a class enemy and not just an outcast. He is weak and cowardly, but Leonov is obviously at pains to hint at some redeeming feature in his make-up. Is it to be found in his instinctive, ineradicable Russianness? He is playing the Germans' game, he serves loyally his German masters, but one can feel that there is no love lost between them, and the Germans simply despise him and treat him like dirt. There is almost a note of admiration in Fayunin's voice when he describes Mrs. Talanov as "an iron old woman" after the scene in which Fyodor pretends he is Kolesnikov.

Of the "positive" characters, the Talanov couple are Leonov's greatest success. Ordinary Russian people, not Communists, they are the "unheroic heroes" of the war. But even in the portrait of Kolesnikov, Leonov has managed to avoid a hagiographic approach. The Germans in the play are deliberately contrasted with the other characters and are shown as mechanical robots, not human beings.

Leonov has a true sense of the theater, but his plays, like Ibsen's, can also be enjoyed as literature. His characters' speech is so sharply individualized that the characters are immediately recognized by their voices. As one Soviet critic put it, "One can listen to his plays with one's eyes shut." His stage remarks are an integral part of the play.

Leonov's second war play, *Lyonushka*, described as "a people's tragedy in four acts," has many points in common with *Invasion* but is even more intensely dramatic. It presents a group of partisans in the German rear, each of them a sharply outlined, individual character. The plot follows two intersecting lines. One of them involves a traitor who appears among the partisans; the other is concerned with the love of Lyonushka, the heroine (the only girl among the partisans), for a handsome tank lieutenant whom she meets as they move out of their village and who is later brought to their headquarters in the woods as a half-burned live corpse. Once more Leonov uses the method of symbolic realism and manages to achieve great dramatic suspense without resorting to declamatory effects.

Konstantin Simonov's play *Russkie lyudi* (*The Russians*, 1942) deals with a war episode on the Southern front. Some of the scenes are laid on the Russian side of the front, some in the German-occupied area. The main characters are a group of ordinary people whose unassuming bravery and contempt of death are symbolic of the whole Russian people. There are also some Germans in the play and a Russian traitor. The title is significant. Throughout the play the stress is on *Russian* patriotism, a fact for which Simonov had to apologize later. The romantic element is furnished by the hero's love for the young girl driver, Valya, whom he has to send on dangerous reconnaissance work behind enemy lines.

Simonov's play is much simpler than Leonov's, written along straightforward realistic lines. Its chief merit lies in its lifelike characterization; several of the minor characters are particularly good. The play was a great success during the war and made Simonov's name familiar outside Russia.

Alexander Korneychuk (b. 1910), a Ukrainian dramatist, caused a sensation with his wartime problem-play *Front* (*The Front*, 1942).[6] Unlike Leonov, Korneychuk is concerned not with deep and tense human conflicts but with a problem of military-political nature. He shows two different types of Red Army commanders. One, Ivan Gorlov, an old soldier of the Revolution, still thinks in the antiquated terms of the Civil War and scorns the modern idea of technical warfare. He has personal courage and a distinguished revolutionary record, but he does not fit in with the new requirements of a total war and surrounds himself with men who also are inadequate. Korneychuk portrays this entourage of Gorlov in a deliberately satirical, even grotesque, vein—even their names are expressive of their character, in the old, eighteenth-century tradition. To Gorlov is opposed Ognyov, a much younger man. Gorlov is inclined to look down on him because he was a mere boy when Gorlov was fighting with Budyonny's Red Cavalry in Poland. Ognyov, however, understands much better what is needed in the war against Nazi Germany, and in the end is appointed in Gorlov's place. Korneychuk intensifies the dramatic conflict by introducing two other Gorlovs into the play, Ivan's son and brother. Both of them are opposed to Ivan and are instrumental in bringing about his downfall.

Korneychuk was praised by the Soviet press for fearlessly tackling an important and topical problem. During the first year of the war many of the older commanders who had acquired experience in the Civil War stuck obstinately to the old notions of revolutionary warfare. They included Marshals Budyonny and Voroshilov, both of whom had to be replaced. Korneychuk's exposure of these romantics of the Civil War at a time when the Soviet Union was suffering serious reverses caused resentment in some

[6] The original Ukrainian spelling of the playwright's name is Korniychuk. Most of his plays were written in Ukrainian and translated into Russian (perhaps by himself; as a rule the name of the translator was not mentioned). It is not clear whether *The Front* was written in Russian or Ukrainian.

quarters. But the play, one of the most widely discussed events of the 1942 theater season, met with official approval. One may even suspect that its writing was suggested in the highest spheres.

War Poetry

Simonov   In poetry, too, patriotic war themes predominated during these years— almost to the exclusion of all other themes.

Among the most popular wartime poets were Konstantin Simonov and Alexey Surkov, both of whom spent the greater part of the war with the Russian armies. The war also took Simonov outside Russia, and when it was over, he visited most of the European countries, as well as the United States and Japan. One of Simonov's most popular and most characteristic war poems (and also one of his best) was dedicated to his friend and fellow poet Surkov. Beginning with the line, "Do you recall, Alyosha, the roads of the Smolensk region?" and recalling poignant scenes of the Russian retreat before the Germans during the early phase of the war, it was full of deep love for one's country, of Russian, rather than Soviet, patriotism (the word Soviet is not once mentioned in the poem), and this explains why it became so popular with Russian *émigrés* outside Russia. As the poet recalled the road of Russian retreat ("Villages, villages, villages and churchyards"), he had a vision of the dead rising from their village graves to pray "for their grandsons who no longer believed in God."[7] And he voiced his pride in being born a Russian:

> Up till now, my friend, the bullets have been kind to us,
>   But three times when I thought that death was at hand,
> I was full of pride that I had been born a Russian,
>   I was proud of our dear, our terrible land,
> Proud it was a Russian mother who gave birth to me,
>   Proud it was my fate for such a land to die,
> Proud that a Russian woman had given me the threefold
>   Embrace in Russian fashion when she bade me goodbye.[8]

Even more widely popular was Simonov's short poem "Zhdi menya" ("Wait for Me"). Its poetic value was slight and its appeal chiefly sentimental, for it voiced, in a simple if somewhat naïve form, the feelings of a soldier at the front who wants his wife (or his beloved) back home to wait for him even when all the others—parents, friends, and relatives—despair of his return.

Like his earlier work, Simonov's war poetry is very uneven. In a poem written during the battles on the Voronezh front, at the height of the Russian retreat in 1942, he succeeds in investing his emotions, bordering on despair, with powerful poetic accent. In "Ubey ego!" ("Kill Him!"), a poem

[7] These two lines were deleted from some later editions.

[8] Translated by V. da Sola Pinto in *The Road to the West: Sixty Soviet War Poems.*

inspired by savage hatred for the enemy, he remains cold and prosaic. Too often his poetry is marred by a tendency toward journalism. His best poems are those where the patriotic and the personal notes are mingled. The volume *S toboy i bez tebya* (*With and Without You,* 1944) is composed mostly of entirely personal love poetry. Some of these poems, for which Simonov—of all people!—was criticized as an "individualist," are good, but in the final analysis Simonov seems to lack that indefinable something, that magic which turns merely good poetry into great poetry.

Surkov, on the contrary, is better when he is more impersonal, when he speaks of collective deeds of heroism. Poems like "Rossiya" ("Russia") and "Rodina" ("My Country") evoke the glorious past of Russia and the wars she fought in olden days. The poet refers to Russia as "immortal, undying, enigmatic in her wise simplicity." He recalls the Battle of the Kulikovo Field and the Polish, Swedish, and French invasions. Like other Soviet poets he voices his hatred for the enemy, and one of the sections of his book *Dekabr' pod Moskvoy* (*December Before Moscow,* 1942), in which the German onslaught on Moscow at the end of 1941 is evoked, is entitled "I Sing Hate." Some poems strike, however, a more personal, intimate note. **Surkov**

Surkov also wrote several popular war songs, such as "Pesnya smelykh" ("The Song of the Bold"), written on the day the Germans invaded Russia, with its famous refrain: "The bold strike fear into bullets,/The bold are unscathed by the bayonet"; "Pesnya zashchitnikov Moskvy" ("The Song of the Defenders of Moscow"), and "Zastolnaya" ("The Drinking Song").

Alexander Prokofyev, Evgeny Dolmatovsky, and Stepan Shchipachov all contributed their quota of patriotic war poetry—much of it rather indifferent "slogan poetry"—each more or less following his personal bent. So did Tvardovsky, the author of *The Land of Muravia,* which he tried to parallel in another humorous epic, *Vasily Tyorkin.* Its hero is a kind of synthetic Russian soldier—cheerful, humorous, resourceful—embodying both the inherently homely wisdom of the Russian people and certain specific Soviet characteristics. The poem deals with his adventures, grave and gay, at the front and follows him almost to the gates of Berlin. It was written and published in installments over a period of several years (1941–45) and lacks the unity of *The Land of Muravia,* but has many of its qualities—its humor, its mastery of racy Russian, its variety of meters, and its wealth of memorable lines. **Prokofyev Dolmatovsky Shchipachov and Tvardovsky**

Special mention should be made of the war output of the two young women poets, Margarita Aliger and Olga Bergholz. Both of them grew in stature during the war. Of the two, Bergholz is perhaps the more accomplished poet. Her best war poems, collected in *Leningradskaya tetrad* (*The Lenin-* **Aliger and Bergholz** *grad Notebook*, 1942), reflect the heroic Siege of Leningrad, throughout which she stayed in the city, doing regular broacasts on the radio while it functioned. She is essentially a lyric poet, and her approach throughout is personal, but it is in the combination of the trivial and the majestic, in the fusion of the personal and the impersonal, that she is at her best. Her poetry reflects not only the misery of the war-ravaged city, where hunger and disease were rampant, not only the nobility of its heroic spirit, but also its historic grandeur. In its austere clarity her poetry is in the classical tradition.

Aliger is more romantic, more emotional, and more spontaneous. Her choice of words is less fastidious, her diction more blurred. One of her best war poems is "Moya pobeda" ("My Victory"), a long lyric poem in which the general theme of the war and the personal theme of a woman's destiny are closely interwoven. In "Zoya" she attempted a nonpersonal narrative poem. Its heroine is Zoya Kosmodemyanskaya, a young girl tortured and executed by the Germans.

Tikhonov and Inber Two older poets, Nikolay Tikhonov and Vera Inber, also found their inspiration in the heroic Siege of Leningrad, its misery and grandeur. Tikhonov's long poem *Kirov s nami* (*Kirov Is with Us*) earned him a Stalin Prize. It described Kirov, the Communist boss of Leningrad who was assassinated in 1934, going the rounds of blockaded Leningrad on a dark, cold night. In another poem, in which he deliberately imitated the majestic numbers of Pushkin and went to Russian history for inspiration, Tikhonov drew a poetic parallel between Leningrad and Moscow.

During the siege Vera Inber, who came to Leningrad at the beginning of the war and stayed there for nearly three years, wrote her long poem *Pulkovsky meridian* (*The Pulkovo Meridian*, 1943), for which she was also awarded a Stalin Prize. Classical in form and realistic in content, this poem of 816 lines, divided into 136 six-line stanzas with sonnetlike rhyming scheme, gives a picture of everyday life in the blockaded city, alternating with the author's comments on the events. The result is somewhat uneven, which is not surprising in a poem of such length. Inber is best when she is most concrete; the weakest parts of the poem are those where she generalizes and rationalizes. Here is one of her typical stanzas:

> How painfully—still worse, how swiftly—can
> Faces grow old these days. The features stand
> Out, cut to birdlike sharpness by the hand,
> It seems, of some ill-omened make-up man.
> A pinch of ashes and a little lead—
> And faces look like faces of the dead.[9]

[9] Translated by A. Kaun and D. P. Radin in Kaun, *Soviet Poets and Poetry*, 197.

Of the other established poets who made their contribution to war poetry, **Pasternak** mention should be made of Pasternak and Anna Akhmatova. As has been **and** said, Pasternak published very little original poetry after the appearance of **Akhmatova** *The Second Birth* in 1932. He concentrated on translations and was also working on a new prose work. In 1938–39 he published in *Literaturnaya Gazeta* and two periodicals (*Ogonyok* and *30 Dney*), and also read at a literary gathering, fragments of a novel in which, in retrospect, one can see the first drafts of the future *Doctor Zhivago*.[10] Before that, in 1936 and 1937, he had had to face repeated attacks in the press and from some of his fellow writers. He was accused of "individualism," of "aloofness," of inability, if not reluctance, to fit into the general stream of Soviet literature.

At a writers' conference in Minsk in February, 1936, Pasternak was called upon by Bezymensky to "quit his chamber" and come out into the wide world. "The Revolution has already solved the problems about which you are still brooding," said Bezymensky. Surkov demanded from Pasternak that he give up "resolutely and consistently" the idealistic philosophy which underlay his poetry. He also called upon Pasternak to learn from Mayakovsky and to chase away various flatterers and false friends, one of whom had mistakenly proclaimed him to be a classic of modern Russian poetry. This was apparently a reference to Mirsky, one of the very few people who resolutely defended Pasternak at the time and spoke of him as a great poet (Mirsky even called him the greatest living poet). Another champion of Pasternak at the Minsk conference was the critic E. Mustangova.

Pasternak replied to some of his critics in a speech which, according to *Literaturnaya Gazeta*, was received with "stormy and prolonged applause." This speech, published under the title "About Modesty and Boldness," was a strange document in which apology alternated with defiance. Pasternak did not deny that he and some of his fellow poets did not speak the same language. He accused some of them of treating poems as though they were parts of a machine, badly or not badly turned. At the same time he announced his intention to "re-educate" himself and warned his friends that for some time he would be writing "very badly."[11]

[10] "Iz novogo romana o 1905 g." ("From a New Novel About the Year 1905"), *Literaturnaya Gazeta*, December 31, 1937; "Uezd v tylu" ("A District in the Rear"), *Literaturnaya Gazeta*, December 15, 1938; "Nadmenny nishchiy" ("A Haughty Beggar"), *Ogonyok*, No. 1 (1939), 14–15; "Tyotya Olya" ("Aunt Olya"), *30 Dney*, No. 8–9 (1939), 31–35. An English translation of the second of these fragments will be found in B. Pasternak, *The Last Summer* (trans. by G. Reavey).

[11] "O skromnosti i smelosti" ("On Modesty and Courage"), *Literaturnaya Gazeta*, February 16, 1936. For other views voiced at the Minsk conference, or by way of reaction to it, see *Literaturnaya Gazeta*, February 16, 24, 29, March 15, 20, 27, 1936. Attacks on Pasternak, more or less along the same lines, were resumed in 1937. See *Literaturnaya Gazeta*, February 26, March 5, 10, 26, May 30, 1937. For Pasternak's own, somewhat veiled comments on this campaign against him see his *Letters to Georgian*

Pasternak was silent during the first two years of the war (he lived part of this time far in the rear, in Chistopol on the Kama, and part of the time in Moscow and Peredelkino). In 1943 his first book of poems since *The Second Birth* was published. Called *Na rannikh poezdakh* (*On Early Trains*), it contained twenty-six poems, of which eleven were written in 1936 and fifteen in 1941. Most of the latter were inspired by the war. In 1945 a new book appeared, entitled *Zemnoy prostor* (*The Terrestrial Expanse*) and consisting of poems from the 1943 volume and some new ones. The chief characteristic of the wartime poems in these two little books was their greater simplicity and directness—of themes, of emotions, and of poetic structure. Some of Pasternak's admirers found them disappointing. As may be seen from *Doctor Zhivago* and the 1956 autobiographical essay (both of which will be dealt with in the sequel to this volume), they reflected a profound change in Pasternak, in his attitude toward poetry, which led to a reappraisal of his own poetic past. At times, indeed, this striving after simplicity at all costs, and the resultant change in poetic method, led to a certain flatness and insipidity. The simplicity in some of the war poems was achieved at the expense of the old magic. Some Soviet critics, however, welcomed Pasternak's "more human attitude toward life." Others continued to accuse him of being too subjective even in his treatment of war themes; still others doubted whether this new "un-Pasternakian" simplicity really suited him.

The former Constructivist Zelinsky praised him for saying, however belatedly, "some intelligent and poetic things" about the war and for having put on record his "love and respect for the Soviet man, the fighter, the victor." Soon, however, the attacks on Pasternak were resumed, and Zelinsky and others who had praised him came in for their share of criticism.

Anna Akhmatova, the only survivor by that time—in Russia—of the second Golden Age of Russian poetry, made her reappearance as a poet in 1940, when several of her poems were published in *Zvezda*.[12] The same year a collected edition of her poetry, entitled *Iz shesti knig* (*From Six Books*) was brought out. It contained selections—with some significant omissions—from all five of her earlier books of poems (the last of which had appeared in 1923). It also included a few previously uncollected poems

---

Friends, 64–69, as well as my review of that book in *Slavic Review*, Vol. XXVIII, No. 4 (1969), 683–86. Pasternak's Georgian friends, the poets Titian Tabidze and Paolo Yashvili became victims of Stalin's purges in 1937.

[12] Akhmatova's name had actually reappeared somewhat earlier. In 1933, *Zvezda* had published her study of the connection between Pushkin's *The Golden Cockerel* and Washington Irving's *The Legends of the Alhambra*, and in 1936 another Pushkin study (about Pushkin's debt to Benjamin Constant's *Adolphe*) had appeared in a scholarly Pushkin publication. It was also in 1936 that *Zvezda* published Akhmatova's translation of a poem by the Armenian poet Daniel Varuzhan (1884–1915).

and those from a new (the sixth) book, called *Iva* (*Willow Tree*), which contained a score or so of poems written between 1924 and 1940, mostly after 1936.[13] These new poems showed no slackening of poetic power. Some, in fact, were among Akhmatova's best. Two poems were dedicated to two such different contemporaries as Pasternak and Mayakovsky (the poem about Mayakovsky was an evocation of the poet at the height of his Futurist fame in 1913). The volume was, on the whole, coolly received by Soviet critics, who emphasized that Akhmatova had remained true to her old self—that the Revolution had had little effect on her. During the war Akhmatova was evacuated to central Asia, and a volume of her poetry was published in Tashkent in 1943. The war inspired her to some poignant patriotic poetry. By 1945 she was back in Leningrad and publishing in local magazines.

Of newcomers of promise there were practically none during the war.

[13] It is not quite clear whether, before the publication of *From Six Books*, the new poems making up "Willow Tree" had been published separately under that title, also in 1940. A review of "Willow Tree" in *Literaturnaya Gazeta* suggests that this might have been the case, but there is no other evidence of the existence of a separate edition. In *The Short Literary Encyclopaedia*, "Willow Tree" is described as a "cycle." In the post-Stalin editions of Akhmatova's *Collected Works* the name of this cycle was changed to "Trostnik" ("Bullrush").

Chapter 26. IN THE MIDST OF WAR

War Reportage and War Diaries

A great many Soviet writers worked as correspondents, and their front-line reports appeared regularly in the Soviet press or were broadcast by Radio Moscow. Among them we find Simonov, Ehrenburg, Evgeny Petrov (of the Ilf-Petrov team), Grossman, Gorbatov, Stavsky, and others. Simonov was one of the most active and prolific; his front-line reports covered the vast extent of the front, as was indicated by the title of the volume in which some of them were collected: *Ot Barentsova morya do Chornogo* (*From the Barents Sea to the Black Sea*). Simonov's *Voennye dnevniki* (*War Diaries*) were published in the magazine *Znamya* and also issued in book form, as was the *Frontovoy dnevnik* (*Front-Line Diary*, 1942) of Evgeny Petrov, who was killed in 1942 near Sevastopol. Grossman's *Stalingradskie ocherki* (*Stalingrad Sketches*), later included in his book *Gody voyny* (*The Years of War*, published in 1946), was one of the earliest coherent accounts of the great Stalingrad battle. The Siege of Leningrad found its documentary reflection, in addition to the stories and poems already mentioned, in Fadeyev's *Leningrad v dni blokady* (*Leningrad in the Days of the Blockade*, 1944) and Inber's *Pochti tri goda. Leningradsky dnevnik* (*Almost Three Years: A Leningrad Diary*, 1945). Inber's *Diary* gives a realistic picture of life in the blockaded city, with its mixture of nightmare and reality; but there is something rather unpleasant about the affected tone and patronizing attitudes the author strikes now and then—for example, when she speaks about the workers of Leningrad. Fadeyev's sketches are more simple, impersonal, and straightforward.

There was also some interesting nonliterary war reportage. One of the earliest works to attract attention and to be published also outside Russia was Polyakov's *V tylu vraga* (*In the Enemy's Rear*, 1942). Alexander Polyakov (1908–42) served as a political commissar in the army and at the same time was a correspondent of the Red Army newspaper, the *Red Star*. He was attached to Major General Galitsky's infantry division, which, after dealing heavy blows to German tank columns in the very early days of the war, was encircled by the enemy and forced to fight its way out of the encirclement, for which purpose it was divided into several detachments. Polyakov accompanied one of these detachments, and his book is a day-by-day account of their eastward march.

Later, partisan activities behind the German lines provided one of the most exciting subjects. In 1944 appeared P. Ignatov's *Dnevnik partizana* (*The Diary of a Partisan*). It described the activities of a guerrilla detachment in the Kuban region, covering the period from 1941 to May, 1943. In 1945 the magazine *Znamya* began publication of the work called *Lyudi s chistoy sovestyu* (*People with a Clear Conscience*), by Petro Vershigora (b. 1905); the next year it appeared in book form. Vershigora, a young Ukrainian film producer, was mobilized at the very beginning of the war. The early chapters of the book give some idea of the military unpreparedness of the Soviet Union and of the summary methods of training. Less than a month after he was mobilized, Vershigora, utterly untrained and inexperienced, was commanding a platoon in action. The bulk of Vershigora's book, however, consists of an interesting and patently truthful account of the raids made behind the enemy lines by the famous partisan army of Sidor Kovpak, which Vershigora joined in 1942. These raids took them through the enemy-occupied Belorussia and Ukraine and as far west as the Carpathians. Their object was to harass the Germans, to disrupt their lines of communication, to undermine their morale, and to boost the spirit of the population.

While pointing out the "romantic" nature of their activities and the fact that those who joined the partisan army were "romantics," Vershigora writes simply and realistically, and his book throws light on one of the most interesting and peculiar aspects of the war on the Soviet-German front, the existence of "Partisania," a separate country within the vast German-occupied Soviet territory. Vershigora himself does not use the term Partisania, but he constantly speaks of "Great Land" ("*Bolshaya Zemlya*") to refer to the nonoccupied part of the Soviet Union, while designating the territory held by the partisans as "Little Land" ("*Malaya Zemlya*"). Contact between the two was maintained almost entirely by radio, though there were also exchanges of flying visits, and Kovpak himself—a colorful old Ukrainian who had taken part as a sergeant in World War I and later distinguished himself in the Civil War—paid a visit to Stalin in the Kremlin to receive instructions. It is interesting to note that here and there Vershigora voices the partisans' resentment against the Red Army on account of its retreats. Thus he writes:

Let us put it bluntly: before the battle of Stalingrad we all tendered our accounts to the Red Army. Many bitter words were said, many bitter thoughts thought. After all, we were battering the Germans in their rear and moving forward, while they still kept retreating. . . .

They abandoned towns, villages, rivers. They abandoned them with a heavy heart, perhaps, but nevertheless behind them lay a country which was being more and more filled with the Stalinist will to victory, and they felt it. They had the rear, the mighty Soviet rear. And we, an army with no rear and no flanks, we saw only the bitter fruits of the retreat, its seamy side. We saw Belorussia thrown into dust, we saw the Ukraine trampled underfoot, bloodstained. And we also knew the thoughts and angry words of a certain Order of the Day, and more than anybody else, we, the civilians, schoolmasters, accountants, collective farmers, and musicians who had taken to arms, we had the right to hurl reproaches at the men who were retreating eastward.

Vershigora adds, however, that many of them understood that they owed their victories to the fact of being opposed by the weakest units of the enemy while the bulk of Hitler's forces and resources was being used against the Red Army.

Like other Soviet writers who wrote about the war, Vershigora abstains from analyzing more closely the causes of the catastrophic Russian retreat in 1941 and 1942. Today, from the revelations of numbers of Russian displaced persons, of so-called "*nevozvrashchentsy*" ("irrepatriates")—Soviet citizens who refused to be repatriated when the war was over—we know (and this is something that many people suspected at the time, but no one dared say aloud) that in 1941 there were mass desertions from the Red Army and that the population of the occupied territories welcomed the Germans with bread and salt and with pealing of church bells. At this time the phrase, "Welcome to you!" upon which Leonov built his play had quite another meaning.[1] The large-scale partisan movement among the people began later, when the Nazis had exasperated the population by their behavior. True, Vershigora does portray "traitors" and hint at disloyal behavior of a village population, but such cases are presented as individual, not as a mass phenomenon. In approaching Soviet war literature—whether fictional or documentary works—we must always bear in mind that, no matter how truthful it is (and Vershigora's book certainly gives the impression of truthfulness), it never tells the whole truth. This limits its documentary value for the future historian. An interesting proof of the fact that some Soviet writers themselves were aware even then of the danger of the optimistic concealment of the whole truth may be seen in an article which

---

[1] It is to be noted that among the great numbers of "displaced persons," many of whom remained voluntarily under the Germans and were what one may call "passive defectors" who later moved to the West, there were no writers with established reputations, although many of the displaced persons belonged to the intelligentsia and were to make a name for themselves in a variety of fields in their countries of adoption. Offhand one may mention perhaps three exceptions: the peasant writer Akulshin, once a member of the Pereval group; Gleb Glinka, also a member of Pereval; and Anna Radlova, a poet well known for her Shakespeare translations. But Mme Radlova and her husband, Sergey, a prominent theatrical director, chose to be repatriated at the end of the war, whereupon both were sent to a concentration camp. Mme Radlova died there; her husband was released in 1956. Akulshin continued to write and publish abroad under the name Rodion Beryozov. Glinka published in the United States a book about Pereval which has been mentioned earlier and a book of poems. Some important literary "defections" were to take place in the post-Stalin period.

Fyodor Panfyorov published in *Oktyabr* in 1946.[2] A loyal and sincere Communist, the author of *Bruski* spoke there of people who tend to simplify the complex problem of the war and of the Soviet victory; who insist that there was no such thing as the retreat of the Red Army, that it was but "a planned withdrawal, wearing down the enemy"; and who, when reminded that there was a time "when the fate of our country hung by a thread," tell you to "forget it."

Panfyorov's frank outburst was subsequently criticized as a manifestation of pessimism and despondency, unworthy of a good Communist.

Wartime Journalism

After the outbreak of the war the Soviet government made full use of the patriotic Russian spirit it had been assiduously fostering since the late thirties. The great national figures of the past—Dmitry Donskoy, Alexander Nevsky, Minin and Pozharsky, Suvorov, Kutuzov—became objects of a veritable patriotic cult. They were all mentioned by Stalin in his first wartime public pronouncement—the radio speech he made on July 3, 1941. In this speech, after the usual "Comrades," he used the truly Russian old form of address: "Brothers and sisters." The war against Germany became officially known as the Second War for the Fatherland (*Vtoraya Otechestvennaya Voyna*)—the first was the one Russia fought against Napoleon in 1812. This stress on Russian, rather than Soviet, patriotism, which we have already noticed in Soviet literature, was no doubt dictated to the government by the realization that to make the war really popular and to arouse the masses it had to be presented as a war for national existence and national heritage. For the first time in many years the word Russia was readmitted into the Communist vocabulary and freely used in the press. The taboo was lifted even from the past achievements of the Russian state. In a wartime broadcast of Pushkin's great poem *The Bronze Horseman* the poem was referred to as a work about St. Petersburg—"that magnificent embodiment of Russian military glory and of Russian statecraft."

Characteristic of this revival of Russian patriotism were the wartime articles of Alexey Tolstoy and Ilya Ehrenburg. Both were pre-Revolutionary writers, both had taken a patriotic attitude during World War I, both had proved themselves to be eminently adaptable opportunists, and both found no difficulty in taking the new line, especially since in the case of Tolstoy it answered his innermost leanings. His acceptance of the Revolution had been, in part at least, dictated by his inborn Russian patriotism, and the task of reconciling the Soviet regime with the historical development of Russia appealed to him. He wrote eloquently of Russia's glorious past, of her epic heroes and her great historical figures, of the "Russian psyche" which was

Tolstoy and Ehrenburg

[2] No. 5 (1946), 151–62.

an unknown quantity to foreigners and even to many Russians and which was now revealed as

the psychology of the Soviet, and above all Russian, man who, having drunk of the drink of freedom, has discovered that . . . under the vivifying sun there exists higher justice inscribed with golden letters in the Stalin Constitution and that there also exists our Soviet Motherland—the country of our fathers and forefathers, destined for the happiness of our children and grandchildren.[3]

Tolstoy's wartime articles were collected in two volumes: *Rodina* (*Motherland*, 1942) and *Chto my zashchishchayem* (*What We Are Defending*, 1942).

Ehrenburg was even more prolific than Tolstoy. The articles he wrote between June, 1941, and March, 1943, were collected in two volumes of nearly four hundred pages each, entitled *Voyna* (*The War*, 1942 and 1943.) The first volume is divided into four sections, entitled "Germans," "Hirelings," "Friends," and "Our War." The second is similarly arranged. Many of his articles were written in defense of the common heritage of European civilization, and many of the things which he said in them were to become highly unpopular four or five years later. Thus, in an article published on July 20, 1941, he spoke of the courage of London as "the first victory of human dignity over the barbarity of Fascism," of England being "left alone in the ranks," and of "the brotherly front of the three great Powers." In another article, dated September 20, 1941, referring to German attempts to sow discord among the allies, he wrote:

We are not going to tell the Germans how much war equipment was and will be delivered to us by our allies. Our business is to kill the Germans—it does not matter how, whether in our fighters or in American, whether in our tanks or in British. Our business is to kill the Germans on our front. The British will see about the second front. . . . There has never been a stronger alliance than the alliance of peoples against Hitler.

On July 14, 1942, Ehrenburg wrote: "Soviet patriotism is a natural continuation of Russian patriotism. The Russians were never given to despising other peoples." And he went on to speak of the Russians' learning from Europe, of Peter the Great's going to school in Holland, of Voltaire's influence on Russian freethinkers, of the Decembrists' debt to the French Revolution, of Pushkin's passionate attachment to foreign poets, of the influence of Hegel on Herzen and Belinsky, of Mechnikov's learning from Pasteur, and even of the Russian proletariat's profiting by the lessons of the European labor movement. True, he also spoke of Europe's debt to Russia, to her literature. But the main idea, which Ehrenburg kept driving home

[3] "Za Sovetskuyu Rodinu " ("For the Soviet Motherland!"), *Pravda*, February 23, 1942. Reprinted in A. Tolstoy, *Rodina* (*Motherland*).

in his articles, was the indivisibility of European cultural heritage. He wrote on March 19, 1943:

We never separated our culture from that of Europe, we are bound up with it not by wires, not by rails, but by blood vessels, by convolutions of the brain. . . . The destinies of European culture are infinitely dear to us. We remember that the Decembrists were inspired by the Declaration of the Rights of Man, that Turgenev was a friend of the best French writers. We cannot look at the tragedy of Europe from the side—

This theme runs through many of Ehrenburg's wartime articles. It was obvious that he was glad to be able to vent his inherent cosmopolitanism and in particular his attachment to French culture. On the other hand, he gave free rein to his hatred for the Germans. His anti-German articles had no equal in their venomous mordancy, Alexey Tolstoy coming in second best. A moment came, however, when a sudden halt was called to these anti-German effusions of Ehrenburg. In the spring of 1945, *Pravda* published an article entitled "Comrade Ehrenburg Exaggerates." It accused Ehrenburg of overdoing the "hate-the-Germans" campaign and pointed out that there were both "bad" and "good" Germans. The article came from a high quarter—it was signed by Georgy Aleksandrov, head of the Propaganda Section of the Central Committee of the Communist party—and Ehrenburg had no alternative but to take the cue and change his tune. For a time he simply stopped writing. The change of tactics implied in Aleksandrov's article was, of course, dictated by military-political considerations. Had Alexey Tolstoy been alive then (he had died a little earlier, in February, 1945), Aleksandrov's injunction would have been applicable to him, too.

Historical Novels and Plays

The vogue for historical novels and plays, as well as for biographies (straightforward or novelized) of national heroes, continued during the war. Heroes of the Napoleonic wars naturally enjoyed great popularity, and there were several biographies of Suvorov, Kutuzov, Bagration, and other Russian generals.

Alexey Tolstoy, in additon to resuming his work on *Peter the First* (see Chapter 12), also wrote two plays about Ivan the Terrible. They formed two parts of *Ivan Grozny* (*Ivan the Terrible*), which was subtitled *A Dramatic Tale*. The first part was called *Oryol i orlitsa* (*The Eagle and His Mate*, 1942); the second, *Trudnye gody* (*The Hard Years*, 1943).[4] Soviet critics spoke of this play as one of the greatest achievements not only of Tolstoy but also of Soviet dramaturgy. In the words of one of them, "For the

---

[4] These were limited, privately printed editions (see Veksler, *A. N. Tolstoy*, 446–47). The play in its revised version was published in *Oktyabr*, No. 11–12 (1943).

first time [Tolstoy] applied the principles of Shakespearean dramaturgy as understood by the founders of Marxism."[5]

The two plays overlap chronologically, covering respectively the periods 1553-69 and 1566-71. In the first the stress is on Ivan the man; in the second, on the statesman who subordinates everything to the interests of the state as he understands them. Tolstoy deliberately commits certain anachronisms and takes some liberties with history, but on the whole his "dramatic tale," like his great novel, is based on a careful study of historical material, and several documents of the period are skillfully incorporated into the play. With great mastery Tolstoy reproduces the spirit of the tsar's language as we know it from his writings, with its combination of biblical solemnity and crude colloquialism. But the tendency to read the present into the past, or at least to suggest a parallel between the two, is much more obvious here than in *Peter the First.*

The play is meant to be an apologia for the cruel and tyrannical tsar not only as a statesman who, in ruthlessly suppressing the boyar aristocracy and in establishing his absolute rule, had at heart the long-range interests of the Russian state but also as a personality. In this, Tolstoy is poles apart from his distant relative for whom he was named, Count Alexey K. Tolstoy (1817-75), who portrayed Ivan in his tragedy *The Death of Ivan the Terrible* and in his novel *Prince Serebryany.* In direct contradiction to the literary and historical tradition, the Soviet author proceeds also to white-wash Ivan's cruelest henchman, Malyuta Skuratov, while presenting in an unfavorable light the noble figure of Metropolitan Philip, one of Ivan's victims. In his interpretation of Ivan's personality Tolstoy is at variance with the nineteenth-century historical tradition and is closest to the more recent interpretation of Ivan the Terrible in the work of R. Wipper, whose book about Ivan, first published in 1923, was reissued in 1944 (an English translation of it appeared in Moscow in 1947). In his literary autobiography, published in 1943 in *Novy Mir* (No. 1), Tolstoy said that the age of Ivan the Terrible attracted him as "one of the tragic and creative epochs during which the Russian character was formed." In a later variant of the same autobiography he pointed out that in writing his play he was stimulated by the humiliations to which the Germans had subjected his country: "I called to life out of nowhere that great and passionate Russian character—Ivan the Terrible—in order to arm my own 'infuriated conscience.' "[6]

In the first part of Tolstoy's dramatic diptych an important place is occupied by the story of Ivan's love for his Circassian wife, Marya Temryukovna,

---

[5] That is, Marx and Engels. See Veksler, *A. N. Tolstoy,* 472.

[6] "Kratkaya avtobiografiya" ("A Short Autobiography"), in A. Tolstoy, *Povesti i rasskazy, 1910–1943* (*Tales and Stories: 1910–1943*). See also Veksler, *A. N. Tolstoy,* 444–45.

in whose portrayal Tolstoy also departs from the historical tradition. In general, while it has many literary merits, viewed as history Tolstoy's play is either a piece of skillful propaganda or a feat of subtle legpulling.

A similar tendency toward whitewashing Ivan can be discerned in Vladimir Solovyov's play *Velikiy Gosudar'* (*The Great Sovereign*) and in the three-volume novel *Ivan Grozny* (*Ivan the Terrible*, 1941–45), by Valentin Kostylyov (1888–1950). The latter focuses attention on the wars that Ivan fought to secure for Russia an outlet to the Baltic.

More recent periods of Russian history also attracted several writers. In the light of the armed conflict with Germany some eyes were naturally turned to World War I. During the war the veteran novelist Sergeyev-Tsensky published three novels dealing with this period: *Brusilovsky proryv* (*Brusilov's Breakthrough*, 1943), *Pushki vydvigayut* (*The Guns Are Brought Out*, 1944), and *Pushki zagovorili* (*The Guns Have Spoken*, 1945). All three form part of the author's *Transfiguration* (see page 147 above), designed as a vast epic of Russian life, comparable in scope to Jules Romains's *Les Hommes de bonne volonté*.

As historical novels, Sergeyev-Tsensky's World War I novels are in the tradition of Leo Tolstoy's *War and Peace*, rather than in that of Alexey Tolstoy's *Peter the First*. Their heroes are fictitious, while historical characters are assigned subordinate roles. *Brusilov's Breakthrough*, which deals with the 1916 offensive of the Russian armies against Austria-Hungary, recaptures very well the atmosphere of "patriotic anxiety" which prevailed in Russia on the eve of the Revolution. The central character is Lieutenant Liventsev (who reappears in the sequels to the novel), a young, intelligent, and sensitive officer. Through his reactions the author presents the events to us. There are also a number of other characters, both historical (Emperor Nicholas, Brusilov, Ivanov, and other generals) and fictitious, but the author is primarily concerned with depicting the social psychology of the Russian people during the war. The novel is remarkable for its objective, and even sympathetic, treatment of the conflict which Lenin and his fellow Bolsheviks (including Stalin) had denounced as "imperialistic"; this would have been unthinkable before 1941. On its publication Sergeyev-Tsensky's novel was warmly acclaimed by Soviet critics, but as soon as the war was over, it was attacked for its "objectivism" and its unorthodox approach.

Brusilov, one of the few old-time war leaders to rally to the Soviet regime and to give his blessing to its war against Poland in 1920, was the hero of another novel (which bears his name) by a pre-Revolutionary writer, Yury Slyozkin (1887–1947). Its first installments appeared in *Oktyabr* in 1944, but for some reason the publication was interrupted, and the complete novel did not appear in book form until 1947. Soviet critics favorably contrasted Slyozkin's political interpretation with that of Sergeyev-Tsensky. Still another work about Brusilov was Selvinsky's play *General Brusilov* (1943). A reissue of Brusilov's *Memoirs* also marked this temporary revival of interest in World War I.

The Russo-Japanese War also came in for its share of attention. It was the subject of *Port Arthur* (1944), a long and rather dull novel by Alexander Stepanov. Inferior to Novikov-Priboy's *Tsushima* as literature, it made up for what the latter lacked in patriotism.

A place apart among the wartime historical novels belongs to *Pugachov* (1943–44), a very long novel by Vyacheslav Shishkov (1873–1945) about the famous eighteenth-century rebel. It is a colorful work, with a multitude of characters, written in the realistic tradition. Shishkov died before completing it. An engineer by profession, Shishkov lived most of his life in Siberia, and many of his earlier works had that part of Russia for their background. One of the most interesting was *Vataga* (*The Gang*, 1923), a novel about a group of Old Believers who became revolutionary partisans during the Civil War.

Non-Russian history provided material for *Staraya Angliya* (*Old England*, 1943), by Evgeny Lann, a novel about Jonathan Swift and the contemporary political struggle in England. This was one of the signs of an increased interest, favored by wartime alliance with the West, in the Anglo-Saxon world.

Zoshchenko, Fedin, and Herman on the Carpet

Zoshchenko Some nine hundred Soviet writers, in one form or another, took part in the war, and it is small wonder that they wrote about almost nothing else. A work dealing with a subject entirely unrelated to the current events, or to something that could be regarded as their antecedent in the past, was a *rara avis* in the Soviet periodicals of those days. Such a rarity was Zoshchenko's "novel" *Pered voskhodom solntsa* (*Before Sunrise*), which began appearing in *Oktyabr* in 1943 (Nos. 6–7 and 8–9). Two installments of it were printed, totaling sixty-eight pages, whereupon the publication was discontinued without any explanation. Issue No. 8–9 of *Oktyabr* was signed for the press on September 27, but No. 10 was not signed until December 27. The delay may have been due to ordinary wartime causes, but it is significant that in the meantime Zoshchenko's work was attacked by a certain L. Dmitriev in *Literatura i Iskusstvo*[7] and made subject for discussion in the Presidium of the Union of Soviet Writers—a not unusual procedure.[8] Dmitriev described Zoshchenko's work as "vulgar," "harmful," and "remote from the life of the people." At the discussion in the Union of Soviet Writers it was criticized by Fadeyev as "antinational" and "antiartistic," while the critic Yudin called

---

[7] "O novom romane Zoshchenko" ("About Zoshchenko's New Novel"), *Literatura i Iskusstvo*, December 4, 1943.

[8] This took place on December 6, 1943.

it "amoral" and said that it "went against the fine traditions of Russian literature." A feeble attempt to defend Zoshchenko was made by Olga Forsh, who evoked Rousseau's *Confessions*.[9] Before long, more guns were brought into action against Zoshchenko. *Bolshevik*, the authoritative party organ specializing in higher exegesis, published a short article signed by four individuals who described themselves as "average Leningrad readers." The article protested against Zoshchenko's "vulgar philistinism" and deliberate disregard of the great struggle in which his country was engaged. In the next number of *Bolshevik*, Tikhonov, in an article about Soviet literature and the war, spoke of Zoshchenko's novel as "a phenomenon profoundly alien to the spirit and character of Soviet literature."[10]

What exactly was Zoshchenko's crime?

Before Sunrise is not an easily definable work. Zoshchenko subtitled it *Povest'*, which is usually translated as "Tale," but is in fact a term used in Russian to designate a genre intermediate between a story and a novel—something like a short novel. Zoshchenko's work is, however, neither a story nor a novel in the accepted sense of the word. It bears a certain resemblance to his *Youth Restored* (see page 158 above), which Zoshchenko himself recalls in his "Introduction." The similarity lies chiefly in the introduction of the element of science. Pavlov's physiological theories form an integral part of the work, while there are also references to Freud's interpretations of dreams. This time, however, the scientific aspect is treated more seriously, while the element of fiction—in the proper sense of the word—is completely absent (at least in the published parts) and is replaced by short autobiographical fragments recalling various incidents in the author's life. These fragments cover first the years 1912–26, then the years 1900–15 (that is, when Zoshchenko was between five and fifteen years of age), then the still earlier childhood, first from the age of two to the age of five and then before the age of two.

Zoshchenko begins by saying, "I am unhappy and I don't know why," and the object of this retrogressive excursion into his past is to discover the true cause of his unhappiness, of his melancholy and life-weariness. But to the reader the real meaning of all this devious probing into his youth and childhood is not very easy to see. Many of the autobiographical incidents are indeed trivial or even vulgar. Very few have a real intrinsic interest. The psychopathological significance of some is doubtful. But what shocked the Soviet critics was the frankly introspective character of the whole work, the author's exclusive and unashamed preoccupation with his ego, coupled with

---

[9] For more details see Reavey, *Soviet Literature Today*, 118–20.

[10] "Ob odnoy vrednoy povesti" ("About a Harmful Story"), *Bolshevik*, No. 2 (January, 1944), 56–58. See also Tikhonov's article "Otechestvennaya voyna i sovetskaya literatura" ("The War for the Fatherland and Soviet Literature"), *Bolshevik*, No. 3–4, (1944).

his flippant attitude toward the "epochal" events of his time. There is nothing in the work, however, to justify the charge of fundamental hostility to the Soviet regime or even of incurable and decadent pessimism. In fact, Zoshchenko hints that he succeeded in the end in curing himself of his melancholy and that he was helped in this by Pavlov and his theory of conditioned reflexes. How this was achieved would probably have been told in the subsequent installments. As for Freud, who is *persona non grata* in the Soviet Union, Zoshchenko showed no leaning toward him; on the contrary, he tried to beat him with Pavlov.

As it stands (though perhaps one should not judge it in this incomplete form), *Before Sunrise* is not one of Zoshchenko's successes. One wonders, however, whether, like *Youth Restored*, it was not meant to be a gigantic hoax. The most interesting thing in it are a few confessions that throw light on Zoshchenko as a writer, Zoshchenko the unhumorous humorist.

Zoshchenko's *Before Sunrise* was to be recalled three years later, when he was "purged" from Soviet literature (see Part VII). At the same time it was pointed out that throughout the war he had stayed in Alma-Ata and made no contribution to the literary war effort. It is true that, but for *Before Sunrise*, the name of Zoshchenko is conspicuously absent from the Soviet wartime periodicals. Zoshchenko himself said a little flippantly that during the first year of the war he was "busy writing various scenarios on subjects needed in the days of the great war for the Fatherland," and in 1942 began working on *Before Sunrise*, for which he had been collecting materials for ten years.[11]

Fedin Another interesting work that had no relation to the war was Fedin's book of literary reminiscences, *Gorky in Our Midst*, which has already been mentioned in connection with the Serapion Brothers. The first part was published in 1943 and was highly praised. Coming as it did from the pen of one of the most distinguished Soviet writers and dealing with the earliest period of Soviet literature, it was of great literary interest. The second volume appeared in 1944, with the subtitle *Ukhodyashchy Peterburg* (*The Vanishing Petersburg*). It contained some interesting portraits of such writers as Sologub, Remizov, and Volynsky. But this time it was Fedin's turn to come under fire. He was accused of being "objective" (a crime from the point of view of Socialist Realism) and "dispassionate," of having completely left out of account the historical-political background. "How can one be outside politics during the war for the Fatherland?" exclaimed Vsevolod Vishnevsky, while I. Lezhnev significantly accused Fedin of having been carried away by the fashionable tendency toward a "revaluation of values" and therefore ready to "revise the very foundations of our out-

[11] *Before Sunrise*, never again published in the Soviet Union, was reissued in its incomplete form in the United States in 1967.

look." Marietta Shaginyan spoke of Fedin's "soft benevolence" and of his "distortion of the past," and Tikhonov reproached Fedin for misinterpreting Gorky's position.[12] The second volume of Fedin's memoirs was accordingly taken off the shelves as a work that, in the official view, reflected no credit on Soviet literature. Later the first volume was included in the condemnation.[13] Fedin, still recognized as one of the best Soviet writers, took it in his stride and in 1945 published an interesting full-length novel—his first since *The Rape of Europe*—which also had nothing to do with current events. Together with its postwar sequel it will be discussed in the next chapter.

A Soviet critic once smugly wrote that for Soviet literature there were no **Herman** "forbidden subjects."[14] Her tacit implication may have been, however, that there were forbidden approaches and forbidden attitudes, and the history of Soviet literature, especially since 1929, affords ample proof and illustration of this. A postwar case of a work by a well-known writer suppressed for being out of tune with the official outlook may be mentioned here. In 1949, *Zvezda* began the publication of a short war novel by Yury Herman, *Pokpolkovnik meditsinskoy sluzhby* (*Lieutenant Colonel of the Medical Corps*). The first installment, of some forty pages, appeared in No. 1, and the conclusion was to follow. It did not, however, appear in No. 2. On the last

[12] All these opinions were voiced at the routine post mortem on Fedin's book in the Presidium of the Union of Soviet Writers and were reported in *Literatura i Iskusstvo*, September 9, 1944. See Reavey, *Soviet Literature Today*, 121. Before that, however, the same L. Dmitriev who had attacked Zoshchenko published an article in the same paper (August 5, 1944), in which he described Fedin's book as "a defense of the attitude of a contemplative artist [and] of apolitical art."

[13] A new edition of *Gorky in Our Midst*, with the subtitle *Kartiny literaturnoy zhizni* (*Pictures of Literary Life*) and a short introduction by the author, was published in 1968. To the original material was added a new section under the title "Za shestnadtsat' let" ("In the Course of Sixteen Years"), covering the period 1920–36 and consisting of the correspondence between Fedin and Gorky during those years. This correspondence was introduced by an interesting letter which A. S. Dolinin (b. 1883), the well-known Dostoyevsky scholar, wrote to Fedin, after the original publication of Part 2 of *Gorky in Our Midst,* on the subject of Gorky's attitude to Dostoyevsky, and Fedin's reply to it, dated April 28, 1947. In the composite volume of essays and biographical materials about Fedin, published two years earlier—*Tvorchestvo Konstantina Fedina* (*The Work of Konstantin Fedin*)—there is an interesting retrospective analysis of Fedin's 1943–44 book about Gorky by the prominent Gorky scholar B. A. Byalik. It is entitled "Kniga trudnoy sudby" ("A Book with a Difficult Destiny"). This volume about Fedin contains a full bibliography of Fedin's published works, including his letters.

[14] E. Knipovich, in *Znamya*, No. 2 (1947), 173. The article was a review of some stories which had appeared in *Novy Mir*. The phrase was used in connection with a story by Andrey Platonov, which Knipovich criticized for its picture of postwar relations in a Soviet family. This was one of the last stories by Platonov to be published. In the post-Stalin period it was revealed that several of his works had remained unpublished, and there came a sharp re-appraisal of his literary reputation.

page of the next number *Zvezda* printed Herman's "Letter to the Editor" in which he wrote that in view of the readers' "just criticisms" he had decided to stop the publication of his novel, which needed "radical reworking from the first chapter to the last." Herman explained:

It has been pointed out that the hero of the novel, Dr. Levin, lived isolated in his tiny circumscribed world, was completely engrossed in his own sufferings, and had no right to be described as a positive character. The psychological self-probing of the decadent hero, the complexity of his attitude toward life—all this taken together had led to a wrong picture of the life of the hospital and the garrison.

To this letter of self-criticism the editors of *Zvezda* added a short postscript to the effect that they now realized the error they had made in publishing Herman's novel, "in which the main character is portrayed as an aloof, decadent, morbidly irritable individualist," and were not going to print any more of it. Of the six members of the editorial board of *Zvezda*, one was Herman himself.

Part VII. **Toeing the New Party Line, 1946–53**

Chapter 27. **TURNING ON THE SCREW**

No sooner was the war over than the tightening of ideological controls in the Soviet Union became apparent to most people. Actually, these controls were never relaxed very much; that is, the government never really let out of sight its long-range aims, and the seeming concessions to popular feelings were of a purely tactical, opportunistic nature.

Even during the war there were enough signs to show that the Communist party would never allow the "revaluation of values" to go too far and that as soon as the proper bounds were overstepped it would clamp down on the transgressors. This was the meaning of the attack on Zoshchenko in 1943 and of the rebuke to Fedin in 1944, as well as that to Ehrenburg in 1945. There were other similar cases. Thus, Aseyev and Selvinsky, one a former Futurist and the other a former Constructivist, were accused of "ideological mistakes" in their poems about Russia. Selvinsky's mistake (in a poem called "Whom Russia Lullabied") consisted in depicting Russia as too "soft" and broad-minded. Pasternak was criticized for keeping aloof from the war and devoting himself almost entirely to new translations of Shakespeare (somewhat inconsistently, another poet, Mikhail Lozinsky, was praised for accomplishing his excellent translation of Dante's *Divine Comedy* to the accompaniment of guns and bombs, and this was even adduced as a proof of the artist's freedom in the U.S.S.R.).

Certainly those in the West who spoke of the "great retreat" (the title of the book published in the United States in 1942 by the well-known Russian-American jurist and sociologist Nicholas Tinashev) of the Soviet regime and expected the war to bring about far-reaching internal changes in Russia were soon undeceived. The concessions which the Soviet government made before the war, and even more so during the war, to Russian patriotism and to Russian national feelings were no doubt dictated by the consideration that patriotism and national feelings could be used to advantage in an all-out conflict with Nazi Germany. Once this new national spirit was aroused, it was not easy to exorcise it, but it was possible to make use of it as a weapon of domestic and international policy, to channel it *ad majorem gloriam* of the Soviet state.

The ever-growing tendency toward statism, the glorification of the Soviet state, endowed with all the attributes of unlimited autocracy, became one of the salient features of the ideological evolution in the Soviet Union. So far as there was a revival and a rehabilitation of the past and its traditions, there appeared a predominant tendency to strengthen the authority and prestige of the state. Old ranks, orders and decorations, uniforms (not only for schoolboys and schoolgirls but even for schoolteachers), strict enforcement of discipline in the army and in schools—such were the characteristic features which distinguished Stalin's Russia from Lenin's. The historical figures that were particularly glorified also represented the same trend: Ivan the Terrible, Peter the Great, Suvorov, Kutuzov, and other great military leaders.

The cult of the state which characterized Stalinite Russia was, of course, in flagrant contradiction not only to the credo of the "revolutionary-democratic" thinkers whom the present-day Russian Communists still pretend to regard as their predecessors, or to the early trends of Russian Bolshevism, but also to the teachings of Marx, Engels, and Lenin about the "withering away" of the state. That this glaring inconsistency was puzzling some minds in the Soviet Union may be seen from the fact that in August, 1950, Stalin deemed it necessary to publish in *Bolshevik* an authoritative explanation of why the Marx-Engels-Lenin thesis was no longer applicable to conditions in the Soviet Union.[1] In his statement he poked fun at the "doctrinaires and Talmudists" who imagined that it was enough to memorize Marxist formulas by heart and recite them forwards and backwards.

During the war many people also made much of the concessions which the Soviet government accorded to religion, and to the Orthodox church in particular. The antireligious campaign was gradually slackened after the mid-thirties. This change of policy—if not of heart—undoubtedly represented a concession to popular feelings which paralleled the concessions to the people's patriotism and was dictated by the interests of the Soviet state in the event of an international conflict. One of the Soviet government's first acts when the war broke out was to close down the antireligious journal *Bezbozhnik* (*The Godless One*), to which Demyan Bedny was a regular contributor, to abolish the society for propagation of atheism, and to seek the support of the church in the all-out national effort. In wartime literature the religious sentiments of the people were often reflected (as in Simonov's poems and in Leonov's dramas). The fact that village priests took part in the guerrilla movement was duly emphasized.

After the war the policy of concessions to the church was continued. To some extent, no doubt, this policy did represent a genuine retreat and an admission, on the part of the Communist leaders, of their defeat on the religious front, the original plan of exterminating religion by open persecution having proved a failure. But the price paid by the church for these partial concessions was a heavy one, for they resulted in making the now officially recognized Orthodox church subservient to the state and even turning it into a useful instrument of the Kremlin's foreign policy in the

[1] *Bolshevik*, No. 15 (August, 1950).

Near East and in the Balkans. The traditional enmity of the Orthodox hierarchy to Roman Catholicism was skillfully fostered by the professedly atheist government of Communist Russia. Unable to indoctrinate the Russian masses with the idea that religion was opium for the people, Stalin took the cue from Ivan the Terrible and Peter the Great and subordinated the church to the state. The important difference between them was that neither Ivan nor Peter professed to be an atheist. With the church well under control it was possible after the war to resume antireligious propaganda, which was now mainly directed toward young Communists, among whom religion seemed to have won many recruits.[2]

With the war at an end it soon became increasingly clear that the precarious and uneasy alliance between Stalin's totalitarian police state and the democracies of the West, known as the alliance of all "freedom-loving" nations, was cracking at the seams. During the war Soviet leaders perforce had to acknowledge the role of their Western allies in the victories won over Nazi Germany. On June 13, 1944, a week after the landings in Normandy, Stalin spoke in glowing terms of the Allied invasion of the Continent, saying that "the history of warfare knows no other undertaking comparable in breadth of conception, grandeur of scale, and mastery of execution."[3] But as the war drew to its conclusion, the achievements of the Western allies began to be played down. The 1946 edition of the officially approved textbook of Soviet history, which was speedily brought out to replace the 1945 edition, spoke briefly and somewhat grudgingly of the Allied contribution to the victory over Germany, representing the Soviet Union as "the savior of civilization and progress in Europe and the whole world."[4] Stalin's tribute to the Allies' invasion of Germany disappeared from the 1946 edition. So did, significantly, the account of the dissolution of the Communist International in 1943, which the West had hailed as the final break with the old Communist policy of fomenting world revolution.

In a speech on February 9, 1946, Stalin outlined the new party line with regard to the war and the victory—the latter was presented as a triumph for the Soviet social and political order and as a proof of its superiority to the non-Soviet order. The speech heralded the return to the old Bolshevik conception of two irreconcilably hostile worlds. The wartime alliance of freedom-loving nations (which in truth was no more than a cobelligerency) was to give place to a total ideological war in which the Soviet Union was to

[2] For an over-all picture of Christian religion and the Church in the Soviet Union see N. Struve, *Les Chrétiens en U.R.S.S.* (an English translation of this book was published in 1967).

[3] I. Stalin, *O Velikoy Otechestvennoy Voyne Sovetskogo Soyuza* (*About the Great War for the Fatherland Waged by the Soviet Union*), 137.

[4] A. M. Pankratova (ed.), *Istoriya SSSR* (*A History of the U.S.S.R.*), 390. This text book for high schools, published under the auspices of the Academy of Sciences of the U.S.S.R., was compiled by K. Bazilevich, S. Bakhrushin, A. Pankratova, and A. Vogt.

stand opposed to its wartime democratic allies. This ideological war was soon to reach an unheard-of pitch of violence and acerbity and to eclipse completely anything that was ever said or written in the Soviet Union against Fascism. Significantly enough, the first attacks in this all-out war of ideologies were launched on the literary front.[5]

The Zhdanov Bombshell

On August 14, 1946, the Central Committee of the Communist party passed a resolution which, although it dealt with some specific cases of literary "heresy," marked the starting point of a new era in Soviet literature which became associated with Andrey Zhdanov.

The resolution, known as the resolution "On the magazines *Zvezda* and *Leningrad*," came to most people outside the Soviet Union as a bolt from the blue; nor was it apparently expected by the Soviet writers. It took many people a long time to understand its full purport. It dealt with the unsatisfactory manner in which the above-named Leningrad literary magazines were run.[6] *Zvezda* was accused of publishing recently several "ideologically harmful" works and specifically of "providing a literary tribune" for Zoshchenko, a writer who had "long since been specializing in writing empty, fatuous and vulgar stuff, and in preaching a rotten lack of ideas [*bezideynost*], vulgarity, and apoliticalness, designed to lead our youth astray and to poison its consciousness." Zoshchenko was described as "scum of literature," and his story "Priklyucheniya obezyany" ("The Adventures of a Monkey"), published in 1946 in *Zvezda* (No. 5–6), was singled out for attack. It was characterized as "a vulgar lampoon on Soviet life and Soviet people." Zoshchenko was accused of "anti-Soviet innuendoes," and his "unworthy behavior" during the war, when he published such a "disgusting" work as "Before Sunrise," was recalled.

The resolution further accused *Zvezda* of "popularizing" the work of Anna Akhmatova, who was described as "a typical representative of vacuous poetry which is devoid of ideas and alien to our people." Her poems were said to be "imbued with the spirit of pessimism and decadence," expressive of "the tastes of the old drawing-room poetry, . . . of bourgeois-aristocratic aestheticism and decadence, of 'art for art's sake,'" and "harmful to the cause of the upbringing of our youth." Akhmatova's poetry, said the resolution, was "not to be tolerated in Soviet literature." By publishing Zoshchenko's and Akhmatova's work, went on the resolution, the magazine had

[5] The switch in the Soviet attitude to the war and to its allies is discussed at some length, with numerous quotations, in G. S. Counts and Nucia Lodge, *The Country of the Blind: The Soviet System of Mind Control.*

[6] *Zvezda* was a monthly founded in 1924. It was regarded as the organ of the Leningrad branch of the Union of Soviet Writers. In the thirties it was one of the best Soviet literary periodicals. *Leningrad* was a fortnightly magazine of more recent origin.

wrought "ideological havoc" among the Leningrad writers. Similar accusations were proffered against the other magazine, *Leningrad*, which also had published Zoshchenko and Akhmatova, as well as "a number of works imbued with the spirit of servility before everything foreign." The editorial boards of both magazines were charged with having forgotten the fundamental maxim of Leninism which proclaims that

our magazines, whether scientific or literary, cannot be apolitical. . . . Our magazines are a powerful weapon of the Soviet state in the task of educating the Soviet people, and especially of the young, and must therefore be guided by that which constitutes the essence of the Soviet order, namely its politics. The Soviet regime cannot tolerate the education of the young in a spirit of indifference to Soviet politics, in a spirit of pooh-poohism and of ideological neutrality. . . . All preaching of ideological neutrality, of apoliticalness, of "art for art's sake," is alien to Soviet literature.

The resolution further accused the Union of Soviet Writers and its chairman, Tikhonov, as well as the Leningrad City Committee of the Communist party, of condoning the political mistakes of *Zvezda* and *Leningrad* and of taking no steps for the improvement of those magazines. The editors of *Zvezda* were ordered to "liquidate" these "mistakes and shortcomings" and to stop printing Zoshchenko, Akhmatova, and "suchlike" writers. A. M. Egolin, deputy chief of the Propaganda Section of the Central Committee of the Communist party, was appointed editor-in-chief of *Zvezda*, while *Leningrad* was simply suppressed.[7]

A week later, Zhdanov—who during the next two years was to play the role of the Communist cultural "boss"[8]—made reports on the situation arising out of the Central Committee's resolution before the Leningrad branch of the Union of Soviet Writers and the Leningrad City Committee of the Communist party, developing and clarifying the main points of the

[7] The resolution of the Central Committee was first published in *Kultura i Zhizr'*. It was reproduced in *Pravda* and other newspapers and in all literary magazines. In some it was accompanied by editorial comments and embroiderings and additions to the list of "harmful" works. Thus *Znamya* attacked its own editorial board, in particular for publishing Grossman's prewar play *Esli verit' pifagoreytsam* (*If One Is to Believe the Pythagoreans*) as reflecting an "alien philosophy." The play is not devoid of interest, but its "philosophy" is not easily detectable. Its moral seems to be that a good old Liberal of the tsar's days who swears by Pythagoras is a more valuable individual than a bad Bolshevik who values his material well-being above everything else. *Znamya* added to the list of "harmful works" Vsevolod Ivanov's novel *Pri vzyatii Berlina* (*At the Taking of Berlin*), Fedin's *Gorky in Our Midst*, Kirsanov's "formalistic" poem about Alexander Matrosov, etc. See "Vyshe znamya ideynosti v literature!" ("Higher the Banner of Ideas in Literature!"), *Znamya*, No. 10 (1946), 27–37.

[8] The fact that at the same time Zhdanov played an important political role and in 1947 was entrusted with the leading part in the revived Communist International (the Cominform) shows what importance was attached at this juncture to the "cultural front."

resolution and laying down the new party line in matters of art and literature.[9]

Zoshchenko and Akhmatova were discussed by Zhdanov at some length. He denounced Zoshchenko as "a vulgarian" who was "accustomed to mocking at Soviet life, Soviet conditions, and Soviet people, while disguising his mockery under a mask of empty entertainment and fatuous facetiousness." Zoshchenko's story about the monkey he characterized as "the epitome of all that is negative in Zoshchenko's literary production," adding that Zoshchenko deliberately portrayed Soviet life as ugly, grotesque, and vulgar "in order to put into the mouth of a monkey the vile, poisonous, anti-Soviet statement to the effect that life in a zoo is better than life at large and that in a cage one can breathe more freely than among Soviet people."[10] Zhdanov then recalled Zoshchenko's contribution to the Serapion Brothers' autobiographies and made a general attack on the Serapions for preaching "rotten apoliticalness, philistinism, and vulgarity."

From Zoshchenko, Zhdanov passed on to Akhmatova, whom he characterized as an out-and-out individualist, a representative of the "reactionary literary morass," a "cross between a nun and a whore." Her poetry was described as "remote from the people," as "the poetry of the upper ten thousand of the old Russia of the landed gentry," a relic of the irrevocable past, which could only breed depression and pessimism and a desire to escape into the narrow world of personal emotions and thus poison the minds of the young people.[11]

Zhdanov went on:

It is not an accident that the literary magazines of Leningrad showed an enthusiasm for the cheap modern bourgeois literature of the West. Some of our writers have come to look upon themselves not as masters but as pupils of the bourgeois-philistine writers, adopting the tone of servility and admiration toward philistine foreign literature. Does this servility become us, Soviet patriots, who have built up the Soviet order, which is a hundred times better than any bourgeois order? Does this servility before the narrow bourgeois-philistine literature of the

[9] A combined and condensed stenographic version of Zhdanov's reports was printed in all Soviet newspapers and most literary periodicals. For a more nearly complete English translation see Counts and Lodge, *The Country of the Blind*, 84–97, where it is, however, mistakenly described as a report made at the First All-Union Congress of Soviet Writers (which took place in 1934). The quotations that follow were translated from the Russian text printed in *Znamya*, No. 10 (1946), 7–26.

[10] Zoshchenko's story described, in his usual satirical vein, the adventures of a monkey which had escaped from a zoo. His quips at Soviet conditions of life were neither more nor less venomous than those in most of his satirical stories. Zhdanov also mentioned and quoted a verse satire on Soviet conditions, by A. Khazin, written in the form of an amusing parody, a sequel to Pushkin's *Eugene Onegin*.

[11] The obvious inference is that the moods voiced by Ahkmatova and by other "pessimists" and "individualists" found a response among Soviet audiences and caused Communist leaders considerable worry.

West become our progressive Soviet literature which is the most revolutionary literature in the world?

At the root of the grave blunders committed by the editors of *Zvezda* and *Leningrad* lay the fact that they had forgotten some of the fundamental Leninist principles, said Zhdanov. And he reminded his audience of Lenin's article of 1905, in which he wrote that literature of the Socialist proletariat must become "Party-minded" (*partiynaya*).

Zhdanov also uttered a warning to those who, spurred no doubt by the encouragement given to Russian patriotism during the war, were going too far in their "revaluation of values." He accused Zoshchenko and Akhmatova of not really loving Leningrad and of seeing in it "the embodiment of a different social-political order, of a different ideology," of substituting for it the old St. Petersburg, with the Bronze Horseman as its symbol.

Zhdanov blamed the Leningrad City Committee of the Communist party for forgetting the importance of the ideological front and emphasized the international aspect of the whole affair. This international aspect was soon to overshadow all the rest. Said Zhdanov:

The bourgeois world resents our successes both at home and in the international arena. As a result of World War II the positions of Socialism have been strengthened. The question of Socialism is on the agenda in many countries in Europe. The imperialists of all breeds resent it. They are afraid of Socialism, they are afraid of our Socialist country which serves as a model to all progressive mankind. The imperialists and their ideological henchmen . . . try their best to slander our country, to show it up in a wrong light, to slander Socialism. . . . The task of Soviet literature is not only to reply, blow for blow, to all these infamous calumnies and attacks . . . but also to castigate and attack boldly bourgeois culture which is in a state of decay and corruption.

It did not become Soviet patriots, went on Zhdanov, to worship at the shrine of bourgeois culture and play the part of its pupils. Soviet literature stood for a higher culture and had the right to teach all the others. Soviet writers were "in the front line of fire" at a moment when the ideological front was becoming more important than ever.

The resolution of the Central Committee concerning *Zvezda* and *Leningrad* initiated a movement that went on gathering momentum and had far-reaching repercussions on Soviet literature. It meant much more than the eclipse of Zoshchenko and Akhmatova or even their expulsion from literature. Before a few weeks had passed, both were in fact officially expelled from the Union of Soviet Writers,[12] and the latter cleansed its administra-

---

[12] As far as it is possible to ascertain, for over three years not a line of Akhmatova's was published in the Soviet press. But in April, 1950, several poems over her signature, all of them very unlike her earlier poetry, appeared in the popular illustrated weekly magazine *Ogonyok*. They bore the title "Iz tsikla 'Slava miru'" ("From the 'Glory to Peace' Cycle"). A few more poems from the same cycle appeared in two later issues

tion, relieving Tikhonov of his presidential post and appointing Alexander Fadeyev as its first secretary, to be assisted by four other secretaries: Simonov, Tikhonov (who was thus demoted but not ostracized), Vishnevsky, and Korneychuk. The Presidium of the Board of the Union of Soviet Writers also passed a resolution in which it voiced its full support of Zhdanov and the Central Committee and listed with gusto its own sins. The Central Committee was right, said the resolution, in pointing out that the Board of the Union of Soviet Writers and its chairman took no steps to improve the working of *Zvezda* and *Leningrad* and that, far from fighting the harmful influences of Zoshchenko and Akhmatova and other "un-Soviet" writers, they encouraged "the infiltration of alien tendencies and morals into Soviet literature." *Literaturnaya Gazeta,* the official organ of the Union of Soviet Writers, was guilty of publishing an interview with Akhmatova in 1945, as well as her portrait. The leadership of the Union was

---

of *Ogonyok*. The land of the Soviets was described as a happy country where "poets' voices have a fuller sound." "Foreign slander" was denounced, and Stalin was hailed as the incarnation of freedom and peace. The poems were meant to be Akhmatova's contribution to the Stockholm Peace Petition. Those who knew Akhmatova well realized at the time that by this abject capitulation before her detractors she was buying not so much the right to re-enter literature as her son's freedom. Her son, Lev Gumilyov, a young and gifted historian, had been arrested and sentenced to prison in 1937. Released during the war, he was rearrested and exiled to Siberia when the war was over. He was finally freed in May, 1956. Akhmatova's poems glorifying Stalin were not included in the three post-1953 editions of her collected works (one slim volume published in 1958, a larger one in 1961, and a still larger one in 1965), though some other poems from the same "peace cycle" are to be found in them. The entire cycle was reprinted, as a "document of the time" and an illustration of the tragic plight of Soviet poets, in Volume II of Akhmatova's *Collected Works* published in the United States (ed. by G. Struve and B. Filippov). This edition includes also the remarkable cycle entitled *Requiem*, which was inspired by the poet's ordeal during her son's imprisonment. The poems of that cycle are a poignant evocation of the sufferings of many nameless Russian mothers and of the Russian people in general during the terrible years of Stalin's rule. The cycle, written between 1935 and 1940, did not become known until 1963, when it was published outside Russia as a separate volume. It was reissued in 1969, but remains taboo in the Soviet Union. Its story, just as the rest of the story of Akhmatova's "rehabilitation" in the late fifties and of her new and important role in Russian literature, belongs to the the post-Stalin period and will be dealt with in the sequel to this book.

As for Zoshchenko, some patriotic war stories of his were published a year after his fall into disfavor in some minor periodicals, but he never regained his position in Soviet literature. After his death in 1958 a volume of heavily censored and slanted selections from his works was published, without an explanatory introduction. This was followed by other editions of selected works. His rehabilitation has been only partial. The *Short Literary Encyclopaedia* (Vol. II, 1964) makes no mention of the Zhdanov episode. In the long entry on Zoshchenko there is only a brief reference to the fact that in the 1940's he "stopped publishing." *Before Sunrise* is not mentioned.

also responsible for the "wide diffusion" given to Pasternak's "apolitical poetry, devoid of ideas and severed from the people's life." It was guilty also of encouraging such "ideologically harmful" works as Sergeyev-Tsensky's *Brusilov's Breakthrough* and of tolerating "the morbid delectation in suffering" which characterized the work of some of the young poets.

The resolution went on to stress the "un-Soviet spirit of servility before the bourgeois culture of the West . . . which was particularly conspicuous in the drama," and lashed out against the dramatic critics. It pointed out that there was no satisfactory program for the teaching of the history of Soviet literature in the Union's Institute of Literature. Harmful "bourgeois-nationalist tendencies" were said to exist in some national republics (the Ukrainian, Tatar, and Bashkir in particular). Several Soviet writers were accused of "keeping aloof from the fundamental problems of the day," of "ignoring the life and the needs of the people," and of "not knowing how to depict the best traits and qualities of the Soviet man." The resolution insisted on a "radical change" in the "ideological life and work" of the Writers' Union, on focusing attention on contemporary themes, and on the necessity to "castigate servility, expose the true nature of the capitalist environment, combat its demoralizing influences, and lay bare the character of modern imperialism with its implied threat of new bloody wars."[13]

Fadeyev made an attack on Pasternak, saying that, although he had grown up under the Soviet regime (which was not accurate—Pasternak was twenty-seven at the outbreak of the Revolution), his work stood for "that individualism which is profoundly alien to the spirit of our society." Surkov accused himself of lack of "vigilance" in allowing the publication of Akhmatova's poems in *Ogonyok*, of which he was editor-in-chief. Vishnevsky, one of the editors of *Znamya*, voiced his amazement at Akhmatova's "silence" in the face of "the judgment of the people and of the Party" and proposed to expel Akhmatova and Zoshchenko from the Union of Soviet Writers, reminding his colleagues what they owed to the party, which had always shown its concern for literature and had always come to its aid.[14]

In the meantime the Central Committee of the Communist party followed up the resolution on *Zvezda* and *Leningrad* by two others. One was entitled "On the Repertoire of Dramatic Theaters and Measures for Its Improvement," and the other, "On the Motion Picture *Big Life*." The resolution on the theaters signalized the unsatisfactory condition of the Soviet theaters, whose main weakness was the almost complete absence of plays by Soviet authors on contemporary themes. The resolution listed some theaters

[13] See *Oktyabr*, No. 9 (1946), 182–87.

[14] It is now known that in 1946, on the eve of Zhdanov's attack on her, a volume of Akhmatova's collected poetry was ready for publication. Most of the printing was destroyed, but a few copies are known to have survived.

and said that out of their 117 current productions only 25 were contemporary Soviet plays. Of these some were described as ideologically worthless.

The authorities responsible for the choice of plays were also criticized for their "passion" for staging historical plays, irrespective of their value, and for "introducing plays by bourgeois foreign dramatists." The Committee on Art Affairs was specifically rebuked for distributing to theaters Somerset Maugham's *The Circle*, Pinero's *The Dangerous Age*, Kaufman and Hart's *The Man Who Came to Dinner*, Bernard's *Le petit café*, and so on. The production of these plays, said the resolution, had turned the Soviet stage into a sounding board for the propaganda of reactionary bourgeois ideology and morals. It meant an attempt "to poison the consciousness of the Soviet people with hostile ideology and to revive the vestiges of capitalism in consciousness and life." This was a gross political error. The resolution called upon the Committee on Art Affairs and the Union of Soviet Writers to concentrate on the creation of a contemporary Soviet repertoire: "Playwrights and theaters must reflect in their plays and performances the life of Soviet society. . . . must contribute in every way to the further development of the best aspects of the character of Soviet man."

The task of Soviet playwrights and producers was described as the training of Soviet youth "in cheerfulness and joyousness, in devotion to their country, and in confidence in the victory of their cause." "At the same time," the resolution continued, "the Soviet theater is called upon to show that these qualities are characteristic not just of a few chosen persons, of heroes, but of many millions of Soviet people."

The second of these resolutions dealt specifically with the shortcomings of Pavel Nilin's film *Big Life*, mentioning also other "unsuccessful and faulty" films, such as the second part of Eisenstein's *Ivan the Terrible*, Pudovkin's *Admiral Nakhimov*, and Kozintsev and Trauberg's *Simple People*. Of Eisenstein's film it was said that he had "exhibited ignorance of historical facts by portraying the progressive army of the *oprichniki*[15] as a band of degenerates, similar to the American Ku Klux Klan, and Ivan the

---

[15] The *oprichniki* (from Oprichnina—the Apart, the Peculium) were a special army or police force created by Ivan the Terrible as part of his policy of exterminating the boyar opposition. Each member carried a dog's head and a broom attached to his saddle as the emblems of his job, which was to "bite and sweep out the traitors to the tsar." The *Soviet Encyclopaedias*, both the *Little* (1930) and the *Great* (1939), while pointing out that the earlier historians had distorted the class nature of the Oprichnina and presented it as a cruel whim of the cruel tsar, emphasized its oppressiveness for the mass of the peasants (*The Great Encyclopaedia*) and spoke of the cruel methods of the *oprichniki*, who did not spare even children (*The Little Encyclopaedia*). By 1946 the Oprichnina had come to be looked upon as a wholly "progressive" phenomenon. Any taunts at it could easily be construed, of course, as veiled attacks on the Soviet secret police.

Terrible, a man of strong will and character, as weak and spineless, resembling Hamlet in his irresolution.

The showing of *Big Life* was prohibited, and its author hastened to recant. Eisenstein, too, made a groveling confession, dutifully agreeing that he had distorted historical truth. The second part of his film was withdrawn. Pudovkin, for his part, refashioned his *Admiral Nakhimov*, removing from it all that was objectionable.

One of the echoes of these resolutions on the drama and the motion pictures was an address made by Simonov at the All-Union Conference of Theater Leaders and Playwrights in November, 1946, in which he declared that "a playwright must be a politician," that "Soviet art" was not a mere "geographical conception," and that not all that was written and performed on the territory of the Soviet Union was thereby automatically Soviet literature: "The struggle with capitalism, with alien ideologies, is not merely an external struggle. It is also our internal struggle with the birthmarks of capitalism within our society."[16]

Simonov also called upon Soviet dramatists "to reveal . . . to the entire world the ideological superiority of our people." His whole speech was a fiery call to arms, to an "active, merciless, and unceasing attack on our enemies." These enemies were to be sought on the "ideological front," where "a tremendous battle is being waged on a world scale and with unparalleled violence."

The response to Zhdanov's new line went on rapidly mounting in pitch and violence.

[16] *Sovetskoye Iskusstvo (Soviet Art)*, November 22, 1946.

Chapter 28. **THE ANTI-WEST WITCH-HUNT**

It was the accusation of "servility before the West" (or even "before every-thing foreign"), contained in the resolution of the Central Committee, elaborated by Zhdanov in his reports, and taken up by the Union of Soviet Writers in its resolution of September 4, that was to become the keynote of the new party line in cultural matters and the "theme" of the Zhdanov era in Soviet literature. The autumn of 1946 marked the beginning of this era. Viewed retrospectively, this beginning appears somewhat modest. The Central Committee resolutions, the Zhdanov reports, and the first reactions of the Soviet writers to them can be compared to a few instruments in an orchestra tuning up. But before long the whole orchestra of Soviet totali-tarian propaganda, obeying its invisible conductor, was performing, in an ever-increasing crescendo, what might be called the "Anti-West Symphony."

To give a detailed account of the anti-West campaign which rapidly permeated all the fields of Soviet life would require a separate volume. All that can be done here is to indicate its main phases and facets as far as literature is concerned and to give some of the more striking illustrations.[1]

The campaign went in three principal directions: (1) the ferreting out of those guilty of "servility before the West," to whom the term "rootless cosmopolitans" (*bezrodnye kosmopolity*)[2] soon came to be applied; (2) di-

[1] From literature the fight against "servility before the West" spread rapidly to other fields: music, art, linguistics, science, etc. In 1949 even Soviet circuses were denounced by the official *Sovetskoyo Iskusstvo* for their tendency toward "bourgeois cosmopoli-tanism" and "Formalism." For more details of this anti-Western witch-hunt in fields other than literature see Counts and Lodge, *Country of the Blind*, especially Chapters V ("Music as a Weapon"), VI ("Science as a Weapon"), and VII ("Education as a Weapon"). In linguistics there was a remarkable about-face when Stalin himself, in the summer of 1950, came up with a denunciation of the linguistic theories of Marr, whose opponents had been hounded for over two years as "bourgeois cosmopolitans." Stalin's "contribution" to linguistics was hailed as "a work of genius" by many Soviet scholars and critics.

[2] The exact rendering of this phrase is "cosmopolitans without kith or kin," and one is almost tempted to translate it as "bastard cosmopolitans." I have not been able to ascertain when, where, or by whom it was first used. It figured in *Pravda*'s editorial on January 28, 1949, with reference to the "plenary meeting" of the Board of the Union of Soviet Writers early that month, at which an attack had been made on "a certain antipatriotic group of theater critics." These critics were described as "bearers of a rootless cosmopolitanism, profoundly repugnant and alien to Soviet man." After that the phrase became common currency. Its possible anti-Semitic implications will be discussed below. The expression "bourgeois cosmopolitanism" had been used earlier

rect attacks on, and denunciations of, the "decadent West," especially of the United States; and (3) glorification of everything Russian and assertion of Russian superiority in every field.

The Hunt for "Rootless Cosmopolitans"

In the spring of 1947 the Board of the Union of Soviet Writers held one of its periodic conferences at which Fadeyev, in his capacity of secretary, read a report on the tasks of Soviet literary theory and literary criticism. He stressed the superiority of Russian realism over its Western European counterpart and attacked those who regarded Russian realistic literature as "a sort of appendix to Western European literature." He spoke with particular venom of a book published in 1941 by one of the most prominent Soviet critics of the thirties, Isaac Nusinov, an orthodox Marxist and Communist. Fadeyev called the book "a very harmful one." The book, entitled *Pushkin i mirovaya literatura* (*Pushkin and World Literature*), discussed the relation between Pushkin's "Little Tragedies" and contemporary European literature. Nusinov advanced the thesis that Pushkin was "a European" and that in his plays he owed a great deal to foreign stimuli. There was nothing novel in Nusinov's ideas, but for Fadeyev they were now tantamount to the crime of lese majesty. Fadeyev quoted a passage from the book in which Nusinov said that Pushkin had not attracted so much attention in the West because he was "incomparably more of a European writer than Tolstoy and Dostoyevsky" who "negated the West, opposing to it their Oriental ideals, the ideals of Russia." Fadeyev's comment upon this rather platitudinous statement was as follows:

The book proceeds from the conception that the light shines from the West and that Russia is an "Oriental" country. Pushkin is denationalized, turned into something universal, pan-European, pan-human . . . . Nusinov is preaching the eternal "universal" themes which seem to have an abstract existence. Pushkin for Nusinov is a genius only because he has his own solutions for these abstractly existing universal themes. Therefore, throughout his chapters, there flashes before us a series of names of writers and poets of Western Europe, and Nusinov hops, carefree, from one century into another . . . . The book has nothing to do with Marxism.[3]

After thus tearing to pieces Nusinov's six-year-old book, which at the time of its publication had aroused no special objections, Fadeyev proceeded to look for the roots of Nusinov's "heresies" and found them in the theories of Alexander Veselovsky, a great nineteenth-century Russian literary scholar and one of the pioneers of the comparative study of literature. Veselovsky

in connection with the attack on "Veselovskyism." Later, "rootless cosmopolitans" were also described as "passportless tramps."

[3] Fadeyev's report as printed in B. Byalik (ed.), *Problemy sotsialisticheskogo realizma* (*Problems of Socialist Realism*), 24.

was looked upon as their master by many leading Soviet literary scholars, especially of the Formalist school.[4] But even outside that school he was held in great esteem. In 1938 the centenary of his birth was commemorated with great pomp, all Russian literary scholars and critics, including orthodox Marxists (such as V. Desnitsky) paying tribute to him. In 1940 one of Veselovsky's major works, *Istoricheskaya poètika* (*Historical Poetics*), was reissued with an introduction by Zhirmunsky, and even as late as 1946 the Leningrad University published a little book by V. Shishmaryov on *Alexander Veselovsky and Russian Literature*, in which Veselovsky was spoken of as a pathbreaker in the field of literary studies.

But now Fadeyev, from the heights of his official position, fulminated against Veselovsky and his followers as the true originators of "servility before the West." His attack unleashed a veritable storm. All leading Soviet periodicals carried a spate of articles against "Veselovskyism" and its survivals in the Soviet Union, many examples of which were cited. The name Veselovsky was bandied about in the Soviet press, and "Veselovskyism," identified with "cosmopolitanism," "comparativism," and "bourgeois liberalism," became a term of abuse, like the earlier "Bogdanovism," "Voronskyism," and "Pereverzevism." At the end of 1947, *Oktyabr* published a long article by the well-known critic Kirpotin, in which the charges against Veselovsky and his school were summed up.[5] In the same number two feeble voices of protest were raised. One belonged to the former Formalist and Futurist Victor Shklovsky; the other, to Shishmaryov, whose booklet on Veselovsky Fadeyev had attacked.[6] Shishmaryov timidly suggested that Veselovsky's detractors might have confused him with his less important brother, Alexey, author of a well-known book on Western influences in Russian literature.

But in the next issue of *Oktyabr* (January, 1948), Kirpotin published a thundering reply under the following long and elaborate title "About Servility Before the Capitalist West, About Alexander Veselovsky, About His Followers, and About Things That Matter Most."[7] There Veselovsky was portrayed as one of the ideologists of the pre-Revolutionary ruling classes (Veselovsky was in fact a democratic liberal, with strong inclinations toward Comtian Positivism). He was blamed for inculcating into the minds of Russian intelligentsia the notion of Russia's inferiority and the idea that the Russians must look upon Western Europeans as their "masters." The

[4] For Veselovsky's influence on the Formalists, see pages 204ff.

[5] See *Oktyabr*, No. 12 (1947). Kirpotin's "big gun" was supported by two smaller-caliber guns, I. Dmitrakov and M. Kuznetsov.

[6] *Ibid.* At this time the editors of *Oktyabr* (who included Kirpotin himself) still regarded a "discussion" about Veselovsky as permissible. Later they were blamed for such misplaced "liberalism."

[7] "O nizkopoklonstve pered kapitalisticheskim Zapadom, ob Aleksandre Veselovskom, o ego posledovatelyakh i o samom glavnom," *Oktyabr*, No. 1 (1948), 3–21.

name Veselovsky, said Kirpotin, was made use of "to blunt the revolutionary and social acuity of the heritage of Russian classical criticism." His followers fell back on it in order to pass off their "mimicry of Marxism" for the genuine article. Under Veselovsky's label "comparativism" was smuggled into Soviet literary scholarship and disguised as Marxism. From Veselovsky a direct line could be traced to "historical fatalism with all its spiritual diseases: passivism, contemplativeness, skepticism, 'pure scholarship.' "

A month later Anatoly Tarasenkov, who had been earlier accused of favoring Pasternak and probably had to make good for his "sin," followed up with an even more violent attack on Veselovsky in *Novy Mir*.[8] Whatever timid voices had been raised in defense of Veselovsky were finally silenced in March, 1948, when *Kultura i Zhizn'*, the official mouthpiece of the Central Committee of the Communist party, authoritatively pronounced the "excommunication" of Veselovsky and his school. But the anti-Veselovsky witch-hunt continued in the Soviet press, and Soviet critics and journalists vied with each other in denouncing various manifestations of "comparativism" (which now became synonymous with "Veselovskyism") in literary history and literary criticism. *Lituraturnaya Gazeta* easily broke all the records in this respect, but even serious scholarly publications tried to keep pace with it. The denouncers were obviously eager to curry favor with those who shaped the literary party line on the higher level, but often were themselves denounced in turn, and no one could feel immune in the face of this inquisitorial competition.[9]

Here are some typical examples, chosen more or less at random, of accusations that were to be found in *Lituraturnaya Gazeta* and other Soviet periodicals during 1948 and 1949. Authors of the first volume of the new *History of French Literature* (published by the Academy of Sciences in 1946), a

---

[8] An. Tarasenkov, "Kosmopolity ot literaturovedeniya" ("Cosmopolitans in Literary Scholarship"), *Novy Mir*, No. 2 (1948), 124–37.

[9] Thus such critics as L. Subotsky, J. Altman, and A. Isbach, all of whom wrote articles against "servility before the West," were later branded in their turn as "rootless cosmopolitans." The examples could be easily multiplied, but the whole matter seems to pertain rather to the field of psychopathology than to that of literary history. Many of the critics attacked in 1948–49 must have recalled the skit which A. Raskin published in *Novy Mir* (No. 10–11, 1946) at the very beginning of the anti-West witch-hunt. It is in the form of extracts from the diary of a Soviet critic who, after waiting for two years and four months for his "indignation" to mature, attacks a book "according to all the rules of etiquette" and then discovers that the book was in fact good and his article a piece of "downright opportunism." The diary contained the "ten commandments" of a Soviet critic, among them the following: "1. Do not be the first to speak out! 2. Do not be the second! 3. Be the third! 4. Confess the mistakes of your fellow critic! 5. Quote! 6. Avoid appraisals! A cheap appraisal may cost you dear. 7. It is better to overblame than to underpraise. 8. If you have been smitten on your right cheek, protect the left." I do not know whether Raskin (himself a Jew) was involved in the subsequent purge.

joint effort of several leading Soviet scholars, were taken to task for constantly referring to the well-established fact of the influence of such French authors as Boileau, Molière, and La Fontaine on Russian eighteenth-century literature. A similar accusation was brought up against the joint authors (again all of them leading specialists in their field) of the new *History of English Literature*. Their crime consisted of mentioning the influence of Swift, Richardson, Fielding, and Sterne on Russian literature. They had even dared speak of Gorky's debt to Fielding—an unpardonable sacrilege![10] Boris Eichenbaum, author of some very good works on Tolstoy, was accused of regarding Schopenhauer, "that reactionary obscurantist," as Tolstoy's principal philosophical master and of looking to the French novels of adultery as one of the sources of *Anna Karenina*.

Authors of a program of courses for Soviet theatrical institutes were accused by *Literaturnaya Gazeta* of "insulting" the great Russian dramatist Ostrovsky by suggesting that in his play *Bez viny vinovatye* (*The Guilty Without Guilt*) he had used the well-worn device of "recognition" which he took from the Greek comedy via Molière and other European dramatists. A certain Veronica Motylevskaya, of whom nobody had heard before, detected dangerous "comparativist" tendencies in the standard history of the Russian theater by Vsevolodsky-Gerngross (first published in 1929). In an article in *Literaturnaya Gazeta* she described the author as "an idealist and a Formalist, an inveterate representative of the 'comparativist' school, . . . a true disciple and follower of Alexey Veselovsky and of Peretts, . . . a fierce, militant champion of foreign, and especially German, influence on the Russian theater." She accused him in particular of associating the origins of the Russian theater in the seventeenth century with the German troupe of Pastor Gregory—a fact that will be found even in most general textbooks of Russian history.

Even the authors of the officially approved *History of the U.S.S.R.*, by Pankratova and others (1947 edition), were found at fault in mentioning the influence of Leibnitz, Helvetius, Rousseau, Mably, Raynal, and other European thinkers on Alexander Radishchev.

No period in the history of Russian literature was left untouched by Zhdanov's witch-hunters. One of the most glaring examples of this literary inquisition was the case of V. Propp, whose book on the sources of magic folk tales was published by the University of Leningrad in 1946 and favor-

---

[10] Whether or not Gorky was influenced by Fielding, the fact remains that his famous article "O tom kak ya uchilsya pisat'" ("On How I Learned to Write"), written in 1932 was a glowing tribute to Western European literature and a frank acknowledgment of the influence exercised on him by French writers. He wrote there: "The real and deeply educative influence on me as a writer was exercised by the 'great' French literature—by Stendhal, Balzac, and Flaubert. I would very much like to advise the 'beginners' to read these authors" (*About Literature*, 215).

ably reviewed at the time by Zhirmunsky and others. But when the witch-hunt was in full swing, Propp's book was brought out of oblivion and its author put on the carpet. He was accused of quoting abundantly from such international authorities on folklore and anthropology as Frazer, Lévy-Bruhl, Boas, Kroeber, Frobenius, and others, and his book was indignantly compared to a London or Berlin telephone directory. His statement that folklore was essentially an international phenomenon was declared to be "un-Marxian" and "a survival of Veselovskyism." His whole conception, it was said, was vitiated by a complete "disregard for nations and classes."

An obscure Soviet critic, one Sergev Ivanov, attacked Leonid Grossman, author of a number of valuable studies of Dostoyevsky, Tyutchev, and other writers, for suggesting that in Lermontov's poetry can be traced many biblical and Oriental motifs.

There is no point in multiplying these examples. It is enough to say that "comparativism" in literary studies came to be regarded in the Soviet Union as a mortal sin. At least this is true so far as foreign influences on Russian literature are concerned. The comparative approach was permitted, however, in reverse, so to speak—that is, in order to demonstrate the influence of Russian, and especially Soviet, writers on Western European and American literature. Soviet scholars and critics were enjoined to study, for instance, the influence of Gorky on Jack London, Upton Sinclair, and Dreiser. In 1948 such a well-known comparativist as Grossman, cut off from his proper field of studies, published an article about the influence of Mayakovsky on Louis Aragon.

An important aspect of the Zhdanov inquisition is to be seen in the sinners' confessions and recantations, which in character and scope far exceeded anything that happened during the 1929–32 period, when Averbach tried to boss Soviet literature. Perhaps the most glaring example of this was the mass recantation of literary scholars accused of "Veselovskyism" in the big auditorium of the University of Leningrad in April, 1948. Zhirmunsky, Eichenbaum, Dolinin, Azadovsky, Propp, and others mounted the rostrum in turn and abjured their comparativist sins, renouncing their old and valuable works and promising to "reform." The most pathetic of all was the declaration made by Dolinin, whose book *V tvorcheskoy laboratorii Dostoevskogo* (*In Dostoyevsky's Creative Laboratory*, 1947), an interesting and stimulating study of the genesis of Dostoyevsky's novel *A Raw Youth*, had been attacked because of his "leniency" toward Dostoyevsky's "reactionary" views. Dolinin, who had devoted most of his career to the study of Dostoyevsky, making a valuable contribution to it, now announced his intention of "giving up" Dostoyevsky and turning his attention to Belinsky, Dobrolyubov, Chernyshevsky, and other "Revolutionary democrats."[11]

[11] A more detailed account of this remarkable university meeting will be found in my article "The Soviets Purge Literary Scholarship," *The New Leader*, April 2, 1949,

The campaign against rootless cosmopolitans reached the highest pitch of intensity during 1949, when literally dozens of literary and dramatic critics were purged. The peculiar feature of these new purges was the divulging of the critics' real names whenever they happened to use pseudonyms. By this process it was revealed that a great many of those who were specifically branded as rootless cosmopolitans bore Jewish names. Since at the same time certain Jewish cultural organizations were subjected to persecution for propagating Jewish cultural separatism and sympathizing with Zionism and the last Jewish newspaper was closed down,[12] it came to be widely believed outside the Soviet Union that the campaign against cosmopolitanism had a definite anti-Semitic cast. While it is not to be denied that in their campaign against the West the Communist rulers of Russia may have deliberately played on the anti-Semitic sentiments of certain sections of the Russian population, especially in the Ukraine (and this must be the explanation of the unprecedented practice of divulging the real names of Jewish critics), the three following facts must also be borne in mind: (1) many of those who were described as rootless cosmopolitans were not Jews; (2) there were also Jews among their accusers; and (3) other national minorities in the Soviet Union were similarly charged with harboring bourgeois-nationalist tendencies, and their cultural organizations were persecuted alongside the Jewish ones. Tatar and other writers were accused of idealizing their historical heroes, many of whom had been historical enemies of Russia, and of thus emphasizing their apartness. When the

---

8–9. One scholar against whom the charge of cosmopolitanism had been leveled and who did not turn up at the mass confession and yet apparently sent no "excuses" (he was then teaching in Saratov) was Grigory Alexandrovich Gukovsky (1902–50), a student of Veselovsky's and an outstanding specialist in eighteenth-century literature. His failure to repent had dire consequences for him. His name was struck off the roster of scholars; it was carefully removed from the 1951 revised edition of *The History of Russian Eighteenth-Century Literature* by his colleague D. Blagoy, who in the earlier edition had paid fulsome tribute to him; his own book on Pushkin and the Russian Romantics, published in 1946, was withdrawn from circulation (it was reissued only in 1966). His personal fate was not made known to the world at large; the man simply vanished. After his "posthumous rehabilitation" it was revealed that he had been "repressed illegally" in 1949, the year of the mass recantation, and had died in 1950. The circumstances of his death were never disclosed.

[12] Among the disbanded Jewish organizations was the Jewish Anti-Fascist Committee. One of its leaders, the great actor Solomon Michoels (1890–1948), director of the Jewish State Theater in Moscow, was posthumously denounced as a cosmopolitan. The Jewish poet Itzek Fefer (1900–52), who accompanied Michoels on his wartime friendship visits to the United States and Great Britain, was also involved in the anti-cosmopolitan purge and disappeared from the literary stage together with a number of other Jewish writers, including Peretz Markish (1895–1952). Some of them were later reported to have been "liquidated." It is now known that such was the fate of Michoels, too.

Russian Jews were accused of considering their literature as part of a general Jewish literature and not as one of the components of Soviet literature, it was a similar phenomenon, and its causes are to be sought not in any specifically *Russian* nationalism, but in the supranational Communist ideology. Whatever its actual anti-Semitic propensities, the Soviet government succeeded in cleverly disguising them. The notorious "plot" involving Jewish doctors, allegedly discovered not long before Stalin's death, was subsequently denounced as a fake and blamed on Beria, and Soviet writers were even permitted to touch upon its anti-Semitic implications.[13]

One of the most vicious attacks was delivered posthumously against Alexander Grin. In an article entitled "Propovednik kosmopolitizma. Nechisty smysl 'chistogo iskusstva' Alexandra Grina" ("A Preacher of Cosmopolitanism: The Impure Meaning of Alexander Grin's 'Pure Art' "), Victor Vazhdayev denounced Grin as a typical cosmopolitan and a worthless imitator of Edgar Allan Poe, Robert Louis Stevenson, and other writers. What Vazhdayev did not understand was that, even if Grin's romances were not great literature, for Soviet readers and for many a Soviet writer, Grin and his Grinland filled a sorely felt gap and that even a third-rate Stevenson (which is probably what Grin was) would have satisfied them. After 1956, Grin regained his earlier popularity, and his works began to reappear in large editions. This was a phenomenon akin to the growing popularity of science fiction in the post-Stalin period. But in the case of the latter, attempts were and are still being made to channel it into the service of Communism.

The anticosmopolitan theme naturally found its reflection in literature, in novels, stories, and plays. A typical example is a novel by a comparative newcomer to Soviet literature, Grigory Konovalov (b. 1908), entitled *Universitet (The University*, 1947). It portrays the life of students in one of the newer Soviet universities. Its hero, Ilya Kozharov, is a young scholar, a scientist turned philosopher, who sees his vocation in demonstrating the

[13] In view of the international implications of the postwar Soviet campaign against "cosmopolitanism," it is possible to presume that certain sections of the Jewish population appeared to the Communist rulers of Russia suspect from the point of view of their Western, and more particularly American, sympathies. It is also significant that many Soviet cartoons depicting "Wall Street warmongers" emphasized exaggerated Semitic facial characteristics. There were also anti-Zionist cartoons which in olden days might well have adorned the pages of some reactionary anti-Semitic publication. The political and international significance of the campaign launched by Zhdanov in 1946 on the literary front was later stressed by himself and by Georgy Malenkov, another member of the Politburo, at the first Cominform meeting in Poland in 1947. In his address there Malenkov said: "Kowtowing and servility before the West represent at this juncture a serious threat to our state inasmuch as the agents of international reaction are endeavoring to make use of people who are infected with the feeling of servility and kowtowing before the bourgeois culture for the purpose of weakening the Soviet state."

originality of Russian philosophy and its superiority over that of the West. By "Russian philosophy" he means primarily the revolutionary-democratic thought of Belinsky, Chernyshevsky, and Dobrolyubov, and the teachings of Russian materialistic scientists. When one of his elder colleagues writes an article about Belinsky, Chernyshevsky, and Dobrolyubov and entitles it "Russian Feuerbachians," Kozharov grows indignant. To describe these thinkers as Feuerbachians is to underrate their original contribution to Russian thought.[14] Some of Kozharov's colleagues, good Communists though they are, sound a little skeptical about his unqualified enthusiasm for Russian philosophy. A great friend of his, a chemist, asks: "But where are the philosophers? Stalin alone, but then he is an all-embracing genius. Name me at least one modern philosopher.... There are chemists, there are biologists, there are constructors, but where are the philosophers?" But the author's sympathy is obviously on Kozharov's side, and he shows him energetically sweeping through the university like a new broom and getting the better of his opponents.

This ideological theme of Konovalov's otherwise rather trite novel anticipated the attack which was launched in 1947 against Georgy Alexandrov, former head of the Red Army Propaganda Section, for his book on Western philosophy, in which he was said to have overrated the influence of Hegel and other Western philosophers on Russian thought.

The anticosmopolitan theme was also exploited by Simonov in his novel *Dym otechestva* (*The Smoke of Home Fires*, 1948), which, however, left Communist critics dissatisfied. But particularly numerous were the plays on this subject, since the theater was always regarded in the Soviet Union as an effective weapon of political propaganda. In Romashov's *Velikaya sila* (*A Great Force*, 1948) the main characters are two scholars. One of them, Lavrov, is a good Soviet patriot; the other, Milyagin, an admirer of things foreign. On his return from the United States, Milyagin is full of admiration for the American way of life. "They have comfort, they know how to live," he says. He also denies the existence of any specific Soviet science. For him science is international, universal; it "belongs to the whole world." In the end Milyagin is, of course, unmasked and removed. In A. Stein's play *Zakon chesti* (*Point of Honor*, 1948) the villain is a Soviet scholar, Professor Losev, who goes to the United States, is feted there, and agrees to sell the secret of his medical discovery (a pain-killing remedy).

---

[14] The influence of Feuerbach, a left-wing German Hegelian and a philosophical precursor of Marx, on the Russian "revolutionary democrats" was previously commonly taken for granted (among others, by Lenin). But the complete originality of Belinsky became the dominant theme of the vast 1948 jubilee literature about him. One Soviet critic went so far as to say that it was high time to stop speaking of Belinsky as a Westerner. Before a year had passed, this unfortunate critic (Johann Altman) was himself denounced as a rootless cosmopolitan.

He is exposed, however, by a colleague of his who accuses him of being ready to "cede the priority of Soviet science to an American firm." Soviet patriotism and vigilance triumph over "cosmopolitan machinations."

Some Soviet critics pointed out the many weaknesses of these plays, especially the unconvincingness of their "villains." For one of them (Efim Kholodov, pseudonym of M. Meyerovich), Milyagin was let off too lightly by the author. But less than a year later Kholodov himself was denounced as a rootless cosmopolitan and his pseudonym duly divulged.

Simonov's play *Chuzhaya ten'* (*Someone Else's Shadow*, 1949), represents a variant on the same theme. Here Professor Trubnikov, an old-fashioned individualist, communicates his scientific discovery—a means to put an end to epidemic disease—to his foreign colleagues. An old-fashioned humanist, he finds it somewhat difficult to believe his "vigilant" collaborators when they point out to him that he has committed a crime. But when it is explained to him that American scientists might avail themselves only of the first part of his discovery and breed microbes for use in future war, he realizes the "monstrosity" of what he has done.

Another cosmopolitan-minded scholar was portrayed by A. Sofronov in his play *Karyera Beketova* (*Beketov's Career*, 1949). Highly praised at first, this play was subsequently denounced as crude and unrealistic. But the anticosmopolitan theme continued to be regarded as topical and important and at the meeting of the Board of the Union of Soviet Writers in January, 1949, Fadeyev said: "Greatly mistaken are those who think that the fight against cosmopolitanism is but a short-term campaign. It is a war of principles and ideas which must be fought continuously and intransigently."

An impartial observer of the Soviet literary scene cannot help reflecting with dismay on the fact that not a single voice of dissent, let alone protest, was raised against this total subjection of literature to the line dictated from the party heights. Yet—as one subservient Soviet critic thought it appropriate to recall in 1947—when in 1925 the Communist party adopted its famous resolution on literary policy whereby a *modus vivendi* was established with the so-called fellow travelers, many writers openly disapproved of it and regarded it as an uncalled-for interference with literature.[15] But when Zhdanov died in 1948, all Soviet literary magazines carried glowing

---

[15] See L. Plotkin, "Partiya i literatura" ("The Party and Literature"), *Zvezda*, No. 10 (1947), 161. Plotkin referred specifically to Veresayev, who had expressed his regret that such pre-Revolutionary writers as Sologub, Voloshin, and Akhmatova were "doomed to silence" under Soviet conditions; to Andrey Sobol, who had written that "tutelage and art were incompatible"; to Ivan Novikov, who had said that the very notion of "guidance" in matters of literature was beyond his comprehension; and to Pasternak, who had "polemized with the resolution of the Central Committee with undisguised hostility, . . . maintaining that we were passing not through a cultural revolution but through a cultural reaction."

obituary tributes to him, and he was hailed as "the great, wise, exacting and benevolent friend of Soviet literature."[16]

Denouncing the "Decadent West"

Parallel with the unmasking of rootless cosmopolitans at home went the denunciation of the decadent bourgeois West, of the "Anglo-American imperialists" and "warmongers" and their "satellites." The memories of the wartime alliance against Hitler were quickly thrown to the winds, and the Western democracies were portrayed as the "capitalist environment," as the implacable enemies of the Soviet Union, plotting day and night for its destruction. If during the First Five-Year Plan, Soviet literature was placed in the service of industrialization, now it was openly made into a weapon of Soviet postwar foreign policy. The purely literary content of *Literaturnaya Gazeta* was reduced to a minimum, and it was filled instead with purely political articles in which Tikhonov, Simonov, Lavrenyov, Surkov, Gorbatov, and many others denounced the United States and Great Britain (and later Tito's Yugoslavia) and fulminated against President Truman, Ernest Bevin, Léon Blum, Jules Moch, and, later, Trygve Lie. Contemporary European and American literature was represented as rotten to the core.

The only exemption from the wholesale condemnation was accorded those writers who showed themselves friendly to the Soviet Union. As soon as this or that writer changed his attitude toward the Soviet Union to an unfavorable one, he lost favor with his Soviet admirers. Thus it was with Lion Feuchtwanger, Upton Sinclair, Sinclair Lewis, Richard Wright, and J. B. Priestley. The last was rather popular in the Soviet Union until his "Open Letter" to Ehrenburg (published in April, 1950), when Simonov denounced him as a "warmonger" for refusing to sign the Stockholm Peace Petition. Jean-Paul Sartre and Henry Miller took the place of Joyce and Proust as the incarnation of all that was evil in modern European culture. But whereas in the thirties there were at least some more or less serious studies of Joyce and Proust in Soviet magazines, sheer abuse was now the only recognized method of polemic. Sartre and Henry Miller and their followers were described as "spiritual lechers," William Faulkner as "flesh of the flesh of a decaying society." John Steinbeck's works were "putrid, lurid, and antihuman." Eugene O'Neill was "a degenerate." And no language was strong enough when it came to former Communists or former Communist sympathizers. Arthur Koestler was described by Ivan Anisimov as "a literary *agent provocateur*" whose writings "stank."[17] George Orwell

[16] See L. Plotkin, "A. A. Zhdanov i voprosy literatury" ("A. A. Zhdanov and Problems of Literature"), *Zvezda*, No. 1 (1949), 121.

[17] *Oktyabr*, No. 10 (1938). Before World War II, Anisimov specialized in Western European literature.

was called "a charlatan," a "suspicious individual," a former police agent and yellow-press correspondent who passed in England for a writer because there was "a great demand for garbage there." André Gide and André Malraux were also denounced as "renegades" and "American agents."

The anti-Western, especially anti-American, theme was exploited by Soviet writers to their hearts' content. Among the plays with such anti-American bias (to put it mildly) may be listed Simonov's *Pod kashtanami Pragi* (*Under the Chestnuts of Prague*, 1947) and *Russkiy vopros* (*The Russian Problem*, 1947)—the former about the liberation of Czechoslovakia, the latter about an American journalist who misinforms his public about the Soviet Union but later repents, with dire consequences to himself; Anatoly Surov's *Nezadachlivy galantereyshchik* (*The Ill-starred Haber-dasher*, 1948), a crude satirical comedy comparing President Truman to Hitler; and Lavrenyov's *Golos Ameriki* (*The Voice of America*, 1949), which is very violent in its denunciation of American "warmongers" but stresses the existence of "two Americas."

In *Ya khochu domoy* (*I Want to Go Home*, 1949), a play by Sergey Mik-halkov,[18] the British were the villains. This crudely sentimental play dealt with the fate of Soviet children in displaced-persons camps whom the British "refused" to repatriate. Both the British and the Americans were shown as treacherous, dishonest, and callous in Vitaly Sobko's *Za vtorym frontom* (*Behind the Second Front*, 1949).

In poetry too anti-Westernism became the staple theme. It was the key-note of Simonov's little book *Druzya i vragi* (*Friends and Foes*, 1948), in which he lashed out mostly at the Americans but made also a savage attack on Léon Blum. The book was an obvious but unsuccessful attempt to imitate the satirical invectives of Mayakovsky. The verse was crude and prosaic. Anti-Americanism also characterized a group of poems by Dolmatovsky entitled "Slovo o zavtrashnem dne" ("The Word About Tomorrow"), which were published in *Novy Mir* (No. 7, 1949). In one of these poems the poet visualizes a new Nuremberg trial which will take place in Moscow (apparently after World War III and a successful Communist revolution in the United States), when the "working class of America will stand by our side," when "neither prayers nor the Bomb will save our enemies," and when the new warmongers will follow in the footsteps of Ribbentrop and Goering. The "exhibits" before the court will include the atom bomb and "an engraved dollar bill—the coin of treachery." The judges—among whom will be Spanish prisoners, Chinese soldiers, and lynched Negroes—will pass a death sentence on the "warmongers," and "this will be the last execution on earth." In another poem Dolmatovsky refers to a mysterious

[18] Sergey Mikhalkov (b. 1913) was the coauthor (with El-Registan) of the new Soviet national anthem. He also wrote some good poetry for children and some clever political fables on topical subjects, imitating the great Russian fabulist Krylov.

explosion somewhere in Soviet Asia, designed to "move mountains" and to serve "as a warning to our enemies on foreign shores." This first poetic hint of the Soviet atomic explosion appeared in print a few months before President Truman's disclosure startled the world.

Anti-Western ingredients also played an important part in Pavlenko's novel *Schastye* (*Happiness*, 1947), which was awarded an annual Stalin Prize. Most of the action is set in the Crimea in 1945. There are chapters dealing with the background of the Yalta Conference of the Big Three, with glimpses of Roosevelt and Churchill. While Roosevelt, in accordance with the view assiduously fostered in the Soviet Union, is portrayed on the whole sympathetically, Pavlenko is much less kind to Churchill. One of the characters, a Soviet wine expert, is used by Pavlenko as a foil to an American visiting journalist, in order to demonstrate the superiority of everything Soviet over everything Western and to pour contempt on the Allies' conduct of the war. In the chapters dealing with the Red Army's march through Europe, the anti-Allied sentiments characteristic of 1947 are clearly voiced. In one scene Pavlenko introduces an American major who is obviously supposed to epitomize the spirit of the United States Army. For this officer, a peacetime businessman, war is just another chance of furthering his business interests. He boasts:

"I have adapted myself well to the front conditions. I always carry with me half a score of prospectuses and price lists and a dozen ready-made contracts. I hit upon it in Alexandria. . . . We flooded the Egyptian market with our goods, right under the enemy fire, so to speak. . . . In North Africa . . . we landed with ammunition and samples of merchandise—we captured towns and conquered markets all in one. In Italy the procedure was, naturally, still further improved. On my tanks I wrote in Italian: 'Buy SANIT soap, the best in the world.' "

The operations of the Allied armies during the final phases of the war are dismissed by Pavlenko in a few colorfully contemptuous sentences:

The Americans were hurrying toward the frontiers of Austria. The British were capturing, in the backyards of the war, some scared Nazi generals and singing praises, both in prose and in verse, to their "Monty," as though Montgomery's soldiers were the only ones on the battlefield.

Pavlenko's novel was first serialized in 1947 and was published in book form in 1948. Later Soviet writers, journalists, and military experts went even further in minimizing the contribution of their erstwhile allies to the common victory over the Germans. In April, 1950, the popular weekly *Ogonyok* published an article about Field Marshal Montgomery by Lev Slavin, author of the Civil War play *Interventsiya* (*Intervention*) and other works. The article, entitled "An Orderly as a Field Marshal," presented Montgomery as an "errand boy" of his American "bosses" and described the famous Dunkirk operation as "Hitler's miracle." According to Slavin, Hitler deliberately let the British escape in the hope of enlisting Great Britain's help against the Soviet Union.

Another minor Soviet writer, Gennady Fish, in a volume of anti-American propaganda entitled *Sovetskaya byl' i amerikanskie skazki* (*Soviet Facts and American Fairy Tales*, 1948), wrote of American Lend-Lease: ". . . the Americans sent us a bit of their harvest. Did their harvest not come from the seeds carried from Russia? So they did not give us a loan; it would be more exact to say they paid their old, old debt . . . of which we did not remind them."[19]

This systematic falsification of recent history reached its culminating point in a film called *Secret Mission*, with music by Aram Khachaturian, exhibited in Moscow in August, 1950. It showed Churchill revealing to the Germans in 1944 the secret of the coming Red Army offensive, which was to save the Allies from their difficulties in the Ardennes, and the Americans concluding a secret deal with Himmler.

It is highly significant that Soviet denunciations of German National Socialism and of Italian Fascism never reached the degree of frenzy and violence of this campaign against the democracies of the West, not even during the Spanish Civil War. Nor were Soviet writers ever made to participate so unreservedly in the anti-Fascist campaign as they were in the campaign against the "Anglo-American warmongers." Back in the thirties *Literaturnaya Gazeta* had still preserved its literary appearance; now at least one page of the four in each issue was almost wholly devoted to frenzied outbursts against the United States and its "lackeys," among whom Marshal Tito held a prominent place.

"Sowjetrussland über Alles"

"Cosmopolitanism," authoritatively wrote the leading Soviet philosophical review in 1948,

is a reactionary ideology which preaches renunciation of national traditions, contempt for the distinctive features in the national development of each people, and renunciation of the feelings of national dignity and national pride. Cos-

---

[19] Quoted by W. W. Kulski in "Can Russia Withdraw from Civilization?" *Foreign Affairs*, Vol. XXVIII (July, 1950), 631. In 1949 a book called *Vot ona Amerika!* (*Here She Is, America!*) was published in Moscow. It contained excerpts from the writings of Gorky, Mayakovsky, and Bill-Belotserkovsky (a Soviet playwright who at one time lived and worked in the United States and published a volume of *American Stories*), as well as from two Soviet journalists. The object of the book was to present the United States in as dark colors as possible. Mikhail Koryakov, a former Soviet journalist, pointed out in an article in *Novoye Russkoye Slovo* (New York) that extracts from Mayakovsky were carefully pruned of all more or less flattering references to things American. The book was suitably illustrated with drawings picturing various "horrors" of American life. The artist received a Stalin Prize of fifty thousand rubles.

mopolitanism preaches a nihilistic attitude of the individual toward his nationality—toward its past, present, and future . . . . The ideology of cosmopolitanism is hostile to, and in radical contradiction with, Soviet patriotism—the basic feature which characterizes the world outlook of Soviet man.[20]

If "Soviet patriotism" was thus proclaimed to be the basic feature of the new Soviet outlook, it was in turn based on the glorification of everything Russian. Russian superiority in every field of human endeavor was broadcast to the world, and Russian priority claimed for nearly every modern—and not so modern—invention.[21] The blowing of its own trumpet, in which the Soviet Union was indulging in those years was the necessary logical counterpart of the denunciation of the West, and was designed to boost Soviet patriotism and to build up the concept of a self-sufficient, superior world.

Soviet writers were expected to glorify everything Russian and to defend the honor of Russian science, just as they had to decry everything foreign. Such was the demand of the party line. Parallel with propagating in their works the idea of Soviet all-round superiority, they were carefully building up the myth of the prevalent anti-Western trend in nineteenth-century Russian literature and progressive thought, to the complete distortion of truth. This anti-Western mythology presided over the 1948 commemoration of the centenary of Belinsky's death and the 1949 sesquicentennial celebrations of Pushkin's birth. The narrow nationalistic approach to Pushkin, the complete denial of his essential "Europeanness," which characterized the 1949 jubilee literature, was particularly significant and contrasted sharply even with the 1937 Pushkin commemoration, although at the time patriotism had already become part of the official Soviet outlook. But it was then more broad-minded and did not imply a wholesale rejection of everything foreign, so that even in 1941 it was possible for Nusinov to describe Pushkin as "a European" and to say that he "continued and deepened Western culture" and could not conceive Russia's future "outside the Western paths." Six years later, as we have seen, these commonplaces were rigged up as dangerous heresies, and Nusinov was ostracized from literature.

[20] See "Protiv burzhuaznoy ideologii kosmopolitizma" ("Against the Bourgeois Ideology of Cosmopolitanism"), *Voprosy Filosofii* (*Problems of Philosophy*), No. 2 (1948).
[21] It was claimed, for instance, that book printing was known in Russia before Gutenberg.

Chapter 29. SELF-GLORIFICATION AND MIND CONTROL

Reappraising Soviet Literature

In their whitewashing of the historical past the Communist leaders of Russia sometimes got involved in inextricable contradictions. They were well aware of the risk of Soviet patriotism being confused with Russian patriotism and that of the good points of the "good old times" being exaggerated. From time to time writers were warned of these dangers. Immediately after the war there was a sharp revulsion from the indiscriminate hero worship practiced during the war. Writers were sharply reminded that it would not do to seek escape in historical themes, that such themes must be chosen with great discretion, and that it was imperative for them to pay more attention to contemporary Soviet subjects, to the portrayal of postwar reconstruction problems and of peacetime home-front heroes. A number of novels were, indeed, written in response to this injunction—some of them will be mentioned in a later section.

A characteristic echo of the overdoing of the historical-rehabilitation theme is found in the already mentioned novel by Grigory Konovalov, *The University*. After its hero, Ilya Kozharov, wins his academic battle and is appointed to supervise the work of doctoral candidates, he is shocked by the general trend of doctoral theses submitted to the faculty, their remoteness from the realities of the day, their concentration on minor issues of the past, and especially their lack of that

concretely historical, scholarly approach which we are wont to describe as party-mindedness. He just couldn't put up with it. In this respect one thesis stood out. . . . [Its author] was writing about poetry at the time of Peter the Great. . . . Coming across dithyrambs to Peter, Ilya could not help thinking: "All this was written not by a candidate who had lived in a Soviet family and studied in a Soviet school and was engaged in propaganda work at a factory, but by some sort of a Liberal."

Proceeding along this path, Kozharov thought, one might easily arrive even at whitewashing Nicholas I.

In 1949 the Soviet critic A. Leites published a study of university dissertations submitted during the preceding five years, pointing out that, while 212 of them dealt with Russian pre-Revolutionary literature and 158 with foreign literature, only 24 dealt with Soviet literature. Leites ridiculed the choice of subject for her dissertation of a certain T. Vasilyeva, who wrote about "the little-known English writer [Walter Savage] Landor." Referring later to this dissertation in his report at the conference of Soviet writers in January, 1950, Fadeyev said: "I also think that our young people could do for the time being without Landor." Apropos of another dissertation, on Rainer Maria Rilke and Russian literature, Fadeyev exclaimed: "And who is Rilke? An extreme mystic and reactionary in poetry."

Some thorny problems were also involved in the Soviet claim to the classical heritage of Russian literature. In 1948 an interesting discussion took place in the course of which Soviet literary historians and critics were reminded that the Soviet period of Russian literature must not be treated as just another link in a continuous chain of development (this was known as the "theory of a single stream"), that the October Revolution of 1917 represented a sharp break with the past and the beginning of a new era. In a report "On the Teaching of Soviet Literature in High Schools," read at a meeting of the Presidium of the Leningrad branch of the Union of Soviet Writers early in 1948, A. Dementyev and E. Naumov came out with a sharp attack on L. Timofeyev's standard high-school textbook of Soviet literature.[1] He was accused of the fundamental fallacy of regarding Soviet literature as part of modern literature, or "so-called 'contemporary literature' which continues the Russian classical literature of the nineteenth century," and of ignoring it as "a completely new phase in the development of Russian and world literature." Timofeyev was also accused of denying the very existence of a history of Soviet literature; for him, said Dementyev and Naumov, only a few Soviet writers existed, such as Gorky, Alexey Tolstoy, Mayakovsky, Sholokhov, and Fadeyev, but there was "no history of Soviet literature." The same accusation was leveled against the Russian literature curricula in Soviet universities. The authors concluded their report by suggesting that the literature curricula should be "refashioned" by the Ministry of Education "in such a way as to give Soviet literature its rightful place in schools" and that a new textbook of Soviet literature should be produced: "It must be competent, bright, and lively and must teach our youth to love the re-

---

[1] A shortened version of this report was printed in *Zvezda*, No. 3 (1948), 182–88, under the title "Uluchshit' prepodavanie sovetskoy literatury" ("Improve the Teaching of Soviet Literature"). The so-called theory of the single stream was mentioned again by Fadeyev in his 1950 report "On the Tasks of Literary Criticism," *Literaturnaya Gazeta*, February 4, 1950. He claimed that it had been successfully disposed of and that in doing so Soviet writers and critics had had to repeat that Dostoyevsky was a reactionary writer, that there were also reactionary sides to Tolstoy's work, that it was wrong to gloss over Chekhov's "apoliticalness," and that even Gorky had made big mistakes which he set straight "under the enormous ideological influence of Lenin and Stalin." At the same time Fadeyev made several thrusts at the well-known Hungarian Marxist critic Georg Lukács for "denying the possibility of Party guidance in literature" and for being too lenient to Existentialism and other hostile movements in the capitalist world.

markable Soviet literature—the most progressive, the richest in ideas, the most revolutionary literature in the world."

For many years the necessity of producing a competent and comprehensive *History of Soviet Literature* had been urged in official and literary circles. Before World War II a special committee was set up under the chairmanship of Alexey Tolstoy for this purpose, but it never made any real progress; and if we discount some textbooks for high schools, in which very few writers were discussed individually, there was no survey of post-Revolutionary Russian literature in the Soviet Union until after Stalin's death.[2] This was understandable inasmuch as the process of revision and obliteration of the recent past was going on all the time, and not only were well-established literary reputations suddenly questioned or blown to pieces but also a number of writers were constantly becoming Orwellian unpersons.

Most of these disappearances, both literary and physical, occurred in the late thirties, during the great purges associated with Yagoda, Ezhov, and Beria. But more names were struck out of the annals of Soviet literature during the postwar period. When Ilf and Petrov's *The Twelve Chairs* was reissued in 1948 after a long interval, *Literaturnaya Gazeta* took the publishers to task and said that had the authors been alive they would never have allowed their novel to be published without substantial revision. The book was then apparently withdrawn from circulation. Later the soundness of Bagritsky's romantic poetry was questioned, and particular aspersions were cast on his once popular work *The Lay of Opanas*. In 1949 even the validity of Mayakovsky for the new generation of Soviet poets came to be questioned, and there was a long and bitter controversy about him in *Literaturnaya Gazeta*. The argument was resolved in favor of Mayakovsky with the reminder of Stalin's verdict on him as "the greatest and most talented poet of the Revolutionary era."

When it came to writers who were still living, there was a tendency to keep silent about their past transgressions, but occasionally zealous watchdogs among the critics reminded them and their editors that "history is history" and that there was no use concealing certain facts—that even such eminent Soviet writers as Ehrenburg, Fedin, and Aseyev had written dubious or harmful works in the past and that Fedin, for instance, had belonged to the Serapion Brotherhood, the true "un-Soviet" nature of which was now exposed by Zhdanov.

---

[2] The latest survey of Soviet literature available to its students was Gorbachov's *Contemporary Literature*, the second edition of which had appeared in 1929. A new printing of it was dated 1931, although by that time Gorbachov had already been denounced as a Trotskyite and his book must have been withdrawn from circulation and made inaccessible in libraries (a usual procedure in the Soviet Union).

"Stalin the Great"

The picture of Soviet literature between 1947 and 1953 would be incomplete without another reference to the cult of Stalin the Leader (the Russian *vozhd'*—Leader—is, by the way, the exact equivalent of the German *Führer* and the Italian *Duce*). After the war this cult acquired unprecedented dimensions and penetrated deeply into Soviet literature. "The Greatest Man of Our Time," "the Teacher," "the Father of the Peoples," "the Coryphaeus of All Sciences," "the All-embracing Genius"—such were the titles which Soviet writers freely bestowed on Stalin. Parallel examples of such abject adulation would be difficult to find in modern history. There was hardly a novel, a story, a play, or a poem on a contemporary Soviet theme which did not illustrate this truly Oriental worship of the all-powerful ruler who is endowed with all imaginable qualities and faculties. A few instances should suffice here.

In Pavlenko's novel *Happiness*, the hero, Voropayev, is received by Stalin in Livadia, the former Imperial residence in the Crimea, during the Yalta Conference. The chapter describing their meeting is a real gem of Communist hagiography. When Voropayev, a Communist of long standing with an excellent war record, first saw Stalin at a little distance, "he could not budge—his legs did not obey him." Stalin was engaged in a friendly conversation with an old gardener and advising him to "experiment boldly" with grapes and lemons. The gardener looked at Stalin "in bewilderment and at the same time with a kind of childish admiration." This idyllic scene was interrupted by Voropayev's appearance, and suddenly Voropayev saw "with horror" (?) that Stalin

was going toward him, with outstretched arms, smiling his all-pervading smile. . . . Stalin was calm to the point of improbability. . . . Voropayev thought that Stalin had not aged since he had seen him last at the parade on November 7, 1941, but had changed sharply in a different sense. His face, still the same, familiar to its slightest fold, had acquired new features, features of solemnity, and Voropayev was glad when he noticed them. Stalin's face could not but change and become a little different, because the nation had changed and had become even more majestic.

Molotov, who happened to be present at the interview, though busy with diplomatic papers, helped Stalin and Voropayev break the ice. During the conversation Stalin of course revealed his warm and kindly nature, his interest in men, his amazing grasp of the situation.

The finale of the scene is quite priceless and deserves being quoted at least in part in Pavlenko's own words:

Moved infinitely by this soul-burning conversation Voropayev put his hand into the pocket of his greatcoat and, together with the handkerchief, pulled out and dropped on the ground the morning posy of snowdrops. . . .

[The posy had been given to Voropayev that morning by a little girl he met on the road "for Stalin." On hearing the story, Stalin ordered a basket of cookies for the girl and after it was brought dismissed Voropayev with a few encouraging words.]

And as he looked straight into Voropayev's eyes, his face seemed to sparkle as though a ray of sun had whisked across it.

The tone of Pavlenko's description, as though parodied from Tolstoy, makes the whole scene sound still more incongruous.

A different aspect of the Stalin cult will be found in I. Popov's play *Semya* (*The Family*, published in *Novy Mir*, No. 1, 1950). Here we have a deliberate attempt to enhance the historical importance of Stalin in the Bolshevik movement and to link him more closely than ever with Lenin. The action of the play takes place between 1886 and 1897, partly in Simbirsk during Lenin's school years and partly in St. Petersburg. The last scene shows a group of Social Democratic workers discussing the tactics of the labor movement and the strike that is breaking out in Petersburg, and the name of Stalin is introduced in a conversation between several Bolshevik party members as the name of someone who "at the other end of the country" follows the same line as Lenin, advocates the creation of a centralized workers' party, and "denounces without mercy everything that stands in the way to our great goal."

Just before the curtain falls Lenin himself makes a dramatic entry—he has just been released from prison—and Stalin's name is once more brought in:

Vladimir Ilyich . . . (*with sudden ardor*): And have you heard about Transcaucasia?
Voices: We know, we know! We have just heard it from Babushkin.
Vladimir Ilyich: But do you know all about Transcaucasia?
Voices: Stalin is there!
Vladimir Ilyich: Splendid. Ivan Vasilyevich, pass on my firm and friendly handshake to comrade Stalin.

The play ends with Lenin's announcing the coming foundation of "a great, powerful and unshakable party." But one is almost inclined to suspect that Mr. Popov wrote his play about Lenin with the object of outdoing his fellow writers and firmly affixing Stalin's star on the historical firmament alongside Lenin's as far back as 1897 (when Stalin was seventeen years old) —a matchless example of Communist mythmaking. At least, in reviewing the first performance of the play in *Literaturnaya Gazeta* (January 21, 1950), the novelist Vera Smirnova wrote: "Thus for the first time, at the cradle of the Party, are linked together the two great names dear to us."

When earlier works of fiction were revised by Soviet writers, one found inserted in them the previously absent references to Stalin. Thus, in Slonim-

sky's *First Years,* the revised version of *The Lavrovs* (see page 121), a conversation between two characters is introduced in which Stalin is mentioned
as Lenin's right-hand man in the October, 1917, coup d'état. Slonimsky also
took an opportunity to remove from *The Lavrovs* some disparaging references to Lenin and some complimentary ones to Plekhanov.

As for poetry, the poems and songs that sang and extolled Stalin the
Great in all the languages of the Soviet Union were countless, and few
were the poets who did not make their contribution to this treasury of
Staliniana. Among the more curious examples may be cited a poem by
Vsevolod Azarov entitled "Velikaya kniga" ("The Great Book"), published
by *Zvezda* in 1949 (No. 5). It is a twenty-four-line paean to the official
History of the Communist Party, in which "every word was created by
Stalin" and which is described as

> The simple, the great, the wise book,
> The immortal chronicle of our victories.

The Postwar Novel

That literature could still exist under the above-described conditions of relentless mind control from above and continuous mind reading by fellow
writers and critics is not a little surprising. Yet, in quantity at least, the output of the years that followed Zhdanov's bombshell is considerable, though
the quality is mostly very low. No more than a brief catalogue of the more
important works which appeared during this period can be given here.

Several of the older Soviet writers added to their output of novels. Among
them may be mentioned Fedin, Kaverin, Katayev, Ehrenburg, Grossman,
and Panfyorov.

Fedin   Fedin's two novels, *Pervye radosti (Early Joys,* 1946) and *Neobyknovennoe
leto (No Ordinary Summer,* 1948), were conceived as the first two parts of
a trilogy (the third part was added to them much later, in the 1960's). They
belong undoubtedly among the most important literary events of the
postwar period (the first of the two novels was written and even published
before the advent of the Zhdanov era). They are written in the nineteenth-
century tradition of social-psychological realism. A long span of time is
covered, and they introduce a great number of characters from different
walks of life, against the background of Russian life before and during the
Revolution.

In *Early Joys* most of the action takes place in Fedin's native town on the
Volga, Saratov, not long before the outbreak of World War I. The main
protagonist is Kirill Izvekov, shown first as a boy and then as a young man
whose political interests and concerns are awakened early and in whom the

reader can sense at once a future revolutionary. Of particular importance to him is his meeting and friendship with Ragozin, a workman and revolutionary who seems to have stepped out of the pages of Gorky's autobiography. Gorky's influence is also felt in the portrayal of the Parabukin family, to which belongs the future heroine of the novel. There is also another important female character, the daughter of a local merchant and Kirill's first love. In the hero's relationship with the two girls the personal and the class conflicts are neatly paralleled.

An important role in both novels is played by two representatives of the intelligentsia, the actor Tsvetukhin and the writer Pastukhov. Through the latter Fedin voices some of his own *earlier* attitudes toward the Revolution, his questionings and hesitations, as well as—in the first novel which is laid entirely in the pre-Revolutionary period—his views on art and on the writer's craft. There are also many episodic figures, and Fedin succeeds in creating a sufficiently varied picture of life in a large and prosperous Russian provincial city. The first part of the trilogy ends with the arrest of Kirill and Ragozin for their underground revolutionary activities.

In the second novel the action is confined to the summer of 1919. Kirill Izvekov is now a full-fledged Bolshevik, an army commissar happily married to Annochka Parabukina. Much place is given by Fedin to the inner evolution of Tsvetukhin and Pastukhov, who, unlike Fedin's earlier intellectual heroes Startsov and Karev, and like Fedin himself, end by accepting the Revolution, adjusting themselves to its demands, and reconciling it with their artistic vocation. In the case of Pastukhov this evolution takes a rather twisted course, and Fedin avoids simplifying or schematizing the issues. In a large measure Pastukhov must be seen as Fedin's alter ego, and the novel may be viewed as a sort of hidden confession by a capitulating intellectual.

Though lacking the freshness and novelty of style and composition of *Cities and Years*, both novels are examples of fine writing. The conservative trend in Soviet literature, with its reversion to the nineteenth-century tradition, may be seen in them at its best. This back-to-the-tradition element is particularly noticeable in *No Ordinary Summer*, whose period and setting (at the height of the Civil War, the "Unforgettable Year Nineteen," as it was sometimes called) are much the same as in *Cities and Years*. Unfortunately, even Fedin, whose reputation as a writer was well established, felt obliged to pay tribute to the Stalin myth and introduce a passage in which, contrary to historical evidence, the final defeat of General Denikin's White Army was credited to Stalin's genius, while Trotsky was shown as a traitor. In general, Fedin's handling of the Civil War lacks the color and the dynamic urgency of Sholokhov's. As Simmons has rightly pointed out in his study of Fedin, the latter "has little interest in the excitement of violence, in the thrill of a cavalry charge, or in the stirring spectacle of clashing armies."[3]

Kaverin   Kaverin's novel *Otkrytaya kniga* (*The Open Book*) in the course of writing also assumed the dimensions of a trilogy. The first part was serialized in 1949 in *Novy Mir*. A few years later appeared the second volume, entitled *Doktor Vlasenkova*, and this was followed in 1956 by a third volume, *Poiski i nadezhdy* (*Quests and Hopes*). As in Fedin's trilogy, the period covered extends from before the Revolution to World War II. The heroine of the novel (the story is told in the form of her own memoirs and diary) is a girl who becomes a famous Soviet bacteriologist. As in his *Fulfillment of Desires*, Kaverin introduces into the framework of a social-psychological novel elements of an adventure story. In the first part of the trilogy an important role is played by an old and eccentric doctor with a revolutionary past. To him is attributed an epoch-making discovery in virus bacteriology which for various reasons he cannot make public. After his death the heroine inherits his notes, and their disappearance plays an important part in the plot.

Kaverin's description of the life of Soviet students brought forth some sharp criticisms. *Literaturnaya Gazeta* published a letter from a group of Leningrad students who protested against the author's "one-sided" and "distorted" picture of Soviet youth as being interested only in love and other personal matters. Kaverin was therefore obliged to revise the first volume. The last volume, which was first published in the almanac *Literaturnaya Moskva* (destined to become an important landmark in the post-Stalin "Thaw") was criticized for a different reason. In it Kaverin made the husband of the heroine a victim of a false denunciation. He is arrested and sent to a concentration camp. At the time this was one of the most outspoken references to a previously forbidden subject. The final part of the trilogy belongs, in fact, to the post-Stalin period.

Katayev   Another work that was severely criticized on its appearance in *Oktyabr* was Katayev's novel *Za vlast' Sovetov* (*For the Power of the Soviets*, 1949). The novel portrayed the underground wartime activities of the Odessa partisans, whose headquarters were located in the famous catacombs under the city. Katayev introduced into it the two principal characters of his *The Lone White Sail*, the boys Petya Bachey and Gavrik, both of them middle-aged men now, Petya with a son of his own, very much like the boy hero of the earlier novel. The novel lacks the peculiar attraction of *The Lone White Sail*, but is well written and has an exciting story. The criticism of it came

[3] E. Simmons, *Russian Fiction and Soviet Ideology: Introduction to Fedin, Leonov, and Sholokhov*, 82. In subsequent editions of Fedin's novel the passage about "Stalin's genius" was removed.

from a fellow writer, Mikhail Bubennov, who wrote a letter to the editor of *Oktyabr* charging Katayev with minimizing, and even disfiguring, the role of the Communist party in the partisan movement. Several other critics chimed in somewhat belatedly, and at the plenary conference of the Board of the Union of Soviet Writers early in 1950 the novel was described as a "political blunder," and, like Fadeyev with his *Young Guard*, Katayev had to revise the novel. In its final form it constituted the last part of the tetralogy about the Bachey family, begun with *The Lone White Sail*, the other parts being *Khutorok v stepi* (*The Little Farm in the Steppe*, 1956) and *Zimniy veter* (*The Winter Wind*, 1960–61), dealing with the Civil War.

Grossman

The first parts of a long and ambitious war novel by Vasily Grossman, called *Za pravoe delo* (*For the Just Cause*), were serialized in *Novy Mir* in 1952. Its military focal point was the battle for Stalingrad, but it involved also various complex family and personal relationships. Some critics, including the writer M. Bubennov, attacked Grossman for "distorting" the picture of the war. A revised version of the first parts of the novel was published in 1954, but the sequel never appeared. Officially the novel is described as "unfinished," but there are reasons to suppose that the manuscript of the sequel was confiscated by the KGB in 1963, together with some other manuscripts (see also below, page 389).

Gladkov

Gladkov's main contribution to postwar literature was his three-volume autobiography, *Povest' o detstve* (*Story of My Childhood*, 1949), *Volnitsa* (*Free Gang*, 1950), and *Likhaya godina* (*Hard Times*, 1954). Although written in the third person, its autobiographical character is beyond doubt. Free from most of Gladkov's usual defects, it will probably come to be regarded as his most satisfactory work, forming in this respect a parallel to Gorky's autobiographical series. And the older writer's influence is felt in it very strongly.

Ehrenburg

Ehrenburg's two long novels, *Burya* (*The Storm*, 1948) and *Devyaty val* (*The Ninth Wave*, 1953), are frankly political. They constitute a sequel to *The Fall of Paris*, not only because they give a general picture of Europe and the world at large, first during World War II and then in the grip of the Cold War, but also because they bring back some of the major characters of *The Fall of Paris* and trace their fortunes in the rapidly changing world. In *The Storm* the action shifts from France to Russia and back. The characters include Soviet people from all walks of life, Frenchmen, British and American officers, and Germans. It is a colorful transposition of daily journalism into fictional terms. The narrative moves at a rapid pace, and Ehrenburg displays his knack for happy phrases and for a quick summing up of a situation, as well as his matchless ability to respond when necessary to the prevalent official line. As one of the Soviet critics who praised Ehrenburg's novel put it, speaking of his portrayal of the British and the Americans: "The reader unmistakably recognizes [in them] the familiar faces of people who have sold their honor, their conscience, and their opinions for those ringing dollars."[4] This was not, of course, Ehrenburg's attitude at the time of the events described by him (as may be seen from his wartime articles), but it did reflect accurately the official Soviet attitude in 1948.

The same is true of *The Ninth Wave*. It was written by Ehrenburg in his capacity as the Soviet campaigner for world peace, the role he assumed in the early fifties. The propaganda object of the novel is obvious: to portray the Soviet Union as the greatest force for peace and to expose the United States in all its iniquity by laying stress on all the seamy aspects of its life— racial discrimination, venality of politicians, general decline of morals, and so on. The events of the Cold War are presented in part through the spectacles of a French journalist, a kind of French Ehrenburg who begins to see the light and changes his skeptical, or even negative, attitude toward the Soviet Union to one of great admiration. Sympathies for the Soviet Union among the uncommitted European intellectuals are made much of, and the arguments of all sorts of "neutralists" are presented objectively. Scattered here and there are some sharply formulated negative views and judgments of the Soviet Union and its policies which Ehrenburg may or may not have shared but which are put into the mouths of "enemies." Nevertheless, they make strange reading in a Soviet novel.

The geographical range of the novel is very wide. The action takes place in Moscow and elsewhere in the Soviet Union, in Paris and in Prague, in Bonn and in the streets of American cities. While Ehrenburg knew Europe, and especially France, well and at first hand and portrayed its life and its people convincingly, his picture of the United States is a grotesque travesty and his portraits of Americans, especially of a senator and his daughter who are involved in large-scale anti-Soviet intrigues, are caricatures. There is also a one-sided picture of West Germany as a country well on the way to the inevitable revival of National Socialism.

Panfyorov   Fyodor Panfyorov's long novel *V strane poverzhennykh* (*In the Land of the Vanquished*, 1948), a sequel to his earlier *Borba za mir* (*The Struggle for Peace*, 1946–47), has an improbable, melodramatic plot involving the diversionary work of a young and beautiful Soviet girl among the Germans. The characters are equally unreal, especially the Germans, who are portrayed as vile and inhuman in the extreme.

[4] Dmitrevsky, in *Zvezda*, No. 6 (1948).

Of the newcomers to Soviet literature Vera Fyodorovna Panova attracted attention with her short novel *Sputniki* (*Traveling Companions*, 1947). This unpretentious tale, describing a group of people working together during the war on an ambulance train which evacuates the wounded from the front, struck a genuinely human note and was remarkable for its objective characterization and its detached tone reminiscent of Chekhov. Panova's next work, *Kruzhilikha* (1948; the title is the name of a factory), dealt with some problems of transition from wartime to peacetime conditions in Soviet industry, but Panova's chief concern was again with human beings and their relationships. Though not as good as the earlier work, it had the same quality of detachment and understatement. *Kruzhilikha* led to a curious and typical controversy, during which some critics blamed Panova for this very quality. One of them complained, with naïve earnestness, that Panova did not "decipher" her characters enough, that no sooner did the reader come to like a character than he discovered that the author meant that character to be a "negative" one, and vice versa, thus "shouldering upon the reader the responsibility for appraising her characters": "Why is Panova so merciless to good people as to floodlight all their shortcomings, making us several times change our attitude toward her characters and in the end remain perplexed? Why is she so kind to wicked people as to floodlight their slightest good characteristics?"

Literaturnaya Gazeta complained that at a critical discussion of *Kruzhilikha* the novel was used by some critics "to preach non-Party spirit in literature." The critic Munblit was quoted as saying that the principal charm of Panova's novel lay in the fact that "one cannot tell which character is positive and which negative. . . . I find it interesting to meet such imperfect people who change and toward whom my attitude changes." This, said *Literaturnaya Gazeta*, was the statement of an aesthete, "aimed at the principle of Party-mindedness in our literature." Although both of Panova's novels were singled out for Stalin awards, several critics maintained that her "detachment" was incompatible with Socialist Realism.

Panova's third short novel, *Yasny Bereg* (*The Clear Shore*, 1949), described life on a large state stockbreeding farm. She was awarded another Stalin Prize for it.

Other newcomers who attracted attention after the war were Mikhail Bubennov (b. 1909), Semyon Babayevsky (b. 1909), and Vasily Azhayev (b. 1915). Bubennov's *Belaya beryoza* (*The White Birch*, 1948) is a long and tedious war novel, with conventional characters and situations. Babayevsky received the Stalin Prize in 1948 and 1949 for his *Kavaler zolotoy zvezdy* (*The Knight of the Golden Star*) and its sequel, *Svet nad zemlyoy* (*Light over the Land*). The hero of the novels is a war veteran who returns to his native village and engages in collective farm work. These novels responded to the insistently voiced demand for the portrayal of postwar reconstruction and peacetime heroes and are characteristic examples of conscientious and orthodox Socialist Realism, of little literary distinction. The same may be said of Azhayev's *Dalyoko ot Moskvy* (*Far from Moscow*, 1948), which describes the heroic feat of the building of an oil pipeline in eastern Siberia within one year in 1941. The novel is naïve, long (over seven hundred pages), and formless.

Since the interest in contemporary Soviet themes was particularly encouraged at that time, six similar novels were awarded the Stalin Prize in 1949 (in addition to Babayevsky's *Light over the Land*, which had the distinction of a first prize). They were *Zemlya Kuznetskaya* (*The Land of Kuznetsk*), about the life of Siberian coal miners, by Alexander Voloshin (b. 1912); *Marya*, about women's part in collective farming, by Grigory Medynsky (pseudonym of Pokrovsky, b. 1909); *U nas uzhe utro* (*With Us It Is Morning Already*), about fishermen's life in southern Saghalien, by Alexander Chakovsky; *Ivan Ivanovich*, about an ordinary Soviet family in the Far North, by Antonina Koptyaeva (b. 1909); and *Bolshaya doroga* (*The Highway*), by Vasily Ilyenkov (b. 1897). On the other hand, only one war novel had the distinction of a Stalin Prize—*Vesna na Odere* (*Spring on the Oder*), which describes the last stages of the Soviet offensive against Germany, by Emmanuel Kazakevich (1913–62).

Boris Polevoy's *Povest' o nastoyashchem cheloveke* (*The Tale of a Real Man*, 1947), enthusiastically acclaimed by the critics, told the dramatic story of the adventures of one of the real heroes of the war, a Soviet airman who lost his legs in a forced landing but managed to crawl out of the enemy lines and later rejoined the air force. Polevoy's volume of sketches *My, sovetskie lyudi* (*We, the Soviet People*, 1948) was also based on true-life stories.

To the documentary literature about the partisan movement were added *V Krymskom podpolye* (*In the Crimean Underground*, 1947), by Ivan Kozlov (1888–1957); Leonid Korobov's *Malaya zemlya* (*The Little Land*, 1948), the impressions of a *Pravda* correspondent with Kovpak's army, supplementing Vershigora's book; and A. Fyodorov's *Podpolny obkom deystvuyet* (*The Underground Regional Committee Is in Action*, 1947).

The vogue for historical fiction continued after the war, even though writers were enjoined not to withdraw too much into the past. In postwar historical novels the stress was on the great military (and naval) exploits of the past. Typical examples are Leonty Rakovsky's *Generalissimo Suvorov* (1947); Marianna Yakhontova's *Korabli vykhodyat v more* (*The Ships Sail Out*, 1948), dealing with the Russo-Turkish War under Catherine II; and Alexander Yugov's *Ratobortsy* (*The Champions*, 1949), a long parallel novel about two Russian medieval princes, Alexander Nevsky and Daniel of Galicia. In Rakovsky's novel about Suvorov the anti-British bias is very prominent. The anti-American theme was exploited by Ivan Kratt (1899–1950) in his novel *Koloniya Ross* (*The Ross Colony*, 1950), about the Russians in California, with Colonel Rezanov as its hero.[5] There were also many historical, literary, and scientific biographies, permeated with anti-foreign spirit and designed to foster the sense of Russian national superiority. Typical of them is *Povest' ob ukradennoy idee* (*The Story of a Stolen Idea*, 1948), by Yury Weber, a biography of Alexander Popov, from whom Marconi is alleged to have stolen the idea of radio.[6]

The Drama

Many postwar dramas have already been mentioned in the sections dealing with the fight against the West and with new Soviet nationalism. These anti-Western and anticosmopolitan plays constitute the bulk of postwar dramatic production. To those that have been mentioned before may be added Nikolay Virta's *Zagovor obrechonnykh* (*The Conspiracy of the Doomed*, 1949) and Sergey Mikhalkov's *Ilya Golovin* (1949). The action of Virta's play takes place in Czechoslovakia and exposes the "intrigues" of the American "warmongers" in "People's democracies." Mikhalkov's drama denounces a cosmopolitan-minded artist. The same anticosmopolitan spirit colors many biographical plays about Russian artists, writers, and scientists. *Literaturnaya Gazeta* complained of the overproduction of these biographical plays and of the dearth of good plays on contemporary Soviet themes— a complaint of which Soviet leaders and critics never seemed to tire. One such topical play, *Ognennaya reka* (*River of Fire*, 1949), by Vadim Kozhevnikov (b. 1909), was praised by most critics until *Kultura i Iskusstvo* came down upon Kozhevnikov and his flatterers with a thundering article, denouncing his ignorance of Soviet life and of the technicalities of his subject (the play dealt with some new technological invention in Soviet metallurgy), as well as his conventional characters and pretentious style. With wonted alacrity, all Soviet critics, as well as fellow writers, took their cue from *Kultura i Iskusstvo* and began to speak of Kozhevnikov's play and its publication as "a big mistake."

Yet a look at the last page of *Pravda* or *Izvestia* of those days would show that most Moscow theaters were still showing pre-Revolutionary plays, either Russian or foreign. Thus, for instance, on March 7, 1950, *Pravda* listed plays by Gogol, Ostrovsky, Naydyonov, Goldoni, Oscar Wilde (*The Ideal Husband*), Shaw (*Pygmalion*), and so on, as against no more than two or three plays by Soviet writers, not one of them dealing with a contemporary subject. The inference seems inevitable that Soviet theatergoers preferred plays by Gogol and Goldoni, by Ostrovsky and Shaw, to plays about "Soviet realities."

[5] The same author's earlier novel about the Russians in Alaska, *Ostrov Baranova* (*Baranov's Island*, 1945), was free of anti-American bias.
[6] For the true facts of the case see C. Süsskind, *Popov and the Beginnings of Radio-telegraphy* (San Francisco, 1962).

Poetry

In poetry the deadening influence of the party line was particularly telling. Pasternak published no original poetry after 1945. Akhmatova, as we saw, after three years of enforced silence had to toe the line and extol in verse the Soviet peace campaign and even Stalin. Tikhonov, Bergholz, Aliger, and Inber wrote nothing that could match their war poetry. Simonov, who as late as 1947 had shown enough mettle to defend Margarita Aliger from those who accused her of writing poetry that was "too personal" and "despondent," confined himself after that to writing propaganda verse and plays with a strong anticosmopolitan bias. Prokofyev, Dolmatovsky, and Shchipachov (among whom Prokofyev is probably the only true poet, limited though his range is) were more than eager to conform to the latest party line and fell below even their prewar and wartime levels. Tvardovsky's long poem *Dom u dorogi* (*The House by the Road*, 1946) was written before the advent of Zhdanovism. Complementing his *Vasily Tyorkin*, it narrated the peregrinations and sufferings of a simple soldier's wife captured by the Germans and sent to a labor camp. Written in the same popular vein reminiscent of Nekrasov, it was refreshingly free from party politics, though orthodox in spirit.

The new stars to appear on the Soviet poetic horizon in the late forties were Nikolay Matveevich Gribachov (b. 1910), Alexander Yashin (pseudonym of Alexander Yakovlevich Popov, b. 1913), and Alexey Ivanovich Nedogonov (1914–48). All three were awarded the Stalin Prize, Gribachov and Nedogonov in 1948 for narrative poems about postwar collective farms, and Yashin in 1949 for his *Alyona Fomina*, another kolkhoz poem glorifying the work of women in collective farming. Gribachov showed a certain amount of sophistication and some influence of Mayakovsky and Pasternak, while Yashin drew very much of his technique from folk poetry. All three poems were greatly inferior to Tvardovsky's *Land of Muravia*, but while lacking true poetic merit, they made up for it by their "healthy," buoyant optimism and their heroic spirit. This was what had been expected of Soviet writers ever since Zhdanov's attack on pessimism and "morbid" preoccupation with personal problems and what they vied with each other to produce. All three poems also contributed to Stalin mythology, especially Nedogonov's *Flag nad selsovetom* (*The Flag over the Village Council*).

Literary Criticism and Literary Scholarship

After all that has been said in this chapter there is no need to explain why nothing of real value could be added, in those postwar years, to literary criticism, or why even literary research into the past was most unfavorably affected. In both, the theme of anti-Westernism and anticosmopolitanism effectively drowned everything else, and even the publication of literary documentation—a field in which much had been done in the Soviet Union in the first twenty years—was governed by the same bias. To give an example, three literary critics and historians were awarded the Stalin Prize of the second magnitude in 1949. The choice fell upon works that complied with the prescribed party line. One of them was Ermilov's revised version of a book on Chekhov. The revision consisted in bringing into due prominence Chekhov's deficiencies, especially his political neutrality. Another was Yakov Elsberg's book on Herzen, which, by stressing one-sidedly Herzen's hostility to bourgeois Europe, duly met the demands of the Zhdanov era. The third work awarded a prize was S. Makashin's study of Saltykov-Shchedrin.

The meaning of Socialist Realism, even after so many years of its enforced practice as the only admissible artistic method, continued to be a subject of heated discussion. In 1948 an attempt was made to bring Socialist Realism in line with Zhdanov's 1946 directives. For this purpose a volume of studies was published under the title *Problemy sotsialisticheskogo realisma* (*Problems of Socialist Realism*).[7] It contained, besides Fadeyev's address denouncing Veselovsky, an essay by Tamara Motylyova arguing the superiority of Soviet literature over that of the bourgeois world and Yakov Fried's paper on decadent European literature.[8] There was also a long essay by B. Byalik on Gorky and Socialist Realism,[9] in which Gorky's thesis about Socialist Realism as a combination of realism and revolutionary romanticism was revamped and developed. This led to a further rather futile debate on this stale subject. The consensus went against Byalik—for the time being, romanticism was still in discredit. Byalik was accused of having misunderstood and misinterpreted Gorky's view.

There is no need to go into the details of that controversy here. Some interest attaches, however, to an article by A. Belik, a minor critic who

---

[7] A reference to this volume has been made earlier in connection with Fadeyev's attack on Veselovsky.

[8] "Sotsialisticheskiy realizm i sovremennaya dekadentskaya literatura" ("Socialist Realism and Modern Decadent Literature"), 347–93. This is a comparatively serious, though biased, study of certain trends in modern European literature, without any attacks on "American warmongers" and without a specific anti-American bias, most of the writers discussed being French or British. There are, of course, inevitable references to Proust, Joyce, Dos Passos, and Sartre, but a number of other writers are brought in, too, as "decadent," among them Paul Valéry, François Mauriac, Valery Larbaud, Jean Giraudoux, Henry de Montherlant, André Gide, Jules Romains, Julien Benda, André Malraux, Albert Camus, André Breton, Romain Gary, Franz Kafka, Stephen Spender, Edwin Muir, and William Faulkner. To these "decadents" the author opposed Soviet writers and a few Western "progressives," such as Romain Rolland, Theodore Dreiser, J. B. Priestley, Jean-Richard Bloch, Jean Cassou, Louis Aragon, and Paul Eluard. It was obvious that the principal criterion of "progressivity" was the writer's Soviet sympathies, and soon thereafter the name of J. B. Priestley was struck off this list.

[9] "Gorky i sotsialisticheskiy realizm," 115–16.

managed to survive the anticosmopolitan purge.[10] Belik said that he was
interested not in what had been achieved by Soviet literary scholars but in
"what has not yet been done or what is being done in a wrong way." Soviet
literary scholars lagged behind life because they had failed to grasp fully
Lenin's teaching. Belik laid much of the blame at the door of Georgy
Alexandrov, whose book on Western philosophy, even though denounced
by Zhdanov and the party, continued to exercise a baneful influence. Several
well-known Soviet literary scholars and critics were said to share with
Alexandrov his sin—that of "vicious objectivism." Among those named by
Belik were Kirpotin, Tarasenkov, Belchikov, Isaac Lezhnev (in his book
on Sholokhov), Veksler (in his book on Alexey Tolstoy), and Timofeyev
(in his *Theory of Literature*).

Even such a party stalwart as Egolin (1896–1959), who had been a faithful
supporter of Zhdanov, was attacked by Belik.[11] Belik appealed to Stalin's
supreme authority in literary matters and advised literary scholars and
critics to take guidance from the recently published letters of Stalin to
Gorky and to Felix Kohn, in which all the problems facing Soviet literature
had been neatly solved. It was Lenin and Stalin, said Belik, who had "laid
down the firm theoretical foundations of Socialist literature by formulating
the principle of Party-mindedness as the fundamental law of Socialist
Realism." With the aid of some quotations from Lenin and Stalin, Belik
wound up by frankly equating Socialist Realism with "Party-minded attitude toward Socialist realities." It was clear, therefore, said Belik, that by no
means everything published in the Soviet Union was in accord with
Socialist Realism. As an example of a work that came short of the mark
Belik cited Katayev's *For the Power of the Soviets*. He also attacked the
critic Tarasenkov for his broad interpretation of Socialist Realism as allowing of "different literary techniques"[12] and reminded his readers that as late
as 1945 Tarasenkov had praised Pasternak as a true Soviet poet. While not
denying that writers were free to follow "different creative paths," Belik
suggested that if Socialist Realism was "the true and dominant method of
Socialist literature" then "there must exist techniques, media of expression,
laws of composition, of the plot, of image building, and so on, which

[10] "O nekotorykh oshibkakh v literaturovedenii" ("About Certain Mistakes in
Literary Scholarship"), *Oktyabr*, No. 2 (1950), 150–64.

[11] In 1946, Egolin had been entrusted with the reorganization of Zvezda. In 1948
his lecture pamphlet *Za vysokuyu ideynost 'sovetskoy literatury (For the High Ideological Content of Soviet Literature)* was given wide publicity as an authoritative statement of the official party line in literature (there was an American edition of it). An
earlier work by Egolin, *Osvoboditelnye i patrioticheskie idei russkoy literatury XIX
veka (The Ideas of Liberation and Patriotism in Nineteenth-Century Russian Literature*, 1946), was criticized by Belik for its "cryptoliberalism."

[12] In his book *Idei i obrazy sovetskoy literatury (Ideas and Images in Soviet Literature)*.

correspond to that method," just as, conversely, "there exist techniques, media of expression, and so on, which contradict Socialist Realism."

Belik was probably too frank in his equation of Socialist Realism with party-mindedness, too blatant and tactless in his Stalinist zeal. Before long his article came under the fire of the big guns of party leadership. On March 31, 1950, *Kultura i Zhizn'* printed an editorial accusing Belik of attempting to go back to the evil days of RAPP and Averbach. No more was heard of Belik. His name does not figure in *The Short Literary Encyclopaedia*. But, as time went on, party-mindedness came to be invoked more and more often, alongside Socialist Realism, as one of the mainstays of Soviet art.

The full story of the persecution of "rootless cosmopolitans" and of its connection with the over-all policies of the Soviet government during the last years of Stalin's rule is still to be written and unraveled. It seemed to abate after 1949, but there was another flare-up in 1951–52, this time with clear anti-Semitic overtones. A number of prominent Jewish writers (Markish, Fefer, Bergelson, Hofstein, Kvitko, and others) were arrested and apparently liquidated. It seems to be no coincidence that for all those named above 1952 is given as the year of their deaths.[13]

The episode culminated in the notorious "Jewish doctors' plot" to do away with prominent Soviet leaders by poisoning them. The discovery of this "plot" was officially announced on January 13, 1953, and that announcement became the "signal for the opening of an all-out campaign against foreign and domestic enemies," with much of the blame being put on the United States as the real force behind the "plotters."[14] It is impossible to say what would have been the outcome of this affair had not Stalin died two months later. The "doctors' plot" found a reflection in Ehrenburg's *Ottepel* (*The Thaw*), one of the first important fiction works of the post-Stalin period. References to it, together with an effective general picture of the Zhdanov period, will also be found in Vasily Grossman's short "novel" *Vsyo techot* (*Everything Flows*), written between 1955 and 1963 and smuggled out of Russia in 1970. It is the first known work by a Soviet writer in which Lenin is denounced as the "murderer of Russian freedom" (and of the true democratic revolution): Stalin merely continued Lenin's work. A more detailed analysis of Grossman's "novel" will be presented in the sequel to this book.

[13] The article on modern Jewish literature in Russia by G. Remenik in *The Short Literary Encyclopaedia* speaks of "the heavy blow dealt to Jewish literature during the period of the cult of Stalin's personality" and describes those writers as innocent victims of repression.

[14] See Boris I. Nicolaevsky, *Power and the Soviet Elite*, 151.

Part VIII. Conclusion

Part VII. Conclusion

Chapter 30. LOOKING TOWARD THE THAW

The six years which preceded the death of Stalin—the period associated with the name of Andrey Zhdanov, although the bearer of that name had died long before this period was over—were the most barren years in the history of Soviet literature, literary criticism, and literary scholarship.[1] During this period strict adherence to Socialist Realism—tantamount in practice to an undeviating toeing of the current party line—was expected of artists in every field of creative endeavor. Rigid thought control was exercised by the party. An impenetrable iron curtain was lowered to shut off the Soviet Union from "pernicious" influences seeping through from the "decadent" bourgeois West. Denunciations of "rootless cosmopolitans" in literature and other fields of cultural activity became an everyday occurrence and were followed either by abject recantations or by disappearances from the literary, artistic, or academic scene. Gloom and darkness had descended upon Soviet art and letters. The literary output of those years was marked by drab uniformity.

Certain misgivings about this state of affairs in Soviet literature began to be voiced before Stalin's death. In 1952, *Pravda* initiated a debate about what came to be known as "theory of conflictlessness." Soviet writers, particularly the playwrights, were accused of holding the erroneous view that in the period of transition from Socialism to Communism there was no longer any room for social conflicts and contradictions and that therefore a new type of dramatic literature was demanded. They were reminded that there were still enough survivals of capitalism in the consciousness of the Soviet man, that conditions were still far from ideal in the Soviet Union, that there was enough evil in Soviet life and plenty of "negative" characters. "We need not fear showing up our shortcomings and difficulties. We need Gogols and Shchedrins," wrote *Pravda*.[2] In his report to the Nineteenth Congress of the Communist party at the end of 1952, this theme was de-

---

[1] When Zhdanov died, *Literaturnaya Gazeta* published (on September 1, 1948) an editorial in his memory entitled "A Friend of Soviet Writers." The University of Leningrad was renamed for him. Until quite recently the First State Printing Office in Moscow bore his name. His name does not, however, figure in the *Short Literary Encyclopaedia* although he deserves a place in it because of his nefarious role in postwar literature.

[2] "Preodolet' otstavanie dramaturgii" ("To Overcome the Lagging Behind of Dramaturgy"), *Pravda*, April 7, 1952.

veloped at some length by Georgy Malenkov, who at that time appeared to be Stalin's second-in-command and successor-designate.

Several Soviet writers responded with wonted alacrity to this official demand for satirical works. Sergey Mikhalkov wrote a play, called *Raki* (*The Crayfish*), in which he deliberately transposed the characters of Gogol's *The Government Inspector* into contemporary Soviet life and setting. In another satirical play, *Gosti* (*The Guests*), Leonid Zorin (b. 1924) exposed the would-be classless Soviet society by portraying in the blackest possible colors the new, degenerate upper stratum of Soviet bureaucracy. A similarly satirical exposé of the seamy side of Soviet life and society was to be found in such plays as *Bolshie khlopoty* (*Great Cares*), by Leonid Lench (pseudonym of Leonid Sergeevich Popov, b. 1905), and *Nasledny prints* (*The Heir Apparent*), by Anatoly Marienhof (1897–1962), a former friend of Esenin's and a fellow leader of Imaginism. As had happened more than once before, although written in response to an official demand, most of these plays were soon attacked for overdoing the satire and slandering the Soviet society. This was the case with the plays by Zorin and Marienhof. In a retrospective appraisal of this rebirth of satirical literature the officially sponsored *Outline History of Soviet Literature*, published in 1955, spoke of those plays as being inspired by "petit bourgeois" sentiments and going out of their way to portray with gusto the alleged evils of Soviet life under the cover of exposing its negative aspects.[3]

When Stalin died on March 5, 1953, Soviet writers shared outwardly in what was at the time presented to the outside world as the unanimous grief of the Soviet people for their "Great, Beloved Leader and Teacher." In their April, 1953, issues, Soviet literary magazines carried poems by Russian and non-Russian Soviet poets, as well as by some poets from the so-called People's Democracies, voicing their deep sorrow. One of the characteristic features was the absence of any truly personal element. Stalin's name was hardly ever mentioned; these poems seemed to have been written about some impersonal, abstract, lofty being. And, just as during the last year of Stalin's life, there was in them a tendency to deification. In one of the typical poems Nikolay Aseyev spoke of the light which "*he*" had lit for thousands of years to come and which would never be extinguished.

In the April issue of *Novy Mir* appeared a selection of opinions about Stalin expressed by famous writers of different nationalities. The list included Gorky, Alexey Tolstoy, Romain Rolland, Barbusse, Louis Aragon, and Martin Andersen-Nexö. In the same issue Fadeyev paid a short tribute to Stalin, describing him as "the greatest humanist the world ever knew."[4]

---

[3] *Ocherk istorii russkoy sovetskoy literatury, ii,* 305.

[4] A. Fadeyev, "Gumaniszm Stalina" ("Stalin's Humanism"), *Novy Mir,* No. 4 (1953), 167. The verse tributes to Stalin in the same issue included poems by such well-known poets as Aseyev, Aliger, and Tvardovsky.

Who could have foreseen then that in less than three years' time Stalin would be denounced as a tyrant and dethroned, while a little later the author of that tribute, one of Zhdanov's faithful literary henchmen and—who knows?—perhaps a sincere admirer of Stalin, would take his own life?

But the literary wake for Stalin, on the whole, not only lacked sincerity and spontaneity—it was also short-lived. Before long, adapting themselves to the new regime and the newly proclaimed slogan "Collective Leadership," poets began to extol the party and its collective brains.[5] At the same time the first signs of a change in the literary weather became discernible. The long Zhdanovite winter was to give place to the Thaw. A new period in Soviet literature began in 1953.

[5] See, for example, a poem by Gleb Pagiryov in the August, 1953, issue of *Novy Mir.*

BIBLIOGRAPHY

Section I of this bibliography lists those book-length works referred to in the footnotes, as well as a few selected articles of unusual significance.

In Section II are listed important and useful bibliographical sources of both a general and a specific nature, in Russian and in the principal Western languages. Information about all books published in the Soviet Union may be obtained from the monthly *Knizhnaya Letopis* (*Book Records*), issued by the State Publishing House, Moscow.

Section III contains a selective bibliography of the major general works about Russia, her history, her culture, and her social life and similar works on the Soviet Union. Only works in English, including translations from Russian and other languages, have been included. In making the selection from what is a vast and rapidly growing body of secondary literature of unequal value, I paid special attention to those works, irrespective of their points of view, which have a bearing on the facts and issues discussed in this book. With a few exceptions, only works published before 1963 have been included in this section.

Section IV is divided into two subsections: *A*, a descriptive note on works in Russian; and *B*, as nearly complete a list as possible of works available in English which deal with Soviet literature before 1953. Articles and papers published in periodicals have not been included, but a note has been added, listing the most important Western periodicals in which such articles will be found. A few of the more important works in languages other than English have also been included.

Section V represents the most nearly complete listing available to date of Soviet literature in English translations—again, of works published before 1953. Those published later, even though written earlier, are not included. They will be discussed in the sequel to this book. Whenever possible, account has been taken of both American and British editions, but no attempt has been made to include systematically all the translations published by the Foreign Languages Publishing House in Moscow. Some of its editions paralleled those published in the West, but there were also many others, mostly of works by minor writers. For the list in this section I relied heavily on the bibliographies of Philip Grierson and A. Attlinger and J. Gladstone, as well as on those published subsequently. No attempt has been made to list translations of Soviet authors which appeared in periodicals, nor have the stories included in various anthologies and collections been listed separately, though in many cases the names of the authors thus included are given in brackets. When the title of the English translation differs considerably from the Russian, the exact English rendering of the original title is supplied in brackets. In the case of some of the major Soviet writers, including literary critics and scholars who are mentioned in the book, their nonfictional works (critical, autobiographical, and so on) have also been included. The same

396

applies to the authors of some documentary books about World War II which are often mentioned in the text.

The names of publishing houses in bibliographical references to works published in the Soviet Union have been omitted, other than the Foreign Languages Publishing House, for publications in English. Except for a short period in the early 1920's all those houses were and are part of the vast state publishing complex, and there is little point in distinguishing among them.

SECTION I. BOOKS CITED IN FOOTNOTES

Akhmatova. *Sochineniya* (*Works*). 2 vols. [Washington, D.C.], Inter-Language Literary Associates, 1965–68. Vol. I, Intro. in English by G. Struve, Intro. in Russian by B. Filippov, 1965; 2d ed., rev. and enl., 1967. Vol. II, Intro. in English by A. Rannit, Intros. in Russian by V. Frank and B. Filippov, Appendix by N. Struve, "Vosem' chasov s Annoy Akhmatovoy" ("Eight Hours with Anna Akhmatova"), 1968.

Antologiya russkoy sovetskoy poèzii v dvukh tomakh: 1917–1957 (*An Anthology of Soviet Russian Poetry in Two Volumes: 1917–1957*). Moscow, 1957.

Balukhaty, S. *Teoriya literatury. Annotirovannaya bibliografiya. I. Obshchie voprosy* (*Theory of Literature: An Annotated Bibliography. I. General Problems*). Leningrad, 1929.

———, and K. Muratova. *M. Gorky. Spravochnik* (*M. Gorky: A Reference Guide*). Leningrad, 1938.

Barghoorn, F. C. *The Soviet Image of the United States: A Study in Distortion.* New York, Harcourt, Brace, 1950.

Bely, A. *Masterstvo Gogolya* (*Gogol's Craftsmanship*). Leningrad, 1934.

———. *Ritm kak dialektika i "Medny Vsadnik." Issledovanie* (*Rhythm as Dialectics and "The Bronze Horseman": A Research Study*). Moscow, 1929.

Berberova, N. *The Italics Are Mine.* Auth. trans. by Philippe Radley. New York, Harcourt, Brace and World, 1969.

Berkovsky, N. *Tekuschaya literatura* (*Current Literature*). Moscow, 1930.

Borland, H. *Soviet Literary Theory and Practice During the First Five-Year Plan: 1928–1923.* New York, King's Crown Press, 1950.

Brodsky, N. L., V. Lvov-Rogachevsky, and N. P. Sidorov, eds. *Literaturnye manifesty* (*Literary Manifestoes*). Moscow, 1929.

Brown, E. J. *The Proletarian Episode in Russian Literature: 1928–1932.* New York, Columbia University Press, 1953.

———. *Russian Literature Since the Revolution.* New York, Collier Books, 1963; 2d ed., 1968.

Bukharin, N. *Poèziya, poètika i zadachi poèticheskogo tvorchestva v SSSR* (*Poetry, Poetics and Tasks of Poetic Creation in the U.S.S.R.*). [Moscow], 1934.

Byalik, B., ed. *Problemy sotsialisticheskogo realizma* (*Problems of Socialist Realism*). Moscow, 1948.

Chukovsky, K. *Aleksandr Blok kak chelovek i poèt* (*Alexander Blok as Man and Poet*). Petrograd, 1924.

———. *Repin. Gorky. Mayakovsky. Bryusov. Vospominaniya* (*Repin, Gorky, Mayakovsky, Bryusov: Memoirs*). Moscow, 1940.

————, ed. Introduction to Walt Whitman, *Listya travy* (*Leaves of Grass*), Leningrad, 1935.

————, ed. "Uitman i Mayakovsky" ("Whitman and Mayakovsky"), in Walt Whitman, *Izbrannye stikhotvoreniya i proza* (*Selected Poems and Prose Writings*). Moscow, 1944.

Chuzhak, N. F., ed. *Literatura fakta. Pervy sbornik materialov rabotnikov LEF'a* (*Literature of Fact: The First Collection of Materials of the Workers of LEF*). Moscow, 1929.

Counts, G. S., and N. Lodge. *The Country of the Blind: The Soviet System of Mind Control*. Boston, Houghton Mifflin, 1949.

Dymshits, A. L., and O. V. Tsekhnovitser, eds. *Vladimir Mayakovsky. Sbornik I. Vladimir Mayakovsky: Collection I.* Moscow-Leningrad, 1940.

Eastman, M. *Artists in Uniform: A Study of Literature and Bureaucratism*. London, Allen & Unwin, 1934; New York, Knopf, 1934.

Egolin, A. M. *Osvoboditelnye i patrioticheskie idei russkoy literatury XIX veka* (*The Ideas of Liberation and Patriotism in Nineteenth-Century Russian Literature*). [Leningrad], 1946.

————. *Za vysokuyu ideynost' sovetskoy literatury* (*For the High Ideological Content of Soviet Literature*). Moscow, 1946. In English: *The Ideological Content of Soviet Literature*. Trans. by M. Kriger. Washington, D.C., Public Affairs Press, [1948].

Engelhardt, B. *Formalny metod v istorii literatury* (*The Formal Method in the History of Literature*). Leningrad, 1927.

Ermolaev, H. *Soviet Literary Theories, 1917–1934: The Genesis of Socialist Realism*. Berkeley and Los Angeles, University of California Press, 1963.

Fadeyev, A. *Literatura i zhizn'* (*Literature and Life*). [Moscow], 1939.

————. *Stolbovaya doroga proletarskoy literatury* (*The Highway of Proletarian Literature*). Leningrad, 1929.

Fedin, K. *Gorky sredi nas* (*Gorky in Our Midst*). Chast' 1. Dvadtsatye gody (Part I: *The Twenties*), 1943. Chast' 2. *Kartiny literaturnoy zhizni, 1921–1928* (Part II: *Pictures of Literary Life, 1921–1928*), 1944.

————. *Gorky sredi nas. Kartiny literaturnoy zhizni.* (*Gorky in Our Midst: Pictures of Literary Life*). Moscow, 1968.

————. *Tvorchestvo Konstantina Fedina. Statyi. Soobshcheniya. Documentalnye materialy. Vstrechi s Fedinym. Bibliografiya.* (*The Work of Konstantin Fedin: Articles, Communications, Documentary Materials, Meetings with Fedin, Bibliography*). Moscow, 1966.

Gayev, A. *Tsenzura sovetskoy pechati* (*Censorship of the Soviet Press*). Munich, Institute for the Study of the U.S.S.R., 1955.

Glinka, G. *Na Perevale* (*At the Pass*). New York, Chekhov Publishing House, 1954.

Gorbachov, G. *Ocherki sovremennoy russkoy literatury* (*Studies of Contemporary Russian Literature*). 2d enl. ed. Leningrad, 1925.

————. *Sovremennaya russkaya literatura* (*Contemporary Russian Literature*). 2d ed., rev. and enl. [Leningrad], 1929.

Gorbov, D. *Poiski Galatei* (*In Search of Galatea*). Moscow, 1928.

Gorky, M. *O literature. Statyi i rechi 1928–1936* (*About Literature: Articles and Addresses, 1928–1936*). Moscow, 1937. In English (incomplete): *Literature and Life: A Selection from the Writings of Maxim Gorki*. Trans. by Edith Bone. London and New York, Hutchinson International Authors, 1946.

Gumilyov, N. *Sobranie sochineniy* (*Collected Works*). 4 vols. Ed. by G. Struve and B. Filippov. Washington, D.C., Victor Kamkin, Inc., 1962–68.

Harvard Slavic Studies, Vol. I. Cambridge, Harvard University Press, 1953. [Gorky's letters to V. F. Khodasevich, tr. and ed. by H. McLean.]

Herling, G. *Da Gorki a Pasternak: Considerazioni sulla letteratura sovietica.* Rome, 1958.

Ivanov-Razumnik, R. *Pisatelskie sudby* (*Writers' Destinies*). New York, Literaturny Fond, 1951.

Jackson, R. L. *The Underground Man in Russian Literature*. The Hague, Mouton, 1958.

Jakobson, R. *Noveyshaya russkaya poeziya* (*Recent Russian Poetry*). Prague, 1921.

Karlinsky, S. *Marina Cvetaeva: Her Life and Art*. Berkeley and Los Angeles, University of California Press, 1966.

Katanyan, V. *Mayakovsky. Literaturnaya khronika* (*Mayakovsky: A Literary Chronicle*). 4th ed. Moscow, 1956.

Kaun, A. *Soviet Poets and Poetry*. Berkeley and Los Angeles, University of California Press, 1943.

Kaverin, V. *The Unknown Artist* [in the same volume with *Envy*, by Yu. Olesha]. Trans. by P. Ross, Intro. by G. Struve. London, Westhouse, 1947.

Klyuev, N. *Polnoe sobranie sochineniy* (*Complete Works*). 2 vols. Ed. by B. Filippov. New York, Chekhov Publishing House, 1954.

———. *Sobranie sochineniy* (*Collected Works*). 2 vols. Ed. by G. Struve and B. Filippov. [Munich], A. Neimanis Verlag, 1969.

Konovalov, S., ed. *Bonfire: Stories Out of Soviet Russia*. London, Benn, 1932.

Lelevich, G. *Tvorcheskie puti proletarsky literatury* (*The Creative Paths of Proletarian Literature*). Leningrad, 1925.

Lezhnev, A. *Literaturnye budni* (*Literary Weekdays*). Moscow, 1929.

———. *Ob iskusstve* (*About Art*). Moscow, 1935.

———. *Sovremenniki. Literaturno-kriticheskie ocherki* (*Contemporaries: Literary-Critical Studies*). [Moscow], 1927.

———. *Voprosy literatury i kritiki* (*Problems of Literature and Criticism*). Moscow-Leningrad, [1924–25?].

———, and D. Gorbov. *Literatura revolyutsionnogo desyatiletiya* (*Literature of the Revolutionary Decade*). Kharkov, 1929.

Lezhnev, I. *Mikhail Sholokhov*. [Leningrad], 1948.

Lidin, Vl., ed. *Pisateli. Avtobiografii i portrety sovremennykh russkikh prozaikov* (*Writers: Autobiographies and Portraits of Contemporary Russian Prose-Fiction Authors*). 2d ed., enl. and rev. Moscow, 1928.

Literaturnoe Nasledstvo (*Literary Heritage*), Vol. 70. *Gorky i sovetskie pisateli. Neizdannaya perepiska* (*Gorky and Soviet Writers: Unpublished Correspondence*). Moscow, 1963.

Literaturnye otkliki (*Literary Echoes*). Moscow, [1923].

Littlepage, J., and D. Bess. *In Search of Soviet Gold*. New York, Harcourt, Brace, 1938.

Maguire, R. A. *Red Virgin Soil: Soviet Literature in the 1920's*. Princeton, Princeton University Press, 1968.

Mandelstam, O. *Razgovor o Dante* (*Talking About Dante*). Postface by L. E. Pinsky. Moscow, 1967. In English: in *Books Abroad* [special issue, *A Homage to Dante*, May, 1965]. In Spanish: in *Dante en su centenario*. Madrid, Taurus, 1965.

———. *Sobranie sochineniy* (*Collected Works*). 3 vols. Ed. by G. Struve and B. Filippov. Washington, D.C., Inter-Language Literary Associates, 1964–69. Vol. I, *Poetry*, Intros. by C. Brown, G. Struve, and E. Rais, 1964; 2d ed., rev. and enl., 1967. Vol. II, *Poetry, Prose*, Intro. by B. Filippov, 1966. Vol. III, *Essays, Letters*, Intros. by G. Ivask, N. Struve, and B. Filippov, 1969.

Markov, Vl. "O Khlebnikove. Popytka apologii i soprotivleniya" ("On Khlebnikov: An Attempted Apology and Retort"), *Grani* (Frankfurt), No. 2 (1954).

———. *Russian Futurism: A History*. Berkeley and Los Angeles, University of California Press, 1968.

———, ed. *The Longer Poems of Velimir Khlebnikov*. Berkeley and Los Angeles, University of California Press, 1962.

———, ed. *Priglushonnye golosa. Poèziya za zheleznym zanavesom* (*Subdued Voices: Poetry Behind the Iron Curtain*). New York, Chekhov Publishing House, 1952.

[Mayakovsky, V.] *Smert' Vladimira Mayakovskogo* (*The Death of Vladimir Mayakovsky*). Berlin, Petropolis, 1931.

Maynard, Sir J. *Russia in Flux*. Ed. and abr. by S. H. Guest from *Russia in Flux* and *The Russian Peasants and Other Studies*. New York, Macmillan, 1948.

Mirsky, D. S. *Contemporary Russian Literature: 1881–1925*. New York, Knopf, 1926; London, Routledge, 1925.

Mosely, P. E., ed. *The Soviet Union Since World War II*. Special issue of *Annals of the American Academy of Political and Social Sciences*, Vol. CCLXIII (May, 1949).

Nicolaevsky, B. I. *Power and the Soviet Elite: "The Letter of an Old Bolshevik" and Other Essays*. Intro. by G. F. Kennan. New York, Praeger, 1965.

Nikitin, N. *Sobranie sochineniy* (*Collected Works*). Vol. I. Kharkov, 1925.

Nikulina, N. *A. A. Fadeyev: Seminariy* (*A. A. Fadeyev: A. Seminar*). Leningrad, 1958.

Nusinov, I. *Pushkin i mirovaya literatura* (*Pushkin and World Literature*). Moscow, 1941.

Ocherk istorii russkoy sovetskoy literatury (*An Outline History of Soviet Russian Literature*). Vol. II. Moscow, 1955.

Oksyonov, I., ed. *Sovremennaya russkaya kritika: 1918–1924* (*Contemporary Russian Criticism: 1918–1924*). Leningrad, 1925.

Olesha, Yu. *Envy* [in the same volume with V. Kaverin, *The Unknown Artist.*] Trans. by P. Ross, Intro. by G. Struve. London, Westhouse, 1947.

————. *Izbrannye sochineniya (Selected Works)*. Moscow, 1956.

Orwell, George. *The Collected Essays, Journalism and Letters*. Ed. by Sonia Orwell and Ian Angus. Vol. 3, *As I Please, 1943–1945*. Vol. 4, *In Front of Your Nose, 1945–1950*. New York, Harcourt, Brace & World, 1968.

Oulanoff, H. *The Serapion Brothers: Theory and Practice*. The Hague, Mouton, 1966.

Pankratova, A. M., ed. *Istoriya SSSR (A History of the U.S.S.R.)*. 3 vols. Moscow, 1946–48. In English: *A History of the U.S.S.R.* Moscow, Foreign Languages Publishing House,[1] 1947–48.

Pasternak, B. "A District in the Rear," in *The Last Summer*. Trans. by G. Reavey. New York, Hearst Corp., 1958.

————. *Letters to Georgian Friends*. Trans. and ed. by D. Magarshack. New York, Harcourt, Brace and World, 1967.

Petrov, E. "Vospominaniya ob Ilfe" ("Recollections of Ilf"), in Ilya Ilf. *Zapisnye knizhki (Notebooks)*. Moscow, [1939].

Pilnyak, B. *Kamni i korni (Rocks and Roots)*. Moscow, 1935.

Pisateli ob iskusstve i o sebe. Sbornik statey No. I (Writers About Art and About Themselves. Collection of Essays No. I). Moscow-Leningrad, 1924.

Poggioli, R. *The Phoenix and the Spider*. Cambridge, Mass., Harvard University Press, 1957.

Pozner, V. *Panorama de la littérature russe contemporaine*. Paris, Kra, 1929.

Proletariat i literatura. Sbornik statey (Proletariat and Literature: A Collection of Articles). Leningrad, 1925.

Radek, K. *Sovremennaya mirovaya literatura i zadachi proletarskogo iskusstva (Contemporary World Literature and the Tasks of Proletarian Art)*. Moscow, 1934. In English: In H. G. Scott, ed. *Problems of Soviet Literature* [see below].

Reavey, G. *Soviet Literature Today*. London, Lindsay Drummond, 1946; New Haven, Yale University Press, 1947.

Richards, D. J. *Zamyatin: A Soviet Heretic*. London and New York, Hillary, 1962.

Ripellino, A. M. "Chlebnikov e il futurismo russo," *Convivium*, No. 5 (1949).

Russian Formalist Criticism: Four Essays. Trans. and ed. by L. T. Lemon and M. J. Reis. Lincoln, University of Nebraska Press, 1965. [Includes two essays by Shklovsky and one each by Eichenbaum and Tomashevsky.]

Russkiy Literaturny Arkhiv (Russian Literary Archives). Ed. by D. Cizevsky and M. Karpovich. New York, published under the auspices of the Department of Slavic Languages and Literatures of Harvard University and the Harvard College Library, 1956.

Sakulin, P. N. *Russkaya literatura. Sotsiologo-sinteticheskiy obzor literaturnykh stiley (Russian Literature: A Sociological Synthetic Survey of Literary Styles)*. Moscow, 1929.

[1] Henceforth abbreviated FLHP.

————. *Russkaya literatura i sotsializm* (*Russian Literature and Socialism*). Moscow, 1924.

Scott, H. G., ed. *Problems of Soviet Literature: Reports and Speeches at the First Writers' Congress*. London, Lawrence, 1935.

Seidel, R., and M. Zwieback. *Klassovy vrag na istoricheskom fronte. Tarle i Platonov i ikh shkoly* (*The Class Enemy on the History Front: Tarle and Platonov and Their Schools*). Moscow-Leningrad, 1931.

Serebryansky, M. *Sovetskiy istoricheskiy roman* (*The Soviet Historical Novel*). Moscow, 1936.

Shane, A. M. *The Life and Works of Evgenij Zamjatin*. Berkeley and Los Angeles, University of California Press, 1968.

Shulgin, V. *Tri stolitsy* (*Three Capitals*). Berlin, [1927].

Simmons, E. J. *Russian Fiction and Soviet Ideology: Introduction to Fedin, Leonov, and Sholokhov*. New York, Columbia University Press, 1958.

Stalin, I. *O velikoy Otechestvennoy Voyne Sovetskogo Soyuza* (*About the Great War for the Fatherland Waged by the Soviet Union*). Moscow, 1944.

————. *Sochineniya* (*Works*). Vol. 12. Moscow, 1949.

Struve, G. *Russkaya literatura v izgnani* (*Russian Literature in Exile*). New York, Chekhov Publishing House, 1956.

Struve, N. *Les Chrétiens en Russie*. Paris, Editions du Seuil, 1963. In English: N. Struve. *Christians in Contemporary Russia*. New York, Scribner's, 1967.

Süsskind, C. *Popov and the Beginnings of Radiotelegraphy*. San Francisco, San Francisco Press, 1962.

Tarasenkov, A. *Idei i obrazy sovetskoy literatury* (*Ideas and Images in Soviet Literature*). Moscow, 1949.

Tarsis, V. *Sovremennye russkie pisateli* (*Contemporary Russian Writers*). Ed. by I. Oksyonov. Leningrad, 1930.

Tolstoy, A. N. *Chetvert' veka sovetskoy literatury. Doklad na yubileynoy sessii Akademii Nauk SSSR 18 noyabrya 1942 goda* (*A Quarter of a Century of Soviet Literature: Report read at the Jubilee Session of the Academy of Sciences of the U.S.S.R. on November 18, 1942*). Moscow, 1943.

Tomashevsky, B. *Teoriya literatury. Poètika* (*Theory of Literature: Poetics*). 3d rev. ed. Moscow-Leningrad, 1927.

Trotsky, L. *Literature and Revolution*. Trans. by R. Strunsky. New York, International Publishers, 1925; London, Allen & Unwin, 1925; new ed., Ann Arbor, University of Michigan Press, 1960.

Veksler, I. I. *Alexey Nikolayevich Tolstoy. Zhiznenny i tvorcheskiy put* (*Alexey Nikolayevich Tolstoy: His Life and Work*). Moscow, 1947.

Vladislavlev, I. *Russkie pisateli* (*Russian Writers*). Moscow-Leningrad, 1924.

Voronsky, A. *Literaturnye portrety* (*Literary Portraits*). 2 vols. Moscow, 1928–29.

Zabolotsky, N. *Stikhotvoreniya* (*Poems*). Ed. by G. Struve and B. Filippov, Intros. by A. Rannit, B. Filippov, and E. Rais. [Washington, D.C.], Inter-Language Literary Associates, 1965.

Zamyatin, E. *Litsa* (*Faces*). New York, Chekhov Publishing House, 1955; new ed., Intro. by M. Koryakov, postface by V. Bondarenko, New York, Inter-Language Literary Associates, 1967.

————. *A Soviet Heretic: Essays by Yevgeny Zamyatin.* Trans. and ed. by M. Ginsburg. Chicago and London, University of Chicago Press, 1970.

Zavalishin, V. *Early Soviet Writers.* New York, Praeger, 1958.

Zazubrin, V. *Dva mira (Two Worlds).* Intro. by M. Gorky. Leningrad, 1930, 1958.

Zelinsky, K. *A. A. Fadeev: Kritiko-biograficheskiy ocherk (A. A. Fadeyev: A Critical-Biographical Study).* Moscow, 1956.

Zhdanov, A. *Sovetskaya literatura—samaya ideynaya, samaya peredovaya literatura v mire (Soviet Literature—the Richest in Ideas, the Most Progressive Literature in the World).* Moscow, 1934. In English: In H. G. Scott, ed. *Problems of Soviet Literature* [see above].

Žirmunskij, V. *Introduction to Metrics: The Theory of Verse.* Ed. by E. Stankiewicz and W. N. Vickery. The Hague, London, and Paris, Mouton, 1966.

Zoshchenko, M. *Pered voskhodom solntsa (Before Sunrise).* Ed. by E. Zhiglevich, Intros. by V. von Wiren-Garchinskaya and B. Filippov. New York, Inter-Language Literary Associates, 1967.

SECTION II. BIOGRAPHICAL, BIBLIOGRAPHICAL, AND OTHER REFERENCE WORKS

A. IN RUSSIAN

Balukhaty, S. *Teoriya literatury. Annotirovannaya bibliografiya. I. Obshchie voprosy (Theory of Literature: An Annotated Bibliography. I. General Problems).* Leningrad, 1929.

Kozmin, B., ed. *Pisateli sovremennoy èpokhi. Bio-bibliograficheskiy slovar' russkikh pisateley XX veka (Writers of the Contemporary Period. A Biobibliographical Dictionary of Russian Writers of the Twentieth Century).* Vol. 1 [no more were published]. Moscow, 1928.

"Letopis' sovetskoy literatury 1917–1932" ("Chronicle of Soviet Literature, 1917–1932"), *Literaturny Kritik,* Nos. 7–12 (1937), No. 1 (1938).

Lidin, Vl., ed. *Literaturnaya Rossiya (Literary Russia).* Moscow, 1924.

————, ed. *Pisateli. Avtobiografii i portrety (Writers: Autobiographies and Portraits)* [see Section I].

Matsuyev, N. *Khudozhestvennaya literatura, russkaya i perevodnaya. Ukazatel' statey i retsenziy (Imaginative Literature, Russian and Translated: A Guide to Articles and Book Reviews).* 4 vols. Moscow, 1926–40.

————. *Tri goda sovetskoy literatury (Three Years of Soviet Literature).* Moscow, 1934.

Muratova, K. *Periodika po literature i iskusstvu za gody Revolyutsii: 1917–1932 (Periodical Literature about Literature and Art During The Years of the Revolution: 1917–1932).* Ed. by S. D. Balukhaty. Leningrad, 1933.

Nikitina, E. *Russkaya literatura ot simvolizma do nashikh dney. Literaturno-sotsiologicheskiy seminariy (Russian Literature from Symbolism to Our Days: A Literary-Sociological Seminar).* Moscow, 1926.

Rogozhin, N. P. *Literaturno-khudozhestvennye almanakhi i sborniki. 1918–1927 gody (Literary-Artistic Almanacs and Collections: 1918–1927).* Moscow, 1960.

Rozanov, I. N. *Putevoditel' po sovremennoy russkoy literature* (*A Guide to Contemporary Russian Literature*). Moscow, 1929.

Tarasenkov, A. *Russkie poety XX veka: 1900–1955. Bibliografiya* (*Russian Poets of the 20th Century: 1900–1955: A Bibliography*). Moscow, 1966.

Tarsis, V. *Sovremennye russkie pisateli* (*Contemporary Russian Writers*) [See Section I].

Troitsky, N. A. *Boris Leonidovich Pasternak, 1890–1960: A Bibliography of the Works of Pasternak and Literature About Him Printed in Russia*. Ithaca, Cornell University Press, 1969.

Vitman, A. M., N. D. Pokrovskaya, and M. E. Ettinger. *Vosem' let russkoy khudozhestvennoy literatury* (*1917–1925*). *Bibliograficheskiy spravochnik* (*Eight Years of Russian Imaginative Literature* (*1917–1925*): *A Bibliographical Reference Guide*). Moscow, 1926.

Vladislavlev, I. *Literatura velikogo desyatiletiya, 1917–1927* (*Literature of the Great Decade, 1917–1927*). Vol. 1. Moscow-Leningrad, 1928.

———. *Russkie pisateli* (*Russian Writers*) [See Section I].

B. IN ENGLISH AND OTHER WESTERN LANGUAGES

The American Bibliography of Slavic and East European Studies. 7 vols. [covering the years 1959–65]. Bloomington, Indiana University Press, 1960–68. [Year 1959 ed. by J. R. Shaw and D. Djaparidze; year 1960 ed. by J. T. Shaw, A. Todd, and S. Viederman; years 1961 and 1962 ed. by A. Todd and S. Viederman; year 1963 ed. by F. Epstein, A. Todd, and S. Viederman; years 1964 and 1965 ed. by F. Epstein.]

Boutchik, V. *Bibliographie des oeuvres littéraires russes traduites en français*. Paris, Orobitg, 1935; 2d no., 1936; supplement, 1938; 2d supplement, 1941; 3d supplement, 1943.

———. *La Littérature russe en France*. Paris, Champion, 1947.

Dana, H. W. L. *Handbook on Soviet Drama: Lists of Theatres, Plays, Operas, Ballets, Films and Books and Articles About Them*. New York, American-Russian Institute, 1938.

Ettlinger, A., and J. Gladstone. *Russian Literature, Theatre and Art: A Bibliography of Works in English Published 1900–1945*. London, Hutchinson, 1947.

Florinsky, M. T., ed. *McGraw-Hill Encyclopaedia of Russia and the Soviet Union*. New York, McGraw-Hill, 1961.

Gibian, G., ed. *Soviet Russian Literature in English: A Checklist Bibliography*. Ithaca, Cornell University Press, 1967.

Grierson, P. *Books on Soviet Russia: 1917–1942: A Bibliography and A Guide to Reading*. London, Methuen, 1943. [For a continuation of this bibliography see "Books and Pamphlets on Russia," *Slavonic and East European Review*, Vol. XXIV (1946), 133–47; Vol. XXV (1947), 508–17; Vol. XXVI (1948), 512–18; Vol. XXVII (1949), 556–62; Vol. XXVIII (1950), 486–92.]

Harkins, W. E. *Dictionary of Russian Literature*. New York, Littlefield, 1959 [Paperback.]

Horecky, P. L. *Basic Russian Publications: An Annotated Bibliography on Russia and the Soviet Union*. Chicago, University of Chicago Press, 1962.

————. *Russia and the Soviet Union: A Bibliographical Guide to Western-Language Publications*. Chicago and London, University of Chicago Press, 1965.

Kerner, R. J. *Slavic Europe: A Selected Bibliography in the Western European Languages. Comprising History, Languages and Literature*. Cambridge, Mass., Harvard University Press; London, Humphrey Milford, 1918.

Kolarz, W., ed. *Books on Communism: A Bibliography*. 2d ed. New York, Oxford University Press, 1964.

Maichel, K. *Guide to Russian Reference Books*. 2 vols. Ed. by J. S. G. Simmons. Stanford, Hoover Institution, 1962, 1964.

————, comp. *Soviet and Russian Newspapers at the Hoover Institution. . . . A Catalog*. Stanford, Hoover Institution, 1966.

Martianov, N. *Books Available in English by Russians and on Russia, Published in the United States*. 4th ed. New York, privately printed, 1950.

Mehnert, K., ed. *Die Sovet Union, 1917–1932. Systematische, mit Kommentaren versehene Bibliographie der 1917–1932 in deutscher Sprache ausserhalb der Sovet-Union veröffentlichten 1900 wichtigsten Bücher und Aufsätze über den Bolschewismus und die Sovet-Union*. Königsberg Province and Berlin, Ost-Europa Verlag, 1933.

Messina, G. L. "Le traduzioni dal russo nel 1920–1943," *Belfagor*, Vol. IV, No. 6 (1949), 693–703.

Mohrenschildt, D. S. von. "Books in English on Russian Literature, 1917–42," *Russian Review*, Vol. II, No. 1 (Autumn, 1942), 122–28.

Ruggles, M., and V. Mostecky. *Russian and East-European Publications in the Libraries of the United States*. New York, Columbia University Press, 1960.

Slavic Review. *Index to the* Slavic Review *and Its Predecessors, 1941–1964*. Seattle, University of Washington Press, 1965.

Thomson, R. D. B. "Bibliography of the Works of Leonid Leonov," *Oxford Slavonic Papers*, Vol. XI (1964), 137–50.

Thorlby, A., ed. *The Penguin Companion of Literature. 2: European*. Baltimore, Penguin Books, 1959.

U.S.S.R. Handbook. London, Gollancz, 1936. [Contains a chapter on literature and "Who's Who."]

Victorof-Toporoff, V. *Rossica et Sovietica: Bibliographie des ouvrages parus en français de 1917 à 1930 inclus relatifs à la Russie et à l'URSS*. Saint-Cloud, Editions documentaires et bibliographiques, 1930.

SECTION III. GENERAL BACKGROUND WORKS IN ENGLISH ABOUT RUSSIA, THE SOVIET UNION, AND COMMUNISM

Alliluyeva, S. *Only One Year*. Trans. by P. Chavchavadze. New York, Harper & Row, 1969.

Backer, G. *The Deadly Parallel: Stalin and Ivan the Terrible*. New York, Random House, 1950.

Barghoorn, F. C. *The Soviet Cultural Offensive*. Princeton, Princeton University Press, 1960.

————. *The Soviet Image of the United States: A Study in Distortion*. New York, Harcourt, Brace, 1950.

Baring, M. *Landmarks in Russian Literature*. London, Methuen, 1916.
———. *The Russian People*. London, Methuen, 1911.
Basily, N. de., ed. *Russia Under Soviet Rule: Twenty Years of Bolshevik Experiment*. London, Allen & Unwin, 1938.
Beloff, M. *The Foreign Policy of Soviet Russia*. 2 vols. London and New York, Oxford University Press, 1947–49.
Black, C. E., ed. *Rewriting Russian History*. New York, Praeger, 1956.
Borkenau, F. *The Communist International*. London, Faber & Faber, 1938.
Brown, D. *Soviet Attitudes Toward American Writing*. Princeton, Princeton University Press, 1962.
Brzezinski, Z. K. *The Permanent Purge*. Cambridge, Mass., Harvard University Press, 1962.
Carr, E. H. *A History of Soviet Russia*. 7 vols. in 8. London and New York, Macmillan, 1950–64.
———. *The October Revolution: Before and After*. New York, Knopf, 1969; London, Macmillan, 1969.
———. *The Soviet Impact on the Western World*. London, Macmillan, 1946; New York, Macmillan, 1947.
———. *Studies in Revolution*. London, Macmillan, 1950.
Chamberlin, W. H. *The Russian Enigma*. New York, Scribner's, 1944.
———. *The Russian Revolution*. New York, Macmillan, 1935; London, Duckworth, 1935.
———. *Russia's Iron Age*. Boston, Little, Brown, 1934; London, Duckworth, 1935.
———. *World Order or Chaos?* London, Duckworth, 1946. American ed.: *The European Cockpit*. New York, Macmillan, 1947.
Chesterton, Mrs. C. *Sickle or Swastika?* London, Stanley Paul, 1938.
Conquest, R. *The Great Terror: Stalin's Purges of the Thirties*. New York, Macmillan, 1968.
Counts, G. S. *The Challenge of Soviet Education*. New York, McGraw-Hill, 1957.
Crossman, R. H. S., ed. *The God That Failed*. New York, Harper, 1949; London, Hamish Hamilton, 1950. [Essays by A. Koestler, I. Silone, and others.]
Curtiss, J. S. *The Russian Church and the Soviet State, 1917–1950*. Boston, Little, Brown, 1953.
Dallin, D. *The Real Soviet Russia*. Rev. ed. New Haven, Yale University Press, 1947.
———, and B. Nicolaevsky. *Forced Labor in Soviet Russia*. New Haven, Yale University Press, 1947.
Daniels, R. V. *The Conscience of the Revolution: Communist Opposition in Soviet Russia*. Cambridge, Mass., Harvard University Press, 1960.
Deane, J. R. *Strange Alliance: The Story of our Efforts at Wartime Co-operation with Russia*. New York, Viking Press, 1947.
Deutscher, I. *The Prophet Armed: Trotsky, 1879–1921*. New York, Oxford University Press, 1954.
———. *Stalin: A Political Biography*. New York, Oxford University Press, 1949.

Drachkovitch, M. M. *Fifty Years of Communism in Russia.* University Park and London, Pennsylvania State University Press, 1968.

Ehrenburg, I. *Memoirs: 1921–1941.* Trans. by T. Shebunina and Y. Kapp. Cleveland, World Publishing Co., 1964.

————. *People and Life: Memoirs of 1891–1917.* Trans. by A. Bostock and Y. Kapp. London, McGibbon & Kee, 1961.

————. *People and Life: 1891–1921.* Trans. by A. Bostock and Y. Kapp. New York, Knopf, 1962. [Vols. II–VI of Ehrenburg's memoirs, entitled *Lyudi, gody, zhizn'* (*Men, Years, Life*) have also been published under the following titles: Vol. II, *First Years of Revolution: 1918–1921,* trans. by A. Bostock and Y. Kapp; Vol. III, *Truce: 1921–33,* trans. by T. Shebunina and Y. Kapp; Vol. IV, *Eve of War: 1933–1941,* trans. by T. Shebunina and Y. Kapp; Vol. V, *The War: 1941–45,* trans. by T. Shebunina and Y. Kapp; Vol. VI, *Post–War Years: 1945–1954,* trans. by T. Shebunina and Y. Kapp. The British edition was published by McGibbon & Kee; the American, by World Publishing Co. They appeared between 1961 and 1966.]

Fainsod, M. *How Russia Is Ruled.* Cambridge, Mass., Harvard University Press, 1954.

Fischer, G. *Soviet Opposition to Stalin.* Cambridge, Mass., Harvard University Press, 1952.

Fischer, L. *Machines and Men in Russia.* New York, Harrison Smith, 1932; London, Cape, 1932.

Fletcher, W. C. *A Study in Survival: The Church in Russia, 1927–1943.* New York, Macmillan, 1965.

Florinsky, M. T. *Russia: A History and an Interpretation.* 2 vols. New York, Macmillan, 1953.

Fülop-Muller, R., and J. Gregor. *Mind and Face of Bolshevism: An Examination of Cultural Life in Soviet Russia.* Trans. by S. Flint and D. F. Tait. London, Putnam, 1927.

Gerschenkron, A. *Economic Backwardness in Historical Perspective: A Book of Essays.* Cambridge, Mass., Belknap Press of Harvard University, 1962. [Includes three essays on Soviet novels as "a neglected source of economic information on Soviet Russia."]

Gray, C. *The Great Experiment: Russian Art, 1863–1922.* New York, Abrams, 1962.

Griffith, H., ed. *Playtime in Russia.* London, Methuen, 1935.

Haimson, L. H. *The Russian Marxists and the Origins of Bolshevism.* Cambridge, Mass., Harvard University Press, 1955.

Hart, B. H. L. *The Soviet Army.* London, Weidenfeld & Nicolson, 1956.

Hill, C. *Lenin and the Russian Revolution.* London, Hodder and Stoughton for the English Universities Press, 1947.

Hunt, R. N. C. *The Theory and Practice of Communism.* London and New York, Macmillan, 1950.

Inkeles, A. *Public Opinion in Soviet Russia.* Cambridge, Mass., Harvard University Press, 1950.

Jaworskij, M. ed. *Soviet Political Thought: An Anthology*. Baltimore, Johns Hopkins Press, 1968.

Kaplan, F. I. *Bolshevik Ideology and the Ethics of Soviet Labor: 1917–1920, the Formative Years*. New York, Philosophical Library, 1969.

Kennell, R. E. *Theodore Dreiser and the Soviet Union, 1927–1945: A First-Hand Chronicle*. New York, International Publishers, 1969.

Koestler, A. *The Yogi and the Commissar and Other Essays*. London and New York, Macmillan, 1946.

Kolarz, W. *Myths and Realities in Eastern Europe*. London, Lindsay Drummond, 1946.

———. *Religion in the Soviet Union*. New York, St. Martin's Press, 1961.

Koriakov, M. *I'll Never Go Back: A Red Officer Talks*. Trans. by N. Wreden. London and New York, Harrap, 1949.

Kravchenko, V. *I Chose Freedom*. New York, Scribner's, 1946.

Langdon-Davies, J. *Russia Puts the Clock Back: A Study of Soviet Science and Some British Scientists*. London, Gollancz, 1949.

Lawrence, J. *Life in Russia*. London, Allen, 1947.

Levine, I. D. *I Rediscover Russia: 1924–1964*. New York, Duell, Sloan & Pearce, 1964.

Lovel, M. *The Soviet Way of Life: An Examination*. London, Methuen, 1948.

Lyons, E. *Assignment in Utopia*. New York, Harcourt, Brace, 1937; London, Harrap, 1938.

———. *Modern Moscow*. London, Hurst and Blackett, 1935. American ed.: *Moscow Carrousel*. New York, Knopf, 1935.

Mandelstam, N. *Hope Against Hope: A Memoir*. Intro. by C. Brown. New York, Athenaeum Publishers, 1970.

Marcuse, H. A. *Soviet Marxism: A Critical Analysis*. New York, Columbia University Press, 1957.

Masaryk, T. G. *The Spirit of Russia*. 2 vols. Trans. by E. and C. Paul. London, Allen and Unwin, 1919; New York, Macmillan, 1919.

Maynard, Sir J. *Russia in Flux Before October*. London, Gollancz, 1941.

———. *Russian Peasant and Other Studies*. London, Gollancz, 1942.

Mehnert, K. *Soviet Man and His World*. Trans. by Maurice Rosenbaum. New York, Praeger, 1962.

Meyendorff, Baron A. *The Background of the Russian Revolution*. New York, Henry Holt, 1929.

Miliukov, P. N. *Outlines of Russian Culture*. 3 vols. Trans. by V. Ughet and E. Davis, ed. by M. Karpovich. Philadelphia, University of Pennsylvania Press, 1943.

Mirsky, D. S. *A History of Russian Literature*. Ed. by F. J. Whitfield. New York, Knopf, 1949.

Moore, B., Jr. *Soviet Politics—The Dilemma of Power*. Cambridge, Mass., Harvard University Press, 1950.

Muggeridge, M. *Winter in Moscow*. London, Eyre and Spottiswoode, 1934; Boston, Little, Brown, 1934.

Pares, Sir B. *A History of Russia*. 4th ed. New York, Knopf, 1946; London, Cape, 1946.

——. *Russia*. London, Penguin Books, 1941; Washington and New York, Penguin Books, 1944.

——. *Russia and the Peace*. New York, Macmillan, 1944.

Rauch, G. von. *A History of Soviet Russia*. Rev. ed. Trans. by P. and A. Jacobsohn. New York, Praeger, 1958.

Reshetar, J. S., ed. *The Communist Party of the Soviet Union*. New York, Praeger, 1956.

Riasanovsky, N. V. *A History of Russia*. New York, Oxford University Press, 1963; 2d ed., 1968.

Rigby, T. H. *Communist Party Membership in the USSR, 1917–1967*. Princeton, Princeton University Press, 1968.

Ritvo, H., ed. *The New Soviet Society: Final Text of the Program of the Communist Party of the Soviet Union*. New York, New Leader Press, 1962. [Original paperback.]

Rostow, W. W. *Dynamics of Soviet Society*. New York, Mentor Books, 1954.

Schapiro, L. *The Origin of the Communist Autocracy, 1917–1922*. Cambridge, Mass., Harvard University Press, 1955.

Schlesinger, R. *Spirit of Post-War Russia: Soviet Ideology, 1917–1946*. New York, Universal Distributors, 1947.

——., ed. *Changing Attitudes in Soviet Russia: The Family in the U.S.S.R. Documents and Readings*. London, Routledge and Kegan Paul, 1949.

Serge, V. *From Lenin to Stalin*. Trans. by R. Manheim. New York, Pioneer Publications, 1937.

Seton-Watson, H. *From Lenin to Malenkov: The History of World Communism*. New York, Praeger, 1957.

Shub, D. *Lenin: A Biography*. Garden City, Doubleday, 1948.

Simmons, E. J., ed. *U.S.S.R.: A Concise Handbook*. Ithaca, Cornell University Press, 1947.

Smith, W. B. *My Three Years in Moscow*. Philadelphia, Lippincott, 1949.

Sorlin, P. *The Soviet People and Their Society*. New York, Praeger, 1969.

Souvarine, B. *Stalin: A Critical Survey of Bolshevism*. Trans. by C. L. R. James. London, Secker and Warburg, 1939; New York, Longmans, Green, 1939.

Soviet Comes of Age. "By 28 of the foremost citizens of the U.S.S.R." Foreword by S. and B. Webb. London, Hodge, 1938.

Soviet Foreign Policy During the Patriotic War: Documents and Materials. Trans. by A. Rothstein. London, Hutchinson, 1946.

Soviet Union Year Book, 1930. Ed. by A. A. Santalov and L. Segal. London, Allen & Unwin, 1930. [Contains "Who's Who in Literature."]

Spinka, M. *The Church in Soviet Russia*. New York, Oxford University Press, 1956.

[Stalin, J.]. *Joseph Stalin*. New York, International Publishers, 1950.

——. *War Speeches, Orders of the Day, and Interviews to Foreign Correspondents During the Great Patriotic War, July 3, 1941–June 22, 1945*. London, Hutchinson, 1946.

Steinberg, J., ed. *Verdict of Three Decades*. New York, Duell, Sloan & Pearce, 1950.

Stevens, E. *This Is Russia Uncensored: Everyday Life Under the Soviet Regime*. New York, Didier, 1950.

Sumner, B. H. *Survey of Russian History*. 2d ed. London, Duckworth, 1948. American ed.: *A Short History of Russia*. New York, Reynal and Hitchcock, 1943.

Tchernavin, V. V. *I Speak for the Silent Prisoners of the Soviets*. Trans. by N. Oushakoff. Boston and New York, Hale, Cushman and Flint, 1935.

Terrell, R. *Soviet Understanding*. London, Heinemann, 1937.

Timasheff, N. *The Great Retreat: The Growth and Decline of Communism in Russia*. New York, Dutton, 1946.

———. *Religion in Soviet Russia: 1917–1942*. New York, Sheed and Ward, 1942.

Treadgold, D. W., ed. *The Development of the U.S.S.R.: An Exchange of Views*. Seattle, University of Washington Press, 1964.

———. *Twentieth Century Russia*. Chicago, Rand-McNally, 1959. [Contains a valuable critical bibliography.]

Trotsky, L. *The History of the Russian Revolution*. 3 vols. Trans. by M. Eastman. New York, Simon and Schuster, 1932.

———. *The Revolution Betrayed*. Trans. by M. Eastman. London, Secker and Warburg, 1937; New York, Doubleday, 1937.

———. *Stalin: An Appraisal of the Man and His Influence*. Trans. by C. Malamuth. New York and London, Harper, 1941.

Valentinov, N. [N. V. Volsky]. *The Early Years of Lenin*. Trans. and ed. by R. W. Theen, Intro. by B. D. Wolfe. Ann Arbor, University of Michigan Press, 1969.

———. *Encounters with Lenin*. Trans. by P. Rosta and B. Pearce, Foreword by L. Schapiro. London, New York, and Toronto, Oxford University Press, 1968.

Vernadsky, G. *A History of Russia*. New Haven, Yale University Press, 1944.

Voigt, F. A. *Unto Caesar*. London, Constable, 1938.

Walsh, W. B. *Russia and the Soviet Union: A Modern History*. Ann Arbor, University of Michigan Press, 1958.

Webb, S., and B. Webb. *Soviet Communism: A New Civilization*. 2 vols. London and New York, Longmans, Green, 1935.

Weidlé, W. *Russia: Absent and Present*. Trans. by A. Gordon Smith. London, Hollis & Carter, 1952; New York, D. Day Co., 1960. The original edition, in French: *La Russie absente et présente*. Paris, Gallimard, 1949.

Werth, A. *Musical Uproar in Moscow*. London, Turnstile Press, 1949.

Williams, A. R. *The Russians: The Land, the People and Why They Fight*. London, Harrap, 1943.

———. *The Soviets*. New York, Harcourt, Brace, 1937. [Contains a valuable bibliography.]

Williams, H. W. *Russia of the Russians*. London, Pitman, 1914.

Wolfe, B. D. *The Bridge and the Abyss: The Troubled Friendship of Maxim*

Gorky and Vladimir Lenin. New York, Praeger for the Hoover Institution, 1969.

——. *Six Keys to the Soviet System.* Boston, Beacon Press, 1956.

——. *Three Who Made a Revolution: A Biographical History.* New York, Dial Press, 1948.

Woytinsky, W. S. *Stormy Passage: A Personal History Through Two Russian Revolutions to Democracy and Freedom: 1905–1960.* Intro. by A. A. Berle. New York, Vanguard Press, 1961.

Zenkovsky, V. V. *A History of Russian Philosophy.* 2 vols. Trans. by G. L. Kline. New York, Columbia University Press, 1953.

SECTION IV. WORKS ABOUT SOVIET LITERATURE

A. A NOTE ON WORKS IN THE RUSSIAN LANGUAGE

The number of such works published since 1951, and especially in the last ten or twelve years, has grown so large that any idea of providing an exhaustive list had to be abandoned for reasons of space. In view of the noticeable improvements—by comparison with the period between 1930 and 1956—of this literary-historical and critical output, the presentation of a selective list was also found to be impractical. Some of the important and/or symptomatic works published during the period covered in this book and referred to or quoted in the text will be found in Section I above.

In 1958–61 the Soviet Academy of Sciences at last brought out the first comprehensive *Istoriya russkoy sovetskoy literatury* (*History of Soviet Russian Literature*) in three volumes. Volume I, covering the period from 1917 to 1928, was edited by L. Timofeyev and A. Dementyev; Volume II, covering the period from 1929 to 1940, was also edited by Timofeyev and Dementyev; Volume III, covering the period from 1941 to 1957 was edited by Dementyev alone. Soon after the publication of the last volume it became clear that this monumental *History* was already hopelessly out of date, having failed to keep pace with developments in the post-Stalin era, which involved, among other things, a rewriting of the history of Soviet literature. A new edition, not only enlarged and brought up to date but also "revised," was called for. Such an edition, this time planned for four volumes, began to appear in 1967 under the editorship of A. Dementyev, assisted by L. Polyak and L. Timofeyev. Three volumes were published in 1967–68. Volume I covers the years 1917–29; Volume II, the years 1930–41; Volume III, the years 1941–53. Volume IV is to bring the story up to 1965. Each volume contains a signed general introductory survey of the period,[2] as well as some articles of special nature. In Volume I there are articles on "Lenin and Soviet Art," by V. Shcherbina, and on "Lunacharsky and Problems of Soviet Literature," by A. Dementyev and I. Satz. In Volume II there is an article on "Community of National Cultures," by G. Lomidze. In Volume III there is no such special article at the beginning, but there is one at the end (on writers in the front-line press). Each volume has a series of monographs on individual writers, written by indi-

[2] In Volume II there are two such surveys, one dealing with wartime literature, the other with the 1946–53 period. Both are collectively authored.

vidual scholars and critics; a survey of journalism and literary criticism for the period; a similar survey of the "international ties" of Soviet literature; and a detailed "Chronicle" of literary life, year by year.

While in the first edition separate chapters were allotted to forty-three writers, in the second edition only thirty-nine are represented. There are, however, significant additions in the second edition: in Volume I, Isaac Babel and Alexander Grin; in Volume II, Tynyanov and Zoshchenko; in Volume III, Pasternak. Of those whose names have disappeared from the second edition, four will probably be included in Volume IV: Sholokhov, Fedin, Leonov, and Simonov. The same may be true of Ehrenburg, Paustovsky, and Tvardovsky, about whom there are chapters in Volume III of the first edition, but who do not figure in the second edition. On the other hand, it looks as though Aseyev and Pogodin (both discussed in Volume II of the first edition) must have been dropped by the way. The two important names one misses in both editions are those of Olesha and Kaverin, and the probable inclusion of the former in Volume IV would appear to be rather strange from the purely chronological point of view. The important role he played in Soviet literature is part of the earlier scene. In a number of cases the order, the arrangement, and the authors of chapters on individual writers differ in the two editions.

In 1929 the publishing house of the Communist Academy (not to be confused with the Soviet Academy of Sciences) began publishing a literary encyclopaedia (*Literaturnaya Entsiklopediya*). Eleven volumes were published, covering the greater part of the alphabet, but publication was discontinued in the late thirties, and the whole edition was later withdrawn from circulation. Some of its editors and principal contributors turned out to be either "Trotskyites" or other "enemies of the people." A reprint of the existing volumes was issued in the 1950's in the United States by the American Council of Learned Societies. A new *Kratkaya Literaturnaya Entsiklopediya (Short Literary Encyclopaedia)*, in six volumes, was launched under Khrushchev to replace the old one, under the general editorship of the poet A. Surkov. Five volumes appeared between 1962 and 1968, when it looked as though more than six volumes would be needed to complete the alphabet. With all its deficiencies and gaps, it is a valuable source of biographical and bibliographical information and, in its own way, a symptomatic literary phenomenon, to be discussed and evaluated in the proper context in the sequel to this book.

The following principal Soviet periodicals, now defunct, are invaluable for the study of Soviet literature: *Kniga i Revolyutsiya* (1920–23), *Pechat' i Revolyutsiya* (1921–30; continued as *Literatura i Iskusstvo* in 1930–31 and as *Marksistskoye Iskusstvoznanie* in 1932–33), *Krasnaya Nov* (1921–42), *Krasnaya Niva* (1923–31), *LEF* (1923–25), (resumed as *Novy LEF*, 1927–28), *30 Dney* (1925–41), *Russkiy Sovremennik* (1924), *Literatura i Marksizm* (1928–31), *Literaturny Kritik* (1933–41), *Literaturny Sovremennick* (1933–41), and *Literaturnoye Obozrenie* (1936–41). Similarly invaluable among those periodicals still existing are *Oktyabr* (founded in 1924), *Novy Mir* (1925), *Literaturnaya Gazeta* (1929), *Zvezda* (1926), *Znamya* (1935), and *Moskva* (1957).

Two periodicals, both devoted entirely to the study of literature and literary history, were started in 1958: *Russkaya Literatura* (*Russian Literature*) and *Voprosy Literatury* (*Problems of Literature*). The former is of a more scholarly nature, is more historically oriented, and is confined to Russian literature. The latter devotes more space to criticism of contemporary literature and is more eclectic; but neither is exclusive.

A great deal of interesting material on earlier Soviet literature has appeared in recent years in some provincial literary periodicals, such as *Podyom* (Voronezh, started in 1931), *Prostor* (Alma Ata, 1933), *Literaturnaya Armeniya* (Erevan, 1960), *Literaturnaya Gruziya* (Tbilisi, 1957), and *Zvezda Vostoka* (Tashkent, 1945).

For the earliest period, *Russkaya Kniga*, continued as *Novaya Russkaya Kniga* and published in Berlin in 1921–23, is of considerable interest. The same is true of Russian *émigré* newspapers and magazines, both before World War II—such as *Rul'* (Berlin), *Poslednie Novosti* (Paris), *Vozrozhdenie* (Paris), *Segodnya* (Riga), *Russkaya Mysl'* (Sofia-Prague-Berlin), *Chisla* (Paris), *Vstrechi* (Paris), and *Russkie Zapiski* (Paris)—and after the war—such as *Novy Zhurnal* (New York), *Vozrozhdenie* (Paris), *Grani* (Frankfurt), *Novoye Russkoye Slovo* (New York), *Posev* (Frankfurt), and *Russkaya Mysl'* (Paris).

B. WORKS ABOUT SOVIET LITERATURE IN ENGLISH AND OTHER WESTERN LANGUAGES[1]

Alexandrova, V. *A History of Soviet Literature*. Trans. by M. Ginsburg. Garden City, Doubleday, 1963.

Apletin, M. *Literature of the Peoples of the USSR*. Moscow, 1934.

Arseniew, N. von. *Die russische Literatur der Neuzeit und Gegenwart in ihren geistigen Zusammenhängen*. Mainz, Dioskuren-Verlag, 1929.

Aucouturier, M. *Pasternak par lui-même*. Paris, Editions du Seuil, 1963.

Berger, Y. *Boris Pasternak*. Paris, Seghers, 1958.

Bonnard, A. *Vers un Humanisme nouveau: Refléxions sur la littérature soviétique (1917–1947)*. Lausanne, Association Suisse-URSS, 1948.

Bradshaw, M., ed. *Soviet Theaters 1917–1941*. New York, Research Program on the USSR, 1954.

Brainina, B. *Konstantin Fedin*. Trans. by T. Stein, ed. by G. Stein. Berlin, Verlag Kultur und Fortschritt, 1954.

Carter, H. *The New Spirit in the Russian Theatre, 1917–1928*. New York, Brentano's, 1929; London, Shaylor, 1929.

Dana, H. W. L. *Drama in Wartime Russia*. New York, National Council of American-Soviet Friendship, 1943.

Davie, D., and A. Livingstone. *Modern Judgements: Pasternak*. London, Macmillan, 1968.

De Graaf, F. *Sergej Esenin: A Biographical Sketch*. The Hague, Mouton, 1966.

Dickinson, T. H., et al. *The Theatre in a Changing Europe*. New York, Henry Holt, 1937; London, Putnam, 1938. [Articles on the theater in Russia by G. Gregor and H. W. L. Dana.]

Egolin, A. M. *The Ideological Content of Soviet Literature*. Trans. by M. Kriger. Washington, D.C., Public Affairs Press, 1948.

---

[1] Those works listed in Section I are not repeated here.

————. *J. W. Stalin und die Sowjetliteratur*. Berlin, Dietz, 1952.

————. *Die Sowjetliteratur*. Trans. by I. Nebenzahl. Berlin-Leipzig, SWA-Verlag, 1949.

Ehrenburg, I. *Uber die Arbeit des Schriftstellers*. Trans. by G. Stein. Berlin, Verlag Kultur und Fortschritt, 1954.

Erlich, V. *The Double Image: Concepts of the Poet in Slavic Literatures*. Baltimore, Johns Hopkins Press, 1964. [Contains essays on Pasternak and Mayakovsky.]

————. *Russian Formalism: History—Doctrine*. The Hague, Mouton, 1955, 1969.

Flores, A., ed. *Literature and Marxism: A Controversy by Soviet Critics*. New York, Critics Group, 1938.

Folejewski, Z. *Studies in Modern Slavic Poetry. I*. Uppsala, Almqvist & Wicksells Boktryckeri, 1955. [Esenin and Mayakovsky.]

Freeman, J., J. Kunitz, and L. Lozowick. *Voices of October: Art and Literature in Soviet Russia*. New York, Vanguard Press, 1930.

Friedberg, M. *Russian Classics in Soviet Jackets*. New York, Columbia University Press, 1962.

Gasiorowska, X. *Women in Soviet Fiction, 1917–1964*. Madison, University of Wisconsin Press, 1968.

Geheimnis der Dichtkunst, Das. Aufsätze und Reden sowjetischer Schriftsteller. Trans. by W. Rathfelder. Berlin, Verlag Kultur und Fortschritt, 1955.

Gifford, H. *The Novel in Russia: From Pushkin to Pasternak*. London, Hutchinson, 1964.

Ginzburg, L. *Scrittori russi*. Turin, 1948.

Goriély, B. *La nouvelle poésie en U.R.S.S.* Brussels, Editions du Canard Sauvage, 1928.

————. *Les Poètes dans la révolution russe*. Paris, Gallimard, 1934.

————. *Science des lettres soviétiques*. Paris, Editions des Portes de France, 1947.

Gourfinkel, N. *Gorky*. New York, Evergreen, 1960.

————. *Le Théatre russe contemporain*. Paris, 1931.

Grindea, M., ed. *Soviet Literature, Art, Music*. London, Practical Press, 1942.

Gruzdev, I. *Das Leben des jungen Maxim Gorki*. Trans. by G. Kischke, Berlin, Zech, 1948.

————. *Das Leben Maxim Gorkis. Biographie*. Trans. by E. Boehme. Berlin, Malik-Verlag, 1928.

————. *Leben und Abenteuer des jungen Maxim Gorki*. Trans. by M. Einstein. Leipzig, Volk und Wissen, 1946.

Guenther, J. von. *Alexander Block: Das Versuch einer Dartstellung*. Munich, Weissmann, 1948.

Gyseghem, A. van. *Theatre in Soviet Russia*. London, Faber, 1943.

Hare, R. *Maxim Gorky: Romantic Realist and Conservative Revolutionary*. New York, Oxford University Press, 1962.

————. *Russian Literature from Pushkin to the Present Day*. London, Methuen, 1947.

Hayward, M., and L. Labedz, eds. *Literature and Revolution in Soviet Russia, 1917–1962: A Symposium.* New York, Oxford University Press, 1963.

Holthusen, J. *Russische Gegenwartsliteratur.* Vol. I: *1890–1940. Die literarische Avantgarde.* Bern and Munich, Francke Verlag, 1963.

Houghton, N. *Moscow Rehearsals: An Account of Methods of Production in the Soviet Theatre.* New York, Harcourt, Brace, 1936; London, Allen & Unwin, 1938.

Isakovskij, M. *Von der Meisterschaft der Poeten.* Trans. by A. E. Thoss. Berlin, Verlag Volk und Welt, 1954.

Jung, F. *Der neue Mensch im neuen Russland: Rückblick über die erste Etappe proletarischer Erzählkunst.* Vienna, Verlag für Literatur und Politik, 1924.

Kiparsky, V. *English and American Characters in Russian Fiction.* Wiesbaden, 1964.

Kisch, C. H. *Alexander Blok, Prophet of Revolution.* New York, Roy, 1961.

Kossuth, L. *Das sowjetische Leben im Schaffen Maxim Gorkis.* Berlin, Aufbau-Verlag, 1954.

Kuckhoff, A.-G. *Sowjetische Dramatik: 1946–1962. Eine Bilanz.* Berlin, Verlag Kultur und Fortschritt, 1953.

Lavrin, J. *From Pushkin to Mayakovsky: A Study in the Evolution of a Literature.* London, Sylvan Press, 1948.

———. *An Introduction to the Russian Novel.* London, Methuen, 1942; New York, McGraw-Hill, 1947.

Lettenbauer, W. *Russische Literaturgeschichte.* Frankfurt, Humboldt-Verlag, 1955.

Lo Gatto, E. *Dall' epica alla cronaca nella Russia sovietista.* Rome, 1929.

———. *Histoire de la littérature russe des origines à nos jours.* Trans. by M. Cabrini and A.-M. Cabrini. [Paris], Desclée de Brouwer, 1965.

———. *La Letteratura sovietista.* Rome, 1929.

———. *Storia del teatro russo.* 2 vols. Florence, Sansoni, 1952.

London, K. *The Seven Soviet Arts.* London, Faber & Faber, 1937; New Haven, Yale University Press, 1938.

McLean, H. "The Development of Modern Russian Literature," in *The Development of the USSR: An Exchange of Views,* 1964. [See Section III.]

McLeod, J. *The Actors Cross the Volga: A Study of the 19th Century Russian Theatre and of Soviet Theatres in War.* London, Allen & Unwin, 1946.

———. *The New Soviet Theatre.* London, Allen & Unwin, 1943.

Mallac, G. de. *Boris Pasternak.* Paris, Editions Universitaires, 1963.

Markov, P. A. *The Soviet Theatre.* London, Gollancz, 1934.

Markov, V., ed. *Manifesty i programmy russkikh futuristov (Manifestoes and Programs of the Russian Futurists).* Munich, Fink Verlag, 1967. [Texts in Russian, introduction and commentary in English.]

Messina, G. L. *La letteratura sovietica.* Florence, Le Monnier, 1950.

Miliukov, P. *Outlines of Russian Culture.* Trans. by V. Ughet and E. Davis, ed. by M. Karpovich. Philadelphia, University of Pennsylvania Press, 1943. [Part II: "Literature."]

Mjasnikov, A. *Maxim Gorki und Fragen der Literatur*. Berlin, Verlag Kultur und Fortschritt, 1952.

Muchnic, H. *From Gorky to Pasternak: Six Writers in Soviet Russia*. New York, Random House, 1961; London, Methuen, 1963.

Nilsson, N. A. *Sovjetrysk Litteratur 1917–1947*. Stockholm, Forum, 1948.

Ozerov, V. *Das Problem des Typischen in der sowjetischen Literatur*. Trans. by R. Krickmann. Berlin, Dietz, 1954.

———. *Das Schaffen Alexander Fadejews*. Trans. by U. Kuhirt. Berlin, Aufbau-Verlag, 1953; Leipzig-Jena, Urania-Verlag, 1954.

Patrick, G. Z. *Popular Poetry in Soviet Russia*. Berkeley, University of California Press, 1929.

Payne, R. *The Three Worlds of Boris Pasternak*. New York, Coward-McCann, 1961.

Plank, D. L. *Pasternak's Lyric: A Study of Sound and Imagery*. The Hague and Paris, Mouton, 1966.

Poggioli, R. *Pietre di paragone*. Florence, 1939. [Essays on Gorky, Zamyatin, Mandelstam, Esenin, and Mayakovsky.]

———. *The Poets of Russia: 1890–1930*. Cambridge, Mass., Harvard University Press, 1960.

———. *Politica letteraria sovietica: Bilancio d'un ventennio*. Rome, 1937.

Proyart, J. de. *Pasternak*. Paris, Gallimard, 1964. [Contains valuable bibliographical information.]

Reeve, F. D. *Aleksandr Blok: Between Image and Idea*. New York, Columbia University Press, 1962.

Revjakin, A. *Das Problem des Typischen in der schönen Literatur*. Trans. by H. Tautz. Berlin, Dietz, 1955.

Ripellino, Angelo Maria. *Poesie di Chlébnikov. Saggio, antologia, commento*. Turin, Einaudi, 1968. [Translations of Khlebnikov's selected poems, with an introductory essay, "Tentative di esplorazione del continente Chlébnikov," and a detailed commentary.]

Roberts, S. E. *Soviet Historical Drama: Its Role in the Development of a National Mythology*. The Hague, Nijhoff, 1965.

Roskin, A. *Maxim Gorki*. Trans. by A. Wagner. Berlin-Leipzig, SWA-Verlag, 1947.

Ruge, G. *Pasternak: Eine Bildbiographie*. Munich, Kindler Verlag, 1958. Also in French: Text by G. Toucoulov-Tachovères. Paris, Hachette, 1959.

Rühle, J. *Das gefesselte Theater*. Cologne, Kiepenheuer und Witsch, 1957.

———. *Literature and Revolution: A Critical Study of the Writer and Communism in the Twentieth Century*. Trans. and ed. by J. Steinberg. New York, Praeger, 1969.

Sayler, O. M. *Inside the Moscow Art Theatre*. New York, Brentano's, 1925; London, 1928.

———. *Russian Theatre Under the Revolution*. New York and London, Brentano's, 1922.

Sčerbina, V. *Alexej Tolstoj*. Trans. by Harold Cossack. Weimer, Böhlau, 1954.

Setschkareff, V. *Geschichte der russischen Literatur*. Stuttgart, Reclam, 1962.

Simmons, E. J. *Introduction to Russian Realism: Pushkin, Gogol, Dostoevsky, Tolstoy, Chekhov, Sholokhov*. Bloomington, Indiana University Press, 1967.

——, ed. *Through the Glass of Soviet Literature*. New York, Columbia University Press, 1953.

Šklovskij, V. *Una teoria della prosa*. Trans. by M. Olsoufieva. Bari, De Donato, 1966.

Slonim, M. *Russian Theatre: From the Empire to the Soviets*. Trans. with an essay by D. Magarshack. New York, Atheneum, 1961.

——. *Soviet Russian Literature: Writers and Problems*. New York, Oxford University Press, 1964; new ed., 1967.

Soviet Writers' Reply to English Writers' Questions. Foreword by J. B. Priestley. London, Society for Cultural Relations, 1948.

Sowjetische Literaturkritik: Eine Auswahl. Ed. and Intro. by A. Antkowiak. Berlin, Verlag Kultur und Fortschritt, 1953.

Stanislavsky, C. *Building a Character*. Trans. by E. Hapgood. London, Reinhardt & Evans; New York, Theatre Art Books, 1950.

——. *Stanislavsky on the Art of the Stage*. London, Faber & Faber, 1950.

Stewart, D. H. *Mikhail Sholokhov: A Critical Introduction*. Ann Arbor, University of Michigan Press, 1967.

Strada, V. *Tradizione e rivoluzione nella letteratura russa*. Turin, Einaudi, 1969.

Striedter, J., ed. *Texte der russischen Formalisten*. Vol. I: *Theorie und Geschichte der Literatur und der schönen Künste*. Munich, Fink Verlag, 1969.

Struve, G. *Geschichte der Sowjetliteratur*. Munich, Isar Verlag, 1957; new ed., Munich, Wilhelm Goldmann Verlag, [1964].

——. *Histoire de la littérature soviétique*. Paris, Editions du Chêne, 1946.

——. *Soviet Russian Literature*. London, Routledge, 1935.

——. *25 Years of Soviet Russian Literature*. London, Routledge, 1944.

Swayze, H. *Political Control of Literature in the USSR: 1946–1959*. Cambridge, Mass., Harvard University Press, 1962.

Tairov, A. *Das entfesselte Theater: Aufzeichnungen eines Regisseurs*. Trans. by E. K. Wieber. Potsdam, G. Kiepenheuer, 1923, 1927.

The Theatre in the U.S.S.R. Moscow, 1934.

Thorgevsky, I. *De Gorki à nos jours: la nouvelle littérature russe*. Paris, La Renaissance, 1945.

Timofejew, L. *Geschichte der Sowjetliteratur*. Vol. III of *Geschichte der russischen Literatur*. Trans. by W. Hoepp and H. Asemissen. Berlin, Verlag Kultur und Fortschritt, 1953.

——. *Sowjetische Literatur*. Leipzig, 1949.

——. *Uber den sozialistischen Realismus*. Trans. by E. Jeran, Berlin, Verlag Kultur und Fortschritt, 1953.

Tolstoy, A. N. "Trends in Soviet Literature," *Science and Society*, Vol. VII, No. 3 (Summer, 1943), 233–50.

Vengrov, N., and N. M. Efros. *Ein Mensch wie Du: Das Leben Nikolaj Ostrowskijs*. Trans. by K. Roose. Berlin, Verlag Kultur und Fortschritt, 1950.

Vickery, W. *The Cult of Optimism: Political and Ideological Problems of Recent Soviet Literature*. Bloomington, Indiana University Press, 1963.

Volkov, A. *Alexander Serafimowitsch*. Trans. by L. Kossuth. Berlin, Verlag
    Kultur und Fortschritt, 1953.
Walpole, H., ed. *Tendencies of the Modern Novel*. London, Allen & Unwin,
    1934. [D. S. Mirsky on the Soviet Russian novel.]
Weil, I. *Gorky: His Literary Development and Influence on Soviet Intellectual
    Life*. New York, Random House, [1966].
Wilczkowski, C. *Ecrivains soviétiques*. Paris, Editions de la Revue des Jeunes,
    1949.
Wolf, M. *Maxim Gorki: Revolutionärer Romantiker und sozialistischer Realist*.
    Berlin, Henschel Verlag, 1953.
Yarmolinsky, A. *Literature Under Communism*. Bloomington, Indiana Uni-
    versity Press, [1960].
Yershov, P. *Comedy in the Soviet Theatre*. New York, Praeger, 1956.
Zhdanov, A. A. *Essays on Literature, Philosophy and Music*. New York, Inter-
    national Publishers, 1950.
Zveteremich, P., ed. *Narratori Russi moderni*. Milano, Bompian, 1963.

Articles about Soviet literature, its problems, and individual authors will be
found in various academic publications, such as *Slavonic and East European
Review* (London), *American Slavic and East European Review* (later renamed
Slavic Review), *Russian Review* (United States), *Slavic and East European
Journal* (United States), *Canadian Slavic Studies* (Montreal), *Canadian Slavonic
Papers* (Toronto), *Revue des Études Slaves* (Paris), *Die Welt der Slaven* (Wiesbaden), *Slavische Zeitschrift* (Berlin), *Annali: Sezione slava* (Naples), *Ricerche
Slavistiche* (Rome), and *Scando-Slavica* (Copenhagen and Stockholm), as well
as in such publications as *Survey* (London) and *Problems of Communism*
(Washington, D.C.) and also in the English-language Moscow monthly *International Literature* (1933–45, thereafter continued as *Soviet Literature*). Articles
published in the United States after 1959 are listed in *The American Bibliography of Slavic and East European Studies* (see Section II).
    For English translations of the more important papers and articles published
in Soviet periodicals see *Soviet Studies in Literature* and similar series published
by International Arts and Sciences Publications (IASP), New York, as well as
Current Digest of the Soviet Press, published by Ohio State University, Columbus.

SECTION V. SOVIET LITERATURE IN ENGLISH TRANSLATION

A.   ANTHOLOGIES AND COLLECTIONS

Binyon, T. J., ed. *A Soviet Verse Reader*. New York, Pitman, 1965.
Blake, B., ed. *Four Soviet Plays*. Trans. by A. Wixley, H. G. Scott, and R. S.
    Carr. London, Lawrence and Wishart, 1937; New York, International Pub-
    lishers, 1937. [Plays by Gorky, Vishnevsky, Pogodin, and Kocherga.]
Blake, P., and M. Hayward, eds. *Dissonant Voices in Soviet Literature*. Intro. by
    M. Hayward. New York, Pantheon Books, 1962. [Pasternak, Zamyatin,
    Shklovsky, Esenin, Babel, Grin, Pilnyak, Zoshchenko, and others.]

Bowra, C. M., ed. *A Second Book of Russian Verse*. London, Macmillan, 1948.

Carlisle, O., ed. *Poets on Street Corners*. New York, Random House, 1968.

Cournos, J., comp. and trans. *Short Stories out of Soviet Russia*. London, Dent, 1929; New York, Dutton, 1929.

———, ed. *A Treasury of Russian Life and Humor*. New York, Coward-McCann, 1943.

Deutsch, B., and A. Yarmolinsky. *Russian Poetry: An Anthology*. Rev. ed. New York, International Publishers, 1930.

Dutt, V. L., trans. *Soviet Science Fiction*. New York, Collier, 1962.

Fineberg, J., ed. *Heroic Leningrad: Documents, Sketches and Stories*. Moscow, FLPH, 1945. [Tikhonov, Fadeyev, Vishnevsky, Bergholz, and others.]

Flying Osip: Stories of New Russia. Trans. by L. S. Friedland and J. R. Piroshnikoff. London, Fisher Unwin, 1925.

Four Soviet War Plays. London, Hutchinson, 1943. [Plays by Korneychuk, Leonov, and Simonov.]

Friedberg, M., ed. *A Bilingual Collection of Russian Short Stories*. New York, Random House, 1965. [Stories by Kaverin, Babel, Ivanov, Olesha, Pilnyak, and Tynyanov.]

Ginsburg, M., ed. and trans. *The Fatal Eggs and Other Soviet Satire*. New York, Macmillan, 1965.

Graham, S., ed. *Russian Great Short Stories*. London, Benn, 1929.

Guerney, B. G., ed. *An Anthology of Russian Literature in the Soviet Period from Gorki to Pasternak*. New York, Random House, 1960. [Includes Zamyatin's *We*.]

———, ed. *New Russian Stories*. Norfolk, Conn., New Directions, n.d. [Stories by Tynyanov, Yakovlev, Sobol, Grin, Gorky, Zoshchenko, Ivanov, Tolstoy, Pasternak, Zamyatin, Babel, Pilnyak, and others.]

———, ed. *Portable Russian Reader*. New York, Viking Press, 1947. [Selections by Gorky, Tolstoy, Ilf and Petrov, Babel, Ehrenburg, Katayev, and Zoschenko.]

———, ed. *A Treasury of Russian Literature*. New York, Vanguard Press, 1947; London, Bodley Head, 1948.

Kapp, V., ed. *Short Stories of Russia Today*. Trans. by T. Shebunina. Boston, Houghton Mifflin, 1959. [Stories by Paustovsky, Prishvin, Ilyenkov, Tikhonov, Lavrenyov, Simonov, Inber, Gorbatov, and others.]

Konovalov, S., ed. *Bonfire: Stories out of Soviet Russia*. London, Benn, 1932.

Kunitz, J., ed. *Azure Cities: Stories of New Russia*. Trans. by J. J. Robbins. New York, International Publishers, 1929; London, Modern Books, 1929.

———, ed. *Russian Literature Since the Revolution*. New York, Boni and Gaer, 1948.

Laughlin, J., ed. *New Directions in Prose and Poetry, 1941*. Norfolk, Conn., New Directions, 1941.

Lavrin, J. ed. *Russian Humorous Stories*. London, Sylvan Press, 1946.

Lemon, L. T., and M. J. Ries, eds. and trans. *Russian Formalist Criticism*. Lincoln, University of Nebraska Press, 1965.

Lindsay, J., trans. *Modern Russian Poetry*. London, Vista Books, 1960.

Lyons, E., ed. *Six Soviet Plays*. Boston and New York, Houghton Mifflin, 1934; London, Gollancz, 1935.

MacAndrew, A., trans. and ed. *Four Soviet Masterpieces*. Toronto, New York, and London, Bantam Books, 1965.

————, trans. and ed. *20th Century Russian Drama*. New York, Bantam Books, 1963. [Mayakovsky, *The Bathouse*; Olesha, *A List of Assets*.]

Magidoff, R., ed. *Russian Science Fiction: An Anthology*. Trans. by D. Johnson. New York, New York University Press, 1964.

Markov, Vl., and M. Sparks, eds. *Modern Russian Poetry: An Anthology with Verse Translations*. Intro. by V. Markov. New York, Bobbs Merrill, 1966; London, McGibbon & Kee, 1966.

Milner-Gulland, R. R., ed. *Soviet Russian Verse: An Anthology*. New York, Macmillan, 1964.

Modern Poets from Russia. Trans. by G. Shelley. London, Allen & Unwin, 1942.

Modern Russian Stories. Selected and trans. by E. Fen. London, Methuen, 1943.

Montagu, I., and H. Marshall, eds. *Soviet Short Stories, 1942*. London, Pilot Press, 1942.

————, and ————, eds. *Soviet Short Stories, 1942–43*. London, Pilot Press, 1943.

————, and ————, eds. *Soviet Short Stories, 1944*. London, Pilot Press, 1944.

Newnham, R., ed. *Soviet Short Stories*. London, Dobson, 1962; Baltimore, Penguin Books, 1963.

Noyes, G. R., ed. *Masterpieces of the Russian Drama*. New York and London, Appleton, 1933. [Includes Mayakovsky, *Mystery-Bouffe*.]

Obolensky, D., ed. *The Penguin Book of Russian Verse*. Balitmore, Penguin Books, 1962.

Patrick, L. A., ed. *Six Soviet One-Act Plays*. New York, Pitman, 1963.

Reavey, G., ed. *14 Great Short Stories by Soviet Writers*. New York, Avon Books, 1959. [Stories by Gorky, Tolstoy, Zamyatin, Ehrenburg, Ivanov, Babel, Zoshchenko, Olesha, Prishvin, Pasternak, and Sholokhov.]

————, ed. *Modern Soviet Short Stories*. New York, Grosset & Dunlap, 1961.

————, and M. Slonim, eds. *Soviet Literature: An Anthology*. London, Wishart, 1933; New York, Covici-Friede, 1934.

Reeve, F. D., ed. *An Anthology of Russian Plays*. Vol. II. New York, Random House, 1963.

————, ed. *Great Soviet Short Stories*. New York, Dell, 1962. [Stories by Babel, Bulgakov, Fadeyev, Fedin, Ilf and Petrov, Ivanov, I. Katayev, V. Katayev, Kaverin, Leonov, Nikitin, Olesha, Pasternak, Pilnyak, Romanov, Sholokhov, Tynyanov, Zamyatin, Zoshchenko, and others.]

Road to Victory: Twelve Tales of the Red Army. London, Hutchinson, [1945].

The Road to the West: Sixty Soviet War Poems. Selected and trans. by A. M. Williams and V. de Sola Pinto. London, F. Muller, 1945.

Rodker, J., ed. *Soviet Anthology*. Trans. by A. Brown, S. Garry, and others. London, Cape, 1943.

Russian Short Stories. London, Faber & Faber, [1943?].

Snow, C. P., and P. H. Johnson, eds. *Stories from Modern Russia: Winter's*

Tales 7. New York, St. Martin's Press, 1962. [Stories by Tvardovsky, Paustovsky, Sholokhov, and others.]

Soviet Scene: Six Plays of Russian Life. Trans. by A. Bakshy. New Haven, Yale University Press, 1946.

Soviet Short Stories. Moscow, FLPH, 1947.

Soviet Stories of the Last Decade. Selected and trans. by E. Fen. London, Methuen, 1945.

Soviet War Stories. London, Hutchinson, 1943.

Struve, G., ed. *Russian Stories*. Bantam Dual-Language Book. Toronto, London, and New York, Bantam Books, 1961. [Stories by Babel, Zamyatin, and Zoshchenko.]

Three Soviet Plays. London, Penguin Books, 1966. [Mayakovsky, *The Bedbug*, trans. by M. Hayward; Babel, *Mariya*, trans. by M. Glenny and H. Shukman; Schwartz, *The Dragon*, trans. by M. Hayward and H. Shukman; Intros. by M. Glenny, P. Blake, and H. Shukman.]

We Carry On: Tales of the War. Moscow, FLPH, 1942.

Yarmolinsky, A., ed. *Soviet Short Stories*. Garden City, Doubleday Anchor Books, 1960. [Stories by Zamyatin, Pasternak, Romanov, Zoshchenko, Olesha, Katayev, Paustovsky, Yashin, and others.]

———, ed. *A Treasury of Russian Verse*. New York, Macmillan, 1949.

———, ed. *Two Centuries of Russian Verse: An Anthology from Lomonosov to Voznesensky*. Trans. by B. Deutsch. New York, Random House, 1966.

B. WORKS BY INDIVIDUAL AUTHORS[1]

Afinogenov, A. *Distant Point*. Trans. and adapted by H. Griffith. London, Pushkin Press, 1941. [Translation of the play *Dalyokoye*.]

———. *Fear*. In Lyons, ed. *Six Soviet Plays* [see Section V-A]. Also: Trans. by N. Strelsky, D. B. Colman, and A. Greene. Poughkeepsie, 1934.

———. *Listen, Professor!* American acting version by P. Phillips. New York and Los Angeles, French, 1944. [Adaptation of *Mashenka*.]

Akhmatova, A. *Forty-seven Love Poems*. Trans. by N. Duddington. London, Cape, 1927.

———. *Selected Poems*. Trans. by R. McKane. New York, Oxford University Press, 1969.

Arseniev, V. K. *Dersu, the Trapper: A Hunter's Life in Ussuria*. Trans. by M. Burr. London, Secker and Warburg, 1939; New York, Dutton, 1941.

Avdeyenko, A. *I Love*. Trans. by A. Wixley. London, Lawrence, 1935; New York, International Publishers, 1935.

Averbakh, L., ed. *Belomor: An Account of the Construction of the New Canal Between the White Sea and the Baltic Sea*. New York, Smith and Haas, 1935.

Babel, I. *Benia Krik: A Film Novel*. Trans. by I. Montagu and S. Nalbandov. London, Collet's, 1935.

———. *Benya Krik, the Gangster, and Other Stories*. Ed. by A. Yarmolinsky. New York, Schocken Books, 1948.

---

[1] Only translations of works published before 1953 are included here.

————. *Collected Stories*. Trans. and ed. by W. Morrison, Intro. by L. Trilling, New York, Criterion Books, 1955.

————. *Isaac Babel: The Lonely Years, 1925–1939*. Trans. by A. R. MacAndrew and M. Hayward, ed., with Intro., by N. Babel. New York, Farrar, Straus, 1964. [Unpublished stories and private correspondence.]

————. *Red Cavalry*. Trans. by N. Helstein. New York and London, Knopf, 1929.

————. *Sunset*. New York, Noonday, 1961.

————. *You Must Know Everything: Stories 1917–1937*. Trans. by M. Hayward, ed. by N. Babel. New York, Farrar, Straus & Giroux, 1969. Also: Trans. by M. Hayward. New York, Harper & Row, 1969.

Bazhov, P. *The Malachite Casket: Tales from the Urals*. Trans. by A. M. Williams. London and New York, Hutchinson, 1944.

Beck, A. *On the Forward Fringe: A Novel of General Panfilov's Division*. London, Hutchinson, 1945.

Bill-Belotserkovsky, V. *Life Is Calling: A Play in Four Acts*. Trans. by A. Wixley. London, Lawrence and Wishart, 1938; New York, International Publishers, 1938.

Blok, A. *The Spirit of Music*. Trans. by I. Freiman. London, Lindsay Drummond, 1946. [Includes several of Blok's post-Revolutionary essays.]

————. *The Twelve*. Trans. by C. E. Bechhofer. London, Chatto and Windus, 1920. Also: Trans. by B. Deutsch and A. Yarmolinsky. New York, Rudge, 1931.

Bulgakov, M. *Days of the Turbins*. In Lyons, ed. *Six Soviet Plays* [see Section V-*A*].

Chapygin, A. *Stepan Razin*. Trans. by C. Paul. London and New York, Hutchinson, 1946.

Chukovsky, K. *Crocodile*. Trans. by B. Deutsch. New York, Lippincott, 1931; London, Mathews, 1932.

————. *From Two to Five*. Trans. and ed. by M. Morton. Berkeley, University of California Press, 1963.

Chumandrin, M. *White Star*. London, Lawrence, 1933.

Efremov, I. *Andromeda: A Space-Age Tale*. Trans. by G. Hanna. Moscow, FLPH, [1960].

————. *A Meeting over Tuscarora and Other Adventures*. Trans. by M. and N. Nichols. London, Hutchinson, 1946.

Ehrenburg, I. *European Crossroad: A Soviet Journalist in the Balkans*. Trans. by A. Markov. New York, Knopf, 1947. [Translation of *Roads to Europe*.]

————. *The Extraordinary Adventures of Julio Jurenito and His Disciples . . . .* Trans. by U. Vanzler. New York, Covici-Friede, 1930. Also: *Julio Jurenito*. Trans. by A. Bostock and Y. Kapp. London, MacGibbon, 1958; Chester Springs, Pa., Du Four, 1963.

————. *The Fall of Paris*. Trans. by G. Shelley. London, Hutchinson, 1942; New York, Knopf, 1943; new ed., London, May Fair, 1962.

————. *The Love of Jeanne Ney*. Trans. by H. C. Mathewson. London, Peter Davies, 1929.

———. *The Ninth Wave*. Trans. by T. Shebunina and J. Castle. London, Lawrence, 1955.

———. *Out of Chaos*. Trans. by A. Bakshy. New York, Henry Holt, 1934. [Translation of *The Second Day*.]

———. *Russia at War*. Trans. by G. Shelley. Intro. by J. B. Priestley. London, Hutchinson, 1943.

———. *A Soviet Writer Looks at Vienna*. Trans. by I. Montagu. London, Lawrence, 1934.

———. *The Storm*. Trans. by E. Hartley and T. Shebunina. London and New York, Hutchinson, 1949.

———. *Stormy Life of Lazik Roitschwantz*. Trans. by L. Barocowicz and G. Flor. New York, Polyglot, 1960. Also: *The Stormy Life of Laz Roitshvantz*. Trans. by A. Brown. London, Elek Books, 1965.

———. *A Street in Moscow*. Trans. by S. Volochova. New York, Covici-Friede, 1932; London, Grayson & Grayson, 1933. [Translation of *In Protochny Lane*.]

———. *The Tempering of Russia*. Trans. by A. Kaun. New York, Knopf, 1944.

Ejxenbaum, B. M. *O'Henry and the Theory of the Short Story*. Trans. and ed. by I. Titunik. Ann Arbor, University of Michigan Press, 1968.

Emelyanova, N. *The Surgeon*. Trans. by J. Fineberg. London, Hutchinson, 1945.

Fadeyev, A. *Leningrad in the Days of the Blockade*. Trans. by R. D. Charques. London, 1946.

———. *The Nineteen*. Trans. by R. D. Charques. London, Lawrence, 1929; New York, International Publishers, 1929. Also: *The Rout*. Trans. by O. Gorchakov. Moscow, FLHP, 1956.

———. *Young Guard*. Trans. by V. Dutt, ed. by D. Skvirsky. London, Universal Distributors, 1959.

Fedin, K. *Cities and Years*. Trans. by M. Scammell. New York, Dell, 1962.

———. *Early Joys*. Trans. by H. Kazanina, Intro. by E. J. Simmons. New York, Random House, 1960.

———. *No Ordinary Summer*. 2 vols. Trans. by M. Wettlin. Moscow, FLHP, 1950.

Furmanov, D. *Chapayev*. London, Lawrence, 1935; New York, International Publishers, 1935. Also: Trans. by G. and J. Kittell. Moscow, FLHP, 1959.

Gaydar, A. *Timur and His Comrades*. Trans. by R. Renbourn. London, Pilot Press, 1942. Also: *Timur and His Gang*. New York, Scribner's, 1943.

Gladkov, F. *Cement*. Trans. by A. S. Arthur and C. A. Ashleigh. London, Lawrence, 1929; New York, International Publishers, 1929.

———. *Restless Youth*. Trans. by R. Parker and V. Scott. Moscow, FLPH, 1959.

Glebov, A. *Inga: A Play in Four Acts*. In Lyons, ed. *Six Soviet Plays* [see Section V-A].

Gorky, M. *The Artamonov Business*. Trans. by A. Brown. London, Hamilton, 1948; New York, Pantheon Books, 1948.

———. *The Autobiography of Maxim Gorky*. New York, Collier, 1962.

———. *Best Short Stories*. Ed. by A. Yarmolinsky and M. Budberg. London, Cape, 1939; New York, Grayson, 1939.

————. *Bystander*. Trans. by B. G. Guerney. New York, Cape and Smith, 1930; London, Cape. 1930. [Vol. I of *The Life of Klim Samgin*.]

————. *Culture and the People*. London, Lawrence and Wisehart, 1939.

————. *Days with Lenin*. London, Lawrence, 1933.

————. *Decadence*. Trans. by V. Dewey. New York, McBride, 1927; London, Cassell, 1927. [Translation of *The Artamonov Business*.]

————. *The Judge: A Play in Four Acts*. Trans. by M. Zakrevsky and B. H. Clark. New York, McBride, 1924.

————. *The Last Plays*. Adapted by Gibson-Cowan. London, Lawrence and Wishart, 1937. [*Egor Bulychev and Others* and *Dostigayev and Others*.]

————. *Lenin: A Biographical Essay*. Intro. by Z. A. B. Zeman. Edinburgh, Oxford University Press, 1967.

————. *The Life of Matvey Kozhemyakin*. Trans. by M. Wettlin. Moscow, FLPH, 1960.

————. *Literary Portraits*. Trans. by I. Litvinov. Moscow, FLPH, n.d.

————. *Literature and Life*. Trans. by E. Bone. London, Hutchinson, 1946.

————. *The Magnet*. Trans. by A. Bakshy. New York, Cape and Smith, 1931; London, Cape, 1931. [Vol. II of *The Life of Klim Samgin*.]

————. *On Guard for the Soviet Union*. London, Lawrence, 1931; New York, International Publishers, 1933.

————. *On Literature: Selected Articles*. Trans. by J. Katzer and I. Litvinov. Moscow, FLPH, 1960.

————. *Orphan Paul*. Trans. by L. Turner and M. Strever. New York, Boni and Gaer, 1946. [Also includes "How I Became a Writer."]

————. *Other Fires*. Trans. by A. Bakshy. New York and London, Appleton, 1933. [Vol. III of *The Life of Klim Samgin*.]

————. *Reminiscences of Leonid Andreyev*. Trans. by K. Mansfield and S. S. Koteliansky. London, Heinemann, 1931.

————. *Reminiscences of My Youth*. Trans. by V. Dewey. London, Heinemann, 1924.

————. *Reminiscences of Tolstoy, Chekov and Andreyev*. New ed. Trans. by K. Mansfield, S. S. Koteliansky, and L. Woolf. London, Hogarth Press, 1949.

————. *Seven Plays by Maxim Gorky*. Trans. by A. Bakshy. New Haven, Yale University Press, 1945.

————. *A Sky-Blue Life and Selected Stories*. Trans. with Foreword by G. Reavey. New York, New American Library, 1964.

————. *The Specter*. Trans. by A. Bakshy. New York and London, D. Appleton-Century, 1938. [Vol. IV of *The Life of Klim Samgin*.]

————. *The Story of the Novel and Other Stories*. Trans. by M. Zakrevsky. New York, Dial Press, 1925.

————. *To American Intellectuals*. New York, International Pamphlets, 1932.

————. *Unrequited Love and Other Stories*. Trans. by M. Budberg. London, Weidenfeld & Nicolson, 1949.

————. *Untimely Thoughts: Essays on Revolution, Culture and the Bolsheviks, 1917–1918*. Trans. with Intro. by H. Ermolaev. New York, P. S. Eriksson, 1968.

——, ed. *History of the Civil War in the U.S.S.R.* Vol. II: *The Great Proletarian Revolution, October-November, 1917.* Trans. by J. Fineberg. London, Lawrence, 1947.

Grossman, V. *No Beautiful Nights.* New York, Julian Messner, 1944. [Translation of *The People Immortal.*]

——. *The People Immortal.* Trans. by E. Donnelly. Moscow, FLPH, 1943.

——. *Stalingrad Hits Back.* Trans. by A. Fineberg and D. Fromberg. Moscow, FLPH, 1942.

——. *The Years of War (1941–1945).* Trans. by E. Donnelly and R. Prokofiev. Moscow, FLPH, 1946.

Herman, Yu. *Alexei the Gangster.* Trans. by S. Garry. London, Routledge, 1940. [Translation of "Alexey Zhmakin" and "Lapshin."]

——. *Antonina.* Trans. by S. Garry. London, Routledge, 1937. American ed.: *Tonia.* New York, Knopf, 1938. [Translation of *Nashi znakomye.*]

Ignatov, P. K. *Partisans of the Kuban.* Trans. by J. Fineberg. London, Hutchinson, 1945.

Ilf, I., and E. Petrov. *Diamonds to Sit on.* Trans. by E. Hill and D. Mudie. London, Methuen, 1930. Also: *The Twelve Chairs.* Trans. by J. Richardson, Intro. by M. Friedberg. New York, Random House, 1961.

——, and ——. *The Little Golden America: Two Famous Humorists Survey These United States.* New York, Farrar & Rinehart, 1937.

——, and ——. *The Little Golden Calf: A Satiric Novel.* Trans. by C. Malamuth. London, Grayson & Grayson; New York, Farrar & Rinehart, 1932. Also: *The Golden Calf.* Trans. by J. H. C. Richardson. New York, Random House, 1962; London, F. Muller, 1964.

Ilyenkov, V. *Driving Axle: A Novel of Socialist Reconstruction.* London, Lawrence, 1933; New York, International Publishers, 1933.

Ivanov, V. *The Adventures of a Fakir.* New York, Vanguard Press, n.d. Also: *Patched Breeches.* Toronto, Macmillan, [1936]; *I Live a Queer Life: An Extraordinary Biography.* London, Lovat Dickson, 1936.

——. *Armoured Train 14–69.* Trans. by Gibson-Cowan and A. T. K. Grand. London, Lawrence, 1933.

Kalinin, A. *In the South.* Trans. by S. Garry. London, Hutchinson, 1946.

Kallinikov, I. *Land of Bondage.* Trans. by P. Kirwin. London, Grayson, 1931.

——. *Women and Monks.* Trans. by P. Kirwin. London, Secker, 1930; New York, Harcourt, Brace, 1930.

Kassil, L. *Brother of the Hero.* Trans. by A. T. White. New York, Braziller, 1968.

——. *Land of Shvambrania: A Novel with Maps, a Coat of Arms and a Flag.* Trans. by S. Glass and N. Guterman. New York, Viking Press, 1935.

——. *The Story of Alesha-Ryazan and Uncle White-Sea.* London, Lawrence, 1935; New York, Co-operative Publishing Society, 1935.

Katayev, V. *The Embezzlers.* Trans. by L. Zarine. London, Benn, 1929; New York, Dial Press, 1929.

——. *Lonely White Sail, or Peace Is Where the Tempests Blow.* Trans. by C.

Malamuth. London, Allen & Unwin, 1937; New York, Farrar & Rinehart, 1937.

———. *Small Farm in the Steppe*. Trans. by A. Bostock. London, Lawrence, 1958.

———. *Squaring the Circle*. Trans. by N. Goold-Verschoyle. London, Wishart, 1934. Also: Rev. ed. by A. Dukes. New York, 1935. In Lyons, ed. *Six Soviet Plays* [see Section V-*A*].

———. *Time, Forward!* Trans. by C. Malamuth. New York, Farrar & Rinehart, 1933. British ed.: *Forward, Oh Time!* London, Gollancz, 1934.

———. *The Wife*. London, Hutchinson, 1946.

Kaverin, V. *The Larger View*. Trans. by E. Swan. New York, Stackpole Sons; London, Collins, 1938. [Translation of *Fulfillment of Desires*.]

———. *An Open Book*. Trans. by Brian Pearce. London, Lawrence, 1955.

———. *Two Captains*. Trans. by E. Swan. London, Cassell, 1938; New York, Modern Age, 1942.

———. *The Unknown Artist*. Trans. by P. Ross. London, Westhouse, 1947. [In the same volume with Yu. Olesha, *Envy*. Intro. by G. Struve.]

Kirshon, V. *Bread: A Play in Five Acts*. In Lyons, ed. *Six Soviet Plays* [see Section V-*A*].

———, and A. V. Ouspensky. *Red Rust*. Trans. by V. Vernon and F. Vernon. New York, Brentano's, 1930.

Kocherga, I. *Masters of Time: A Play in Four Acts*. In Blake, ed. *Four Soviet Plays* [see Section V-*A*]. [Translation of *The Watchmaker and the Hen*.]

Kollontay, A. *Red Love*. New York, Seven Arts, 1927. Also: *Great Love*. Trans. by L. Lore. New York, Vanguard Press, 1929; and *Free Love*. Trans. by C. J. Hogarth. London, Dent, 1934. [Translations of *The Love of Toiling Bees*.]

Korneychuk, A. *The Front*. In *Four Soviet War Plays* [see Section V-*A*].

———. *Guerrillas in the Ukrainian Steppes*. In *Four Soviet War Plays* [see Section V-*A*].

Krymov, Y. *Tanker Derbent*. Trans. by B. Kagan. Kuybyshev, 1940.

Larry, Y. *The Extraordinary Adventures of Karik and Valda*. Trans. by J. P. Mandeville. London, Hutchinson, 1945.

Leonov, L. *The Badgers*. London, Hutchinson, 1946.

———. *Chariot of Wrath*. Trans. by N. Guterman. New York, Fischer, 1946. [Translation of *The Taking of Velikoshumsk*.]

———. *The Invasion*. In *Four Soviet War Plays* [see Section V-*A*].

———. *Road to the Ocean*. Trans. by N. Guterman. New York, Fischer, 1944.

———. *The Russian Forest*. Trans. by B. Isaacs. Moscow, 1966.

———. *Skutarevsky*. Trans. by A. Brown. London, Lovat Dickson, 1936; New York, Harcourt, Brace, 1936.

———. *Sot*. Trans. by I. Montagu and S. Nalbandov. London and New York, Putnam, 1931. [American ed. under the title *Soviet River*.]

———. *The Thief*. Trans. by H. Butler. London, Secker, 1931; New York, Dial Press, 1931; new ed., Intro. by R. Mathewson, Jr., New York, Random House, 1960.

————. *Tuatamur*. Trans. by I. Montagu and S. Nalbandov. London, Collet's, 1935.

Libedinsky, Yu. *A Week*. London, Allen & Unwin, 1923; New York, Huebsch, 1923.

Lidin, V. *The Apostate*. Trans. by H. C. Matheson. London, Cape, 1931. American ed.: *The Price of Life*. New York, Harper and Brothers, 1932.

Lunacharsky, A. *The Bear's Wedding*. Trans. by Z. Zamkovsky and N. Borudin. London, 1926.

————. *On Literature and Art*. Moscow, 1965.

————. *Revolutionary Silhouettes*. Trans. and ed. by M. Glenny, Intro. by I. Deutscher. London, Penguin Press, 1967.

————. *Three Plays (Faust and the City, Vasilisa the Wise, The Magi)*. Trans. by L. A. Magnus and K. Walter. London, Routledge, 1923.

Luntz, L. *The City of Truth: A Play in Three Acts*. Trans. by J. Silver. London, 1929.

Makarenko, A. *The Collective Family: A Handbook for Russian Parents*. Trans. by R. Daglish, Intro. by U. Bronfenbrenner. Garden City, Doubleday, 1967.

————. *Road to Life*. Trans. by S. Garry. London, Nott, 1936. Also: *Road to Life*. 3 vols. Trans. by I. Litvinov and T. Litvinov. London, Collet's, 1952. [Translation of *Educational Epic*.]

Mandelstam, O. *The Prose of Osip Mandelstam: The Noise of Time—Theodosia —The Egyptian Stamp*. Trans. with Intro. by C. Brown. Princeton, Princeton University Press, 1965.

Marienhoff, A. *Cynics*. Trans. by V. D. Bell and L. Coleman. New York, Boni, 1930.

Marshak, S. *At Life's Beginning: Some Pages of Reminiscence*. Trans. by K. H. Blair, Foreword by M. Budberg. New York, Dutton, 1964.

Matveyev, V. *Bitter Draught*. Trans. by D. Flower. London, Collins, 1935.

————. *Commissar of the Gold Express: An Episode in the Civil War*. London, Lawrence, 1933; New York, International Publishers, 1933. [Translation of *The Golden Train*.]

Mayakovsky, V. *The Bathhouse*. In *Three Soviet Plays* [see Section V-A].

————. *The Bedbug and Selected Poetry*. Trans. by M. Hayward and G. Reavey, ed. by P. Blake. New York, Meridian Books, 1960.

————. *The Complete Plays*. Trans. by G. Daniels, Intro. by Robert Payne. [1968].

————. *Mayakovsky and His Poetry*. Comp. by H. Marshall. London, Pilot Press, 1942; rev. ed., 1945; 3d ed., Bombay, Current Book House, 1955; new ed., New York, Hill & Wang, 1965.

————. *Mystery-Bouffe*. Trans. by G. R. Noyes and A. Kaun. In Noyes, ed. *Masterpieces of the Russian Drama* [see Section V-A].

Neverov, A. *City of Bread*. Trans. anonymous. New York, Doran, 1927. Also: *Tashkent*. Trans. by R. Morton and W. G. Walton. London, Gollancz, 1930.

Nilin, P. *Comrade Venka*. Trans. by J. Barnes. New York, Simon and Schuster, 1959.

————. *Cruelty*. New York, Macmillan, 1963.

Nizovoy, P. *The Ocean.* Trans. by J. Cournos. New York and London, Harper and Brothers, 1936.

Novikov-Priboy, A. *The Captain.* London, Hutchinson, 1946.

———. *Tsushima.* Trans. by E. and C. Paul. London, Allen & Unwin, 1936.

Ognyov, N. *The Diary of a Communist Schoolboy.* Trans. by A. Werth. London, Gollancz, 1928; New York, Payson & Clarke, 1928.

———. *The Diary of a Communist Undergraduate.* Trans. by A. Werth. London, Gollancz, 1929; New York, Payson & Clarke, 1929.

Olesha, Yu. *Envy.* Trans. by A. Wolfe. London, Hogarth Press, 1936. Also: Trans. by P. Ross. London, Westhouse, 1947. [In the same volume with V. Kaverin, *The Unknown Artist.* Intro. by G. Struve.]

———. *Love and Other Stories.* Trans. with Intro. by R. Payne. New York, Washington Square Press, 1967.

———. *The Wayward Comrade and the Commissars.* Trans. by A. R. Mac-Andrew. New York, Signet Books, 1960. [Translation of *Envy*; also includes some stories.]

Ostrovsky, N. *Born of the Storm.* Trans. by L. L. Hiler. New York, Critics Group, 1939.

———. *The Making of a Hero.* Trans. by A. Brown. New York, Dutton, 1937.

Panfyorov, F. *Bruski: A Story of Peasant Life in Soviet Russia.* Trans. by Z. Mitrov and J. Tabrisky. New York, International Publishers, 1930; London, Lawrence, 1930.

Panova, V. *Factory.* Trans. by M. Budberg. Toronto, McClelland, 1950.

———. *Span of the Year.* Trans. by V. Traill. London, Harvill, 1957. [Translation of *Four Seasons.*]

———. *Time Walked.* Cambridge, Mass., Arlington Books, 1959. [Translation of *A Summer to Remember.*] Also: *A Summer to Remember.* New York, Yoseloff, 1962.

———. *The Train.* Trans. by M. Budberg. New York, Knopf, 1949.

Pasternak, B. *The Adolescence of Zhenya Luvers.* Trans. by I. Langnas. New York, Citadel, 1961.

———. *Childhood.* Trans. by R. Payne. Singapore, Straits Times Press, 1941. [Unsatisfactory translation of *The Childhood of Luvers.*]

———. *The Collected Prose Works.* Trans. by R. Payne and B. Scott. London, Lindsay Drummond, 1945. [*Safe Conduct* and four short stories.]

———. *Fifty Poems.* Trans., with Intro., by L. Pasternak-Slater. London, Allen & Unwin, 1963.

———. *Five Lyric Poems.* Trans. by L. Pasternak-Slater. London, Elek Books, 1959.

———. *In the Interlude: Poems 1945–1960.* Trans. by H. Kamen, Foreword by Sir M. Bowra, notes by G. Katkov. London, Oxford University Press, 1962.

———. *The Last Summer.* Trans. with Intro. by G. Reavey. New York, Hearst Corporation, Avon Book Division, [1959]. [Also contains "A District Behind the Front."] Also: Intro. by Lydia Slater. London, Penguin Books, 1960.

————. *Letters to Georgian Friends.* Trans. with Intro. by D. Magarshack. New York, Harcourt, Brace and World, 1968.

————. *Poems.* Trans. by L. Slater. Foreword by H. Macdiarmid. Fairwarp, Sussex, Peter Russell, 1957, 1959.

————. *Poems.* Trans. by E. M. Kayden. Ann Arbor, University of Michigan Press, 1959; 2d ed., rev. and enl., Yellow Springs, Ohio, 1964.

————. *The Poetry of Boris Pasternak 1917–1959.* Trans. and ed. by G. Reavey. New York, Putnam, 1959. [Contains an essay on the life and writings of Pasternak and a bibliography by G. Reavey, as well as three important prose pieces by Pasternak.]

————. *Safe Conduct: An Early Autobiography and Other Works.* Trans. by A. Brown. *Five Lyric Poems.* Trans. by L. Pasternak-Slater. London, Elek Books, 1959.

————. *Selected Poems.* Trans. by J. M. Cohen. London, Lindsay Drummond, 1947.

————. *Selected Writings.* Norfolk, Conn., New Directions, 1949; new ed., 1958. Also: London, Benn, 1959. [*Safe Conduct,* four stories, and selected poems.]

————. *Sister My Life: Summer 1917.* Trans. by P. C. Flayderman. New York, Washington Square Press, 1967.

————. *Three Letters from Boris Pasternak.* Trans. by D. Magarshack. New York, Harcourt, Brace and World, 1967.

Paustovsky, K. *The Black Gulf: Stories.* Trans. by E. Schimanskaya. London, Hutchinson, 1946.

————. *The Golden Rose.* Trans. by S. Rosenberg. Moscow, FLPH, 1961.

Pavlenko, P. *Flames of Vengeance.* Moscow, FLPH, 1942. [Translation of *A Russian Tale.*]

————. *Red Planes Fly East.* Trans. by S. Garry. London, Routledge, 1938. [Translation of *In the East.*]

Perventsev, A. *Cossack Commander.* Trans. by S. Garry. London, Routledge, 1939. [Translation of *Kochubey.*]

————. *The Ordeal.* New York and London, Harper and Brothers, 1944. British ed.: *The Test.*

Pilnyak, B. *Ivan Moscow.* Trans. by A. S. Schwartzmann. New York, Christopher, 1935.

————. *Mother Earth and Other Stories.* Trans. and ed. by V. T. Reck and M. Green. New York, Praeger, 1968.

————. *The Naked Year.* Trans. by A. Brown. New York, Payson and Clarke, 1928; London, Putnam, 1928.

————. *The Tale of the Unextinguished Moon and Other Stories.* Trans. by B. Scott, Intro. by R. Payne. New York, Washington Square Press, 1967.

————. *Tales of the Wilderness.* Trans. by F. O'Dempsey. New York, Knopf, 1925.

————. *The Volga Flows to the Caspian Sea.* Trans. by C. Malamuth. New York, Farrar & Rinehart, 1931; London, Davies, 1932.

Platonov, A. *The Fierce and Beautiful World.* Trans. by J. Barnes, Intro. by Y. Yevtushenko. New York, Dutton, 1970. [Translations of several stories.]

Pogodin, N. *Aristocrats: A Comedy in Four Acts*. In Blake, ed. *Four Soviet Plays* [see Section V-*A*]. Also: acting ed. London, Lawrence, 1937.

———. *Tempo*. In Lyons, ed. *Six Soviet Plays* [see Section V-*A*].

Polevoy, B. *A Russian Looks at Reborn Europe*. London, Soviet News, 1946.

———. *To the Last Breath*. London, Hutchinson, 1945.

Polyakov, A. *Russians Don't Surrender*. Trans. by N. Guterman. New York, Dutton, 1942.

———. *White Mammoths: The Dramatic Story of Russian Tanks*. Trans. by N. Guterman. New York, Dutton, 1943. British ed.: *Westbound Tanks*. London, Hutchinson, 1943.

———. *With a Soviet Unit Through the Nazi Lines*. London, Hutchinson, 1944.

Prishvin, M. *Jen Sheng: The Root of Life*. Trans. by G. Walton and P. Gibbons. London, Melrose, 1936.

———. *The Lake and the Woods, or Nature's Calendar*. Trans. by W. L. Goodman. New York, Pantheon, 1952.

———. *Shiptimber Grove*. Trans. by D. Fry. London, Lawrence, 1957.

———. *Treasure Trove of the Sun*. Trans. by R. Balkoff-Drowne. New York, Viking Press, 1952.

Romanov, P. *Diary of a Soviet Marriage*. Trans. by J. Furnivall and R. Parmenter. London, Nutt, 1936.

———. *The New Commandment*. Trans. by V. Snow. New York, Scribner's, 1933; London, Benn, 1933.

———. *On the Volga and Other Stories*. Trans. by A. Gretton. New York, Scribner's, 1931; London, Benn, 1931.

———. *Three Pairs of Silk Stockings*. Trans. by L. Zarine. New York, Scribner's, 1931; London, Benn, 1931. [Translation of *Comrade Kislyakov*.]

———. *Without Cherry Blossom*. Trans. by L. Zarine. London, Benn, 1930.

Ryss, E. *Before the Shadows Fell*. London, Hutchinson, 1946.

Serafimovich, A. *The Iron Flood*. London, Lawrence, 1935.

Sergeyev-Tsensky, S. *Transfiguration*. Trans. by M. Budberg. Ed. with Intro. by M. Gorky. New York, McBride, 1926. [Translation of *Valya*.]

Shiryaev, P. *Taglioni's Grandson: The Story of a Russian Horse*. Trans. by A. Fremantle. London, Putnam, 1937. American ed.: *Flattery's Foal*. New York, Knopf, 1938.

Shishkov, V. *Children of Darkness*. London, Gollancz, 1931.

Shkvarkin, V. *Father Unknown*. [Translation of *Another Man's Child*.] In *Soviet Scene* [see Section V-*A*].

Sholokhov, M. *And Quiet Flows the Don*. Trans. by S. Garry. London, Putnam, 1934; New York, Knopf, 1935. [Vols. I and II of *The Quiet Don*.]

———. *The Don Flows Home to the Sea*. Trans. by S. Garry. London, Putnam, 1940; New York, Knopf, 1941. [Continuation of *And Quiet Flows the Don*.]

———. *One Man's Destiny and Other Stories, Articles, and Sketches: 1923–1963*. Trans. by H. C. Stevens. New York, Knopf, 1967.

———. *Tales of the Don*. Trans. by H. C. Stevens. New York, Knopf, 1962.

———. *Virgin Soil Upturned.* Trans. by S. Garry. London, Putnam, 1935, American ed.: *Seeds of Tomorrow.* New York, Knopf, 1942.

Simonov, K. *Days and Nights.* Trans. by J. Barnes. New York, Simon and Schuster, 1945. Also: Trans. by J. Fineberg. London, Hutchinson, 1945.

———. *The Russians.* In *Four Soviet War Plays* [see Section V-*A*].

Smirnov, V. *Sons.* Trans. by N. Y. Yohel. New York, Doubleday, 1947.

Smirnova, N. *Marfa: A Siberian Novel.* Trans. by M. Burr. London, Boriswood, 1932.

Sobol, A. *Freak Show.* Trans. by J. Cowan. New York and London, Kendall, 1930.

Sobolev, L. *Soul of the Sea.* Trans. by N. Orloff. Philadelphia and New York, Lippincott, 1946.

———. *Storm Warning.* Trans. by A. Fremantle. London, 1935. American ed.: *Romanoff.* New York, Longmans, Green, 1935. [Abridged version of *Capital Refitting.*]

Tarasov-Rodionov, A. *February 1917.* Trans. by W. A. Drake. New York, Covici-Friede, 1931.

———. *Chocolate.* Trans by C. Malamuth. New York, Doubleday, 1932; London, Heinemann, 1933.

Teleshov, N. *A Writer Remembers.* Trans. by L. Britton. London, Hutchinson, 1946.

Tolstoy, A. N. *Bread.* Trans. by S. Garry. London, Gollancz, 1937.

———. *Daredevils and Other Stories.* Trans. by D. Fromberg. Moscow, FLPH, 1942.

———. *Darkness and Dawn.* Trans. by E. Bone and E. Burns. London, Gollancz, 1935; New York, Longmans, Green, 1936. [The first two parts of *The Way Through Hell.*]

———. *The Death Box.* Trans. by B. G. Guerney. London, Methuen, 1936. Also: *The Garin Death Ray.* Trans. by Y. Rakuzin. Moscow, FLPH, 1961.

———. *Imperial Majesty.* Trans. by H. C. Matheson. London, Mathews and Marrot, 1932. American ed.: *Peter the Great.* New York, Covici-Friede, 1932. [Vol. I of *Peter the First.*]

———. *Nikita's Childhood.* Trans. by V. Lansbury-Dutt. London, Hutchinson, n.d.

———. *Peter the First.* Trans. by T. Shebunina. New York, Macmillan, 1959.

———. *Peter the Great.* Trans. by E. Bone and E. Burns. London, Gollancz, 1936. [Vols. I and II of *Peter the First.*]

———. *The Road to Calvary.* Trans. by Mrs. R. S. Townsend. New York, Boni and Liveright, 1923. [The first part of *The Way Through Hell.*]

———. *Road to Calvary.* Trans. by E. Bone. New York, Knopf, 1946. [Complete version of *The Way Through Hell.*]

Trenyov, K. *Lyubov Yarovaya.* In *Soviet Scene: Six Plays of Russian Life* [see Section V-*A*].

Tretyakov, S. *Chinese Testament: The Autobiography of Tan-Shih-hua as Told to Tretyakov.* London, Gollancz, 1934.

————. *Roar, China!* Trans. by E. Polianovska and B. Nixon. London, Lawrence, 1931.

Tynyanov, Yu. *Death and Diplomacy in Persia.* Trans. by A. Brown. London, Boriswood, 1938. [Translation of *The Death of Wazir-Muchtar.*]

Veresayev, V. *The Deadlock.* Trans. by N. Vissotsky and C. Coventry. London, Faber and Gwyer, 1927. [Translation of *In a Blind Alley.*]

————. *The Sisters.* Trans. by J. Soskice. London, Hutchinson, 1934.

Vigdorova, F. *Diary of a Russian Schoolteacher.* Trans. by R. Prokofieva. Evergreen, 1960. [Paperback.]

Vinogradov, A. *The Black Consul.* Trans. by E. Burns. London, Gollancz, 1935; New York, Viking Press, 1935.

————. *The Condemnation of Paganini.* Trans. by S. Garry. London, Hutchinson, 1946.

————. *Three Colours of Time.* London, Hutchinson, 1946.

Vishnevsky, V. *An Optimistic Tragedy. A Play in Three Acts.* In Blake, ed. *Four Soviet Plays* [see Section V-A].

Voronsky, A. *Waters of Life and Death.* Trans. by L. Zarine. London, Allen & Unwin, 1936. [Voronsky's novelized autobiography.]

Voynova, A. *Semi-Precious Stones.* Trans. by V. Snow. New York, Cape and Smith, 1931. British ed.: *Glittering Stones.* London, Heinemann, 1933.

Voytekhov, B. *Last Days of Sevastopol.* Trans. by R. Parker and V. M. Genne. New York, Knopf, 1943; London, Cassell, 1943.

Yugov, A. *Immortality.* Trans. by D. Magarshack. London, Hutchinson, 1946.

Zamyatin, E. *The Dragon: Fifteen Stories.* Trans. and ed. by M. Ginsburg. New York, Random House, 1967. [Includes all Zamyatin's major stories.]

————. *A Soviet Heretic: Essays by Yevgeny Zamyatin.* Trans. and ed. by M. Ginsburg. Chicago, University of Chicago Press, 1970. [Critical essays from *Litsa* and other works.]

————. *We.* Trans. by G. Zilboorg. New York, Dutton, 1924. New ed., Foreword by G. Zilboorg, Intro. by P. Rudy, and Preface by M. Slonim, 1959. Also: by B. G. Guerney, ed. *An Anthology of Russian Literature in the Soviet Period from Gorki to Pasternak* [see Section V-A].

Zoshchenko, M. *Nervous People and Other Stories.* Trans. by M. Gordon and H. McLean. New York, Pantheon, 1963.

————. *Russia Laughs.* Trans. by H. Clayton. Boston, Lothrop Lee & Shepard, 1935.

————. *Scenes from "The Bathhouse" and Other Stories of Communist Russia.* Trans. with Intro. by S. Monas. Ann Arbor, University of Michigan Press, 1961; paperback ed., 1962.

————. *The Woman Who Could Not Read and Other Tales.* Trans. by E. Fen. London, Methuen, 1940.

————. *The Wonderful Dog and Other Tales.* Trans. by E. Fen. London, Methuen, 1942.

NOTE: *The tonic stress is indicated throughout the index to help readers with the pronunciation of Russian names; it is, however, omitted from the first names given in English forms.*

The paper on which this book is printed bears the watermark of the University of Oklahoma Press and has an effective life of at least three hundred years.